Y0-BQU-019

HOMERS ODYSSES.
Translated according to yͤ Greeke.
By. Geo: Chapman
At mihi qd viuo detraxerit Inuida Turba
Post obitum duplici fœnore reddet Honos.
Solus sapit hic homo.
Reliqui vero.
Umbræ mouentur.
Pallas
Vlysses
Imprinted at London by
Rich: Field, for Nath-
aniell Butter.

CHAPMAN'S HOMER

THE ILIAD · THE ODYSSEY AND THE LESSER HOMERICA

Edited, with Introductions, Textual Notes, Commentaries, and Glossaries, by

ALLARDYCE NICOLL

VOLUME TWO

THE ODYSSEY & THE LESSER HOMERICA

BOLLINGEN SERIES XLI

PANTHEON BOOKS

PUBLISHED FOR BOLLINGEN FOUNDATION, INC.
BY PANTHEON BOOKS INC., NEW YORK, N.Y.
Published simultaneously in Canada by McClelland & Stewart Ltd., Toronto

THIS IS THE FORTY-FIRST
IN A SERIES OF WORKS
SPONSORED BY AND PUBLISHED
FOR BOLLINGEN FOUNDATION

LIBRARY OF CONGRESS CATALOGUE CARD NUMBER: 55–10027
MANUFACTURED IN THE UNITED STATES OF AMERICA
BY KINGSPORT PRESS, INC., KINGSPORT, TENN.

CONTENTS

The Odyssey

The Lesser Homerica

The Crowne of all Homers Workes

THE ODYSSEY

INTRODUCTION

IN SOME RESPECTS the text of the *Odysses* presents a much simpler problem than that of the *Iliads*. The latter moves from the early *Seven Books* on through the *Twelve Books* to the final version of 1611, and consequently the listing of variants is bound to be both complex and lengthy. Here, in the *Odysses*, we are concerned with one single text, printed in two parts presumably within a space of a couple of years, 1614–1615.

If, however, this fact makes the editing of the *Odysses* a simpler task, Chapman himself has introduced problems of a different kind in his verses. For some reason, after having declared emphatically that the fourteener was the ideal measure for dealing with the Homeric Greek, he has turned the text of the *Odyssey* into rimed decasyllabic couplets. Perhaps he wished to emphasise the difference between the wrath which forms the theme of the *Iliad* and the patient suffering celebrated in the story of Ulysses. Whatever the cause, the result is that his involved sentence structure tends to be even more involved, and frequently we stumble on passages so obscure that we become utterly lost—the more so since he has now allowed himself much greater licence than in his earlier translation. Again and again, generally for the purpose of stressing his own philosophic interpretation of Ulysses' fate, he completely abandons the Greek: and consequently, when we are confronted with obscurities in these sections, there is no possibility of seeking light from the Homeric original, from the Latin version given in the Spondanus folio or from Spondanus' own lengthy commentary.

There can be no doubt but that, as he advanced in age and in his task, Chapman permitted stylistic mannerisms to grow upon him. His sentences drift on to almost irritating length; he repeats and repeats once more the trick of telling his story by means of phrase multiplied upon phrase; he frequently causes confusion by using 'who,' 'whom' or 'whose' as the subject or object noun of a new sentence; and, similarly, 'when' is often employed in a positive sense at the beginning of sentences, even of paragraphs, with the significance of 'at this time' or 'while this action had been proceeding.'

There are weaknesses in the style of the translation, undoubtedly, yet the Chapman *Odysses* are by no means to be despised. No doubt, the fourteeners that thunder out Achilles' tale are a more characteristic accomplishment than the decasyllabic couplets which narrate Ulysses' fate; no doubt, the *Odysses* depart farther from Homer than do the *Iliads*. At the same time, Chapman does succeed, despite all his obscurities and digressions, in telling his story forcefully and well. He may miss his effect when he comes to deal with the famous episode of Ulysses and his dog, but when he treats of his hero on shipboard or when he narrates the result of battle there can be no hesitation in saying that he has achieved masterfully what he set out to accomplish. The winds whistle round the patient Ulysses and the surge of the sea is in the lines that describe his wanderings.

*

The volume that commonly is thought of first when Chapman's name is mentioned is the complete *Whole Works of Homer,* issued in folio some time between 1614 and 1616. This volume, however, is in reality a kind of patchwork. The first part consists of unsold sheets of the *Iliads,* as originally issued in 1611; the second part is made up of two distinct sets of sheets containing the *Odysses.*

Apparently Chapman, following his earlier practice when he was dealing with the *Iliads,* paused when he reached the conclusion of the twelfth book of the *Odysses* and allowed this half of the complete work to be published separately by Nathaniel Butter. 'Odisses 24 books' was entered on November 2, 1614, and the first twelve books were apparently printed before the end of the year—ready, indeed, to form a New Year's gift to the Earl of Somerset, who had only recently been made Lord Chamberlain. The titlepage is a particularly interesting example of contemporary engraving. In a tablet at the top is the title itself: "HOMER'S ODYSSES. / Translated according to y[e] Greeke / By Geo: Chapman / At mihi q[d] viuo detraxerit Inuida Turba / Post obitum duplici fœnore reddet Honos." This is surrounded by a floral ornament supported by two angels. In the centre stands Homer, with the inscription: "Solus sapit hic homo": at his sides, faintly delineated, are the figures of other poets, with the inscription: "Reliqui vero. Vmbræ mouentur." At the bottom "Pallas" is seated left, her finger raised as in admonition, facing "Ulysses," at whose knees a dog is fawning. A rounded tablet between these characters reads: "Imprinted at London by Rich: Field for Nathaniell Butter."

This volume was dedicated to Robert Carr, Earl of Somerset, in an epistle that mingles prose and verse. It opens with the following lines:

TO THE MOST NOBLE,

NOW LIVING RESTORER

OF THE VLYSSEAN TEMPER;

OF SOLIDE VERTVE

The most secret, and therein sacred Sustainer;

OF POPVLAR VAPOR

The most open, profest, and Heroicall Contemner;

OF ALL TRVE HONOR

The most Truth-like, vnalterable, and inuincible Deseruer,

ROBERT, *Earle of Somerset,*

Lord Chamberlaine, &c.

His Lo[ps]

Euer most deseruedly deuoted

GEO. CHAPMAN

Humbly celebrates this New-yeares Light; *with discouerie of that long hidden Relict; for whose presentment* Macedon *would haue giuen a kingdome;*

HOMER reuiu'd:

Here follow the verse lines, beginning "That he to his unmeasur'd mightie Acts," as they appear in the text of this edition.

The printing of this section of the *Odysses* is particularly good, with few literal errors. Each book ends with a Latin conclusion of the form 'Finis libri primi (secundi etc.) Hom. Odyss.'; while the corresponding conclusion to Book 12 adds a perplexing note—'Opus novem dierum. Σὺν Θεῷ.' This appears to suggest that the entire twelve books were finished in a period of nine days—an absolute impossibility unless the reference is merely to a revision of work already done. It has been suggested that the Latin conclusion is based on the practice of Thomas Phaer, who, in his version of the *Æneid* (1558–92), had dated most of his books and indicated the number of days occupied in each task;[1] and possibly the explanation is that Chapman, rejoicing at the completion of his labour in so short a time, gleefully ended the twelfth book with a note to the effect that this—and not all the twelve books—was done within a space of nine days. Whatever the explanation, however, we have reason to believe that the author regretted his enthusiastic tag. In the Douce collection is a copy of the excessively rare 'twelve books,' presented by the author to Sir Henry Fanshawe: "For y[e] righte worthie Knighte / My exceeding Noble ffreinde; / S[r.] Henry ffanshawe," runs his autograph inscription, "A pore Homericall New yeares gifte." Presumably it was Chapman himself who, in this copy, heavily inked out the puzzling words at the conclusion.

That the twelfth book was hurriedly translated is suggested by another fact. Throughout the greater part of this first section of the *Odysses* the marginalia are numerous and lengthy—so lengthy that on several occasions a note that springs from a particular word in the text trickles down the edge of the page, gathering volume as it goes until it spreads out into a

[1] Phyllis Brooks Bartlett, 'Chapman and Phaer' (*Modern Language Notes,* lvi, 1941, 599–601).

vast lake of small italic print at the foot. So far as line 120 of the twelfth book this practice is continued and then there follow some eleven or twelve pages in which the margins remain suspiciously blank. The likelihood is that, after having gone slowly and laboriously through the larger part of his task, Chapman suddenly hurried on, for some reason or other, towards its end.

At first glance the entire *Odysses* might have been thought to have been printed as a whole at one time: and this no doubt was the impression that the publishers wished to convey. A second glance, however, rapidly demonstrates that Books 1–12 and Books 13–24 belong to two utterly different settings. The signatures of the former run in sixes: Book 12 starts on the recto of Q 6 (p. 179), followed by seven leaves of print. The fifth of these is marked R 5, although elsewhere in the volume the fifth and sixth leaves of a folding remain unsignatured: thus the end of the book is made up of signature R (six leaves), an unsignatured leaf and a blank. The text ends on the recto of the unsignatured leaf (p. 193), and, had there been continuous printing, Book 13 would have started on the verso: actually it is made to begin on the recto of a new leaf, paginated 195, with the signature S—the blank leaf being retained between the two books.

In general, an attempt has been made to make the setting of Books 13–24 follow the pattern of the first part, but there are obvious differences between them. In the headings, the earlier books have 'HOMERS ODYSSES,' where the later have 'HOMERS ODYSSES'; the conclusions to the former are in Latin (e.g. *'Finis duodecimi libri Hom. Odyss.'*), where those of the latter are in English (e.g. *'The End of the Thirteenth Booke of Homers Odysses'*); when ornaments are used, they are of a different kind; the initial capitals in the former printing are frameless, set in a conventional foliage pattern, where those of the latter have frames, with a pattern usually introducing animal or human figures.

In addition to these variations it is obvious that the composition is different. The setting-up of Books 1–12 is excellent and one has the impression that the compositor in the main followed and understood Chapman's manuscript: literal errors are few and the punctuation, although erratic, rarely makes nonsense of the text. When we turn to Books 13–24 we realise that another hand is at work—a rather mechanical hand which seems to have been controlled by a brain that moved uncomprehendingly through many passages of the verse. New sentences are started in the very midst of phrases; what must have been intended as separate sentences are run into one. Quite clearly, the printing of these later books was a less competent job than that of the earlier books—and with this the quality of the paper agrees. Up to the end of signature R the paper (of which the watermark is a vase) is good and strong; the rest of the paper is of poor quality (with a different watermark), porous and thin.

At the same time as the second set of twelve books was printed, a change was made in the opening of the dedicatory epistle. The recto of signature

A3 was reset, and the reference to the Earl of Somerset altered to the form given in the present edition. No doubt the reason for this was the desire to cut out the allusion to New Year's day—no longer appropriate; although two later allusions in the epistle remained without change.

It seems almost impossible to say whether the twenty-four books of the *Odysses* were issued for sale separately in any quantity. The probability is that most of the sheets were used to make up the *Whole Works.* In this form they no doubt appeared in various guises. For some copies the engraved titlepage was retained; for others a printed title was substituted, reading "HOMERS / ODYSSES. / TRANSLATED ACCORDING / TO THE GREEKE. / [line] / BY / *GEORGE CHAPMAN.* / [line] / *At mihi quod vivo detraxerit Invida turba / Post obitum duplici fœnore reddet Honos.* / [line; ornament; line] / *LONDON,* / Printed for *Nathaniel Butter.*". Still others omitted any separate title for the *Odysses;* and it seems that at least a few copies were issued without any title or dedicatory lines, the text of the *Odysses* immediately following that of the *Iliads* (separated only by the blank leaf at its conclusion).

*

In the main, the editorial treatment of the *Odysses* in the present edition follows the plan adopted for the *Iliads,* but in view of certain textual differences in the original some comments, applying specifically to the former, must be added here:

1. Long ſ has been levelled under short *s;* the *u-v* usage has been brought into accordance with modern practice; and, in similar manner, *j* has been substituted for *i*—with one exception, the word 'Troian (Troians),' which is here printed (as it is once in the *Odysses,* XI. 217) as 'Troyan (Troyans).' No *j* forms, it may be noted, appear in the original (except for certain Latin words in the marginalia).

2. Since Chapman never has the spelling 'than' and since this word, in the form of 'then,' is of frequent occurrence alongside of 'then' in a time sense, I have altered 'then' to 'than' in all comparative clauses.

3. The quotations from Greek are given, without comment, as in modern texts, with appropriate accents.

4. So far as punctuation is concerned, the same comments apply to the *Odysses* as were made on the *Iliads.* It should, however, be observed that, while the original punctuation of Books 1–12 probably reproduces much of Chapman's own pointing, that of Books 13–24 is so erratic, and so erroneous by any standards, as to make possible only one assumption—that the person responsible for most of it was a not very intelligent compositor.

5. As in the *Iliads,* direct speeches are indicated by single quotation marks, none of these being present in the folio text. So, too, I have in-

serted an apostrophe to mark the possessive case in nouns. In the *Iliads* no such apostrophes appear, but I have noted a few in the *Odysses* (i, Argument, 2, Calypso's, 7, Menta's; xiv, 297, *Pluto's;* xiv, 575, supper's; xiv, 631, wil's; xv, 20, Father's; xv, 145, *Juno's;* xv, 152, *Sydonia's;* xvi, 304, *Minerua's;* xvii, 441, *Man's;* xix, 27, *Wrath's;* xix, 267, *Lucina's;* xx, 103, *Pluto's;* xx, 421, *Apollo's;* xxi, 151, *Mycena's;* xxiv, 346, *life's*). These sporadic apostrophes are almost certainly due to the compositor, who has introduced others falsely in verbal forms: 'hel'd' for 'held' may serve as an example. Neither the quotation marks nor the possessive apostrophes are listed in the Textual Notes, but the use of 'I'le' for the original 'Ile' or, occasionally, 'Il'e' is recorded in each case.

6. As in the *Iliads,* the original italicization of certain words has been disregarded. At the same time it should be observed that in the first twelve books and erratically in the second twelve the printer has italicized not only proper names but also a considerable number of words (e.g., *Contention, Tumult, Sleepe*) which might be taken to have a personified sense. In addition, some other words (e.g., *Portico*) appear in italics, and some of these have been listed in the Textual Notes.

7. The marginalia or glosses in the folio are commonly (but not absolutely regularly) indicated either by an * or by the use of an a, b or c. These have all been omitted silently.

8. In the *Iliads* the second 'Arguments' are headed 'Another Argument'; in the *Odysses* the corresponding heads read simply 'Another.' For the sake of uniformity 'Another Argument' has been substituted throughout.

Apart from the above exceptions, all other changes are recorded in the Textual Notes. As for the *Iliads,* so for the *Odysses* I have been most conservative in the introduction of emendations. Such emendations as have previously been suggested by G. G. Loane are acknowledged in each instance immediately after the original reading in the Textual Notes, but several among his numerous proposed emendations, even although all of them are fully justified and possibly do reproduce what Chapman wrote, have not been followed: if the original text makes sense I have let it stand.

The text itself is based on my own copy of the *Odysses,* and the readings in the second column of the Textual Notes are from that edition. In the Glossary an * marks words or meanings for which I can find no record before 1614–15 and which Chapman himself in all probability invented.

Homer's Odysses

TO THE MOST WORTHILY HONORED, MY SINGULAR GOOD LORD, ROBERT, EARLE OF SOMERSET, Lord Chamberlaine, &c

I have adventured, Right Noble Earle, out of my utmost
and ever-vowed service to your Vertues, to entitle their Merits
to the Patronage of Homer's English life—whose wisht naturall
life the great Macedon would have protected as the spirit
of his Empire— 5

That he to his unmeasur'd mightie Acts
Might adde a Fame as vast, and their extracts,
In fires as bright and endlesse as the starres,
His breast might breathe and thunder out his warres.
But that great Monark's love of fame and praise 10
Receives an envious Cloud in our foule daies—
For, since our Great ones ceasse themselves to do
Deeds worth their praise, they hold it folly too
To feed their praise in others. But what can
(Of all the gifts that are) be given to man 15
More precious than Eternitie and Glorie,
Singing their praises in unsilenc't storie
Which no blacke Day, no Nation, nor no Age,
No change of Time or Fortune, Force nor Rage,
Shall ever race? All which the Monarch knew 20
Where Homer liv'd entitl'd would ensew:
—Cuius de gurgite vivo
Combibit arcanos vatum omnis turba furores, &c.—

Ex Angeli Politiani Ambra.

From whose deepe Fount of life the thirstie rout
Of Thespian Prophets have lien sucking out 25
Their sacred rages. And as th'influent stone
Of Father Jove's great and laborious Sonne
Lifts high the heavie Iron and farre implies
The wide Orbs that the Needle rectifies
In vertuous guide of every sea-driven course, 30

To all aspiring his one boundlesse force:
So from one Homer all the holy fire
That ever did the hidden heate inspire
In each true Muse came cleerly sparkling downe,
And must for him compose one flaming Crowne. 35
He, at Jove's Table set, fils out to us
Cups that repaire Age sad and ruinous,
And gives it Built of an eternall stand
With his all-sinewie Odyssean hand—
Shifts Time and Fate, puts Death in Life's free state 40
And Life doth into Ages propagate.
He doth in Men the Gods' affects inflame,
His fuell Vertue, blowne by Praise and Fame,
And, with the high soule's first impulsions driven,
Breakes through rude Chaos, Earth, the Seas and Heaven. 45
The Nerves of all things hid in Nature lie
Naked before him, all their Harmonie
Tun'd to his Accents, that in Beasts breathe Minds.
What Fowles, what Floods, what Earth, what Aire, what Winds,
What fires Æthereall, what the Gods conclude 50
In all their Counsels, his Muse makes indude
With varied voices, that even rockes have mov'd.
And yet for all this, naked Vertue lov'd,
Honors without her he as abject prises,
And foolish Fame deriv'd from thence despises— 55
When, from the vulgar taking glorious bound
Up to the Mountaine where the Muse is crownd,
He sits and laughs to see the jaded Rabble
Toile to his hard heights, t'all accesse unable, &c.

Thus far Angel. Politianus, for the most part translated.

And that your Lordship may in his Face take view of his 60
Mind, the first word of his Iliads *is* μῆνιν,wrath; *the first*
word of his Odysses, ἄνδρα, Man—*contracting in either word*
his each worke's Proposition. In one, Predominant
Perturbation; in the other, over-ruling Wisedome; in one, the
Bodie's fervour and fashion of outward Fortitude to all 65
possible height of Heroicall Action; in the other, the Mind's
inward, constant and unconquerd Empire, unbroken,
unalterd with any most insolent and tyrannous infliction. To
many most soveraigne praises is this Poeme entitled, but to
that Grace *in chiefe which sets on the Crowne both of Poets* 70
and Orators, τὸ τὰ μικρὰ μεγάλως, καὶ τὰ κοινά καινῶς—*that is,*
Parva magnè dicere, pervulgata novè, jejuna plenè: *To*

speake things litle, greatly; things commune, rarely; things
barren and emptie, fruitfully and fully. The returne of a
man into his Countrie is his whole scope and object, which in 75
itselfe, your Lordship may well say, is jejune and fruitlesse
enough, affoording nothing feastfull, nothing magnificent.
And yet even this doth the divine inspiration render vast,
illustrous and of miraculous composure. And for this, my
Lord, is this Poeme preferred to his Iliads; for therein much 80
magnificence, both of person and action, gives great aide to his
industrie, but in this are these helpes exceeding sparing or
nothing; and yet is the Structure so elaborate and pompous
that the poore plaine Groundworke (considered together)
may seeme the naturally rich wombe to it and produce it 85
needfully. Much wonderd at, therefore, is the Censure of
Dionysius Longinus (a man otherwise affirmed, grave and of
elegant judgement), comparing Homer in his Iliads to the
Sunne rising, in his Odysses to his descent or setting, or to
the Ocean robd of his aesture, many tributorie flouds and 90
rivers of excellent ornament withheld from their observance
—when this his worke so farre exceeds the Ocean, with all his
Court and concourse, that all his Sea is onely a serviceable
streame to it. Nor can it be compared to any One power to be
named in nature, being an entirely wel-sorted and digested 95
Confluence of all—where the most solide and grave is made as
nimble and fluent as the most airie and firie, the nimble and
fluent as firme and well-bounded as the most grave and solid.
And (taking all together) of so tender impression, and of such
Command to the voice of the Muse, that they knocke 100
heaven with her breath and discover their foundations as
low as hell. Nor is this all-comprising Poesie phantastique, or
meere fictive, but the most material and doctrinall illations
of Truth, both for all manly information of Manners in the
yong, all prescription of Justice, and even Christian pietie, 105
in the most grave and high-governd. To illustrate both which
in both kinds, with all height of expression, the Poet creates
both a Bodie and a Soule in them—wherein, if the Bodie
(being the letter, or historie) seemes fictive and beyond
Possibilitie to bring into Act, the sence then and Allegorie 110
(which is the Soule) is to be sought—which intends a more
eminent expressure of Vertue, for her lovelinesse, and of
Vice, for her uglinesse, in their severall effects, going beyond
the life than any Art within life can possibly delineate. Why
then is Fiction to this end so hatefull to our true Ignorants? 115
Or why should a poore Chronicler of a Lord Maior's naked

Truth (that peradventure will last his yeare) include more
worth with our moderne wizerds than Homer for his naked
Ulysses, clad in eternall Fiction? But this Prozer Dionysius
and the rest of these grave and reputatively learned (that 120
dare undertake for their gravities the headstrong censure of
all things, and challenge the understanding of these Toyes in
their childhoods, when even these childish vanities retaine
deepe and most necessarie learning enough in them to make
them children in their ages and teach them while they live) are 125
not in these absolutely divine Infusions allowd either voice or
relish—for Qui Poeticas ad fores accedit, &c., *sayes the Divine*
Philosopher, he that knocks at the Gates of the Muses, sine
Musarum furore, *is neither to be admitted entrie nor a touch*
at their Thresholds, his opinion of entrie ridiculous and his 130
presumption impious. Nor must Poets themselves (might I a
litle insist on these contempts, not tempting too farre your
Lordship's Ulyssean patience) presume to these doores without
the truly genuine and peculiar induction—there being in
Poesie a twofold rapture (or alienation of soule, as the 135
abovesaid Teacher termes it), one Insania, *a disease of the*
mind and a meere madnesse, by which the infected is thrust
beneath all the degrees of humanitie, et ex homine Brutum
quodammodo redditur *(for which poore Poesie in this*
diseasd and impostorous age is so barbarously vilified); 140
the other is Divinus furor, *by which the sound and divinely*
healthfull supra hominis naturam erigitur, et in Deum transit:
one a perfection directly infused from God, the other an
infection obliquely and degenerately proceeding from man.
Of the divine Furie, my Lord, your Homer hath ever bene 145
both first and last Instance, being pronounced absolutely
τὸν σοφώτατον καὶ τὸν θειότατον ποιητήν, *the most wise and most*
divine Poet—against whom whosoever shall open his prophane
mouth may worthily receive answer with this of his divine
defender (Empedocles, Heraclitus, Protagoras, Epicharmus, 150
&c. *being of Homer's part)* τίς οὖν, *&c., who against such an*
Armie and the Generall Homer dares attempt the assault
but he must be reputed ridiculous? And yet against this hoast
and this invincible Commander shall we have every Besogne
and foole a Leader—the common herd (I assure myself) readie 155
to receive it on their hornes, their infected Leaders

Such men as sideling ride the ambling Muse,
Whose saddle is as frequent as the stuse,
Whose Raptures are in every Pageant seene,

In every Wassall rime and Dancing greene— 160
When he that writes by any beame of Truth
Must dive as deepe as he past shallow youth.
Truth dwels in Gulphs, whose Deepes hide shades so rich
That Night sits muffl'd there in clouds of pitch,
More Darke than Nature made her, and requires, 165
To cleare her tough mists, Heaven's great fire of fires,
To whom the Sunne it selfe is but a Beame.
For sicke soules then (but rapt in foolish Dreame)
To wrestle with these Heav'n-strong mysteries
What madnesse is it—when their light serves eies 170
That are not worldly in their least aspect
But truly pure and aime at Heaven direct.
Yet these none like but what the brazen head
Blatters abroad, no sooner borne but dead.

Holding then in eternal contempt, my Lord, those 175
short-lived Bubbles, eternize your vertue and judgement with
the Grecian Monark, esteeming not us the least of your
New-yeare's Presents

Homer, three thousand yeares dead, now reviv'd
Even from that dull Death that in life he liv'd, 180
When none conceited him, none understood,
That so much life in so much death as blood
Conveys about it could mixe. But when Death
Drunke up the bloudie Mist that humane breath
Pour'd round about him (Povertie and Spight 185
Thickning the haplesse vapor), then Truth's light
Glimmerd about his Poeme; the pincht soule
(Amidst the Mysteries it did enroule)
Brake powrefully abroad. And as we see
The Sunne, all hid in clouds, at length got free, 190
Through some forc't covert, over all the wayes
Neare and beneath him, shootes his vented rayes
Farre off and stickes them in some litle Glade,
All woods, fields, rivers left besides in shade:
So your Apollo, from that world of light 195
Closde in his Poem's bodie, shot to sight
Some few forc't Beames, which neare him were not seene
(As in his life or countrie), Fate and Spleene
Clouding their radiance, which, when Death had clear'd,
To farre-off Regions his free beames appear'd— 200
In which all stood and wonderd, striving which
His Birth and Rapture should in right enrich.

Twelve Labours of your Thespian Hercules
I now present your Lorship. Do but please
To lend Life meanes till th' other Twelve receave 205
Equall atchievement—and let Death then reave
My life now lost in our Patrician Loves
That knocke heads with the herd, in whom there moves
One blood, one soule, both drownd in one set height
Of stupid Envie and meere popular Spight, 210
Whose loves with no good did my least veine fill,
And from their hates I feare as little ill.
Their Bounties nourish not when most they feed,
But where there is no Merit or no Need;
Raine into rivers still; and are such showres 215
As bubbles spring and overflow the flowres.
Their worse parts and worst men their Best subornes,
Like winter Cowes, whose milke runnes to their hornes.
And as litigious Clients' bookes of Law
Cost infinitely, taste of all the Awe 220
Bencht in our kingdome's Policie, Pietie, State,
Earne all their deepe explorings, satiate
All sorts there thrust together by the heart
With thirst of wisedome spent on either part,
Horrid examples made of Life and Death 225
From their fine stuffe woven—yet, when once the breath
Of sentence leaves them, all their worth is drawne
As drie as dust and weares like Cobweb Lawne:
So these men set a price upon their worth
That no man gives but those that trot it forth 230
Through Need's foule wayes, feed Humors with all cost
Though Judgement sterves in them, Rout State-engrost
(At all Tabacco benches, solemne Tables,
Where all that crosse their Envies are their fables)
In their ranke faction, Shame and Death approv'd 235
Fit Penance for their Opposites, none lov'd
But those that rub them, not a Reason heard
That doth not sooth and glorifie their preferd
Bitter Opinions—when, would Truth resume
The cause to his hands, all would flie in fume 240
Before his sentence, since the innocent mind
Just God makes good, to whom their worst is wind.
For that I freely all my Thoughts expresse
My Conscience is my Thousand witnesses,
And to this stay my constant Comforts vow: 245
You for the world I have, or God for you.

CERTAINE ANCIENT GREEKE EPIGRAMMES TRANSLATED

All starres are drunke up by the firie Sunne,
And in so much a flame lies shrunke the Moone:
Homer's all-liv'd Name all Names leaves in Death,
Whose splendor onely Muses' Bosomes breath.

Another

Heav'ns fires shall first fall darkn'd from his Sphere;
Grave Night the light weed of the Day shall weare;
Fresh streames shall chace the Sea, tough Plowes shall teare
Her fishie bottomes; Men in long date dead
Shall rise and live—before Oblivion shed
Those still-greene leaves that crowne great Homer's head.

Another

The great Mæonides doth onely write,
And to him dictates the great God of Light.

Another

Seven kingdomes strove in which should swell the wombe
That bore great Homer, whom Fame freed from Tombe—
Argos, Chius, Pylos, Smyrna, Colophone,
The learn'd Athenian and Ulyssean Throne.

Another

'Art thou of Chius?' 'No.' 'Of Salamine?'
'As little.' 'Was the Smyrnean Countrie thine?'
'Nor so.' 'Which then? Was Cumas? Colophone?'
'Nor one, nor other.' 'Art thou then of none
That Fame proclames thee?' 'None.' 'Thy Reason call.'
'If I confesse of one, I anger all.'

THE FIRST BOOKE
of
HOMER'S ODYSSES

THE ARGUMENT

The Gods in counsaile sit, to call
Ulysses from Calypso's thrall,
And order their high pleasures thus:–
Gray Pallas to Telemachus
(In Ithaca) her way addrest, 5
And did her heavenly lims invest
In Mentas' likenesse, that did raigne
King of the Taphians (in the Maine
Whose rough waves neare Leucadia runne),
Advising wise Ulysses' sonne 10
To seeke his father, and addresse
His course to yong Tantalides
That govern'd Sparta. Thus much said,
She shewd she was Heav'ns martiall Maid,
And vanisht from him. Next to this 15
The Banquet of the wooers is.

Another Argument

Ἄλφα *The Deities sit;*
The Man retir'd;
Th'Ulyssean wit
By Pallas fir'd.

The information or fashion of an absolute man, and necessarie (or fatal) passage through many afflictions

The Man, O Muse, informe, that many a way
Wound with his wisedome to his wished stay;
That wanderd wondrous farre when He the towne
Of sacred Troy had sackt and shiverd downe.

(according with the most sacred Letter) to his naturall haven and countrey, is the whole argument and scope of this inimitable and miraculous Poeme. And therefore is the epithete πολύτροπον *given him in the first verse;* πολύτροπος *signifying* Homo cuius ingenium velut per multas, et varias vias, vertitur in verum.

The cities of a world of nations, 5
With all their manners, mindes and fashions,
He saw and knew; at Sea felt many woes,
Much care sustaind, to save from overthrowes
Himselfe and friends in their retreate for home.
But so their fates he could not overcome, 10
Though much he thirsted it. O men unwise,
They perisht by their owne impieties,
That in their hunger's rapine would not shunne
The Oxen of the loftie-going Sunne,
Who therefore from their eyes the day bereft 15
Of safe returne. These acts, in some part left,
Tell us, as others, deified seed of Jove.

Now all the rest that austere Death out-strove
At Troy's long siege at home safe anchor'd are,
Free from the malice both of sea and warre; 20
Onely Ulysses is denide accesse
To wife and home. The Grace of Goddesses,
The reverend Nymph Calypso, did detaine
Him in her Caves, past all the race of men
Enflam'd to make him her lov'd Lord and Spouse. 25
And when the Gods had destin'd that his house,
Which Ithaca on her rough bosome beares,
(The point of time wrought out by ambient yeares)
Should be his haven, Contention still extends
Her envie to him, even amongst his friends. 30
All Gods tooke pitie on him: onely he
That girds Earth in the cincture of the sea
Divine Ulysses ever did envie,
And made the fixt port of his birth to flie.

Neptune's progresse to the Æthiops.

But he himselfe solemniz'd a retreate 35
To th'Æthiops, farre dissunderd in their seate
(In two parts parted, at the Sunne's descent
And underneath his golden Orient
The first and last of men), t'enjoy their feast
Of buls and lambes in Hecatombs addrest: 40
At which he sat, given over to Delight.

These notes following, I am inforced to insert (since the words they containe, differ from all other translations), lest I be thought to erre out of that ignorance, that may perhaps possesse my depraver.

The other Gods in Heaven's supreamest height
Were all in Councell met—to whom began
The mightie Father, both of God and man,
Discourse, inducing matter that inclin'd 45
To wise Ulysses, calling to his mind

'Αμύμονος *translated in this place* inculpabilis, *and made the epithete of Ægisthus, is from the true sence of the word as it is here to be understood—which is quite contrary. As* ἀντίθεος *is to be expounded in some place* Divinus, *or* Deo similis, *but in another (soone after)* contrarius Deo—*the person to whom the Epithete is given giving reason to distinguish it. And so* δλοόφρων, *an Epithete given to Atlas, instantly following, in one place signifies* Mente perniciosus; *in the next,* qui universa mente gerit.

Faultfull Ægisthus, who to death was done
By yong Orestes, Agamemnon's sonne.
His memorie to the Immortals then
Mov'd Jove thus deeply: 'O how falsly men 50
Accuse us Gods as authors of their ill,
When by the bane their owne bad lives instill
They suffer all the miseries of their states—
Past our inflictions and beyond their fates.
As now Ægisthus past his fate did wed 55
The wife of Agamemnon, and (in dread
To suffer death himselfe) to shunne his ill
Incurr'd it by the loose bent of his will,
In slaughtering Atrides in retreate—
Which we foretold him would so hardly set 60
To his murtherous purpose, sending Mercurie
(That slaughterd Argus) our considerate spie
To give him this charge: "Do not wed his wife,
Nor murther him, for thou shalt buy his life
With ransome of thine owne, imposde on thee 65
By his Orestes, when in him shall be
Atrides' selfe renewd, and but the prime
Of youth's spring put abroad, in thirst to clime
His haughtie Father's throne by his high acts."
These words of Hermes wrought not into facts 70
Ægisthus' powres; good counsell he despisde,
And to that Good his ill is sacrifisde.'

Pallas to Jupiter.

Pallas (whose eyes did sparkle like the skies)
Answerd: 'O Sire! supreame of Deities!
Ægisthus past his Fate and had desert 75
To warrant our infliction; and convert
May all the paines such impious men inflict
On innocent sufferers to revenge as strict,
Their owne hearts eating. But that Ithacus
(Thus never meriting) should suffer thus 80
I deeply suffer. His more pious mind
Divides him from these fortunes. Though unkind
Is Pietie to him, giving him a fate
More suffering than the most infortunate,
So long kept friendlesse in a sea-girt soile, 85
Where the sea's navile is a sylvane Ile,
In which the Goddesse dwels that doth derive
Her birth from Atlas, who of all alive
The motion and the fashion doth command,

With his wise mind, whose forces understand 90
The inmost deepes and gulfes of all the seas,
Who (for his skill of things superiour) stayes
The two steepe Columnes that prop earth and heaven.
His daughter tis who holds this homelesse-driven
Still mourning with her—evermore profuse 95
Of soft and winning speeches that abuse
And make so languishingly and possest
With so remisse a mind, her loved guest
Manage the action of his way for home.
Where he (though in affection overcome) 100
In judgement yet more longs to shew his hopes,
His countrie's smoke leape from her chimney tops,
And death askes in her armes. Yet never shall
Thy lov'd heart be converted on his thrall,
Austere Olympius. Did not ever he 105
In ample Troy thy altars gratifie,
And Grecians' Fleete make in thy offerings swim?
O Jove, why still then burnes thy wrath to him?'
The Cloud-assembler answerd: 'What words flie,
Bold daughter, from thy Pale of Ivorie? 110
As if I ever could cast from my care
Divine Ulysses, who exceeds so farre
All men in wisedome, and so oft hath given
To all th'Immortals thron'd in ample heaven
So great and sacred gifts? But his decrees, 115
That holds the earth in with his nimble knees,
Stand to Ulysses' longings so extreme,
For taking from the God-foe Polypheme
His onely eye—a Cyclop, that excell'd
All other Cyclops, with whose burthen swell'd 120
The Nymph Thoosa, the divine increase
Of Phorcys' seed, a great God of the seas.

In this place is Atlas given the Epithete ὀλοόφρων, *which signifies* qui universa mente agitat *—here given him for the power the starres have in all things. Yet this receives other interpretation in other places, as abovesaid.*

94 Δύστηνος *is here turned by others* infelix *in the generall collection: when it hath here a particular exposition, applied to expresse Ulysses' desert errors,* παρὰ τὸ στῆναι, ut sit, qui vix locum invenire potest ubi consistat.

97 *This is thus translated the rather to expresse and approve the Allegorie driven through the whole* Odysses*—deciphering the intangling of the wisest in his affections and the torments that breede in every pious minde, to be thereby hindred to arrive so directly as he desires at the proper and onely true naturall countrie of every worthy man, whose haven is heaven and the next life, to which this life is but a sea in continuall æsture and vexation. The words occasioning all this are* μαλακοῖσι λόγοισιν, μαλακὸς *signifying* qui languide, et animo remisso rem aliquam gerit*—which being the effect of Calypso's sweete words in Ulysses is here applied passively to his owne sufferance of their operation.*

109 *Jupiter to Pallas.* 110 Ἕρκος ὀδόντων *viz.* vallum *or* claustrum dentium, *which for the better sound in our language is here turned 'Pale of Ivorie'—the teeth being that rampier or pale given us by nature in that part, for restraint and compression of our speech, till the imagination, appetite and soule (that ought to rule in their examination before their deliverie) have given worthy passe to them. The most grave and divine Poet teaching therein that not so much for the necessarie chewing of our sustenance our teeth are given us as for their stay of our words, lest we utter them rashly.*

She mixt with Neptune in his hollow caves
And bore this Cyclop to that God of waves.
For whose lost eye th'Earth-shaker did not kill 125
Erring Ulysses, but reserves him still
In life for more death. But use we our powres
And round about us cast these cares of ours,
All to discover how we may preferre
His wisht retreate, and Neptune make forbeare 130
His sterne eye to him—since no one God can
In spite of all prevaile, but gainst a man.'
To this, this answer made the gray-eyd Maide:
'Supreame of rulers, since so well apaide
The blessed Gods are all then, now, in thee 135
To limit wise Ulysses' miserie,
And that you speake as you referd to me
Prescription for the meanes, in this sort be
Their sacred order:—Let us now addresse
With utmost speed our swift Argicides, 140
To tell the Nymph that beares the golden Tresse *Calypso.*
In th'ile Ogygia that tis our will
She should not stay our lov'd Ulysses still,
But suffer his returne: and then will I
To Ithaca, to make his sonne apply 145
His Sire's inquest the more, infusing force
Into his soule to summon the concourse
Of curld-head Greekes to counsaile, and deterre
Each wooer that hath bene the slaughterer
Of his fat sheepe and crooked-headed beeves 150
From more wrong to his mother, and their leaves
Take in such termes as fit deserts so great.
To Sparta then, and Pylos, where doth beate
Bright Amathus, the flood and epithete
To all that kingdome, my advice shall send 155
The spirit-advanc'd Prince, to the pious end
Of seeking his lost father, if he may
Receive report from Fame where rests his stay—
And make, besides, his owne successive worth
Knowne to the world and set in action forth.' 160
This said, her wingd shooes to her feete she tied, *The preparation of Pallas for Ithaca.*
Formd all of gold and all eternified,
That on the round earth or the sea sustaind
Her ravisht substance swift as gusts of wind.
Then tooke she her strong Lance, with steele made keene, 165
Great, massie, active, that whole hoasts of men

(Though all Heroes) conquers, if her ire
Their wrongs inflame, backt by so great a Sire.
Downe from Olympus' tops she headlong div'd,
And swift as thought in Ithaca arriv'd, 170
Close at Ulysses' gates; in whose first court
She made her stand, and for her breast's support
Leand on her iron Lance; her forme imprest
Pallas like Mentas. With Mentas' likenesse, come as being a guest.
There found she those proud wooers, that were then 175
Set on those Oxe-hides that themselves had slaine,
Before the gates, and all at dice were playing.
To them the heralds and the rest, obaying,
Fill'd wine and water; some, still as they plaid,
And some, for solemne supper's state, purvaid 180
With porous sponges, clensing tables, serv'd
With much rich feast; of which to all they kerv'd.
God-like Telemachus amongst them sat,
Griev'd much in mind; and in his heart begat
All representment of his absent Sire— 185
How (come from far-off parts) his spirits would fire
With those proud wooers' sight, with slaughter parting
Their bold concourse, and to himselfe converting
The honors they usurpt, his owne commanding.
In this discourse, he first saw Pallas standing, 190
Unbidden entrie; up rose and addrest
His pace right to her, angrie that a guest
Should stand so long at gate; and, coming neare,
Her right hand tooke, tooke in his owne her speare,
And thus saluted: 'Grace to your repaire, 195
Faire guest, your welcome shall be likewise faire.
Enter and (chear'd with feast) disclose th'intent
That causde your coming.' This said, first he went,
And Pallas followd. To a roome they came,
Steepe, and of state; the Javelin of the Dame 200
He set against a pillar vast and hie,
Amidst a large and bright-kept Armorie,
Which was, besides, with woods of Lances grac'd
Of his grave father's. In a throne he plac'd
The man-turnd Goddesse, under which was spred 205
A Carpet, rich and of devicefull thred,
A footstoole staying her feete; and by her chaire
Another seate (all garnisht wondrous faire,
To rest or sleepe on in the day) he set
Farre from the prease of wooers, lest at meate 210

The noise they still made might offend his guest,
Disturbing him at banquet or at rest,
Even to his combat, with that pride of theirs
That kept no noble forme in their affaires.
And these he set farre from them, much the rather 215
To question freely of his absent father.
A Table fairely polisht then was spread,
On which a reverend officer set bread,
And other servitors all sorts of meate
(Salads, and flesh, such as their haste could get), 220
Serv'd with observance in. And then the Sewre
Powr'd water from a great and golden Ewre,
That from their hands t'a silver Caldron ran.
Both washt and seated close, the voicefull man
Fetcht cups of gold and set by them, and round 225
Those cups with wine with all endevour crownd.
Then rusht in the rude wooers; themselves plac't;
The heralds water gave; the maids in haste
Serv'd bread from baskets—when of all prepar'd
And set before them the bold wooers shar'd, 230
Their Pages plying their cups past the rest.
But lustie wooers must do more than feast;
For now (their hungers and their thirsts allaid)
They call'd for songs and Dances. Those, they said,
Were th'ornaments of feast. The herald strait 235
A Harpe, carv'd full of artificiall sleight,
Thrust into Phemius' (a learnd singer's) hand,
Who till he much was urg'd on termes did stand,
But, after, plaid and sung with all his art.

Telemachus to Pallas.

Telemachus to Pallas then (apart, 240
His eare inclining close, that none might heare)
In this sort said: 'My Guest, exceeding deare,
Will you not sit incenst with what I say?
These are the cares these men take—feast and play—
Which easly they may use, because they eate, 245
Free and unpunisht, of another's meate,
And of a man's whose white bones wasting lie
In some farre region, with th'incessancie
Of showres powr'd downe upon them, lying ashore,
Or in the seas washt nak'd. Who, if he wore 250
Those bones with flesh and life and industrie,
And these might here in Ithaca set eye
On him returnd, they all would wish to be
Either past other in celeritie

Of feete and knees, and not contend t'exceed 255
In golden garments. But his vertues feed
The fate of ill death, nor is left to me
The least hope of his life's recoverie–
No, not if any of the mortall race
Should tell me his returne; the chearfull face 260
Of his returnd day never will appeare.
But tell me–and let Truth your witnesse beare–
Who, and from whence you are, what citie's birth,
What parents? In what vessell set you forth,
And with what mariners arriv'd you here? 265
I cannot thinke you a foote passenger.
Recount then to me all, to teach me well
Fit usage for your worth. And if it fell
In chance now first that you thus see us here,
Or that in former passages you were 270
My father's guest? For many men have bene
Guests to my father. Studious of men
His sociable nature ever was.'

On him againe the grey-eyd Maide did passe

Pallas to Telemachus.

This kind reply: 'I'le answer passing true 275
All thou hast askt. My birth his honour drew
From wise Anchialus. The name I beare
Is Mentas, the commanding Ilander
Of all the Taphians, studious in the art
Of Navigation, having toucht this part 280
With ship and men, of purpose to maintaine
Course through the darke seas t'other-languag'd men.
And Temesis sustaines the citie's name
For which my ship is bound, made knowne by fame
For rich in brasse, which my occasions need; 285
And therefore bring I shining steele in steed,
Which their use wants, yet makes my vessel's freight,
That neare a plowd field rides at anchor's weight,
Apart this citie, in the harbor calld
Rhethrus, whose waves with Neius' woods are walld. 290
Thy Sire and I were ever mutuall guests
At either's house, still interchanging feasts.
I glorie in it. Aske, when thou shalt see
Laertes, th'old Heroe, these of mee
From the beginning. He, men say, no more 295
Visits the Citie, but will needs deplore
His sonne's beleev'd losse in a private field–
One old maide onely at his hands to yeeld

Foode to his life, as oft as labour makes
His old limbs faint; which, though he creepes, he takes 300
Along a fruitfull plaine, set all with vines,
Which husbandman-like (though a King) he proines.
But now I come to be thy father's guest.
I heare he wanders while these wooers feast.
And (as th'Immortals prompt me at this houre) 305
I'le tell thee, out of a prophetique powre—
Not as profest a Prophet, nor cleare seene
At all times what shall after chance to men—
What I conceive for this time will be true:—
The Gods' inflictions keepe your Sire from you. 310
Divine Ulysses yet abides not dead
Above earth, nor beneath, nor buried
In any seas (as you did late conceive),
But, with the broad sea sieg'd, is kept alive
Within an Ile by rude and up-land men, 315
That in his spite his passage home detaine.
Yet long it shall not be before he tred
His countrie's deare earth, though solicited
And held from his returne with iron chaines,
For he hath wit to forge a world of traines, 320
And will of all be sure to make good one
For his returne, so much relide upon.
But tell me, and be true: Art thou indeed
So much a sonne as to be said the seed
Of Ithacus himselfe? Exceeding much 325
Thy forehead and faire eyes at his forme touch,
For oftentimes we met, as you and I
Meete at this houre, before he did apply
His powres for Troy, when other Grecian States
In hollow ships were his associates. 330
But since that time mine eyes could never see
Renowmd Ulysses, nor met his with me.'

Τόσος παῖς, Tantus filius, *Pallas thus enforcing her question to stirre up the son the more to the father's worthinesse.*

The wise Telemachus againe replide:
'You shall with all I know be satisfide.

Telemachus to Pallas.

My mother, certaine, sayes I am his sonne: 335
I know not, nor was ever simply knowne
By any child the sure truth of his Sire.
But would my veines had tooke in living fire
From some man happie, rather than one wise,
Whom age might see seizd of what youth made prise. 340
But he, whoever of the mortall race
Is most unblest, he holds my father's place.

This, since you aske, I answer.' She, againe:
Pallas to Telemachus. 'The Gods sure did not make the future straine
Both of thy race and dayes obscure to thee, 345
Since thou wert borne so of Penelope.
The stile may by thy after acts be wonne,
Of so great Sire the high undoubted sonne.
Say truth in this then: What's this feasting here?
What all this rout? Is all this nuptiall cheare? 350
Or else some friendly banquet made by thee?
For here no shots are, where all sharers be.
Past measure contumeliously this crew
Fare through thy house; which should th'ingenuous view
Of any good or wise man come and find, 355
(Impietie seeing playd in every kind)
He could not but through every veine be mov'd.'
Againe Telemachus: 'My guest much lov'd,
Since you demand and sift these sights so farre,
I grant twere fit a house so regular, 360
Rich and so faultlesse once in government,
Should still at all parts the same forme present
That gave it glorie while her Lord was here.
But now the Gods, that us displeasure beare,
Have otherwise appointed, and disgrace 365
My father most of all the mortall race.
For whom I could not mourne so were he dead,
Amongst his fellow Captaines slaughtered
By common enemies, or in the hands
Of his kind friends had ended his commands, 370
After he had egregiously bestow'd
His powre and order in a warre so vow'd,
And to his tombe all Greekes their grace had done,
That to all ages he might leave his sonne
Immortall honor: but now Harpies have 375
Digg'd in their gorges his abhorred grave.
Obscure, inglorious, Death hath made his end,
And me (for glories) to all griefes contend.
Nor shall I any more mourne him alone,
The Gods have given me other cause of mone. 380
For looke how many Optimates remaine
In Samos, or the shoares Dulichian,
Shadie Zacynthus; or how many beare
Rule in the rough browes of this Iland here;
So many now my mother and this house 385
At all parts make defam'd and ruinous.

And she her hatefull nuptials nor denies,
Nor will dispatch their importunities,
Though she beholds them spoile still as they feast
All my free house yeelds, and the little rest 390
Of my dead Sire in me, perhaps intend
To bring, ere long, to some untimely end.'
This Pallas sigh'd, and answerd: 'O,' said she,
'Absent Ulysses is much mist by thee,
That on these shamelesse suiters he might lay 395
His wreakfull hands. Should he now come and stay
In thy Court's first gates, armd with helme and shield,
And two such darts as I have seene him wield
When first I saw him in our Taphian Court,
Feasting and doing his deserts disport 400
When from Ephyrus he returnd by us
From Ilus, sonne to Centaur Mermerus—
To whom he traveld through the watrie dreads
For bane to poison his sharpe arrowes' heads,
That death, but toucht, causde; which he would not give, 405
Because he fear'd the Gods that ever live
Would plague such death with death, and yet their feare
Was to my father's bosome not so deare
As was thy father's love (for what he sought,
My loving father found him to a thought)— 410
If such as then Ulysses might but meete
With these proud wooers, all were at his feete
But instant dead men, and their nuptials
Would prove as bitter as their dying galls.
But these things in the Gods' knees are reposde, 415
If his returne shall see with wreake inclosde
These in his house, or he returne no more.
And therefore I advise thee to explore
All waies thy selfe to set these wooers gone;
To which end give me fit attention. 420
Tomorrow into solemne councell call
The Greeke Heroes, and declare to all
(The Gods being witnesse) what thy pleasure is:
Command to townes of their nativities
These frontlesse wooers. If thy mother's mind 425
Stands to her second nuptials so enclinde,
Returne she to her royall father's towers,
Where th'one of these may wed her, and her dowers
Make rich, and such as may consort with grace
So deare a daughter of so great a race. 430

And thee I warne as well (if thou as well
Wilt heare and follow) take thy best built saile,
With twentie owers mann'd, and haste t'enquire
Where the abode is of thy absent Sire—
If any can informe thee, or thine eare 435
From Jove the fame of his retreate may heare
(For chiefly Jove gives all that honours men).
'To Pylos first be thy addression then
To god-like Nestor. Thence to Sparta haste
To gold-lockt Menelaus, who was last 440
Of all the brasse-armd Greekes that saild from Troy.
And trie from both these, if thou canst enjoy
Newes of thy Sire's returnd life any where,
Though sad thou sufferst in his search a yeare.
If of his death thou hear'st, returne thou home, 445
And to his memorie erect a tombe,
Performing parent-rites of feast and game,
Pompous, and such as best may fit his fame;
And then thy mother a fit husband give.
These past, consider how thou maist deprive 450
Of worthlesse life these wooers in thy house,
By open force, or projects enginous.
Things childish fit not thee; th'art so no more.
Hast thou not heard how all men did adore
Divine Orestes, after he had slaine 455
Ægisthus, murthering by a trecherous traine
His famous father? Be then, my most lov'd,
Valiant and manly, every way approv'd
As great as he. I see thy person fit,
Noble thy mind, and excellent thy wit— 460
All given thee so to use and manage here
That even past death they may their memories beare.
In meane time I'le descend to ship and men,
That much expect me. Be observant then
Of my advice, and carefull to maintaine 465
In equall acts thy royall father's raigne.'
Telemachus replide: 'You ope, faire Guest,
A friend's heart in your speech, as well exprest
As might a father serve t' informe his sonne:
All which sure place have in my memorie wonne. 470
Abide yet, though your voyage calls away,
That, having bath'd and dignifide your stay
With some more honour, you may yet beside
Delight your mind by being gratifide

With some rich Present taken in your way, 475
That, as a Jewell, your respect may lay
Up in your treasurie, bestowd by me,
As free friends use to guests of such degree.'
'Detaine me not,' said she, 'so much inclinde
To haste my voyage. What thy loved minde 480
Commands to give, at my returne this way
Bestow on me, that I directly may
Convey it home; which (more of price to mee)
The more it askes my recompence to thee.'
This said, away gray-eyd Minerva flew, 485
Like to a mounting Larke; and did endue
His mind with strength and boldnesse, and much more
Made him his father long for than before.
And weighing better who his guest might be,
He stood amaz'd, and thought a Deitie 490
Was there descended: to whose will he fram'd
His powres at all parts, and went so inflam'd
Amongst the wooers, who were silent set
To heare a Poet sing the sad retreat
The Greekes performd from Troy—which was from thence 495
Proclaimd by Pallas, paine of her offence.
When which divine song was perceiv'd to beare
That mournfull subject by the listning eare
Of wise Penelope (Icarius' seed,
Who from an upper roome had giv'n it heed) 500
Downe she descended by a winding staire—
Not solely, but the State in her repaire
Two Maides of Honour made. And when this Queene
Of women stoopt so low, she might be seene
By all her wooers. In the doore, aloofe 505
(Entring the Hall grac'd with a goodly roofe)
She stood, in shade of gracefull vailes implide
About her beauties: on her either side
Her honor'd women. When, (to teares mov'd) thus
She chid the sacred Singer: 'Phemius, 510
You know a number more of these great deeds
Of Gods and men (that are the sacred seeds
And proper subjects of a Poet's song,
And those due pleasures that to men belong)
Besides these facts that furnish Troy's retreate. 515
Sing one of those to these, that round your seate
They may with silence sit, and taste their wine:
But cease this song, that through these eares of mine

Convey deserv'd occasion to my heart
Of endlesse sorrowes, of which the desert 520
In me unmeasur'd is past all these men,
So endlesse is the memorie I retaine,
And so desertfull is that memorie
Of such a man as hath a dignitie
So broad it spreds it selfe through all the pride 525
Of Greece and Argos.' To the Queene, replide
Inspir'd Telemachus: 'Why thus envies
My mother him that fits societies
With so much harmonie, to let him please
His owne mind in his will to honor these? 530
For these ingenuous and first sort of men
That do immediatly from Jove retaine
Their singing raptures are by Jove as well
Inspir'd with choice of what their songs impell.
Jove's will is free in it, and therefore theirs; 535
Nor is this man to blame that the repaires
The Greekes make homeward sings, for his fresh Muse
Men still most celebrate that sings most newes.
'And therefore in his note your eares employ:
For not Ulysses onely lost in Troy 540
The day of his returne, but numbers more
The deadly ruines of his fortunes bore.
Go you then in, and take your worke in hand,
Your web and distaffe, and your maids command
To plie their fit worke. Words to men are due, 545
And those reproving counsels you pursue,
And most to me of all men, since I beare
The rule of all things that are manag'd here.'
She went amazd away, and in her heart
Laid up the wisedome Pallas did impart 550
To her lov'd sonne so lately, turnd againe
Up to her chamber, and no more would raigne
In manly counsels. To her women she
Applied her sway, and to the wooers he
Began new orders, other spirits bewraid 555
Than those in spite of which the wooers swaid.
And (whiles his mother's teares still washt her eies,
Till gray Minerva did those teares surprise
With timely sleepe, and that her woo'rs did rouse
Rude Tumult up through all the shadie house, 560
Disposde to sleepe because their widow was),

'Ερίηρος ἀοιδός: Cantor, cuius tam apta est societas hominibus. 'Ανδράσιν ἀλφηστῇσιν. 'Αλφηστῇσιν *is an Epithete proper to Poets for their first finding out of Arts and documents tending to elocution and government, inspired onely by Jove: and are here called the first of men, since first they gave rules to manly life, and have their information immediatly from Jove (as Plato in* ῎Ιωνε *witnesseth). The word deduced from* ἄλφα, *which is taken for him,* qui primas teneat aliqua in re. *And will* ἀλφηστῇσιν *then be sufficiently exprest with* ingeniosis *than which no exposition goes further?*

Telemachus in new termes with the wooers.

Telemachus this new-given spirit did passe
On their old insolence: 'Ho! you that are
My mother's wooers! Much too high ye beare
Your petulant spirits! Sit, and, while ye may 565
Enjoy me in your banquets, see ye lay
These loud notes downe, nor do this man the wrong
(Because my mother hath dislikt his song)
To grace her interruption: tis a thing
Honest, and honourd too, to heare one sing 570
Numbers so like the Gods in elegance

'Ἠῶθεν, prima luce.

As this man flowes in. By the morne's first glance
I'le call ye all before me in a Court
That I may cleerly banish your resort
With all your rudenesse from these roofes of mine. 575
Away; and elsewhere in your feasts combine:
Consume your owne goods and make mutuall feast
At either's house. Or if ye still hold best,
And for your humors' more suffised fill,
To feed, to spoile (because unpunisht still) 580
On other findings, spoile; but here I call
Th' eternall Gods to witnesse, if it fall
In my wisht reach once to be dealing wreakes,
(By Jove's high bountie) these your present checks
To what I give in charge shall adde more reines 585
To my revenge hereafter, and the paines
Ye then must suffer shall passe all your pride
Ever to see redrest or qualifide.'

At this all bit their lips, and did admire
His words sent from him with such phrase and fire: 590
Which so much mov'd them, that Antinous
(Eupitheus' sonne) cried out: 'Telemachus!
The Gods, I thinke, have rapt thee to this height
Of elocution, and this great conceit
Of selfe-abilitie. We all may pray 595
That Jove invest not in this kingdome's sway
Thy forward forces, which I see put forth
A hote ambition in thee for thy birth.'

Upon this answer of Telemachus, because it hath so sodain a change, and is so farre let down from his late height of heate, altering and tempering so commandingly

'Be not offended,' he replide, 'if I
Shall say I would assume this emperie, 600
If Jove gave leave. You are not he that sings:
The rule of kingdomes is the worst of things.
Nor is it ill at all to sway a throne:
A man may quickly gaine possession
Of mightie riches, make a wondrous prise 605

his affections, I thought not amisse to insert here Spondanus' further Annotation, which is this: Prudenter Telemachus ioco, furorem Antinoi ac asperitatem emollijt. Nam ita dictum illius interpretatur, ut existimetur censere iocose illa etiam ab Antinoo adversum se pronunciata. Et primum Ironice se Regem esse exoptat propter commoda quæ Reges solent comitari. Ne tamen invidiam in se ambitionis concitet, testatur se regnum Ithacæ non ambire, mortuo Ulysse, cum id alij possidere queant se longe præstantiores ac digniores: hoc unum ait se moliri, ut propriarum ædium et bonorum solus sit dominus, ijs exclusis ac eiectis, qui vi illa occupare ac disperdere conantur.

Set of his vertues, but the dignities
That decke a King, there are enough beside
In this circumfluous Ile that want no pride
To thinke them worthy of, as yong as I,
And old as you are. An ascent so hie 610
My thoughts affect not: dead is he that held
Desert of vertue to have so exceld.
But of these turrets I will take on me
To be the absolute King, and reigne as free
As did my father, over all his hand 615
Left here is this house slaves to my command.'
 Eurymachus, the sonne of Polybus,
To this made this reply: 'Telemachus!
The Girlond of this kingdome let the knees
Of deitie runne for; but the faculties 620
This house is seasd of, and the turrets here,
Thou shalt be Lord of, nor shall any beare
The least part off of all thou doest possesse,
As long as this land is no wildernesse
Nor rul'd by out-lawes. But give these their passe, 625
And tell me, best of Princes, who he was
That guested here so late? From whence? And what
In any region bosted he his state?
His race? His countrie? Brought he any newes
Of thy returning Father? Or for dues 630
Of moneys to him made he fit repaire?
How sodainly he rusht into the aire,
Nor would sustaine to stay and make him knowne!
His Port shewd no debaucht companion.'
 He answerd: 'The returne of my lov'd Sire 635
Is past all hope; and should rude Fame inspire
From any place a flattring messenger
With newes of his survivall, he should beare
No least beliefe off from my desperate love.
Which if a sacred Prophet should approve 640
(Calld by my mother for her care's unrest),
It should not move me. For my late faire guest,
He was of old my Father's, touching here
From Sea-girt Taphos, and for name doth beare
Mentas, the sonne of wise Anchialus, 645
And governes all the Taphians, studious
Of Navigation.' This he said, but knew
It was a Goddesse. These againe withdrew
To dances, and attraction of the song.

And while their pleasures did the time prolong, 650
The sable Even descended, and did steepe
The lids of all men in desire of sleepe.
  Telemachus, into a roome built hie
Of his illustrous Court, and to the eie
Of circular prospect, to his bed ascended, 655
And in his mind much weightie thought contended.
Before him, Euryclea (that well knew
All the observance of a handmaid's due,
Daughter to Opis Pisenorides)
Bore two bright torches—who did so much please 660
Laertes in her prime that for the price
Of twentie Oxen he made merchandize
Of her rare beauties, and Love's equall flame
To her he felt as to his nuptiall Dame.
Yet never durst he mixe with her in bed, 665
So much the anger of his wife he fled.
She, now growne old, to yong Telemachus
Two torches bore, and was obsequious,
Past all his other maids, and did apply
Her service to him from his infancie. 670
His wel-built chamber reacht, she op't the dore;
He on his bed sat, the soft weeds he wore
Put off, and to the diligent old maid
Gave all, who fitly all in thicke folds laid,
And hung them on a beame-pin neare the bed, 675
That round about was rich embrodered.
Then made she haste forth from him, and did bring
The doore together with a silver ring,
And by a string a barre to it did pull.
He, laid, and coverd well with curled wooll 680
Woven in silke quilts, all night emploid his minde
About the taske that Pallas had design'd.

Finis libri primi Hom. Odyss.

THE SECOND BOOKE
of
HOMER'S ODYSSES

THE ARGUMENT

Telemachus to Court doth call
The wooers, and commands them all
To leave his house; and taking then
From wise Minerva ship and men,
And all things fit for him beside 5
That Euryclea could provide
For sea-rites till he found his Sire,
He hoists saile; when heaven stoopes his fire.

Another Argument

Βῆτα. *The old Maid's store*
The voyage cheres;
The ship leaves shore,
Minerva steres.

Now when with rosie fingers, th'early borne
And throwne through all the aire, appear'd the morne,
Ulysses' lov'd sonne from his bed appeard,
His weeds put on, and did about him gird
His sword that thwart his shoulders hung, and tied 5
To his faire feete faire shooes, and all parts plied
For speedie readinesse; who, when he trod
The open earth, to men shewd like a God.
The Heralds then he strait charg'd to consort
The curld-head Greekes with lowd calls to a Court. 10
They summon'd; th'other came in utmost haste;
Who all assembld and in one heape plac't,
He likewise came to councell, and did beare
In his faire hand his iron-headed speare.
Nor came alone, nor with men troopes prepar'd, 15

The Greekes called to councell by Telemachus.

But two fleete dogs made both his traine and Guard.
Pallas supplied with her high wisedome's grace
(That all men's wants supplies) State's painted face.
His entring presence all men did admire;
Who tooke seate in the high throne of his Sire, 20
To which the grave Peeres gave him reverend way—
Amongst whom an Ægyptian Heroe
(Crooked with age, and full of skill) begun
The speech to all; who had a loved sonne
That with divine Ulysses did ascend 25
His hollow fleete to Troy, to serve which end
He kept faire horse and was a man at Armes,
And in the cruell Cyclop's sterne alarmes
His life lost by him in his hollow cave,
Whose entrailes open'd his abhorred grave 30
And made of him (of all Ulysses' traine)
His latest supper, being latest slaine.
His name was Antiphus. And this old man,
This crooked growne, this wise Ægyptian,
Had three sonnes more, of which one, riotous, 35
A wooer was, and calld Eurynomus;
The other two tooke both his owne wisht course.
Yet both the best fates weighd not downe the worse,
But left the old man mindfull still of mone—
Who, weeping, thus bespake the Session: 40
'Heare, Ithacensians, all I fitly say.
Since our divine Ulysses' parting day
Never was councell calld, nor session;
And now by whom is this thus undergone?
Whom did Necessitie so much compell 45
Of yong or old? Hath any one heard tell
Of any coming armie, that he thus now
May openly take boldnesse to avow,
First having heard it? Or will any here
Some motion for the publicke good preferre? 50
Some worth of note there is in this command,
And, me thinkes, it must be some good man's hand
That's put to it, that either hath direct
Meanes to assist, or, for his good affect,
Hopes to be happie in the proofe he makes— 55
And that Jove grant, what ere he undertakes.'
Telemachus (rejoycing much to heare
The good hope and opinion men did beare
Of his yong actions) no longer sat,

Telemachus proposeth his estate to the Greekes.

But longd t'approve what this man pointed at, 60
And make his first proofe in a cause so good.
And in the Councel's chiefe place up he stood,
When strait Pisenor (Herald to his Sire,
And learnd in counsels) felt his heart on fire
To heare him speake, and put into his hand 65
The Scepter that his Father did command.
Then (to the old Ægyptian turnd) he spoke:
'Father, not farre he is that undertooke
To call this councell; whom you soone shall know.
My selfe, whose wrongs my griefes will make me show, 70
Am he that author'd this assembly here.
Nor have I heard of any armie neare,
Of which, being first told, I might iterate,
Nor for the publicke good can aught relate.
Onely mine owne affaires all this procure, 75
That in my house a double ill endure—
One, having lost a Father so renownd,
Whose kind rule once with your command was crownd;
The other is what much more doth augment
His weightie losse, the ruine imminent 80
Of all my house by it, my goods all spent.
And of all this the wooers, that are sonnes
To our chiefe Peeres, are the Confusions,
Importuning my Mother's mariage
Against her will; nor dares their bloud's bold rage 85
Go to Icarius', her father's, Court,
That, his will askt in kind and comely sort,
He may endow his daughter with a dowre,
And she, consenting, at his pleasure's powre
Dispose her to a man that (thus behav'd) 90
May have fit grace, and see her honor sav'd;
But these in none but my house all their lives
Resolve to spend, slaughtring my sheepe and beeves,
And with my fattest goates lay feast on feast,
My generous wine consuming as they list. 95
A world of things they spoile, here wanting one
That like Ulysses quickly could set gone
These peace-plagues from his house, that spoile like warre—
Whom my powres are unfit to urge so farre,
My selfe immartiall. But had I the powre, 100
My will should serve me to exempt this houre
From out my life time. For, past patience,
Base deeds are done here, that exceed defence

Of any honor. Falling is my house,
Which you should shame to see so ruinous. 105
Reverence the censures that all good men give
That dwell about you, and for feare to live
Exposde to heaven's wrath (that doth ever pay
Paines, for joye's forfait), even by Jove I pray,
Or Themis, both which powres have to restraine 110
Or gather Councels, that ye will abstaine
From further spoile, and let me oncly waste
In that most wretched griefe I have embrac't
For my lost Father. And though I am free
From meriting your outrage, yet, if he 115
(Good man) hath ever with a hostile heart
Done ill to any Greeke, on me convert
Your like hostilitie and vengeance take
Of his ill on my life, and all these make
Joyne in that justice; but to see abusde 120
Those goods that do none ill, but being ill usde,
Exceeds all right. Yet better tis for me
My whole possessions and my rents to see
Consum'd by you than lose my life and all;
For on your rapine a revenge may fall 125
While I live, and so long I may complaine
About the Citie, till my goods againe
(Oft askt) may be with all amends repaid.
But in the meane space your mis-rule hath laid
Griefes on my bosome, that can onely speake 130
And are denied the instant powre of wreake.'
This said, his Scepter gainst the ground he threw,
And teares still'd from him; which mov'd all the crew.
The Court strooke silent, not a man did dare
To give a word that might offend his eare. 135
Antinous onely in this sort replied:

Antinous to Telemachus.

'High-spoken, and of spirit unpacified,
How have you sham'd us in this speech of yours?
Will you brand us for an offence not ours?
Your mother (first in craft) is first in cause. 140
Three yeares are past, and neare the fourth now drawes,
Since first she mocked the Peeres Achaian.
All she made hope, and promist every man,
Sent for us ever, left love's shew in nought,
But in her heart conceald another thought. 145
Besides, (as curious in her craft) her loome

The wile of Penelope to her wooers.

She with a web charg'd, hard to overcome,
And thus bespake us: "Youths that seeke my bed,
Since my divine Spouse rests among the dead,
Hold on your suites but till I end, at most, 150
This funerall weed, lest what is done be lost.
Besides, I purpose that when th'austere fate
Of bitter death shall take into his state
Laertes the Heroe, it shall decke
His royall corse, since I should suffer checke 155
In ill report of every common dame,
If one so rich should shew in death his shame."
This speech she usde, and this did soone perswade
Our gentle mindes. But this a worke she made

Telam Penelopes retexere—Proverbium.

So hugely long, undoing still in night 160
(By torches) all she did by daye's broade light,
That three yeares her deceit div'd past our view,
And made us thinke that all she faind was true.
But when the fourth yeare came, and those slie houres
That still surprise at length Dames' craftiest powres, 165
One of her women that knew all disclosde
The secret to us—that she still unlosde
Her whole daie's faire affaire in depth of night.
And then no further she could force her sleight,
But, of necessitie, her worke gave end. 170
And thus, by me, doth every other friend
Professing love to her reply to thee—
That even thy selfe, and all Greeks else, may see
That we offend not in our stay, but shee.
To free thy house then, send her to her Sire, 175
Commanding that her choice be left entire
To his election, and one settl'd will.
Nor let her vexe with her illusions still
Her friends that woo her, standing on her wit,
Because wise Pallas hath given wiles to it, 180
So full of Art, and made her understand
All workes in faire skill of a Ladie's hand.
But (for her working mind) we reade of none
Of all the old world, in which Greece hath showne
Her rarest peeces, that could equall her: 185
Tyro, Alcmena and Mycena were
To hold comparison in no degree
(For solide braine) with wise Penelope.
And yet in her delayes of us she showes
No profit's skill, with all the wit she owes; 190

For all this time thy goods and victuals go
To utter ruine, and shall ever so
While thus the Gods her glorious mind dispose.
Glorie her selfe may gaine, but thou shalt lose
Thy longings even for necessary food, 195
For we will never go where lies our good,
Nor any other where, till this delay
She puts on all she quits with th'endlesse stay
Of some one of us, that to all the rest
May give free farewell with his nuptiall feast.' 200

Telemachus to Antinous.

The wise yong Prince replide: 'Antinous!
I may by no meanes turne out of my house
Her that hath brought me forth and nourisht me.
Besides, if quicke or dead my Father be
In any region, yet abides in doubt. 205
And twill go hard (my meanes being so runne out)
To tender to Icarius againe
(If he againe my mother must maintaine
In her retreate) the dowre she brought with her.
And then a double ill it will conferre, 210
Both from my Father and from God, on me,
When (thrust out of her house) on her bent knee
My Mother shall the horrid Furies raise
With imprecations, and all men dispraise
My part in her exposure. Never then 215
Will I performe this counsell. If your splene
Swell at my courses, once more I command
Your absence from my house. Some other's hand
Charge with your banquets. On your owne goods eate,
And either other mutually intreate 220
At either of your houses with your feast.
But if ye still esteeme more sweete and best
Another's spoile, so you still wreaklesse live,
Gnaw (vermine-like) things sacred, no lawes give
To your devouring—it remaines that I 225
Invoke each ever-living Deitie,
And vow, if Jove shall daigne in any date
Powre of like paines for pleasures so past rate,
From thenceforth looke, where ye have reveld so
Unwreakt, your ruines all shall undergo.' 230

The word is κείρετε—κείρω *signifying,* insatiabili quadam edacitate voro.

Augurium.

Thus spake Telemachus, t'assure whose threat
Farre-seeing Jove upon their pinions set
Two Eagles from the high browes of a hill,
That, mounted on the winds, together still

Their strokes extended. But, arriving now 235
Amidst the Councell, over every brow
Shooke their thicke wings, and (threatning death's cold feares)
Their neckes and cheekes tore with their eager Seres.
Then on the Court's right-hand away they flew,
Above both Court and Citie—with whose view 240
And studie what events they might foretell
The Councell into admiration fell.

Halitherses an Augur.

The old Heroe, Halitherses then,
The sonne of Nestor, that of all old men
(His Peeres in that Court) onely could foresee 245
By flight of fowles man's fixed destinie,
Twixt them and their amaze this interposde:
'Heare, Ithacensians, all your doubts disclosde.
The wooers most are toucht in this ostent,
To whom are dangers great and imminent. 250
For now not long more shall Ulysses beare
Lacke of his most lov'd, but fils some place neare,
Addressing to these wooers Fate and Death.
And many more this mischiefe menaceth
Of us inhabiting this famous Ile. 255
Let us consult yet, in this long forewhile,
How to our selves we may prevent this ill.
Let these men rest secure and revell still—
Though they might find it safer, if with us
They would in time prevent what threats them thus, 260
Since not without sure triall I foretell
These coming stormes, but know their issue well.
For to Ulysses all things have event
As I foretold him, when for Ilion went
The whole Greeke fleete together and with them 265
Th'abundant in all counsels tooke the streame.
I told him that, when much ill he had past
And all his men were lost, he should at last
The twentith yeare turne home, to all unknowne—
All which effects are to perfection growne.' 270
Eurymachus, the sonne of Polybus,
Opposde this man's presage, and answerd thus:

Eurymachus excepts against the prophecie.

'Hence, Great in yeares; go prophecie at home;
Thy children teach to shun their ils to come.
In these superiour farre to thee am I. 275
A world of fowles beneath the Sunne-beames flie
That are not fit t'enforme a prophecie.
Besides, Ulysses perisht long ago—

And would thy fates to thee had destin'd so,
Since so thy so much prophecie had spar'd 280
Thy wronging of our rights, which, for reward
Expected home with thee, hath summon'd us
Within the anger of Telemachus.
But this will I presage, which shall be true,
If any sparke of anger chance t'ensue 285
Thy much old art in these deepe Auguries
In this yong man, incensed by thy lies,
Even to himselfe his anger shall conferre
The greater anguish, and thine owne ends erre
From all their objects: and, besides, thine age 290
Shall feele a paine to make thee curse presage
With worthy cause, for it shall touch thee neare.
But I will soone give end to all our feare,
Preventing whatsoever chance can fall,
In my suite to the yong Prince for us all, 295
To send his mother to her father's house,
That he may sort her out a worthy spouse,
And such a dowre bestow as may befit
One lov'd to leave her friends and follow it.
Before which course be, I beleeve that none 300
Of all the Greekes will cease th'ambition
Of such a match. For, chance what can to us,
We no man feare—no, not Telemachus,
Though ne're so greatly spoken. Nor care we
For any threats of austere prophecie 305
Which thou, old dotard, vantst of so in vaine.
And thus shalt thou in much more hate remaine,
For still the Gods shall beare their ill expence,
Nor ever be disposde by competence,
Till with her nuptials she dismisse our suites. 310
Our whole lives' dayes shall sow hopes for such fruites.
Her vertues we contend to, nor will go
To any other, be she never so
Worthy of us, and all the worth we owe.'

Telemachus to the wooers.

He answerd him: 'Eurymachus, and all 315
Ye generous wooers, now, in generall,
I see your brave resolves, and will no more
Make speech of these points, and, much lesse, implore.
It is enough that all the Grecians here,
And all the Gods besides, just witnesse beare 320
What friendly premonitions have bene spent
On your forbearance, and their vaine event.

Yet with my other friends let love prevaile
To fit me with a vessell free of saile,
And twentie men, that may divide to me 325
My readie passage through the yeelding sea.
For Sparta, and Amathoan Pylos' shore
I now am bound, in purpose to explore
My long-lackt Father and to trie if Fame
(Or Jove, most author of man's honourd name) 330
With his returne and life may glad mine eare,
Though toild in that proofe I sustaine a yeare.
If dead I heare him, nor of more state, here
(Retir'd to my lov'd countrie) I will rere
A Sepulcher to him and celebrate 335
Such royall parent-rites as fits his state.
And then my mother to a Spouse dispose.'

This said, he sat; and to the rest arose
Mentor, that was Ulysses' chosen friend,
To whom, when he set forth, he did commend 340
His compleate family, and whom he willd
To see the mind of his old Sire fulfild,
All things conserving safe till his retreate—
Who (tender of his charge, and seeing so set
In sleight care of their King his subjects there, 345
Suffering his sonne so much contempt to beare),
Thus gravely and with zeale to him began:

Mentor for Telemachus.

'No more let any Scepter-bearing man
Benevolent, or milde, or humane be,
Nor in his minde forme acts of pietie, 350
But ever feed on blood, and facts unjust
Commit even to the full swinge of his lust,
Since of divine Ulysses no man now
Of all his subjects any thought doth show.
All whom he governd, and became to them 355
(Rather than one that wore a diadem)
A most indulgent father. But (for all
That can touch me) within no envie fall
These insolent wooers, that in violent kind
Commit things foule by th'ill wit of the mind, 360
And, with the hazard of their heads, devoure
Ulysses' house, since his returning houre
They hold past hope. But it affects me much,
Ye dull plebeians, that all this doth touch
Your free States nothing, who (strooke dumbe) afford 365
These wooers not so much wreake as a word,

Though few, and you with onely number might
Extinguish to them the prophaned light.'

Leocritus to Mentor.

Evenor's sonne, Leocritus, replide:
'Mentor! the railer, made a foole with pride! 370
What language giv'st thou that would quiet us
With putting us in storme, exciting thus
The rout against us?—who, though more than we,
Should find it is no easie victorie
To drive men habited in feast from feasts— 375
No, not if Ithacus himselfe such guests
Should come and find so furnishing his Court
And hope to force them from so sweete a fort.
His wife should little joy in his arrive,
Though much she wants him: for, where she alive 380
Would hers enjoy, there Death should claime his rights:
He must be conquerd that with many fights.
Thou speakst unfit things. To their labours then
Disperse these people, and let these two men,
Mentor and Halitherses, that so boast 385
From the beginning to have governd most
In friendship of the Father, to the sonne
Confirme the course he now affects to runne.
But my mind sayes that, if he would but use
A little patience, he should here heare newes 390
Of all things that his wish would understand,
But no good hope for of the course in hand.'

This said, the Councell rose, when every Peere
And all the people in dispersion were
To houses of their owne; the wooers yet 395
Made to Ulysses' house their old retreat.

Telemachus, apart from all the prease,
Prepar'd to shore, and (in the aged seas
His faire hands washt) did thus to Pallas pray:

Telemachus prayes to Pallas.

'Heare me, O Goddesse, that but yesterday 400
Didst daigne accesse to me at home and lay
Grave charge on me to take ship and enquire
Along the darke seas for mine absent Sire—
Which all the Greekes oppose, amongst whom, most
Those that are proud still at another's cost, 405
Past measure and the civill rights of men,
My mother's wooers, my repulse maintaine.'

Thus spake he praying, when close to him came
Pallas, resembling Mentor both in frame
Of voice and person, and advisde him thus: 410

Minerva in the person of Mentor, exhorts to the voyage.

'Those wooers well might know, Telemachus,
Thou wilt not ever weake and childish be,
If to thee be instilld the facultie
Of mind and bodie that thy Father grac't.
And if (like him) there be in thee enchac't 415
Vertue to give words works, and works their end,
This voyage that to them thou didst commend
Shall not so quickly, as they idly weene,
Be vaine, or given up for their opposite spleene.
But if Ulysses nor Penelope 420
Were thy true parents, I then hope in thee
Of no more urging thy attempt in hand;
For few that rightly bred on both sides stand
Are like their parents, many that are worse,
And most-few, better. Those then that the nurse 425
Or mother call true-borne, yet are not so,
Like worthy Sires much lesse are like to grow.
But thou shewst now that in thee fades not quite
Thy Father's wisedome, and that future light
Shall therefore shew thee farre from being unwise 430
Or toucht with staine of bastard cowardize.
Hope therefore sayes that thou wilt to the end
Pursue the brave act thou didst erst intend.
But for the foolish wooers, they bewray
They neither counsell have nor soule, since they 435
Are neither wise nor just, and so must needs
Rest ignorant how blacke above their heads
Fate hovers, holding Death, that one sole day
Will make enough to make them all away.
For thee, the way thou wishest shall no more 440
Flie thee a step; I that have bene before
Thy Father's friend thine likewise now will be,
Provide thy ship my selfe, and follow thee.
Go thou then home, and sooth each wooer's vaine,
But under hand fit all things for the Maine— 445
Wine, in as strong and sweete casks as you can,
And meale, the very marrow of a man,
Which put in good sure lether sacks, and see
That with sweete foode sweete vessels still agree.
I from the people straite will presse for you 450
Free voluntaries, and, for ships, enow
Sea-circl'd Ithaca containes both new
And old built; all which I'le exactly view
And chuse what one soever most doth please;

Which riggd, wee'l strait lanch and assay the seas.' 455
This spake Jove's daughter, Pallas; whose voice heard,
No more Telemachus her charge deferd,
But hasted home, and, sad at heart, did see
Amidst his Hall, th'insulting wooers flea
Goates and rost swine. Mongst whom, Antinous 460
Carelesse (discovering in Telemachus
His grudge to see them) laught, met, tooke his hand,

Antinous to Telemachus.

And said: 'High spoken! with the mind so mannd!
Come, do as we do; put not up your spirits
With these low trifles, nor our loving merits 465
In gall of any hatefull purpose steepe,
But eate egregiously, and drinke as deepe.
The things thou thinkst on, all at full shall be
By th'Achives thought on, and performd to thee—
Ship and choise Oares that in a trice will land 470
Thy hastie Fleete on heav'nly Pylos' sand,
And at the fame of thy illustrous Sire.'

Telemachus answers.

He answerd: 'Men whom Pride doth so inspire
Are no fit consorts for an humble guest,
Nor are constraind men merrie at their feast. 475
Is't not enough that all this time ye have
Op't in your entrailes my chiefe goods a grave,
And while I was a child made me partake?
My now more growth more grown my mind doth make.
And (hearing speake more judging men than you) 480
Perceive how much I was misgovernd now.
I now will trie if I can bring ye home
An ill Fate to consort you, if it come
From Pylos, or amongst the people here.
But thither I resolve, and know that there 485
I shall not touch in vaine. Nor will I stay,
Though in a merchant's ship I stere my way—
Which shewes in your sights best, since me ye know
Incapable of ship or men to row.'
This said, his hand he coily snatcht away 490
From forth Antinous' hand. The rest the day
Spent through the house with banquets, some with jests
And some with railings dignifying their feasts.
To whom a jest-proud youth the wit began:

The wit of the wooers upon the purpose of Telemachus to seeke his Father.

'Telemachus will kill us every man. 495
From Sparta or the very Pylian sand
He will raise aides to his impetuous hand.
O he affects it strangely! Or he meanes

To search Ephyra's fat shores and from thence
Bring deathfull poisons, which amongst our bowls 500
Will make a generall shipwracke of our soules.'
Another said: 'Alas, who knowes but he
Once gone, and erring like his Sire at sea,
May perish like him farre from aide of friends?
And so he makes us worke, for all the ends 505
Left of his goods here we shall share, the house
Left to his mother and her chosen Spouse.'
Thus they—while he a roome ascended, hie
And large, built by his Father, where did lie
Gold and brasse heapt up, and in coffers were 510
Rich robes, great store of odorous oiles, and there
Stood Tuns of sweete old wines along the wall,
Neate and divine drinke, kept to cheare withall
Ulysses' old heart, if he turnd againe
From labors fatall to him to sustaine. 515
The doores of Planke were, their close exquisite,
Kept with a double key, and day and night
A woman lockt within, and that was she
Who all trust had for her sufficiencie,
Old Euryclea (one of Opis' race, 520
Sonne to Pisenor, and in passing grace
With gray Minerva). Her, the Prince did call,
Telemachus to Euryclea.
And said: 'Nurse! draw me the most sweete of all
The wine thou keepst, next that which for my Sire
Thy care reserves, in hope he shall retire. 525
Twelve vessels fill me forth, and stop them well.
Then into well-sewd sacks, of fine ground meale
Powre twentie measures. Nor to any one
But thou thy selfe let this designe be knowne.
All this see got together; I it all 530
In night will fetch off, when my mother shall
Ascend her high roome and for sleepe prepare.
Sparta and Pylos I must see, in care
To find my Father.' Out Euryclea cried,
Euryclea's answer.
And askt with teares: 'Why is your mind applied, 535
Deare sonne, to this course? Whither will you go?
So farre off leave us, and beloved so,
So onely? And the sole hope of your race?
Royall Ulysses, farre from the embrace
Of his kind countrie, in a land unknowne 540
Is dead, and you from your lov'd countrie gone,
The wooers will with some deceit assay

To your destruction, making then their prey
Of all your goods. Where in your owne y'are strong,
Make sure abode. It fits not you, so yong, 545
To suffer so much by the aged seas
And erre in such a waylesse wildernesse.'

Telemachus comforts Euryclea.

'Be chear'd, lov'd nurse,' said he, 'for not without
The will of God go my attempts about.
Sweare therefore not to wound my mother's eares 550
With word of this before from heaven appeares
Th'eleventh or twelfth light, or her selfe shall please
To aske of me, or heares me put to seas—
Lest her faire bodie with her woe be wore.'
To this the great oath of the Gods she swore; 555
Which having sworne, and of it every due
Performd to full, to vessels wine she drew,
And into well-sewd sacks powr'd foodie meale.
In meane time he (with cunning to conceale
All thought of this from others) himselfe bore 560
In broade house, with the wooers, as before.

The care of Minerva for Telemachus.

Then grey-eyd Pallas other thoughts did owne,
And (like Telemachus) trod through the Towne,
Commanding all his men in th'even to be
Aboord his ship. Againe then question'd she 565
Noemon (fam'd for aged Phronius' sonne)
About his ship, who all things to be done
Assur'd her freely should. The Sunne then set,
And sable shadowes slid through every streete,
When forth they lancht, and soone aboord did bring 570
All Armes and choice of every needfull thing
That fits a well-riggd ship. The Goddesse then
Stood in the Port's extreame part, where her men
(Nobly appointed) thicke about her came,
Whose every breast she did with spirit enflame. 575
Yet still fresh projects laid the grey-eyd Dame.
Strait to the house she hasted, and sweete sleepe
Powr'd on each wooer, which so laid in steepe
Their drowsie temples that each brow did nod
As all were drinking; and each hand his lode 580
(The cup) let fall. All start up, and to bed,
Nor more would watch when sleepe so surfeted
Their leaden ey-lids. Then did Pallas call
Telemachus (in bodie, voice, and all
Resembling Mentor) from his native nest, 585
And said that all his arm'd men were addrest

To use their Oares, and all expected now
He should the spirit of a souldier show.
'Come then,' said she, 'no more let us deferre
Our honor'd action.' Then she tooke on her 590
A ravisht spirit and led as she did leape,
And he her most haste tooke out, step by step.
Arriv'd at sea and ship, they found ashore
The souldiers, that their fashiond long haire wore,
Telemachus to his souldiers.
To whom the Prince said: 'Come, my friends, let's bring 595
Our voyage's provision: everything
Is heapt together in our Court, and none
(No, not my mother, nor her maids) but one
Knowes our intention.' This exprest, he led;
The souldiers close together followed, 600
And all together brought aboord their store.
Aboord the Prince went, Pallas still before
Sat at the Sterne, he close to her, the men
Up hasted after. He and Pallas then
Put from the shore. His souldiers then he bad 605
See all their Armes fit, which they heard and had.
Navigatur.
A beechen Mast then in the hollow base
They put, and hoisted, fixt it in his place
With cables, and with well-wreath'd halsers hoise
Their white sailes, which gray Pallas now employes 610
With full and fore-gales through the darke deep maine.
κῦμα πορφύρεον.
The purple waves (so swift cut) roar'd againe
Against the ship sides, that now ranne and plowd
The rugged seas up. Then the men bestowd
Their Armes about the ship, and sacrifice 615
With crownd wine cups to th'endlesse Deities
They offerd up. Of all yet thron'd above,
They most observ'd the grey-eyd seed of Jove,
Who from the evening till the morning rose,
And all day long, their voyage did dispose. 620

Finis libri secundi Hom. Odyss.

THE THIRD BOOKE
of
HOMER'S ODYSSES

THE ARGUMENT

Pallas.

Telemachus and heav'ns wise Dame,
That never husband had, now came
To Nestor, who his either guest
Receiv'd at the religious feast
He made to Neptune on his shore. 5
And there told what was done before
The Troyan turrets, and the state
Of all the Greekes since Ilion's fate.
This booke these three of greatest place
Doth serve with many a varied grace. 10
Which past, Minerva takes her leave.
Whose state when Nestor doth perceive,
With sacrifice he makes it knowne,
Where many a pleasing rite is showne.
Which done, Telemachus had gaind 15
A chariot of him, who ordaind
Pisistratus, his sonne, his guide
To Sparta, and when starrie eyd
The ample heav'n began to be,
All house-rites to affoord them free 20
(In Pheris) Diocles did please,
His sirname Ortilochides.

Vid. Minerva, Nestor and Telemachus.

Another Argument

Γάμμα. *Ulysses' sonne*
With Nestor lies;
To Sparta gone,
Thence Pallas flies.

The Sunne now left the great and goodly Lake,
And to the firme heav'n bright ascent did make,

To shine as well upon the mortall birth
Inhabiting the plowd life-giving earth
As on the ever-tredders upon Death. 5
And now to Pylos, that so garnisheth
Her selfe with buildings, old Neleus' towne,
The Prince and Goddesse come, had strange sights showne—
For on the Marine shore the people there
To Neptune, that the Azure lockes doth weare, 10
Beeves that were wholy blacke gave holy flame.
Nine seates of State they made to his high name,
And every Seate set with five hundred men,
And each five hundred was to furnish then
With nine blacke Oxen every sacred Seate. 15
These of the entrailes onely pleasd to eate,
And to the God enflam'd the fleshie thies.
By this time Pallas, with the sparkling eies,
And he she led within the haven bore,
Strooke saile, cast anchor, and trod both the shore, 20
She first, he after. Then said Pallas: 'Now
No more befits thee the least bashfull brow;
T'embolden which this act is put on thee
To seeke thy Father, both at shore and sea,
And learne in what Clime he abides so close, 25
Or in the powre of what Fate doth repose.
'Come then; go right to Nestor; let us see,
If in his bosome any counsell be
That may informe us. Pray him not to trace
The common courtship and to speake in grace 30
Of the Demander, but to tell the truth—
Which will delight him—and commend thy youth
For such prevention, for he loves no lies,
Nor will report them, being truly wise.'
He answerd: 'Mentor! how alas shall I 35
Present my selfe, how greete his gravitie?
My youth by no meanes that ripe forme affords
That can digest my mind's instinct in words
Wise and beseeming th'eares of one so sage.
Youth of most hope blush to use words with Age.' 40
She said: 'Thy mind will some conceit impresse,
And something God will prompt thy towardnesse.
For I suppose thy birth and breeding too
Were not in spite of what the Gods could do.'
This said, she swiftly went before, and he 45
Her steps made guides, and followd instantly.

Minerva to Telemachus.

Telemachus to Minerva.

When soone they reacht the Pylian throngs and seates,
Where Nestor with his sonnes sate, and the meates
That for the feast serv'd round about them were
Adherents dressing, all their sacred cheare 50
Being rost and boyld meates. When the Pylians saw
These strangers come, in thrust did all men draw
About their entrie, tooke their hands, and praid
They both would sit—their entrie first assaid
By Nestor's sonne, Pisistratus, in grace 55
Of whose repaire he gave them honor'd place
Betwixt his Sire and brother Thrasymed,
Who sate at feast on soft Fels that were spred
Along the sea sands, kerv'd, and reacht to them
Parts of the inwards, and did make a streame 60
Of spritely wine into a golden boule,
Which to Minerva, with a gentle soule
He gave, and thus spake: 'Ere you eate, faire guest,
Invoke the Sea's King, of whose sacred feast
Your travell hither makes ye partners now; 65
When (sacrificing as becomes) bestow
This boule of sweete wine on your friend, that he
May likewise use these rites of pietie—
For I suppose his youth doth prayers use,
Since all men need the Gods. But you I chuse 70
First in this cup's disposure, since his yeares
Seeme short of yours, who more like me appeares.'
Thus gave he her the cup of pleasant wine;
And since a wise and just man did designe
The golden boule first to her free receit, 75
Even to the Goddesse it did adde delight,
Who thus invokt: *'Heare, thou whose vast embrace*
Enspheres the whole earth, nor disdaine thy grace
To us that aske it in performing this.
To Nestor first, and these faire sonnes of his, 80
Vouchsafe all honor; and, next them, bestow
On all these Pylians, that have offerd now
This most renowmed Hecatomb to thee,
Remuneration fit for them, and free;
And lastly daigne Telemachus and me 85
(The worke performd for whose effect we came)
Our safe returne both with our ship and fame.'
Thus praid she, and her selfe her selfe obaid,
In th'end performing all for which she praid.
And now to pray, and do as she had done, 90

They are received as guests.

The humanitie of Pisistratus to strangers.

Minerva's grace.

She gave the faire round boule t'Ulysses' sonne.
The meate then drest and drawne, and serv'd t'each guest,
They celebrated a most sumptuous feast,
When (appetite to wine and food allaid)
Horse-taming Nestor then began, and said: 95
Nestor to the strangers. 'Now life's desire is serv'd as farre as fare,
Time fits me to enquire what guests these are.
Faire guests, what are ye, and for what Coast tries
Your ship the moist deepes? For fit merchandize?
Or rudely coast ye like our men of prize, 100
The rough seas tempting, desperatly erring,
The ill of others in their good conferring?'
The wise Prince now his boldnesse did begin,
For Pallas' selfe had hardned him within,
By this device of travell, to explore 105
His absent Father; which two Girlonds wore—
His good, by manage of his spirits, and then
To gaine him high grace, in th'accounts of men.
Telemachus answers. 'O Nestor! still in whom Neleus lives,
And all the glorie of the Greeks survives! 110
You aske from whence we are, and I relate.
From Ithaca (whose seate is situate
Where Neius, the renowmed Mountaine, reares
His haughtie forehead and the honor beares
To be our Sea-marke) we assaid the waves. 115
The businesse, I must tell, our owne good craves,
And not the publicke. I am come t'enquire
If in the fame that best men doth inspire
Of my most-suffering Father I may heare
Some truth of his estate now, who did beare 120
The name (being joynd in fight with you alone)
To even with earth the height of Ilion.
Of all men else that any name did beare
And fought for Troy, the severall ends we heare;
But his death Jove keepes from the world unknowne, 125
The certaine fame thereof being told by none—
If on the Continent by enemies slaine,
Or with the waves eat of the ravenous Maine.
For his love tis that to your knees I sue,
That you would please out of your owne cleare view 130
T'assure his sad end, or say if your eare
Hath heard of the unhappie wanderer,
To too much sorrow whom his mother bore.
You, then, by all your bounties I implore

(If ever to you deed or word hath stood, 135
By my good Father promist, renderd good
Amongst the Troyans, where ye both have tried
The Grecian sufferance) that in nought applied
To my respect or pitie you will glose,
But unclothd Truth to my desires disclose.' 140

Nestor to Telemachus.

'O my much lov'd,' said he, 'since you renew
Remembrance of the miseries that grew
Upon our still-in-strength-opposing Greece
Amongst Troy's people, I must touch a peece
Of all our woes there, either in the men 145
Achilles brought by sea and led to gaine
About the Country, or in us that fought
About the Citie, where to death were brought
All our chiefe men, as many as were there.
There Mars-like Ajax lies; Achilles there; 150

Patroclus.

There the in-counsell-like-the-Gods, his friend;
There my deare sonne Antilochus tooke end,
Past measure swift of foote, and staid in fight.
A number more that ils felt infinite:
Of which to reckon all, what mortall man 155
(If five or sixe yeares you should stay here) can
Serve such enquirie? You would backe againe,
Affected with unsufferable paine,
Before you heard it. Nine yeares siegd we them
With all the depth and sleight of stratagem 160
That could be thought. Ill knit to ill, past end:
Yet still they toild us, nor would yet Jove send
Rest to our labors—nor will scarcely yet.
But no man liv'd that would in publicke set
His wisedome by Ulysses' policie 165
(As thought his equall): so excessively
He stood superiour all wayes. If you be
His sonne indeed, mine eyes even ravish me
To admiration. And, in all consent,
Your speech puts on his speeche's ornament, 170
Nor would one say that one so yong could use
(Unlesse his sonne) a Rhetorique so profuse.
And while we liv'd together, he and I
Never in speech maintaind diversitie—
Nor set in counsell but (by one soule led) 175
With spirit and prudent counsell furnished
The Greeks at all houres that, with fairest course,
What best became them they might put in force.

But when Troy's high Towres we had leveld thus,
We put to sea, and God divided us. 180
And then did Jove our sad retreat devise;
For all the Greeks were neither just nor wise,
And therefore many felt so sharpe a fate,
Sent from Minerva's most pernicious hate,
Whose mightie Father can do fearfull things. 185
By whose helpe she betwixt the brother Kings
Let fall Contention; who in councell met (De Græcorum dissidio.)
In vaine, and timelesse, when the Sunne was set,
And all the Greeks calld, that came chargd with wine.
Yet then the Kings would utter their designe, 190
And why they summond. Menelaus, he
Put all in mind of home, and cried, "To sea!"
But Agamemnon stood on contraries,
Whose will was they should stay and sacrifise
Whole Hecatombs to Pallas, to forgo 195
Her high wrath to them. Foole, that did not know
She would not so be wonne—for not with ease
Th'eternall Gods are turnd from what they please.
So they (divided) on foule language stood.
The Greekes in huge rout rose, their wine-heate bloud 200
Two wayes affecting. And that night's sleepe too
We turnd to studying either other's wo—
When Jove besides made readie woes enow.
Morne came, we lancht, and in our ships did stow
Our goods, and faire-girt women. Halfe our men 205 (Discors navigatio Græcorum.)
The people's guide, Atrides, did containe,
And halfe (being now aboord) put forth to sea.
A most free gale gave all ships prosperous way.
God settld then the huge whale-bearing lake,
And Tenedos we reacht, where, for time's sake, 210
We did divine rites to the Gods. But Jove
(Inexorable still) bore yet no love
To our returne, but did againe excite
A second sad Contention, that turnd quite
A great part of us backe to sea againe— 215
Which were th'abundant-in-all-counsels men,
Your matchlesse Father, who (to gratifie
The great Atrides) backe to him did flie.
But I fled all, with all that followd me,
Because I knew God studied miserie 220
To hurle amongst us. With me likewise fled
Martiall Tydides. I the men he led

Gat to go with him. Winds our fleete did bring
To Lesbos, where the yellow-headed King,
Though late, yet found us, as we put to choise 225
A tedious voyage—if we saile should hoise
Above rough Chius (left on our left hand)
To th'Ile of Psyria, or that rugged land
Saile under, and for windie Mimas stere.
We askt of God that some ostent might cleare 230
Our cloudie businesse, who gave us signe
And charge that all should (in a middle line)
The sea cut for Eubœa, that with speed
Our long-sustaind infortune might be freed.
Then did a whistling wind begin to rise, 235
And swiftly flew we through the fishie skies
Till to Geræstus we in night were brought,
Where (through the broad sea since we safe had wrought)
At Neptune's altars many solid thies
Of slaughterd buls we burnd for sacrifise. 240
'The fourth day came, when Tydeus' sonne did greete
The haven of Argos with his complete Fleete.
But I for Pylos strait ster'd on my course,
Nor ever left the wind his fore-right force,
Since God fore-sent it first. And thus I came, 245
Deare sonne, to Pylos uninformd by fame,
Nor know one sav'd by Fate, or overcome,
Whom I have heard of since (set here at home)
As fits thou shalt be taught, nought left unshowne.
'The expert speare-men, every Myrmidon, 250
(Led by the brave heire of the mightie-soul'd
Unpeerd Achilles) safe of home got hold;
Safe Philoctetes, Pœan's famous seed;
And safe Idomeneus his men led
To his home, Crete, who fled the armed field— 255
Of whom yet none the sea from him withheld.
'Atrides (you have both heard, though ye be
His farre off dwellers) what an end had he,
Done by Ægisthus to a bitter death—
Who miserably paid for forced breath, 260
Atrides leaving a good sonne, that dide
In bloud of that deceitfull parricide
His wreakfull sword. And thou my friend (as he
For this hath his fame) the like spirit in thee
Assume at all parts. Faire and great I see 265
Thou art in all hope; make it good to th'end,

That after-times as much may thee commend.'

Telemachus Nestori. He answerd: 'O thou greatest grace of Greece,
Orestes made that wreake his master peece,
And him the Greeks will give a master praise, 270
Verse finding him to last all after daies.
And would to God the Gods would favour me
With his performance—that my injurie
Done by my mother's wooers, being so foule,
I might revenge upon their every soule, 275
Who (pressing me with contumelies) dare
Such things as past the powre of utterance are!
But heaven's great Powres have grac't my destinie
With no such honor. Both my Sire and I
Are borne to suffer everlastingly.' 280

Nestor Telemacho. 'Because you name those wooers, Friend,' said he,
'Report sayes many such, in spite of thee,
(Wooing thy mother) in thy house commit
The ils thou nam'st. But say:—proceedeth it
From will in thee to beare so foule a foile, 285
Or from thy subjects' hate, that wish thy spoile
And will not aide thee, since their spirits relie
(Against thy rule) on some grave Augurie?
What know they, but at length thy Father may
Come, and with violence their violence pay— 290
Or he alone, or all the Greeks with him?
But if Minerva now did so esteeme
Thee as thy Father in times past, whom, past
All measure, she with glorious favours grac't
Amongst the Troyans, where we suffered so— 295
(O! I did never see in such cleare show
The Gods so grace a man as she to him,
To all our eyes, appeard in all her trim)—
If so, I say, she would be pleasd to love,
And that her mind's care thou so much couldst move 300
As did thy Father, every man of these
Would lose in death their seeking mariages.'

Telemachus. 'O Father,' answerd he, 'you make amaze
Seise me throughout. Beyond the height of phrase
You raise expression; but twill never be 305
That I shall move in any Deitie
So blest an honour—not by any meanes,
If Hope should prompt me, or blind Confidence
(The God of Fooles), or every Deitie
Should will it, for tis past my destinie.' 310

Minerva.

The burning-eyd Dame answerd: 'What a speech
Hath past the teeth-guard Nature gave to teach
Fit question of thy words before they flie!
God easily can (when to a mortall eie
Hee's furthest off) a mortall satisfie: 315
And does, the more still. For thy car'd-for Sire,
I rather wish that I might home retire
After my sufferance of a world of woes
Farre off, and then my glad eyes might disclose
The day of my returne, than strait retire   320
And perish standing by my houshold fire—
As Agamemnon did, that lost his life
By false Ægisthus and his falser wife.
'For Death to come at length, tis due to all;
Nor can the Gods themselves, when Fate shall call   325
Their most lov'd man, extend his vitall breath
Beyond the fixt bounds of abhorred Death.'

Volente Deo, nihil est difficile.

Telemachus.

'Mentor!' said he, 'let's dwell no more on this,
Although in us the sorrow pious is.
No such returne as we wish Fates bequeath   330
My erring Father, whom a present death
The deathlesse have decreed. I'le now use speech
That tends to other purpose, and beseech
Instruction of grave Nestor, since he flowes
Past shore in all experience, and knowes   335
The sleights and wisedomes to whose heights aspire
Others as well as my commended Sire,
Whom Fame reports to have commanded three
Ages of men and doth in sight to me
Shew like th'Immortals. Nestor! the renowne   340
Of old Neleius! make the cleare truth knowne
How the most great in Empire, Atreus' sonne,
Sustaind the act of his destruction.
Where then was Menelaus? How was it,
That false Ægisthus, being so farre unfit   345
A match for him, could his death so enforce?
Was he not then in Argos—or his course
With men so left, to let a coward breathe
Spirit enough to dare his brother's death?'
'I'le tell thee truth in all, faire sonne,' said he.   350
'Right well was this event conceiv'd by thee.
If Menelaus in his brother's house
Had found the idle liver with his spouse
(Arriv'd from Troy), he had not liv'd, nor dead

Nestor Telemacho de Ægisthi adulterio.

Had the diggd heape powrd on his lustfull head, 355
But fowles and dogs had torne him in the fields
Farre off of Argos. Not a Dame it yeelds
Had given him any teare, so foule his fact
Shewd even to women. Us Troy's warres had rackt
To every sinewe's sufferance, while he 360
Ægisthus. In Argos' uplands liv'd, from those workes free,
And Agamemnon's wife with force of word
Flatterd and softn'd, who, at first abhord
A fact so infamous. The heav'nly Dame
A good mind had, but was in blood to blame. 365
ἀοιδὸς ἀνήρ. There was a Poet to whose care the King
His Queene committed, and in every thing
(When he for Troy went) charg'd him to apply
Himselfe in all guard to her dignitie.
But when strong Fate so wrapt-in her affects 370
That she resolv'd to leave her fit respects,
Into a desart Ile her Guardian led,
(There left) the rapine of the Vultures fed.
Then brought he willing home his will's wonne prize,
On sacred Altars offerd many Thies, 375
Hung in the Gods' Phanes many ornaments,
Garments and gold, that he the vast events
Of such a labor to his wish had brought
As neither fell into his hope nor thought.
'At last, from Troy saild Sparta's king and I, 380
Both holding her untoucht. And (that his eie
Might see no worse of her), when both were blowne
To sacred Sunium (of Minerva's towne
The goodlie Promontorie), with his shafts severe
Augur Apollo slue him that did stere 385
Atrides' ship, as he the sterne did guide,
And she the full speed of her saile applide.
He was a man that nations of men
Exceld in safe guide of a vessell, when
A tempest rusht in on the ruffld seas: 390
His name was Phrontis Onetorides.
And thus was Menelaus held from home,
Whose way he thirsted so to overcome,
To give his friend the earth being his pursuite,
And all his exequies to execute. 395
Οἴνοπα πόντον: οἴνοψ, cuius facies vinum representat. But sailing still the wine-hewd seas, to reach
Some shore for fit performance, he did fetch
The steepe Mount of the Malians, and there

With open voice offended Jupiter
Proclaimd the voyage his repugnant mind, 400
And powr'd the puffes out of a shreeking wind
That nourisht billowes heightned like to hils;
And with the Fleet's division fulfils
His hate proclaimd, upon a part of Crete
Casting the Navie, where the sea-waves meete 405
Rough Jardanus, and where the Cydons live.
'There is a Rocke on which the Sea doth drive,
Bare and all broken, on the confines set
Of Gortys, that the darke seas likewise fret;
And hither sent the South a horrid drift 410
Of waves against the top, that was the left
Of that torne cliffe, as farre as Phæstus' Strand.
A litle stone the great sea's rage did stand.
The men here driven scapt hard the ships' sore shocks,
The ships themselves being wrackt against the rocks, 415
Save onely five, that blue fore-castles bore,
Which wind and water cast on Ægypt's shore—
When he (there victling well, and store of gold
Aboord his ships brought) his wilde way did hold,
And t'other languag'd men was forc't to rome. 420
Meane space Ægisthus made sad worke at home
And slue his brother, forcing to his sway (Agamemnonis interitus.)
Atrides' subjects, and did seven yeares lay
His yoke upon the rich Mycenean State.
But in the eighth (to his affrighting fate) 425
Divine Orestes home from Athens came,
And what his royall Father felt, the same (Orestes patrem ulciscitur.)
He made the false Ægisthus grone beneath:
Death evermore is the reward of Death.
'Thus having slaine him, a sepulchrall feast 430
He made the Argives for his lustfull guest
And for his mother, whom he did detest.
The selfe-same day upon him stole the King
(Good-at-a-martiall-shout) and goods did bring
As many as his freighted Fleete could beare. 435
But thou, my sonne, too long by no meanes erre,
Thy goods left free for many a spoilfull guest,
Lest they consume some and divide the rest,
And thou (perhaps besides) thy voyage lose.
To Menelaus yet thy course dispose 440
I wish and charge thee, who but late arriv'd
From such a shore and men, as to have liv'd

In a returne from them he never thought,
And whom blacke whirlwinds violently brought
Within a sea so vast that in a yeare 445
Not any fowle could passe it any where,
So huge and horrid was it. But go thou
With ship and men (or, if thou pleasest now
To passe by land, there shall be brought for thee
Both horse and chariot, and thy guides shall be 450
My sonnes themselves) to Sparta the divine,
And to the King whose locks like Amber shine.
Intreate the truth of him; nor loves he lies;
Wisedome in truth is, and hee's passing wise.'
This said, the Sunne went downe and up rose Night, 455
Pallas Nestori.
When Pallas spake: 'O Father, all good right
Beare thy directions. But divide we now
The sacrifise's tongues, mixe wine, and vow
To Neptune and the other ever-blest,
That, having sacrifisd, we may to rest. 460
The fit houre runnes now; light dives out of date;
At sacred feasts we must not sit too late.'
She said; they heard; the Herald water gave;
The youths crownd cups with wine, and let all have
Their equall shares, beginning from the cup 465
Their parting banquet. All the Tongues cut up,
The fire they gave them, sacrifisde, and rose,
Wine and divine rites usde to each dispose.
Minerva and Telemachus desirde
They might to ship be, with his leave, retirde. 470
He (mov'd with that) provokt thus their abodes:
'Now Jove forbid, and all the long-liv'd Gods,
Your leaving me to sleepe aboord a ship—
As I had drunke of poore Penia's whip,
Even to my nakednesse, and had nor sheete 475
Nor covering in my house, that warme nor sweete
A guest, nor I my selfe, had meanes to sleepe—
Where I both weeds and wealthy coverings keepe
For all my guests; nor shall Fame ever say
The deare sonne of the man Ulysses lay 480
All night a ship boord here while my dayes shine,
Or in my Court whiles any sonne of mine
Enjoyes survivall—who shall guests receive,
Whom ever my house hath a nooke to leave.'
'My much lov'd Father,' said Minerva, 'well 485
All this becomes thee. But perswade to dwell

This night with thee thy sonne Telemachus,
For more convenient is the course for us,
That he may follow to thy house and rest,
And I may boord our blacke saile, that addrest 490
At all parts I may make our men and cheare
All with my presence, since of all men there
I boast my selfe the senior; th'others are
Youths, that attend in free and friendly care
Great-soul'd Telemachus and are his peeres 495
In fresh similitude of forme and yeeres.
For their confirmance I will therefore now
Sleepe in our blacke Barke. But, when Light shall shew
Her silver forehead, I intend my way
Amongst the Caucons, men that are to pay 500
A debt to me, nor small, nor new. For this,
Take you him home—whom in the morne dismisse
With chariot and your sonnes, and give him horse
Ablest in strength and of the speediest course.'

Disparet Minerva.

This said, away she flew, formd like the fowle 505
Men call the Ossifrage—when every soule
Amaze invaded; even th'old man admir'd,

Nestor Telemacho.

The youth's hand tooke, and said: 'O most desir'd,
My hope sayes thy proofe will no coward show,
Nor one unskild in warre, when Deities now 510
So yong attend thee and become thy guides—
Nor any of the heaven-housde States besides,
But Tritogenia's selfe, the seed of Jove,
The great in prey, that did in honor move
So much about thy Father amongst all 515
The Grecian armie. Fairest Queene, let fall
On me like favours: give me good renowne,
Which, as on me, on my lov'd wife let downe,
And all my children. I will burne to thee
An Oxe right bred, brode-headed and yoke-free, 520
To no man's hand yet humbled. Him will I
(His hornes in gold hid) give thy Deitie.'

Thus praid he, and she heard; and home he led
His sonnes and all his heapes of kindered,
Who, entring his Court royall, every one 525
He marshald in his severall seate and throne.
And every one, so kindly come, he gave
His sweet-wine cup, which none was let to have
Before this leventh yeare landed him from Troy,
Which now the Butleresse had leave t'employ— 530

Who therefore pierst it and did give it vent.
Of this, the old Duke did a cup present
To every guest, made his maid many a praire
That weares the Shield fring'd with his nurse's haire,
And gave her sacrifise. With this rich wine 535
And food suffisde, Sleepe all eyes did decline,
And all for home went; but his Court alone
Telemachus, divine Ulysses' sonne,
Must make his lodging, or not please his heart.
A bed, all chequerd with elaborate Art, 540
Within a Portico that rung like brasse,
He brought his guest to; and his bedfere was
Pisistratus, the martiall guide of men,
That liv'd, of all his sonnes, unwed till then.
Himselfe lay in a by-roome, farre above, 545
His bed made by his barren wife, his love.

The rosie-fingerd morne no sooner shone
But up he rose, tooke aire, and sat upon
A seate of white and goodly polisht stone,
That such a glosse as richest ointments wore, 550
Before his high gates, where the Counsellor
That matcht the Gods (his Father) usde to sit—
Who now (by Fate forc't) stoopt as low as it.
And here sate Nestor, holding in his hand
A Scepter, and about him round did stand 555
(As early up) his sonnes' troope—Perseus,
The God-like Thrasymed, and Aretus,
Echephron, Stratius, the sixt and last
Pisistratus, and by him (halfe embrac't
Still as they came) divine Telemachus. 560
To these spake Nestor, old Gerenius:

Nestoris filij patris jussu Minervæ sacrum apparant.

'Haste, loved sonnes, and do me a desire,
That (first of all the Gods) I may aspire
To Pallas' favour, who vouchsaft to me
At Neptune's feast her sight so openly. 565
Let one to field go, and an Oxe with speed
Cause hither brought, which let the Heardsman leade.
Another to my deare guest's vessell go,
And all his souldiers bring, save onely two.
A third the Smith that works in gold command 570
(Laertius) to attend and lend his hand
To plate the both hornes round about with gold.
The rest remaine here close. But first, see told

The maids within, that they prepare a feast,
Set seates through all the Court, see strait addrest 575
The purest water, and get fuell feld.'
This said, not one but in the service held
Officious hand. The Oxe came led from field;

The forme of the Sacrifice.

The Souldiers troopt from ship; the Smith he came
And those tooles brought that serv'd the actuall frame 580
His Art conceiv'd, brought Anvile, hammers brought,
Faire tongs, and all with which the gold was wrought.
Minerva likewise came to set the Crowne
On that kind sacrifice and mak't her owne.
Then th'old Knight Nestor gave the Smith the gold, 585
With which he strait did both the hornes infold,
And trimm'd the Offering so, the Goddesse joyd.
About which thus were Nestor's sonnes employd:
Divine Echephron and faire Stratius
Held both the hornes; the water odorous 590
In which they washt what to the rites was vowd
Aretus (in a caldron all bestrowd
With herbes and flowres) serv'd in from th'holy roome
Where all were drest and whence the rites must come.
And after him a hallowd virgin came, 595
That brought the barlet cake, and blew the flame.
The axe with which the Oxe should both be feld
And cut forth, Thrasymed stood by and held.
Perseus the vessell held that should retaine
The purple licour of the offering slaine. 600
Then washt the pious Father, then the Cake
(Of barley, salt and oile made) tooke, and brake,
Askt many a boone of Pallas, and the state
Of all the offering did initiate,
In three parts cutting off the haire, and cast 605
Amidst the flame. All th'invocation past
And all the Cake broke, manly Thrasymed
Stood neare and sure, and such a blow he laid
Aloft the offring that to earth he sunke,
His neck-nerves sunderd and his spirits shrunke. 610
Out shriekt the daughters, daughter in lawes and wife
Of three-ag'd Nestor (who had eldest life
Of Clymen's daughters)—chast Eurydice.
The Oxe on broad earth then layd laterally
They held, while Duke Pisistratus the throte 615
Dissolv'd and set the sable blood afflote,

And then the life the bones left. Instantly
They cut him up; apart flew either Thie,
That with the fat they dubd, with art alone,
The throte-briske and the sweet-bread pricking on. 620
Then Nestor broild them on the cole-turnd wood,
Powr'd blacke wine on, and by him yong men stood,
That spits five-pointed held, on which (when burnd
The solid Thies were) they transfixt and turnd
The inwards, cut in cantles—which (the meate 625
Vowd to the Gods consum'd) they rost and eate.
In meane space, Polycaste (calld the faire,
Nestor's yongst daughter) bath'd Ulysses' heire,
Whom having cleansd and with rich balmes bespred,
She cast a white shirt quickly o're his head, 630
And then his weeds put on, when forth he went
And did the person of a God present,
Came, and by Nestor tooke his honourd seate,
This pastor of the people. Then, the meate
Of all the spare parts rosted, off they drew, 635
Sate, and fell to. But soone the temperate few
Rose, and in golden bolles filld others wine,
Till, when the rest felt thirst of feast decline,
Nestor his sonnes bad fetch his high-man'd horse
And them in chariot joyne, to runne the course 640
The Prince resolv'd. Obaid as soone as heard
Was Nestor by his sonnes, who strait prepar'd
Both horse and chariot. She that kept the store,
Both bread and wine, and all such viands more
As should the feast of Jove-fed Kings compose, 645
Pourvaid the voyage. To the rich Coach rose
Ulysses' sonne, and close to him ascended
The Duke Pisistratus, the reines intended,
And scourg'd, to force to field who freely flew,
And left the Towne, that farre her splendor threw— 650
Both holding yoke, and shooke it all the day.
But now the Sunne set, darkning every way,
When they to Pheris came, and in the house
Of Diocles (the sonne t'Ortilochus,
Whom flood Alpheus got) slept all that night— 655
Who gave them each due hospitable rite.
But when the rosie-fingerd morne arose,
They went to Coach and did their horse inclose,
Drave forth the fore-court and the porch that yeelds
Each breath a sound, and to the fruitfull fields 660

Telemachus proficiscitur ad Menelaum.

Rode scourging still their willing flying Steeds,
Who strenuously performd their wonted speeds,
Their journey ending just when Sunne went downe,
And shadowes all wayes through the earth were throwne.

Finis libri tertij Hom. Odyss.

THE FOURTH BOOKE
of
HOMER'S ODYSSES

THE ARGUMENT

Receiv'd now in the Spartan Court,
Telemachus preferres report
To Menelaus of the throng
Of wooers with him, and their wrong.
Atrides tels the Greekes' retreate 5
And doth a Prophecie repeate
That Proteus made—by which he knew
His brother's death—and then doth shew
How with Calypso liv'd the sire
Of his yong guest. The woo'rs conspire 10
Their Prince's death: whose trechery knowne,
Penelope in teares doth drowne—
Whom Pallas by a dreame doth cheare
And in similitude appeare
Of faire Iphthima, knowne to be 15
The sister of Penelope.

Menelaus.

Another Argument

Δέλτα. *Here of the Sire*
The Sonne doth heare:
The woo'rs conspire;
The mother's feare.

In Lacedæmon now, the nurse of Whales,
These two arriv'd, and found at festivals
(With mightie concourse) the renowmed King,
His sonne and daughter joyntly marrying.
Alector's daughter he did give his sonne, 5
Strong Megapenthes, who his life begunne
By Menelaus' bondmaid; whom he knew

Λακεδαίμονα κητώεσσαν, *which is expounded* Spartam amplam, *or* μεγάλην, magnam: *where* κητώεσσαν *signifies properly* plurima cete nutrientem.

In yeares, when Helen could no more renew
In issue like divine Hermione,
Who held in all faire forme as high degree 10
As golden Venus. Her he married now
To great Achilles' sonne, who was by vow
Bethrothd to her at Troy. And thus the Gods
To constant loves give nuptiall periods.
Whose state here past, the Myrmidons' rich towne 15
(Of which she shar'd in the Imperiall Crowne)
With horse and chariots he resign'd her to.
Meane space, the high huge house with feast did flow
Of friends and neighbours, joying with the King.
Amongst whom did a heavenly Poet sing 20
And touch his Harpe. Amongst whom likewise danc't
Two, who, in that dumbe motion advanc't,

Μολπῆς ἐξάρχοντες— Cantum auspicantes: *of which place, the Critiks affirme, that* saltatores motu suo indicant cantori, quo genere cantus saltaturi forent.

Would prompt the Singer what to sing and play.
All this time in the utter Court did stay,
With horse and chariot, Telemachus 25
And Nestor's noble sonne, Pisistratus.
Whom Eteoneus, coming forth, descried,
And, being a servant to the King most tried
In care and his respect, he ranne and cried:
'Guests! Jove-kept Menelaus! two such men 30
As are for forme of high Saturnius' straine!
Informe your pleasure, if we shall unclose
Their horse from coach, or say they must dispose
Their way to some such house as may embrace
Their knowne arrivall with more welcome grace?' 35

The rapture of Eteoneus at sight of Telemachus and Pisistratus.

Menelaus rebukes his servant for his doubt to entertaine guests worthy.

He (angry) answerd: 'Thou didst never show
Thy selfe a foole, Boethides, till now,
But now (as if turnd child) a childish speech
Vents thy vaine spirits. We our selves now reach
Our home by much spent hospitalitie 40
Of other men, nor know if Jove will trie
With other after wants our state againe.
And therefore from our feast no more detaine
Those welcome guests, but take their Steeds from Coach
And with attendance guide in their approach.' 45
This said, he rusht abroad and calld some more
Tried in such service, that together bore
Up to the guests and tooke their Steeds, that swet
Beneath their yokes, from Coach, at mangers set,
Wheate and white barley gave them mixt, and plac't 50
Their Chariot by a wall so cleare it cast

A light quite thorough it. And then they led
Their guests to the divine house, which so fed
Their eyes at all parts with illustrous sights
That Admiration seisd them. Like the lights 55
The Sunne and Moone gave, all the Pallace threw
A luster through it. Satiate with whose view,
Downe to the King's most bright-kept Baths they went,
Where handmaids did their services present,
Bath'd, balmd them, shirts and well-napt weeds put on, 60
And by Atrides' side set each his throne.
Then did the handmaid royall water bring,
And to a Laver, rich and glittering,
Of massie gold, powr'd; which she plac't upon
A silver Caldron, into which might runne 65
The water as they washt. Then set she neare
A polisht table, on which all the cheare
The present could affoord, a reverend Dame
That kept the Larder set. A Cooke then came
And divers dishes, borne thence, serv'd againe, 70
Furnisht the boord with bolles of gold. And then
(His right hand given the guests) Atrides said:
'Eate, and be chearfull; appetite allaid,
I long to aske of what stocke ye descend—
For not from parents whose race namelesse end 75
We must derive your ofspring. Men obscure
Could get none such as you. The pourtraiture
Of Jove-sustaind and Scepter-bearing Kings
Your either person in his presence brings.'
An Oxe's fat chine then they up did lift 80
And set before the guests—which was a gift
Sent as an honor to the King's owne tast.
They saw yet twas but to be eaten plac't,
And fell to it. But food and wine's care past,
Telemachus thus prompted Nestor's sonne 85
(His eare close laying, to be heard of none):
'Consider (thou whom most my mind esteemes)
The brasse-worke here, how rich it is in beames,
And how, besides, it makes the whole house sound.
What gold, and amber, silver, ivorie, round 90
Is wrought about it! Out of doubt, the Hall
Of Jupiter Olympius hath of all
This state the like. How many infinites
Take up to admiration all men's sights!'
Atrides over-heard, and said: 'Lov'd sonne, 95

Telemachus to Pisistratus, in observation of the house, not so much that he hartily admired it, as to please Menelaus, who he knew heard, though he seemd desirous he shold not heare.

Menelaus relates his travels to his guests.

No mortall must affect contention
With Jove, whose dwellings are of endlesse date.
Perhaps (of men) some one may emulate
(Or none) my housc, or me. For I am one
That many a grave extreme have undergone, 100
Much error felt by sea, and till th'eighth yeare
Had never stay, but wanderd farre and neare—
Cyprus, Phœnicia, and Sidonia,
And fetcht the farre-off Æthiopia,
Reacht the Erembi of Arabia 105
And Lybia, where with hornes Ewes yeane their Lambs,
Where every full yeare Ewes are three times dams,
Where neither King nor shepheard want comes neare
Of cheese, or flesh, or sweete milke. All the yeare
They ever milke their Ewes. And here, while I 110
Errd, gathering meancs to live, one murtherously,
Unwares, unseene, bereft my brother's life,
Chiefly betraid by his abhorred wife.
So hold I (not enjoying) what you see.
And of your Fathers (if they living be) 115
You must have heard this, since my suffrings were
So great and famous—from this Pallace herc
(So rarely-well-built, furnished so well,
And substanced with such a precious deale
Of well-got treasure) banisht by the doome 120
Of Fate, and erring as I had no home.
And now I have and usc it, not to take
Th'entire delight it offers, but to make
Continuall wishes that a triple part
Of all it holds were wanting, so my heart 125
Were easde of sorrowes (taken for their deaths
That fell at Troy) by their revived breaths.
And thus sit I here, weeping, mourning still
Each least man lost, and sometimes make mine ill
(In paying just teares for their losse) my joy. 130
Sometimes I breathe my woes; for in annoy,
The pleasure soone admits satietie.
But all these men's wants wet not so mine eie
(Though much they move me) as one sole man's misse—
For which my sleepe and meate even lothsome is 135
In his renewd thought, since no Greeke hath wonne
Grace for such labours as Laertes' sonne
Hath wrought and sufferd—to himselfe nought else
But future sorrowes forging, to me hels

Intending Ulysses.

For his long absence, since I cannot know 140
If life or death detaine him, since such woe
For his love, old Laertes, his wise wife,
And poore yong sonne sustaines, whom new with life
He left as sirelesse.' This speech griefe to teares
(Powrd from the sonne's lids on the earth) his eares 145
(Told of the Father) did excite, who kept
His cheekes drie with his red weed as he wept,
His both hands usde therein. Atrides then
Began to know him, and did strife retaine,
If he should let himselfe confesse his Sire, 150
Or with all fitting circumstance enquire.

While this his thoughts disputed, forth did shine
Diana. (Like to the golden distaffe-deckt divine),
From her bed's high and odoriferous roome,
Helen's reparance and ornament. Helen. To whom (of an elaborate loome) 155
Adresta set a chaire; Alcippe brought
A peece of Tapestrie, of fine wooll wrought;
Phylo a silver Cabinet conferd
(Given by Alcandra, Nuptially endeard
To Lord Polybius, whose abode in Thebes, 160
Th'Ægyptian citie, was, where wealth in heapes
His famous house held, out of which did go
In gift t'Atrides silver bath-tubs two,
Two Tripods, and of fine gold talents ten).
His wife did likewise send to Helen then 165
Faire gifts, a Distaffe that of gold was wrought,
And that rich Cabinet that Phylo brought,
Round and with gold ribd, now of fine thred full,
On which extended (crownd with finest wooll
Of violet glosse) the golden Distaffe lay. 170

She tooke her State-chaire, and a foot-stoole's stay
Had for her feete: and of her husband thus
Helen to Menelaus concerning the guests. Askt to know all things: 'Is it knowne to us,
King Menelaus, whom these men commend
Themselves for, that our Court now takes to friend? 175
I must affirme (be I deceiv'd or no)
I never yet saw man nor woman so
Like one another as this man is like
Ulysses' sonne. With admiration strike
His lookes my thoughts, that they should carrie now 180
Powre to perswade me thus, who did but know
When newly he was borne the forme they bore.
But tis his Father's grace, whom more and more

His grace resembles, that makes me retaine
Thought that he now is like Telemachus then, 185
Left by his Sire when Greece did undertake
Troy's bold warre for my impudencie's sake.'
He answerd: 'Now, wife, what you thinke, I know.
The true cast of his Father's eye doth show
In his eyes' order. Both his head and haire, 190
His hands and feete, his very father's are.
Of whom (so well rememberd) I should now
Acknowledge for me his continuall flow
Of cares and perils, yet still patient.
But I should too much move him, that doth vent 195
Such bitter teares for that which hath bene spoke,
Which (shunning soft shew) see how he would cloke,
And with his purple weed his weepings hide.'

Pisistratus tels who they are.

Then Nestor's sonne, Pisistratus, replide:
'Great Pastor of the people, kept of God! 200
He is Ulysses' sonne, but his abode
Not made before here, and he modest too,
He holds it an indignitie to do
A deed so vaine, to use the boast of words
Where your words are on wing—whose voice affords 205
Delight to us, as if a God did breake
The aire amongst us and vouchsafe to speake.
But me, my father, old Duke Nestor, sent
To be his consort hither, his content,
Not to be heightned so as with your sight, 210
In hope that therewith words and actions might
Informe his comforts from you, since he is
Extremely griev'd and injur'd by the misse
Of his great Father, suffering even at home,
And few friends found to helpe him overcome 215
His too weake sufferance, now his Sire is gone—
Amongst the people not affoorded one
To checke the miseries that mate him thus.
And this the state is of Telemachus.'

Menelaus' joy for Telemachus, and mone for Ulysses' absence.

'O Gods,' said he, 'how certaine, now, I see 220
My house enjoyes that friend's sonne, that for me
Hath undergone so many willing fights!
Whom I resolv'd, past all the Grecian Knights,
To hold in love, if our returne by seas
The farre-off Thunderer did ever please 225
To grant our wishes. And to his respect
A Pallace and a Citie to erect,

My vow had bound me—whither bringing then
His riches and his sonne and all his men
From barren Ithaca (some one sole Towne 230
Inhabited about here batterd downe)
All should in Argos live. And there would I
Ease him of rule, and take the Emperie
Of all on me. And often here would we
(Delighting, loving either's companie) 235
Meete and converse; whom nothing should divide
Till death's blacke veile did each all over hide.
But this perhaps had bene a meane to take
Even God himselfe with envie—who did make
Ulysses therefore onely the unblest, 240
That should not reach his loved countrie's rest.'
These woes made every one with woe in love;
Even Argive Helen wept (the seed of Jove);
Menelaus. Ulysses' sonne wept; Atreus' sonne did weepe;
And Nestor's sonne his eyes in teares did steepe. 245
But his teares fell not from the present cloud
Pisistratus weeps with remembrance of his brother Antilochus. Vid. Memnon. That from Ulysses was exhal'd, but flowd
From brave Antilochus' rememberd due,
Whom the renowmd Sonne of the Morning slue.
Which yet he thus excusde: 'O Atreus' sonne! 250
Old Nestor sayes there lives not such a one
Amongst all mortals as Atrides is
For deathlesse wisedome. Tis a praise of his,
Still given in your remembrance, when at home
Our speech concernes you. Since then overcome 255
You please to be with sorrow, even to teares,
That are in wisedome so exempt from peres,
Vouchsafe the like effect in me excuse
(If it be lawfull). I affect no use
Of teares thus after meales—at least, at night; 260
But when the morne brings forth, with teares, her light,
It shall not then empaire me to bestow
My teares on any worthie's overthrow.
It is the onely right that wretched men
Can do dead friends, to cut haire and complaine. 265
But Death my brother tooke, whom none could call
The Grecian coward, you best knew of all.
I was not there, nor saw; but men report,
Antilochus exceld the common sort
For footmanship, or for the Chariot race, 270
Or in the fight for hardie hold of place.'

'O friend,' said he, 'since thou hast spoken so
At all parts as one wise should say and do,
And like one farre beyond thy selfe in yeares,
Thy words shall bounds be to our former teares. 275
O he is questionlesse a right-borne sonne,
That of his Father hath not onely wonne
The person but the wisedome; and that Sire
(Complete himselfe) that hath a sonne entire,
Jove did not onely his full Fate adorne 280
When he was wedded, but when he was borne.
As now Saturnius, through his life's whole date,
Hath Nestor's blisse raisd to as steepe a state—
Both in his age to keepe in peace his house,
And to have children wise and valorous. 285
But let us not forget our rere Feast thus.
Let some give water here. Telemachus!
The morning shall yeeld time to you and me
To do what fits, and reason mutually.'
This said, the carefull servant of the King, 290
Asphalion, powr'd on th'issue of the Spring,
And all to readie feast set readie hand.
But Helen now on new device did stand,

Helen's potion against Cares.

Infusing strait a medcine to their wine,
That (drowning Cares and Angers) did decline 295
All thought of ill. Who drunke her cup could shed
All that day not a teare—no, not if dead
That day his father or his mother were,
Not if his brother, child or chiefest deare
He should see murtherd then before his face. 300
Such usefull medcines (onely borne in grace
Of what was good) would Helen ever have.
And this Juyce to her Polydamma gave,
The wife of Thoon, an Æygptian borne,
Whose rich earth herbes of medicine do adorne 305
In great abundance. Many healthfull are,
And many banefull. Every man is there
A good Physition out of nature's grace,
For all the nation sprung of Pæon's race.
When Helen then her medicine had infusde, 310
She bad powre wine to it, and this speech usde:

Helen of Ulysses and the sacke of Troy.

'Atrides, and these good men's sonnes, great Jove
Makes good and ill one after other move
In all things earthly: for he can do all.

The woes past, therefore, he so late let fall, 315
The comforts he affoords us let us take,
Feast, and with fit discourses merrie make.
Nor will I other use. As then our blood
Griev'd for Ulysses, since he was so good,
Since he was good, let us delight to heare 320
How good he was, and what his suffrings were—
Though every fight, and every suffring deed,
Patient Ulysses underwent exceed
My woman's powre to number or to name.
But what he did and sufferd, when he came 325
Amongst the Troyans (where ye Grecians all
Tooke part with sufferance) I in part can call
To your kind memories. How with ghastly wounds
Himselfe he mangl'd, and the Troyan bounds
(Thrust thicke with enemies) adventured on, 330
His royall shoulders having cast upon
Base abject weeds, and enterd like a slave.
Then (begger-like) he did of all men crave,
And such a wretch was as the whole Greeke fleete
Brought not besides. And thus through every streete 335
He crept discovering, of no one man knowne.
And yet through all this difference I alone
Smok't his true person, talkt with him—but he
Fled me with wiles still. Nor could we agree
Till I disclaimd him quite, and so (as mov'd 340
With womanly remorse of one that prov'd
So wretched an estate, what ere he were)
Wonne him to take my house. And yet even there,
Till freely I (to make him doubtlesse) swore
A powrefull oath to let him reach the shore 345
Of ships and tents before Troy understood,
I could not force on him his proper good.
But then I bath'd and sooth'd him, and he then
Confest and told me all. And (having slaine
A number of the Troyan guards) retirde 350
And reacht the Fleete, for slight and force admirde.
Their husbands' deaths by him the Troyan wives
Shriekt for, but I made triumphs for their lives.
For then my heart conceiv'd that once againe
I should reach home, and yet did still retaine 355
Woe for the slaughters Venus made for me,
When both my husband, my Hermione,

And bridall roome, she robd of so much right
And drew me from my countrie with her sleight—
Though nothing under heaven I here did need 360
That could my Fancie or my Beautie feed.'

Menelaus to Helen and his guests.

Her husband said: 'Wife! what you please to tell
Is true at all parts, and becomes you well.
And I my selfe, that now may say have seene
The minds and manners of a world of men 365
And great Heroes, measuring many a ground,
Have never (by these eyes that light me) found
One with a bosome so to be belov'd
As that in which th'accomplisht spirit mov'd
Of patient Ulysses. What, brave man, 370
He both did act and suffer, when we wan
The towne of Ilion in the brave-built horse,
When all we chiefe States of the Grecian force
Were housde together, bringing Death and Fate
Amongst the Troyans, you, wife, may relate. 375
For you, at last, came to us; God, that would
The Troyans glorie give, gave charge you should
Approch the engine, and Deiphobus
(The god-like) followd. Thrice ye circl'd us,
With full survay of it, and often tried 380
The hollow crafts that in it were implied.

Helen counterfetted the wives' voices of those Kings of Greece that were in the woodden horse, and calls their husbands.

When all the voices of their wives in it
You tooke on you, with voice so like and fit,
And every man by name so visited
That I, Ulysses and King Diomed 385
(Set in the midst, and hearing how you calld)
Tydides and my selfe (as halfe appalld
With your remorceful plaints) would passing faine
Have broke our silence rather than againe
Endure, respectlesse, their so moving cries. 390
But Ithacus our strongest fantasies
Containd within us from the slendrest noise,
And every man there sat without a voice.
Anticlus onely would have answerd thee,
But his speech Ithacus incessantly 395
With strong hand held in, till (Minerva's call
Charging thee off) Ulysses sav'd us all.'

Telemachus to Menelaus.

Telemachus replide: 'Much greater is
My griefe for hearing this high praise of his.
For all this doth not his sad death divert— 400
Nor can, though in him swelld an iron heart.

Prepare, and leade then (if you please) to rest:
Sleepe (that we heare not) will content us best.'
Then Argive Helen made her handmaids go
And put faire bedding in the Portico, 405
Lay purple blankets on, Rugs warme and soft,
And cast an Arras coverlet aloft.
Itur ad lectum. They torches tooke, made haste, and made the bed.
When both the guests were to their lodgings led
Within a Portico without the house. 410
Atrides and his large-traine-wearing Spouse
(The excellent of women) forth the way,
In a retir'd receit, together lay.
The morne arose; the King rose, and put on
His royall weeds, his sharpe sword hung upon 415
His ample shoulders, forth his chamber went,
And did the person of a God present.
Telemachus accosts him, who begun
Speech of his journey's proposition:
Menelaus enquires the cause of his voyage. 'And what, my yong Ulyssean Heroe, 420
Provokt thee on the broad backe of the sea
To visit Lacedæmon the Divine?
Speake truth—some publicke cause, or onely thine?'
'I come,' said he, 'to heare if any fame
Breath'd of my Father to thy notice came. 425
My house is sackt; my fat workes of the field
Are all destroid; my house doth nothing yeeld
But enemies that kill my harmlesse sheepe
And sinewie Oxen, nor will ever keepe
Their steeles without them. And these men are they } 430
That wooe my Mother, most inhumanely }
Committing injurie on injurie. }
To thy knees therefore I am come, t'attend
Relation of the sad and wretched end
My erring Father felt, if witnest by 435
Your owne eyes, or the certaine newes that flie
From others' knowledges. For more than is
The usuall heape of humane miseries
His Mother bore him to. Vouchsafe me then
(Without all ruth of what I can sustaine) 440
The plaine and simple truth of all you know. }
Let me beseech so much. If ever vow }
Was made and put in good effect to you }
At Troy (where suffrance bred you so much smart)

Upon my Father good Ulysses' part, 445
And quit it now to me (himselfe in youth)
Unfolding onely the unclosed truth.'
He (deeply sighing) answerd him: 'O shame,
That such poore vassals should affect the fame
To share the joyes of such a Worthie's Bed! 450
As when a Hinde (her calves late farrowed
To give sucke) enters the bold Lion's den,
He rootes of hils and herbie vallies then
For food (there feeding) hunting, but at length,
Returning to his Caverne, gives his strength 455
The lives of both the mother and her brood
In deaths indecent; so the wooers' blood
Must pay Ulysses' powres as sharpe an end.
O would to Jove, Apollo and thy friend
(The wise Minerva) that thy Father were 460
As once he was, when he his spirits did rere
Against Philomelides, in a fight
Performd in well-built Lesbos, where downe-right
He strooke the earth with him and gat a shout
Of all the Grecians! O, if now full out 465
He were as then and with the wooers cop't,
Short-liv'd they all were, and their nuptials hop't
Would prove as desperate. But for thy demand
Enforc't with prayrs, I'le let thee understand
The truth directly, nor decline a thought, 470
Much lesse deceive or sooth thy search in ought.
But what the old and still-true-spoken God,
That from the sea breathes oracles abroad,
Disclosde to me, to thee I'le all impart,
Nor hide one word from thy sollicitous heart. 475

Menelai navigatio.

'I was in Ægypt, where a mightie time
The Gods detaind me, though my naturall clime
I never so desir'd, because their homes
I did not greete with perfect Hecatomes.
For they will put men evermore in mind 480
How much their masterly commandments bind.
'There is (besides) a certaine Iland, calld
Pharos, that with the high-wav'd sea is walld,
Just against Ægypt, and so much remote
As in a whole day, with a fore-gale smote, 485
A hollow ship can saile. And this Ile beares
A Port most portly, where sea-passengers
Put in still for fresh water, and away

To sea againe. Yet here the Gods did stay
My Fleete full twentie dayes; the winds (that are 490
Masters at sea) no prosprous puffe would spare
To put us off; and all my victles here
Had quite corrupted, as my men's minds were,
Had not a certaine Goddesse given regard
And pittide me in an estate so hard— 495
And twas Idothea, honourd Proteus' seed,
That old sea-farer. Her mind I made bleed
With my compassion, when (walkt all alone
From all my souldiers, that were ever gone
About the Ile on fishing with hookes bent, 500
Hunger their bellies on her errand sent)
She came close to me, spake, and thus began:
' "Of all men, thou art the most foolish man,
Or slacke in businesse, or stayst here of choice
And doest in all thy suffrances rejoyce, 505
That thus long liv'st detaind here, and no end
Canst give thy tarriance. Thou doest much offend
The minds of all thy fellowes." I replied:
' "Who ever thou art of the Deified,
I must affirme that no way with my will 510
I make abode here, but, it seemes, some ill
The Gods inhabiting broad heaven sustaine
Against my getting off. Informe me then,
(For Godheads all things know) what God is he
That stayes my passage from the fishie sea?" 515

Idothea to Menelaus.

' "Stranger," said she, "I'le tell thee true: there lives
An old Sea-farer in these seas, that gives
A true solution of all secrets here—
Who deathlesse Proteus is, th'Ægyptian Peere,
Who can the deepes of all the seas exquire, 520
Who Neptune's Priest is, and (they say) the Sire
That did beget me. Him if any way
Thou couldst inveagle, he would cleare display
Thy course from hence, and how farre off doth lie
Thy voyage's whole scope through Neptune's skie— 525
Informing thee (O God-preserv'd) beside
(If thy desires would so be satisfide)
What ever good or ill hath got event
In all the time thy long and hard course spent,
Since thy departure from thy house." This said, 530
Againe I answerd: "Make the sleights displaid
Thy Father useth, lest his foresight see,

Or his foreknowledge taking note of me,
He flies the fixt place of his usde abode.
Tis hard for man to countermine with God." 535
'She strait replide: "I'le utter truth in all.

Idothea's counsell to take her father Proteus.

When heaven's supremest height the Sunne doth skall,
The old Sea-tell-truth leaves the deepes and hides
Amidst a blacke storme when the West wind chides,
In caves still sleeping. Round about him sleepe 540
(With short feete swimming forth the fomie deepe)
The Sea-calves (lovely Halosydnes calld)
From whom a noisome odour is exhalld,
Got from the whirle-pooles on whose earth they lie.
Here, when the morne illustrates all the skie, 545
I'le guide, and seate thee in the fittest place
For the performance thou hast now in chace.
In meane time reach thy Fleete, and chuse out three
Of best exploit to go as aides to thee.

The sleights of Proteus.

'"But now I'le shew thee all the old God's sleights. 550
He first will number and take all the sights
Of those his guard, that on the shore arrives—
When, having viewd and told them forth by fives,
He takes place in their midst, and there doth sleepe
Like to a shepheard midst his flocke of sheepe. 555
In his first sleepe call up your hardiest cheare,
Vigor and violence, and hold him there,
In spite of all his strivings to be gone.
He then will turne himselfe to every one
Of all things that in earth creepe and respire, 560
In water swim, or shine in heavenly fire.
Yet still hold you him firme, and much the more
Presse him from passing. But when as before
(When sleepe first bound his powres) his forme ye see,
Then ceasse your force and th'old Heroe free, 565
And then demand which heaven-borne it may bee
That so afflicts you, hindring your retreate
And free sea-passage to your native seate."
'This said, she div'd into the wavie seas,
And I my course did to my ships addresse, 570
That on the sands stucke; where arriv'd, we made
Our supper readie. Then th'Ambrosian shade
Of night fell on us, and to sleepe we fell.
Rosie Aurora rose; we rose as well;
And three of them, on whom I most relied 575
For firme at every force I chusde, and hied

Strait to the many-river-served seas,
And all assistance askt the Deities.
'Meane time Idothea the sea's broad brest
Embrac't, and brought for me, and all my rest, 580
Foure of the sea-calves' skins, but newly flead,
To worke a wile which she had fashioned
Upon her Father. Then (within the sand
A covert digging) when these Calves should land,
She sate expecting. We came close to her; 585
She plac't us orderly, and made us weare
Each one his Calve's skin. But we then must passe
A huge exploit. The sea-calves' savour was
So passing sowre (they still being bred at seas)
It much afflicted us—for who can please 590

Ironicè.

To lie by one of these same sea-bred whales?
But she preserves us, and to memorie calls
A rare commoditie: she fetcht to us
Ambrosia, that an aire most odorous
Beares still about it—which she nointed round 595
Our either nosthrils, and in it quite drownd
The nastie whale-smell. Then the great event
The whole morne's date, with spirits patient,
We lay expecting. When bright Noone did flame
Forth from the sea, in Sholes the sea-calves came, 600
And orderly at last lay downe and slept
Along the sands. And then th'old sea-god crept
From forth the deepes, and found his fat calves there,
Survaid and numberd, and came never neare
The craft we usde, but told us five for calves. 605
His temples then diseasd with sleepe he salves;
And in rusht we with an abhorred crie,
Cast all our hands about him manfully—
And then th'old Forger all his formes began.
First was a Lion, with a mightie mane; 610
Then next a Dragon; a pide Panther then;
A vast Boare next; and sodainly did straine
All into water. Last, he was a tree,
Curld all at top, and shot up to the skie.
'We, with resolv'd hearts, held him firmly still, 615

Proteus taken by Menelaus.

When th'old one (held too streight for all his skill
To extricate) gave words, and questiond me:
' "Which of the Gods, O Atreus' sonne," said he,
"Advisde and taught thy fortitude this sleight,
To take and hold me thus in my despight? 620

What asks thy wish now?" I replide: "Thou knowst.
Why doest thou aske? What wiles are these thou showst?
I have within this Ile bene held for winde
A wondrous time, and can by no meanes find
An end to my retention. It hath spent 625
The very heart in me. Give thou then vent
To doubts thus bound in me—ye Gods know all—
Which of the Godheads doth so fowly fall
On my addression home, to stay me here,
Avert me from my way, the fishie cleare 630
Barr'd to my passage?" He replide: "Of force
(If to thy home thou wishest free recourse)
To Jove, and all the other Deities,
Thou must exhibite solemne sacrifice,
And then the blacke sea for thee shall be cleare, 635
Till thy lov'd countrie's settl'd reach. But where
Aske these rites thy performance? Tis a fate
To thee and thy affaires appropriate,
That thou shalt never see thy friends, nor tred
Thy Countrie's earth, nor see inhabited 640
Thy so magnificent house, till thou make good
Thy voyage backe to the Ægyptian flood,
Whose waters fell from Jove, and there hast given
To Jove, and all Gods housd in ample heaven,
Devoted Hecatombs; and then free wayes 645
Shall open to thee, cleard of all delayes."
'This told he; and, me thought, he brake my heart,
In such a long and hard course to divert
My hope for home, and charge my backe retreat
As farre as Ægypt. I made answer yet: 650
' "Father, thy charge I'le perfect; but, before,
Resolve me truly, if their naturall shore,
All those Greeks and their ships do safe enjoy,
That Nestor and my selfe left, when from Troy
We first raisde saile? Or whether any died 655
At sea a death unwisht? Or (satisfied)
When warre was past, by friends embrac't, in peace
Resign'd their spirits?" He made answer: "Cease
To aske so farre; it fits thee not to be
So cunning in thine owne calamitie. 660
Nor seeke to learne what, learnd, thou shouldst forget.
Men's knowledges have proper limits set,
And should not prease into the mind of God.
But twill not long be (as my thoughts abode)

Before thou buy this curious skill with teares. 665
Many of those whose states so tempt thine eares
Are stoopt by Death, and many left alive:
One chiefe of which in strong hold doth survive
Amidst the broad sea. Two in their retreate
Are done to death. I list not to repeate 670
Who fell at Troy; thy selfe was there in fight.
But in returne swift Ajax lost the light
In his long-oard ship. Neptune yet a while
Saft him unwrackt to the Gyræan Ile,

The wracke of Ajax Oileus.

A mightie Rocke removing from his way. 675
And surely he had scapt the fatall day
In spite of Pallas, if to that foule deed
He in her Phane did (when he ravished
The Troyan Prophetesse) he had not here

Cassandra.

Adjoynd an impious boast—that he would beare 680
(Despite the Gods) his ship safe through the waves
Then raisde against him. These his impious braves
When Neptune heard, in his strong hand he tooke
His massie Trident and so soundly strooke
The rocke Gyræan that in two it cleft, 685
Of which, one fragment on the land he left,
The other fell into the troubld seas;
At which first rusht Ajax Oiliades
And split his ship, and then himselfe aflote
Swum on the rough waves of the world's vast mote, 690
Till having drunke a salt cup for his sinne,
There perisht he. Thy brother yet did winne
The wreath from Death while in the waves they strove,
Affected by the reverend wife of Jove.
But when the steepe Mount of the Malian shore 695
He seemd to reach, a most tempestuous blore
Farre to the fishie world, that sighes so sore,
Strait ravisht him againe—as farre away
As to th'extreme bounds where the Agrians stay,
Where first Thyestes dwelt, but then his sonne 700
Ægisthus Thyestiades liv'd. This done,
When his returne untoucht appeard againe,
Backe turnd the Gods the wind, and set him then
Hard by his house. Then, full of joy, he left
His ship, and close t'his countrie earth he cleft, 705
Kist it, and wept for joy, powrd teare on teare
To set so wishedly his footing there.
But see: a Sentinell that all the yeare

Craftie Ægisthus in a watchtowre set
To spie his landing, for reward as great 710
As two gold talents, all his powres did call
To strict remembrance of his charge, and all
Discharg'd at first sight which at first he cast
On Agamemnon, and with all his hast
Informd Ægisthus. He an instant traine 715
Laid for his slaughter. Twentie chosen men
Of his Plebeians he in ambush laid.
His other men he charg'd to see purvaid
A Feast, and forth, with horse and chariots grac't,
He rode t'invite him, but in heart embrac't 720
Horrible welcomes, and to death did bring,
With trecherous slaughter, the unwary King—
Receiv'd him at a Feast, and (like an Oxe
Slaine at his manger) gave him bits and knocks.
No one left of Atrides' traine; nor one 725
Sav'd to Ægisthus but himselfe alone:
All strowd together there the bloudie Court."

Agamemnon's slaughter by Ægisthus' trechery.

This said, my soule he sunke with his report;
Flat on the sands I fell, teares spent their store;
I light abhord; my heart would live no more. 730
'When drie of teares, and tir'd with tumbling there,
Th'old Tel-truth thus my danted spirits did cheare:
'"No more spend teares nor time, O Atreus' sonne;
With ceaslesse weeping never wish was wonne.
Use uttermost assay to reach thy home, 735
And all unwares upon the murtherer come,
(For torture) taking him thy selfe alive;
Or let Orestes, that should farre out-strive
Thee in fit vengeance, quickly quit the light
Of such a darke soule, and do thou the right 740
Of buriall to him with a Funerall feast."
'With these last words I fortifide my breast,
In which againe a generous spring began
Of fitting comfort, as I was a man;
But, as a brother, I must ever mourne. 745
Yet forth I went, and told him the returne
Of these I knew, but he had nam'd a third,
Held on the broad sea, still with life inspir'd—
Whom I besought to know, though likewise dead,
And I must mourne alike. He answered: 750
'"He is Laertes' sonne, whom I beheld
In Nymph Calypso's Pallace, who compeld

His stay with her: and since he could not see
His countrie earth, he mournd incessantly.
For he had neither ship instruct with oares, 755
Nor men to fetch him from those stranger shores.
Where leave we him and to thy selfe descend,
Whom not in Argos Fate nor Death shall end;
But the immortall ends of all the earth,
So rul'd by them that order death by birth 760

Elysium described.

(The fields Elysian) Fate to thee will give—
Where Rhadamanthus rules, and where men live
A never-troubld life, where snow, nor showres,
Nor irksome Winter spends his fruitlesse powres,
But from the Ocean Zephyr still resumes 765
A constant breath, that all the fields perfumes—
Which, since thou marriedst Helen, are thy hire,
And Jove himselfe is by her side thy Sire."

Proteus leaveth Menelaus.

'This said, he div'd the deepsome watrie heapes.
I and my tried men tooke up to our ships, 770
And worlds of thoughts I varied with my steps.
'Arriv'd and shipt, the silent solemne Night
And Sleepe bereft us of our visuall light.
At morne, masts, sailes reard, we sate, left the shores,
And beate the fomie Ocean with our oares. 775
'Againe then we the Jove-falne flood did fetch
As farre as Ægypt, where we did beseech
The Gods with Hecatombs—whose angers ceast,
I toomb'd my brother, that I might be blest.
'All rites performd, all haste I made for home, 780
And all the prosprous winds about were come;
I had the Pasport now of every God,
And here closde all these labours' period.
'Here stay then till th'eleventh or twelfth daie's light,
And I'le dismisse thee well, gifts exquisite 785
Preparing for thee—Chariot, horses three,
A Cup of curious frame to serve for thee
To serve th'immortall Gods with sacrifice,
Mindfull of me while all Sunnes light thy skies.'

Telemachus to Menelaus.

He answerd: 'Stay me not too long time here, 790
Though I could sit attending all the yeare:
Nor should my house, nor parents, with desire
Take my affections from you, so on fire
With love to heare you are my thoughts: but so
My Pylian friends I shall afflict with wo, 795
Who mourne even this stay. Whatsoever be

The gifts your Grace is to bestow on me,
Vouchsafe them such as I may beare and save
For your sake ever. Horse, I list not have
To keepe in Ithaca, but leave them here 800
To your soile's dainties, where the broad fields beare
Sweet Cypers grasse, where men-fed Lote doth flow,
Where wheate-like Spelt and wheate it selfe doth grow,
Where Barley, white and spreading like a tree—

Ithaca described by Telemachus.

But Ithaca hath neither ground to be 805
(For any length it comprehends) a race
To trie a horse's speed, nor any place
To make him fat in—fitter farre to feed
A Cliffe-bred Goate than raise or please a Steed.
Of all Iles Ithaca doth least provide 810
Or meades to feed a horse, or wayes to ride.'
He, smiling, said: 'Of good bloud art thou, sonne.
What speech, so yong! What observation
Hast thou made of the world! I well am pleasde
To change my gifts to thee, as being confessd 815
Unfit indeed: my store is such, I may.
Of all my house-gifts, then, that up I lay
For treasure there, I will bestow on thee
The fairest and of greatest price to me.
I will bestow on thee a rich carv'd Cup 820
Of silver all, but all the brims wrought up
With finest gold: it was the onely thing
That the Heroicall Sydonian King
Presented to me, when we were to part
At his receit of me, and twas the Art 825
Of that great Artist that of heaven is free;
And yet even this will I bestow on thee.'
This speech thus ended, guests came and did bring
Muttons (for Presents) to the God-like King,
And spirit-prompting wine, that strenuous makes. 830
Their Riband-wreathed wives brought fruit and cakes.
Thus in this house did these their Feast apply.

The wooers' conspiracie against Telemachus.

And in Ulysses' house, Activitie
The wooers practisde—Tossing of the Speare,
The Stone, and hurling: thus delighted, where 835
They exercisde such insolence before,
Even in the Court that wealthy pavements wore.
Antinous did still their strifes decide,
And he that was in person deifide
Eurymachus, both ring-leaders of all, 840

For in their vertues they were principall.
These by Noemon (sonne to Phronius)
Were sided now, who made the question thus:
'Antinous! does any friend here know
When this Telemachus returnes, or no, 845
From sandie Pylos? He made bold to take
My ship with him; of which I now should make
Fit use my selfe, and saile in her as farre
As spacious Elis, where of mine there are
Twelve delicate Mares, and under their sides go 850
Laborious Mules that yet did never know
The yoke, nor labour; some of which should beare
The taming now, if I could fetch them there.'
This speech the rest admir'd, nor dreamd that he
Neleian Pylos ever thought to see, 855
But was at field about his flocks' survay,
Or thought his heardsmen held him so away.
Eupitheus' sonne, Antinous, then replied:
'When went he, or with what Traine dignified
Of his selected Ithacensian youth? 860
Prest men, or Bond men were they? Tell the truth.
Could he effect this? Let me truly know.
To gaine thy vessell did he violence show,
And usde her gainst thy will, or had her free,
When fitting question he had made with thee?' 865
Noemon answerd: 'I did freely give
My vessell to him. Who deserves to live
That would do other, when such men as he
Did in distresse aske? He should churlish be
That would denie him. Of our youth the best 870
Amongst the people, to the interest
His charge did challenge in them, giving way,
With all the tribute all their powres could pay.
Their Captaine (as he tooke the ship) I knew,
Who Mentor was, or God. A deitie's shew 875
Maskt in his likenesse. But to thinke twas he,
I much admire, for I did clearly see,
But yester morning, God-like Mentor here;
Yet, th'other evening, he tooke shipping there,
And went for Pylos.' Thus went he for home, 880
And left the rest with envie overcome,
Who sate, and pastime left. Eupitheus' sonne
(Sad, and with rage his entrailes overrunne)
His eyes like flames, thus interposde his speech:

Antinous' anger for the scape of Telemachus.

'Strange thing, an action of how proud a reach 885
Is here committed by Telemachus!
A boy, a child—and we a sort of us,
Vowd gainst his voyage, yet admit it thus,
With ship and choise youth of our people too!
But let him on, and all his mischiefe do; 890
Jove shall convert upon himselfe his powres.
Before their ill presum'd he brings on ours.
Provide me then a ship, and twentie men
To give her manage, that against again
He turnes for home, on th'Ithacensian seas 895
Or Cliffie Samian, I may interprease,
Way-lay, and take him, and make all his craft
Saile with his ruine for his Father saf't.'
  This all applauded, and gave charge to do,
Rose, and to greete Ulysses' house did go. 900
But long time past not ere Penelope
Had notice of their far-fetcht trecherie.
Medon the Herald told her, who had heard
Without the Hall how they within conferd,
And hasted strait to tell it to the Queene, 905
Who, from the entrie having Medon seene,

Penelope to Medon.

Prevents him thus: 'Now, Herald, what affaire
Intend the famous woo'rs in your repaire?
To tell Ulysses' maids that they must ceasse
From doing our worke, and their banquets dresse? 910
I would to heaven that (leaving wooing me,
Nor ever troubling other companie)
Here might the last Feast be, and most extreme,
That ever any shall addresse for them.
They never meete but to consent in spoile 915
And reape the free fruites of another's toile.
O did they never, when they children were,
What to their Fathers was Ulysses, heare—
Who never did gainst any one proceed
With unjust usage, or in word or deed? 920
Tis yet with other Kings another right,
One to pursue with love, another spight;
He still yet just, nor would, though might, devoure,
Nor to the worst did ever taste of powre.
But their unruld acts shew their minds' estate: 925
Good turnes receiv'd once, thanks grow out of date.'

Medon to Penelope relates the voyage of Telemachus.

  Medon, the learn'd in wisedome, answerd her:
'I wish, O Queene, that their ingratitudes were

Their worst ill towards you: but worse by farre,
And much more deadly, their endevours are, 930
Which Jove will faile them in. Telemachus
Their purpose is (as he returnes to us)
To give their sharpe steeles in a cruell death—
Who now is gone to learne if Fame can breathe
Newes of his Sire, and will the Pylian shore 935
And sacred Sparta in his search explore.'

This newes dissolv'd to her both knees and heart;
Long silence held her ere one word would part;
Her eyes stood full of teares; her small soft voice
All late use lost, that yet at last had choice 940
Of wonted words, which briefly thus she usde:

'Why left my sonne his mother? Why refusde
His wit the solid shore, to trie the seas
And put in ships the trust of his distresse,
That are at sea to men unbridld horse, 945
And runne, past rule, their farre-engaged course
Amidst a moisture past all meane unstaid?
No need compeld this: did he it, afraid
To live and leave posteritie his name?'

'I know not,' he replide, 'if th'humor came 950
From current of his owne instinct, or flowd
From others' instigations; but he vowd
Attempt to Pylos, or to see descried
His Sire's returne, or know what death he died.'

This said, he tooke him to Ulysses' house 955
After the wooers; the Ulyssean Spouse
(Runne through with woes) let Torture seise her mind,
Nor in her choice of state-chaires stood enclin'd
To take her seate, but th'abject threshold chose
Of her faire chamber for her loth'd repose, 960
And mournd most wretch-like. Round about her fell
Her handmaids, joynd in a continuate yell.
From every corner of the Pallace, all
Of all degrees tun'd to her comfort's fall
Their owne dejections—to whom her complaint 965
She thus enforc't: 'The Gods beyond constraint
Of any measure urge these teares on me,
Nor was there ever Dame of my degree
So past degree griev'd. First, a Lord so good,
That had such hardie spirits in his blood 970
That all the vertues was adornd withall,
That all the Greeks did their Superiour call,

To part with thus, and lose! And now a sonne,
So worthily belov'd, a course to runne
Beyond my knowledge, whom rude tempests have 975
Made farre from home his most inglorious grave!

Penelope rebuketh her Ladies for not telling her of Telemachus.

Unhappie wenches, that no one of all
(Though in the reach of every one must fall
His taking ship) sustaind the carefull mind
To call me from my bed, who this designd 980
And most vowd course in him had either staid
(How much soever hasted) or dead laid
He should have left me. Many a man I have
That would have calld old Dolius my slave
(That keepes my Orchard, whom my Father gave 985
At my departure) to have runne and told
Laertes this, to trie if he could hold
From running through the people, and from teares,
In telling them of these vowd murtherers—
That both divine Ulysses' hope, and his, 990
Resolve to end in their conspiracies.'

His Nurse then, Euryclea, made reply:

Euryclea's pious comfort of Penelope.

'Deare Soveraigne, let me with your owne hands die,
Or cast me off here; I'le not keepe from thee
One word of what I know. He trusted me 995
With all his purpose, and I gave him all
The bread and wine for which he pleasd to call.
But then a mightie oath he made me sweare,
Not to report it to your royall eare
Before the twelfth day either should appeare, 1000
Or you should aske me when you heard him gone.
Empaire not then your beauties with your mone,
But wash and put unteare-staind garments on:
Ascend your chamber with your Ladies here,
And pray the seed of Goat-nurst Jupiter 1005
(Divine Athenia) to preserve your sonne,
And she will save him from confusion.
Th'old King, to whom your hopes stand so inclin'd
For his grave counsels, you perhaps may find
Unfit affected, for his age's sake. 1010
But heaven-kings waxe not old, and therefore make
Fit pray'rs to them; for my thoughts never will
Beleeve the heavenly powres conceit so ill
The seed of righteous Arcesiades
To end it utterly, but still will please 1015
In some place evermore some one of them

Laertes sonne to Arcesius the son of Jupiter.

To save, and decke him with a Diadem,
Give him possession of erected Towres
And farre-stretcht fields, crownd all of fruits and flowres.'
This easd her heart and dride her humorous eies, 1020
When having washt, and weeds of sacrifise
(Pure, and unstaind with her distrustfull teares)
Put on, (with all her women-ministers)
Up to a chamber of most height she rose,
And cakes of salt and barly did impose 1025
Within a wicker basket—all which broke
In decent order, thus she did invoke:

Penelope to Pallas.

'Great Virgin of the Goat-preserved God,
If ever the inhabited abode
Of wise Ulysses held the fatted Thies 1030
Of sheepe and Oxen, made thy sacrifice
By his devotion, heare me, nor forget
His pious services, but safe see set
His deare sonne on these shores, and banish hence
These wooers, past all meane in insolence.' 1035

This said, she shriekt, and Pallas heard her praire.
The wooers broke with tumult all the aire
About the shadie house; and one of them,
Whose pride his youth had made the more extreme,
Said: 'Now the many-wooer-honourd Queene 1040
Will surely satiate her delayfull spleene,
And one of us in instant nuptials take.
Poore Dame, she dreames not what designe we make
Upon the life and slaughter of her sonne.'

So said he; but so said was not so done;— 1045
Whose arrogant spirit in a vaunt so vaine

Antinous to the rest.

Antinous chid, and said: 'For shame, containe
These braving speeches! Who can tell who heares?
Are we not now in reach of others' eares?
If our intentions please us, let us call 1050
Our spirits up to them, and let speeches fall.
By watchfull Danger men must silent go:
What we resolve on, let's not say, but do.'
This said, he chusde out twentie men that bore
Best reckning with him, and to ship and shore 1055
All hasted, reacht the ship, lancht, raisd the mast,
Put sailes in, and with leather loopes made fast
The oares, Sailes hoisted; Armes their men did bring,
All giving speed and forme to every thing.

Then to the high-deepes their riggd vessell driven, 1060
They supt, expecting the approching Even.
  Meane space, Penelope her chamber kept
And bed, and neither eate, nor dranke, nor slept—
Her strong thoughts wrought so on her blamelesse sonne,
Still in contention, if he should be done 1065
To death, or scape the impious wooers' designe.
Looke how a Lion, whom men-troopes combine
To hunt and close him in a craftie ring,
Much varied thought conceives, and feare doth sting
For urgent danger: so far'd she till sleepe 1070
All juncture of her joynts and nerves did steepe
In his dissolving humor. When (at rest)
Pallas her favours varied, and addrest
An Idoll, that Iphthima did present
In structure of her every lineament, 1075
Great-sould Icarius' daughter, whom for Spouse
Eumelus tooke, that kept in Pheris house.
This to divine Ulysses' house she sent,
To trie her best meane how she might content
Mournfull Penelope, and make Relent 1080
The strict addiction in her to deplore.
This Idoll (like a worme, that lesse or more
Contracts or straines her) did it selfe convey
Beyond the wards or windings of the key
Into the chamber, and, above her head 1085
Her seate assuming, thus she comforted
Distrest Penelope: 'Doth sleepe thus sease
Thy powres, affected with so much disease?
The Gods, that nothing troubles, will not see
Thy teares nor griefes in any least degree 1090
Sustaind with cause, for they will guard thy sonne
Safe to his wisht and native mansion,
Since he is no offender of their States,
And they to such are firmer than their Fates.'
  The wise Penelope receiv'd her thus 1095
(Bound with a slumber most delicious,
And in the Port of dreames): 'O sister, why
Repaire you hither, since so farre off lie
Your house and houshold? You were never here
Before this houre, and would you now give cheare 1100
To my so many woes and miseries,
Affecting fitly all the faculties

Δέμας, membrorum structura.

παρὰ κληῖδος, ἱμάντα. Ἱμὰς, affectus curculionis significat quod longior et gracilior evaserit.

Minerva sub Iphthimæ persona, solatur Penelopen in somnis.

Penelope to the Dreame.

My soule and mind hold, having lost before
A husband, that of all the vertues bore
The Palme amongst the Greeks, and whose renowne 1105
So ample was that Fame the sound hath blowne
Through Greece and Argos to her very heart?
And now againe, a sonne, that did convert
My whole powres to his love, by ship is gone—
A tender Plant, that yet was never growne 1110
To labour's taste nor the commerce of men—
For whom more than my husband I complaine,
And lest he should at any sufferance touch
(Or in the sea, or by the men so much
Estrang'd to him, that must his consorts be) 1115
Feare and chill tremblings shake each joynt of me.
Besides, his danger sets on foes profest
To way-lay his returne, that have addrest
Plots for his death.' The scarce-discerned Dreame
Said: 'Be of comfort, nor feares so extreme 1120
Let thus dismay thee; thou hast such a mate
Attending thee as some at any rate
Would wish to purchase, for her powre is great:
Minerva pities thy delight's defeate,
Whose Grace hath sent me to foretell thee theese.' 1125

Penelope to the Idoll.

'If thou,' said she, 'be of the Goddesses,
And heardst her tell thee these, thou mayst as well
From her tell all things else. Daigne then to tell
If yet the man to all misfortunes borne
(My husband) lives, and sees the Sunne adorne 1130
The darksome earth, or hides his wretched head
In Pluto's house and lives amongst the dead?'
'I will not,' she replide, 'my breath exhale
In one continude and perpetuall tale,
Lives he or dies he. Tis a filthy use 1135
To be in vaine and idle speech profuse.'
This said, she through the key-hole of the dore
Vanisht againe into the open blore.
Icarius' daughter started from her sleepe,
And Joye's fresh humor her lov'd brest did steepe, 1140
When now so cleare, in that first watch of night,
She saw the seene dreame vanish from her sight.
The wooers (shipt) the sea's moist wayes did plie,
And thought the Prince a haughtie death should die.
There lies a certaine Iland in the sea, 1145

Twixt rockie Samos and rough Ithaca,
That cliffie is it selfe, and nothing great,
Yet holds convenient havens that two wayes let
Ships in and out, calld Asteris: and there
The wooers hop't to make their massakere. 1150

Finis libri quarti Hom. Odyss.

THE FIFTH BOOKE
of
HOMER'S ODYSSES

THE ARGUMENT

A Second Court on Jove attends,
Who Hermes to Calypso sends,
Commanding her to cleare the wayes
Ulysses sought; and she obayes.
When Neptune saw Ulysses free, 5
And so in safetie plow the sea,
Enrag'd, he ruffles up the waves,
And splits his ship. Leucothea saves
His person yet, as being a Dame
Whose Godhead governd in the frame 10
Of those seas' tempers. But the meane
By which she curbs dread Neptune's splene
Is made a Jewell, which she takes
From off her head, and that she makes
Ulysses on his bosome weare; 15
About his necke she ties it there,
And, when he is with waves beset,
Bids weare it as an Amulet,
Commanding him that not before
He toucht upon Phæacia's shore 20
He should not part with it, but then
Returne it to the sea agein
And cast it from him. He performes;
Yet, after this, bides bitter stormes,
And in the rockes sees Death engrav'd; 25
But on Phæacia's shore is sav'd.

Another Argument

E. *Ulysses builds*
A ship, and gaines
The Glassie fields;
Payes Neptune paines.

Aurora rose from high-borne Tithon's Bed,
That men and Gods might be illustrated:
And then the Deities sate. Imperiall Jove,
That makes the horrid murmure beate above,
Tooke place past all, whose height for ever springs 5
And from whom flowes th'eternall powre of things.
Then Pallas (mindfull of Ulysses) told
The many Cares that in Calypso's hold
He still sustaind—when he had felt before
So much affliction and such dangers more. 10

Pallas to the Gods.

'O Father,' said she, 'and ye everblest!
Give never King hereafter interest
In any aide of yours by serving you,
By being gentle, humane, just, but grow
Rude, and for ever scornfull of your rights, 15
All justice ordring by their appetites,
Since he that rul'd as it in right behov'd,
That all his subjects as his children lov'd,
Finds you so thoughtlesse of him and his birth.
Thus men begin to say, ye rule in earth, 20
And grudge at what ye let him undergo,
Who yet the least part of his sufferance know—
Thralld in an Iland, shipwrackt in his teares,
And in the fancies that Calypso beares
Bound from his birthright, all his shipping gone, 25
And of his souldiers not retaining one.
And now his most-lov'd Sonne's life doth inflame
Their slaughterous envies; since his Father's fame
He puts in pursuite, and is gone as farre
As sacred Pylos, and the singular 30
Dame-breeding Sparta.' This, with this reply,

Jove to Pallas.

The Cloud-assembler answerd: 'What words flie
Thine owne remembrance, daughter? Hast not thou
The counsell given thy selfe, that told thee how
Ulysses shall with his returne addresse 35
His wooers' wrongs? And, for the safe accesse
His Sonne shall make to his innative Port,
Do thou direct it in as curious sort
As thy wit serves thee—it obeys thy powers—
And in their ship returne the speedlesse wowers.' 40
Then turnd he to his issue Mercurie,

Jove to Mercury.

And said: 'Thou hast made good our Ambassie
To th'other Statists. To the Nymph then now
On whose faire head a tuft of gold doth grow

Beare our true-spoken counsell, for retreat 45
Of patient Ulysses—who shall get
No aide from us, nor any mortall man;
But in a patcht-up skiffe (built as he can,
And suffering woes enow) the twentith day
At fruitfull Scheria let him breathe his way, 50
With the Phæacians, that halfe Deities live,
Who like a God will honour him, and give
His wisedome clothes, and ship, and brasse, and gold,
More than for gaine of Troy he ever told—
Where, at the whole division of the prey, 55
If he a saver were, or got away
Without a wound (if he should grudge) twas well.
But th'end shall crowne all; therefore Fate will deale
So well with him, to let him land, and see
His native earth, friends, house and family.' 60

ἐπὶ σχεδίης πολυδέσμου—in rate multis vinculis ligatus.

Thus charg'd he; nor Argicides denied,
But to his feete his faire wingd shooes he tied,
Ambrosian, golden, that in his command
Put either sea or the unmeasur'd land
With pace as speedie as a puft of wind. 65
Then up his Rod went, with which he declin'd
The eyes of any waker, when he pleasd,
And any sleeper, when he wisht, diseasd.

Mercurij descriptio.

This tooke, he stoopt Pieria, and thence
Glid through the aire, and Neptune's Confluence 70
Kist as he flew, and checkt the waves as light
As any Sea-Mew in her fishing flight,
Her thicke wings soucing in the savorie seas.
Like her, he past a world of wildernesse,
But when the far-off Ile he toucht, he went 75
Up from the blue sea to the Continent,
And reacht the ample Caverne of the Queene,
Whom he within found—without, seldome seene.
A Sun-like fire upon the harth did flame,
The matter precious, and divine the frame, 80
Of Cedar cleft, and Incense was the Pile,
That breath'd an odour round about the Ile.
Her selfe was seated in an inner roome,
Whom sweetly sing he heard, and at her loome
About a curious web, whose yarne she threw 85
In with a golden shittle. A Grove grew
In endlesse spring about her Caverne round,
With odorous Cypresse, Pines, and Poplars crownd,

Descriptio specus Calypsus.

Where Haulks, Sea-owles, and long-tongu'd Bittours bred,
And other birds their shadie pinions spred— 90
All Fowles maritimall; none roosted there
But those whose labours in the waters were.
A Vine did all the hollow Cave embrace,
Still greene, yet still ripe bunches gave it grace.
Foure Fountaines one against another powrd 95
Their silver streames, and medowes all enflowrd
With sweete Balme-gentle and blue Violets hid,
That deckt the soft brests of each fragrant Mead.
Should any one (though he immortall were)
Arrive and see the sacred objects there, 100
He would admire them and be over-joyd.
And so stood Hermes' ravisht powres employd.
But having all admir'd, he enterd on
The ample Cave, nor could be seene unknowne
Of great Calypso (for all Deities are 105
Prompt in each other's knowledge, though so farre
Severd in dwellings), but he could not see
Ulysses there within. Without was he
Set sad ashore, where twas his use to view
Th'unquiet sea, sigh'd, wept, and emptie drew 110
His heart of comfort. Plac't here in her throne
(That beames cast up to Admiration)
Divine Calypso question'd Hermes thus:

Calypso to Mercurie.

'For what cause, deare, and much-esteem'd by us,
Thou golden-rod-adorned Mercurie, 115
Arriv'st thou here? Thou hast not usde t'apply
Thy passage this way. Say, what ever be
Thy heart's desire, my mind commands it thee,
If in my meanes it lie or powre of fact.
But first, what hospitable rights exact, 120
Come yet more neare and take.' This said, she set
A Table forth, and furnisht it with meate
Such as the Gods taste, and serv'd in with it
Vermilion Nectar. When with banquet fit
He had confirmd his spirits, he thus exprest 125

Mercurie to Calypso.

His cause of coming: 'Thou hast made request,
Goddesse of Goddesses, to understand
My cause of touch here: which thou shalt command,
And know with truth. Jove causd my course to thee
Against my will, for who would willingly 130
Lackey along so vast a lake of Brine,
Neare to no Citie that the powres divine

Receives with solemne rites and Hecatombs?
But Jove's will ever all law overcomes;
No other God can crosse or make it void. 135
And he affirmes that one, the most annoid
With woes and toiles of all those men that fought
For Priam's Citie, and to end hath brought
Nine yeares in the contention, is with thee.
For in the tenth yeare, when roy Victorie 140
Was wonne to give the Greeks the spoile of Troy,
Returne they did professe, but not enjoy,
Since Pallas they incenst, and she the waves
By all the winds' powre, that blew ope their graves.
And there they rested. Onely this poore one 145
This Coast both winds and waves have cast upon:
Whom now forthwith he wils thee to dismisse,
Affirming that th'unalterd destinies
Not onely have decreed he shall not die
Apart his friends, but of Necessitie 150
Enjoy their sights before those fatall houres,
His countrie earth reach, and erected Towres.'
This strook a love-checkt horror through her powres,
When (naming him) she this reply did give:

Calypso's displeased reply to Mercurie.

'Insatiate are ye Gods past all that live 155
In all things you affect—which still converts
Your powres to Envies. It afflicts your hearts
That any Goddesse should (as you obtaine
The use of earthly Dames) enjoy the men,
And most in open mariage. So ye far'd 160
When the delicious-fingerd Morning shar'd
Orion's bed: you easie-living States
Could never satisfie your emulous hates
Till in Ortygia the precise-liv'd Dame
(Gold-thron'd Diana) on him rudely came, 165
And with her swift shafts slue him. And such paines,
When rich-haird Ceres pleasd to give the raines
To her affections, and the grace did yeeld
Of love and bed amidst a three-cropt field
To her Iasion, he paid angrie Jove, 170
Who lost no long time notice of their love,
But with a glowing lightning was his death.
And now your envies labour underneath
A mortal's choice of mine; whose life I tooke
To liberall safetie, when his ship Jove strooke 175
With red-hote flashes, peece-meale in the seas,

And all his friends and souldiers succourlesse
Perisht but he. Him, cast upon this coast
With blasts and billowes, I (in life given lost)
Preserv'd alone, lov'd, nourisht, and did vow 180
To make him deathlesse, and yet never grow
Crooked or worne with age his whole life long.
But since no reason may be made so strong
To strive with Jove's will, or to make it vaine—
No, not if all the other Gods should straine 185
Their powres against it—let his will be law,
So he affoord him fit meanes to withdraw
(As he commands him) to the raging Maine:
But meanes from me he never shall obtaine,
For my meanes yeeld nor men, nor ship, nor oares, 190
To set him off from my so envied shores.
But if my counsell and goodwill can aide
His safe passe home, my best shall be assaid.'
'Vouchsafe it so,' said heaven's Ambassador,
'And daigne it quickly. By all meanes abhorre 195
T'incense Jove's wrath against thee—that with grace
He may hereafter all thy wish embrace.'

Mercurie leaves Calypso.

Thus tooke the Argus-killing God his wings.
And since the reverend Nymph these awfull things
Receiv'd from Jove, she to Ulysses went: 200
Whom she ashore found, drownd in discontent;
His eyes kept never drie he did so mourne,
And waste his deare age for his wisht returne—
Which still without the Cave he usde to do,
Because he could not please the Goddesse so. 205
At night yet (forc't) together tooke their rest,
The willing Goddesse and th'unwilling Guest.
But he all day in rockes and on the shore
The vext sea viewd, and did his Fate deplore.
Him, now, the Goddesse (coming neare) bespake: 210

Calypso to Ulysses.

'Unhappie man, no more discomfort take
For my constraint of thee, nor waste thine age.
I now will passing freely disengage
Thy irksome stay here. Come then, fell thee wood,
And build a ship to save thee from the flood. 215
I'le furnish thee with fresh wave, bread, and wine,

Hunger.

Ruddie and sweet, that will the Piner pine,
Put garments on thee, give thee winds foreright,
That every way thy home-bent appetite
May safe attaine to it, if so it please 220

At all parts all the heaven-housd Deities,
That more in powre are, more in skill, than I,
And more can judge what fits humanitie.'
He stood amaz'd at this strange change in her,
Ulysses to Calypso. And said: 'O Goddesse! thy intents preferre 225
Some other project than my parting hence,
Commanding things of too high consequence
For my performance. That my selfe should build
A ship of powre, my home-assaies to shield
Against the great Sea of such dread to passe— 230
Which not the best-built ship that ever was
Will passe exulting, when such winds as Jove
Can thunder up their trims and tacklings prove.
But could I build one, I would ne're aboord
(Thy will opposde) nor (won) without thy word, 235
Given in the great oath of the Gods to me,
Not to beguile me in the least degree.'
The Goddesse smilde, held hard his hand, and said:
'O y'are a shrewd one, and so habited
In taking heed thou knowst not what it is 240
To be unwary, nor use words amisse.
How hast thou charmd me, were I ne're so slie!
Calypso's oath. Let earth know then, and heaven, so broad, so hie,
And th'under-sunke waves of th'infernall streame
(Which is an oath as terribly supreame 245
As any God sweares) that I had no thought
But stood with what I spake, nor would have wrought,
Nor counseld, any act against thy good;
But ever diligently weighd, and stood
On those points in perswading thee, that I 250
Would use my selfe in such extremitie.
For my mind simple is, and innocent,
Not given by cruell sleights to circumvent,
Nor beare I in my breast a heart of steele,
But with the Sufferer willing sufferance feele.' 255
This said, the Grace of Goddesses led home;
He tract her steps; and (to the Caverne come)
In that rich Throne, whence Mercurie arose,
He sate. The Nymph her selfe did then appose
For food and bevridge to him all best meate 260
And drinke that mortals use to taste and eate.
Then sate she opposite, and for her Feast
Was Nectar and Ambrosia addrest
By handmaids to her. Both, what was prepar'd

Did freely fall to. Having fitly far'd, 265
The Nymph Calypso this discourse began:
'Jove-bred Ulysses! many-witted man!
Still is thy home so wisht? So soone, away?
Be still of cheare, for all the worst I say.
But if thy soule knew what a summe of woes 270
For thee to cast up thy sterne Fates impose
Ere to thy country earth thy hopes attaine,
Undoubtedly thy choice would here remaine,
Keepe house with me, and be a liver ever.
Which (me thinkes) should thy house and thee dissever, 275
Though for thy wife there thou art set on fire,
And all thy dayes are spent in her desire—
And though it be no boast in me to say,
In forme and mind I match her every way.
Nor can it fit a mortall Dame's compare 280
T'affect those termes with us that deathlesse are.'

Calypso's promise of immortalitie to Ulysses.

The great in counsels made her this reply:
'Renowm'd and to be reverenc'd Deitie!
Let it not move thee that so much I vow
My comforts to my wife, though well I know 285
All cause my selfe why wise Penelope
In wit is farre inferiour to thee,
In feature, stature, all the parts of show,
She being a mortall, an Immortall thou,
Old ever growing, and yet never old. 290
Yet her desire shall all my dayes see told,
Adding the sight of my returning day,
And naturall home. If any God shall lay
His hand upon me as I passe the seas,
I'le beare the worst of what his hand shall please, 295
As having given me such a mind as shall
The more still rise, the more his hand lets fall.
In warres and waves my sufferings were not small.
I now have sufferd much; as much before;
Hereafter let as much result, and more.' 300

This said, the Sunne set, and earth shadowes gave,
When these two (in an in-roome of the Cave
Left to themselves) left Love no rites undone.
The early Morne up, up he rose, put on
His in and out weed. She her selfe inchaces 305
Amidst a white robe, full of all the Graces,
Ample and pleated, thicke, like fishie skales.
A golden girdle then her waste empales;

Her head a veile decks; and abroad they come.
And now began Ulysses to go home. 310
A great Axe first she gave, that two wayes cut,
In which a faire wel-polisht helme was put
That from an Olive bough receiv'd his frame.
A plainer then. Then led she till they came
To loftie woods that did the Ile confine. 315
The Firre tree, Poplar and heaven-scaling Pine
Had there their ofspring. Of which those that were
Of driest matter and grew longest there,
He chusde for lighter saile. This place thus showne,
The Nymph turnd home. He fell to felling downe, 320
And twentie trees he stoopt in litle space,
Plaind, usde his Plumb, did all with artfull grace.
In meane time did Calypso wimbles bring.
He bor'd, closde, naild, and orderd every thing.
And looke how much a ship-wright will allow 325
A ship of burthen (one that best doth know
What fits his Art), so large a Keele he cast—
Wrought up her decks and hatches, side-boords, mast,
With willow watlings armd her to resist
The billowes' outrage, added all she mist— 330
Sail-yards and sterne for guide. The Nymph then brought
Linnen for sailes, which with dispatch he wrought—
Gables, and halsters, tacklings. All the Frame
In foure dayes' space to full perfection came.
The fifth day they dismist him from the shore, 335
Weeds, neate and odorous, gave him, victles' store,
Wine and strong waters, and a prosperous wind.
To which Ulysses (fit to be divin'd)
His sailes exposd, and hoised. Off he gat;
And chearfull was he. At the Sterne he sat 340
And ster'd right artfully. No sleepe could seise
His ey-lids: he beheld the Pleiades,
The Beare, surnam'd the Waine, that round doth move
About Orion, and keepes still above
The billowie Ocean, the slow-setting starre, 345
Boötes calld, by some the Waggonar.
Calypso warnd him he his course should stere
Still to his left hand. Seventeene dayes did cleare
The cloudie Night's command in his moist way,
And by the eighteenth light he might display 350
The shadie hils of the Phæacian shore,
For which, as to his next abode, he bore.

This foure dayes' worke (you will say) is too much for one man: and Plinie affirmes that Hiero (a king of Sicilie) in five and forty dayes built two hundred and twentie ships, rigged them, and put to sea with them.

The countrie did a pretie figure yeeld,
And lookt from off the darke seas like a shield.
  Imperious Neptune (making his retreate   355
From th'Æthiopian earth, and taking seate
Upon the mountaines of the Solymi,
From thence farre off discovering) did descrie
Ulysses his fields plowing. All on fire
The sight strait set his heart, and made desire   360
Of wreake runne over, it did boile so hie.
When (his head nodding): 'O impietie!'
He cried out, 'Now the Gods' inconstancie
Is most apparent, altring their designes
Since I the Æthiops saw, and here confines   365
To this Ulysses' fate his misery.
The great marke on which all his hopes rely
Lies in Phæacia. But I hope he shall
Feele woe at height ere that dead calme befall.'
This said, he (begging) gatherd clouds from land,   370

συναγείρω—
Mendicando colligo.

Frighted the seas up, snatcht into his hand
His horrid Trident, and aloft did tosse
(Of all the winds) all stormes he could engrosse.
All earth tooke into sea with clouds; grim Night
Fell tumbling headlong from the cope of Light.   375
The East and Southwinds justld in the aire;
The violent Zephyr and North making-faire
Rould up the waves before them: and then bent
Ulysses' knees; then all his spirit was spent.
In which despaire, he thus spake: 'Woe is me!   380
What was I borne to, man of miserie?
Feare tels me now that all the Goddesse said
Truth's selfe will author, that Fate would be paid
Griefe's whole summe due from me at sea, before
I reacht the deare touch of my countrie's shore.   385
With what clouds Jove heaven's heightned forehead binds!
How tyrannize the wraths of all the winds!
How all the tops he bottomes with the deepes!
And in the bottomes all the tops he steepes!
Thus dreadfull is the presence of our death.   390
Thrice foure times blest were they that sunke beneath
Their Fates at Troy, and did to nought contend
But to renowme Atrides with their end!
I would to God my houre of death and Fate
That day had held the power to terminate,   395
When showres of darts my life bore undeprest

About divine Æacides' deceast.
Then had I bene allotted to have died
By all the Greeks with funerals glorified
(Whence Death, encouraging good life, had growne) 400
Where now I die by no man mournd, nor knowne.'
This spoke, a huge wave tooke him by the head
And hurld him o're-boord: ship and all it laid
Inverted quite amidst the waves, but he
Farre off from her sprawld, strowd about the sea, 405
His Sterne still holding, broken off; his Mast
Burst in the midst, so horrible a blast
Of mixt winds strooke it. Sailes and saile-yards fell
Amongst the billowes, and himselfe did dwell
A long time under water, nor could get 410
In haste his head out—wave with wave so met
In his depression, and his garments too
(Given by Calypso) gave him much to do,
Hindring his swimming; yet he left not so
His drenched vessell, for the overthrow 415
Of her nor him, but gat at length againe
(Wrestling with Neptune) hold of her, and then
Sate in her Bulke, insulting over Death—
Which (with the salt streame prest to stop his breath)
He scap't and gave the sea againe to give 420
To other men. His ship so striv'd to live,
Floting at randon, cufft from wave to wave,
As you have seene the Northwind when he drave
In Autumne heapes of thorne-fed Grashoppers
Hither and thither; one heape this way beares, 425
Another that, and makes them often meete
In his confusde gales; so Ulysses' fleete
The winds hurl'd up and downe: now Boreas
Tost it to Notus, Notus gave it passe
To Eurus; Eurus Zephyr made pursue 430
The horrid Tennis. This sport calld the view
Of Cadmus' daughter, with the narrow heele,
(Ino Leucothea) that first did feele
A mortall Dame's desires, and had a tongue,
But now had th'honor to be nam'd among 435
The marine Godheads. She with pitie saw
Ulysses justl'd thus from flaw to flaw;
And (like a Cormorand in forme and flight)
Rose from a whirl-poole, on the ship did light,

Leucothea to Ulysses.

And thus bespeake him: 'Why is Neptune thus 440
In thy pursuite extremely furious,
Oppressing thee with such a world of ill
Even to thy death? He must not serve his will,
Though tis his studie. Let me then advise
As my thoughts serve: thou shalt not be unwise 445
To leave thy weeds and ship to the commands
Of these rude winds, and worke out with thy hands
Passe to Phæacia, where thy austere Fate
Is to pursue thee with no more such hate.
Take here this Tablet with this riband strung, 450
And see it still about thy bosome hung–
By whose eternall vertue never feare
To suffer thus againe, nor perish here.
But when thou touchest with thy hand the shore,
Then take it from thy necke, nor weare it more, 455
But cast it farre off from the Continent,
And then thy person farre ashore present.'
Thus gave she him the Tablet; and againe
(Turnd to a Cormorand) div'd past sight the Maine.
Patient Ulysses sighd at this, and stucke 460
In the conceit of such faire-spoken Lucke,

Ulysses stil suspicious of faire fortunes.

And said: 'Alas, I must suspect even this,
Lest any other of the Deities
Adde sleight to Neptune's force, to counsell me
To leave my vessell, and so farre off see 465
The shore I aime at. Not with thoughts too cleare
Will I obey her: but to me appeare
These counsels best–as long as I perceive
My ship not quite dissolv'd I will not leave
The helpe she may affoord me, but abide 470
And suffer all woes till the worst be tride.
When she is split, I'le swim: no miracle can,
Past neare and cleare meanes, move a knowing man.'
While this discourse emploid him, Neptune raisd
A huge, a high, and horrid sea, that seisd 475

Neptuni in Ulyssem inclementia.

Him and his ship and tost them through the Lake.
As when the violent winds together take
Heapes of drie chaffe and hurle them every way,
So his long woodstacke Neptune strooke astray.
Then did Ulysses mount on rib, perforce, 480
Like to a rider of a running horse,
To stay himselfe a time, while he might shift
His drenched weeds that were Calypso's gift.

When putting strait Leucothea's Amulet
About his necke, he all his forces set 485
To swim, and cast him prostrate to the seas.
When powrefull Neptune saw the ruthlesse prease
Of perils siege him thus, he mov'd his head,
And this betwixt him and his heart he said:
'So, now feele ils enow, and struggle so, 490
Till to your Jove-lov'd Ilanders you row.
But my mind sayes you will not so avoid
This last taske too, but be with sufferance cloid.'
This said, his rich-man'd horse he mov'd, and reacht
His house at Ægas. But Minerva fetcht 495
The winds from sea, and all their wayes but one
Barrd to their passage; the bleake North alone
She set to blow; the rest she charg'd to keepe
Their rages in, and bind themselves in sleepe.
But Boreas still flew high to breake the seas, 500
Till Jove-bred Ithacus the more with ease
The navigation-skild Phæacian States
Might make his refuge, Death and angrie Fates
At length escaping. Two nights yet, and daies,
He spent in wrestling with the sable seas, 505
In which space often did his heart propose
Death to his eyes. But when Aurora rose
And threw the third light from her orient haire,
The winds grew calme and cleare was all the aire,
Not one breath stirring. Then he might descrie 510
(Raisd by the high seas) cleare, the land was nie.
Simile. And then, looke how to good sonnes that esteeme
Their father's life deare (after paines extreame,
Felt in some sicknesse that hath held him long
Downe to his bed, and with affections strong 515
Wasted his bodie, made his life his lode,
As being inflicted by some angrie God)
When on their praires they see descend at length
Health from the heavens, clad all in spirit and strength,
The sight is precious: so, since here should end 520
Ulysses' toiles, which therein should extend
Health to his countrie (held to him his Sire)
And on which long for him Disease did tire,
And then besides, for his owne sake to see
The shores, the woods so neare, such joy had he, 525
As those good sonnes for their recoverd Sire.
Then labourd feete and all parts to aspire

To that wisht Continent, which, when as neare
He came as Clamor might informe an eare,
He heard a sound beate from the sea-bred rocks 530
Against which gave a huge sea horrid shocks,
That belcht upon the firme land weeds and fome,
With which were all things hid there—where no roome
Of fit capacitie was for any port,
Nor (from the sea) for any man's resort, 535
The shores, the rocks, and cliffes so prominent were.
'O,' said Ulysses then, 'now Jupiter
Hath given me sight of an unhop't for shore,
(Though I have wrought these seas so long, so sore)
Of rest yet no place shewes the slendrest prints, 540
The rugged shore so bristl'd is with flints,
Against which every way the waves so flocke,
And all the shore shewes as one eminent rocke—
So neare which tis so deepe, that not a sand
Is there for any tired foote to stand: 545
Nor flie his death-fast-following miseries,
Lest, if he land, upon him fore-right flies
A churlish wave to crush him gainst a Cliffe,
Worse than vaine rendring all his landing strife.
And should I swim to seeke a haven elsewhere, 550
Or land lesse wave-beate, I may justly feare
I shall be taken with a gale againe
And cast a huge way off into the Maine;
And there the great Earth-shaker (having seene
My so neare landing, and againe his spleene 555
Forcing me to him) will some Whale send out
(Of which a horrid number here about
His Amphitrite breeds) to swallow me.
I well have prov'd with what malignitie
He treds my steps.' While this discourse he held, 560
A curst Surge gainst a cutting rocke impeld
His naked bodie, which it gasht and tore,
And had his bones broke, if but one sea more
Pallas. Had cast him on it. But she prompted him
That never faild, and bad him no more swim 565
Still off and on, but boldly force the shore
And hug the rocke that him so rudely tore.
Which he with both hands sigh'd and claspt till past
The billowes' rage was; which scap't backe, so fast
The rocke repulst it, that it reft his hold, 570
Sucking him from it, and farre backe he rould.

And as the Polypus that (forc't from home
Amidst the soft sea, and neare rough land come
For shelter gainst the stormes that beate on her
At open sea, as she abroad doth erre) 575
A deale of gravill and sharpe little stones
Needfully gathers in her hollow bones:
So he forc't hither (by the sharper ill
Shunning the smoother), where he best hop't, still
The worst succeeded: for the cruell friend, 580
To which he clingd for succour, off did rend
From his broad hands the soken flesh so sore
That off he fell and could sustaine no more.
Quite under water fell he, and, past Fate,
Haplesse Ulysses there had lost the state 585
He held in life, if (still the grey-eyd Maid
His wisedome prompting) he had not assaid
Another course and ceast t'attempt that shore,
Swimming, and casting round his eye, t'explore
Some other shelter. Then the mouth he found 590
Of faire Callicoe's flood, whose shores were crownd
With most apt succors–rocks so smooth they seemd
Polisht of purpose, land that quite redeemd
With breathlesse coverts th'other's blasted shores.
The flood he knew, and thus in heart implores: 595
'King of this River, heare! Whatever name
Makes thee invokt, to thee I humbly frame
My flight from Neptune's furies. Reverend is
To all the ever-living Deities
What erring man soever seekes their aid. 600
To thy both flood and knees a man dismaid
With varied sufferance sues. Yeeld then some rest
To him that is thy suppliant profest.'
This (though but spoke in thought) the Godhead heard,
Her Current strait staid, and her thicke waves cleard 605
Before him, smooth'd her waters, and just where
He praid, halfe drownd, entirely sav'd him there.
Then forth he came, his both knees faltring, both
His strong hands hanging downe, and all with froth
His cheeks and nosthrils flowing, voice and breath 610
Spent to all use; and downe he sunke to Death.
The sea had soakt his heart through: all his vaines
His toiles had rackt t'a labouring woman's paines.
Dead wearie was he. But when breath did find
A passe reciprocall, and in his mind 615

Per asperiora vitare lævia.

Ὤδεε *of* ὠδίνω, a partu doleo.

His spirit was recollected, up he rose
And from his necke did th'Amulet unlose
That Ino gave him, which he hurld from him
To sea. It sounding fell, and backe did swim
With th'ebbing waters till it strait arriv'd 620
Where Ino's faire hand it againe receiv'd.
Then kist he th'humble earth, and on he goes,
Till bulrushes shewd place for his repose,
Where laid, he sigh'd, and thus said to his soule:
'O me, what strange perplexities controule 625
The whole skill of thy powres in this event?
What feele I if till Care-nurse Night be spent
I watch amidst the flood? The sea's chill breath
And vegetant dewes I feare will be my death,
So low brought with my labours. Towards day 630
A passing sharpe aire ever breathes at sea.
If I the pitch of this next mountaine scale
And shadie wood, and in some thicket fall
Into the hands of Sleepe, though there the cold
May well be checkt and healthfull slumbers hold 635
Her sweete hand on my powres, all care allaid,
Yet there will beasts devoure me. Best appaid
Doth that course make me yet; for there some strife,
Strength and my spirit may make me make for life,
Which, though empaird, may yet be fresh applied 640
Where perill possible of escape is tried.
But he that fights with heaven, or with the sea,
To Indiscretion addes Impietie.'
  Thus to the woods he hasted, which he found
Not farre from sea, but on farre-seeing ground, 645
Where two twin under-woods he enterd on,
With Olive trees and oile-trees overgrowne,
Through which the moist force of the loud-voic't wind
Did never beate, nor ever Phœbus shin'd,
Nor showre beate through—they grew so one in one, 650
And had, by turnes, their powre t'exclude the Sunne.
Here enterd our Ulysses, and a bed
Of leaves huge and of huge abundance spred
With all his speed. Large he made it, for there
For two or three men ample Coverings were, 655
Such as might shield them from the Winter's worst,
Though steele it breath'd and blew as it would burst.
  Patient Ulysses joyd that ever day

A metaphoricall Hyperbole, expressing the Winter's extremitie of sharpnesse.

Shewd such a shelter. In the midst he lay,
Store of leaves heaping high on every side. 660
And as in some out-field a man doth hide
Simile. A kindld brand to keepe the seed of fire,
No neighbour dwelling neare, and his desire
Serv'd with selfe store he else would aske of none,
But of his fore-spent sparks rakes th'ashes on: 665
So this out-place Ulysses thus receives;
And thus nak't vertue's seed lies hid in leaves.
Yet Pallas made him sleepe as soone as men
Whom Delicacies all their flatteries daine.
And all that all his labours could comprise 670
Quickly concluded in his closed eies.

Finis libri quinti Hom. Odyss.

THE SIXTH BOOKE

of

HOMER'S ODYSSES

THE ARGUMENT

Minerva in a vision stands
Before Nausicaa, and commands
She to the flood her weeds should beare,
For now her Nuptiall day was neare.
Nausicaa her charge obayes, 5
And then with other virgins playes.
Their sports make wak't Ulysses rise,
Walke to them, and beseech supplies
Of food and clothes. His naked sight
Puts th'other Maids, afraid, to flight. 10
Nausicaa onely boldly stayes,
And gladly his desire obayes.
He (furnisht with her favours showne)
Attends her, and the rest, to Towne.

Another Argument

Ζῆτα. *Here Olive leaves*
T'hide shame began.
The Maide receives
The naked man.

ὕπνῳ καὶ καμάτῳ ἀρημένος—Somno et labore afflictus. *Sleep* (καταχρηστικῶς) *for the want of sleepe.*

The much-sustaining, patient, heavenly Man,
Whom Toile and Sleepe had worne so weake and wan,
Thus wonne his rest. In meane space Pallas went
To the Phæacian citie and descent
That first did broad Hyperia's lands divide 5
Neare the vast Cyclops, men of monstrous pride,
That preyd on those Hyperians since they were
Of greater powre; and therefore longer there

Divine Nausithous dwelt not, but arose,
And did for Scheria all his powres dispose, 10
Farre from ingenious Art-inventing men.
But there did he erect a Citie then.
First, drew a wall round; then he houses builds,
And then a Temple to the Gods, the fields
Lastly dividing. But he (stoopt by Fate) 15
Div'd to th'infernals, and Alcinous sate
In his command, a man the Gods did teach
Commanding counsels. His house held the reach
Of grey Minerva's project, to provide
That great-sould Ithacus might be supplide 20
With all things fitting his returne. She went
Up to the chamber, where the faire descent
Nausicaa. Of great Alcinous slept—a maid whose parts
In wit and beautie wore divine deserts.
Well deckt her chamber was: of which the dore 25
Did seeme to lighten, such a glosse it bore
Betwixt the posts, and now flew ope to find
The Goddesse entrie. Like a puft of wind
She reacht the Virgin bed, neare which there lay
Two maids to whom the Graces did convay 30
Figure and manners. But above the head
Of bright Nausicaa did Pallas tred
The subtle aire, and put the person on
Of Dymas' daughter, from comparison
Exempt in businesse Navall. Like his seed 35
Intending Dymas' daughter. Minerva lookt now, whom one yeare did breed
With bright Nausicaa, and who had gaind
Grace in her love, yet on her thus complaind:
'Nausicaa! why bred thy mother one
So negligent in rites so stood upon 40
By other virgins? Thy faire garments lie
Neglected by thee, yet thy Nuptials nie—
When rich in all attire both thou shouldst be,
And garments give to others honoring thee,
That leade thee to the Temple. Thy good name 45
Growes amongst men for these things; they enflame
Father and reverend Mother with delight.
Come, when the Day takes any winke from Night,
Let's to the river and repurifie
Thy wedding garments: my societie 50
Shall freely serve thee for thy speedier aid,
Because thou shalt no more stand on the Maid.

The best of all Phæacia wooe thy Grace
Where thou wert bred, and ow'st thy selfe a race.
Up, and stirre up to thee thy honourd Sire 55
To give thee Mules and Coach, thee and thy tire,
Veiles, girdles, mantles, early to the flood
To beare in state. It suites thy high-borne blood,
And farre more fits thee than to foote so farre,
For far from towne thou knowst the Bath-founts are.' 60
This said, away blue-eyd Minerva went
Up to Olympus, the firme Continent
That beares in endlesse being the deified kind,
That's neither souc't with showres, nor shooke with wind,
Nor chilld with snow, but where Serenitie flies 65
Exempt from clouds; and ever-beamie skies
Circle the glittering hill, and all their daies
Give the delights of blessed Deitie praise.
And hither Pallas flew, and left the Maid
When she had all that might excite her said. 70
Strait rose the lovely Morne, that up did raise
Faire-veild Nausicaa, whose dreame her praise
To Admiration tooke. Who no time spent
To give the rapture of her vision vent
To her lov'd parents, whom she found within, 75
Her mother set at fire, who had to spin
A Rocke, whose tincture with sea-purple shin'd,
Her maids about her. But she chanc't to find
Her Father going abroad, to Counsell calld
By his grave Senate. And to him exhald 80
Her smotherd bosome was. 'Lov'd Sire,' said she,
'Will you not now command a Coach for me,
Stately and complete, fit for me to beare
To wash at flood the weeds I cannot weare
Before repurified? Your selfe it fits 85
To weare faire weeds, as every man that sits
In place of counsell. And five sonnes you have,
Two wed, three Bachelors, that must be brave
In every daye's shift, that they may go dance;
For these three last with these things must advance 90
Their states in mariage—and who else but I,
Their sister, should their dancing rites supply?'

Olympus described.

This familiar and neare wanton cariage of Nausicaa to her father, joyned with that virgin modestie exprest in her after, is much praised by the gravest of Homer's expositors, with her father's loving allowance of it, knowing her shamefastnes and judgement would not let her exceed at any part. Which note is here inserted, not as if this were more worthy the observation than other every where strewd flowers of precept, but because this more generally pleasing subject may perhaps finde more fitnesse for the stay of most Readers.

This generall cause she shewd, and would not name
Her mind of Nuptials to her Sire, for shame.
He understood her yet, and thus replide: 95
'Daughter! nor these, nor any grace beside,
I either will denie thee or deferre,
Mules, nor a Coach, of state and circular,
Fitting at all parts. Go; my servants shall
Serve thy desires and thy command in all.' 100

The servants then (commanded) soone obaid,
Fetcht Coach, and Mules joynd in it. Then the Maid
Brought from the chamber her rich weeds and laid
All up in Coach, in which her mother plac't
A maund of victles varied well in taste, 105
And other junkets. Wine she likewise filld
Within a goat-skin bottle, and distilld
Sweete and moist oile into a golden Cruse
Both for her daughter's and her handmaids' use,
To soften their bright bodies when they rose 110
Clensed from their cold baths. Up to Coach then goes
Th'observed Maid, takes both the scourge and raines,
And to her side her handmaid strait attaines.
Nor these alone, but other virgins grac't
The Nuptiall Chariot. The whole Bevie plac't, 115
Nausicaa scourgd to make the Coach Mules runne,
That neigh'd, and pac'd their usuall speed, and soone
Both maids and weeds brought to the river side
Where Baths for all the yeare their use supplide—
Whose waters were so pure they would not staine, 120
But still ran faire forth, and did more remaine
Apt to purge staines, for that purg'd staine within,
Which, by the water's pure store, was not seen.

These (here arriv'd) the Mules uncoacht, and drave
Up to the gulphie river's shore, that gave 125
Sweet grasse to them. The maids from Coach then tooke
Their cloaths and steept them in the sable brooke,
Then put them into springs, and trod them cleane
With cleanly feet, adventring wagers then
Who should have soonest and most cleanly done— 130
When, having throughly cleansd, they spred them on
The flood's shore all in order. And then, where
The waves the pibbles washt and ground was cleare
They bath'd themselves, and all with glittring oile
Smooth'd their white skins, refreshing then their toile 135
With pleasant dinner by the river's side—

Yet still watcht when the Sunne their cloaths had dride.
Till which time (having din'd) Nausicaa
With other virgins did at stool-ball play,
Their shoulder-reaching head-tires laying by. 140
Nausicaa (with the wrists of Ivory)
The liking stroke strooke, singing first a song
(As custome orderd), and amidst the throng
Made such a shew, and so past all was seene,
Simile. As when the Chast-borne, Arrow-loving Queene, 145
Along the mountaines gliding, either over
Spartan Taygetus, whose tops farre discover,
Or Eurymanthus, in the wilde Bore's chace
Or swift-hov'd Hart, and with her Jove's faire race
(The field Nymphs) sporting—amongst whom, to see 150
How farre Diana had prioritie
(Though all were faire) for fairnesse, yet of all
(As both by head and forhead being more tall)
Latona triumpht, since the dullest sight
Might easly judge whom her paines brought to light: 155
Nausicaa so (whom never husband tam'd)
Above them all in all the beauties flam'd.
But when they now made homewards, and araid,
Ordring their weeds, disorderd as they plaid,
Mules and Coach ready, then Minerva thought 160
What meanes to wake Ulysses might be wrought
That he might see this lovely sighted maid,
Whom she intended should become his aid,
Bring him to Towne, and his returne advance.
Her meane was this (though thought a stool-ball chance): 165
The Queene now (for the upstroke) strooke the ball
Quite wide off th'other maids, and made it fall
Amidst the whirlpooles. At which out shriekt all,
And with the shrieke did wise Ulysses wake,
Who, sitting up, was doubtfull who should make 170
That sodaine outcrie, and in mind thus striv'd:
'On what a people am I now arriv'd?
At civill hospitable men, that feare
The Gods? Or dwell injurious mortals here,
Unjust, and churlish? Like the female crie 175
Of youth it sounds. What are they? Nymphs bred hie
On tops of hils or in the founts of floods,
In herbie marshes, or in leavy woods?
Or are they high-spoke men I now am neare?
I'le prove, and see.' With this the wary Peere 180

The pietie and wisedome of the Poet was such that (agreeing with the sacred letter) not the least of things he makes come to passe, sine Numinis providentia. *As Spondanus well notes of him.*

Crept forth the thicket, and an Olive bough
Broke with his broad hand, which he did bestow
In covert of his nakednesse, and then
Simile. Put hastie head out. Looke how from his den
A mountaine Lion lookes, that, all embrewd 185
With drops of trees and weather-beaten-hewd,
(Bold of his strength) goes on, and in his eye
A burning fornace glowes, all bent to prey
On sheepe, or oxen, or the upland Hart,
His belly charging him, and he must part 190
Stakes with the Heards-man in his beasts' attempt,
Even where from rape their strengths are most exempt:
So wet, so weather-beate, so stung with Need,
Even to the home-fields of the countrie's breed,
Ulysses was to force forth his accesse, 195
Though meerly naked; and his sight did presse
The eyes of soft-haird virgins. Horrid was
His rough appearance to them: the hard passe
He had at sea stucke by him. All in flight
The Virgins scatterd, frighted with this sight, 200
About the prominent windings of the flood.
All but Nausicaa fled; but she fast stood:
Pallas had put a boldnesse in her brest
And in her faire lims tender Feare comprest.
And still she stood him, as resolv'd to know 205
What man he was, or out of what should grow
His strange repaire to them. And here was he
Put to his wisedome, if her virgin knee
He should be bold, but kneeling, to embrace,
Or keepe aloofe and trie with words of grace, 210
In humblest suppliance, if he might obtaine
Some cover for his nakednes, and gaine
Her grace to shew and guide him to the Towne.
The last he best thought to be worth his owne,
In weighing both well: to keepe still aloofe, 215
And give with soft words his desires their proofe,
Lest pressing so neare as to touch her knee
He might incense her maiden modestie.
This faire and fil'd speech then shewd this was he:
Ulysses to Nausicaa. 'Let me beseech, O Queene, this truth of thee: 220
Are you of mortall or the deified race?
If of the Gods that th'ample heavens embrace,
I can resemble you to none above
So neare as to the chast-borne birth of Jove,

The beamie Cynthia. Her you full present 225
In grace of every God-like lineament—
Her goodly magnitude, and all th'addresse
You promise of her very perfectnesse.
If sprong of humanes that inhabite earth,
Thrice blest are both the authors of your birth, 230
Thrice blest your brothers that in your deserts
Must, even to rapture, beare delighted hearts,
To see so like the first trim of a tree
Your forme adorne a dance. But most blest he
Of all that breathe that hath the gift t'engage 235
Your bright necke in the yoke of mariage,
And decke his house with your commanding merit.
I have not seene a man of so much spirit.
Nor man nor woman I did ever see
At all parts equall to the parts in thee. 240
T'enjoy your sight doth Admiration seise
My eie and apprehensive faculties.
Lately in Delos (with a charge of men
Arriv'd, that renderd me most wretched then,
Now making me thus naked) I beheld 245
The burthen of a Palme, whose issue sweld
About Apollo's Phane; and that put on
A grace like thee, for Earth had never none
Of all her Sylvane issue so adorn'd.
Into amaze my very soule was turnd 250
To give it observation, as now thee
To view, O Virgin, a stupiditie
Past admiration strikes me, joynd with feare
To do a suppliant's due and prease so neare
As to embrace thy knees. Nor is it strange; 255
For one of fresh and firmest spirit would change
T'embrace so bright an object. But, for me,
A cruell habite of calamitie
Prepar'd the strong impression thou hast made;
For this last Day did flie Night's twentith shade 260
Since I, at length, escapt the sable seas,
When in the meane time th'unrelenting prease
Of waves and sterne stormes tost me up and downe,
From th'Ile Ogygia: and now God hath throwne
My wracke on this shore, that perhaps I may 265
My miseries vary here—for yet their stay,
I feare, heaven hath not orderd, though before

These late afflictions it hath lent me store.
O Queene, daine pitie then, since first to you
My Fate importunes my distresse to vow. 270
No other Dame, nor man, that this Earth owne,
And neighbour Citie, I have seene or knowne.
The Towne then shew me; give my nakednes
Some shroud to shelter it, if to these seas
Linnen or woollen you have brought to clense. 275
God give you, in requitall, all th'amends
Your heart can wish: a husband, family,
And good agreement. Nought beneath the skie
More sweet, more worthy, is than firme consent
Of man and wife in houshold government. 280
It joyes their wishers well, their enemies wounds,
But to themselves the speciall good redounds.'

Nausicaa to Ulysses.

She answerd: 'Stranger! I discerne in thee
Nor Sloth nor Folly raignes; and yet I see
Th'art poore and wretched. In which I conclude 285
That Industry nor wisedome make endude
Men with those gifts that make them best to th'eie:
Jove onely orders man's felicitie.
To good and bad his pleasure fashions still
The whole proportion of their good and ill. 290
And he perhaps hath formd this plight in thee,
Of which thou must be patient, as he, free.
But after all thy wandrings, since thy way
Both to our Earth and neare our Citie lay,
As being exposde to our cares to relieve, 295
Weeds and what else a humane hand should give
To one so suppliant and tam'd with woe,
Thou shalt not want. Our Citie I will show,
And tell our people's name. This neighbor Towne
And all this kingdome the Phæacians owne. 300
And (since thou seemdst so faine to know my birth,
And mad'st a question, if of heaven or earth)
This Earth hath bred me, and my Father's name
Alcinous is, that in the powre and frame
Of this Ile's rule is supereminent.' 305

Thus (passing him) she to the Virgins went,
And said: 'Give stay both to your feet and fright.
Why thus disperse ye for a man's meere sight?
Esteeme you him a Cyclop, that long since
Made use to prey upon our Citizens? 310

διερὸς βροτὸς—Cui vitalis vel sensualis humiditas inest. βροτὸς ἀ ῥέω, ut dicatur quasi ῥοτὸς, i.e. ὁ ἐν ῥοῇ ὢν, quod nihil sit magis fluxum quam homo.

315 ἀνὴρ virili animo præditus, fortis, magnanimus. *Nor are those affirmed to be men,* qui servile quidpiam et abiectum faciunt; vel, facere sustinent: *according to this of Herodotus in Poly:* πολλοὶ μὲν ἄνθρωποι εἶεν, ὀλίγοι δὲ ἄνδρες. *Many men's formes sustaine, but few are men.*

330 *According to an other translator:* Ab Iove nam supplex pauper procedit et hospes: Res brevis, at chara est, Magni quoque muneris instar. *Which I cite to shew his good when he keepes him to the Originall, and neare in any degree expounds it.*

This man no moist man is (nor watrish thing,
That's ever flitting, ever ravishing
All it can compasse, and, like it, doth range
In rape of women, never staid in change).
This man is truly manly, wise, and staid, 315
In soule more rich the more to sense decaid,
Who nor will do, nor suffer to be done,
Acts leud and abject; nor can such a one
Greete the Phæacians with a mind envious;
Deare to the Gods they are, and he is pious. 320
Besides, divided from the world we are,
The outpart of it, billowes circulare
The sea revolving round about our shore;
Nor is there any man that enters more
Than our owne countrimen with what is brought 325
From other countries. This man, minding nought
But his reliefe, a poore unhappie wretch,
Wrackt here, and hath no other land to fetch,
Him now we must provide for. From Jove come
All strangers, and the needie of a home, 330
Who any gift, though ne're so small it be,
Esteeme as great and take it gratefully.
And therefore, Virgins, give the stranger food
And wine, and see ye bath him in the flood,
Neare to some shore to shelter most enclin'd: 335
To cold Bath-bathers hurtfull is the wind—
Not onely rugged making th'outward skin,
But by his thin powres pierceth parts within.'

This said, their flight in a returne they set,
And did Ulysses with all grace entreate, 340
Shewd him a shore, wind-proofe and full of shade,
By him a shirt and utter mantle laid,
A golden Jugge of liquid oile did adde,
Bad wash, and all things as Nausicaa bad.

Divine Ulysses would not use their aid, 345
But thus bespake them: 'Every lovely maid,
Let me entreate to stand a litle by,
That I alone the fresh flood may apply
To clense my bosome of the sea-wrought brine,

Ulysses' modestie to the Virgins.

He taught their youths modestie by his aged judgment—as recusing the custome of maids then used to that entertainment of men: notwithstanding the modestie of that age could not be corrupted inwardly, for those outward kind observations of guests and strangers, and was therefore priviledged. It is easie to avoide shew: and those that most curiously avoid the outward construction are ever most tainted with the inward corruption.

And then use oile, which long time did not shine 350
On my poore shoulders. I'le not wash in sight
Of faire-haird maidens. I should blush outright
To bathe all bare by such a virgin light.'
They mov'd, and musde a man had so much grace,
And told their Mistris what a man he was. 355
He clensd his broad soild shoulders, backe and head
Yet never tam'd. But now had fome and weed
Knit in the faire curles. Which dissolv'd, and he
Slickt all with sweet oile, the sweet charitie
The untoucht virgin shewd in his attire 360
He cloth'd him with. Then Pallas put a fire,
More than before, into his sparkling eies,
His late soile set off with his soone fresh guise.
His locks (clensd) curld the more, and matcht (in power
To please an eye) the Hyacinthian flower. 365

Simile.

And as a workman that can well combine
Silver and gold, and make both strive to shine,
As being by Vulcan, and Minerva too,
Taught how farre either may be urg'd to go
In strife of eminence, when worke sets forth 370
A worthy soule to bodies of such worth,
No thought reproving th'act in any place,
Nor Art no debt to Nature's liveliest grace:
So Pallas wrought in him a grace as great
From head to shoulders, and ashore did seate 375
His goodly presence—to which such a guise
He shewd in going that it ravisht eies.
All which (continude) as he sate apart,

Nausicaa's admiration of Ulysses.

Nausicaa's eye strooke wonder through her heart,
Who thus bespake her consorts: 'Heare me, you 380
Faire-wristed Virgins, this rare man (I know)
Treds not our country earth against the will
Of some God thron'd on the Olympian hill.
He shewd to me, till now, not worth the note,
But now he lookes as he had Godhead got. 385
I would to heaven my husband were no worse,
And would be calld no better, but the course
Of other husbands pleasd to dwell out here.
Observe and serve him with our utmost cheare.'
She said; they heard, and did. He drunke and eate 390
Like to a Harpy, having toucht no meate
A long before time. But Nausicaa now
Thought of the more grace she did lately vow,

Had horse to Chariot joynd, and up she rose,
Up chear'd her guest, and said: 'Guest, now dispose 395
Your selfe for Towne, that I may let you see
My Father's Court, where all the Peeres will be
Of our Phæacian State. At all parts then
Observe to whom and what place y'are t'attain,
Though I need usher you with no advice, 400
Since I suppose you absolutely wise.
While we the fields passe and men's labours there,
So long (in these maids' guides) directly beare
Upon my Chariot (I must go before
For cause that after comes, to which this more 405
Be my induction) you shall then soone end
Your way to Towne, whose Towres you see ascend
To such a steepnesse. On whose either side
A faire Port stands, to which is nothing wide
An enterer's passage: on whose both hands ride 410
Ships in faire harbors; which, once past, you win
The goodly market place (that circles in
A Phane to Neptune, built of curious stone
And passing ample) where munition,
Gables, and masts men make, and polisht oares— 415
For the Phæacians are not conquerors
By bowes nor quivers. Oares, masts, ships they are
With which they plow the sea and wage their warre.
And now the cause comes why I leade the way,
Not taking you to Coach. The men that sway 420
In worke of those tooles that so fit our State
Are rude Mechanicals, that rare and late
Worke in the market place, and those are they
Whose bitter tongues I shun; who strait would say,
(For these vile vulgars are extreamly proud 425
And fouly languag'd): "What, is he allowd
To coach it with Nausicaa? So large set,
And fairely fashiond? Where were these two met?
He shall be sure her husband. She hath bene
Gadding in some place, and (of forraine men 430
Fitting her fancie) kindly brought him home
In her owne ship. He must, of force, be come
From some farre region; we have no such man.
It may be (praying hard when her heart ran
On some wisht husband) out of heaven some God 435
Dropt in her lap, and there lies she at rode
Her complete life time. But, in sooth, if she

The Citie's description so far forth as may, in part, induce her promist reason why she tooke not Ulysses to coach with her.

Ranging abroad a husband, such as he
Whom now we saw, laid hand on, she was wise,
For none of all our Nobles are of prise 440
Enough for her: he must beyond-sea come
That wins her high mind and will have her home.
Of our Peeres many have importun'd her,
Yet she will none." Thus these folks will conferre
Behind my backe, or (meeting) to my face 445
The foule-mouth rout dare put home this disgrace.
And this would be reproches to my fame,
For even my selfe just anger would enflame
If any other virgin I should see
(Her parents living) keepe the companie 450
Of any man to any end of love,
Till open Nuptials should her act approve.
And therefore heare me, guest, and take such way
That you your selfe may compasse in your stay
Your quicke deduction by my Father's grace, 455
And meanes to reach the roote of all your race.
'We shall, not farre out of our way to Towne,
A never-felld Grove find that Poplars crowne,
To Pallas sacred, where a fountaine flowes,
And round about the Grove a Medow growes; 460
In which my Father holds a Mannor house
Deckt all with Orchards, greene and odorous,
As farre from Towne as one may heare a shout.
There stay and rest your foote paines, till full out
We reach the Citie—where when you may guesse 465
We are arriv'd and enter our accesse
Within my Father's Court, then put you on
For our Phæacian State, where to be showne
My Father's house desire. Each infant there
Can bring you to it, and your selfe will cleare 470
Distinguish it from others, for no showes
The Citie buildings make compar'd with those
That King Alcinous' seate doth celebrate.
In whose roofs and the Court (where men of state
And suiters sit and stay) when you shall hide, 475
Strait passe it, entring further, where abide
My Mother, with her withdrawne houswiferies,
Who still sits in the fire-shine and applies
Her Rocke, all purple and of pompous show,
Her Chaire plac't gainst a Pillar, all arow 480
Her maids behind her set; and to her here

My Father's dining Throne lookes, seated where
He powres his choice of wine in, like a God.
This view once past, for th'end of your abode,
Addresse suite to my Mother, that her meane 485
May make the day of your redition seene,
And you may frolicke strait, though farre away
You are in distance from your wished stay.
For if she once be won to wish you well,
Your Hope may instantly your Pasport seale, 490
And thenceforth sure abide to see your friends,
Faire house, and all to which your heart contends.'

Not without some litle note of our omnisufficient Homer's generall touch of the least fitnesse lying in his way, may this courtly discretion he describes in Nausicaa be observd, if you please.

This said, she usde her shining scourge and lasht
Her Mules, that soone the shore left where she washt;
And (knowing well the way) their pace was fleet 495
And thicke they gatherd up their nimble feet.
Which yet she temperd so, and usde her scourge
With so much skill, as not to over-urge
The foote behind, and make them straggle so
From close societie. Firme together go 500
Ulysses and her maids. And now the Sunne
Sunke to the waters, when they all had wonne
The never-feld and sound-exciting wood,
Sacred to Pallas, where the God-like good
Ulysses rested, and to Pallas praid: 505

More of our Poet's curious and sweet pietie.

'Heare me, of Goate-kept Jove th'unconquerd Maid,
Now throughly heare me, since in all the time
Of all my wracke my pray'rs could never clime
Thy far-off eares, when noisefull Neptune tost
Upon his watry brissels my imbost 510
And rock-torne body: heare yet now and daine
I may of the Phæacian State obtaine
Pitie and grace.' Thus praid he, and she heard:
By no meanes yet (exposde to sight) appear'd,
For feare t'offend her Unkle, the supreme 515

Neptune.

Of all the Sea-Gods, whose wrath still extreme
Stood to Ulysses, and would never cease
Till with his Country shore he crownd his peace.

Finis libri sexti Hom. Odyss.

THE SEVENTH BOOKE
of
HOMER'S ODYSSES

THE ARGUMENT

Nausicaa arrives at Towne,
And then Ulysses. He makes knowne
His suite to Arete, who view
Takes of his vesture; which she knew,
And asks him from whose hands it came. 5
He tels, with all the haplesse frame
Of his affaires in all the while
Since he forsooke Calypso's Ile.

Another Argument

Ἦτα. *The honord minds*
And welcome things
Ulysses finds
In Scheria's Kings.

Thus praid the wise and God-observing Man.
The Maid, by free force of her Palfreys, wan
Accesse to Towne, and the renowmed Court
Reacht of her Father, where, within the Port,
She staid her Coach; and round about her came 5
Her Brothers (made as of immortall frame),
Who yet disdaind not, for her love, meane deeds,
But tooke from Coach her Mules, brought in her weeds.
And she ascends her chamber, where purvaid
A quicke fire was by her old chamber-maid, 10
Eurymedusa, th'Aperæan borne,
And brought by sea from Apera t'adorne
The Court of great Alcinous, because
He gave to all the blest Phæacians lawes,
And, like a heaven-borne Powre in speech, acquir'd 15

Hæc fuit illius sæculi simplicitas: nam vel fraternus quoque Amor tantus fuit, ut libenter hanc redeunti charissimæ sorori, operam præstiterint. Spondanus.

The people's eares. To one then so admir'd,
Eurymedusa was esteemd no worse
Than worth the gift; yet now, growne old, was Nurse
To Ivory-armd Nausicaa, gave heate
To all her fires, and drest her privie meate. 20
Then rose Ulysses, and made way to Towne;
Which ere he reacht, a mightie mist was throwne
By Pallas round about him, in her Care
Lest in the sway of envies popular
Some proud Phæacian might foule language passe, 25
Justle him up, and aske him what he was.

Ulysses à Minerva in ædes Alcinoi perducitur, septus nebula.

Entring the lovely Towne yet, through the cloud
Pallas appeard, and like a yong wench showd
Bearing a pitcher, stood before him so
As if objected purposely to know 30
What there he needed—whom he questiond thus:
'Know you not, daughter, where Alcinous,
That rules this Towne, dwels? I, a poore distrest
Meere stranger here, know none I may request
To make this Court knowne to me.' She replied: 35
'Strange Father, I will see you satisfied
In that request: my Father dwels just by
The house you seeke for; but go silently,
Nor aske, nor speake to any other; I
Shall be enough to shew your way. The men 40
That here inhabite do not entertain
With ready kindnesse strangers, of what worth
Or state soever, nor have taken forth
Lessons of civill usage or respect
To men beyond them. They (upon their powres 45
Of swift ships building) top the watry towres,
And Jove hath given them ships, for saile so wrought
They cut a fether and command a thought.'

νέες ὠκεῖαι ὡς εἰ, naves veloces veluti penna, atque cogitatio.

This said, she usherd him, and after he
Trod in the swift steps of the Deitie. 50
The free-saild sea-men could not get a sight
Of our Ulysses yet, though he foreright
Both by their houses and their persons past:
Pallas about him such a darknesse cast
By her divine powre and her reverend care, 55
She would not give the Towne-borne cause to stare.
He wonderd, as he past, to see the Ports,
The shipping in them, and for all resorts
The goodly market steds, and Iles beside

For the Heroes, walls so large and wide, 60
Rampires so high and of such strength withall
It would with wonder any eye appall.
At last they reacht the Court, and Pallas said:
'Now, honourd stranger, I will see obaid
Your will to shew our Ruler's house; tis here; 65
Where you shall find Kings celebrating cheare;
Enter amongst them, nor admit a feare.
More bold a man is, he prevailes the more,
Though man nor place he ever saw before.
You first shall find the Queene in Court, whose name 70
Is Arete, of parents borne the same
That was the King her Spouse: their Pedigree
I can report. The great Earth-shaker, he
Of Peribœa (that her sex out-shone,
And yongest daughter was t'Eurymedon, 75
Who of th'unmeasur'd-minded Giants swaid
Th'Imperiall Scepter, and the pride allaid
Of men so impious with cold death, and died
Himselfe soone after) got the magnified
In mind, Nausithous, who the kingdome's state 80
First held in supreame rule. Nausithous gat
Rhexenor and Alcinous, now King.
Rhexenor (whose seed did no male fruite spring,
And whom the silver-bow-grac't Phœbus slue
Yong in the Court) his shed blood did renew 85
In onely Arete, who now is Spouse
To him that rules the kingdome in this house,
And is her Unkle, King Alcinous,
Who honors her past equall. She may boast
More honor of him than the honord most 90
Of any wife in earth can of her Lord,
How many more soever Realmes affoord
That keepe house under husbands. Yet no more
Her husband honors her than her blest store
Of gracious children. All the Citie cast 95
Eyes on her as a Goddesse, and give taste
Of their affections to her in their praires,
Still as she decks the streets. For all affaires
Wrapt in contention she dissolves to men:
Whom she affects, she wants no mind to deigne 100
Goodnesse enough. If her heart stand inclin'd
To your dispatch, hope all you wish to find,
Your friends, your longing family, and all

Arete, the wife of Alcinous.

For the more perspicuitie of this pedigree, I have here set down the Diagram as Spondanus hath it. Neptune begat Nausithous of Peribœa. By Nausithous, Rhexenor, Alcinous, were begot. By Rhexenor, Arete, the wife of her unkle Alcinous.

90 *The honor of Arete (or vertue) alleg.*

That can within your most affections fall.'
This said, away the grey-eyd Goddesse flew 105
Along th'untamed sea, left the lovely hew
Scheria presented, out flew Marathon,
And ample-streeted Athens lighted on,
πυκινὸς, spissus. Where to the house that casts so thicke a shade,
Of Erechtheus, she ingression made. 110
Ulysses to the loftie-builded Court
The Court of Alcinous. Of King Alcinous made bold resort;
Yet in his heart cast many a thought before
The brazen pavement of the rich Court bore
His enterd person. Like heaven's two maine Lights, 115
The roomes illustrated both daies and nights.
On every side stood firme a wall of brasse,
Even from the threshold to the inmost passe,
Which bore a roofe up that all Saphire was;
The brazen thresholds both sides did enfold 120
Silver Pilasters hung with gates of gold,
Whose Portall was of silver; over which
A golden Cornish did the front enrich.
Vulcan. On each side, Dogs, of gold and silver fram'd,
The house's Guard stood, which the Deitie (lam'd) 125
With knowing inwards had inspir'd, and made,
That Death nor Age should their estates invade.
Along the wall stood every way a throne
From th'entry to the Lobbie, every one
Cast over with a rich-wrought cloth of state— 130
Beneath which the Phæacian Princes sate
At wine and food, and feasted all the yeare.
Youths forg'd of gold, at every table there,
Stood holding flaming torches, that, in night,
Gave through the house each honourd Guest his light. 135
And (to encounter feast with houswifry)
In one roome fiftie women did apply
Their severall tasks. Some apple-colourd corne
Ground in faire Quernes, and some did spindles turne,
Some worke in loomes; no hand least rest receives, 140
But all had motion apt, as Aspen leaves.
And from the weeds they wove, so fast they laid,
And so thicke thrust together, thred by thred,
That th'oile (of which the wooll had drunke his fill)
Did with his moisture in light dewes distill. 145
As much as the Phæacian men exceld
All other countrimen in Art to build

A swift-saild ship, so much the women there
For worke of webs past other women were.
Past meane, by Pallas' meanes, they understood 150
The grace of good works, and had wits as good.
Without the Hall, and close upon the Gate,
Hortus Alcinoi memorabilis.
A goodly Orchard ground was situate
Of neare ten Acres, about which was led
A loftie Quickset. In it flourished 155
High and broad fruit trees that Pomegranats bore;
Sweet Figs, Peares, Olives, and a number more
Most usefull Plants did there produce their store,
Whose fruits the hardest Winter could not kill,
Nor hotest Summer wither. There was still 160
Fruite in his proper season all the yeare.
Sweet Zephyr breath'd upon them blasts that were
Of varied tempers: these he made to beare
Ripe fruites, these blossomes; Peare grew after Peare,
Apple succeeded apple, Grape the Grape, 165
Fig after Fig came; Time made never rape
Of any daintie there. A spritely vine
Spred here his roote, whose fruite a hote sun-shine
Made ripe betimes. Here grew another, greene.
Here some were gathering, here some pressing seene. 170
A large-allotted severall each fruite had;
And all th'adornd grounds their apparance made
In flowre and fruite, at which the King did aime
To the precisest order he could claime.
Two Fountaines grac't the garden; of which, one 175
Powrd out a winding streame that over-runne
The grounds for their use chiefly, th'other went
Close by the loftie Pallace gate, and lent
The Citie his sweet benefit. And thus
The Gods the Court deckt of Alcinous. 180
Patient Ulysses stood a while at gaze,
But (having all observ'd) made instant pace
Into the Court, where all the Peeres he found
And Captaines of Phæacia, with Cups crownd,
Mercurie.
Offring to sharp-eyd Hermes, to whom last 185
They usde to sacrifise, when Sleepe had cast
His inclination through their thoughts. But these
Ulysses past, and forth went; nor their eies
Tooke note of him, for Pallas stopt the light
With mists about him, that, unstaid, he might 190
First to Alcinous and Arete

Present his person; and of both them, she
(By Pallas' counsell) was to have the grace
Of foremost greeting. Therefore his embrace
He cast about her knee. And then off flew 195
The heavenly aire that hid him—when his view
With silence and with Admiration strooke
The Court quite through: but thus he silence broake:

Areten, Ulysses supplex orat.

'Divine Rhexenor's ofspring, Arete,
To thy most honourd husband, and to thee, 200
A man whom many labours have distrest
Is come for comfort; and to every guest—
To all whom heaven vouchsafe delightsome lives,
And, after, to your issue that survives
A good resignement of the Goods ye leave, 205
With all the honor that your selves receive
Amongst your people. Onely this of me
Is the Ambition, that I may but see
(By your vouchsaft meanes, and betimes vouchsaft)
My country earth, since I have long bin left 210
To labors and to errors, barrd from end,
And farre from benefit of any friend.'

He said no more, but left them dumbe with that,
Went to the harth and in the ashes sat
Aside the fire. At last their silence brake, 215
And Echeneus, th'old Heroe, spake—
A man that all Phæacians past in yeares,
And in perswasive eloquence all the Peeres,
Knew much, and usde it well. And thus spake he:

Echeneus to Alcinous.

'Alcinous! It shewes not decently, 220
Nor doth your honor what you see admit,
That this your guest should thus abjectly sit,
His chaire the earth, the harth his cushion,
Ashes as if apposde for food. A Throne
Adornd with due rites stands you more in hand 225
To see his person plac't in, and command
That instantly your Heralds fill in wine,
That to the God that doth in lightnings shine
We may do sacrifice: for he is there
Where these his reverend suppliants appeare. 230
Let what you have within be brought abroad
To sup the stranger. All these would have showd
This fit respect to him, but that they stay
For your precedence, that should grace the way.'

When this had added to the well-inclin'd 235

And sacred order of Alcinous' mind,
Then of the great in wit the hand he seisd,
And from the ashes his faire person raisd,
Advanc't him to a well-adorned Throne,
And from his seate raisd his most loved sonne 240
(Laodamas, that next himselfe was set)
To give him place. The handmaid then did get
An Ewre of gold, with water fild, which plac't
Upon a Caldron all with silver grac't,
She powrd out on their hands. And then was spred 245
A Table, which the Butler set with bread,
As others serv'd with other food the boord
In all the choise the present could affoord.
Ulysses meate and wine tooke, and then thus
The King the Herald calld: 'Pontonous! 250
Serve wine through all the house, that all may pay
Rites to the Lightner, who is still in way
With humble suppliants, and them pursues
With all benigne and hospitable dues.'
 Pontonous gave act to all he willd, 255
And hony-sweetnesse-giving-minds wine filld,
Disposing it in cups for all to drinke.
All having drunke what either's heart could thinke
Fit for due sacrifice, Alcinous said:
'Heare me, ye Dukes that the Phæacians leade, 260
And you our Counsellors, that I may now
Discharge the charge my mind suggests to you
For this our guest. Feast past, and this night's sleepe,
Next morne (our Senate summond) we will keepe
Justs sacred to the Gods, and this our Guest 265
Receive in solemne Court with fitting Feast:
Then thinke of his returne, that, under hand
Of our deduction, his naturall land
(Without more toile or care, and with delight,
And that soone given him, how farre hence dissite 270
Soever it can be) he may ascend—
And in the meane time without wrong attend,
Or other want, fit meanes to that ascent.
What, after, austere Fates shall make th'event
Of his life's thred (now spinning, and began 275
When his paind mother freed his roote of man)
He must endure in all kinds. If some God
Perhaps abides with us in his abode,
And other things, will thinke upon then we.

The word that beares this long Epithete is translated only dulce: *which signifies more;* μελίφρονα οἶνον ἐχίρνα— Vinum quod mellea dulcedine animum perfundit, et oblectat.

Ascent to his Countrie's shore.

The Gods' wils stand, who ever yet were free 280
Of their appearance to us when to them
We offerd Hecatombs of fit esteem,
And would at feast sit with us, even where we
Orderd our Session. They would likewise be
Encountrers of us, when in way alone 285
About his fit affaires went any one—
Nor let them cloke themselves in any care
To do us comfort; we as neare them are
As are the Cyclops, or the impious race
Of earthy Giants that would heaven outface.' 290
Ulysses answerd: 'Let some other doubt
Employ your thoughts than what your words give out—
Which intimate a kind of doubt that I
Should shadow in this shape a Deitie.
I beare no such least semblance, or in wit, 295
Vertue, or person. What may well befit
One of those mortals, whom you chiefly know
Beares up and downe the burthen of the woe
Appropriate to poore man, give that to me—
Of whose mones I sit in the most degree; 300
And might say more, sustaining griefes that all
The Gods consent to, no one twixt their fall
And my unpitied shoulders letting downe
The least diversion. Be the grace then showne
To let me taste your free-given food in peace: 305
Through greatest griefe the belly must have ease.
Worse than an envious belly nothing is.
It will command his strict Necessities,
Of men most griev'd in body or in mind,
That are in health, and will not give their kind 310
A desperate wound. When most with cause I grieve,
It bids me still, "Eate, man, and drinke, and live";
And this makes all forgot. What ever ill
I ever beare, it ever bids me fill.
But this ease is but forc't and will not last, 315
Till what the mind likes be as well embrac't.
And therefore let me wish you would partake
In your late purpose: when the Morne shall make
Her next appearance, daigne me but the grace
(Unhappie man) that I may once embrace 320
My country earth: though I be still thrust at

Eustathius will have this comparison of the Phæacians with the Giants and Cyclops to proceede out of the inveterate virulency of Alcinous to the Cyclops, who were cause (as is before said) of their remove from their country; and with great endevour labors the approbation of it—but (under his peace) from the purpose: for the sence of the Poet is cleer, that the Cyclops and Giants being in part the issue of the Gods, and yet afterward their defiers (as Polyp. hereafter dares professe), Alcinous (out of bold and manly reason, even to the face of one that might have bin a God, for the past manly appearance he made there) would tell him, and the rest in him, that if they graced those Cyclops with their open appearance, that, thogh descended from them, durst yet denie them, they might much more do them the honor of their open presence that adored them.

By ancient ils, yet make me but see that,
And then let life go—when (withall) I see
My high-rooft large house, lands and family.'
This all approv'd, and each willd every one: 325
'Since he hath said so fairly, set him gone.'
Feast past, and sacrifice, to sleepe all vow
Their eies at either's house. Ulysses now
Was left here with Alcinous and his Queene,
The all-lov'd Arete. The handmaids then 330
The vessell of the Banquet tooke away—
When Arete set eye on his array,
Knew both his out and underweed, which she
Made with her maids, and musde by what meanes he
Obtaind their wearing: which she made request 335
Arete to Ulysses. To know, and wings gave to these speeches: 'Guest!
First let me aske, what and from whence you are?
And then, who grac't you with the weeds you weare?
Said you not lately you had err'd at seas,
And thence arriv'd here?' Laertiades 340
Ulysses to Arete. To this thus answerd: 'Tis a paine, O Queene,
Still to be opening wounds wrought deepe and greene,
Of which the Gods have opened store in me;
Yet your will must be serv'd. Farre hence, at sea,
There lies an Ile that beares Ogygia's name, 345
Where Atlas' daughter, the ingenious Dame,
Faire-haird Calypso lives—a Goddesse grave,
And with whom men nor Gods societie have.
Yet I (past man unhappie) liv'd alone
(By heav'n's wrath forc't) her house companion. 350
For Jove had with a fervent lightning cleft
My ship in twaine, and farre at blacke sea left
Me and my souldiers—all whose lives I lost.
I in mine armes the keele tooke and was tost
Nine dayes together up from wave to wave. 355
The tenth grim Night the angry Deities drave
Me and my wracke on th'Ile in which doth dwell
Dreadfull Calypso, who exactly well
Receiv'd and nourisht me, and promise made
To make me deathlesse, nor should Age invade 360
My powres with his deserts through all my dayes.
All mov'd not me; and therefore on her stayes
Seven yeares she made me lie: and there spent I
The long time steeping in the miserie
Of ceaslesse teares the Garments I did weare 365

From her faire hand. The eighth revolved yeare
(Or by her chang'd mind, or by charge of Jove)
She gave provokt way to my wisht remove,
And in a many-joynted ship, with wine
(Daintie in savour), bread and weeds divine, 370
Sign'd with a harmlesse and sweet wind my passe.
Then seventeene dayes at sea I homeward was,
And by the eighteenth the darke hils appeard
That your Earth thrusts up. Much my heart was cheard
(Unhappie man) for that was but a beame 375
To shew I yet had agonies extreame
To put in sufferance, which th'Earth-shaker sent,
Crossing my way with tempests violent,
Unmeasur'd seas up-lifting; nor would give
The billowes leave to let my vessell live 380
The least time quiet—that even sigh'd to beare
Their bitter outrage, which, at last, did teare
Her sides in peeces, set on by the winds.
I yet through-swomme the waves that your shore binds,
Till wind and water threw me up to it; 385
When, coming forth, a ruthlesse billow smit
Against huge rocks, and an acceslesse shore,
My mangl'd body. Backe againe I bore,
And swom till I was falne upon a flood,
Whose shores, me thought, on good advantage stood 390
For my receit, rock-free and fenc't from wind.
And this I put for, gathering up my mind.
Then the divine Night came, and, tredding Earth,
Close by the flood that had from Jove her birth,
Within a thicket I reposde—when round 395
I ruffld up falne leaves in heape, and found
(Let fall from heaven) a sleepe interminate.
And here my heart (long time excruciate)
Amongst the leaves I rested all that night,
Even till the morning and meridian light. 400
The Sunne declining then, delightsome sleepe
No longer laid my temples in his steepe,
But forth I went, and on the shore might see
Your daughter's maids play. Like a Deitie
She shin'd above them, and I praid to her: 405
And she in disposition did prefer
Noblesse and wisedome, no more low than might
Become the goodnesse of a Goddesse' height.
Nor would you therefore hope (supposde distrest

As I was then, and old) to find the least 410
Of any Grace from her, being yonger farre.
With yong folkes Wisedome makes her commerce rare.
Yet she in all abundance did bestow
Both wine (that makes the blood in humanes grow)
And food, and bath'd me in the flood, and gave 415
The weeds to me which now ye see me have.
This through my griefes I tell you, and tis true.'

αἴθοψ οἶνος—
Vinum calefaciendi
vim habens.

Alcinous answerd: 'Guest! my daughter knew
Least of what most you give her, nor became
The course she tooke, to let with every Dame 420
Your person lackey, nor hath with them brought
Your selfe home too, which first you had besought.'
'O blame her not,' said he, 'Heroicall Lord,
Nor let me heare against her worth a word.
She faultlesse is, and wisht I would have gone 425
With all her women home: but I alone
Would venture my receit here, having feare
And reverend aw of accidents that were
Of likely issue—both your wrath to move,
And to inflame the common people's love 430
Of speaking ill, to which they soone give place:
We men are all a most suspicious race.'
'My guest,' said he, 'I use not to be stird
To wrath too rashly, and where are preferd
To men's conceits things that may both waies faile, 435
The noblest ever should the most prevaile.
Would Jove our Father, Pallas and the Sunne
That (were you still as now and could but runne
One Fate with me) you would my daughter wed
And be my son-in-law; still vowd to leade 440
Your rest of life here. I a house would give
And houshold goods, so freely you would live
Confin'd with us: but gainst your will shall none
Containe you here, since that were violence done
To Jove our Father. For your passage home, 445
That you may well know we can overcome
So great a voyage, thus it shall succeed:
Tomorrow shall our men take all their heed
(While you securely sleepe) to see the seas
In calmest temper, and (if that will please) 450
Shew you your Country and your house ere night,
Though farre beyond Eubœa be that sight.
And this Eubœa (as our subjects say

That have bin there and seene) is farre away
Farthest from us of all the parts they know, 455
And made the triall when they helpt to row
The gold-lockt Rhadamanth, to give him view
Of Earth-borne Tityus—whom their speeds did shew
(In that far-off Eubœa) the same day
They set from hence, and home made good their way 460
With ease againe, and him they did convay.
Which I report to you to let you see
How swift my ships are and how matchlesly
My yong Phæacians with their oares prevaile
To beate the sea through and assist a saile.' 465
This cheard Ulysses, who in private praid:
'I would to Jove our Father, what he said
He could performe at all parts; he should then
Be glorified for ever, and I gaine
My naturall Country.' This discourse they had, 470
When faire-armd Arete her handmaids bad
A bed make in the Portico, and plie
With cloaths—the Covering Tapestrie,
The Blankets purple. Wel-napt Wastcoates too,
To weare for more warmth. What these had to do, 475
They torches tooke and did. The Bed purvaid,
They mov'd Ulysses for his rest, and said:
'Come, Guest, your Bed is fit; now frame to rest.'
Motion of sleepe was gracious to their Guest,
Which now he tooke profoundly, being laid 480
Within a loop-hole Towre, where was convaid
The sounding Portico. The King tooke rest
In a retir'd part of the house, where drest
The Queene her selfe a Bed and Trundlebed,
And by her Lord reposde her reverend head. 485

Finis libri septimi Hom. Odyss.

THE EIGHTH BOOKE
of
HOMER'S ODYSSES

THE ARGUMENT

The Peeres of the Phæacian State
A Councell call, to consolate
Ulysses with all meanes for Home.
The Councell to a Banquet come
Invited by the king. Which done, 5
Assaies for hurling of the stone
The Youths make with the stranger king.
Demodocus, at feast, doth sing
Th'Adulterie of the God of Armes
With her that rules in Amorous charmes, 10
And after sings the entercourse
Of Acts about th'Epæan Horse.

Another Argument

Θῆτα. *The Councels frame*
At fleete applied;
In strifes of Game
Ulysses tried.

Now when the Rosie-fingerd morne arose,
The sacred powre Alcinous did dispose
Did likewise rise, and like him left his Ease
The Cittie-racer Laertiades.
The Councell at the Navie was design'd, 5
To which Alcinous with the sacred mind
Came first of all. On polisht stones they sate
Neare to the Navie. To increase the state,
Minerva tooke the herald's forme on her
That serv'd Alcinous, studious to prefer 10
Ulysses' Suite for home. About the towne

She made quicke way, and fild with the renowne
Of that designe the eares of every man,
Pallas like the Herald.
Proclaiming thus: 'Peers Phæacensian!
And men of Councell! All haste to the Court, 15
To heare the stranger that made late resort
To king Alcinous, long time lost at Sea,
And is in person like a Deitie.'
This all their powres set up and spirit instild,
And straight the Court and seats with men were fild. 20
The whole State wonderd at Laertes' Son
When they beheld him. Pallas put him on
A supernaturall and heavenly dresse,
Enlarg'd him with a height and goodlinesse
In breast and shoulders that he might appeare 25
Gracious and grave and reverend, and beare
A perfect hand on his performance there
In all the trials they resolv'd t'impose.
All met, and gatherd in attention close,
Alcinous exhorts the Phæacians to the reliefe of Ulysses.
Alcinous thus bespake them: 'Dukes, and Lords, 30
Heare me digest my hearty thoughts in words.
This Stranger here whose travels found my Court
I know not, nor can tell if his resort
From East or West comes. But his suite is this,
That to his Countrey earth we would dismis 35
His hither-forced person, and doth beare
The minde to passe it under every Peere—
Whom I prepare and stirre up, making knowne
My free desire of his deduction.
Nor shall there ever any other man 40
That tries the goodnesse Phæacensian
In me and my Court's entertainement stay
Mourning for passage under least delay.
Come then. A ship into the sacred seas,
New-built, now lanch we, and from out our prease 45
Chuse two and fiftie Youths, of all the best
To use an oare. All which see straight imprest
And in their Oare-bound seates. Let others hie
Home to our Court, commanding instantly
The solemne preparation of a feast, 50
In which provision may for any guest
Be made at my charge. Charge of these low things
I give our Youth. You Scepter-bearing kings,
Consort me home, and helpe with grace to use
This guest of ours: no one man shall refuse. 55

Some other of you haste and call to us
The sacred singer, grave Demodocus,
To whom hath God given song that can excite
The heart of whom he listeth with delight.'
  This said, he led. The Scepter-bearers lent 60
Their free attendance, and with all speede went
The herald for the sacred man in song.
Youths two and fiftie, chosen from the throng,
Went, as was willd, to the untam'd sea's shore;
Where come, they lancht the ship, the Mast it bore 65
Advanc't, sailes hoised, every seate his Ore
Gave with a lether thong: the deepe moist then
They further reacht. The drie streets flowd with men
That troup't up to the king's capacious Court,
Whose Porticos were chok't with the resort, 70
Whose wals were hung with men: yong, old, thrust there
In mighty concourse; for whose promist cheere
Alcinous slue twelve Sheepe, eight white-toothd Swine,
Two crook-hancht Beeves; which flead and drest, divine
The show was of so many a jocund Guest 75
All set together at so set a feast.
To whose accomplisht state the Herald then
The lovely Singer led, who past all men

Demodocus Poeta.

The Muse affected, gave him good and ill—
His eies put out, but put in soule at will. 80
His place was given him in a chaire all grac't
With silver studs and gainst a Pillar plac't,
Where as the Center to the State he rests,
And round about the circle of the Guests.
The Herald on a Pinne above his head 85
His soundfull harpe hung, to whose height he led
His hand for taking of it downe at will,
A Boord set by with food, and forth did fill
A Bowle of wine to drinke at his desire.
The rest then fell to feast, and when the fire 90
Of appetite was quencht, the Muse inflam'd
The sacred Singer. Of men highliest fam'd
He sung the glories, and a Poeme pend
That in applause did ample heaven ascend—
Whose subject was the sterne contention 95
Betwixt Ulysses and Great Thetis' Sonne,

The contention of Achilles and Ulysses.

As at a banket sacred to the Gods
In dreadfull language they exprest their ods.
When Agamemnon sat rejoyc't in soule

To heare the Greeke Peeres jarre in termes so foule, 100
For Augur Phœbus in presage had told
The king of men (desirous to unfold
The war's perplexed end, and being therefore gone
In heavenly Pytho to the Porch of stone)
That then the end of all griefes should begin 105
Twixt Greece and Troy when Greece (with strife to winne
That wisht conclusion) in her kings should jarre,
And pleade if force or wit must end the warre.

This brave contention did the Poet sing,
Expressing so the spleene of either king 110
That his large purple weede Ulysses held
Before his face and eies, since thence distilld
Teares uncontaind, which he obscur'd, in feare
To let th'observing Presence note a teare.
But when his sacred song the meere Divine 115
Had given an end, a Goblet crownd with wine
Ulysses (drying his wet eies) did seise,
And sacrifisde to those Gods that would please
T'inspire the Poet with a song so fit
To do him honour and renowme his wit. 120
His teares then staid. But when againe began
(By all the kings' desires) the moving man,
Againe Ulysses could not chuse but yeeld
To that soft passion, which againe withheld
He kept so cunningly from sight that none 125
(Except Alcinous himselfe alone)
Discern'd him mov'd so much. But he sat next,
And heard him deeply sigh—which his pretext
Could not keepe hid from him. Yet he conceal'd
His utterance of it, and would have it held 130
From all the rest, brake off the song, and this
Said to those Ore-affecting Peeres of his:

'Princes and Peeres! we now are satiate
With sacred song that fits a feast of state,
With wine, and food. Now then to field, and try 135
In all kinds our approv'd activity,
That this our Guest may give his friends to know
In his returne that we as little owe
To fights and wrestlings, leaping, speede of race,
As these our Court-rites, and commend our grace 140
In all to all superiour.' Foorth he led
The Peeres and people, troup't up to their head.
Nor must Demodocus be left within,

Ulyssi movetur fletus.

The continued pietie of Ulysses through all places, times and occasions.

Whose harpe the Herald hung upon the pinne,
His hand in his tooke, and abroad he brought 145
The heavenly Poet, out the same way wrought
That did the Princes; and what they would see
With admiration with his companie
They wisht to honour. To the place of Game
These throng'd, and after routs of other came 150
Of all sort infinite. Of Youths that strove,
Many and strong rose to their trial's love.
Up rose Acroneus and Ocyalus,
Elatreus, Prymneus and Anchialus,
Nauteus, Eretmeus, Thoon, Proreus, 155
Ponteus and the strong Amphialus,
Sonne to Tectonides, Polyneus.
Up rose to these, the great Euryalus,
In action like the homicide of warre,
Naubolides, that was for person farre 160
Past all the rest, but one he could not passe
Nor any thought improve, Laodamas.
Up Anabesineus then arose,
And three sonnes of the Scepter state, and those
Were Halius, and fore-praisde Laodamas, 165
And Clytoneus, like a God in grace.
These first the foote-game tride, and from the lists
Tooke start together. Up the dust in mists
They hurld about as in their speede they flew;
But Clytoneus first of all the crew 170
A Stiche's length in any fallow field
Made good his pace, when where the Judges yeeld
The prise and praise his glorious speed arriv'd.
Next for the boistrous wrestling Game they striv'd,
At which Euryalus the rest outshone. 175
At leape, Amphialus, at the hollow stone
Elatreus exceld. At buffets, last,
Laodamas, the king's faire sonne, surpast.

Since the Phæacians were not only dwellers by sea, but studious also of sea quallities, their names seeme to usurpe their faculties therein. All consisting of sea-faring signification, except Laodamas. As Acroneus, summa seu extrema Navis pars. *Ocyalus,* velox in mari. *Elatreus, or* Ἐλατὴρ, ἐλατῆρος, Remex.&c.

When all had striv'd in these assaies their fill,
Laodamas said: 'Come, friends, let's prove what skill 180
This Stranger hath attaind to in our sport;
Me thinks he must be of the active sort.
His calves, thighs, hands and well-knit shoulders show
That Nature disposition did bestow
To fit with fact their forme. Nor wants he prime. 185
But sowre Affliction, made a mate with Time,
Makes Time the more seene. Nor imagine I

A worse thing to enforce debilitie
Than is the Sea, though nature ne're so strong
Knits one together.' 'Nor conceive you wrong,' 190
Replied Euryalus, 'but prove his blood
With what you question.' In the midst then stood
Renowm'd Laodamas, and prov'd him thus:

Laodamas urgeth Ulysses to their sports.

'Come, stranger Father, and assaie with us
Your powrs in these contentions. If your show 195
Be answerd with your worth, tis fit that you
Should know these conflicts, nor doth glorie stand
On any worth more in a man's command
Than to be strenuous both of foote and hand.
Come, then, make proofe with us; discharge your mind 200
Of discontentments, for not farre behind
Comes your deduction. Ship is ready now,
And men and all things.' 'Why,' said he, 'dost thou
Mocke me, Laodamas, and these strifes bind
My powrs to answer? I am more inclind 205
To cares than conflict. Much sustaind I have,
And still am suffering. I come here to crave
In your assemblies meanes to be dismist,
And pray both Kings and subjects to assist.'

The word is πομπή signifying: deductio qua transvehendum curamus cum qui nobiscum aliquando est versatus.

Euryalus an open brawle began, 210
And said: 'I take you, Sir, for no such man
As fits these honord strifes. A number more
Strange men there are that I would chuse before.
To one that loves to lie a ship-boord much,
Or is the Prince of sailours, or to such 215
As traffique farre and neare, and nothing minde
But freight and passage and a foreright winde,
Or to a victler of a ship, or men
That set up all their powrs for rampant Gaine,
I can compare or hold you like to be— 220
But for a wrestler, or of qualitie
Fit for contentions noble, you abhor
From worth of any such competitor.'

Euryalus upbraids Ulysses.

κερδέων θ' ἁρπαλέων.

Ulysses (frowning) answerd: 'Stranger! farre
Thy words are from the fashions regular 225
Of kinde or honour. Thou art in thy guise
Like to a man that authors injuries.
I see the Gods to all men give not all
Manly addiction, wisedome, words that fall
(Like dice) upon the square still. Some man takes 230
Ill forme from parents, but God often makes

Ulysses angry.

ἀτάσθαλος— Damnorum magnorum auctor.

That fault of forme up with observ'd repaire
Of pleasing speech: that makes him held for faire,
That makes him speake securely, makes him shine
In an assembly with a grace divine. 235
Men take delight to see how evenly lie
His words asteepe in honey modestie.
Another, then, hath fashion like a God,
But in his language he is foule and broad.
And such art thou. A person faire is given, 240
But nothing else is in thee sent from heaven,
For in thee lurkes a base and earthy soule—
And t'hast compelld me with a speech most foule
To be thus bitter. I am not unseene
In these faire strifes, as thy words overweene, 245
But in the first ranke of the best I stand.
At least, I did when youth and strength of hand
Made me thus confident, but now am worne
With woes and labours, as a humane borne
To beare all anguish. Sufferd much I have. 250
The warre of men and the inhumane wave
Have I driven through at all parts: but, with all
My waste in sufferance, what yet may fall
In my performance at these strifes I'le trie.
Thy speech hath mov'd and made my wrath runne hie.' 255
This said, with robe and all, he graspt a stone
A little graver than was ever throwne
By these Phæacians in their wrestling rout,
More firme, more massie, which (turnd round about)
He hurried from him with a hand so strong 260
It sung and flew, and over all the throng
(That at the others' markes stood) quite it went:
Yet downe fell all beneath it, fearing spent
The force that drave it flying from his hand,
As it a dart were, or a walking wand. 265
And farre past all the markes of all the rest
His wing stole way. When Pallas straight imprest
A marke at fall of it, resembling then
One of the navy-given Phæacian men,
And thus advanc't Ulysses: 'One (though blinde), 270
O stranger, groping, may thy stone's fall finde;
For not amidst the rout of markes it fell
But farre before all. Of thy worth thinke well,
And stand in all strifes: no Phæacian here,
This bound can either better or come nere.' 275

Ulysses joyd to heare that one man yet
Usde him benignly and would Truth abet
In those contentions. And then thus smooth
He tooke his speech downe: 'Reach me that now, Youth:
You shall (and straight I thinke) have one such more, 280
And one beyond it too. And now, whose Core
Stands sound and great within him (since ye have
Thus put my splene up), come againe and brave
The Guest ye tempted with such grosse disgrace,
At wrestling, buffets, whirlbat, speed of race. 285
At all, or either, I except at none,
But urge the whole State of you; onely one
I will not challenge in my forced boast,
And that's Laodamas, for hee's mine Host—
And who will fight, or wrangle with his friend? 290
Unwise he is, and base, that will contend
With him that feedes him in a forreigne place,
And takes all edge off from his owne sought grace.
None else except I here, nor none despise,
But wish to know and prove his faculties 295
That dares appeare now. No strife ye can name
Am I unskilld in (reckon any game
Of all that are, as many as there are
In use with men); for Archerie I dare
Affirme my selfe not meane. Of all a troupe 300
I'le make the first foe with mine arrow stoupe,
Though with me ne're so many fellowes bend
Their bowes at markt men and affect their end.
Onely was Philoctetes with his bow
Still my superiour, when we Greekes would show 305
Our Archerie against our foes of Troy.
But all that now by bread fraile life enjoy
I farre hold my inferiours. Men of old
None now alive shall witnesse me so bold
To vant equality with such men as these— 310
Œchalian Eurytus, Hercules,
Who with their bowes durst with the Gods contend.
And therefore caught Eurytus soone his end,
Nor di'd at home, in age, a reverend man,
But by the Great incensed Delphian 315
Was shot to death, for daring competence
With him in all an Archer's excellence.
A Speare I'le hurle as farre as any man
Shall shoote a shaft. How at a race I can

He names Laodamas onely for all the other brothers, since in his exception the others' envies were curbd: for brothers either are or should be of one acceptation in all fit things. And Laodamas he calles his host, being eldest son to Alcinous, the heire being ever the yong master; nor might he conveniently prefer Alcinous in his exception, since he stood not in competition at these contentions.

Apollo.

Bestirre my feete I onely yeeld to Feare, 320
And doubt to meete with my superiour here.
So many seas so too much have misusde
My lims for race, and therefore have diffusde
A dissolution through my loved knees.'
This said, he stilld all talking properties. 325

The ingenuous and roiall speech of Alcinous to Ulysses.

Alcinous onely answerd: 'O my Guest,
In good part take we what you have bene prest
With speech to answer. You would make appeare
Your vertues therefore, that will still shine where
Your onely looke is. Yet must this man give 330
Your worth ill language, when he does not live
In sort of mortals (whence so ere he springs
That judgement hath to speake becoming things)
That will deprave your vertues. Note then now
My speech and what my love presents to you, 335
That you may tell Heroes, when you come
To banquet with your Wife and Birth at home,
(Mindfull of our worth) what deservings Jove
Hath put on our parts likewise, in remove
From Sire to Sonne, as an inherent grace 340
Kinde and perpetuall. We must needs give place
To other Countreymen and freely yeeld
We are not blamelesse in our fights of field,
Buffets, nor wrestlings: but in speede of feete
And all the Equipage that fits a fleete 345
We boast us best—for table ever spred
With neighbour feasts, for garments varied,
For Poesie, Musique, Dancing, Baths and Beds.
And now, Phæacians, you that beare your heads
And feete with best grace in enamouring dance, 350
Enflame our guest here, that he may advance
Our worth past all the worlds to his home friends,
As well for the unmatcht grace that commends
Your skills in footing of a dance as theirs
That flie a race best. And so all affaires 355
At which we boast us best he best may trie,
As Sea-race, Land-race, Dance and Poesie.
Some one with instant speede to Court retire
And fetch Demodocus his soundfull lyre.'
This said the God-grac't king, and quicke resort 360
Pontonous made for that faire harpe to Court.
Nine of the lot-chusde publique Rulers rose,
That all in those contentions did dispose,

Commanding a most smooth ground, and a wide,
And all the people in faire game aside. 365
 Then with the rich harpe came Pontonous,
And in the midst tooke place Demodocus.
About him then stood foorth the choise yong men
That on man's first youth made fresh entrie then,
Had Art to make their naturall motion sweete 370
And shooke a most divine dance from their feete,
That twinckld Star-like, mov'd as swift and fine,
And beate the aire so thinne they made it shine.
Ulysses wonderd at it, but amazd
He stood in minde to heare the dance so phras'd. 375
For, as they danc't, Demodocus did sing
The bright-crownd Venus' love with Battaile's king,
As first they closely mixt in t'house of fire.
What worlds of gifts wonne her to his desire,
Who then the night-and-day-bed did defile 380
Of good king Vulcan. But in little while
The Sunne their mixture saw, and came, and told.
The bitter newes did by his eares take hold
Of Vulcan's heart. Then to his Forge he went,
And in his shrewd mind deepe stuffe did invent. 385
His mightie Anvile in the stocke he put,
And forg'd a net that none could loose or cut,
That when it had them it might hold them fast.
Which having finisht, he made utmost haste
Up to the deare roome where his wife he wowd, 390
And (madly wrath with Mars) he all bestrowd
The bed and bed-posts, all the beame above
That crost the chamber, and a circle strove
Of his device to wrap in all the roome.
And twas as pure as of a Spider's loome 395
The woofe before tis woven. No man nor God
Could set his eie on it, a sleight so odde
His Art shewd in it. All his craft bespent
About the bed, he faind as if he went
To well-built Lemnos, his most loved towne 400
Of all townes earthly. Nor left this unknowne
To golden-bridle-using Mars, who kept
No blinde watch over him, but, seeing stept
His rivall so aside, he hasted home
With faire-wreath'd Venus' love stung, who was come 405
New from the Court of her most mightie Sire.
Mars enterd, wrung her hand, and the retire

μαρμαρυγὰς ποδῶν. μαρμαρυγὴ *signifies* splendor vibrans; *a twinckld splendor:* μαρμαρύσσειν—Vibrare veluti radios solares.

373 *Ayre rarefied turns fire.*

The matter whereof none can see.

χρυσήνιος Ἄρης.

Her husband made to Lemnos told, and said:
'Now, Love, is Vulcan gone; let us to bed;
Hee's for the barbarous Sintians.' Well appaid 410
Was Venus with it, and afresh assaid
Their old encounter. Downe they went, and straight
About them clingd the artificiall sleight
Of most wise Vulcan, and were so ensnar'd
That neither they could stirre their course prepar'd 415
In any lim about them, nor arise.
And then they knew they could no more disguise
Their close conveiance, but lay, forc't, stone still.
Backe rusht the both-foote-crook't, but straight in skill
From his neare skout-hole turnd, nor ever went 420
To any Lemnos; but the sure event
Left Phœbus to discover, who told all.
Then home hopt Vulcan, full of griefe and gall,
Stood in the Portall, and cried out so hie

Vulcan's complaint.

That all the Gods heard: 'Father of the skie, 425
And every other deathlesse God,' said he,
'Come all, and a ridiculous object see,
And yet not sufferable neither. Come
And witnesse, how, when still I step from home
(Lame that I am) Jove's daughter doth professe 430
To do me all the shamefull offices,
Indignities, despites, that can be thought;
And loves this all-things-making-come-to-nought
Since he is faire forsooth, foote-sound, and I
Tooke in my braine a little, leg'd awrie— 435
And no fault mine, but all my parents' fault
Who should not get, if mocke me with my halt.
But see how fast they sleepe while I, in mone,
Am onely made an idle looker on.
One bed their turne serves, and it must be mine. 440
I thinke yet I have made their selfe-loves shine.
They shall no more wrong me and none perceive:
Nor will they sleepe together, I beleeve,
With too hote haste againe. Thus both shall lie
In craft and force, till the extremitie 445
Of all the dowre I gave her Sire (to gaine
A dogged set-fac't Girle, that will not staine
Her face with blushing though she shame her head)
He paies me backe. She's faire, but was no maide.'
While this long speech was making, all were come 450
To Vulcan's wholie-brazen-founded home—

Earth-shaking Neptune, usefull Mercurie,
And far-shot Phœbus. No She-Deitie,
For shame, would show there. All the give-good Gods
Stood in the Portall, and past periods 455
Gave length to laughters; all rejoyc't to see
That, which they said that no impietie
Finds good successe at th'end. 'And now,' said one,
'The slow outgoes the swift. Lame Vulcan, knowne
To be the slowest of the Gods, outgoes 460
Mars the most swift. And this is that which growes
To greatest justice, that Adulterie's sport,
Obtain'd by craft, by craft of other sort
(And lame craft too) is plagu'd—which grieves the more
That sound lims turning lame the lame restore.' 465

Intending them sound of foote when they outgoe the soundest.

This speech amongst themselves they entertaind,
When Phœbus thus askt Hermes: 'Thus enchaind
Would'st thou be, Hermes, to be thus disclosde,
Though with thee golden Venus were repos'de?'
He soone gave that an answer: 'O,' said he, 470
'Thou king of Archers, would twere thus with me,
Though thrice so much shame—nay, though infinite
Were powrd about me, and that every light
In great heaven shining witnest all my harmes—
So golden Venus slumberd in mine Armes.' 475
The Gods againe laught; even the watry state
Wrung out a laughter, but propitiate
Was still for Mars, and praid the God of fire
He would dissolve him, offering the desire
He made to Jove to pay himselfe, and said 480
All due debts should be by the Gods repaid.
'Pay me no words,' said he, 'where deeds lend paine;
Wretched the words are given for wretched men.
How shall I binde you in th'Immortals' sight
If Mars be once loos'd, nor will pay his right?' 485
'Vulcan,' said he, 'if Mars should flie, nor see
Thy right repaid, it should be paid by me.'
'Your word, so given, I must accept,' said he—
Which said, he loosd them. Mars then rusht from skie
And stoop't cold Thrace. The laughing Deity 490
For Cyprus was, and tooke her Paphian state
Where she a Grove ne're cut hath consecrate,
All with Arabian odors fum'd, and hath
An Altar there at which the Graces bathe
And with immortall Balms besmooth her skin, 495

This is τὸ τὰ μικρὰ μεγάλως, &c. Parva magne dicere; *grave sentence out of lightest vapor.*

Fit for the blisse Immortals solace in,
Deckt her in to-be-studied attire
And apt to set beholders' hearts on fire.
  This sung the sacred Muse, whose notes and words
The dancers' feete kept, as his hands his cords. 500
Ulysses much was pleased, and all the crew.
  This would the king have varied with a new
And pleasing measure, and performed by
Two with whom none would strive in dancerie.
And those his sonnes were, that must therefore dance 505
Alone, and onely to the harp advance,
Without the words. And this sweete couple was
Yong Halius and divine Laodamas,
Who danc't a Ball dance. Then the rich-wrought Ball
(That Polybus had made, of purple all) 510
They tooke to hand: one threw it to the skie
And then danc't backe; the other (capring hie)
Would surely catch it ere his foote toucht ground
And up againe advanc't it, and so found
The other cause of dance; and then did he 515
Dance lofty trickes till next it came to be
His turne to catch and serve the other still.
When they had kept it up to either's will,
They then danc't ground tricks, oft mixt hand in hand,
And did so gracefully their change command 520
That all the other Youth that stood at pause
With deafning shouts gave them the great applause.

Ulysses to Alcinous.

  Then said Ulysses: 'O past all men here
Cleare, not in powre but in desert as clere,
You said your dancers did the world surpasse, 525
And they performe it cleare, and to amaze.'
  This wonne Alcinous' heart, and equall prise
He gave Ulysses, saying: 'Matchlesse wise,
Princes and Rulers, I perceive our guest,
And therefore let our hospitable best 530
In fitting gifts be given him. Twelve chiefe kings
There are that order all the glorious things
Of this our kingdome, and the thirteenth I
Exist as Crowne to all: let instantly
Be thirteene garments given him, and of gold, 535
Precious and fine, a Talent. While we hold
This our assembly, be all fetcht and given,
That to our feast prepar'd, as to his heaven,
Our guest may enter. And that nothing be

Left unperformd that fits his dignity, 540
Euryalus shall here conciliate
Himselfe with words and gifts, since past our rate
He gave bad language.' This did all commend
And give in charge, and every king did send
His Herald for his gift. Euryalus 545
(Answering for his part) said: 'Alcinous!
Our chiefe of all, since you command, I will
To this our guest by all meanes reconcile,
And give him this entirely mettald sword,
The handle massie silver, and the bord 550
That gives it cover all of Ivorie,
New, and in all kinds worth his qualitie.'
 This put he strait into his hand, and said:
'Frolicke, O Guest and Father; if words, fled,
Have bene offensive, let swift whirlwinds take 555
And ravish them from thought. May all Gods make
Thy wife's sight good to thee, in quicke retreate
To all thy friends and best-lov'd breeding seate,
Their long misse quitting with the greater joy—
In whose sweet, vanish all thy worst annoy.' 560
 'And frolicke thou to all height, Friend,' said he,
'Which heaven confirme with wisht felicitie.
Nor ever give againe desire to thee
Of this sword's usc, which with affects so free,
In my reclaime, thou hast bestowd on me.' 565
 This said, athwart his shoulders he put on
The right faire sword. And then did set the Sunne,
When all the gifts were brought, which backe againe
(With King Alcinous in all the traine)
Were by the honourd Heralds borne to Court, 570
Which his faire sonnes tooke, and from the resort
Laid by their reverend Mother. Each his throne
Of all the Peeres (which yet were overshone
In King Alcinous' command) ascended:
Whom he to passe as much in gifts contended, 575
And to his Queene said: 'Wife! see brought me here
The fairest Cabinet I have, and there
Impose a well-cleansd in and utter weed.
A Caldron heate with water, that with speed
Our Guest well bath'd, and all his gifts made sure, 580
It may a joyfull appetite procure
To his succeeding Feast, and make him heare
The Poet's Hymne with the securer eare.

To all which I will adde my boll of gold,
In all frame curious, to make him hold 585
My memory alwaies deare and sacrifise
With it at home to all the Deities.'
  Then Arete her maids charg'd to set on
A well-siz'd Caldron quickly. Which was done,
Cleare water powr'd in, flame made so entire 590
It gilt the brasse and made the water fire.
In meane space, from her chamber brought the Queene
A wealthy Cabinet, where (pure and cleane)
She put the garments and the gold bestowd
By that free State, and then the other vowd 595
By her Alcinous, and said: 'Now, Guest,
Make close and fast your gifts, lest when you rest
A ship-boord sweetly, in your way you meet
Some losse that lesse may make your next sleepe sweet.'
  This when Ulysses heard, all sure he made, 600
Enclosde and bound safe, for the saving trade
The Reverend-for-her-wisedome (Circe) had
In foreyeares taught him. Then the handmaid bad
His worth to bathing; which rejoyc't his heart,
For since he did with his Calypso part 605
He had no hote baths. None had favourd him,
Nor bin so tender of his kingly lim.
But all the time he spent in her abode,
He liv'd respected as he were a God.
  Cleansd then and balmd, faire shirt and robe put on, 610
Fresh come from bath and to the Feasters gone,
Nausicaa, that from the Gods' hands tooke
The soveraigne beautie of her blessed looke,
Stood by a well-carv'd Columne of the roome,
And through her eye her heart was overcome 615
With admiration of the Port imprest
In his aspect, and said: 'God save you, Guest!

Nausicaa enflamed with Ulysses.

Be chearfull, as in all the future state
Your home will shew you in your better Fate.
But yet, even then, let this rememberd be, 620
Your life's price I lent and you owe it me.'
  The varied-in-all-counsels gave reply:
'Nausicaa! flowre of all this Empery!
So Juno's husband, that the strife for noise
Makes in the clouds, blesse me with strife of Joyes 625
In the desir'd day that my house shall show,
As I, as I to a Goddesse, there shall vow

To thy faire hand that did my Being give,
Which I'le acknowledge every houre I live.'
This said, Alcinous plac't him by his side. 630
Then tooke they feast, and did in parts divide
The severall dishes, filld out wine, and then
The striv'd-for, for his worth, of worthy men
And reverenc't of the State, Demodocus,
Was brought in by the good Pontonous. 635
In midst of all the guests they gave him place
Against a loftie Pillar, when this grace
The grac't-with-wisedome did him. From the Chine
That stood before him of a white-tooth'd Swine
(Being farre the daintiest joynt), mixt through with fat, 640
He carv'd to him and sent it where he sat
By his old friend, the Herald, willing thus:
'Herald! reach this to grave Demodocus.
Say, I salute him and his worth embrace.
Poets deserve past all the humane race 645
Reverend respect and honor, since the Queene
Of knowledge and the supreme worth in men,
The Muse, informes them and loves all their race.'
This reacht the Herald to him, who the grace
Receiv'd encourag'd: which, when feast was spent, 650
Ulysses amplified to this ascent:
'Demodocus! I must preferre you farre
Past all your sort, if or the Muse of warre,
Jove's daughter, prompts you (that the Greeks respects),
Or if the Sunne, that those of Troy affects 655
For I have heard you, since my coming, sing
The Fate of Greece to an admired string—
How much our sufferance was, how much we wrought,
How much the actions rose to when we fought,
So lively forming as you had bin there, 660
Or to some free relator lent your eare.
Forth then, and sing the wooden horse's frame,
Built by Epeus, by the martiall Dame
Taught the whole Fabricke; which, by force of sleight,
Ulysses brought into the Citie's height 665
When he had stuft it with as many men
As leveld loftie Ilion with the Plaine.
With all which if you can as well enchant
As with expression quicke and elegant
You sung the rest, I will pronounce you cleare 670
Inspir'd by God, past all that ever were.'

ἐρίηρον ἀοιδὸν—Poetam cuius hominibus digna est societas.

This said, even stird by God up, he began,
And to his Song fell, past the forme of man,
Beginning where the Greeks a ship-boord went
And every Chiefe had set on fire his Tent, 675
When th'other Kings, in great Ulysses' guide,
In Troy's vast market place the horse did hide,
From whence the Troyans up to Ilion drew
The dreadfull Engine—where sate all arew
Their Kings about it, many counsels given 680
How to dispose it. In three waies were driven
Their whole distractions: first, if they should feele
The hollow wood's heart (searcht with piercing steele),
Or from the battlements (drawne higher yet)
Deject it headlong, or that counterfet 685
So vast and novell set on sacred fire,
Vowd to appease each angerd Godhead's ire.
On which opinion they thereafter saw
They then should have resolv'd, th'unalterd law
Of Fate presaging that Troy then should end 690
When th'hostile horse she should receive to friend;
For therein should the Grecian Kings lie hid,
To bring the Fate and death they after did.
He sung, besides, the Greeks' eruption
From those their hollow crafts, and horse forgone; 695
And how they made Depopulation tred
Beneath her feete so high a Citie's head.
In which affaire, he sung in other place
That of that ambush some man else did race
The Ilian Towres than Laertiades— 700

Ulysses.

But here he sung that he alone did seise
(With Menelaus) the ascended roofe
Of Prince Deiphobus, and Mars-like proofe
Made of his valour, a most dreadfull fight
Daring against him; and there vanquisht quite 705
In litle time (by great Minerva's aid)
All Ilion's remnant, and Troy levell laid.

As by the divine fury directly inspired so, for Ulysses' glory.

This the divine Expressor did so give
Both act and passion that he made it live,
And to Ulysses' facts did breathe a fire 710
So deadly quickning that it did inspire
Old death with life, and renderd life so sweet
And passionate that all there felt it fleet—
Which made him pitie his owne crueltie,
And put into that ruth so pure an eie 715

In that the slaughters he made were exprest so lively.

τήκετο 'Οδυσσεύς. τήκω *Metaphorically signifying,* consumo, tabesco.

Simile.

Of humane frailtie, that to see a man
Could so revive from Death, yet no way can
Defend from death, his owne quicke powres it made
Feele there death's horrors, and he felt life fade.
In teares his feeling braine swet: for in things 720
That move past utterance, teares ope all their springs.
Nor are there in the Powres that all life beares
More true interpreters of all than teares.
And as a Ladie mournes her sole-lov'd Lord,
That, falne before his Citie by the sword, 725
Fighting to rescue from a cruell Fate
His towne and children, and in dead estate
Yet panting seeing him, wraps him in her armes,
Weeps, shriekes and powres her health into his armes,
Lies on him, striving to become his shield 730
From foes that still assaile him, speares impeld
Through backe and shoulders, by whose points embrude
They raise and leade him into servitude,
Labor and languor—for all which the Dame
Eates downe her cheekes with teares, and feeds life's flame 735
With miserable sufferance: so this King
Of teare-swet anguish op't a boundlesse spring—
Nor yet was seene to any one man there
But King Alcinous, who sate so neare
He could not scape him, sighs (so chok't) so brake 740
From all his tempers, which the King did take
Both note and grave respect of, and thus spake:
'Heare me, Phæacian Counsellers and Peeres,
And ceasse, Demodocus; perhaps all eares
Are not delighted with his song, for ever 745
Since the divine Muse sung our Guest hath never
Containd from secret mournings. It may fall
That something sung he hath bin griev'd withall,
As touching his particular. Forbeare,
That Feast may joyntly comfort all hearts here, 750
And we may cheare our Guest up; tis our best
In all due honor. For our reverend Guest
Is all our celebration, gifts, and all;
His love hath added to our Festivall.
A Guest, and suppliant, too, we should esteeme 755
Deare as our brother; one that doth but dreame
He hath a soule, or touch but at a mind
Deathlesse and manly, should stand so enclin'd.
Nor cloke you longer with your curious wit,

Lov'd Guest, what ever we shall aske of it. 760
It now stands on your honest state to tell;
And therefore give your name, nor more conceale
What of your parents and the Towne that beares
Name of your native, or of forreiners
That neare us border, you are calld in fame. 765
There's no man living walkes without a name,
Noble nor base, but had one from his birth
Imposde as fit as to be borne. What earth,
People, and citie owne you? Give to know.
Tell but our ships all, that your way must show; 770
For our ships know th'expressed minds of men,
And will so most intentively retaine
Their scopes appointed that they never erre,
And yet use never any man to stere,
Nor any Rudders have, as others need. 775
They know men's thoughts and whither tends their speed,
And there will set them. For you cannot name
A Citie to them, nor fat Soile, that Fame
Hath any notice given, but well they know,
And will flie to them, though they ebbe and flow 780
In blackest clouds and nights, and never beare
Of any wracke or rocke the slendrest feare.
But this I heard my Sire Nausithous say
Long since, that Neptune, seeing us convay
So safely passengers of all degrees, 785
Was angry with us; and upon our seas
A well-built ship we had (neare harbor come
From safe deduction of some stranger home)
Made in his flitting billowes sticke stone still,
And dimm'd our Citie, like a mightie hill 790
With shade cast round about it. This report
The old King made; in which miraculous sort,
If God had done such things, or left undone,
At his good pleasure be it. But now, on,
And truth relate us, both from whence you errd 795
And to what Clime of men would be transferrd,
With all their faire Townes, be they as they are,
If rude, unjust, and all irregular,
Or hospitable, bearing minds that please
The mightie Deitie. Which one of these 800
You would be set at, say, and you are there.
And therefore what afflicts you? Why to heare
The Fate of Greece and Ilion mourne you so?

This τεϱατολογία or affirmation of miracles, how impossible soever in these times assured, yet in those ages they were neither absurd nor strange. Those inanimate things having (it seemd) certain Genij, *in whose powers they supposed their ships' faculties. As others have affirmed Okes to have sence of hearing: and so the ship of Argos was said to have a Mast made of Dodone—an Oke that was vocall and could speake.*

Intending his father Nausithous.

The Gods have done it; as to all they do
Destine destruction, that from thence may rise 805
A Poeme to instruct posterities.
Fell any kinsman before Ilion?
Some worthy Sire-in-law, or like-neare sonne,
Whom next our owne blood and self-race we love?
Or any friend, perhaps, in whom did move 810
A knowing soule, and no unpleasing thing?
Since such a good one is no underling
To any brother: for what fits true friends
True wisedome is, that blood and birth transcends.

True wisedome fits true friends.

Finis libri octavi Hom. Odyss.

THE NINTH BOOKE
of
HOMER'S ODYSSES

THE ARGUMENT

Ulysses here is first made knowne;
Who tels the sterne contention
His powres did gainst the Cicons trie;
And thence to the Lotophagi
Extends his conquest: and from them 5
Assayes the Cyclop Polypheme,
And, by the crafts his wits apply,
He puts him out his onely eye.

Another Argument

Ἰῶτα. *The strangely fed*
Lotophagi.
The Cicons fled.
The Cyclop's eye.

Ulysses thus resolv'd the King's demands:
'Alcinous (in whom this Empire stands),
You should not of so naturall right desherit
Your princely feast as take from it the spirit.
To heare a Poet that in accent brings 5
The Gods' brests downe, and breathes them as he sings,
Is sweet and sacred; nor can I conceive,
In any common weale, what more doth give
Note of the just and blessed Empery
Than to see Comfort universally 10
Cheare up the people, when in every roofe
She gives observers a most humane proofe

He begins where Alcinous commanded Demodocus to end.

Of men's contents. To see a neighbour's Feast
Adorne it through, and thereat heare the breast
Of the divine Muse, men in order set, 15
οἰνοχόος.
A wine-page waiting, tables, crownd with meate,
Set close to guests that are to use it skilld,
The Cup-boords furnisht and the cups still filld—
This shewes (to my mind) most humanely faire.
Nor should you, for me, still the heavenly aire 20
That stirrd my soule so, for I love such teares
As fall from fit notes beaten through mine eares
With repetitions of what heaven hath done,
And breake from heartie apprehension
Of God and goodnesse, though they shew my ill. 25
And therefore doth my mind excite me still
To tell my bleeding mone; but much more now
To serve your pleasure, that to over-flow
My teares with such cause may by sighs be driven,
Though ne're so much plagu'd I may seeme by heaven. 30
'And now my name; which way shall leade to all
My miseries after, that their sounds may fall
Through your eares also, and shew (having fled
So much affliction), first, who rests his head
In your embraces, when (so farre from home) 35
I knew now where t'obtaine it resting roome.
'I am Ulysses Laertiades,
The feare of all the world for policies,
For which my facts as high as heaven resound.
I dwell in Ithaca, Earth's most renownd, 40
εἰνοσίφυλλον—quatientem seu agitantem frondes.
All over-shadow'd with the Shake-leafe hill,
Tree-fam'd Neritus, whose neare confines fill
Ilands a number, well inhabited,
Quædam quibus corpus alitur et vita sustentatur ὕλη appellantur.
That under my observance taste their bread—
Dulichius, Samos, and the full-of-food 45
Zacynthus, likewise grac't with store of wood.
But Ithaca, though in the seas it lie,
Yet lies she so aloft she casts her eye
Quite over all the neighbour Continent—
Farre Norward situate, and (being lent 50
But litle favour of the Morne and Sunne)
With barren rocks and cliffes is over-runne,
And yet of hardie youths a Nurse of Name.
Nor could I see a Soile, where ere I came,
More sweete and wishfull. Yet from hence was I 55
Withheld with horror by the Deitie,

Divine Calypso, in her cavie house,
Enflam'd to make me her sole Lord and Spouse.
Circe Ææa, too, (that knowing Dame,
Whose veines the like affections did inflame) 60
Detaind me likewise. But to neither's love
Could I be tempted—which doth well approve

Amor patriæ.

Nothing so sweete is as our countrie's earth
And joy of those from whom we claime our birth.
Though roofes farre richer we farre off possesse, 65
Yet (from our native) all our more is lesse.
'To which, as I contended, I will tell
The much-distress-conferring facts that fell
By Jove's divine prevention since I set
From ruin'd Troy my first foote in retreat. 70
'From Ilion ill winds cast me on the Coast
The Cicons hold, where I emploid mine hoast
For Ismarus, a Citie built just by
My place of landing, of which Victory
Made me expugner, I depeopl'd it, 75
Slue all the men, and did their wives remit,
With much spoile taken, which we did divide
That none might need his part. I then applide
All speed for flight; but my command therein
(Fooles that they were) could no observance win 80
Of many souldiers, who, with spoile fed hie,
Would yet fill higher, and excessively
Feel to their wine, gave slaughter on the shore
Cloven-footed beeves and sheepe in mightie store.
In meane space, Cicons did to Cicons crie, 85
When, of their nearest dwellers, instantly
Many and better souldiers made strong head,
That held the Continent and managed
Their horse with high skill, on which they would fight,
When fittest cause serv'd, and againe alight 90
(With soone seene vantage) and on foote contend.
Their concourse swift was, and had never end;
As thicke and sodaine twas as flowres and leaves
Darke Spring discovers when she Light receaves.

After Night, in the first of the Morning.

And then began the bitter Fate of Jove 95
To alter us unhappie, which even strove
To give us suffrance. At our Fleet we made
Enforced stand, and there did they invade
Our thrust-up Forces: darts encountred darts,
With blowes on both sides, either making parts 100

Good upon either, while the Morning shone
And sacred Day her bright increase held on,
Though much out-matcht in number. But as soone
As Phœbus Westward fell, the Cicons wonne
Much hand of us; sixe proved souldiers fell 105
(Of every ship), the rest they did compell
To seeke of Flight escape from Death and Fate.
'Thence (sad in heart) we saild: and yet our State
Was something chear'd, that (being over-matcht so much
In violent number) our retreate was such 110
As sav'd so many, our deare losse the lesse
That they surviv'd, so like for like successe.
Yet left we not the Coast before we calld
Home to our country earth the soules exhald
Of all the friends the Cicons overcame. 115

The ancient custome of calling home the dead.

Thrice calld we on them, by their severall name,
And then tooke leave. Then from the angry North,
Cloud-gathering Jove a dreadfull storme calld forth
Against our Navie, coverd shore and all
With gloomie vapors. Night did headlong fall 120
From frowning Heaven. And then hurld here and there
Was all our Navie; the rude winds did teare
In three, in foure, parts, all their sailes; and downe
Driven under hatches were we, prest to drowne.
Up rusht we yet againe, and with tough hand 125
(Two daies, two nights entoild) we gat nere land,
Labours and sorrowes eating up our minds.
The third cleare day yet, to more friendly winds
We masts advanc't, we white sailes spred, and sate.
Forewinds and guides againe did iterate 130
Our ease and home-hopes; which we cleare had reacht,
Had not, by chance, a sodaine North-wind fetcht,
With an extreame sea, quite about againe
Our whole endevours, and our course constraine
To giddie round, and with our bowd sailes greete 135
Dreadfull Maleia, calling backe our fleete
As farre forth as Cythera. Nine dayes more
Adverse winds tost me, and the tenth, the shore
Where dwell the blossome-fed Lotophagi
I fetcht, fresh water tooke in, instantly 140
Fell to our food aship-boord, and then sent
Two of my choice men to the Continent
(Adding a third, a Herald) to discover
What sort of people were the Rulers over

The Lotophagi.

The land next to us. Where the first they met 145
Were the Lotophagi, that made them eate
Their Country diet—and no ill intent
Hid in their hearts to them, and yet th'event
To ill converted it, for, having eate
Their daintie viands, they did quite forget 150
(As all men else that did but taste their feast)
Both country-men and country, nor addrest
Any returne t'informe what sort of men
Made fixt abode there; but would needs maintaine
Abode themselves there, and eate that food ever. 155
I made out after, and was faine to sever
Th'enchanted knot by forcing their retreate,
That striv'd, and wept, and would not leave their meate
For heaven it selfe. But, dragging them to fleete,
I wrapt in sure bands both their hands and feete 160
And cast them under hatches, and away
Commanded all the rest, without least stay,
Lest they should taste the Lote too, and forget
With such strange raptures their despisde retreate.
'All then aboord, we beate the sea with Ores, 165
And still with sad hearts saild by out-way shores,

The idle Cyclops.

Till th'out-lawd Cyclops' land we fetcht—a race
Of proud-liv'd loiterers, that never sow,
Nor put a plant in earth, nor use a Plow,
But trust in God for all things; and their earth 170
(Unsowne, unplowd) gives every of-spring birth
That other lands have—Wheate and Barley, Vines
That beare in goodly Grapes delicious wines.
And Jove sends showres for all: no counsels there,
Nor counsellers, nor lawes, but all men beare 175
Their heads aloft on mountaines, and those steepe,
And on their tops too; and there houses keepe
In vaultie Caves, their housholds governd all
By each man's law, imposde in severall;
Nor wife, nor child awd, but as he thinks good, 180
None for another caring. But there stood
Another litle Ile, well stor'd with wood,
Betwixt this and the entry; neither nie
The Cyclops' Ile, nor yet farre off doth lie.
Men's want it sufferd, but the men's supplies 185
The Goates made with their inarticulate cries.
Goates beyond number this small Iland breeds,
So tame that no accesse disturbs their feeds.

No hunters (that the tops of mountaines scale
And rub through woods with toile) seeke them at all. 190
Nor is the soile with flocks fed downe, nor plowd,
Nor ever in it any seed was sowd.
Nor place the neighbour Cyclops their delights
In brave Vermilion prow-deckt ships—nor wrights
Usefull and skilfull in such works as need 195
Perfection to those trafficks that exceed
Their naturall confines, to flie out and see
Cities of men, and take in mutually
The prease of others. To themselves they live
And to their Iland, that enough would give 200
A good inhabitant, and time of yeare
Observe to all things Art could order there.
There, close upon the sea, sweet medowes spring,
That yet of fresh streames want no watering
To their soft burthens, but of speciall yeeld 205
Your vines would be there and your common field
But gentle worke make for your plow, yet beare
A loftie harvest when you came to sheare.
For passing fat the soile is. In it lies
A harbor so opportune that no ties, 210
Halsers, or gables need, nor anchors cast.
Whom stormes put in there are with stay embrac't,
Or to their full wils safe, or winds aspire
To Pilots' uses their more quicke desire.
At entry of the haven a silver foord 215
Is from a rock-impressing fountaine pow'rd,
All set with sable Poplars. And this Port
Were we arriv'd at, by the sweet resort
Of some God guiding us, for twas a night
So gastly darke all Port was past our sight, 220
Clouds hid our ships and would not let the Moone
Affoord a beame to us, the whole Ile wonne
By not an eye of ours. None thought the Blore
That then was up shov'd waves against the shore,
That then to an unmeasur'd height put on; 225
We still at sea esteemd us, till alone
Our fleet put in it selfe. And then were strooke
Our gatherd sailes: our rest ashore we tooke,
And day expected. When the Morne gave fire,
We rose, and walkt, and did the Ile admire, 230
The Nymphs, Jove's daughters, putting up a heard
Of mountaine Goates to us, to render cheard

The descriptions of all these countries have admirable allegories, besides their artly and pleasing relation.

My fellow souldiers. To our Fleet we flew,
Our crooked bowes tooke, long-pil'd darts, and drew
Our selves in three parts out—when, by the grace 235
That God vouch-saft we made a gainfull chace.
Twelve ships we had, and every ship had nine
Fat Goates allotted it, ten onely mine.
Thus all that day, even till the Sunne was set,
We sate and feasted, pleasant wine and meate 240
Plenteously taking, for we had not spent
Our ruddie wine aship-boord: supplement
Of large sort each man to his vessell drew,
When we the sacred Citie overthrew
That held the Cicons. Now then saw we neare 245
The Cyclops' late-praisd Iland, and might heare
The murmure of their sheepe and goates, and see
Their smokes ascend. The Sunne then set, and we
(When Night succeeded) tooke our rest ashore.
And when the world the Morning's favour wore, 250
I calld my friends to councell, charging them
To make stay there, while I tooke ship and streame
With some associates, and explor'd what men
The neighbour Ile held—if of rude disdaine,
Churlish and tyrannous, or minds bewraid 255
Pious and hospitable. Thus much said,
I boorded, and commanded to ascend
My friends and souldiers, to put off, and lend
Way to our ship. They boorded, sate, and beate
The old sea forth, till we might see the seate 260
The greatest Cyclop held for his abode,
Which was a deepe Cave neare the common rode
Of ships that toucht there, thicke with Lawrels spred,
Where many sheepe and goates lay shadowed:
And neare to this a Hall of torne-up stone, 265
High built with Pines, that heaven and earth attone,
And loftie-fronted Okes: in which kept house
A man in shape immane and monsterous,
Fed all his flocks alone, nor would affoord
Commerce with men, but had a wit abhord, 270
His mind his body answering. Nor was he
Like any man that food could possibly
Enhance so hugely, but (beheld alone)
Shewd like a steepe hil's top, all overgrowne
With trees and brambles; litle thought had I 275
Of such vast objects. When, arriv'd so nie,

Some of my lov'd friends I made stay aboord
To guard my ship, and twelve with me I shor'd,
The choice of all. I tooke besides along
A Goat-skin flagon of wine, blacke and strong, 280
That Maro did present, Euantheus' sonne
And Priest to Phœbus, who had mansion
In Thracian Ismarus (the Towne I tooke).
He gave it me since I (with reverence strooke
Of his grave place, his wife and children's good) 285
Freed all of violence. Amidst a wood
Sacred to Phœbus stood his house, from whence
He fetcht me gifts of varied excellence,
Seven talents of fine gold, a boll all fram'd
Of massie silver. But his gift most fam'd 290
Was twelve great vessels filld with such rich wine
As was incorruptible and divine.
He kept it as his jewell, which none knew
But he himselfe, his wife, and he that drew.
It was so strong that never any filld 295
A cup, where that was but by drops instilld,
And drunke it off, but twas before allaid
With twentie parts in water; yet so swaid
The spirit of that litle that the whole
A sacred odour breath'd about the boll. 300
Had you the odour smelt and sent it cast,
It would have vext you to forbeare the taste.
But then (the taste gaind too) the spirit wrought
To dare things high set up an end my thought.

Vinum Maroneum memorabile.

'Of this a huge great flagon full I bore, 305
And in a good large knapsacke victles' store;
And longd to see this heape of fortitude,
That so illiterate was and upland rude
That lawes divine nor humane he had learnd.
With speed we reacht the Caverne, nor discernd 310
His presence there. His flocks he fed at field.
'Entring his den, each thing beheld did yeeld
Our admiration—shelves with cheeses heapt,
Sheds stuft with Lambs and Goates, distinctly kept,
Distinct the biggest, the more meane distinct, 315
Distinct the yongest. And in their precinct
(Proper and placefull) stood the troughs and pailes
In which he milkt; and what was given at meales
Set up a creaming, in the Evening still
All scouring bright as deaw upon the hill. 320

'Then were my fellowes instant to convay
Kids, cheeses, lambs, aship boord, and away
Saile the salt billow. I thought best not so,
But better otherwise; and first would know
What guest-gifts he would spare me. Little knew 325
My friends on whom they would have preyd: his view
Prov'd after that his inwards were too rough
For such bold usage: we were bold enough
In what I sufferd, which was there to stay,
Make fire and feed there, though beare none away. 330
There sate we till we saw him feeding come
And on his necke a burthen lugging home,
Most highly huge of Sere-wood, which the pile
That fed his fire supplide all supper while.
Downe by his den he threw it, and up rose 335
A tumult with the fall. Afraid, we close
Withdrew our selves, while he into a Cave
Of huge receit his high-fed cattell drave,
All that he milkt; the males he left without
His loftie roofes, that all bestrowd about 340
With Rams and buck-goates were. And then a rocke
He lift aloft, that damd up to his flocke
The doore they enterd: twas so hard to wield
That two and twentie Waggons, all foure-wheeld,
(Could they be loaded and have teames that were 345
Proportion'd to them) could not stirre it there.
Thus, making sure, he kneeld and milkt his Ewes
And braying Goates with all a milker's dues.
Then let in all their yong: then quicke did dresse
His halfe milke up for cheese and in a presse 350
Of wicker prest it, put in bolls the rest,
To drinke and eate and serve his supping feast.
'All works dispatcht thus, he began his fire,
Which blowne, he saw us, and did thus enquire:
' "Ho! Guests! what are ye? Whence saile ye these seas? 355
Trafficke, or rove ye, and like theeves oppresse
Poore strange adventurers, exposing so
Your soules to danger and your lives to wo?"
'This utterd he, when Feare from our hearts tooke
The very life, to be so thunder-strooke 360
With such a voice and such a monster see.
But thus I answerd: "Erring Grecians, we
From Troy were turning homewards, but by force

This his relation of Agamemnon, and his glory and theirs for Troye's sacke, with the pietie of supplicant's receit to him that was so barbarous and impious, must be intended spoken by Ulysses with supposition that his hearers wold note, still as he spake, how vaine they would shew to the Cyclops—who respected litle Agamemnon or their valiant exploit against Troy, or the Gods themselves. For otherwise the serious observation of the words (though good and grave, if spoken to another) want their intentional sharpnesse and life.

Of adverse winds, in far-diverted course,
Such unknowne waies tooke and on rude seas tost 365
(As Jove decreed) are cast upon this Coast.
Of Agamemnon (famous Atreus' sonne)
We boast our selves the souldiers—who hath wonne
Renowme that reacheth heaven, to overthrow
So great a Citie and to ruine so 370
So many nations. Yet at thy knees lie
Our prostrate bosomes, forc't with praires to trie
If any hospitable right or Boone
Of other nature (such as have bin wonne
By lawes of other houses) thou wilt give. 375
Reverence the Gods, thou greatst of all that live.
We suppliants are, and hospitable Jove
Poures wreake on all whom praires want powre to move,
And with their plagues together will provide
That humble Guests shall have their wants supplide." 380
'He cruelly answerd: "O thou foole," said he,
"To come so farre and to importune me
With any God's feare or observed love.
We Cyclops care not for your Goat-fed Jove
Nor other Blest ones; we are better farre. 385
To Jove himselfe dare I bid open warre,
To thee, and all thy fellowes, if I please.
But tell me: where's the ship that by the seas
Hath brought thee hither? If farre off, or neare,
Informe me quickly." These his temptings were. 390
But I too much knew not to know his mind,
And craft with craft paid, telling him the wind
(Thrust up from sea by him that shakes the shore)
Had dasht our ship against his rocks and tore
Her ribs in peeces close upon his Coast, 395
And we from high wracke sav'd, the rest were lost.
'He answerd nothing, but rusht in and tooke
Two of my fellowes up from earth and strooke
Their braines against it. Like two whelps they flew
About his shoulders, and did all embrew 400
The blushing earth. No mountaine Lion tore
Two Lambs so sternly, lapt up all their gore
Gusht from their torne-up bodies, lim by lim,
(Trembling with life yet) ravisht into him.
Both flesh and marrow-stuffed bones he eate 405
And even th'uncleansed entrails made his meate.

We, weeping, cast our hands to heaven to view
A sight so horrid. Desperation flew
With all our after lives to instant death
In our beleev'd destruction. But when breath 410
The fury of his appetite had got .
Because the gulfe his belly reacht his throte,
Man's flesh and Goate's milke laying laire on laire,
Till neare chokt up was all the passe for aire,
Along his den, amongst his cattell, downe 415
He rusht, and streakt him—when my mind was growne
Desperate to step in, draw my sword and part
His bosome where the strings about the heart
Circle the Liver, and adde strength of hand.
But that rash thought, more staid did countermand; 420
For there we all had perisht, since it past
Our powres to lift aside a log so vast
As barrd all outscape; and so sigh'd away
The thought all Night, expecting active Day.
Which come, he first of all his fire enflames, 425
Then milks his Goates and Ewes, then to their dams
Lets in their yong, and wondrous orderly,
With manly haste, dispatcht his houswifery.
Then to his Breakfast, to which other two
Of my poore friends went; which eate, out then go 430
His heards and fat flocks, lightly putting by
The churlish barre and closde it instantly;
For both those works with ease as much he did,
As you would ope and shut your Quiver lid.
'With stormes of whistlings then his flocks he drave 435
Up to the mountaines, and occasion gave
For me to use my wits—which to their height
I striv'd to skrew up, that a vengeance might
By some meanes fall from thence, and Pallas now
Affoord a full eare to my neediest vow. 440
This then my thoughts preferd: a huge club lay
Close by his milk-house, which was now in way
To drie and season, being an Olive tree
Which late he feld, and, being greene, must be
Made lighter for his manage. Twas so vast 445
That we resembl'd it to some fit Mast
To serve a ship of burthen that was driven
With twentie Ores, and had a bignesse given
To beare a huge sea. Full so thicke, so tall
We judg'd this club, which I, in part, hewd small 450

And cut a fathome off. The peece I gave
Amongst my souldiers to take downe and shave;
Which done, I sharpn'd it at top, and then
(Hardn'd in fire) I hid it in the den
Within a nastie dunghill reeking there, 455
Thicke, and so moist, it issude every where.
Then made I lots cast by my friends, to trie
Whose fortune serv'd to dare the bor'd out eie
Of that man-eater, and the lot did fall
On foure I wisht to make my aid of all, 460
And I the fift made, chosen like the rest.

'Then came the Even; and he came from the feast
Of his fat cattell, drave in all, nor kept
One male abroad: if, or his memory slept
By God's direct will, or of purpose was 465
His driving in of all then, doth surpasse
My comprehension. But he closde againe
The mightie barre, milkt, and did still maintaine
All other observation as before.
His worke all done, two of my souldiers more 470
At once he snatcht up, and to supper went.
Then dar'd I words to him, and did present
A boll of wine with these words: "Cyclop! take
A boll of wine from my hand, that may make
Way for the man's flesh thou hast eate, and show 475
What drinke our ship held—which in sacred vow
I offer to thee, to take ruth on me
In my dismission home. Thy rages be
Now no more sufferable. How shall men
(Mad and inhumane that thou art) againe 480
Greet thy abode and get thy actions grace,
If thus thou ragest and eatst up their race."

'He tooke, and drunke, and vehemently joyd
To taste the sweet cup; and againe employd
My flagon's powre, entreating more, and said: 485
"Good Guest, againe affoord my taste thy aid,
And let me know thy name, and quickly now,
That in thy recompence I may bestow
A hospitable gift on thy desert,
And such a one as shall rejoyce thy heart. 490
For to the Cyclops too the gentle Earth
Beares generous wine, and Jove augments her birth
In store of such with showres. But this rich wine
Fell from the river that is meere divine,

Of Nectar and Ambrosia." This againe 495
I gave him, and againe; nor could the foole abstaine,
But drunke as often. When the noble Juyce
Had wrought upon his spirit, I then gave use
To fairer language, saying: "Cyclop! now
As thou demandst, I'le tell my name; do thou 500
Make good thy hospitable gift to me.
My name is No-Man; No-Man each degree
Of friends, as well as parents, call my name."
He answerd, as his cruell soule became:
"No-Man! I'le eate thee last of all thy friends; 505
And this is that in which so much amends
I vowd to thy deservings; thus shall be
My hospitable gift made good to thee."
This said, he upwards fell, but then bent round
His fleshie necke, and Sleepe (with all crownes crownd) 510
Subdude the Savage. From his throte brake out
My wine, with man's flesh gobbets, like a spout,
When, loded with his cups, he lay and snor'd.
And then tooke I the club's end up, and gor'd
The burning cole-heape that the point might heate, 515
Confirmd my fellowes' minds, lest Feare should let
Their vowd assay and make them flie my aid.
Strait was the Olive Lever I had laid
Amidst the huge fire, to get hardning, hot,
And glowd extremely, though twas greene—which got 520
From forth the cinders, close about me stood
My hardie friends: but that which did the good
Was God's good inspiration, that gave
A spirit beyond the spirit they usde to have;
Who tooke the Olive sparre, made keene before, 525
And plung'd it in his eye, and up I bore,
Bent to the top close, and helpt poure it in
Simile. With all my forces. And as you have seene
A ship-wright bore a navall beame, he oft
Thrusts at the Augur's Froofe, works still aloft, 530
And at the shanke helpe others with a cord
Wound round about, to make it sooner bor'd,
All plying the round still: so into his eye
The firie stake we labourd to imply.
Out gusht the blood, that scalded; his eye-ball 535
Thrust out a flaming vapour, that scorcht all
His browes and eye-lids, his eye-strings did cracke
As in the sharpe and burning rafter brake—

Simile.

And as a Smith to harden any toole
(Broad Axe, or Mattocke) in his Trough doth coole 540
The red-hote substance, that so fervent is
It makes the cold wave strait to seethe and hisse:
So sod and hizd his eye about the stake.
He roar'd withall, and all his Caverne brake
In claps like thunder. We did frighted flie, 545
Disperst in corners. He from forth his eie
The fixed stake pluckt: after which, the blood
Flowd freshly forth, and, mad, he hurl'd the wood
About his hovill. Out he then did crie
For other Cyclops that in Cavernes by 550
Upon a windie Promontorie dwelld—
Who hearing how impetuously he yelld
Rusht every way about him, and enquir'd
What ill afflicted him, that he expir'd
Such horrid clamors, and in sacred Night, 555
To breake their sleepes so? Askt him, if his fright
Came from some mortall that his flocks had driven?
Or if by craft, or might, his death were given?
He answerd from his den: "By craft, nor might,
No-Man hath given me death." They then said: "Right: 560
If no man hurt thee and thy selfe alone,
That which is done to thee by Jove is done.
And what great Jove inflicts no man can flie;

Neptune.

Pray to thy Father yet, a Deitie,
And prove, from him, if thou canst helpe acquire." 565
Thus spake they, leaving him. When all on fire
My heart with joy was, that so well my wit
And name deceiv'd him; whom now paine did split,
And groning up and downe he groping tride
To find the stone, which found, he put aside— 570
But in the doore sate, feeling if he could
(As his sheepe issude) on some man lay hold,
Esteeming me a foole, that could devise
No stratageme to scape his grosse surprise.
But I, contending what I could invent 575
My friends and me from death so imminent
To get deliverd, all my wiles I wove
(Life being the subject) and did this approve:
Fat fleecie Rams, most faire and great, lay there,

Wooll of a violet colour.

That did a burthen like a Violet beare. 580
These (while this learn'd-in-villanie did sleepe)
I yokt with Osiers cut there, sheepe to sheepe,

Three in a ranke, and still the mid sheepe bore
A man about his belly; the two more
Marcht on his each side for defence. I then, 585
Chusing my selfe the fairest of the den,
His fleecie belly under-crept, embrac't
His backe, and in his rich wooll wrapt me fast
With both my hands, arm'd with as fast a mind.
And thus each man hung till the morning shin'd; 590
Which come, he knew the houre and let abroad
His male-flocks first; the females unmilkt stood
Bleating and braying, their full bags so sore
With being unemptied, but their shepheard more
With being unsighted; which was cause his mind 595
Went not a milking. He (to wreake enclin'd)
The backs felt as they past of those male dams,
(Grosse foole) beleeving we would ride his Rams,
Nor ever knew that any of them bore
Upon his belly any man before. 600
The last Ram came to passe him, with his wooll
And me together, loded to the full,
For there did I hang: and that Ram he staid,
And me withall had in his hands, my head
Troubl'd the while, not causlesly, nor least. 605
This Ram he grop't, and talkt to: "Lazie beast!
Why last art thou now? Thou hast never usde
To lag thus hindmost, but still first hast brusde
The tender blossome of a flowre, and held
State in thy steps, both to the flood and field. 610
First still at Fold at Even, now last remaine?
Doest thou not wish I had mine eye againe
Which that abhord man No-Man did put out,
Assisted by his execrable rout,
When he had wrought me downe with wine? But he 615
Must not escape my wreake so cunningly.
I would to heaven thou knewst, and could but speake,
To tell me where he lurks now; I would breake
His braine about my Cave, strewd here and there,
To ease my heart of those foule ils that were 620
Th'inflictions of a man I prisde at nought."
'Thus let he him abroad; when I (once brought
A litle from his hold) my selfe first losde,
And next, my friends. Then drave we and disposde
His strait-leggd fat-fleece-bearers over land, 625
Even till they all were in my ship's command,

And to our lov'd friends shewd our praid-for sight,
Escap't from death. But for our losse outright
They brake in teares, which with a looke I staid,
And bad them take our Boote in. They obaid, 630
And up we all went, sate, and usde our Ores,
But, having left as farre the savage shores
As one might heare a voice, we then might see
The Cyclop at the haven, when instantly
I staid our Ores, and this insultance usde: 635

Ulysses insults over the Cyclop.

"Cyclop! thou shouldst not have so much abusde
Thy monstrous forces to oppose their least
Against a man immartiall and a guest,
And eate his fellowes: thou mightst know there were
Some ils behind, rude swaine, for thee to beare— 640
That feard not to devoure thy guests and breake
All lawes of humanes. Jove sends therefore wreake,
And all the Gods, by me." This blew the more
His burning furie; when the top he tore
From off a huge Rocke, and so right a throw 645
Made at our ship that just before the Prow
It overflew and fell, mist Mast and all
Exceeding litle, but about the fall
So fierce a wave it raisd that backe it bore
Our ship so farre it almost toucht the shore. 650
A bead-hooke then (a far-extended one)
I snatcht up, thrust hard, and so set us gone
Some litle way, and strait commanded all
To helpe me with their Ores, on paine to fall
Againe on our confusion. But a signe 655
I with my head made, and their Ores were mine
In all performance. When we off were set,
(Then first, twice further) my heart was so great
It would againe provoke him, but my men
On all sides rusht about me to containe, 660
And said: "Unhappie! why will you provoke
A man so rude that with so dead a stroke
Given with his Rock-dart made the sea thrust backe
Our ship so farre, and neare hand forc't our wracke?
Should he againe but heare your voice resound 665
And any word reach, thereby would be found
His Dart's direction, which would in his fall
Crush peece-meale us, quite split our ship and all,
So much dart weilds the monster." Thus urg'd they
Impossible things in feare; but I gave way 670

To that wrath which so long I held deprest
(By great Necessitie conquerd) in my brest.

Ulysses' continued insolence, no more to repeate what he said to the Cyclop than to let his hearers know his Epithetes, and estimation in the world.

' "Cyclop! if any aske thee who imposde
Th'unsightly blemish that thine eye enclosde,
Say that Ulysses (old Laertes' sonne, 675
Whose seate is Ithaca, and who hath wonne
Surname of Citie-racer) bor'd it out."
'At this he braid so loud that round about
He drave affrighted Ecchoes through the Aire,
And said: "O beast! I was premonisht faire 680
By aged Prophecie in one that was
A great and good man, this should come to passe;
And how tis prov'd now! Augur Telemus,
Surnam'd Eurymides (that spent with us
His age in Augurie and did exceed 685
In all presage of Truth) said all this deed
Should this event take, author'd by the hand
Of one Ulysses; who I thought was mand
With great and goodly personage, and bore
A vertue answerable, and this shore 690
Should shake with weight of such a conqueror,
When now a weakling came, a dwarfie thing,
A thing of nothing, who yet wit did bring
That brought supply to all, and with his wine
Put out the flame where all my light did shine. 695
Come, land againe, Ulysses! that my hand
May Guest-rites give thee, and the great command
That Neptune hath at sea I may convert
To the deduction where abides thy heart,
With my sollicitings—whose sonne I am, 700
And whose fame boasts to beare my Father's name.
Nor thinke my hurt offends me, for my Sire
Can soone repose in it the visuall fire
At his free pleasure; which no powre beside
Can boast, of men or of the deifide." 705
'I answerd: "Would to God I could compell
Both life and soule from thee, and send to hell
Those spoiles of nature. Hardly Neptune then
Could cure thy hurt and give thee all again."

Polyphem's imprecation against Ulysses.

'Then flew fierce vowes to Neptune, both his hands 710
To starre-borne heaven cast: "O thou that all lands
Girdst in thy ambient Circle, and in aire
Shak'st the curld Tresses of thy Saphire haire,
If I be thine, or thou maist justly vant

Thou art my Father, heare me now, and grant 715
That this Ulysses (old Laertes' sonne,
That dwels in Ithaca, and name hath wonne
Of Citie-ruiner) may never reach
His naturall region. Or if to fetch
That and the sight of his faire roofes and friends 720
Be fatall to him, let him that amends
For all his miseries long time and ill
Smart so and faile of; nor that Fate fulfill
Till all his souldiers quite are cast away
In others' ships. And when at last the day 725
Of his sole-landing shall his dwelling show,
Let Detriment prepare him wrongs enow."

'Thus praid he Neptune, who, his Sire, appeard,
And all his praire to every syllable heard.
But then a Rocke, in size more amplified 730
Than first, he ravisht to him, and implied
A dismall strength in it, when (wheeld about)
He sent it after us; nor flew it out
From any blind aime, for a litle passe
Beyond our Fore-decke from the fall there was— 735
With which the sea our ship gave backe upon
And shrunke up into billowes from the stone,
Our ship againe repelling neare as neare
The shore as first. But then our Rowers were
(Being warnd) more armd and stronglier stemd the flood 740
That bore backe on us, till our ship made good
The other Iland where our whole Fleet lay,
In which our friends lay mourning for our stay
And every minute lookt when we should land.
Where (now arriv'd) we drew up to the sand, 745
The Cyclop's sheepe dividing, that none there
(Of all our privates) might be wrung, and beare
Too much on powre. The Ram yet was alone,
By all my friends, made all my portion
Above all others; and I made him then 750
A sacrifice for me and all my men
To cloud-compelling Jove, that all commands—
To whom I burnd the Thighs; but my sad hands
Receiv'd no grace from him, who studied how
To offer men and fleete to Overthrow. 755

No occasion let passe to Ulysses' pietie in our Poet's singular wit and wisedome.

'All day, till Sun-set yet, we sate and eate,
And liberall store tooke in of wine and meate.
The Sunne then downe and place resign'd to shade,

We slept. Morne came, my men I raisd, and made
All go aboord, weigh Anker, and away. 760
They boorded, sate and beate the aged sea;
And forth we made saile, sad for losse before,
And yet had comfort since we lost no more.

Finis libri noni Hom. Odyss.

THE TENTH BOOKE
of
HOMER'S ODYSSES

THE ARGUMENT

Ulysses now relates to us
The grace he had with Æolus,
Great Guardian of the hollow winds;
Which in a leather bag he binds
And gives Ulysses; all but one, 5
Which Zephyr was, who filld alone
Ulysses' sailes. The Bag once seene
(While he slept) by Ulysses' men,
They, thinking it did gold inclose,
To find it all the winds did lose— 10
Who backe flew to their guard againe.
Forth saild he, and did next attaine
To where the Læstrygonians dwell,
Where he eleven ships lost, and fell
On the Ææan coast, whose shore 15
He sends Eurylochus t'explore,
Dividing with him halfe his men—
Who go, and turne no more againe
(All save Eurylochus, to swine
By Circe turnd.) Their stayes encline 20
Ulysses to their search, who got
Of Mercurie an Antidote,
(Which Moly was) gainst Circe's charmes,
And so avoids his souldiers' harmes.
A yeare with Circe all remaine, 25
And then their native formes regaine.
On utter shores a time they dwell,
While Ithacus descends to hell.

Another Argument

Κάππα. *Great Æolus*
And Circe, friends
Finds Ithacus;
And Hell descends.

'To the Æolian Iland we attaind,
That swumme about still on the sea, where raign'd
The God-lov'd Æolus Hippotades.
A wall of steele it had, and in the seas
A wave-beat-smooth rocke mov'd about the wall. 5
Twelve children in his house imperiall
Were borne to him; of which, sixe daughters were
And sixe were sonnes, that youth's sweet flowre did beare.
His daughters to his sonnes he gave as wives,
Who spent in feastfull comforts all their lives, 10
Close seated by their Sire and his grave Spouse.
Past number were the dishes that the house
Made ever savour, and still full the Hall
As long as day shin'd; in the night-time all
Slept with their chaste wives, each his faire carv'd bed 15
Most richly furnisht; and this life they led.
'We reacht the Cittie and faire roofes of these,
Where, a whole moneth's time, all things that might please
The King vouchsaf't us—of great Troy enquir'd,
The Grecian fleete, and how the Greekes retir'd. 20
To all which I gave answer as behov'd.
'The fit time come when I dismission mov'd,
He nothing would denie me, but addrest
My passe with such a bountie as might best
Teach me contentment. For he did enfold 25
Within an Oxe hide, flead at nine yeares old,
All th'airie blasts that were of stormie kinds.
Jupiter. Saturnius made him Steward of his winds,
And gave him powre to raise and to asswage;
And these he gave me, curbd thus of their rage. 30
Which in a glittering silver band I bound
And hung up in my ship, enclosd so round
That no egression any breath could find.
Onely he left abroad the Westerne wind,
To speede our ships and us with blasts secure. 35
But our securities made all unsure,
Nor could he consummate our course alone,
When all the rest had got egression.
Which thus succeeded. Nine whole daies and nights
We saild in safetie, and the tenth, the lights 40
Borne on our Countrey earth we might descrie,
So neere we drew; and yet even then fell I
(Being overwatcht) into a fatall sleepe,
For I would suffer no man else to keepe

πόδα νηὸς—
He calles the Sterne the foote of the ship.

The foote that rul'd my vessel's course, to leade 45
The faster home. My friends then Envy fed
About the bag I hung up, and supposde
That gold and silver I had there enclosde,
As gift from Æolus, and said: "O heaven!
What grace and grave price is by all men given 50
To our Commander, whatsoever coast
Or towne he comes to! How much he engrost
Of faire and precious prey, and brought from Troy!
We the same voiage went, and yet enjoy
In our returne these emptie hands for all. 55
This bag now Æolus was so liberall
To make a Guest-gift to him. Let us trie
Of what consists the faire-bound Treasurie,
And how much gold and silver it containes."
Ill counsaile present approbation gaines. 60
They op't the bag and out the vapours brake,
When instant tempest did our vessell take,
That bore us backe to Sea, to mourne anew
Our absent Countrey. Up amazd I flew,
And desperate things discourst—if I should cast 65
My selfe to ruine in the seas, or taste
Amongst the living more mone and sustaine.
Silent, I did so, and lay hid againe
Beneath the hatches, while an ill winde tooke
My ships backe to Æolia, my men strooke 70
With woe enough. We pumpt and landed then,
Tooke foode for all this, and (of all my men)
I tooke a Herald to me and away
Went to the Court of Æolus, where they
Were feasting still, he, wife and children set 75
Together close. We would not (at their meate)
Thrust in, but humbly on the threshold sat.
He then, amazd, my presence wonderd at,
And calld to me: "Ulysses! how thus backe
Art thou arriv'd here? What foule spirit brake 80
Into thy bosome to retire thee thus?
We thought we had deduction curious
Given thee before, to reach thy shore and home.
Did it not like thee?" I (even overcome
With worthy sorrow) answerd: "My ill men 85
Have done me mischiefe, and to them hath bene
My sleepe th'unhappie motive. But do you,
Dearest of friends, daigne succour to my vow:

Your powres command it." Thus endevord I
With soft speech to repaire my misery. 90
The rest with ruth sat dumbe. But thus spake he:
"Avant, and quickly quit my land of thee,
Thou worst of all that breathe; it fits not me
To convoy and take in whom heavens expose.
Away, and with thee go the worst of woes, 95
That seek'st my friendship, and the Gods thy foes."
'Thus he dismist me, sighing. Foorth we saild,
At heart afflicted: and now wholy faild
The minds my men sustaind, so spent they were
With toiling at their oares, and worse did beare 100
Their growing labours that they causd their grought
By selfe-willd follies, nor now ever thought
To see their Countrey more. Six nights and daies
We saild; the seventh, we saw faire Lamos raise
Her loftie Towres (the Læstrygonian State) 105
That beares her Ports so farre disterminate,
Where Shepheard Shepheard calls out, he at home
Is calld out by the other that doth come
From charge abroad, and then goes he to sleepe,
The other issuing. He whose turne doth keepe 110
The Night observance hath his double hire,
Since Day and Night in equall length expire
About that Region, and the Night's watch weigh'd
At twice the Daie's ward, since the charge that's laid
Upon the Nights-man (besides breach of sleepe) 115
Exceeds the Daies-man's: for one oxen keepe,
The other sheepe. But when the haven we found
(Exceeding famous, and environd round
With one continuate rocke, which so much bent
That both ends almost met, so prominent 120
They were, and made the haven's mouth passing streight)
Our whole fleete in we got; in whole receipt
Our Ships lay anchord close, nor needed we
Feare harme on any staies. Tranquillitie
So purely sate there that waves great nor small 125
Did ever rise to any height at all.
And yet would I no entrie make, but staid

This place suffers different construction in all the Commentors—in which all erre from the mind of the Poet, as in a hundred other places (which yet I want time to approve) especially about ἐγγὺς γὰρ νυκτὸς, &c. Prope enim noctis et diei sunt viæ (*or* similiter *which* ἐγγὺς *signifies)—which they will have to be understood that the daies in that region are long and the nights short; where Homer intends, that the Equinoctiall is there (for how else is the course of day and night neare or equall?). But therefore the nights-man hath his double hire, being as long about his charge as the other, and the night being more dangerous, etc. And if the day were so long, why should the nights man be preferred in wages?*

124 *For being cast on the staies, as ships are by weather.*

Alone without the haven, and thence survaid
From out a loftie watch-towre raised there
The Countrie round about: nor any where 130
The worke of man or beast appeard to me;
Onely a smoke from earth breake I might see.
I then made choice of two, and added more,
A Herald for associate, to explore
What sort of men liv'd there. They went, and saw 135
A beaten way through which carts usde to draw
Wood from the high hils to the Towne, and met
A maid without the Port, about to get
Some neare spring-water. She the daughter was
Of mightie Læstrygonian Antiphas, 140
And to the cleare spring cald Artacia went,
To which the whole Towne for their water sent.
To her they came, and askt who governd there,
And what the people whom he orderd were?
She answerd not, but led them through the Port, 145
As making haste to shew her father's Court.
Where enterd, they beheld (to their affright)
A woman like a mountaine top in height,
Who rusht abroad, and from the Counsaile place
Cald home her horrid husband Antiphas— 150

Antiphas was king there.

Who (deadly minded) straight he snatcht up one,
And fell to supper. Both the rest were gone,
And to the fleete came. Antiphas a crie
Drave through the Citie; which heard, instantly
This way and that innumerable sorts, 155
Not men, but Gyants, issued through the Ports,
And mightie flints from rocks tore, which they threw
Amongst our ships, through which an ill noise flew
Of shiverd ships and life-expiring men,
That were like fishes by the monsters slaine 160
And borne to sad feast. While they slaughterd these
That were engag'd in all th'advantages
The close-mouth'd and most dead-calme haven could give,
I (that without lay) made some meanes to live—
My sword drew, cut my gables, and to oares 165
Set all my men, and from the plagues those shores
Let flie amongst us we made haste to flie,
My men close working, as men loth to die.
My ship flew freely off, but theirs that lay
On heapes in harbors could enforce no way 170
Through these sterne fates that had engag'd them there.

Forth our sad remnant saild, yet still retaind
The joyes of men that our poore few remaind.
'Then to the Ile Ææa we attaind,
Where faire-haird, dreadfull, eloquent Circe raignd, 175
Æetes' sister, both by Dame and Sire,
Both daughters to heaven's man-enlightning fire
And Perse, whom Oceanus begat.
The ship-fit Port here soone we landed at,
Some God directing us. Two daies, two nights, 180
We lay here pining in the fatall spights
Of toile and sorrow. But the next third day
When faire Aurora had informd, quicke way
I made out of my ship, my sword and lance
Tooke for my surer guide, and made advance 185
Up to a prospect, in assay to see
The works of men, or heare mortalitie
Expire a voice. When I had climb'd a height
Rough and right hardly accessible, I might
Behold from Circe's house (that in a grove 190
Set thicke with trees stood) a bright vapor move.
I then grew curious in my thought to trie
Some fit enquirie, when so spritely flie
I saw the yeallow smoke. But my discourse
A first retiring to my ship gave force 195
To give my men their dinner, and to send
(Before th'adventure of my selfe) some friend.
Being neare my ship, of one so desolate
Some God had pittie, and would recreate
My woes a little, putting up to me 200
A great and high-palmd Hart, that (fatallie,
Just in my way it selfe, to taste a flood)
Was then descending: the Sunne heate had sure
Importun'd him, besides the temperature
His naturall heate gave. Howsoever, I 205
Made up to him and let my Javelin flie,
That strooke him through the mid-part of his chine,
And made him (braying) in the dust confine
His flying forces. Forth his spirit flew,
When I stept in, and from the death's wound drew 210
My shrewdly-bitten lance; there let him lie
Till I of cut-up Osiers did imply
A With a fathome long, with which his feete
I made together in a sure league meete,
Stoop't under him, and to my necke I heav'd 215

μερμαίρω, curiose cogito.

αἴθοπα καπνόν—αἴθοψ *signifying* rutilus: *by reason of the fire mixt with it.* Fumus qui fit dum aliquid accenditur.

The mightie burthen; of which I receav'd
A good part on my lance, for else I could
By no meanes with one hand alone uphould
(Joynd with one shoulder) such a deathfull lode.
And so to both my shoulders both hands stood 220
Needfull assistents, for it was a Deare
Goodly-wel-growne: when (coming something neare
Where rode my ships) I cast it downe, and rer'd
My friends with kind words, whom by name I cheer'd
In note particular, and said: "See, friends, 225
We will not yet to Pluto's house; our ends
Shall not be hastend, though we be declind
In cause of comfort, till the day design'd
By Fate's fixt finger. Come, as long as food
Or wine lasts in our ship, let's spirit our blood 230
And quit our care and hunger both in one."
'This said, they frolikt, came, and lookt upon
With admiration the huge-bodied beast;
And when their first-serv'd eyes had done their feast,
They washt, and made a to-be-striv'd-for meale 235
In point of honour. On which all did dwell
The whole day long. And, to our venzon's store,
We added wine till we could wish no more.
'Sunne set, and darknesse up, we slept till light
Put darknesse downe: and then did I excite 240
My friends to counsaile, uttering this: "Now, friends,
Affoord unpassionate eare, though ill Fate lends
So good cause to your passion; no man knowes
The reason whence and how the darknesse growes;
The reason how the Morne is thus begunne; 245
The reason how the Man-enlightning Sunne
Dives under earth; the reason how againe
He reres his golden head. Those counsailes then
That passe our comprehension we must leave
To him that knowes their causes, and receave 250
Direction from him in our acts as farre
As he shall please to make them regular
And stoope them to our reason. In our state,
What then behoves us? Can we estimate,
With all our counsailes, where we are, or know 255
(Without instruction past our owne skils) how
(Put off from hence) to stere our course the more?
I thinke we can not. We must then explore
These parts for information—in which way

ἐρικυδέα δαῖτα. *The whole end of this counsaile was to perswade his souldiers to explore those parts: which he knew would prove a most unpleasing motion to them, for their fellowes' terrible entertainement with Antiphas and Polypheme, and therefore he prepares the little he hath to say with this long circumstance, implying a necessitie of that service, and necessary resolution to adde the triall of the event to their other adventures.*

We thus farre are: last Morne I might display 260
(From off a high-raisd cliffe) an Iland lie
Girt with th'unmeasur'd Sea, and is so nie
That in the midst I saw the smoke arise
Through tufts of trees. This rests then to advise
Who shall explore this." This strooke dead their hearts, 265
Remembring the most execrable parts
That Læstrygonian Antiphas had plaid
And that foule Cyclop, that their fellowes braid
Betwixt his jawes; which mov'd them so, they cried.
But idle teares had never wants supplied. 270
I in two parts divided all, and gave
To either part his Captaine: I must have
The charge of one, and one of God-like looke,
Eurylochus, the other. Lots we shooke
(Put in a caske together), which of us 275
Should leade th'attempt, and twas Eurylochus.
He freely went, with two and twenty more:
All which tooke leave with teares, and our eyes wore
The same wet badge of weake humanity.

Circe's house.

These in a dale did Circe's house descrie, 280
Of bright stone built in a conspicuous way;
Before her gates hill-wolves and Lyons lay,
Which with her virtuous drugs so tame she made
That Wolfe nor Lyon would one man invade
With any violence, but all arose, 285
Their huge long tailes wagd, and in fawnes would close

Simile.

As loving dogs when masters bring them home
Relicks of feast—in all observance come
And sooth their entries with their fawnes and bounds,
All guests still bringing some scraps for their hounds: 290
So, on these men the Wolves and Lyons rampt,
Their horrid paws set up. Their spirits were dampt
To see such monstrous kindnesse, staid at gate,
And heard within the Goddesse elevate
A voice divine, as at her web she wrought, 295
Subtle and glorious, and past earthly thought.
As all the houswiferies of Deities are.
To heare a voice so ravishingly rare,
Polites (one exceeding deare to me,
A Prince of men, and of no meane degree 300

κεδνός—Cuius animus curas prudentes versat.

In knowing vertue, in all Acts whose mind
Discreete cares all wayes usde to turne and wind)
Was yet surprisd with it, and said: "O friends,

Some one abides within here that commends
The place to us and breathes a voice divine 305
As she some web wrought, or her spindle's twine
She cherisht with her song; the pavement rings
With imitation of the tunes she sings;
Some woman, or some Goddesse tis. Assay
To see with knocking." Thus said he, and they 310
Both knockt, and calld; and straight her shining gates
She opened, issuing, bade them in to cates—
Led, and unwise they follow'd, all but one,
Which was Eurylochus, who stood alone
Without the gates, suspicious of a sleight. 315
They enterd, she made sit; and her deceit
She cloakt with Thrones and goodly chaires of State,
Set hearby honey and the delicate
Wine brought from Smyrna to them, meale and cheese;
But harmefull venoms she commixt with these, 320
That made their Countrey vanish from their thought.
Which eate, she toucht them with a rod that wrought
Their transformation farre past humane wunts;
Swines' snowts, swines' bodies tooke they, bristles, grunts,
But still retaind the soules they had before, 325
Which made them mourne their bodies' change the more.
She shut them straight in sties, and gave them meate—
Oke-mast and beech and Cornell fruite they eate,
Groveling like swine on earth in fowlest sort.
Eurylochus straight hasted the report 330
Of this his fellowes' most remorcefull fate,
Came to the ships, but so excruciate
Was with his woe he could not speake a word:
His eyes stood full of teares, which shew'd how stor'd
His mind with mone remaind. We all admir'd, 335
Askt what had chanc't him, earnestly desir'd
He would resolve us. At the last, our eyes
Enflam'd in him his fellowes' memories,

Seeing them, he thought of his fellowes.

And out his griefe burst thus: "You willd we went
Through those thicke woods you saw; when a descent 340
Shew'd us a faire house in a lightsome ground,
Where (at some worke) we heard a heavenly sound
Breath'd from a Goddesse, or a woman's brest.
They knockt, she op't her bright gates; each her guest
Her faire invitement made, nor would they stay 345
(Fooles that they were) when she once led the way.
I enterd not, suspecting some deceit—

When all together vanisht, nor the sight
Of any one (though long I lookt) mine eye
Ulysses mov'd for his souldiers. Could any way discover." Instantly, 350
(My sword and bow reacht) I bad shew the place,
When downe he fell, did both my knees embrace,
Eurylochus. And praid with teares thus: "O thou kept of God,
Do not thy selfe lose, nor to that aboad
Leade others rashly; both thy selfe, and all 355
Thou ventur'st thither, I know well must fall
In one sure ruine: with these few then flie.
We yet may shunne the others' destinie."
'I answerd him: "Eurylochus! stay thou
And keepe the ship then, eate and drinke. I now 360
Will undertake th'adventure; there is cause
In great Necessitie's unalterd lawes."
This said, I left both ship and seas, and on
Along the sacred vallies all alone
Went in discovery, till at last I came 365
Where of the manie-medcine-making Dame
I saw the great house, where encounterd me
Ulysses encounters Mercurie. The golden-rod-sustaining Mercurie,
Even entring Circe's doores. He met me in
A yong man's likenesse, of the first-flowr'd chin, 370
Whose forme hath all the grace of one so yong.
He first cald to me, then my hand he wrung,
And said: "Thou no-place-finding-for-repose,
Whither, alone, by these hill-confines goes
Thy erring foote? Th'art entring Circe's house, 375
Where (by her medcines blacke and sorcerous)
Thy souldiers all are shut in well-armd sties,
And turned to swine. Art thou arriv'd with prise
Fit for their ransomes? Thou com'st out no more
If once thou enterst, like thy men before 380
Made to remaine here. But I'le guard thee free,
And save thee in her spite: receive of me
This faire and good receipt, with which once arm'd,
Enter her roofes, for th'art to all proofe charm'd
Against the ill day. I will tell thee all 385
Her banefull counsaile. With a festivall
Shee'le first receive thee, but will spice thy bread
With flowrie poysons: yet unaltered
Shall thy firme forme be, for this remedy
Stands most approv'd gainst all her Sorcery— 390
Which thus particularly shunne: when she

Shall with her long rod strike thee, instantly
Draw from thy thigh thy sword, and flie on her
As to her slaughter. She, (surprisde with feare
And love) at first will bid thee to her bed; 395
Nor say the Goddesse nay, that welcomed
Thou maist with all respect be, and procure
Thy fellowes' freedomes. But before, make sure
Her favours to thee and the great oath take
With which the blessed Gods assurance make 400
Of all they promise, that no prejudice
(By stripping thee of forme and faculties)
She may so much as once attempt on thee."
This said, he gave his Antidote to me,
Which from the earth he pluckt, and told me all 405
The vertue of it, with what Deities call
The name it beares—and Moly they impose
For name to it. The roote is hard to loose
From hold of earth by mortals, but Gods' powre
Can all things do. Tis blacke, but beares a flowre 410
As white as milke. And thus flew Mercurie
Up to immense Olympus, gliding by
The sylvan Iland. I made backe my way
To Circe's house, my mind of my assay
Much thought revolving. At her gates I staid 415
And cald: she heard and her bright doores displaid,
Invited, led; I followed in, but tract
With some distraction. In a Throne she plac't
My welcome person. Of a curious frame
Twas and so bright I sate as in a flame. 420
A foote-stoole added. In a golden boule
She then subornd a potion, in her soule
Deformd things thinking, for amidst the wine
She mixt her man-transforming medicine—
Which when she saw I had devourd, she then 425
No more observ'd me with her soothing vaine
But strooke me with her rod, and to her Sty
Bad—"Out, away, and with thy fellowes lie."
I drew my sword and charg'd her as I ment
To take her life—when out she cri'd, and bent 430
Beneath my sword her knees, embracing mine,
And (full of teares) said: "Who? Of what high line
Art thou the issue? Whence? What shores sustaine
Thy native Citie? I amaz'd remaine
That, drinking these my venomes, th'art not turnd. 435

The herbe Moly which, with Ulysses' whole Narration, hath in chiefe an Allegoricall exposition. Notwithstanding I say with our Spondanus, Credo in hoc vasto mundi ambitu extare res innumeras mirandæ facultatis: adeo, ut ne quidem ista quæ ad transformanda corpora pertinet, iure e mundo eximi possit, &c.

Never drunke any this cup but he mournd
In other likenesse if it once had past
The ivorie bounders of his tongue and taste.
All but thy selfe are brutishly declind:
Thy breast holds firme yet and unchang'd thy mind. 440
Thou canst be, therefore, none else but the man
Of many virtues—Ithacensian,
Deepe-soul'd Ulysses: who, I oft was told
By that slie God that beares the rod of gold,
Was to arrive here in retreat from Troy. 445
Sheath then thy sword, and let my bed enjoy
So much a man, that, when the bed we prove,
We may beleeve in one another's love."
'I then: "O Circe, why entreat'st thou me
To mixe in any humane league with thee, 450
When thou my friends hast beasts turnd?—and thy bed
Tenderst to me, that I might likewise leade
A beast's life with thee, softn'd, naked stript,
That in my blood thy banes may more be steept?
I never will ascend thy bed before 455
I may affirme that in heaven's sight you swore
The great oath of the Gods, that all attempt
To do me ill is from your thoughts exempt."
'I said; she swore—when, all the oath-rites said,
I then ascended her adorned bed, 460
But thus prepar'd: foure handmaids serv'd her there,
That daughters to her silver fountaines were,
To her bright-sea-observing sacred floods,
And to her uncut consecrated woods.
One deckt the Throne-tops with rich clothes of state, 465
And did with silkes the foote-pace consecrate.
Another, silver tables set before
The pompous Throne, and golden dishes' store
Serv'd in with severall feast. A third fild wine;
The fourth brought water, and made fewell shine 470
In ruddy fires beneath a wombe of brasse.
Which heat, I bath'd; and odorous water was
Disperpled lightly on my head and necke,
That might my late heart-hurting sorrowes checke
With the refreshing sweetnesse; and, for that, 475
Men sometimes may be something delicate.
Bath'd and adorn'd, she led me to a Throne
Of massie silver, and of fashion
Exceeding curious. A faire foote-stoole set,

Water apposde, and every sort of meate 480
Set on th'elaborately polisht boord.
She wisht my taste emploid, but not a word
Would my eares taste of taste: my mind had food
That must digest; eye-meate would do me good.
Circe (observing that I put no hand 485
To any banquet, having countermand
From weightier cares than light cates could excuse)
Bowing her neare me, these wing'd words did use:
'"Why sits Ulysses like one dumbe, his mind
Lessening with languors? Nor to food enclind, 490
Nor wine? Whence comes it? Out of any feare
Of more illusion? You must needs forbeare
That wrongful doubt, since you have heard me sweare."
'"O Circe!" I replied, "what man is he,
Awd with the rights of true humanitie, 495
That dares taste food or wine before he sees
His friends redeem'd from their deformities?
If you be gentle, and indeed incline
To let me taste the comfort of your wine,
Dissolve the charmes that their forc't formes encheine 500
And shew me here my honord friends like men."
'This said, she left her Throne, and tooke her rod,
Went to her Stie and let my men abroad,
Like swine of nine yeares old. They opposite stood,
Observ'd their brutish forme, and look't for food; 505
When, with another medicine (every one
All over smeer'd) their bristles all were gone,
Produc't by malice of the other bane,
And every one afresh lookt up a man,
Both yonger than they were, of stature more, 510
And all their formes much goodlier than before.
All knew me, clingd about me, and a cry
Of pleasing mourning flew about so hie
The horrid roofe resounded, and the Queene
Her selfe was mov'd to see our kinde so keene— 515
Who bad me now bring ship and men ashore,
Our armes and goods in caves hid, and restore
My selfe to her with all my other men.
I granted, went, and op't the weeping veine
In all my men, whose violent joy to see 520
My safe returne was passing kindly free
Of friendly teares, and miserably wept.
You have not seene yong Heiffers (highly kept,

Filld full of daisies at the field, and driven
Home to their hovels, all so spritely given 525
That no roome can containe them, but about
Bace by the Dams, and let their spirits out
In ceasselesse bleating) of more jocund plight
Than my kind friends, even crying out with sight
Of my returne so doubted—circl'd me 530
With all their welcomes, and as cheerfully
Disposde their rapt minds as if there they saw
Their naturall Countrie, cliffie Ithaca,
And even the roofes where they were bred and borne,
And vowd as much, with teares: "O your returne 535
As much delights us as in you had come
Our Countrie to us and our naturall home.
But what unhappie fate hath reft our friends?"
I gave unlookt-for answer, that amends
Made for their mourning; bad them first of all 540
Our ship ashore draw, then in Caverns stall
Our foodie cattell, hide our mutuall prise;
"And then," said I, "attend me, that your eies
In Circe's sacred house may see each friend,
Eating and drinking banquets out of end." 545
'They soone obeid—all but Eurylochus,
Who needes would stay them all, and counselld thus:
' "O wretches! whither will ye? Why are you
Fond of your mischiefs, and such gladnesse show
For Circe's house, that will transforme ye all 550
To Swine, or Wolves, or Lions? Never shall
Our heads get out if once within we be,
But stay compelld by strong Necessitie.
So wrought the Cyclop, when t'his cave our friends
This bold one led on, and brought all their ends 555
By his one indiscretion." I, for this,
Thought with my sword (that desperate head of his
Hewne from his necke) to gash upon the ground
His mangld bodie, though my blood was bound
In neare alliance to him. But the rest 560
With humble suite containd me, and request
That I would leave him with my ship alone
And to the sacred Pallace leade them on.
'I led them, nor Eurylochus would stay
From their attendance on me, our late fray 565
Strooke to his heart so. But meane time my men
In Circe's house were all in severall baine

φράσσαντό τε πάντα—Commemorabantque omnia. *Intending all their miseries, escapes, and meetings.*

Studiously sweetn'd, smugd with oile, and deckt
With in and outweeds: and a feast select
Serv'd in before them—at which close we found 570
They all were set, cheer'd, and carousing round.
When (mutuall sight had, and all thought on) then
Feast was forgotten, and the mone againe
About the house flew, driven with wings of joy.
But then spake Circe: "Now, no more annoy. 575
I know my selfe what woes by sea and shore
And men unjust have plagu'd enough before
Your injur'd vertues: here then, feast as long,
And be as cheerfull, till ye grow as strong
As when ye first forsooke your Countrie earth. 580
Ye now fare all like exiles, not a mirth
Flasht in amongst ye but is quencht againe
With still-renewd teares—though the beaten vaine
Of your distresses should (me thinke) be now
Benumb with sufferance." We did well allow 585
Her kind perswasions, and the whole yeare staid
In varied feast with her. When now arraid
The world was with the Spring, and orbie houres
Had gone the round againe through herbs and flowres,
The moneths absolv'd in order till the daies 590
Had runne their full race in Apollo's raies,
My friends rememberd me of home, and said,
If ever Fate would signe my passe, delaid
It should be now no more. I heard them well,
Yet that day spent in feast till darknesse fell, 595
And sleepe his virtues through our vapours shed—
When I ascended sacred Circe's bed,
Implor'd my passe and her performed vow,
Which now my soule urg'd, and my souldiers now
Afflicted me with teares to get them gone. 600
All these I told her, and she answerd these:
"Much-skilld Ulysses Laertiades!
Remaine no more against your wils with me,
But take your free way: onely this must be
Perform'd before you stere your course for home. 605
You must the way to Pluto overcome
And sterne Persephone, to forme your passe
By th'aged Theban Soule Tiresias,
The dark-browd Prophet, whose soule yet can see
Clearely and firmely: grave Persephone 610

(Even dead) gave him a mind that he alone
Might sing Truth's solide wisedome, and not one
Prove more than shade in his comparison."

'This broke my heart; I sunke into my bed,
Mourn'd, and would never more be comforted 615
With light, nor life. But having now exprest
My paines enough to her in my unrest,
That so I might prepare her ruth, and get
All I held fit for an affaire so great,
I said: "O Circe, who shall stere my course 620
To Pluto's kingdome? Never ship had force
To make that voiage." The divine in voice
Said: "Seeke no guide, raise you your Mast, and hoice
Your ship's white sailes, and then sit you at peace.
The fresh North spirit shall waft ye through the seas. 625
But, having past th'Ocean, you shall see
A little shore that to Persephone
Puts up a consecrated wood, where growes
Tall Firres, and Sallowes that their fruits soone loose.
Cast anchor in the gulphes, and go alone 630
To Pluto's darke house, where to Acheron
Cocytus runnes and Pyriphlegethon,
Cocytus borne of Styx; and where a Rocke
Of both the met floods beares the roring shocke,
The darke Heroe, great Tiresias, 635
Now coming neare, to gaine propitious passe,
Dig (of a cubit every way) a pit,
And powre (to all that are deceast) in it
A solemne sacrifice. For which, first take
Honey and wine, and their commixtion make; 640
Then sweete wine, neate; and thirdly, water powre;
And lastly, adde to these the whitest flowre.
Then vow to all the weake necks of the dead
Offerings a number, and, when thou shalt tread
The Ithacensian shore, to sacrifice 645
A Heifer never tam'd and most of prise,
A pyle of all thy most-esteemed goods
Enflaming to the deare streames of their bloods.
And in secret Rites to Tiresias vow
A Ram cole blacke at all parts, that doth flow 650
With fat and fleece, and all thy flockes doth leade.
When the all-calling nation of the dead
Thou thus hast praid to, offer on the place
A Ram and Ewe all blacke, being turn'd in face

κλυτὰ ἔθνεα νεκρῶν—*Which is expounded* Inclyta

examina mortuorum. *But* κλυτὸς *is the Epithete of Pluto, and by Analogie belongs to the dead,* quod ad se omnes advocat.

To dreadfull Erebus, thy selfe aside 655
The flood's shore walking. And then gratified
With flocks of Soules, of Men and Dames deceast,
Shall all thy pious Rites be. Straight addrest
See then the offering that thy fellowes slew
Flayd and imposde in fire, and all thy Crew 660
Pray to the state of either Deitie,
Grave Pluto and severe Persephone.
Then draw thy sword, stand firme, nor suffer one
Of all the faint shades of the dead and gone
T'approch the blood till thou hast heard their king, 665
The wise Tiresias—who thy offering
Will instantly do honour, thy home wayes,
And all the measure of them, by the seas
Amply unfolding." This the Goddesse told;
And then the morning in her Throne of gold 670
Survaid the vast world, by whose orient light
The Nymph adorn'd me with attires as bright,
Her owne hands putting on both shirt and weede,
Robes fine and curious; and upon my head
An ornament that glitterd like a flame 675
Girt me in gold; and forth betimes I came
Amongst my souldiers, rousd them all from sleepe,
And bad them now no more observance keepe
Of ease and feast, but straight a shipboard fall—
For now the Goddesse had inform'd me all. 680
Their noble spirits agree'd, nor yet so cleare
Could I bring all off, but Elpenor there
His heedlesse life left: he was yongest man
Of all my company, and one that wanne
Least fame for armes, as little for his braine; 685
Who (too much steept in wine, and so made faine
To get refreshing by the coole of sleepe,
Apart his fellowes plung'd in vapors deepe,
And they as high in tumult of their way)
Sodainly wak't, and (quite out of the stay 690
A sober mind had given him) would descend
A huge long Ladder, forward, and an end
Fell from the very roofe, full pitching on
The dearest joynt his head was plac't upon—
Which (quite dissolv'd) let loose his soule to hell. 695
I to the rest, and Circe's meanes did tell
Of our returne (as crossing cleane the hope
I gave them first) and said: "You thinke the scope

Of our endevours now is straight for home.
No: Circe otherwise design'd, whose doome 700
Enjoynd us first to greet the dreadfull house
Of Austere Pluto and his glorious spouse,
To take the counsaile of Tiresias
(The reverend Theban) to direct our passe."
'This brake their hearts, and griefe made teare their haire— 705
But griefe was never good at great affaire.
It would have way yet. We went wofull on
To ship and shore, where was arriv'd as soone
Circe unseene, a blacke Ewe and a Ram
Binding for sacrifice; and, as she came, 710
Vanisht againe, unwitnest by our eyes;
Which griev'd not us, nor checkt our sacrifice—
For who would see God, loath to let us see?
This way or that bent, still his waies are free.

Finis decimi libri Hom. Odyss.

THE ELEVENTH BOOKE
of
HOMER'S ODYSSES

THE ARGUMENT

Ulysses' way to Hell appeares,
Where he the grave Tiresias heares,
Enquires his owne and others' fates,
His mother sees and th'after states
In which were held by sad Decease 5
Heroes and Heroesses
A number, that at Troy wag'd warre,
As Ajax that was still at jarre
With Ithacus for th'armes he lost,
And with the great Achilles' Ghost. 10

Another Argument

Λάμβδα. *Ulysses here*
Invokes the dead;
The lives appeare
Hereafter led.

'Arriv'd now at our ship, we lancht, and set
Our Mast up, put forth saile, and in did get
Our late-got Cattell. Up our sailes, we went,
My wayward fellowes mourning now th'event.
They mournd the event before they knew it.
A good companion yet, a foreright wind, 5
Circe (the excellent utterer of her mind)
Supplied our murmuring consorts with, that was
Both speed and guide to our adventurous passe.
All day our sailes stood to the winds, and made
Our voiage prosprous. Sunne then set, and shade 10
All wayes obscuring, on the bounds we fell
Of deepe Oceanus, where people dwell
Whom a perpetuall cloud obscures outright,

To whom the cheerfull Sunne lends never light,
Nor when he mounts the star-sustaining heaven, 15
Nor when he stoopes earth and sets up the Even;
But Night holds fixt wings, fetherd all with Banes,
Above those most unblest Cimmerianes.
Here drew we up our ship, our sheepe with-drew,
And walkt the shore till we attaind the view 20
Of that sad region Circe had foreshow'd;
And then the sacred offerings, to be vow'd,
Eurylochus and Perimedes bore.
When I my sword drew, and earth's wombe did gore
Till I a pit digg'd of a cubite round, 25
Which with the liquid sacrifice we crown'd—
First, honey mixt with wine, then sweete wine neate,
Then water powr'd in, last the flowre of wheate.
Much I importun'd then the weake-neckt dead,
And vowd, when I the barren soile should tread 30
Of cliffie Ithaca, amidst my hall
To kill a Heifer, my cleare best of all,
And give in offering on a Pile composd
Of all the choise goods my whole house enclosd—
And to Tiresias himselfe alone 35
A sheepe cole-blacke and the selectest one
Of all my flockes. When to the powres beneath,
The sacred nation that survive with Death,
My prayrs and vowes had done devotions fit,
I tooke the offrings, and upon the pit 40
Bereft their lives. Out gusht the sable blood,
And round about me fled out of the flood
The Soules of the deceast. There cluster'd then
Youths, and their wives, much suffering aged men,
Soft tender virgins that but new came there 45
By timelesse death, and greene their sorrowes were.
There men at Armes, with armors all embrew'd,
Wounded with lances and with faulchions hew'd,
In numbers up and downe the ditch did stalke,
And threw unmeasur'd cries about their walke, 50
So horrid that a bloodlesse feare surprisde
My daunted spirits. Straight then I advisde
My friends to flay the slaughter'd sacrifice,
Put them in fire, and to the Deities,
Sterne Pluto and Persephone, apply 55
Excitefull prayrs. Then drew I from my Thy
My well-edg'd sword, stept in, and firmely stood

Betwixt the prease of shadowes and the blood,
And would not suffer any one to dip
Within our offring his unsolide lip 60
Before Tiresias, that did all controule.
The first that preast in was Elpenor's soule,
His body in the broad-waid earth as yet
Unmournd, unburied by us, since we swet
With other urgent labours. Yet his smart 65
I wept to see, and ru'd it from my heart,
Enquiring how he could before me be
That came by ship? He, mourning, answerd me:
"In Circe's house, the spite some Spirit did beare
And the unspeakable good licour there 70
Hath bene my bane. For being to descend
A ladder much in height, I did not tend
My way well downe, but forwards made a proofe
To tread the rounds, and from the very roofe
Fell on my necke and brake it. And this made 75
My soule thus visite this infernall shade.
And here, by them that next thy selfe are deare,
Thy Wife and Father, that a little one
Gave food to thee, and by thy onely Sonne
At home behind thee left, Telemachus, 80
Do not depart by stealth and leave me thus,
Unmourn'd, unburied, lest neglected I
Bring on thy selfe th'incensed Deitie.
I know that, saild from hence, thy ship must touch
On th'Ile Ææa, where vouchsafe thus much, 85
Good king, that, landed, thou wilt instantly
Bestow on me thy royall memory
To this grace, that my body, armes and all,
May rest consum'd in firie funerall.
And on the fomie shore a Sepulchre 90
Erect to me, that after times may heare
Of one so haplesse. Let me these implore,
And fixe upon my Sepulcher the Ore
With which alive I shooke the aged seas,
And had of friends the deare societies." 95

Misenus apud Virgilium, ingenti mole, etc.

'I told the wretched Soule I would fulfill
And execute to th'utmost point his will;
And all the time we sadly talkt, I still
My sword above the blood held, when aside
The Idoll of my friend still amplified 100
His plaint, as up and downe the shades he err'd.

Then my deceased mother's Soule appeard,
Faire daughter of Autolycus the Great,
Grave Anticlea, whom, when forth I set
For sacred Ilion, I had left alive. 105
Her sight much mov'd me, and to teares did drive
My note of her deceasse; and yet not she
(Though in my ruth she held the highest degree)
Would I admit to touch the sacred blood
Till from Tiresias I had understood 110
What Circe told me. At the length did land
Theban Tiresias' soule, and in his hand
Sustaind a golden Scepter, knew me well,
Tiresias to Ulysses. And said: "O man unhappy, why to hell
Admitst thou darke arrivall and the light 115
The Sunne gives leav'st, to have the horrid sight
Of this blacke region and the shadowes here?
Now sheath thy sharpe sword and the pit forbeare,
That I the blood may taste, and then relate
The truth of those acts that affect thy Fate." 120
'I sheath'd my sword, and left the pit, till he,
The blacke blood tasting, thus instructed me:
"Renoum'd Ulysses! all unaskt, I know
That all the cause of thy arrivall now
Is to enquire thy wisht retreate for home— 125
Which hardly God will let thee overcome,
Since Neptune still will his opposure trie,
With all his laid-up anger, for the eye
His lov'd Sonne lost to thee. And yet through all
Thy suffring course (which must be capitall) 130
If both thine owne affections and thy friends'
Thou wilt containe, when thy accesse ascends
The three-forckt Iland, having scap't the seas,
(Where ye shall find fed, on the flowrie leas,
Fat flocks and Oxen which the Sunne doth owne, 135
To whom are all things as well heard as showne,
And never dare one head of those to slay,
But hold unharmefull on your wished way)
Though through enough affliction, yet secure
Your Fates shall land ye. But Presage saies sure, 140
If once ye spoile them, spoile to all thy friends,
Spoile to thy Fleete; and if the justice ends
Short of thy selfe, it shall be long before,
And that length forc't out with infliction's store—
When, losing all thy fellowes, in a saile 145

Of forreigne built (when most thy Fates prevaile
In thy deliverance) thus th'event shall sort:
Thou shalt find shipwracke raging in thy Port,
Proud men thy goods consuming and, thy Wife
Urging with gifts, give charge upon thy life. 150
But all these wrongs Revenge shall end to thee,
And force, or cunning, set with slaughter free
Thy house of all thy spoilers. Yet againe
Thou shalt a voyage make, and come to men
That know no Sea, nor ships, nor oares, that are 155
Wings to a ship, nor mixe with any fare

Men that never eate salt with their foode.

Salt's savorie vapor. Where thou first shalt land,
This cleare-given signe shall let thee understand
That there those men remaine: assume ashore
Up to thy roiall shoulder a ship oare, 160
With which, when thou shalt meete one on the way
That will in Countrey admiration say—
"What dost thou with that wanne upon thy necke?"—
There fixe that wanne, thy oare, and that shore decke
With sacred Rites to Neptune: slaughter there 165
A Ram, a Bull, and (who for strength doth beare
The name of husband to a herd) a Bore.
And, coming home, upon thy naturall shore
Give pious Hecatombs to all the Gods
(Degrees observ'd). And then the Periods 170
Of all thy labors in the peace shall end
Of easie death, which shall the lesse extend
His passion to thee that thy foe, the Sea,

γήρᾳ ὕπο λιπαρῷ *Which all translate* senectute sub molli. *The Epethete* λιπαρῷ *not of* λιπαρός, viz. pinguis; *or* λιπαρῶς, pinguiter: *But* λιπαρῶς *signifying* flagitanter orando. *To which pious age is ever altogether addicted.*

Shall not enforce it, but Death's victory
Shall chance in onely-earnest-prayr-vow'd age, 175
Obtaind at home, quite emptied of his rage,
Thy subjects round about thee, rich and blest.
And here hath Truth summ'd up thy vitall rest."
'I answerd him: "We will suppose all these
Decreed in Deity; let it likewise please 180
Tiresias to resolve me, why so neare
The blood and me my mother's Soule doth beare,
And yet nor word nor looke vouchsafe her Sonne?
Doth she not know me?" "No," said he, "nor none
Of all these spirits but my selfe alone 185
Knowes any thing till he shall taste the blood.
But whomsoever you shall do that good
He will the truth of all you wish unfold;
Who you envy it to will all withhold."

'Thus said the kingly soule, and made retreate 190
Amidst the inner parts of Pluto's Seate,
When he had spoke thus by divine instinct.
Still I stood firme till to the blood's precinct
My mother came and drunke; and then she knew
I was her Sonne, had passion to renew 195
Her naturall plaints, which thus she did pursew:
"How is it, O my Sonne, that you alive
This deadly-darksome region underdive?
Twixt which and earth so many mighty seas
And horrid currents interpose their prease— 200
Oceanus in chief—which none (unlesse
More helpt than you) on foote now can transgresse?
A well built ship he needs that ventures there.
Com'st thou from Troy but now, enforc't to erre
All this time with thy souldiers? Nor hast seene, 205
Ere this long day, thy Countrey and thy Queene?"
'I answerd that a necessary end
To this infernall state made me contend,
That from the wise Tiresias' Theban Soule
I might an Oracle involv'd unrowle— 210
For I came nothing neare Achaia yet,
Nor on our lov'd earth happy foote had set,
But (mishaps suffering) err'd from Coast to Coast
Ever since first the mighty Grecian hoast
Divine Atrides led to Ilion, 215
And I his follower, to set warre upon
The rapefull Troyans: and so praid she would
The Fate of that ungentle death unfould
That forc't her thither—if some long disease,
Or that the Splene of her that arrowes please 220
(Diana, envious of most eminent Dames)
Had made her th'object of her deadly aimes?
My Father's state and sonne's I sought—if they
Kept still my goods, or they became the prey
Of any other, holding me no more 225
In powre of safe returne, or if my store
My wife had kept together, with her Sonne?
If she her first mind held, or had bene wonne
By some chiefe Grecian from my love and bed?
'All this she answerd—that Affliction fed 230
On her blood still at home, and that to griefe
She all the dayes and darknesse of her life
In teares had consecrate. That none possest

My famous kingdome's Throne, but th'interest
My sonne had in it still he held in peace— 235
A Court kept like a Prince, and his increase
Spent in his subjects' good, administring lawes
With justice and the generall applause
A king should merit, and all calld him king.
My Father kept the upland, labouring, 240
And shun'd the Citie, usde no sumptuous beds,
Wonderd-at furnitures, nor wealthy weeds,
But in the Winter strew'd about the fire
Lay with his slaves in ashes, his attire
Like to a begger's—when the Sommer came, 245
And Autumne all fruits ripend with his flame,
Where Grape-charg'd vines made shadows most abound,
His couch with falne leaves made upon the ground.
And here lay he, his Sorrowe's fruitfull state
Increasing, as he faded, for my Fate. 250
And now the part of age that irksome is
Lay sadly on him. And that life of his
She led, and perish in, not slaughterd by
The Dame that darts lov'd and her archerie,
Nor by disease invaded, vast and foule, 255
That wasts the body and sends out the soule
With shame and horror: onely in her mone
For me and my life she consum'd her owne.
'She thus; when I had great desire to prove
My armes the circle where her soule did move. 260
Thrice prov'd I, thrice she vanisht like a sleepe
Or fleeting shadow, which strooke much more deepe
The wounds my woes made, and made aske her why
She would my Love to her embraces flie,
And not vouchsafe that even in hell we might 265
Pay pious Nature her unalterd right,
And give Vexation here her cruell fill?
"Should not the Queene here, to augment the ill
Of every sufferance (which her office is),
Enforce thy idoll to affoord me this?" 270
' "O Sonne," she answerd, "of the race of men
The most unhappy, our most equall Queene
Will mocke no solide armes with empty shade,
Nor suffer empty shades againe t'invade
Flesh, bones, and nerves; nor will defraud the fire 275
Of his last dues, that, soone as spirits expire
And leave the white bone, are his native right,

Proserpina or Persephone.

When, like a dreame, the soule assumes her flight.
The light then of the living with most haste,
O Sonne, contend to: this thy little taste 280
Of this state is enough; and all this life
Will make a tale fit to be told thy wife."
'This speech we had; when now repair'd to me
The old Heroesses appeare to Ulysses.
More female spirits, by Persephone
Driven on before her. All t'heroes' wives 285
And daughters, that led there their second lives,
About the blacke blood throngd. Of whom yet more
My mind impell'd me to enquire, before
I let them altogether taste the gore,
For then would all have bene disperst and gone 290
Thicke as they came. I, therefore, one by one
Let taste the pit, my sword drawne from my Thy
And stand betwixt them made, when severally
All told their stockes. The first that quencht her fire
Tyro.
Was Tyro, issu'd of a noble Sire. 295
She said she sprong from pure Salmoneus' bed,
And Cretheus, Sonne of Æolus, did wed,
Yet the divine flood Enipeus lov'd,
Who much the most faire streame of all floods mov'd.
Neare whose streames Tyro walking, Neptune came 300
Like Enipeus and enjoyd the Dame:
Like to a hill the blew and Snakie flood
Above th'immortall and the mortall stood,
And hid them both as both together lay
Just where his current falles into the Sea. 305
Her virgine wast dissolv'd, she slumberd then;
But when the God had done the worke of men,
Her faire hand gently wringing, thus he said:
"Woman! Rejoyce in our combined bed,
For when the yeare hath runne his circle round 310
(Because the Gods' loves must in fruite abound)
My love shall make (to cheere thy teeming mones)
Thy one deare burthen beare two famous Sonnes.
Love well and bring them up: go home, and see
That, though of more joy yet I shall be free, 315
Thou dost not tell to glorifie thy birth:
Thy Love is Neptune, shaker of the earth."
This said, he plung'd into the sea, and she
(Begot with child by him) the light let see
Great Pelias and Neleus, that became 320
In Jove's great ministrie of mighty fame.

Pelias in broad Iolcus held his Throne,
Wealthy in cattell; th'other roiall Sonne
Rul'd sandy Pylos. To these issue more
This Queene of women to her husband bore— 325
Æson and Pheres, and Amythaon,
That for his fight on horsebacke stoopt to none.

Antiope like Tyro.

'Next her I saw admir'd Antiope,
Asopus' daughter, who (as much as she
Boasted attraction of great Neptune's love) 330
Boasted to slumber in the armes of Jove,
And two Sonnes likewise at one burthen bore
To that her all-controlling Paramore—
Amphion and faire Zethus, that first laid
Great Thebes' foundations and strong wals convaid 335
About her turrets, that seven Ports enclosde.
For though the Thebans much in strength reposde,
Yet had not they the strength to hold their owne
Without the added aides of wood and stone.

Alcmena.

'Alcmena next I saw, that famous wife 340
Was to Amphitryo, and honor'd life
Gave to the Lyon-hearted Hercules,
That was of Jove's embrace the great increase.

Megara.

'I saw besides proud Creon's daughter there,
Bright Megara, that nuptiall yoke did weare 345
With Jove's great Sonne, who never field did try
But bore to him the flowre of victory.

Epicasta, the mother of Œdipus.

'The mother then of Œdipus I saw,
Faire Epicasta, that beyond all law
Her owne Sonne maried, ignorant of kind, 350
And he (as darkly taken in his mind)
His mother wedded, and his father slew—
Whose blind act heaven exposde at length to view,
And he in all-lov'd Thebes the supreame state
With much mone manag'd, for the heavy Fate 355
The Gods laid on him. She made violent flight
To Pluto's darke house from the lothed light,
Beneath a steepe beame strangl'd with a cord,
And left her Sonne, in life, paines as abhord
As all the furies powr'd on her in hell. 360

Chloris.

Then saw I Chloris, that did so excell
In answering beauties that each part had all;
Great Neleus married her, when gifts not small
Had wonne her favour, term'd by name of dowre.
She was of all Amphion's seed the flowre 365

(Amphion, calld Iasides, that then
Ruld strongly Minyæan Orchomen),
And now his daughter rul'd the Pylian Throne
Because her beautie's Empire overshone.
She brought her wise-awd husband Neleus, 370
Nestor much honord, Periclymenus,
And Chromius, Sonnes with soveraigne vertues grac't;
But after brought a daughter that surpast,
Rare-beautied Pero, so for forme exact
That Nature to a miracle was rackt 375
In her perfections, blaz'd with th'eyes of men,
That made of all the Countries' hearts a chaine
And drew them suiters to her. Which her Sire
Tooke vantage of, and (since he did aspire
To nothing more than to the broad-browd herd 380
Of Oxen which the common fame so rer'd,
Own'd by Iphicles) not a man should be
His Pero's husband that from Phylace
Those never-yet-driven Oxen could not drive—
Yet these a strong hope held him to atchieve 385
Because a Prophet that had never err'd
Had said that onely he should be prefer'd
To their possession. But the equall Fate
Of God withstood his stealth—inextricate
Imprisoning Bands and sturdy churlish Swaines 390
That were the Heardsmen, who withheld with chaines
The stealth attempter: which was onely he
That durst abet the Act with Prophecie;
None else would undertake it, and he must.
The king would needs a Prophet should be just; 395
But when some daies and moneths expired were
And all the Houres had brought about the yeare,
The Prophet did so satisfie the king
(Iphicles all his cunning questioning)
That he enfranchisde him, and (all worst done) 400
Jove's counsaile made th'all-safe conclusion.

Leda.

'Then saw I Leda (linkt in nuptiall chaine
With Tyndarus) to whom she did sustaine
Sonnes much renowm'd for wisedome; Castor one,
That past for use of horse comparison, 405
And Pollux, that exceld in whirlbat fight,
Both these the fruitfull Earth bore while the light
Of life inspir'd them—after which they found
Such grace with Jove that both liv'd under ground

By change of daies: life still did one sustaine, 410
While th'other died; the dead then liv'd againe,
The living dying, both of one selfe date
Their lives and deaths made by the Gods and Fate.

Iphimedia.

'Iphimedia after Leda came,
That did derive from Neptune too the name 415
Of Father to two admirable Sonnes.
Life yet made short their admirations,
Who God-opposed Otus had to name
And Ephialtes farre in sound of Fame.
The prodigall Earth so fed them that they grew 420
To most huge stature and had fairest hew
Of all men but Orion, under heaven;
At nine yeares old nine cubits they were driven
Abroad in breadth, and sprung nine fathomes hie.
They threatn'd to give battell to the skie 425
And all th'Immortals. They were setting on
Ossa upon Olympus, and upon
Steepe Ossa leavie Pelion, that even
They might a high-way make with loftie heaven—
And had perhaps perform'd it had they liv'd 430
Till they were Striplings. But Jove's Sonne depriv'd
Their lims of life before th'age that begins
The flowre of youth and should adorne their chins.

Phædra and Procris.

'Phædra and Procris, with wise Mino's flame,
(Bright Ariadne) to the offring came. 435
Whom whilom Theseus made his prise from Crete
That Athens' sacred soile might kisse her feete,
But never could obtaine her virgin Flowre
Till in the Sea-girt Dia Dian's powre
Detain'd his homeward haste, where (in her Phane, 440
By Bacchus witnest) was the fatall wane

Mæra and Clymene.

Of her prime Glorie. Mæra, Clymene,
I witnest there, and loth'd Eriphyle,

Amphiaraus was her husband, whom she betrayd to his ruine at Thebes for gold taken of Adrastus her brother.

That honour'd gold more than she lov'd her Spouse.
'But all th'Heroesses in Pluto's house 445
That then encounterd me exceeds my might
To name or number, and Ambrosian Night
Would quite be spent, when now the formall houres
Present to Sleepe our all-disposed powres—
If at my ship, or here. My home-made vow 450
I leave for fit grace to the Gods and you.'
This said, the silence his discourse had made
With pleasure held still through the house's shade,

When white-arm'd Arete this speech began:
'Phæacians! how appeares to you this man, 455
So goodly person'd and so matcht with mind?
My guest he is, but all you stand combin'd
In the renowne he doth us. Do not then
With carelesse haste dismisse him, nor the maine
Of his dispatch to one so needie maime; 460
The Gods' free bountie gives us all just claime
To goods enow.' This speech the oldest man
Of any other Phæacensian,
The grave Heroe Echeneus, gave
All approbation, saying: 'Friends! ye have 465
The motion of the wise Queene in such words
As have not mist the marke, with which accords
My cleare opinion. But Alcinous
In word and worke must be our rule.' He thus,
And then Alcinous said: 'This then must stand, 470
If while I live I rule in the command
Of this well-skild-in-Navigation State.
Endure then, Guest, though most importunate
Be your affects for home. A litle stay
If your expectance beare, perhaps it may 475
Our gifts make more complete. The cares of all
Your due deduction asks, but Principall
I am therein the ruler.' He replied:
'Alcinous! the most duly glorified
With rule of all of all men, if you lay 480
Commandment on me of a whole yeare's stay,
So all the while your preparations rise,
As well in gifts as time, ye can devise
No better wish for me; for I shall come
Much fuller handed and more honourd home, 485
And dearer to my people, in whose loves,
The richer evermore the better proves.'

Venustè et salsè dictum.

He answerd: 'There is argude in your sight
A worth that works not men for benefit,
Like Prollers or Impostors; of which crew 490
The gentle blacke Earth feeds not up a few,
Here and there wanderers, blanching tales and lies,
Of neither praise nor use. You move our eies
With forme, our minds with matter, and our eares
With elegant oration, such as beares 495
A musicke in the orderd historie
It layes before us. Not Demodocus

With sweeter straines hath usde to sing to us
All the Greeke sorrowes, wept out in your owne.
But say; of all your worthy friends were none 500
Objected to your eyes that Consorts were
To Ilion with you, and serv'd destinie there?
This Night is passing long, unmeasur'd; none
Of all my houshold would to bed yet. On,
Relate these wondrous things. Were I with you, 505
If you would tell me but your woes, as now,
Till the divine Aurora shewd her head,
I should in no night relish thought of bed.'
'Most eminent King,' said he, 'Times all must keepe;
There's time to speake much, time as much to sleepe. 510
But would you heare still, I will tell you still,
And utter more, more miserable ill
Here he begins his other relation.
Of Friends than yet that scap't the dismall warres
And perisht homewards and in houshold jarres
Wag'd by a wicked woman. The chaste Queene 515
Proserpina.
No sooner made these Ladie-ghosts unseene
(Here and there flitting) but mine eie-sight wonne
The Soule of Agamemnon (Atreus' sonne)—
Sad, and about him all his traine of friends
That in Ægisthus' house endur'd their ends 520
With his sterne Fortune. Having drunke the blood,
He knew me instantly, and forth a flood
Of springing teares gusht. Out he thrust his hands
With will t'embrace me, but their old commands
Flowd not about him, nor their weakest part. 525
I wept to see, and mon'd him from my heart,
And askt: "O Agamemnon! King of men!
What sort of cruell death hath renderd slaine
Thy royall person? Neptune in thy Fleete
Heaven and his hellish billowes making meete, 530
Rowsing the winds? Or have thy men by land
Done thee this ill for using thy command
Past their consents, in diminution
Of those full shares their worths by lot had wonne
Of sheepe or oxen? Or of any towne, 535
In covetous strife to make their rights thine owne
In men or women prisoners?" He replied:
"By none of these in any right I died,
But by Ægisthus and my murtherous wife
(Bid to a banquet at his house) my life 540
Hath thus bene reft me—to my slaughter led

Like to an Oxe pretended to be fed.
So miserably fell I, and with me
My friends lay massacred, as when you see
At any rich man's nuptials, shot, or feast, 545
About his kitchin white-tooth'd swine lie drest.
The slaughters of a world of men thine eies,
Both private and in prease of enemies,
Have personally witnest, but this one
Would all thy parts have broken into mone, 550
To see how strewd about our Cups and Cates,
As Tables set with Feast, so we with Fates,
All gasht and slaine lay, all the floore embrude
With blood and braine. But that which most I ru'd
Flew from the heavie voice that Priam's seed, 555
Cassandra, breath'd, whom she that wit doth feed
With banefull crafts, false Clytemnestra, slew,
Close sitting by me; up my hands I threw
From earth to heaven, and tumbling on my sword,
Gave wretched life up—when the most abhord 560
By all her sexe's shame forsooke the roome,
Nor daind (though then so neare this heavie home)
To shut my lips, or close my broken eies.
Nothing so heapt is with impieties
As such a woman that would kill her Spouse, 565
That maried her a maid, when to my house
I brought her, hoping of her love in heart,
To children, maids, and slaves. But she (in th'Art
Of onely mischiefe heartie) not alone
Cast on her selfe this foule aspersion, 570
But loving Dames hereafter to their Lords
Will beare for good deeds her bad thoughts and words."
'"Alas," said I, "that Jove should hate the lives
Of Atreus' seed so highly for their wives.
For Menelaus' wife a number fell; 575
For dangerous absence thine sent thee to hell."
'"For this," he answerd, "be not thou more kind
Than wise to thy wife; never all thy mind
Let words expresse to her. Of all she knowes,
Curbs for the worst still in thy selfe repose. 580
But thou by thy wife's wiles shalt lose no blood;
Exceeding wise she is, and wise in good.
Icarius' daughter, chaste Penelope,
We left a yong Bride when for battell we
Forsooke the Nuptiall peace, and at her brest 585

Her first child sucking—who, by this houre, blest,
Sits in the number of surviving men.
And his blisse she hath, that she can containe,
And her blisse thou hast, that she is so wise;
For by her wisedome thy returned eies 590
Shall see thy sonne, and he shall greete his Sire
With fitting welcomes—when in my retire
My wife denies mine eyes my sonne's deare sight,
And, as from me, will take from him the light
Before she addes one just delight to life, 595
Or her false wit one truth that fits a wife.
For her sake, therefore, let my harmes advise,
That though thy wife be ne're so chaste and wise,
Yet come not home to her in open view

This advice he followed at his coming home.

With any ship or any personall shew, 600
But take close shore disguisde, nor let her know—
For tis no world to trust a woman now.
But what sayes Fame? Doth my Sonne yet survive
In Orchomen or Pylos? Or doth live
In Sparta with his Unkle? Yet I see 605
Divine Orestes is not here with me."
'I answerd, asking: "Why doth Atreus' sonne
Enquire of me, who yet arriv'd where none
Could give to these newes any certaine wings?
And tis absurd to tell uncertaine things." 610
'Such sad speech past us; and as thus we stood,
With kind teares rendring unkind fortunes good,
Achilles' and Patroclus' Soule appear'd,
And his Soule, of whom never ill was heard,
The good Antilochus, and the Soule of him 615
That all the Greeks past both for force and lim,
Excepting the unmatcht Æacides,
Illustrous Ajax. But the first of these
That saw, acknowledg'd, and saluted me

Achilles.

Was Thetis' conquering Sonne, who (heavily 620
His state here taking) said: "Unworthy breath!
What act yet mightier imagineth
Thy ventrous spirit? How doest thou descend
These under regions, where the dead man's end
Is to be lookt on, and his foolish shade?" 625
'I answerd him: "I was induc'd t'invade
These under parts, most excellent of Greece,
To visite wise Tiresias, for advice
Of vertue to direct my voyage home

To rugged Ithaca; since I could come 630
To note in no place where Achaia stood,
And so liv'd ever tortur'd with the blood
In man's vaine veines. Thou therefore, Thetis' sonne,
Hast equald all that ever yet have wonne
The blisse the earth yeelds, or hereafter shall. 635
In life thy eminence was ador'd of all,
Even with the Gods. And now, even dead, I see
Thy vertues propagate thy Emperie
To a renewd life of command beneath.
So great Achilles triumphs over death." 640
This comfort of him this encounter found:
"Urge not my death to me, nor rub that wound.

Achilles of the next life.

I rather wish to live in earth a Swaine
Or serve a Swaine for hire, that scarce can gaine
Bread to sustaine him, than (that life once gone) 645
Of all the dead sway the Imperiall throne.
But say, and of my Sonne, some comfort yeeld,
If he goes on in first fights of the field,
Or lurks for safetie in the obscure Rere?
Or of my Father if thy royall eare 650
Hath bene advertisde, that the Phthian Throne
He still commands as greatest Myrmidon?
Or that the Phthian and Thessalian rage
(Now feete and hands are in the hold of Age)
Despise his Empire? Under those bright rayes 655
In which heaven's fervour hurles about the dayes
Must I no more shine his revenger now,
Such as of old the Ilian overthrow
Witnest my anger, th'universall hoast
Sending before me to this shadie Coast 660
In fight for Grecia. Could I now resort
(But for some small time) to my Father's Court,
In spirit and powre as then, those men should find
My hands inaccessible, and of fire my mind,
That durst with all the numbers they are strong 665
Unseate his honour and suborne his wrong."
'This pitch still flew his spirit, though so low;
And this I answerd thus: "I do not know
Of blamelesse Peleus any least report,
But of your sonne in all the utmost sort 670
I can informe your care with truth, and thus:—

Ulysses' report of Neoptolemus, the son of Achilles.

'"From Scyros princely Neoptolemus
By Fleete I convaid to the Greeks, where he

Was Chiefe at both parts—when our gravitie
Retir'd to councell, and our youth to fight. 675
In councell still (so firie was Conceit
In his quicke apprehension of a cause)
That first he ever spake, nor past the lawes
Of any grave stay in his greatest hast.
None would contend with him, that counseld last, 680
Unlesse illustrous Nestor, he and I
Would sometimes put a friendly contrary
On his opinion. In our fights the prease
Of great or common he would never sease,
But farre before fight ever. No man there 685
For force he forced. He was slaughterer
Of many a brave man in most dreadfull fight.
But one and other whom he reft of light
(In Grecian succour) I can neither name,
Nor give in number. The particular fame 690
Of one man's slaughter yet I must not passe:
Eurypylus Telephides he was
That fell beneath him, and with him the falls
Of such huge men went that they shewd like whales,
Rampir'd about him. Neoptolemus 695
Set him so sharply, for the sumptuous
Favours of Mistresses he saw him weare;
For past all doubt his beauties had no peere
Of all that mine eies noted, next to one,
And that was Memnon, Tithon's Sun-like sonne. 700
Thus farre for fight in publicke may a tast
Give of his eminence. How farre surpast
His spirit in private, where he was not seene,
Nor glorie could be said to praise his spleene,
This close note I excerpted. When we sate 705
Hid in Epeus' horse, no Optimate
Of all the Greeks there had the charge to ope
And shut the Stratageme but I. My scope
To note then each man's spirit in a streight
Of so much danger much the better might 710
Be hit by me than others, as, provokt,
I shifted place still—when in some I smokt
Both privie tremblings and close vent of teares.
In him yet not a soft conceit of theirs
Could all my search see, either his wet eies 715
Plied still with wipings, or the goodly guise
His person all waies put forth in least part

This place (and a number more) is most miserably mistaken by all translators and commentors.

The horse above-said.

By any tremblings shewd his toucht-at heart.
But ever he was urging me to make
Way to their sally, by his signe to shake 720
His sword hid in his scabberd, or his Lance
Loded with iron, at me. No good chance
His thoughts to Troy intended. In th'event
(High Troy depopulate) he made ascent
To his faire ship with prise and treasure store, 725
Safe, and no touch away with him he bore
Of farre-off hurl'd Lance or of close-fought sword,
Whose wounds for favours Warre doth oft affoord,
Which he (though sought) mist in warre's closest wage.
In close fights Mars doth never fight, but rage." 730
'This made the soule of swift Achilles tred
A March of glorie through the herbie meade,
For joy to heare me so renowme his Sonne,
And vanisht stalking. But with passion
Stood th'other Soules strooke, and each told his bane. 735
Onely the spirit Telamonian
Ajax, the sonne of Telamon.
Kept farre off, angrie for the victorie
I wonne from him at Fleete, though Arbitrie
Of all a Court of warre pronounc't it mine,
And Pallas' selfe. Our prise were th'armes divine 740
Of great Æacides, proposde t'our fames
Achilles.
By his bright Mother at his funerall Games.
Thetis.
I wish to heaven I ought not to have wonne,
Since for those Armes so high a head so soone
The base earth coverd—Ajax, that of all 745
The hoast of Greece had person capitall
And acts as eminent, excepting his
Whose armes those were, in whom was nought amisse.
I tride the great Soule with soft words, and said:
"Ajax! great sonne of Telamon, arraid 750
In all our glories! What? Not dead resigne
Thy wrath for those curst Armes? The Powres divine
In them forg'd all our banes, in thine owne One,
In thy grave fall our Towre was overthrowne.
We mourne (for ever maimd) for thee as much 755
As for Achilles; nor thy wrong doth touch
In sentence any but Saturnius' doome,
Jupiter.
In whose hate was the hoast of Greece become
A very horror—who exprest it well
In signing thy Fate with this timelesse Hell. 760
Approch then, King of all the Grecian merit,

Represse thy great mind and thy flamie spirit,
And give the words I give thee worthy eare."
'All this no word drew from him, but lesse neare
The sterne Soule kept. To other Soules he fled, 765
And glid along the River of the dead.
Though Anger mov'd him, yet he might have spoke,
Since I to him. But my desires were strooke
With sight of other Soules. And then I saw
Minos. Minos, that ministred to Death a law, 770
And Jove's bright sonne was. He was set, and swaid
A golden Scepter, and to him did pleade
A sort of others, set about his Throne
In Pluto's wide-door'd house; when strait came on,
Orion. Mightie Orion, who was hunting there 775
The heards of those beasts he had slaughterd here
In desart hils on earth. A Club he bore,
Entirely steele, whose vertues never wore.
Tityus. 'Tityus I saw, to whom the glorious Earth
Opened her wombe and gave unhappie birth; 780
Upwards and flat upon the Pavement lay
His ample lims, that spred in their display
Nine Acres compasse. On his bosome sat
Two Vultures digging through his caule of fat
Into his Liver with their crooked Beakes; 785
And each by turnes the concrete entraile breakes
(As Smiths their steele beate) set on either side.
Nor doth he ever labour to divide
His Liver and their Beakes, nor with his hand
Offer them off, but suffers by command 790
Of th'angrie Thunderer, offring to enforce
His love Latona in the close recourse
She usde to Pytho through the dancing land,
Smooth Panopeus. I saw likewise stand,
Up to the chin amidst a liquid lake, 795
Tormented Tantalus, yet could not slake
His burning thirst. Oft as his scornfull cup
Th'old man would taste, so oft twas swallowd up,
And all the blacke earth to his feete descried;
Divine powre (plaguing him) the lake still dried. 800
About his head, on high trees clustering, hung
Peares, Apples, Granets, Olives, ever yong,
Delicious Figs, and many fruite trees more
Of other burthen, whose alluring store
When th'old Soule striv'd to pluck, the winds from sight 805

In gloomie vapours made them vanish quite.
Sisyphus. 'There saw I Sisyphus in infinite mone,
With both hands heaving up a massie stone,
And on his tip-toes racking all his height
To wrest up to a mountaine top his freight; 810
When prest to rest it there (his nerves quite spent)
Downe rusht the deadly Quarrie, the event
Of all his torture new to raise againe;
To which strait set his never-rested paine.
The sweate came gushing out from every Pore, 815
And on his head a standing mist he wore,
Reeking from thence as if a cloud of dust
Were raisd about it. Downe with these was thrust
Hercules. The Idoll of the force of Hercules—
But his firme selfe did no such Fate oppresse; 820
He feasting lives amongst th'immortall States,
White-ankled Hebe and himselfe made mates
In heavenly Nuptials—Hebe, Jove's deare race,
And Juno's, whom the golden Sandals grace.
About him flew the clamors of the dead 825
Like Fowles, and still stoopt cuffing at his head.
He with his Bow, like Night, stalkt up and downe,
His shaft still nockt, and hurling round his frowne
At those vext hoverers, aiming at them still,
And still, as shooting out, desire to still. 830
A horrid Bawdricke wore he thwart his brest,
The Thong all gold, in which were formes imprest
Where Art and Miracle drew equall breaths,
In Beares, Bores, Lions, Battels, Combats, Deaths.
Who wrought that worke did never such before, 835
Nor so divinely will do ever more.
Soone as he saw he knew me, and gave speech:
"Sonne of Laertes, high in wisedome's reach,
And yet unhappie wretch, for in this heart,
Of all exploits atchiev'd by thy desert, 840
Thy worth but works out some sinister Fate,
As I in earth did. I was generate
By Jove himselfe, and yet past meane opprest
By one my farre inferiour, whose proud hest
Imposde abhorred labours on my hand. 845
Of all which, one was to descend this Strand,
And hale the dog from thence. He could not thinke
An act that Danger could make deeper sinke—
And yet this depth I drew, and fetcht as hie

As this was low the dog. The Deitie 850
Of sleight and wisedome, as of downe-right powre,
Both stoopt, and raisd, and made me Conquerour."
'This said, he made descent againe as low
As Pluto's Court; when I stood firme, for show
Of more Heroes of the times before, 855
And might perhaps have seene my wish of more
(As Theseus and Pirithous, deriv'd
From rootes of Deitie), but before th'atchiev'd
Rare sight of these the rank-soul'd multitude
In infinite flocks rose, venting sounds so rude 860
That pale Feare tooke me, lest the Gorgon's head
Rusht in amongst them, thrust up, in my dread,
By grim Persephone. I therefore sent
My men before to ship, and after went—
Where, boorded, set, and lancht, th'Ocean wave 865
Our Ores and forewinds speedie passage gave.

Finis libri undecimi Hom. Odyss.

THE TWELFTH BOOKE
of
HOMER'S ODYSSES

THE ARGUMENT

He shewes from Hell his safe retreate
To th'Ile Ææa, Circe's seate;
And how he scapt the Sirens' calls,
With th'erring Rockes and waters' falls,
That Scylla and Charybdis breake; 5
The Sunne's stolne Herds, and his sad wreake
Both of Ulysses' ship and men,
His owne head scaping scarce the paine.

Another Argument

Mῦ. *The Rockes that errd;*
The Sirens' call;
The Sunne's stolne Herd;
The souldiers' fall.

'Our Ship now past the streights of th'Ocean flood;
She plowd the broad sea's billowes, and made good
The Ile Ææa, where the Pallace stands
Of th'early Riser with the rosie hands,
Active Aurora—where she loves to dance, 5
And where the Sunne doth his prime beames advance.
'When here arriv'd, we drew her up to land,
And trod our selves the resaluted sand,
Found on the shore fit resting for the Night,
Slept, and expected the celestiall light. 10
'Soone as the white-and-red-mixt-fingerd Dame
Had guilt the mountaines with her Saffron flame,
I sent my men to Circe's house before,
To fetch deceast Elpenor to the shore.

Reditur ab inferis ad Circen.

'Strait swelld the high banks with feld heapes of trees, 15
And (full of teares) we did due Exequies
Elpenor tumulatur. To our dead friend—whose Corse consum'd with fire
And honourd Armes, whose Sepulcher entire,
And, over that, a Columne raisd, his Ore,
Curiously carv'd (to his desire before) 20
Upon the top of all his Tombe we fixt.
Of all Rites fit his Funerall Pile was mixt.
'Nor was our safe ascent from hell conceald
From Circe's knowledge, nor so soone reveald
But she was with us, with her bread and food 25
And ruddie wine, brought by her sacred brood
Of woods and Fountaines. In the midst she stood,
And thus saluted us: "Unhappie men,
That have (inform'd with all your sences) bene
In Pluto's dismall mansion! You shall die 30
Twice now, where others, that Mortalitie
In her faire armes holds, shall but once decease.
But eate and drinke out all conceit of these,
And this day dedicate to food and wine,
The following Night to Sleepe. When next shall shine 35
The chearfull Morning, you shall prove the seas.
Your way, and every act ye must addresse,
My knowledge of their order shall designe,
Lest with your owne bad counsels ye encline
Events as bad against ye, and sustaine 40
By sea and shore the wofull ends that raigne
In wilfull actions." Thus did she advise,
And for the time our Fortunes were so wise
To follow wise directions. All that day
We sate and feasted. When his lower way 45
The Sunne had enterd, and the Even the hie,
My friends slept on their Gables; she and I
(Led by her faire hand to a place apart,
By her well sorted) did to sleepe convert
Our timed powres—when all things Fate let fall 50
In our affaire she askt. I told her all,
To which she answerd: "These things thus tooke end.
And now to those that I informe attend,
Which (you remembring) God himselfe shall be
Circe præsagit futura pericula. The blessed author of your memorie. 55
'"First to the Sirens ye shall come, that taint
The minds of all men whom they can acquaint

With their attractions. Whosoever shall
Sirenarum descriptio. (For want of knowledge mov'd) but heare the call
Of any Siren, he will so despise 60
Both wife and children for their sorceries,
That never home turnes his affection's streame,
Nor they take joy in him, nor he in them.
The Sirens will so soften with their song
(Shrill, and in sensuall appetite so strong) 65
His loose affections that he gives them head.
And then observe: They sit amidst a meade,
And round about it runnes a hedge or wall
Of dead men's bones, their witherd skins and all
Hung all along upon it; and these men 70
Were such as they had fawnd into their Fen,
And then their skins hung on their hedge of bones.
Saile by them therefore, thy companions
Before hand causing to stop every eare
With sweete soft waxe so close that none may heare 75
A note of all their charmings. Yet may you
(If you affect it) open eare allow
To trie their motion: but presume not so
To trust your judgement when your senses go
So loose about you, but give straight command 80
To all your men to bind you foote and hand
Sure to the Mast, that you may safe approve
How strong in instigation to their love
Their rapting tunes are. If so much they move
That, spite of all your reason, your will stands 85
To be enfranchisde both of feete and hands,
Charge all your men before to sleight your charge
And rest so farre from fearing to enlarge
That much more sure they bind you. When your friends
Have outsaild these, the danger that transcends 90
Rests not in any counsaile to prevent,
Unlesse your owne mind finds the tract and bent
Of that way that avoids it. I can say
That in your course there lies a twofold way,
The right of which your owne taught, present wit 95
And grace divine must prompt. In generall yet
Let this informe you: Neare these Sirens' shore
Move two steepe Rocks, at whose feete lie and rore
The blacke sea's cruell billowes: the blest Gods
Call them the Rovers. Their abhord abods 100

πέλειαι τρήρωνες—Columbæ timidæ. *What these Doves were, and the whole minde of this place, the Great Macedon asking Chiron Amphipolites, he answered: They were the Pleiades or seven Stares. One of which (besides his proper imperfection, of being* ἀμυδρός, i.e. adeo exilis, vel subobscurus, ut vix appareat) *is utterly obscured or let by these Rocks. Why then, or how, Jove still supplied the lost one, that the number might be full? Athenæus falles to it, and helps the other out, interpreting it to be affirmed of their perpetuall septenary number, though there appeared but sixe. But how lame and loathsome these Prozers shew in their affected expositions of the Poeticall Minde, this and an hundred others, spent in meere presumptuous guesse at this inaccessible Poet, I hope will make plaine enough to the most envious of any thing done, besides their owne set censures and most arrogant over weenings. In the 23. of the Iliads, (being* ψ) *at the Games celebrated at Patroclus' funerals they tied to the top of a Mast* πέλειαν τρήρωνα, timidam Columbam, *to shoote at for a game: so that (by these great men's abovesaid expositions) they shot at the Pleiades.*

No bird can passe—no, not the Doves, whose feare
Sire Jove so loves, that they are said to beare
Ambrosia to him, can their ravine scape,
But one of them falles ever to the rape
Of those slie rocks. Yet Jove another still 105
Adds to the rest, that so may ever fill
The sacred number. Never ship could shunne
The nimble perill wing'd there, but did runne
With all her bulke and bodies of her men
To utter ruine. For the seas retaine 110
Not onely their outragious æsture there,
But fierce assistents of particular feare
And supernaturall mischiefe they expire—
And those are whirlewinds of devouring fire
Whisking about still. Th'Argive ship alone 115
(Which bore the care of all men) got her gone,
Come from Æeta. Yet perhaps even she
Had wrackt at those Rocks if the Deitie
That lies by Jove's side had not lent her hand
To their transmission, since the man that mann'd 120
In chiefe that voyage she in chiefe did love.
Of these two spitefull Rocks, the one doth shove
Against the height of heaven her pointed brow.
A blacke cloud binds it round, and never show
Lends to the sharp point: not the cleare blew skie 125
Lets ever view it, not the Sommer's eye,

116 νηῦς πᾶσι μέλουσα, &c.—Nauis omnibus Curæ: *the ship that held the care of all men, or of all things: which our Critickes will needs restraine,* omnibus heroibus Poetis omnibus, vel Historicis, *when the care of all men's preservation is affirmed to be the freight of it: as if Poets and Historians comprehended all things, when I scarce know any that makes them any part of their care. But this likewise is garbige good enough for the monster. Nor wil I tempt our spic't consciences with expressing the divine mind it includes, being afraid to affirme any good of poore Poesie, since no man gets any goods by it. And notwithstanding many of our bird-eyd starters at prophanation are for nothing so afraid of it as that lest their galled consciences (scarce beleeving the most reall truth, in approbation of their lives) should be rubbed with the confirmation of it, even in these contemned vanities (as their impieties please to call them,) which by much more learned and pious than themselves, have ever bene called the raptures of divine inspiration—by which,* Homo supra humanam naturam erigitur, et in Deum transit. Plat.

Not fervent Autumne's. None that Death could end
Could ever skale it, or, if up, descend,
Though twenty hands and feete he had for hold:
A polisht ice-like glibnesse doth enfold 130
The rocke so round, whose midst a gloomie cell
Shrowds so farre Westward that it sees to hell.
From this keepe you as farre as from his bow
An able yong man can his shaft bestow.
For here, the whuling Scylla shrowds her face, 135
That breaths a voice, at all parts no more base
Than are a newly-kitn'd kitling's cries—
Her selfe a monster yet of boundlesse sise,
Whose sight would nothing please a mortal's eies—
No, nor the eyes of any God, if he 140
(Whom nought should fright) fell foule on her, and she
Her full shape shew'd. Twelve foule feete beare about
Her ougly bulke. Sixe huge long necks looke out
Of her ranke shoulders; every necke doth let
A ghastly head out; every head three set, 145
Thicke thrust together, of abhorred teeth;
And every tooth stucke with a sable death.
'"She lurkes in midst of all her denne, and streakes
From out a ghastly whirle-poole all her necks;
Where (gloting round her rocke) to fish she falles, 150
And up rush Dolphins, Dogfish, somewhiles Whales,
If got within her when her rapine feeds—
For ever-groning Amphitrite breeds
About her whirlepoole an unmeasur'd store;
No Sea-man ever boasted touch of shore 155
That there toucht with his ship, but still she fed
Of him and his, a man for every head

δεινὸν λελακυῖα, &c.—Graviter vociferans, *as all most untruly translate it. As they do in the next verse these words,* σκύλακος νεογιλῆς, Catuli Leonis—*no Lion being here dreamed of, nor any vociferation*— δεινὸν λελακυῖα *signifying* indignam, dissimilem, *or* horribilem vocem edens. *But in what kind* horribilem? *Not for the gravitie or greatnesse of her voice, but for the unworthy or disproportionable small whuling of it, she being in the vast frame of her body, as the very words* πέλωρ κακὸν *signifie,* monstrum ingens; *whose disproportion and deformitie is too Poetically (and therein elegantly) ordered for fat and flat Prozers to comprehend. Nor could they make the Poet's words serve their comprehension, and therefore they adde of their owne,* λάσκω, *from whence* λελακυῖα *is derived, signifying* crepo, *or* stridule clamo. *And* σκύλακος νεογιλῆς *is to be expounded* catuli nuper *or* recens nati, *not* Leonis. *But thus they botch and abuse the incomparable expressor, because they knew not how otherwise to be monstrous enough themselves to helpe out the Monster—imagining so huge a great body must needs have a voice as huge. And then would not our Homer have likened it to a Lion's whelp's voyce, but to the Lion's owne; and all had bene much too little to make a voyce answerable to her hugenesse. And therefore found our inimitable master a new way to expresse her monstrous disproportion, performing it so as there can be* nihil supra. *And I would faine learne of my learned Detractor, that will needs have me onely translate out of the Latine, what Latine translation telles me this? or what Grecian hath ever found this and a hundred other such? Which may be some poore instance or proofe of my Grecian faculty, as far as old Homer goes in his two simple Poems, but not a sillable further will my sillie spirit presume.*

Spoiling his ship of. You shall then descrie
The other humbler Rocke, that moves so nie
Your dart may mete the distance. It receaves 160
A huge wilde Fig-tree, curl'd with ample leaves,
Beneath whose shades divine Charybdis sits
Supping the blacke deepes. Thrice a day her pits
She drinkes all dry, and thrice a day againe
All up she belches, banefull to sustaine. 165
When she is drinking, dare not neare her draught,
For not the force of Neptune (if once caught)
Can force your freedome. Therefore, in your strife
To scape Charybdis, labour all for life
To row neare Scylla, for she will but have 170
For her sixe heads sixe men, and better save
The rest than all make offerings to the wave."
'This Neede she told me of my losse, when I
Desir'd to know, if that Necessitie
(When I had scap't Charybdis' outrages) 175
My powres might not revenge, though not redresse?
She answerd: "O unhappy! art thou yet
Enflam'd with warre, and thirst to drinke thy swet?
Not to the Gods give up both Armes and will?
She deathlesse is, and that immortall ill 180
Grave, harsh, outragious, not to be subdu'd,
That men must suffer till they be renew'd.
Nor lives there any virtue that can flie
The vicious outrage of her crueltie.
Shouldst thou put Armes on, and approch the Rocke, 185
I feare sixe more must expiate the shocke.
Sixe heads sixe men aske still. Hoise saile, and flie;
And in thy flight aloud on Cratis crie
(Great Scylla's Mother, who exposde to light
That bane of men) and she will do such right 190
To thy observance that she downe will tread
Her daughter's rage, nor let her shew a head.
'"From thenceforth then, for ever past her care,
Thou shalt ascend the Ile Triangulare,
Where many Oxen of the Sunne are fed, 195
And fatted flocks. Of Oxen fifty head
In every herd feed, and their herds are seven,
And of his fat flocks is their number Even.
Increase they yeeld not, for they never die.
There every shepherdesse a Deitie: 200
Faire Phaethusa and Lampetie

The lovely Nymphs are that their Guardians be,
Who to the daylight's lofty-going flame
Had gracious birthright from the heavenly Dame,
Still yong Neæra; who (brought forth and bred) 205
Farre off dismist them, to see duly fed
Their Father's herds and flocks in Sicilie.
These herds and flocks if to the Deitie
Ye leave, as sacred things, untoucht, and on
Goe with all fit care of your home, alone 210
(Though through some sufferance) you yet safe shall land
In wished Ithaca. But if impious hand
You lay on those herds to their hurts, I then
Presage sure ruine to thy ship and men.
If thou escap'st thy selfe, extending home 215
Thy long'd-for landing, thou shalt loded come
With store of losses, most exceeding late,
And not consorted with a saved mate."
'This said, the golden-thron'd Aurora rose;
She her way went, and I did mine dispose 220
Up to my ship, weigh'd Anchor, and away—
When reverend Circe helpt us to convaie
Our vessell safe, by making well inclind
A Sea man's true companion, a forewind,
With which she filld our sailes—when, fitting all 225
Our Armes close by us, I did sadly fall
To grave relation what concernd in Fate
My friends to know, and told them that the state
Of our affaire's successe, which Circe had
Presag'd to me alone, must yet be made 230
To one nor onely two knowne, but to all;
That since their lives and deaths were left to fall
In their elections, they might life elect,
And give what would preserve it fit effect.
'I first inform'd them that we were to flie 235
The heavenly-singing Sirens' harmony
And flowre-adorned Medow. And that I
Had charge to heare their song, but fetterd fast
In bands unfavor'd to th'erected Mast;
From whence if I should pray or use command 240
To be enlarg'd, they should with much more band
Containe my struglings. This I simply told
To each particular, nor would withold
What most enjoyn'd mine owne affection's stay,
That theirs the rather might be taught t'obay. 245

'In meane time flew our ship, and straight we fetcht
The Sirens' Ile, a spleenelesse wind so stretcht
Her wings to waft us and so urg'd our keele.
But, having reacht this Ile, we could not feele
The least gaspe of it: it was striken dead, 250
And all the Sea in prostrate slumber spread:
The Sirens' divell charm'd all. Up then flew
My friends to worke, strooke saile, together drew
And under hatches stowd them, sat and plicd
Their polisht oares, and did in curls divide 255
The white-head waters. My part then came on;
A mighty waxen Cake I set upon,
Chopt it in fragments with my sword, and wrought
With strong hand every peece till all were soft.
The great powre of the Sunne, in such a beame 260
As then flew burning from his Diademe,
To liquefaction helpt us. Orderlie
I stopt their eares, and they as faire did ply
My feete and hands with cords, and to the Mast
With other halsers made me soundly fast. 265
'Then tooke they seate, and forth our passage strooke—
The fomie Sea beneath their labour shooke—
Rowd on in reach of an erected voice;
The Sirens soone tooke note without our noice,
Tun'd those sweete accents that made charmes so strong 270
And these learn'd numbers made the Sirens' song:
' "Come here, thou, worthy of a world of praise,
That dost so high the Grecian glory raise.
Ulysses! stay thy ship, and that song heare
That none past ever but it bent his eare, 275
But left him ravishd and instructed more
By us than any ever heard before.
For we know all things whatsoever were
In wide Troy labour'd, whatsoever there
The Grecians and the Troyans both sustain'd 280
By those high issues that the Gods ordain'd:
And whatsoever all the earth can show
T'informe a knowledge of desert, we know."
'This they gave accent in the sweetest straine
That ever open'd an enamour'd vaine— 285
When my constrain'd heart needs would have mine eare
Yet more delighted, force way forth, and heare.
To which end I commanded with all signe
Sterne lookes could make (for not a joynt of mine

Had powre to stirre) my friends to rise, and give 290
My limbs free way. They freely striv'd to drive
Their ship still on. When (farre from will to lose)
Eurylochus and Perimedes rose
To wrap me surer, and opprest me more
With many a halser than had use before. 295
When, rowing on without the reach of sound,
My friends unstopt their eares and me unbound,
And that Ile quite we quitted. But againe
Fresh feares emploid us. I beheld a maine
Of mighty billows, and a smoke ascend, 300
A horrid murmure hearing. Every friend
Astonisht sat: from every hand his oare
Fell quite forsaken: with the dismall Rore,
Where all things there made Echoes, stone still stood
Our ship it selfe, because the ghastly flood 305
Tooke all men's motions from her in their owne:
I through the ship went, labouring up and downe
My friends' recoverd spirits. One by one
I gave good words, and said that well were knowne
These ills to them before: I told them all; 310
And that these could not prove more capitall
Than those the Cyclop blockt us up in, yet
My vertue, wit, and heaven-helpt Counsailes set
Their freedomes open. I could not beleeve
But they rememberd it, and wisht them give 315
My equall care and meanes now equall trust:
The strength they had for stirring up they must
Rouze and extend, to trie if Jove had laid
His powres in theirs up, and would adde his aid
To scape even that death. In particular then 320
I told our Pylot that past other men
He most must beare firme spirits, since he swaid
The Continent that all our spirits convaid
In his whole guide of her. He saw there boile
The fierie whirlpooles that to all our spoile 325
Inclosde a Rocke, without which he must stere,
Or all our ruines stood concluded there.

'All heard me, and obaid, and little knew
That, shunning that Rocke, sixe of them should rue
The wracke another hid. For I conceal'd 330
The heavy wounds that never would be heal'd,
To be by Scylla opened—for their feare
Would then have robd all of all care to stere

Or stirre an oare, and made them hide beneath,
When they, and all, had died an idle death. 335
But then even I forgot to shunne the harme
Circe forewarnd—who willd I should not arme,
Nor shew my selfe to Scylla, lest in vaine
I ventur'd life. Yet could not I containe,
But arm'd at all parts, and two lances tooke, 340
Up to the foredecke went, and thence did looke
That Rockie Scylla would have first appear'd
And taken my life, with the friends I feard.
'From thence yet no place could afford her sight,
Though through the darke rocke mine eye threw her light, 345
And ransackt all waies. I then tooke a streight
That gave my selfe and some few more receipt
Twixt Scylla and Charybdis; whence we saw
How horridly Charybdis' throat did draw
The brackish sea up, which when all abroad 350
She spit againe out, never Caldron sod
With so much fervor, fed with all the store
That could enrage it. All the Rocke did rore
With troubl'd waters: round about the tops
Of all the steepe crags flew the fomy drops. 355
But when her draught the sea and earth dissunderd,
The troubl'd bottoms turnd up, and she thunderd,
Farre under shore the swart sands naked lay—
Whose whole sterne sight the startl'd blood did fray
From all our faces. And while we on her 360
Our eyes bestowd thus to our ruine's feare,
Sixe friends had Scylla snatcht out of our keele,
In whom most losse did force and virtue feele—
When, looking to my ship, and lending eye
To see my friends' estates, their heeles turnd hie 365
And hands cast up I might discerne, and heare
Their calles to me for helpe, when now they were
To try me in their last extremities.
And as an Angler medcine for surprise
Of little fish sits powring from the rocks, 370
From out the crookt horne of a fold-bred Oxe,
And then with his long Angle hoists them hie
Up to the Aire, then sleightly hurles them by,
When helplesse sprauling on the land they lie:
So easely Scylla to her Rocke had rapt 375
My wofull friends, and so unhelpt, entrapt,
Strugling they lay beneath her violent rape,

Who in their tortures, desperate of escape,
Shriekt as she tore, and up their hands to me
Still threw for sweete life. I did never see, 380
In all my sufferance ransacking the seas,
A spectacle so full of miseries.
'Thus having fled these rocks (these cruell dames
Scylla, Charybdis), where the king of flames
Hath offerings burnd to him our ship put in 385
The Iland that from all the earth doth winne
The Epithete Faultlesse, where the broad of head
And famous Oxen for the Sunne are fed,
With many fat flocks of that high-gone God.
Set in my ship, mine eare reacht, where we rod, 390
The bellowing of Oxen and the bleate
Of fleecie sheepe, that in my memorie's seate
Put up the formes that late had bene imprest
By dread Ææan Circe and the best
Of Soules and Prophets, the blind Theban Seer, 395
The wise Tiresias, who was grave decreer
Of my returne's whole meanes. Of which, this one
In chiefe he urg'd, that I should alwaies shunne
The Iland of the Man-delighting Sunne.
When (sad at heart for our late losse) I praid 400
My friends to heare fit counsaile (though dismaid
With all ill fortunes) which was given to me
By Circe's and Tiresias' Prophecie—
That I should flie the Ile where was ador'd
The Comfort of the world, for ills abhorr'd 405
Were ambusht for us there; and therefore willd
They should put off and leave the Ile. This kill'd
Their tender spirits; when Eurylochus
A speech that vext me utter'd, answering thus:
'"Cruell Ulysses! Since thy nerves abound 410
In strength, the more spent, and no toyles confound
Thy able lims, as all beate out of steele,
Thou ablest us to, as unapt to feele
The teeth of Labor and the spoile of Sleepe,
And therefore still wilt wast us in the deepe, 415
Nor let us land to eate, but madly now
In Night put forth, and leave firme land to strow
The Sea with errors. All the rabide flight
Of winds that ruine ships are bred in Night.
Who is it that can keepe off cruell Death, 420
If suddainly should rush out th'angry breath

Of Notus, or the eager-spirited West,
That cuffe ships dead, and do the Gods their hest?
Serve black Night still with shore, meate, sleepe, and ease,
And offer to the Morning for the seas." 425
'This all the rest approv'd, and then knew I
That past all doubt the divell did apply
His slaughterous works. Nor would they be withheld;
I was but one, nor yeelded but compell'd.
But all that might containc them I assaid: 430
A sacred oath on all their powres I laid,
That if with herds or any richest flocks
We chanc't t'encounter, neither sheepe nor Oxe
We once should touch, nor (for that constant ill
That followes folly) scorne advice and kill, 435
But quiet sit us downe, and take such food
As the immortall Circe had bestowd.
'They swore all this in all severest sort;
And then we ancord in the winding Port
Neare a fresh River, where the longd-for shore 440
They all flew out to, tooke in victles' store,
And, being full, thought of their friends, and wept
Their losse by Scylla, weeping till they slept.
'In Night's third part, when stars began to stoope,
The Cloud-assembler put a Tempest up. 115
A boistrous spirit he gave it, drave out all
His flocks of clouds, and let such darknesse fall
That Earth and Seas for feare to hide were driven;
For with his clouds he thrust out Night from heaven.
'At Morne, we drew our ship into a cave, 450
In which the Nymphs that Phœbus' cattaile drave
Fairc dancing Roomes had, and their seates of State.
I urg'd my friends then, that, to shunne their Fate,
They would observe their oath, and take the food
Our ship afforded, nor attempt the blood 455
Of those faire Herds and Flocks, because they were
That dreadfull God's that all could see and heare.
'They stood observant, and in that good mind
Had we bene gone, but so adverse the wind
Stood to our passage that we could not go. 460
For one whole moneth perpetually did blow
Impetuous Notus; not a breath's repaire
But his and Eurus' rul'd in all the Aire.
As long yet as their ruddy wine and bread

Stood out amongst them, so long not a head 465
Of all those Oxen fell in any strife
Amongst those students for the gut and life.
But when their victles faild, they fell to prey:
Necessitie compell'd them then to stray
In rape of fish and fowle: what ever came 470
In reach of hand or hooke, the bellie's flame
Afflicted to it. I then fell to praire;
And (making to a close Retreate repaire,
Free from both friends and winds) I washt my hands,
And all the Gods besought that held commands 475
In liberall heaven to yeeld some meane to stay
Their desperate hunger, and set up the way
Of our returne restraind. The Gods, in steed
Of giving what I prayd for, powre of deed,
A deedlesse sleepe did on my lids distill, 480
For meane to worke upon my friends their fill.
For whiles I slept, there wak't no meane to curb
Their headstrong wants, which he that did disturb
My rule in chiefe at all times, and was chiefe
To all the rest in counsaile to their griefe, 485
Knew well, and of my present absence tooke
His fit advantage, and their iron strooke
At highest heate. For (feeling their desire
In his owne Entrailes, to allay the fire
That Famine blew in them) he thus gave way 490
To that affection: "Heare what I shall say
(Though words will stanch no hunger): every death
To us poore wretches that draw temporall breath
You know is hatefull; but all know, to die
The Death of Famine is a miserie 495
Past all Death loathsome. Let us therefore take
The chiefe of this faire herd, and offerings make
To all the Deathlesse that in broad heaven live,
And in particular vow, if we arrive
In naturall Ithaca, to strait erect 500
A Temple to the haughtie in aspect,
Rich, and magnificent, and all within
Decke it with Relicks many and divine.
If yet he stands incenst, since we have slaine
His high-browd herd, and therefore will sustaine 505
Desire to wracke our ship, he is but one;
And all the other Gods that we attone

With our divine Rites will their suffrage give
To our design'd returne and let us live.
If not, and all take part, I rather crave 510
To serve with one sole Death the yawning wave
Than in a desert Iland lie and sterve,
And with one pin'd life many deaths observe."
'All cried: "He counsailes nobly"; and all speed
Made to their resolute driving. For the feed 515
Of those coleblacke, faire, broad-browd, Sun-lov'd Beeves
Had place close by our ships. They tooke the lives
Of sence, most eminent, about their fall
Stood round, and to the States celestiall
Made solemne vowes. But other Rites their ship 520
Could not afford them; they did therefore strip
The curld-head Oke of fresh yong leaves, to make
Supply of service for their Barly cake.
And on the sacredly enflam'd, for wine
Powrd purest water, all the parts divine 525
Spitting and rosting; all the Rites beside
Orderly using. Then did light divide
My low and upper lids; when my repaire
Made neare my ship, I met the delicate ayre
Their rost exhal'd. Out instantly I cried, 530
And said: "O Jove, and all ye Deified,
Ye have opprest me with a cruell sleepe,
While ye conferd on me a losse as deepe
As Death descends to. To themselves alone
My rude men left ungovernd, they have done 535
A deed so impious (I stand well assur'd)
That you will not forgive though ye procur'd."
'Then flew Lampetie with the ample Robe
Up to her Father with the golden Globe,
Ambassadresse t'informe him that my men 540
Had slaine his Oxen. Heart-incensed then,
He cried: "Revenge me, Father, and the rest
Both ever-living and for ever blest!
Ulysses' impious men have drawne the blood
Of those my Oxen that it did me good 545
To looke on, walking all my starrie round
And when I trod earth, all with medowes crown'd.
Without your full amends I'le leave heaven quite,
Dis and the Dead adorning with my light."
'The Cloud-herd answerd: "Son! thou shalt be ours, 550

And light those mortals in that Mine of flowres.
My red hote flash shall grase but on their ship
And eate it, burning, in the boyling deepe."
'This by Calypso I was told, and she
Inform'd it from the verger Mercurie. 555
' "Come to our ship," I chid, and told by name
Each man how impiously he was to blame.
But chiding got no peace; the Beeves were slaine—
When straight the Gods fore-went their following paine
With dire Ostents. The hides the flesh had lost 560
Crept all before them. As the flesh did rost
It bellowd like the Oxe it selfe, alive.
And yet my souldiers did their dead Beeves drive
Through all these Prodigies in daily feasts.
Sixe daies they banqueted and slue fresh beasts, 565
And when the seventh day Jove reduc't, the wind
That all the moneth rag'd and so in did bind
Our ship and us, was turnd and calm'd, and we
Lancht, put up Masts, Sailes hoised, and to Sea.
'The Iland left so farre that land no where 570
But onely sea and skie had powre t'appeare,
Jove fixt a cloud above our ship, so blacke
That all the sea it darkned. Yet from wracke
She ranne a good free time, till from the West
Came Zephyr ruffling forth, and put his breast 575
Out in a singing tempest so most vast
It burst the Gables that made sure our Mast;
Our Masts came tumbling downe, our tackle downe
Rusht to the Pump, and by our Pylot's crowne
The maine Mast past his fall, pasht all his Skull— 580
And all this wracke but one flaw made at full.
Off from the Sterne the Sternesman diving fell,
And from his sinews flew his Soule to hell.
Together, all this time Jove's Thunder chid,
And through and through the ship his lightning glid 585
Till it embrac't her round; her bulke was filld
With nasty sulphur, and her men were killd,
Tumbl'd to Sea, like Sea-mews swumme about,
And there the date of their returne was out.
'I tost from side to side still, till all broke 590
Her Ribs were with the storme, and she did choke
With let-in Surges, for the Mast, torne downe,
Tore her up pecemeale, and for me to drowne

Left little undissolv'd. But to the Mast
There was a lether Thong left, which I cast 595
About it and the keele, and so sat tost
With banefull weather till the West had lost
His stormy tyranny. And then arose
The South, that bred me more abhorred woes—
For backe againe his blasts expelld me quite 600
On ravenous Charybdis. All that Night
I totter'd up and downe, till Light and I
At Scylla's Rocke encounterd, and the nie
Dreadfull Charybdis. As I drave on these,
I saw Charybdis supping up the seas, 605
And had gone up together if the tree
That bore the wilde figs had not rescu'd me—
To which I leapt and left my keele, and, hie
Clambring upon it, did as close imply
My brest about it as a Reremouse could. 610
Yet might my feete on no stub fasten hold
To ease my hands, the roots were crept so low
Beneath the earth, and so aloft did grow
The far-spred armes that (though good height I gat)
I could not reach them. To the maine Bole flat 615
I therefore still must cling, till up againe
She belcht my Mast, and after that amaine
My keele came tumbling. So at length it chanc't
To me as to a Judge, that, long advanc't
To judge a sort of hote yong fellowes' jarres, 620
At length time frees him from their civill warres,
When glad he riseth, and to dinner goes:
So time at length releast with joyes my woes,
And from Charybdis' mouth appear'd my keele.
To which (my hand now loosd, and now my heele) 625
I altogether with a huge noise dropt,
Just in her midst fell, where the Mast was propt,
And there rowd off, with owers of my hands.
God and Man's Father would not from her sands
Let Scylla see me, for I then had died 630
That bitter death that my poore friends supplied.
'Nine Daies at Sea I hover'd: the tenth Night
In th'Ile Ogygia, where abode the bright
And right renoum'd Calypso, I was cast
By powre of Deitie—where I liv'd embrac't 635
With Love and feasts. But why should I relate
Those kind occurrents? I should iterate

What I in part to your chaste Queene and you
So late imparted. And for me to grow
A talker over of my tale againe 640
Were past my free contentment to sustaine.'

Finis duodecimi libri Hom. Odyss.

Opus novem dierum.
Σὺν Θεῷ

THE THIRTEENTH BOOKE
of
HOMER'S ODYSSES

THE ARGUMENT

Ulysses (shipt but in the Even,
With all the Presents he was given,
And sleeping then) is set next Morne
In full scope of his wisht returne,
And treads unknown his Country shore, 5
Whose search so many winters wore.
The Ship (returning and arriv'd
Against the City) is depriv'd
Of Forme, and all her motion gone,
Transform'd by Neptune to a stone. 10
Ulysses (let to know the Strand
Where the Phæacians made him Land)
Consults with Pallas for the life
Of every Woer of his Wife.
His Gifts she hides within a Cave, 15
And him into a man more Grave,
All hid in wrinkles, crooked, gray,
Transform'd; who so goes on his way.

Another Argument

Nῦ. *Phæacia*
Ulysses leaves—
Whom Ithaca,
Unwares, receaves.

He said, and silence all their Tongues contain'd
(In admiration) when with pleasure chain'd
Their eares had long bene to him. At last brake
Alcinous silence, and in this sort spake
To th'Ithacensian, Laertes' Sonne: 5

'O Ithacus! How ever over-runne
With former sufferings in your way for home,
Since 'twas, at last, your happy Fate to come
To my high-rooft and Brasse-foundation'd house,
I hope such speede and passe auspicious 10
Our Loves shall yeeld you that you shall no more
Wander, nor suffer, homewards as before.
'You then, whoever that are ever grac'st
With all choise of authoriz'd power to tast
Such wine with me as warmes the sacred Rage, 15
And is an Honorarie given to Age,
With which ye likewise heare Divinely sing
(In Honor's praise) the Poet of the King—
I move, by way of my command, to this:
That where, in an elaborate Chist, there lies 20
A Present for our Guest, Attires of price,
And Gold engraven with infinite device,
I wish that each of us should adde beside
A Tripod and a Caldron, amplified
With size, and Mettall of most rate, and great. 25
For we (in counsaile of taxation met)
Will from our Subjects gaine their worth againe,
Since 'tis unequall one man should sustaine
A charge so waighty, being the grace of all,
Which borne by many is a waight but small.' 30
Thus spake Alcinous, and pleas'd the rest;
When each man clos'd with home and sleep his feast.
But when the colour-giving light arose,
All to the Ship did all their speeds dispose,
And wealth (that honest men makes) broght with them. 35
All which even he that wore the Diadem
Stow'd in the Ship himselfe beneath the seats
The Rowers sate in—stooping, lest their lets
In any of their labors he might prove.
Then home he turn'd, and after him did move 40
The whole assembly to expected Feast.
Amongst whom he a sacrifice addrest,
And slue an Oxe to weather-wielding Jove,
Beneath whose Empire all things are and move.
The thighs then rosting, they made glorious chere, 45
Delighted highly; and amongst them there
The honor'd of the people us'd his voice,
Divine Demodocus. Yet through this choice
Of Cheere and Musicke had Ulysses still

γερούσιος οἶνος—quod pro Honorario senibus datur. *And because the worde so Englisht hath no other to expresse it, sounding wel, and helping our Language, it is here usde.*

Intending in chiefe the Senators, with every man's addition of gift.
εὐήνορα χαλκόν—Bene-honestos-faciens-æs.

An Eye directed to the Easterne hill, 50
To see Him rising that illustrates all—
For now into his minde a fire did fall
Of thirst for home. And as in hungry vow
To needfull food a man at fixed Plow
(To whom the black Oxe all day long hath turn'd 55
The stubborne fallowes up, his stomacke burn'd
With empty heate and appetite to food,
His knees afflicted with his spirit-spent blood)
At length the long-expected Sun-set sees,
That he may sit to foode and rest his knees: 60
So to Ulysses set the friendly light
The Sun affoorded with as wish't a sight.
Who straight bespake that Ore-affecting State,
But did in chiefe his speech appropriate
To him by Name that with their Rule was crown'd: 65

Ulysses to Alcinous.

'Alcinous, of all men most renown'd!
Dismisse me with as safe passe as you vow
(Your offering past), and may the Gods to you
In all contentment use as full a hand:
For now my landing heere and stay shall stand 70
In all perfection with my heart's desire,
Both my so safe deduction to aspire,
And loving gifts; which may the Gods to me
As blest in use make as your acts are free,
Even to the finding firme in love and life, 75
With all desir'd event, my friends and wife—
When, as my selfe shall live delighted there,
May you, with your wives, rest as happy here,
Your Sonnes and Daughters (in particular State)
With every vertue rendred consummate, 80
And in your generall Empire may ill never
Approch your Land, but good your good quit ever.'
This all applauded, and all joyntly cried:
'Dismisse the Stranger: he hath dignified
With fit speech his dismission.' Then the King 85

Alcinous to the Herrald.

Thus charg'd the Herrald: 'Fill for offering
A bowl of wine, which through the whol large house
Dispose to all men, that, propitious
Our Father Jove made with our prayers, we may
Give home our Guest in full and wished way.' 90
This said, Pontonous commixt a Bowle
Of such sweete wine as did delight the soule—
Which making sacred to the blessed Gods

That hold in broad heaven their supreame abodes,
God-like Ulysses from his chaire arose, 95
And in the hands of th'Empresse did impose
The all-round Cup—to whom (faire spoke) he saide:

Ulysses to Arete.

'Rejoyce, O Queene, and be your joyes repaide
By heaven, for me, till age and death succeede—
Both which inflict their most unwelcome neede 100
On Men and Dames alike. And first (for me)
I must from hence to both. Live you heere free,
And ever may all living blessings spring
Your joy in Children, Subjects, and your King.'
This saide, divine Ulysses tooke his way: 105
Before whom the unalterable sway
Of King Alcinous' virtue did command
A Herald's fit attendance to the Strand
And Ship appointed. With him likewise went
Handmaids, by Arete's injunction sent. 110
One bore an Out and In-weede, faire and sweete,
The other an embroider'd Cabinet,
The third had Bread to beare and ruddy wine;
All which (at Sea and Ship arriv'd) resigne
Their Freight confer'd—with faire attendants then 115
The sheets and bedding of the Man of men
Within a Cabin of the hollow Keele
Spred and made soft, that sleepe might sweetly seele
His restfull eyes. He enter'd, and his Bed
In silence tooke. The Rowers ordered 120
Themselves in severall seates, and then set gone
The Ship, the Gable from the hollow stone
Dissolv'd and weigh'd up. Altogether close
Then beate the Sea. His lids in sweete repose

The sound sleepe of Ulysses.
Similitude.

Sleepe bound so fast it scarce gave way to breath, 125
Inexcitable, most deare, next of all to death.
And as amids a faire field foure brave horse
Before a Chariot, stung into their course
With fervent lashes of the smarting Scourge,
That all their fire blowes high and makes them urge 130
To utmost speede the measure of their ground:
So bore the Ship aloft her fiery Bound—
About whom rusht the billowes, blacke and vast,
In which the Sea-roares burst. As firme as fast
She ply'd her Course yet, nor her winged speede 135
The Faulcon gentle could for pace exceede.
So cut she through the waves, and bore a Man

Even with the Gods in counsailes, that began
And spent his former life in all misease,
Battailes of men, and rude waves of the Seas, 140
Yet now securely slept, forgetting all.
And when heaven's brightest star, that first doth call
The early morning out, advanc't her head,
Then neere to Ithaca the Billow-bred
Phæacian Ship approch't. There is a Port 145
That th'aged Sea-God Phorcys makes his Fort,
Whose earth the Ithacensian people owne,
In which two Rockes inaccessible are growne
Farre forth into the Sea, whose each strength binds
The boistrous waves in from the high-flowne winds 150
On both the out-parts so that all within
The well-built Ships, that once their harbour win
In his calme bosome, without Anchor rest
Safe and unstir'd. From forth the haven's high crest
Branch the well-brawn'd armes of an Olive tree; 155
Beneath which runs a Cave from all Sun free,
Coole and delightsome, sacred to th'accesse
Of Nymphs whose sur-names are the Naiades;
In which flew humming Bees, in which lay throwne
Stone cups, Stone vessels, Shittles, all of stone, 160
With which the Nymphs their purple Mantles wove,
In whose contexture Art and wonder strove;
In which pure Springs perpetually ran;
To which two entries were—the one for man
(On which the North breath'd), th'other for the gods 165
(On which the South), and that bore no abodes
For earthy men, but onely deathlesse feete
Had there free way. This Port these men thoght meet
To Land Ulysses, being the first they knew,
Drew then their Ship in, but no further drew 170
Than halfe her bulke reach't, by such cunning hand
Her course was manag'd. Then her men tooke land,
And first brought forth Ulysses, bed and all
That richly furnisht it, he still in thrall
Of all-subduing sleepe. Upon the sand 175
They set him softly downe, and then the Strand
They strew'd with all the goods he had, bestow'd
By the renown'd Phæacians, since he show'd
So much Minerva. At the Olive roote
They drew them then in heape, most far from foote 180
Of any Travailer, least ere his eyes

The description of Phorcys' Haven.

Resum'd their charge they might be others' prize.
These then turn'd home: nor was the sea's supreme
Forgetful of his threats for Polypheme
Bent at divine Ulysses, yet would prove 185
(Ere their performance) the decree of Jove:

Neptune to Jupiter.

'Father! No more the Gods shall honor me,
Since men despise me, and those men that see
The Light in Linage of mine owne lov'd race.

The Phæacians were descended Originally from Neptune.

I vow'd Ulysses should, before the grace 190
Of his returne, encounter woes enow
To make that purchase deare—yet did not vow
Simply against it, since thy Brow had bent
To his reduction in the fore-consent
Thou hadst vouchsaf't it. Yet before my minde 195
Hath full powre on him, the Phæacians finde
Their owne minds' satisfaction with his Passe—
So farre from suffering what my pleasure was
That ease and softnesse now is habited
In his secure brest, and his carelesse head 200
Return'd in peace of sleepe to Ithaca,
The Brasse and Gold of rich Phæacia
Rocking his Temples, Garments richly woven,
And worlds of Prize more than was ever stroven
From all the conflicts he sustain'd at Troy, 205
If safe he should his full share there injoy.'

Jupiter to Neptune.

The Showre-dissolver answerd: 'What a speech
Hath past thy Pallate, O thou great in Reach
Of wrackfull Empire? Farre the Gods remaine
From scorne of thee, for 'twere a worke of paine, 210
To prosecute with ignominies One
That swaies our ablest and most ancient Throne.
For men, if any so beneath in power
Neglect thy high will, now, or any houre
That moves heereafter, take revenge to thee, 215
Soothe all thy will, and be thy pleasure free.'

Neptune to Jupiter.

'Why then,' said he, 'thou blacker of the fumes
That dimme the Sun, my licenst power resumes
Act from thy speech: but I observe so much
And feare thy pleasure, that I dare not touch 220
At any inclination of mine owne
Till thy consenting influence be knowne.
But now, this curious-built Phæacian Ship,
Returning from her Convoy, I will strip
Of all her fleeting matter, and to stone 225

Transforme and fixe it (just when she hath gone
Her full time home, and jets before their prease
In all her trim) amids the Sable Seas—
That they may cease to convoy strangers still,
When they shall see so like a mighty Hill 230
Their glory sticke before their Citie's grace,
And my hands cast a maske before her face.'
'O friend,' said Jove, 'it shewes to me the best
Of al earth's objects, that their whole prease, drest
In all their wonder, neere their Towne shall stand 235
And stare upon a Stone, so neere the Land,
So like a Ship, and dam up all their lights
As if a Mountaine interposde their sights.'
When Neptune heard this, he for Scheria went,
Whence the Phæacians tooke their first descent. 240
Which when he reacht, and in her swiftest pride
The water-treader by the Citie's side
Came cutting close, close he came swiftly on,
Tooke her in violent hand, and to a Stone
Turnd all her sylvane substance, all below 245
Firmd her with Rootes and left her. This strange show
When the Phæacians saw, they stupid stood,
And askt each other who amids the flood
Could fixe their Ship so in her full speed home,
And quite transparant make her bulke become? 250
Thus talkt they, but were farre from knowing how
These things had issue. Which their King did show,
And saide: 'O friends, the ancient Prophesies
My Father told to me to all our eyes
Are now in proofe: he saide the time would come 255
When Neptune, for our safe conducting home
All sorts of Strangers (out of envy fir'd)
Would meete our fairest Ship as she retir'd,
And all the goodly Shape and speed we bost
Should like a Mountaine stand before us lost 260
Amids the moving waters—which we see
Perform'd in full end to our prophesie.
Heare then my counsaile, and obey me then:
Renounce henceforth our convoy home of men,
Who ever shall heereafter greete our Towne; 265
And to th'offended Deitie's Renowne
Twelve chosen Oxen let us sacred make,
That he may pitty us, and from us take
This shady Mountaine.' They in feare obaide,

ἀμφικαλύπτω—
Superinijcio aliquid
tanquam tegmen seu
operimentum.

Alcinous tels his people how the Ship became a Stone.

Slew all the Beeves, and to the Godhead praide, 270
The Dukes and Princes all enspearing round
The sacred Altar. While whose Tops were croun'd,
Divine Ulysses (on his Countrie's brest
Laid bound in sleepe) now rose out of his rest,
Nor (being so long remov'd) the Region knew. 275
Besides which absence yet, Minerva threw
A cloud about him, to make strange the more
His safe arrivall, lest upon his Shore
He should make knowne his face and utter all
That might prevent th'event that was to fall— 280
Which she prepar'd so well that not his wife
(Presented to him) should perceive his life,
No Citizen, no Friend, till righteous Fate
Upon the wooers' wrongs were consummate.
Through which cloud all things show'd now to the King 285
Of forreign fashion—the enflowred Spring
Amongst the Trees there, the perpetuall wayes,
The Rockes, that did more high their foreheads raise
To his Rapt eye than naturally they did,
And all the Haven, in which a man seem'd hid 290
From winde and weather when storms loudest chid.

He therefore, being risen, stood and viewd
His countrey earth: which (not perceiv'd) he rew'd,
And, striking with his hurld-downe hands his Thyes,
He mourn'd, and saide: 'O me! Againe where lyes 295
My desart way? To wrongfull men, and rude,
And with no Lawes of humane right indu'de?
Or are they humane, and of holy minds?
What fits my deede with these so many kinds
Of goods late given? What with my selfe wil floods 300
And Errors do? I would to God these Goods
Had rested with their Owners, and that I
Had falne on Kings of more Regality
To grace out my returne, that lov'd indeed,
And would have given me Consorts of fit speed 305
To my distresses' ending! But as now
All knowledge flyes me where I may bestow
My labour'd purchase, heere they shall not stay,
Lest what I car'd for others make their prey.
O Gods! I see the great Phæacians then 310
Were not all just and understanding men,
That land me elsewhere than their vants pretended,
Assuring me my countrey should see ended

My miseries told them, yet now eate their vants.
O Jove! great Guardian of poore Suppliants, 315
That others sees and notes too, shutting in
All in thy plagues that most presume on Sin,
Revenge me on them. Let me number now
The goods they gave, to give my minde to know
If they have stolne none in their close retreat.' 320
The goodly Caldrons then and Tripods (set
In severall rankes from out the heape) he told,
His rich wrought garments too, and all his Gold:
And nothing lack't—and yet this Man did mourne
The but supposd misse of his home returne. 325
And, creeping to the shore with much complaint,
Minerva (like a Shepheard, yong and quaint,
As Kings' sonnes are, a double Mantle cast
Athwart his Shoulders, his faire goers grac'st
With fitted shooes, and in his hand a Dart) 330
Appear'd to him whose sight rejoyc't his hart,
To whom he came, and saide: 'O Friend! Since first
I meete your sight heere, be all good the worst
That can joyne our encounter. Fare you Faire,
Nor with adverse minde welcome my repaire, 335
But guard these goods of mine, and succour me.
As to a God I offer prayers to thee,
And low accesse make to thy loved knee.
Say truth, that I may know, what countrey then,
What commune people live heere, and what men? 340
Some famous Isle is this? Or gives it vent
(Being neere the Sea) to some rich Continent?'
She answer'd: 'Stranger, what so ere you are,
Y'are either foolish or come passing farre,
That know not this Isle, and make that doubt troble, 345
For 'tis not so exceedingly ignoble
But passing many know it, and so many
That of all Nations there abides not any,
From where the Morning rises and the Sun,
To where the Even and Night their courses run, 350
But know this countrey. Rocky 'tis, and rough,
And so for use of horse unapt enough,
Yet with sad Barrennesse not much infested
Since clowds are heere in frequent raines digested
And flowry dewes. The compasse is not great, 355
The little yet well fild with wine and wheat.
It feeds a Goat and Oxe well, being still

Minerva like a Shepheard (such as Kings' sonnes usde at those times to be) appears to Ulysses.

Pallas to Ulysses.

λυπρός—Velut tristis jejunaque natura.

Water'd with floods that ever over-fill
With heaven's continual showers, and wooded so
It makes a Spring of all the kindes that grow. 360
And therefore, Stranger, the extended name
Of this Dominion makes accesse by Fame
From this extreame part of Achaia
As farre as Ilion; and 'tis Ithaca.'
This joy'd him much, that so unknowne a Land 365
Turn'd to his countrey. Yet so wise a hand
He carried, even of this joy flowne so hye,
That other end he put to his reply
Than straight to shew that joy, and lay abrode
His life to Strangers. Therefore he bestowd 370
A veile on Truth. For evermore did winde
About his bosome a most crafty minde,
Ulysses to Pallas. Which thus his words shew'd: 'I have farre at Sea,
In spacious Crete, heard speake of Ithaca,
Of which my selfe (it seemes) now reach the shore 375
With these my Fortunes—whose whole value more
I left in Crete amongst my children there,
From whence I flye for being the slaughterer
Of royall Idomen's most loved Son,
Swift-foote Orsilochus, that could out-run 380
Profest men for the race. Yet him I slue,
Because he would deprive me of my due
In Troyan prize: for which I suffer'd so
(The rude waves piercing) the redoubled wo
Of minde and body in the warres of men: 385
Nor did I gratifie his Father then
With any service, but as well as he
Sway'd in command of other Souldiery.
So, with a friend withdrawne, we way-laide him
When gloomy Night the cope of heaven did dim, 390
And no man knew. But (we lodg'd close) he came,
And I put out to him his vitall flame—
Whose slaughter having author'd with my sword,
I instant flight made, and straight fell aboord
A Ship of the renown'd Phœnician State, 395
When prayer and pay at a sufficient rate
Obtain'd my Passe of men in her command,
Whom I injoyn'd to set me on the land
Of Pylos, or of Elis the divine,
Where the Epeians in great Empire shine. 400
But force of weather check't that course to them,

Though (loath to faile me) to their most extreme
They spent their willing pow'rs. But, forc't from thence,
We err'd, and put in heere with much expence
Of Care and Labour, and in dead of Night, 405
When no man there serv'd any appetite
So much as with the Memory of food,
Though our estates exceeding Needy stood.
But, going ashore, we lay; when gentle sleepe
My weary pow'rs invaded, and from Ship 410
They, fetching these my Riches, with just hand
About me laide them, while upon the sand
Sleepe bound my senses; and for Sidon they
(Put off from hence) made saile, while heere I lay,
Left sad alone.' The Goddesse laught, and tooke 415
His hand in hers, and with another looke
(Assuming then the likenesse of a Dame
Lovely and goodly, expert in the frame
Of vertuous Huswiferies) she answerd thus:

Pallas to Ulysses.

'He should be passing slie, and covetous 420
Of stealth in men's deceits that coted thee
In any craft, though any God should be
Ambitious to exceede in subtilty.

ἐπίκλοπος—
furandi avidus.

Σχέτλιε,
ποκιλομῆτα—
varia et multiplicia
habens consilia.

Thou still-wit-varying wretch! Insatiate
In over-reaches! Not secure thy state 425
Without these wiles, though on thy Native shore
Thou setst safe footing, but upon thy store
Of false words still spend, that even from thy byrth
Have bene thy best friends? Come: our either worth
Is knowne to either. Thou of Men art far 430
(For words and counsailes) the most singular,
But I above the Gods in both may bost
My still-tried Faculties. Yet thou hast lost
The knowledge even of me, the seede of Jove,
Pallas Athenia, that have still out-strove 435
In all thy Labors their extremes, and stood
Thy sure guard ever, making all thy good
Knowne to the good Phæacians, and receiv'd.
And now againe I greete thee, to see weav'd
Fresh Counsailes for thee, and will take on me 440
The close reserving of these goods for thee,
Which the renown'd Phæacian States bestow'd
At thy deduction homewards, onely mov'd
With my both spirit and counsell. All which grace
I now will amplifie, and tell what case 445

Thy houshold stands in, uttering all those paines
That of meere need yet still must racke thy vaines.
Do thou then freely beare, nor one word give
To Man nor Dame to shew thou yet dost live,
But silent suffer over all againe 450
Thy sorrowes past, and beare the wrongs of Men.'

Ulysses to Pallas.

'Goddesse,' said he, 'unjust men and unwise,
That author injuries and vanities,
By vanities and wrongs should rather be
Bound to this ill-abearing destiny 455
Than just and wise men. What delight hath heaven,
That lives unhurt it selfe, to suffer given
Up to all domage those poore few that strive
To imitate it and like the Deities live?
But where you wonder that I know you not 460
Through all your changes, that skill is not got
By sleight or Art, since thy most hard-hit face
Is still distinguisht by thy free-given grace.
And therefore truly to acknowledge thee
In thy encounters is a maistery 465
In men most knowing. For to all men thou
Tak'st severall likenesse. All men thinke they know
Thee in their wits. But, since thy seeming view
Appeares to all and yet thy truth to few,
Through all thy changes to discern thee right 470
Askes chiefe Love to thee, and inspired light.
But this I surely know—that some yeares past
I have beene often with thy presence grac'st,
All time the sonnes of Greece wag'd warre at Troy;
But when Fate's full houre let our swords enjoy 475
Our vowes in sacke of Priam's lofty Towne,
Our Ships all boorded, and when God had blowne
Our Fleete in sunder, I could never see
The seede of Jove, nor once distinguish thee
Boording my Ship to take one woe from me— 480
But onely in my proper spirit involv'd,
Err'd here and there quite slaine, til heaven dissolv'd
Me and my ill: which chanc't not, till thy grace
By open speech confirm'd me, in a place
Fruitfull of people, where, in person, thou 485
Didst give me guide and all their City show;
And that was the renown'd Phæacian earth.
Now then, even by the author of thy Birth,
Vouchsafe my doubt the Truth (for farre it flies

My thoughts, that thus should fall into mine eies 490
Conspicuous Ithaca, but feare I touch
At some farre Shore, and that thy wit is such
Thou dost delude me). Is it sure the same
Most honor'd earth that beares my countrie's name?'
'I see,' sayd she, 'thou wilt be ever thus 495
In every worldly good incredulous,
And therefore have no more the power to see
Fraile life more plagu'd with infelicity
In one so eloquent, ingenious, wise.
Another man, that so long miseries 500
Had kept from his lov'd home, and thus return'd
To see his house, wife, children, would have burn'd
In headlong lust to visit. Yet t'enquire
What states they hold affects not thy desire,
Till thou hast tried if in thy wife there be 505
A Sorrow, wasting dayes and nights for thee
In Loving teares, that then the sight may prove
A full reward for either's mutuall Love.
But I would never credit in you both
Least cause of sorrow, but well knew the troth 510
Of this thine owne returne, though all thy Friends,
I knew as well, should make returnlesse ends—
Yet would not crosse mine Unkle Neptune so
To stand their safeguard, since so high did go
His wrath for thy extinction of the eye 515
Of his lov'd sonne. Come then, I'le shew thee why
I call this Isle thy Ithaca. To ground
Thy credit on my words—this haven is own'd
By th'aged Sea god Phorcys, in whose Brow
This is the Olive with the ample bow, 520
And heere, close by, the pleasant-shaded Cave
That to the Fount-Nymphs th'Ithacensians gave
As Sacred to their pleasures. Heere doth run
The large and cover'd den where thou hast done
Hundreds of Offerings to the Naiades. 525
Here Mount Neritus shakes his curled Tresse
Of shady woods.' This sayd, she cleer'd the clowd
That first deceyv'd his eyes, and all things show'd
His countrey to him. Glad he stood with sight
Of his lov'd Soile, and kist it with delight. 530
And instantly to all the Nymphs hee paide
(With hands held up to heaven) these vowes, and said:
'Ye Nymphs the Naiades, great seed of Jove,

I had conceite that never more should move
Your sight in these spheres of my erring eyes; 535
And therefore, in the fuller Sacrifice
Of my heart's gratitude, rejoyce, till more
I pay your Names in Offerings as before.
Which heere I vow, if Jove's benigne descent
(The mighty Pillager) with life convent 540
My person home and to my sav'd decease
Of my lov'd sonne's sight adde the sweet increase.'
'Be confident,' saide Pallas, 'nor oppresse
Thy spirits with care of these performances;
But these thy fortunes let us straight repose 545
In this divine Cave's bosome, that may close
Reserve their value, and we then may see
How best to order other acts to thee.'
Thus entred she the light-excluding Cave,
And through it sought some inmost nooke to save 550
The Gold, the great Brasse, and robes richly wrought,
Given to Ulysses. All which in he brought,
Laid downe in heape, and she impos'd a stone
Close to the caverne's mouth. Then sat they on
The sacred Olive's roote, consulting how 555
To act th'insulting wooers' overthrow—
When Pallas saide: 'Examine now the means
That best may lay hand on the impudence
Of those proud wooers, that have now three yeares
Thy Roofe's rule swai'd and bene bold Offerers 560
Of suite and gifts to thy renowned wife—
Who for thy absence all her desolate life
Dissolves in teares till thy desir'd returne.
Yet all her wooers, while shee thus doth mourne,
She holds in hope, and every one affords 565
(In fore-sent message) promise. But her words
Beare other utterance than her heart approves.'
'O Gods,' said Ithacus, 'it now behoves
My Fate to end me in the ill deceasse
That Agamemnon underwent, unlesse 570
You tell me, and in time, their close intents.
Advise then meanes to the reveng'd events
We both resolve on. Be thy selfe so kinde
To stand close to me, and but such a minde
Breath in my bosome as when th'Ilian Towres 575
We tore in Cinders. O if equall powres
Thou wouldst enflame amids my Nerves as then,

I could encounter with three hundred men—
Thy onely selfe, great Goddesse, had to friend
In those brave ardors thou wer't wont t'extend.' 580
'I will be strongly with thee,' answer'd she,
'Nor must thou faile, but do thy part with me—
When both whose pow'rs combine, I hope the bloods
And braines of some of these that waste thy goods
Shall strew thy goodly Pavements. Joyne we then: 585
I first will render thee unknowne to men,
And on thy solid Lineaments make dry
Thy now smooth skin, thy bright-brown curles imply
In hoary mattings, thy broad shoulders cloath
In such a cloake as every eye shall loath, 590
Thy bright eyes bleare and wrinkle—and so change
Thy forme at all parts that thou shalt be strange
To all the Wooers, thy yong sonne, and wife.
But to thy Herdsman first present thy life,
That guards thy Swine and wisheth well to thee, 595
That loves thy sonne and wife Penelope.
Thy search shall finde him set aside his Heard,
That are with tast-delighting Acornes rear'd
And drinke the darke-deepe water of the Spring
Bright Arethusa, the most nourishing 600
Raiser of Heards. There stay, and (taking seate
Aside thy Heardsman) of the whole State treate
Of home occurrents, while I make accesse
To faire-dame-breeding Sparta for regresse
Of lov'd Telemachus, who went in quest 605
Of thy lov'd fame and liv'd the welcome Guest
Of Menelaus.' The much-knower saide:
'Why wouldst not thou (in whose grave brest is bred
The Art to order all acts) tell in this
His error to him? Let those yeares of his 610
Amids the rude seas wander and sustaine
The woes there raging, while unworthy men
Devoure his fortunes?' 'Let not care extend
Thy heart for him,' said she, 'my selfe did send
His person in thy search, to set his worth 615
(By good fame blowne) to such a distance forth.
Nor suffers he in any least degree
The griefe you feare, but all variety
That Plenty can yeeld in her quietst fare
In Menelaus' Court doth sit and share. 620
In whose returne from home the Wooers yet

Σπάρτην ἐς καλλιγύναικα.

Lay bloudy ambush, and a Ship have set
To Sea to intercept his life before
He touch againe his birth's attempted shore.
All which my thoughts say they shall never do, 625
But rather that the earth shall overgo
Some one at least of these Love-making men
By which thy goods so much empaire sustain.'
Thus using certaine secret words to him,
She toucht him with her rod, and every lim 630
Was hid all over with a wither'd skin,
His bright eies blear'd, his brown curles white and thin,
And all things did an aged man present.
Then (for his owne weeds) Shirt and coat all rent,
Tann'd, and all sootied with noisome smoke, 635
She put him on, and, over all, a cloke
Made of a Stag's huge hide of which was worne
The haire quite off, a scrip all patcht and torne,
Hung by a cord oft broke and knit againe,
And with a staffe did his old limbes sustaine. 640
Thus, having both consulted of th'event,
They parted both: and forth to Sparta went
The gray-ey'd Goddesse, to see all things done
That appertain'd to wise Ulysses' sonne.

The End of the Thirteenth Booke of Homer's Odysses

THE FOURTEENTH BOOKE
of
HOMER'S ODYSSES

THE ARGUMENT

Ulysses meets amids the Field
His Swaine Eumæus; who doth yeild
Kinde Guest-rites to him, and relate
Occurrents of his wrong'd estate.

Another Argument

Ξι. *Ulysses faines*
for his true Good:
His pious Swaine's
faith understood.

But he the rough way tooke from forth the Port
Through woods and hill tops, seeking the resort
Where Pallas said divine Eumæus liv'd:
Who of the fortunes that were first atchiev'd
By God-like Ithacus in houshold rights, 5
Had more true care than all his Prosylites.
He found him sitting in his Cottage dore,
Where he had rais'd to every ayry Blore
A Front of great height, and in such a place
That round ye might behold of circular grace 10
A walke so wound about it, which the Swain
(In absence of his farre-gone Soveraine)
Had built himselfe, without his Queene's supply
Or old Laertes', to see safely lye
His housed herd. The inner part he wrought 15
Of stones, that thither his owne labors brought,
Which with an hedge of Thorn he fenc't about
And compast all the hedge with pales cleft out
Of sable Oake, that here and there he fixt

προσυλος—materiæ adhærens: Item, qui rebus Mundanis deditus est.

Frequent and thicke. Within his yard he mixt 20
Twelve Sties to lodge his Heard, and every Sty
Had roome and use for fifty Swine to lye—
But those were females all. The male Swine slept
Without doores ever. Nor was their Herd kept
Faire like the Females, since they suffer'd still 25
Great diminution, he being forc't to kill
And send the fattest to the dainty Feasts
Affected by th'ungodly wooing guests.
Their number, therefore, but three hundred were
And sixty. By them Mastives as austere 30
As savage beasts lay ever, their fierce straine
Bred by the Herdsman, a meere Prince of Men:
Their number, foure. Himselfe was then appli'de
In cutting forth a faire hew'd Oxe's hide,
To fit his feete with shooes. His servants held 35
Guard of his Swine—three here and there at field,
The fourth he sent to City with a Sow,
Which must of force be offer'd to the Vow
The Woowers made to all saciety,
To serve which still they did those Offrings ply. 40

ὑλακόμωρος—
Ad latrandum fato
quodam Natus.

The Fate-borne-Dogs-to-Barke tooke sodaine view
Of Odysseus, and upon him flew
With open mouth. He (cunning to appall
A fierce Dog's fury) from his hand let fall
His staffe to earth, and sat him carelesse downe. 45
And yet to him had one foule wrong bene showne
Where most his Right lay, had not instantly
The Herdsman let his hide fall, and his cry
(With frequent stones flung at the dogges) repeld
This way and that their eager course they held— 50
When, through the entry past, he thus did mourne:

Eumæus to Ulysses.

'O Father! How soone had you neere bene torne
By these rude Dogges—whose hurt had branded me
With much neglect of you! But Deity
Hath given so many other sighes and cares 55
To my attendant state that well unwares
You might be hurt for me: for heere I lie
Grieving and mourning for the Majestie
That God-like wonted to be ruling heere,
Since now I fat his Swine for others' cheere, 60
Where he, perhaps, errs hungry up and downe
In Countries, Nations, Cities, all unknowne,
If any where he lives yet and doth see

The Sunne's sweet beames. But, Father, follow mee,
That (cheer'd with wine and foode) you may disclose 65
From whence you truly are, and all the woes
Your age is subject to.' This said, he led
Into his Cottage, and of Osiers spred
A thickned hurdle, on whose top he strow'd
A wilde Goat's shaggy skin, and then bestow'd 70
His owne Couch on it, that was soft and great.
Ulysses joy'd to see him so entreat
His uncouth Presence, saying: 'Jove requite,
And all th'immortall Gods, with that delight
Thou most desir'st thy kinde receite of me, 75
O Friend to humane Hospitality!'
Eumæus answer'd: 'Guest! If one much wurse
Arriv'd here than thy selfe, it were a curse
To my poore meanes to let a Stranger tast
Contempt for fit food. Poore men, and unplac'st 80
In free seats of their owne, are all from Jove
Commended to our entertaining Love.
But poore is th'entertainment I can give,
Yet free and loving. Of such men as live
The lives of servants and are still in feare 85
Where yong Lords governe, this is all the cheare
They can affoord a Stranger. There was One
That usde to manage this now desart Throne,
To whom the Gods deny returne, that show'd
His curious favour to me and bestow'd 90
Possessions on me, a most wished wife,
A house, and portion, and a Servant's life
Fit for the gift a gracious King should give—
Who still tooke pains himselfe; and God made thrive
His personall endevour, and to me 95
His worke the more increast, in which you see
I now am conversant. And therefore much
His hand had help't me, had heaven's wil beene such
He might have heere growne old. But he is gone,
And would to God the whole succession 100
Of Helen might go with him, since for her
So many men di'de, whose Fate did confer
My Liege to Troy in Agamemnon's grace,
To spoile her People and her Turrets race.'
This said, his coate to him he streight did gird 105
And to his Sties went, that contain'd his Herd—
From whence he tooke out two, slew both, and cut

Both fairely up, a fire enflam'd, and put
To spit the joynts; which, roasted well, he set
With spit and all to him, that he might eat 110
From thence his food in all the sindging heat.
Yet dreg'd it first with Flowre: then fil'd his Cup
With good sweet wine, sate then, and cheard him up.
'Eate now, my guest, such leane Swine as are meate
For us poore Swaines. The fat the wooers eate— 115
In whose minds no shame, no remorse, doth move,
Though well they know the blest Gods doe not love
Ungodly actions, but respect the right,
And in the workes of pious men delight.
But these are worse than impious: for those 120
That vow t'injustice, and professe them foes
To other Nations, enter on their Land,
And Jupiter (to shew his punishing hand
Upon th'invaded, for their pennance then)
Gives favour to their foes (though wicked men) 125
To make their prey on them—who, having freight
Their ships with spoile enough, weigh ancor streight
And each man to his house (and yet even these
Doth powrefull feare of God's just vengeance seize
Even for that prize in which they so rejoyce): 130
But these men, knowing (having heard the voyce
Of God by some meanes) that sad Death hath reft
The Ruler heere, will never suffer left
Their unjust wooing of his wife, nor take
Her often answere, and their owne Roofes make 135
Their fit retreats, but (since uncheck't they may)
They therefore wil make still his goods their pray
Without all spare or end. There is no day
Nor night sent out from God that ever they
Prophane with one beast's blood, or onely two, 140
But more make spoile of; and the wrongs they do
In meate's excesse to Wine as well extend,
Which as excessively their ryots spend,
Yet still leave store. For sure his meanes were great,
And no Heroe that hath choisest seate 145
Upon the fruitfull neighbour Continent
Or in this Isle it selfe so opulent
Was as Ulysses—no, nor twenty such
Put altogether did possesse so much.

Ulysses' Wealth. 'Whose Herds and Flockes I'le tell to every Head: 150
Upon the Continent he daily fed

Twelve Herds of Oxen, no lesse Flockes of Sheepe,
As many Herds of Swine, Stals large and steepe,
And equall sort of Goats, which Tenants there
And his owne Sheepherds kept. Then fed he here 155
Eleven faire stalles of Goats, whose food hath yeilde
In the extreame part of a neighbor Field.
Each Stall his Herdsman hath, an honest Swaine,
Yet every one must every day sustaine
The load of one Beast (the most fat and best 160
Of all the Stall-fed) to the Woers' Feast.
And I (for my part) of the Swine I keepe
(With foure more Herdsmen) every day help steep
The Wooers' appetites in blood of one,
The most select our choise can fall upon.' 165

Ulysses incenst against the wooers, with newes of their spoyle.

To this Ulysses gave good eare, and fed,
And drunke his wine, and vext, and ravished
His food for meere vexation. Seeds of ill
His Stomacke sow'd, to heare his goods go still
To glut of wooers. But his dinner done 170
And Stomacke fed to satisfaction,
He drunke a full Bowle all of onely wine,
And gave it to the Guardian of his Swine,
Who tooke it, and rejoyc't. To whom he said:
'O Friend, who is it that (so rich) hath paid 175
Price for thy service, whose commended pow'r,
Thou sayst (to grace the Grecian Conquerour)
At Ilion perisht? Tell me; it may fall
I knew some such. The great God knowes, and all
The other deathlesse Godheads, if I can 180
(Farre having travail'd) tell of such a man.'

Eumæus answer'd: 'Father, never one
Of all the Strangers that have touch't upon
This Coast with his life's Newes could ever yet
Of Queene, or lov'd sonne, any credit get. 185
These Travailers, for cloathes or for a meale,
At all adventures any lye will tell.
Nor do they trade for truth: not any man
That saw the people Ithacensian
Of all their sort, and had the Queene's supplies, 190
Did ever tell her any newes but lies.
She graciously receives them yet, enquires
Of all she can, and all in teares expires.
It is th'accustom'd Law that women keepe,
Their husbands elsewhere dead, at home to weepe. 195

But do thou quickly, Father, forge a Tale;
Some Coat or cloake to keepe thee warme withall
Perhaps some one may yeeld thee. But for him,
Vultures and Dogges have torne from every lim
His porous skin, and forth his soule is fled, 200
His coarse at Sea to Fishes forfeited,
Or on the Shore lies hid in heapes of sand;
And there hath he his ebbe, his Native Strand
With friends' teares flowing. But to me past all
Were teares created. For I never shall 205
Finde so humane a royall Mayster more,
What ever Sea I seeke, what ever Shore.
Nay, to my Father or my Mother's love
Should I returne, by whom I breath and move,
Could I so much joy offer; nor these eyes 210
(Though my desires sustaine extremities
For their sad absence) would so faine be blest
With sight of their lives, in my native Nest,
As with Ulysses dead: in whose last rest,
O friend, my soule shall love him. Hee's not here, 215
Nor do I name him like a Flatterer,
But as one thankfull for his Love and care
To me a poore man, in the rich so rare.
And be he past all shores where Sun can shine,
I will invoke him as a soule divine.' 220
'O Friend,' sayd he, 'to say and to beleeve
He cannot live doth too much license give
To incredulity. For (not to speake
At needy randon, but my breath to breake
In sacred Oath) Ulysses shall returne. 225
And when his sight recomforts those that mourne
In his owne roofes, then give me cloake and cote
And garments worthy of a man of note.
Before which, though neede urg'd me never so
I'le not receive a thred, but naked go. 230
No lesse I hate him than the gates of hell
That poorenesse can force an untruth to tell.
Let Jove then (heaven's chiefe God) just witnes beare,
And this thy hospitable Table heere,
Together with unblam'd Ulysses' house, 235
In which I finde receipt so gracious,
What I affirm'd of him shall all be true.
This instant yeare thine eyes even heere shall view
Thy Lord Ulysses. Nay, ere this moneth's end

(Return'd full home) he shall revenge extend 240
To every one whose ever deed hath done
Wrong to his wife and his illustrous Sonne.'
'O Father,' he replied, 'I'le neither give
Thy newes reward, nor doth Ulysses live.
But come, enough of this; let's drinke and eate, 245
And never more his memory repeate.
It greeves my heart to be remembred thus
By any one of one so glorious.
But stand your oath in your assertion strong,
And let Ulysses come, for whom I long, 250
For whom his wife, for whom his aged Sire,
For whom his Son consumes his God-like fire,
Whose chance I now must mourne, and ever shall—
Whom when the Gods had brought to be as tall
As any upright plant, and I had saide 255
He would amongst a Court of men have swaide
In counsailes, and for forme have bene admir'd
Even with his Father, some God misinspir'd,
Or man tooke from him his owne equall minde,
And past him for the Pylian Shore, to finde 260
His long-lost Father. In returne from whence
The Wooers' pride way-layes his innocence,
That of divine Arcesius all the race
May fade to Ithaca, and not the grace
Of any Name left to it. But leave we 265
His state, however, if surpriz'd he be,
Or if he scape. And may Saturnius' hand
Protect him safely to his native Land.
Do you then, Father, shew your griefes and cause
Of your arrivall heere; nor breake the Lawes 270
That Truth prescribes you, but relate your name,
And of what race you are, your Father's fame
And native Citie's; Ship and men unfold
That to this Isle convaid you, since I hold
Your heere arrivall was not all by shore, 275
Nor that your feete your aged person bore.'
He answer'd him: 'I'le tell all strictly true,
If time and foode and wine enough acrue
Within your roofe to us, that freely we
May sit and banquet. Let your businesse be 280
Discharg'd by others. For, when all is done,
I can not easly, while the yeare doth runne
His circle round, run over all the woes

Beneath which (by the course the Gods dispose)
My sad age labours. First, I'le tell you, then, 285
From ample Crete I fetch my Native straine;
My Father wealthy, whose house many a life
Brought forth and bred besides by his true wife—
But me a Bond-maid bore, his Concubine.
Yet tender'd was I as his lawfull line 290
By him, of whose race I my life profes.
Castor his name, surnam'd Hylacides,
A man in fore-times by the Cretan State,
For goods, good children, and his fortunate
Successe in all acts, of no meane esteem. 295
But death-conferring Fates have banisht him
To Pluto's kingdome. After whom, his sons
By Lots divided his possessions
And gave me passing little, yet bestow'd
A house on me, to which my vertues woo'd 300
A wife from rich men's roofes—nor was borne low,
Nor last in sight, though all Nerves faile me now.
But I suppose that you by thus much seene
Know by the stubble what the Corne hath bene.
For past all doubt affliction past all meane 305
Hath brought my age on; but, in seasons past
Both Mars and Pallas have with boldnesse grac'st,
And Fortitude, my fortunes; when I chus'd
Choise men for ambush, prest to have produc'd
Ill to mine enemies, my too ventrous spirit 310
Set never death before mine eyes for merit.
But (farre the first advanc't still) still I strooke
Dead with my Lance whoever overtooke
My speed of foot. Such was I then for warre.
But rusticke actions ever fled me farre 315
And houshold thrift, which breeds a famous race.
In Ore-driven Ships did I my pleasures place,
In Battailes, light Darts, Arrowes—sad things all,
And into others' thoughts with horror fall.
'But what God put into my minde, to me 320
I still esteem'd as my felicity.
As men of severall Mettals are addrest,
So severall formes are in their soules imprest.
'Before the sonnes of Greece set foot in Troy,
Nine times in Chiefe I did Command enjoy 325
Of Men and Ships against our forreigne foe,
And all I fitly wish't succeeded so.

Yet after this I much exploit atchiev'd—
When straight my house in all possessions thriv'd.
Yet, after that, I great and Reverend grew 330
Amongst the Cretans, till the Thunderer drew
Our Forces out in his foe-Troy decrees,
A hatefull service, that dissolv'd the knees
Of many a Soldier. And to this was I
And famous Idomen enjoyn'd t'apply 335
Our ships and pow'rs. Nor was there to be heard
One reason for deniall, so prefer'd
Was the unreasonable people's rumor.
Nine yeares we therefore fed the martiall humor,
And in the tenth (de-peopling Priam's Towne) 340
We sail'd for home. But God had quickly blowne
Our Fleete in peeces, and to wretched mee
The Counsailor Jove did much mishap decree.
For onely one month I had leave t'enjoy
My wife and children, and my goods t'employ. 345
But, after this, my minde for Egypt stoode,
When nine faire ships I rig'd forth for the flood,
Mann'd them with noble souldiers; all things fit
For such a voyage soone were won to it.
Yet sixe dayes after staid my friends in feast, 350
While I in banquets to the Gods addrest
Much sacred matter for their sacrifice.
The seaventh, we boorded, and the Northerne skies
Lent us a franke and passing prosperous gale,
Fore which we bore as free and easie saile 355
As we had back't a full and frolicke tide;
Nor felt one Ship misfortune for her pride,
But safe we sat, our Sailors and the winde
Consenting in our convoy. When heaven shin'de
In sacred radiance of the fift faire day, 360
To sweetly-water'd Egypt reach't our way,
And there we anchor'd, where I charg'd my men
To stay aboord, and watch. Dismissing then
Some scouts to get the hill-tops and discover,
They (to their owne intemperance given over) 365
Straight fell to forrage the rich fields, and thence
Enforce both wives and infants, with th'expence
Of both their bloods. When straight the rumor flew
Up to the City: (which heard) up they drew
By daie's first breake, and all the field was fild 370
With foot and horse, whose Armes did all things gild.

And then the Lightning-loving Deity cast
A foule flight on my soldiers, nor stood fast
One man of all. About whom Mischiefe stood,
And with his stern steele drew in streames the blood 375
The greater part fed in their dissolute vaines;
The rest were sav'd and made enthralled Swaines
To all the basest usages there bred.
And then even Jove himselfe supplyed my head
With saving counsaile; (though I wisht to dye, 380
And there in Egypt with their slaughters lye,
So much griefe seiz'd me) but Jove made me yeild,
Dishelme my head, take from my necke my shield,
Hurle from my hand my Lance, and to the troop
Of horse the King led instantly made up, 385
Embrace and kisse his knees—whom pitty wun
To give me safety, and (to make me shun
The people's outrage, that made in amaine,
All joyntly fir'd with thirst to see me slaine)
He tooke me to his Chariot, weeping, home— 390
Himselfe with feare of Jove's wrath overcome,
Who yeelding soules receives, and takes most ill
All such as well may save yet love to kill.
Seven yeares I sojourn'd heere, and treasure gat
In good abundance of th'Egyptian state, 395
For all would give. But when th'eight yeare began,
A knowing Fellow (that would gnaw a man
Like to a Vermine with his hellish braine,
And many an honest soule even quicke had slaine,
Whose name was Phœnix) close accosted me, 400
And with insinuations such as he
Practis'd on others my consent he gain'd
To go into Phœnicia, where remain'd
His house and living. And with him I liv'd
A compleat yeare. But, when were all arriv'd 405
The months and daies and that the yeare againe
Was turning round and every season's raigne
Renew'd upon us, we for Libya went;
When (still inventing crafts to circumvent)
He made pretext that I should onely go 410
And helpe convey his freight; but thought not so,
For his intent was to have sold me there
And made good gaine, for finding me a yeare.
Yet him I follow'd, though suspecting this,
For, being aboord his Ship, I must be his 415

'Ανὴρ ἀπατήλια εἰδώς, τρώκτης.

Of strong Necessity. She ran the flood
(Driven with a Northerne gale, right free and good)
Amids the full streame, full on Crete. But then
Jove plotted death to him and all his men.
For (put off quite from Crete, and so farre gone 420
That Shore was lost, and we set eye on none,
But all shew'd heaven and sea) above our Keele
Jove pointed right a cloud as blacke as hell—
Beneath which all the sea hid, and from whence
Jove thunder'd as his hand would never thence. 425
And thicke into our Ship he threw his flash,
That 'gainst a Rocke or Flat her Keele did dash
With headlong Rapture. Of the sulphure all
Her bulke did savour, and her men let fall
Amids the Surges, on which all lay tost 430
Like Sea-guls round about her sides, and lost.
And so God tooke all home-returne from them.
But Jove himselfe (though plung'd in that extream)
Recover'd me, by thrusting on my hand
The Ship's long Mast. And (that my life might stand 435
A little more up) I embrac't it round,
And on the rude windes, that did ruines sound,
Nine dayes we hover'd. In the tenth blacke night
A huge Sea cast me on Thesprotia's height,
Where the Heroe Pheidon, that was chiefe 440
Of all the Thesprotes, gave my wracke reliefe,
Without the price of that redemption
That Phœnix fish't for—where the King's lov'd son
Came to me, tooke me by the hand and led
Into his Court, my poore life surffetted 445
With cold and labour; and because my wrack
Chanc't on his Father's Shore, he let not lack
My plight or coate or cloake or any thing
Might cherish heate in me. And heere the King
Said he receiv'd Ulysses as his Guest, 450
Observ'd him Friend-like and his course addrest
Home to his country, shewing there to me
Ulysses' goods—a very Treasurie
Of Brasse, and Gold, and Steele of curious frame.
And to the tenth succession of his name 455
He laid up wealth enough to serve beside
In that King's house, so hugely amplified
His treasure was. But from his Court the King
Affirm'd him ship't for the Dodonean Spring,

ἐλελίχθη—
qui terram rapido
motu concutit.

ἀπριάτην—
sine emptionis
seu redemptionis
precio.

To heare from out the high-hair'd Oake of Jove 460
Counsaile from him for meanes to his remove
To his lov'd country, whence so many a yeare
He had bene absent—if he should appeare
Disguisd or manifest: and further swore
In his mid Court, at Sacrifice, before 465
These very eyes, that he had ready there
Both Ship and Souldiers to attend and beare
Him to his country. But, before, it chanc't
That a Thesprotean Ship was to be lanch't
For the much-corne-renown'd Dulichian Land, 470
In which the King gave to his men command
To take and bring me under tender hand
To King Acastus. But in ill designe
Of my poore life did their desires combine
So farre forth as might ever keepe me under 475
In fortune's hands, and teare my state in sunder.
And when the water-treader farre away
Had left the Land, then plotted they the day
Of my long servitude, and tooke from me
Both coate and cloake and all things that might be 480
Grace in my habit, and, in place, put on
These tatter'd rags which now you see upon
At Sunne set. My wretched bosom. When heaven's light took sea,
They fetcht the Field-workes of faire Ithaca,
And in the arm'd Ship with a wel-wreath'd cord 485
They streightly bound me, and did all disbord
To shore to supper in contentious rout.
Yet straight the Gods themselves tooke from about
My pressed limbes the bands with equall ease,
And I (my head in rags wrapt) tooke the Seas, 490
Descending by the smooth sterne, using then
My hands for Oares, and made from these bad men
Long way in little time. At last I fetcht
A goodly Grove of Okes, whose Shore I recht,
And cast me prostrate on it. When they knew 495
My thus-made scape, about the Shores they flew,
But (soone not fiinding) held it not their best
To seeke me further, but return'd to rest
Aboord their Vessell. Me the Gods lodg'd close,
Conducting me into the safe repose 500
A good man's stable yeelded. And thus Fate
This poore houre added to my living date.'
'O wretch of Guests,' said he, 'thy Tale hath stirr'd

My minde to much ruth, both how thou hast err'd
And suffer'd hearing, in such good parts showne. 505
But what thy chang'd relation would make knowne
About Ulysses, I hold neither true,
Nor will beleeve. And what need'st thou pursue
A Lye so rashly, since he sure is so
As I conceive, for which my skill shall go? 510
The safe returne my King lackes cannot be,
He is so envied of each Deity
So cleere, so cruelly. For not in Troy
They gave him end, nor let his Corpse enjoy
The hands of Friends (which well they might have done, 515
He manag'd armes to such perfection,
And should have had his Sepulcher and all,
And all the Greekes to grace his Funerall—
And this had given a glory to his Son
Through all times future.) But his head is run 520
Unseene, unhonor'd, into Harpies' mawes.
For my part, I'le not meddle with the cause:
I live a separate life amongst my Swine,
Come at no Towne for any need of mine,
περίφρων. Unlesse the circularly-witted Queene 525
(When any farre-come guest is to be seene
That brings her newes) commands me bring a Brawn—
About which (all things being in question drawne
That touch the King) they sit, and some are sad
For his long absence, some againe are glad 530
To waste his goods unwreak't, all talking still.
But, as for me, I nourish't little will
T'enquire or question of him, since the man
That faign'd himselfe the fled Ætolian
(For slaughtering one, through many Regions straid) 535
In my Stall (as his diversory) staide.
Where well entreating him, he told me then,
Amongst the Cretans with King Idomen
He saw Ulysses at his Ship's repaire,
That had bene brush't with the enraged aire; 540
And that in Summer, or in Autumne, sure
With all his brave friends and rich furniture
He would be heere—and nothing so, nor so.
But thou, an old man, taught with so much wo
As thou hast suffer'd to be season'd true, 545
And brought by his fate, do not heere pursue
His gratulations with thy cunning Lies.

Thou canst not soake so through my Faculties,
For I did never either honor thee
Or give thee love to bring these tales to me. 550
But in my feare of Hospitable Jove
Thou didst to this passe my affections move.'
'You stand exceeding much incredulous,'
Reply'd Ulysses, 'to have witnest thus
My word and Oath, yet yeeld no trust at all. 555
But make we now a covenant here, and call
The dreadfull Gods to witnesse that take seat
In large Olympus—if your King's retreat
Prove made even hither, you shall furnish me
With cloake and coate and make my passage free 560
For lov'd Dulichius. If (as fits my vow)
Your King returne not, let your servants throw
My old limbes headlong from some rock most hye,
That other poore men may take feare to lye.'
The Herdsman, that had gifts in him divine, 565
Replied: 'O Guest, how shal this Fame of mine
And honest vertue amongst men remaine
Now, and heereafter, without worthy staine,
If I, that led thee to my Hovell heere
And made thee fitting hospitable cheere, 570
Should after kill thee, and thy loved minde
Force from thy bones? Or how should stand enclin'd
With any Faith my will t'importune Jove
In any prayer heereafter for his love?
'Come, now 'tis supper's houre, and instant hast 575
My men wil make home, when our sweet repast
Wee'le taste together.' This discourse they held
In mutual kinde, when from a neighbor field
His Swine and Swine-herds came, who in their coats
Inclosd their Herds for sleepe, which mighty throats 580
Laid out in entring. Then the God-like Swaine
His men enjoyn'd thus: 'Bring me to be slaine
A chiefe Swine female for my stranger Guest,
When altogether we wil take our Feast,
Refreshing now our spirits, that all day take 585
Paines in our Swines' good, who may therefore make
For our paines with them all amends with one,
Since others eate our Labors, and take none.'
This said, his sharpe steele hew'd down wood, and they
A passing fat Swine hal'd out of the Sty, 590
Of five yeares old, which to the fire they put.

When, first, Eumæus from the Front did cut
The sacred haire and cast it in the fire,
Then pray'd to heaven, for stil, before desire
Was serv'd with food, in their so rude abods, 595
Not the poore Swine-herd would forget the Gods.
Good soules they bore, how bad soever were
The habits that their bodies' parts did beare.
When all the deathlesse Deities besought
That wise Ulysses might be safely brought 600
Home to his house, then with a logge of Oke
Left lying by (high lifting it) a stroke
He gave so deadly it made life expire.
Then cut the rest her throat, and all in fire
They hid and sindg'd her, cut her up, and then 605
The Maister tooke the office from the men,
Who on the Altar did the parts impose
That serv'd for sacrifice—beginning close
About the belly, thorough which he went,
And (all the chiefe fat gathering) gave it vent 610
(Part dreg'd with Flowre) into the sacred flame.
Then cut they up the joynts, and roasted them,
Drew all from spit, and serv'd in dishes all.
Then rose Eumæus (who was General
In skill to guide each act his fit event) 615
And (all in seven parts cut) the first part went
To service of the Nymphs and Mercury,
To whose names he did Rites of piety
In vowes particular; and all the rest
He shar'd to every one, but his lov'd Guest 620
He grac't with all the Chine, and of that King
To have his heart chear'd set up every string—
Which he observing, saide: 'I would to Jove,
Eumæus, thou liv'dst in his worthy love
As great as mine, that giv'st to such a guest 625
As my poore selfe of all thy goods the best.'
Eumæus answer'd: 'Eate, unhappy wretch,
And to what heere is at thy pleasure reach.
This I have; this thou want'st: thus God will give, — θεὸς δὲ τὸ μὲν δώσει, τὸ δ'ἐάσει.
Thus take away in us, and all that live. 630
To his wil's equall center all things fall;
His minde he must have, for he can do all.' — δύναται γὰρ ἅπαντα.
Thus having eate and to his wine descended,
Before he serv'd his owne thirst, he commended
The first use of it in fit sacrifice 635

(As of his meate) to all the Deities,
Ulysses. And to the City-racer's hand applide
The second cup, whose place was next his side:
Mesaulius did distribute the meate
(To which charge was Eumæus solely set, 640
In absence of Ulysses, by the Queene
And old Laertes) and this man had beene
Bought by Eumæus, with his faculties,
Employ'd then in the Taphian Merchandise.
But now to food apposde, and order'd thus, 645
All fell. Desire suffic'd, Mesaulius
Did take away. For bed then next they were,
All throughly satisfied with compleat cheare.
The night then came, ill, and no Taper shind:
Ζέφυρος μέγας αἰὲν ἔφυδρος. Jove rain'd her whole date, th'ever watry wind 650
Zephyr blew lowd; and Laertiades
(Approving kinde Eumæus' carefulnes
For his whole good) made farre about assay
To get some cast-off Cassocke (least he lay
That rough night cold) of him, or any one 655
Of those his servants: when he thus begun:
'Heare me, Eumæus, and my other friends.
I'le use a speech that to my glory tends,
Since I have drunke wine past my usuall guise:
Strong Wine commands the Foole, and moves the wise— 660
Moves and impels him, too, to sing and dance
And breake in pleasant laughters, and (perchance)
Preferre a speech, too, that were better in.
But when my spirits once to speake begin,
I shall not then dissemble. Would to heaven 665
I were as yong and had my forces driven
As close together as when once our powres
We led to ambush under th'Ilian Towres—
Where Ithacus and Menelaus were
The two Commanders, when it pleas'd them there 670
To take my selfe for third; when to the Towne
And lofty wals we led, we couch't close downe
All arm'd amids the Osiers and the Reeds,
Which oftentimes th'ore-flowing River feeds.
The cold night came, and th'Icy Northerne gale 675
Blew bleake upon us: after which did fall
A snow so cold it cut, as in it beate
A frozen water, which was all concrete
About our Shields like Cristall. All made faine

(Above our armes) to cloathe and cloathe again. 680
And so we made good shift (our shields beside
Clapt close upon our cloathes) to rest and hide
From all discovery. But I, poore foole,
Left my weeds with my men, because so coole
I thought it could not prove—which thoght my pride 685
A little strengthen'd, being loth to hide
A goodly glittering garment I had on.
And so I follow'd with my shield alone,
And that brave weed. But when the night nere ended
Her course on earth and that the starres descended, 690
I jog'd Ulysses (who lay passing neare)
And spake to him, that had a nimble eare,
Assuring him that long I could not lye
Amongst the living, for the fervencie
Of that sharpe night would kill me, since as then 695
My evill Angell made me with my men
Leave all weeds but a fine one. "But I know
'Tis vaine to talke; here wants all remedy now."
'This said, he bore that understanding part
In his prompt spirit that still show'd his Art 700
In Fight and counsell, saying (in a word,
And that low whisper'd): "Peace, least you afford
Some Greeke note of your softnes"—no word more,
But made as if his sterne austerity bore
My plight no pitty. Yet (as still he lay 705
His head reposing on his hand) gave way
To this invention: "Heare me, friends, a Dreame
(That was of some celestiall light a beame)
Stood in my sleepe before me, prompting me
With this fit notice: 'We are farre,' saide he, 710
'From out our Fleet. Let one go then, and try
If Agamemnon wil affoord supply
To what we now are strong.'" This stirr'd a speed
In Thoas to th'affaire—whose purple weede
He left for hast, which then I tooke, and lay 715
In quiet after, til the dawne of day.
'This shift Ulysses made for one in neede;
And would to heaven that youth such spirit did feed
Now in my Nerves, and that my joynts were knit
With such a strength as made me then held fit 720
To leade men with Ulysses. I should then
Seeme worth a weed that fits a herdsman's men—
For two respects, to gaine a thankfull frend,

And to a good man's neede a good extend.'
'O Father,' said Eumæus, 'thou hast showne 725
Good cause for us to give thee good renowne,
Not using any word that was not freed
From all least ill. Thou, therefore, shalt not need
Or coate or other thing that aptly may
Beseeme a wretched suppliant, for defray 730
Of this night's neede. But when her golden throne
The Morne ascends, you must resume your owne.
For heere you must not dreame of many weeds,
Or any change at all. We serve our needs,
As you do yours: One backe, one coate. But when 735
Ulysses' loved sonne returnes, he then
Shal give you coat and cassocke, and bestow
Your person where your heart and soule is now.'
This said, he rose, made neere the fire his bed,
Which all with Goats' and Sheep-skins he bespred, 740
All which Ulysses with himselfe did line.
With whom, besides, he chang'd a gabberdine,
Thicke lin'd and soft, which stil he made his shift
When he would dresse him gainst the horrid drift
Of Tempest, when deepe winter's season blowes. 745
Nor pleasde it him to lye there with his Sowes,
But while Ulysses slept there, and close by
The other yonkers, he abroad would ly,
And therefore arm'd him. Which set cheerefull fare
Before Ulysses' heart, to see such care 750
Of his goods taken, how farre off soever
His fate, his person, and his wealth should sever.
First, then, a sharpe-edg'd sword he girt about
His well-spred shoulders, and (to shelter out
The sharpe West wind that blew) he put him on 755
A thick-lin'd Jacket, and yet cast upon
All that the large hide of a Goat, well fed.
A Lance then tooke he, with a keene steele head,
To be his keepe-off both 'gainst Men and Dogges:
And thus went he to rest with his male Hogges, 760
That still abroad lay underneath a Rocke,
Shield to the North-wind's ever eager shocke.

The End of the Fourteenth Booke of Homer's Odysses

THE FIFTEENTH BOOKE
of
HOMER'S ODYSSES

THE ARGUMENT

Minerva to his Native seate
Exhorts Ulysses' sonne's retreate,
In Bed, and waking. He receives
Gifts of Atrides, and so leaves
The Spartan Court. And, going aboord, 5
Doth favourable way affoord,
To Theoclymenus, that was
The Argive Augure, and sought passe,
Fled for a slaughter he had done.
Eumæus tels Laertes' son 10
How he became his Father's Man,
Being sold by the Phœnician
For some agreed on Faculties,
From forth the Syrian Isle made prise.
Telemachus, arriv'd at home, 15
Doth to Eumæus' Cottage come.

Another Argument

O. { *From Sparta's strand makes safe accesse To his owne Land Ulyssides.* }

εὐρύχορον Λακεδαίμονα—In qua ampli ut pulchri chori duci possunt, vel ducuntur: *which the vulgar translation turne therefore,* latam, seu amplam.

In Lacedæmon, large and apt for dances,
Athenian Pallas her accesse advances
Up to the great in soule, Ulysses' seed,
Suggesting his returne now fit for deed.
She found both him and Nestor's noble son 5
In bed, in front of that faire Mansion—
Nestorides surpriz'd with pleasing sleepe
But on the watch Ulysses' sonne did keepe;

Sleepe could not enter, cares did so excite
His soule, through all the solitary night, 10
For his lov'd Father. To him (neere) she said:
'Telemachus! Tis time that now were staid
Thy forreigne travailes, since thy goods are free
For those proud men that all will eate from thee,
Divide thy whole possessions, and leave 15
Thy too-late presence nothing to receive.
Incite the shrill-voic't Menelaus, then,
To send thee to thy Native seat agen,
While thou mayst yet finde in her honor strong
Thy blamelesse Mother 'gainst thy Father's wrong. 20
For both the Father, and the Brothers too,
Of thy lov'd Mother will not suffer so
Extended any more her widdowe's bed,
But make her now her richest wooer wed,
Eurymachus, who chiefly may augment 25
Her gifts and make her joynture eminent.
And therefore hast thee, least in thy despight
Thy house stand empty of thy Native right.
For well thou know'st what mind a woman beares:
The house of him, who ever she endeares 30
Her selfe in Nuptials to, she sees encreast,
The yssue of her first lov'd Lord deceast
Forgotten quite and never thought on more.
In thy returne, then, the re-counted store
Thou find'st reserv'd, to thy most trusted Maid 35
Commit in guard till heaven's pow'rs have purvaid
A wife in vertue and in beautie's grace
Of fit sort for thee, to supply her place.
And this note more I'le give thee, which repose
In sure remembrance: The best sort of those 40
That woo thy Mother watchfull scouts addresse,
Both in the streights of th'Ithacensian Seas
And dusty Samos, with intent t'invade
And take thy life, ere thy returne be made.
Which yet I thinke will faile, and some of them 45
That waste thy fortunes taste of that extream
They plot for thee. But keepe off farre from shore,
And day and night saile, for a fore-right blore
Who ever of th'Immortals that vow guard
And scape to thy returne will see prepar'd. 50
As soone as thou arriv'st, dismisse to Towne
Thy Ship and Men, and first of all make downe

To him that keepes thy Swine, and doth conceive
A tender care to see thee well survive.
There sleepe, and send him to the Towne to tell 55
The chast Penelope that safe and well
Thou liv'st in his charge, and that Pylos' sands
The place contain'd from whence thy person Lands.'
Thus she to large Olympus made ascent—
When with his heele a little touch he lent 60
To Nestor's son, whose sleepe's sweet chains he losde,
Bad rise, and see in Chariot inclosde
Their one-hoov'd horse, that they might strait bee gone.
'No such haste,' he replied. 'Night holds her throne
And dims all way to course of Chariot. 65
The Morne will soone get up. Nor see forgot
The gifts with hast, that will, I know, be rich,
And put into our Coach with gracious speech
By Lance-fam'd Menelaus. Not a Guest
Shall touch at his house but shall store his brest 70
With fit mind of an hospitable man,
To last as long as any daylight can
His eyes re-comfort in such gifts as he
Will proofes make of his hearty royalty.'
He had no sooner said, but up arose 75
Aurora, that the Golden hils repose.
And Menelaus (good at martiall cries)
From Helen's bed raisde, to his Guest applies
His first apparance. Whose repaire made knowne
T'Ulysses' lov'd sonne, on his robe was throwne 80
About his gracious body, his cloake cast
Athwart his ample shoulders, and in hast
Abroad he went and did the King accost:

Telemachus to Menelaus.

'Atrides, guarded with heaven's deified hoste,
Grant now remission to my Native right, 85
My minde now urging mine owne house's sight.'

Menelaus' answere.

'Nor will I stay,' saide he, 'thy person long,
Since thy desires to go are growne so strong.
I should my selfe be angry to sustein
The like detention urg'd by other men. 90
Who loves a guest past Meane, past Meane will hate:
The Meane in all acts beares the best estate.
A like ill 'tis to thrust out such a guest
As would not go as to detaine the rest.
We should a guest love while he loves to stay, 95
And, when he likes not, give him loving way.

Yet suffer so that we may gifts impose
In Coach to thee—which ere our hands enclose,
Thine eies shall see, lest else our loves may glose.
Besides, I'le cause our women to prepare 100
What our house yeelds, and meerely so much fare
As may suffise for health. Both well will do,
Both for our honor and our profit too;
And serving strength with food, you after may
As much earth measure as wil match the day. 105
If you will turne your course from sea and go
Through Greece and Argos (that my selfe may so
Keepe kinde way with thee), I'le joyne horse, and guide
T'our humane Cities. Nor ungratifide
Will any one remit us; some one thing 110
Will each present us, that along may bring
Our passe with love, and prove our vertues blaz'd—
A Caldron or a Tripod, richly braz'd,
Two Mules, a bowle of Gold, that hath his price
Heightn'd with Emblemes of some rare device.' 115

ἄλεισον—poculum emblematis, et cælaturis ornatum.

The wise Prince answer'd: 'I would gladly go
Home to mine owne, and see that govern'd so
That I may keepe what I for certaine hold,
Not hazard that for onely hop't-for Gold:
I left behind me none so all wayes fit 120
To give it guard as mine owne trust with it.
Besides, in this broad course which you propose,
My Father seeking, I my selfe may lose.'

When this the shrill-voic't Menelaus heard,
He charg'd his Queene and Maids to see prepar'd 125
Breakfast of what the whole house held for best.
To him rose Eteoneus from his rest,
Whose dwelling was not farre off from the Court,
And his attendance his command did sort
With kindling fires, and furth'ring all the rost, 130
In act of whose charge heard no time he lost.

Himselfe then to an odorous roome descended,
Whom Megapenthes and his Queene attended.
Come to his treasury, a two-ear'd cup
He chusde of all, and made his Sonne beare up 135
A Silver bowle. The Queene then taking stand
Aside her Chist, where (by her owne faire hand
Lay Vests of all hues wrought) She tooke out one
Most large, most Artfull, chiefly faire, and shone
Like to a Star, and lay of al the last. 140

Then through the house with either's gift they past—
When to Ulysses' sonne, Atrides said:
'Telemachus, since so entirely swaid
Thy thoghts are with thy vow'd return now tender'd,
May Juno's thundring husband see it render'd 145
Perfect at all parts, action answering thought.
Of all the rich gifts, in my treasure sought,
I give thee heere the most in grace and best—
A Bowle, but Silver, yet the brims comprest
With Gold, whose fabricke his desert doth bring 150
From Vulcan's hand, presented by the King
And great Heroe of Sidonia's State,
When at our parting he did consummate
His whole house keeping. This do thou command.'
This said, he put the round Bowle in his hand; 155
And then his strong son Megapenthes plac't
The Silver cup before him, amply grac't
With worke and luster. Helen (standing by,
And in her hand the Robe, her huswifery)
His name remembring, said: 'And I present, 160
Lov'd sonne, this gift to thee, the Monument
Of the so-many-loved Helen's hands,
Which, at the knitting of thy Nuptiall bands,
Present thy wife. In meane space, may it ly
By thy lov'd Mother; but to me apply 165
Thy pleasure in it, and thus take thy way
To thy faire house and Countrie's wished stay.'
Thus gave she to his hands the veile, and he
The acceptation author'd joyfully—
Which in the Chariot's Chist Pisistratus 170
Plac't with the rest, and held miraculous.
The yellow-headed King then led them all
To seates and Thrones plac't in his spacious Hall.
The Hand-maid water brought, and gave it stream
From out a faire and golden Ewre to them, 175
From whose hands to a silver Caldron fled
The troubl'd wave. A bright boord then she spred,
On which another reverend Dame set bread,
To which more servants store of victuals serv'd.
Eteoneus was the man that kerv'd, 180
And Megapenthes fil'd them all their wine.
All fed and dranke, till all felt care decline
For those refreshings. Both the Guests did go
To horse and coach, and forth the Portico

Menelaus to Telemachus.

A little issu'd, when the yellow King 185
Brought wine himselfe, that with an Offering
To all the Gods they might their journey take.
He stood before the horse, and thus he spake:
'Farewell, yong Princes, to grave Nestor's eare
This salutation from my gratitude beare— 190
That I professe in all our Ilian warres
He stood a carefull Father to my cares.'
To him the wise Ulyssides replied:
'With all our utmost shall be signified
(Jove-kept Atrides) your right royall will, 195
And would to God I could as wel fulfill
Mine owne minde's gratitude for your free grace
In telling to Ulysses, in the place
Of my returne, in what accomplish't kind
I have obtain'd the office of a friend 200
At your deservings, whose faire end you crowne
With gifts so many and of such renowne.'
His wish that he might finde in his retreat
His Father safe return'd (to so repeat
The King's love to him) was saluted thus: 205
An Eagle rose, and in her Seres did trusse
A Goose, all white and huge, a houshold one,
Which men and women (crying out upon)
Pursu'd, but she (being neere the guests) her flight
Made on their right hand and kept still fore-right 210
Before their horses—which observ'd by them,
The spirits in all their minds tooke joyes extream,
Which Nestor's son thus question'd: 'Jove-kept King,
Yeild your grave thoughts, if this ostentfull thing
(This Eagle and this Goose) touch us or you?' 215
He put to study, and not knowing how
To give fit answer, Helen tooke on her
Th'ostent's solution, and did this prefer:
'Heare me, and I will play the Prophet's part,
As the immortals cast it in my heart, 220
And (as I thinke) will make the true sense knowne.
As this Jove's Bird, from out the Mountaines flowne
(Where was her Arie, and whence rose her race),
Trust up this Goose that from the house did grase,
So shall Ulysses (coming from the wilde 225
Of Seas and sufferings) reach, unreconcil'd,
His Native home, where even this houre he is,
And on those house-fed woo'rs those wrongs of his

Nestor's sonne to Menelaus—his Ironicall question continuing still Homer's Character of Menelaus.

Helen dissolves the Ostent.

Will shortly wreake with all their miseries.'

Telemachus to Helen.

'O,' said Telemachus, 'if Saturnian Jove 230
To my desires thy deare presage approve,
When I arrive I will performe to thee
My daily vowes as to a Deity.'
This said, he usde his scourge uppon the horse,
That through the City freely made their course 235
To Field, and all day made that first speed good.
But, when the Sun-set and Obscurenes stood
In each man's way, they ended their accesse
At Pheras, in the house of Diocles,
Sonne to Orsilochus, Alpheus' seede, 240
Who gave them guest-rites: and sleep's naturall need
They that night serv'd there. When Aurora rose,
They joyn'd their horse, tooke coach, and did dispose
Their course for Pylos, whose high City soon
They reach't. Nor would Telemachus be woon 245
To Nestor's house, and therefore order'd thus
His speech to Nestor's son, Pisistratus:

Telemachus to Pisistratus.

'How shall I win thy promise to a grace
That I must aske of thee? We both imbrace
The names of Bed-fellowes, and in that name 250
Will glory as an Adjunct of our fame,
Our Fathers' friendship: our owne equall age,
And our joynt travaile, may the more engage
Our mutuall concord. Do not then assay
(My God-lov'd friend) to leade me from my way 255
To my neere Ship, but take a course direct
And leave me there, lest thy old Sire's respect

ἱέμενος φιλέειν—
Cupiens diligere.

(In his desire to love me) hinder so
My way for home, that have such need to go.'
This said, Nestorides held all discourse 260
In his kind soule, how best he might enforce
Both promise and performance; which at last
He vow'd to venture, and directly cast
His horse about to fetch the Ship and Shore—
Where come, his frend's most lovely gifts he bore 265
Aboord the Ship, and in her hin-deck plac't
The vaile that Helen's curious hand had grac't,
And Menelaus' Gold, and said: 'Away,
Nor let thy men in any least date stay,
But quite put off ere I get home and tell 270
The old Duke you are past: for passing well
I know his minde to so exceed all force

Of any pray'r that he wil stay your course,
Himselfe make hither, all your course call backe—
And, when he hath you, have no thought to racke 275
Him from his bounty and to let you part
Without a Present, but be vext at heart
With both our pleadings, if we once but move
The least repression of his fiery love.'
  Thus took he coach, his faire-man'd steeds scourg'd on 280
Along the Pylian City, and anon
His Father's Court reacht—while Ulysses' Sonne
Bad boord and arme, which with a thought was done.
  His Rowers set, and he rich Odors firing
In his hin-decke, for his secure retiring, 285
To great Athenia, to his Ship came flying
Pallas.
A Stranger and a Prophet, as relying
On wished passage, having newly slaine
A man at Argos, yet his Race's vaine
Flow'd from Melampus, who in former date 290
In Pylos liv'd, and had a huge estate—
But fled his countrey and the punishing hand
Of great-soul'd Neleus, in a forreigne Land
From that most famous Mortall, having held
A world of riches, nor could be compeld 295
To render restitution in a yeare.
In meane space, living as close prisoner
In Court of Phylacus, and for the sake
Of Neleus' daughter, mighty cares did take,
Together with a greevous Languor sent 300
From grave Erinnys, that did much torment
One of the Furies of hell.
His vexed conscience; yet his life's expence
He scapt, and drave the loud-voic't Oxen thence
To breed-sheepe Pylos, bringing vengeance thus
Her foule demerit to great Neleus, 305
And to his Brother's house reduc't his wife:
Who yet from Pylos did remove his life
For feed-horse Argos, where his Fate set downe
A dwelling for him, and in much renowne
Made governe many Argives, where a Spouse 310
He tooke to him, and built a famous house.
There had he borne to him Antiphates
And forcefull Mantius. To the first of these
Was great Oicleus borne: Oicleus gate
Amphiaraus, that the popular State 315
Had all their health in, whom, even from his heart

Jove lov'd, and Phœbus in the whole desert
Of friendship held him—yet not blest so much
That Age's threshold he did ever touch,
His wife betraid him for money.
But lost his life by Female bribery. 320
Yet two sonnes author'd his posterity,
Alcmæon, and renown'd Amphilochus.
Mantius had yssue Polyphidius
And Clytus, but Aurora ravish't him
For excellence of his admired lim, 325
And interested him amongst the Gods.
His Brother knew men's good and bad abods
The best of all men, after the decease
Of him that perish't in unnaturall peace
At spacious Thebes. Apollo did inspire 330
His knowing soule with a Propheticke fire—
Who (angry with his Father) tooke his way
To Hyperesia, where (making stay)
He prophesied to all men, and had there
A Sonne call'd Theoclymenus; who here 335
Came to Telemachus, and found abord
Himselfe at Sacrifice, whom in a word
Theoclymenus to Telemachus.
He thus saluted: 'O Friend, since I finde
Even heere at Ship a sacrificing minde
Informe your actions—by your sacrifice, 340
And by that worthy choise of Deities
To whom you offer, by your selfe and all
These men that serve your course maritimall,
Tell one that askes the truth, nor give it glose,
Both who and whence you are? From what seed rose 345
Your royall person? And what Citie's Tow'rs
Hold habitation to your parents pow'rs?'
Telemachus to Theoclymenus.
He answer'd: 'Stranger! The sure truth is this:
I am of Ithaca; my Father is
(Or was) Ulysses, but austere death now 350
Takes his state from him; whose event to know
(Himselfe being long away) I set forth thus
With ship and souldiers.' Theoclymenus
As freely said: 'And I to thee am fled
From forth my country, for a man strooke dead 355
By my unhappy hand, who was with me
Of one selfe-Tribe, and of his pedigree
Are many Friends and Brothers, and the sway
Of Achive Kindred reacheth farre away.
From whom, because I feare their spleenes suborne 360

Blood and blacke fate against me (being borne
To be a wandrer among forreigne men)
Make thy faire ship my rescue, and sustein
My life from slaughter. Thy deservings may
Performe that mercy, and to them I pray.' 365

Telemachus' Reply.

'Nor will I barre,' said he, 'thy will to make
My meanes and equall ship thy ayde, but take
(With what wee have heere, in all friendly use)
Thy life from any violence that pursues.'

Thus tooke he in his Lance, and it extended 370
Aloft the hatches, which himselfe ascended.
The Prince tooke seate at Sterne, on his right hand
Set Theoclymenus, and gave command
To all his men to arme, and see made fast
Amidst the hollow Keele the Beechen Mast 375
With able halsers, hoise saile, lanch—which soone
He saw obay'd. And then his Ship did runne
A merry course. Blew-ey'd Minerva sent
A fore-right gale, tumultuous, vehement,
Along the aire, that her waie's utmost yeeld 380
The ship might make and plough the brackish field.

Then set the Sun, and Night black't all the waies.
The ship (with Jove's wind wing'd) wher th'Epean swaies
Fetcht Pheas first, then Elis the divine,
And then for those Isles made that Sea-ward shine, 385
For forme and sharpnesse like a Lance's head—
About which lay the wooers ambushed.
On which he rush't, to try if he could scape
His plotted death, or serve their treacherous Rape.

The storie's return to Eumæus.

And now returne we to Eumæus' Shed, 390
Where (at their foode with others marshalled)
Ulysses and his noble Herdsman sate;
To try if whose love's curious estate
Stood firme to his abode, or felt it fade,
And so would take each best cause to perswade 395
His Guest to Towne, Ulysses thus contends:

'Heare me, Eumæus, and ye other Friends.
Next Morne to Towne I covet to be gone,
To beg some other's almes, not still charge one.
Advise me well then, and as well provide 400
I may be fitted with an honest guide,
For through the streets (since Need will have it so)
I'le tread, to try if any will bestow
A dish of drinke on me or bit of bread,

Till to Ulysses' house I may be led. 405
And there I'le tell all-wise Penelope newes,
Mix with the wooers' pride, and (since they use
To fare above the full) their hands excite
To some small Feast from out their infinite—
For which I'le waite, and play the Servingman 410
Fairely enough, command the most they can.
For I will tell thee—note me well, and heare—
That if the will be of heaven's Messenger
(Who to the workes of men of any sort
Can grace infuse, and glory) nothing short 415
Am I of him that doth to most aspire
In any service, as to builde a Fire,
To cleave sere wood, to roast or boile their meat,
To waite at boord, mixe wine, or know the Neate,
Or any worke in which the poore-cal'd worst 420
To serve the rich-cal'd best in Fate are forc't.'

Eumæus to Ulysses.

He, angry with him, said: 'Alas, poore Guest,
Why did this counsaile ever touch thy brest?
Thou seek'st thy utter spoyle beyond all doubt,
If thou giv'st venture on the Wooers' rout, 425
Whose wrong and force affects the Iron heaven.
Their light delights are farre from being given
To such grave Servitors. Youths richly trick't
In coats or Cassocks, Lockes divinely slickt,
And lookes most rapting, ever have the gift 430
To taste their crown'd cups and full Trenchers shift.
Their Tables ever like their Glasses shine,
Loaded with bread, with varied flesh, and wine.
And thou go thither? Stay: for heere do none
Grudge at thy presence—nor my selfe, nor one 435
Of all I feed. But when Ulysses' sonne
Againe shall greet us, he shall put thee on
Both coat and cassocke, and thy quicke retreat
Set where thy heart and soule desire thy seat.'

Ulysses' answere to Eumæus.

Industrious Ulysses gave reply: 440
'I still much wish that heaven's chiefe Deity
Lov'd thee as I do, that hast easde my minde
Of woes and wandrings, never yet confin'de.
Nought is more wretched in a humane Race
Than Countrie's want, and shift from place to place. 445
But for the banefull belly men take care
Beyond good counsaile, whosoever are
In compasse of the wants it undergoes

By wandrings' losses or dependant woes.
Excuse me, therefore, if I err'd at home, 450
Which since thou wilt make heere (as overcome
With thy command for stay) I'le take on me
Cares appertaining to this place, like thee.
Does then Ulysses' Sire and Mother breath,
Both whom he left in th'age next doore to death? 455
Or are they breathlesse, and descended where
The darke house is that never day doth cleere?'

Eumæus' answer to Ulysses.

'Laertes lives,' saide he, 'but every howre
Beseecheth Jove to take from him the powre
That joynes his life and limbes, for with a mone 460
That breeds a mervaile he laments his sonne
Depriv'd by death. And addes to that another
Of no lesse depth for that dead sonne's dead Mother—
Whom he a Virgin wedded, which the more
Makes him lament her losse, and doth deplore 465
Yet more her misse, because her wombe the truer
Was to his brave sonne, and his slaughter slue her—
Which last love to her doth his life engage,
And makes him live an undigested age.
O! such a death she died as never may 470
Seize any one that heere beholds the day,
That either is to any man a friend,
Or can a woman kill in such a kind.
As long as she had Being, I would be
A still Inquirer (since t'was deere to me, 475
Though death to her, to heare his name) when she
Heard of Ulysses: for I might be bold;
She brought me up, and in her love did hold
My life compar'd with long-vail'd Ctimene,
Her yongest yssue (in some small degree 480
Her daughter yet prefer'd), a brave yong Dame.

ἥβην πολυήρατον—
Peroptabilem pubem.

But when of youth the dearely loved Flame
Was lighted in us, marriage did prefer
The maide to Samos, whence was sent for her
Infinite riches, when the Queene bestow'd 485
A faire new suite, new shooes and all, and vow'd
Me to the field—but passing loth to part,
As loving me more than she lov'd her hart.
And these I want now; but their businesse growes
Upon me daily, which the Gods impose, 490
To whom I hold all, give account to them—
For I see none left to the Diadem

That may dispose all better. So I drinke
And eate of what is heere, and whom I think
Worthy or reverend I have given to still 495
These kinds of Guest-rites: for the houshold ill
(Which, where the Queene is, ryots) takes her stil
From thought of these things. Nor is it delight
To heare, from her plight, of or worke or word;
The woo'rs spoyle all. But yet my men will bord 500
Her sorrowes often with discourse of all,
Eating and drinking of the Festivall
That there is kept, and after bring to field
Such things as servants make their pleasures yield.'

Ulysses' answere to Eumæus.

'O me, Eumæus,' saide Laertes' sonne, 505
'Hast thou then err'd so, of a little one,
Like me, from friends, and country? Pray thee say
(And say a Truth), doth vast Destruction lay
Her hand upon the wide-way'd Seat of men,

Supposing him to dwel in a Citie.

Where dwelt thy Sire and reverend Mother then, 510
That thou art spar'd there? Or else, set alone
In guard of Beeves, or Sheepe, set th'enemy on,
Surprisde and Shipt, transfer'd, and sold thee heere?
He that bought thee, paid well, yet bought not deere.'

Eumæus relates his birth, &c.

'Since thou enquir'st of that, my guest,' said he, 515
'Heare and be silent: and, meane space, sit free
In use of these cups to thy most delights;

ἀθέσφατοι.

Unspeakable in length now are the Nights.
Those that affect sleepe yet to sleepe have leave;
Those that affect to heare, their hearers give. 520
But sleep not ere your houre. *Much sleep doth grieve.*
Who ever lists to sleepe—away to bed,
Together with the morning raise his head,
Together with his fellowes breake his fast,
And then his Lord's Herd drive to their repast. 525
We two, still in our Tabernacle heere
Drinking and eating, will our bosomes cheere
With memories and tales of our annoyes.
Betwixt his sorrowes every Humane joyes—
He most, who most hath felt and furthest err'd. 530
And now thy wil to act shall be preferr'd.

Eumæus telles Ulysses how hee was bought and sold.

'There is an Isle above Ortygia
(If thou hast heard) they call it Syria—
Where once a day the Sun moves backwards still.
Tis not so great as good, for it doth fill 535
The fields with Oxen, fils them still with Sheepe,

Fils roofes with wine, and makes al Corne there cheap:
No Dearth comes ever there, nor no Disease,
That doth with hate us wretched mortals sease.
But when men's varied Nations, dwelling there 540
In any City, enters th'aged yeare,
The Silver-bow-bearer (the Sun) and she
That beares as much renowne for Archery
Stoope with their painles shafts, and strike them dead,
As one would sleepe, and never keepe the bed. 545
In this Isle stand two Cities, betwixt whome
All things that of the soile's fertility come
In two parts are divided. And both these,
My Father ruld (Ctesius Ormenides),
A man like the immortals. With these States 550
The crosse-biting Phœnicians traffick't rates
Of infinit Merchandize in ships brought there,
In which they then were held exempt from pere.
'There dwelt within my Father's house a Dame
Borne a Phœnician, skilfull in the frame 555
Of Noble Huswiferies, right tall, and faire.
Her the Phœnician great-wench-net-layer
With sweet words circumvented as she was
Washing her Linnen. To his amorous passe
He brought her first, shor'd from his Ship to her, 560
To whom he did his whole life's love prefer,
Which of these brest-exposing Dames the harts
Deceives, though fashion'd of right honest parts.
He askt her after, What she was, and whence?
She passing presently the excellence 565
Told of her Father's Turrets, and that she
Might boast her selfe sprung from the Progeny
Of the rich Sidons, and the daughter was
Of the much-yeare-revennew'd Arybas—
But that the Taphian Pirats made her prize 570
As she return'd from her field-huswiferies,
Transfer'd her hither, and at that man's house
Where now she liv'd for value precious
Sold her to th'Owner. He that stole her love
Bad her againe to her birth's seate remove, 575
To see the faire roofes of her friends againe,
Who still held state and did the port maintaine
Her selfe reported. She said: "Be it so,
So you and al that in your ship shall roe
Sweare to returne me in all safety hence." 580

πολυπαίπαλος— admodum vafer. Der. ex **παλεύω** I. pertraho in retia, et **παῖς**, I. puella.

'All swore; th'Oath past with every consequence,
She bad: "Be silent now, and not a word
Do you or any of your friends afford,
Meeting me afterward in any way,
Or at the washing Fount, lest some display 585
Be made and told the old man, and he then
Keepe me streight bound, to you and to your men
The utter ruine plotting of your lives.
Keepe in firme thought then every word that strives
For dangerous utterance. Haste your ship's ful freight 590
Of what you Trafficke for, and let me streight
Intending the Ship. Know by some sent friend: 'She hath all in hold,'—
And (with my selfe) I'le bring thence all the gold
I can by all meanes finger: and, beside,
I'le do my best to see your freight supplide 595
With some wel-weighing burthen of mine owne.
For I bring up in house a great man's sonne,
As crafty as my selfe, who will with me
Run every way along, and I will be
His Leader till your Ship hath made him sure. 600
He will an infinite great price procure,
Transfer him to what languag'd men ye may."
'This said, she gat her home, and they made stay
A whole yeare with us, Goods of great availe
Their Ship enriching. Which now fit for saile, 605
They sent a Messenger t'informe the Dame:
And to my father's house a fellow came,
Full of Phœnician craft, that to be sold
A Tablet brought, the body all of Gold,
The Verge all Amber. This had ocular view 610
Both by my honor'd Mother and the crew
Of her house-handmaids, handl'd, and the price
Beat, askt, and promist. And while this device
Lay thus upon the Forge, this Jeweller
Made privy signes (by winkes and wiles) to her 615
That was his object, which she tooke, and he
(His signe seeing noted) hied to Ship. When she
(My hand still taking, as she usde to do
To walke abroad with her) convai'd me so
Abroad with her, and in the Portico 620
Found cups, with tasted Viands, which the guests
That usde to flocke about my Father's feasts
Had left. They gone (some to the Counsaile Court,
Some to heare newes amongst the talking sort)

Her Theft three bowles into her lap convaid, 625
And forth she went. Nor was my wit so staid
To stay her, or my selfe. The Sun went downe,
And shadowes round about the world were flowne,
When we came to the haven, in which did ride
The swift Phœnician Ship—whose faire broad side 630
They boorded straight, tooke us up, and all went
Along the moyst waies. Winde Saturnius sent.
Six dayes we day and night sayl'd; but when Jove
Put up the seventh day, She that shafts doth love *Diana.*
Shot dead the woman, who into the pumpe 635
Like to a Dop-chicke div'd, and gave a thumpe
In her sad setling. Forth they cast her then
To serve the Fish and Sea-calves, no more Men—
But I was left there with a heavy hart.
When winde and water drave them quite apart 640
Their owne course, and on Ithaca they fell,
And there poore me did to Laertes sell:
And thus these eyes the sight of this Isle prov'd.'
'Eumæus,' he replyed, 'Thou much hast mov'd
The minde in me with all things thou hast said, 645
And all the sufferance on thy bosome laid:
But (truly) to thy ill hath Jove joyn'd good,
That one whose veines are serv'd with humane blood
Hath bought thy service, that gives competence
Of food, wine, cloth to thee. And sure th'expence 650
Of thy life's date heere is of good desart—
Whose labours not to thee alone impart
Sufficient food and housing, but to me—
Where I through many a heap't humanity
Have hither err'd, where, though (like thee) not sold, 655
Not staid like thee yet, nor nought needfull hold.'
This mutuall speech they usd, nor had they slept
Much time before the much-nere-morning lept
To her faire throne. And now strooke saile the men
That serv'd Telemachus, arriv'd just then 660
Nere his lov'd shore—wher now they stoopt the Mast,
Made to the Port with Oares, and Anchor cast,
Made fast the Ship; and then ashore they went,
Drest supper, fil'd wine; when (their appetites spent)
Telemachus commanded they should yield 665
The Ship to th'owner, while himselfe at field
Would see his shepherds; when light drew to end
He would his gifts see and to Towne descend,

And in the morning at a Feast bestow
Rewards for all their paines. 'And whither, now,' 670
Said Theoclymenus, 'my loved Son,
Shall I addresse my selfe? Whose mansion,
Of all men in this rough-hewne Isle, shall I
Direct my way to? Or go readily
To thy house, and thy Mother?' He replied: 675
'Another time I'le see you satisfied
With my house entertainment: but as now
You should encounter none that could bestow
Your fit entreaty, and (which lesse grace were)
You could not see my Mother, I not there— 680
For shee's no frequent object, but apart
Keepes from her woocrs, woo'd with her desart,
Up in her chamber, at her Huswifery.
But I'le name one to whom you shall apply
Direct repaire, and that's Eurymachus, 685
Renown'd descent to wise Polybius,
A man whom th'Ithacensians looke on now
As on a God, since he of all that wow
Is farre superior man, and likest far
To wed my mother, and as circular 690
Be in that honor as Ulysses was.
But heaven-housd Jove knowes the yet hidden passe
Of her disposure, and on them he may
A blacker sight bring than her Nuptiall day.'
As this he utter'd, on his right hand flew 695
A Saker, sacred to the God of view,
That in his Tallons trust and plum'd a Dove;
The Feathers round about the Ship did rove,
And on Telemachus fell, whom th'Augure then
Tooke fast by th' hand, withdrew him from his men, 700
And said: 'Telemachus, this Hawke is sent
From God; I knew it for a sure Ostent
When first I saw it. Be you well assur'd
There will no woocr be by heaven indur'd
To rule in Ithaca above your Race, 705
But your pow'rs ever fill the Regall place.'
'I wish to heaven,' said he, 'thy word might stand;
Thou then shouldst soon acknowledge from my hand
Such gifts and friendship as would make thee, Guest,
Met and saluted as no lesse than blest.' 710
This said, he call'd Piræus, Clytius' sonne,
His true associate, saying: 'Thou hast done

Theoclymenus to Telemachus.

Telemachus to Theoclymenus.

Telemachus to Piræus.

(Of all my Followers to the Pylian shore)
My will in chiefe in other things. Once more,
Be chiefly good to me: take to thy house 715
This loved stranger, and be studious
T'embrace and greete him with thy greatest fare
Till I my selfe come and take off thy care.'

Piræus' reply.

The famous for his Lance saide: 'If your stay
Take time for life heere, this man's care I'le lay 720
On my performance, nor what fits a Guest
Shall any penury with-hold his Feast.'
Thus tooke he ship, bad them boord, and away.
They boorded, sate, but did their labour stay
Till he had deckt his feete and reacht his Lance. 725
They to the City: he did straight advance
Up to his Sties, where Swine lay for him store,
By whose sides did his honest Swine-herd snore
Till his short cares his longest Nights had ended,
And nothing worse to both his Lords intended. 730

The End of the Fifteenth Booke of Homer's Odysses

THE SIXTEENTH BOOKE
of
HOMER'S ODYSSES

THE ARGUMENT

The Prince at Field, he sends to Towne
Eumæus, to make truly knowne
His safe returne. By Pallas' will
Telemachus is given the skill
To know his Father. Those that lay 5
In Ambush to prevent the way
Of yong Ulyssides for home
Retire, with anger overcome.

Another Argument

Πι. *To his most deere*
Ulysses showes;
The wise Son heere
his Father knowes.

Ulysses and divine Eumæus rose
Soone as the morning could her eyes unclose,
Made fire, brake fast, and to their Pasture send
The gather'd Herds, on whom their Swaines attend.
The selfe-tyre barking Dogs all fawn'd upon, 5
Nor bark't, at first sight of Ulysses' son.
The whinings of their fawnings yet did greet
Ulysses' eares, and sounds of certaine feet,
Who thus bespake Eumæus: 'Sure some friend
Or one well knowne comes, that the Mastives spend 10
Their mouths no lowder. Onely some one neare
They whine and leape about, whose feete I heare.'

Eumæus' amaze and kinde welcome of Telemachus.

Each word of this speech was not spent before
His Son stood in the entry of the dore.
Out-rusht amaz'd Eumæus, and let go 15

The cup to earth that he had labor'd so,
Cleans'd for the neate wine, did the Prince surprise,
Kist his faire forehead, both his lovely eyes,
Both his white hands, and tender teares distil'd.
There breath'd no kind-soul'd Father that was fild 20
Lesse with his sonne's embraces, that had liv'd
Ten years in farre-off earth, now new retriv'd,
His onely childe, too, gotten in his age,
And for whose absence he had felt the rage
Of griefes upon him, than for this divin'd- 25
So-much-for-forme was this divine-for-mind—
Who kist him through, who grew about him kissing,
As fresh from death scapt. Whom (so long time missing)
He wept for joy, and said: 'Thou yet art come
(Sweet light, sweet Sun-rise) to thy cloudy home. 30
O never I look't, when once shipt away
For Pylos' shores, to see thy turning day.
Come, enter, lov'd Son. Let me feast my hart
With thy sweete sight, new come, so farre apart.
Nor, when you liv'd at home, would you walk downe 35
Often enough heere, but staide still at Towne.
It pleas'd you then to cast such forehand view
About your house on that most damned crew.'
'It shall be so then, Friend,' saide he, 'but now
I come to glad mine eyes with thee, and know 40
If still my Mother in her house remaine,
Or if some wooer hath aspir'd to gaine
Of her in Nuptials: for Ulysses' bed,
By this, lies all with Spiders' cobwebs spred,
In penury of him that should supply it.' 45
'She still,' said he, 'holds her most constant quiet
Aloft thine owne house for the bed's respect:
But for her Lord's sad losse sad nights and daies
Obscure her beauties and corrupt their raies.'
This said, Eumæus tooke his brazen Speare, 50
And in he went: when, being enter'd neare
Within the stony threshold, from his seat
His Father rose to him, who would not let
Th'old man remove, but drew him backe and prest
With earnest termes his sitting, saying: 'Guest, 55
Take heere your seate againe; we soon shall get
Within our owne house heere some other seat.
Heere's one will fetch it.' This said, downe againe
His Father sate, and to his sonne his Swaine

ἀΐδηλον ὅμιλον—ἀΐδηλος *of* ἀΐδης, Orcus, *and signifies properly* tenebricosus, *or* infernalis, *so that* perniciosus (*which is the Latine translation*) *is not so fitte as damnd for that crew of dissolute wooers—the phrase being now usde to all so licentious.*

Strew'd faire greene Osiers, and impos'd thereon 60
A good soft Sheepeskin, which made him a Throne.
Then he appos'd to them his last-left Roste,
And in a wicker basket bread engroste,
Fil'd luscious wine, and then tooke opposite seate
To the divine Ulysses—when, the meate 65
Set there before them all fell to, and eate.
When they had fed, the Prince said: 'Pray thee say,
Whence coms this guest? What seamen gave him way
To this our Isle? I hope these feete of his
Could walke no water. Who boasts he he is?' 70
'I'le tell all truly, Son. From ample Crete
He bosts himselfe, and sayes his erring feete
Have many Cities trod, and God was he
Whose finger wrought in his infirmity.
But to my Cottage the last scape of his 75
Was from a Thesprot's Ship. What ere he is,
I'le give him you: do what you please. His vant
Is that he is (at most) a suppliant.'
'Eumæus,' said the Prince, 'to tell me this,
You have afflicted my weake Faculties: 80
For how shall I receive him to my house
With any safety, that suspitious
Of my yong forces (should I be assaide
With any sodaine violence) may want aide
To shield my selfe? Besides, if I go home, 85
My mother is with two doubts overcome—
If she shall stay with me, and take fit care
For all such guests as there seeke guestive fare,
Her husband's bed respecting and her fame
Amongst the people, or her blood may frame 90
A liking to some wooer, such as best
May bed her in his house, not giving least.
And thus am I unsure of all meanes free
To use a Guest there fit for his degree.
But, being thy Guest, I'le be his supply 95
For all weeds such as mere necessity
Shall more than furnish, fit him with a sword,
And set him where his heart would have bene shor'd.
Or (if so pleasd) receive him in thy Shed:
I'le send thee clothes, I vow, and all the bread 100
His wish would eate, that to thy men and thee
He be no burthen. But that I should be
His meane to my house, where a company

Of wrong-professing wooers wildly live,
I will in no sort author, lest they give 105
Foule use to him, and me as gravely grieve.
For what great act can any one atchieve
Against a multitude, although his minde
Retaine a courage of the greatest kinde?
For all minds have not force in one degree.' 110
Ulysses to Telemachus. Ulysses answer'd: 'O Friend, since 'tis free
For any man to change fit words with thee,
I'le freely speake. Me thinkes a wolvish powre
My heart puts on to teare and to devoure,
To heare your affirmation, that (in spite 115
Of what may fall on you) made opposite,
Being one of your proportion, birth and age,
These wooers should in such injustice rage.
What should the cause be? Do you wilfully
Indure their spoile? Or hath your Empery 120
Bene such amongst your people that all gather
In troope and one voice (which even God doth father)
And vow your hate so that they suffer them?
Or blame your Kinsfolks' faiths, before th'extream
Of your first stroke hath tried them—whom a man, 125
When strifes to blowes rise, trusts, though battel ran
In huge and high waves? Would to heaven my spirit
Such youth breath'd as the man that must inherit
Yet-never-toucht Ulysses, or that he
(But wandring this way) would but come and see 130
What my age could atchieve (and there is Fate
For Hope yet left, that he may recreate
His eyes with such an object). This my head
Should any stranger strike off, if starke dead
I strooke not all, the house in open force 135
Entring with challenge. If their great concourse
Did over-lay me, being a man alone
(Which you urge for your selfe), be you that one.
I rather in mine owne house wish to dye
One death for all than so indecently 140
See evermore deeds worse than death applied—
Guests wrong'd with vile words and blow-giving pride,
The women-servants dragg'd in filthy kind
About the faire house, and in corners blind
Made serve the rapes of Ruffins, food devour'd 145
Idely and rudely, wine exhaust, and pour'd
Through throats prophane; and all about a deed

That's ever wooing, and will never speed.'

Telemachus to his Father.

'I'le tell you, Guest, most truly,' saide his Son,
'I do not thinke that all my people ron 150
One hatefull course against me, nor accuse
Kinsfolkes that I in strifes of weight might use:
But Jove will have it so, our Race alone
(As if made singular) to one and one
His hand confining. Onely to the King 155
(Jove-bred Arcesius) did Laertes spring;
Onely to old Laertes did descend
Ulysses; onely to Ulysses' end
Am I the Adjunct—whom he left so yong
That from me to him never comfort sprong. 160
And to all these now (for their race) arise
Up in their house a brood of enemies,
As many as in these Isles bow men's knees,
Samos, Dulichius, and the rich in Trees
Zacynthus, or in this rough Isle's command, 165
So many suiters for the Nuptials stand
That aske my Mother, and meane space prefer
Their lusts to all spoile, that dishonor her.
Nor doth she (though she loaths) deny their suites,
Nor they denials take, though taste their fruites. 170
But all this time the state of all things there
Their throats devoure, and I must shortly beare
A part in all; and yet the periods
Of these designes lye in the knees of Gods.
Of all Loves, then, Eumæus, make quicke way 175
To wise Penelope, and to her say
My safe returne from Pylos, and alone
Returne thou hither, having made it knowne.
Nor let (besides my Mother) any eare
Partake thy Message, since a number beare 180
My safe returne displeasure.' He replied:

Eumæus to Telemachus.

'I know, and comprehend you; you divide
Your minde with one that understands you well.
But, all in one yet, may I not reveale

Laertes.

To th'old hard-fated Arcesiades 185
Your safe returne? Who through his whole distres
Felt for Ulysses did not yet so grieve
But with his houshold he had will to live,
And serv'd his appetite with wine and food,
Surveigh'd his husbandry, and did his blood 190
Some comforts fitting life: but since you tooke

Your ship for Pylos he would never brooke
Or wine, or food, they say, nor cast an eye
On any labour, but sits weeping by
And sighing out his sorrowes, ceasselesse mones 195
Wasting his body, turn'd all skin and bones.'

Telemachus to Eumæus.

'More sad newes still,' said he, 'yet, mourne he still:
For if the rule of all men's workes be will,
And his will his way goes, mine stands inclin'd
T'attend the home-turne of my neerer kind. 200
Do then what I injoyne, which given effect,
Erre not to field to him, but turne direct,
Entreating first my Mother, with most speed
And all the secrecy that now serves Neede,
To send this way their store-house Guardian, 205
And she shall tell all to the aged Man.'

Intending his Father, whose returne, though hee were far from knowing or fully expecting, yet he desir'd to order all things as he were present.

206 Intending to Laertes, all that Eumæus would have told.

He tooke his shooes up, put them on, and went.
Nor was his absence hid from Jove's descent,
Divine Minerva, who tooke straight to view
A goodly woman's shape, that all workes knew, 210
And, standing in the entry, did prefer
Her sight t'Ulysses. But (though meeting her)
His sonne Telemachus nor saw nor knew:
The Gods' cleere presences are knowne to few.
Yet (with Ulysses) even the Dogs did see 215
And would not barke, but, whining lovingly,
Fled to the Stal's farre side, where She her eine
Moov'd to Ulysses. He knew her designe,
And left the house, past the great Sheep-cote's wall,
And stood before her. She bad utter all 220
Now to his sonne, nor keepe the least unlosde,
That, all the wooers' deaths being now disposde,
They might approach the Towne, affirming she
Not long would faile t'assist to victory.

Pallas appeares to Ulysses.

This said, She laide her golden Rod on him, 225
And with his late-worne weeds grac't every lim,
His body straitn'd, and his youth instill'd,
His fresh blood call'd up, every wrinkle fill'd
About his broken eyes, and on his chin
The browne haire spred. When his whole trim wrought in, 230
She yssu'd, and he enter'd to his sonne,
Who stood amaz'd, and thought some God had done
His house that honor, turn'd away his eyes,
And sayd: 'Now, Guest, you grace another guise
Than suites your late shew; other weeds you weare, 235

Pallas restores Ulysses' youth for the time.

Telemachus to his Father.

And other person. Of the starry spheare
You certainly present some deathlesse God.
Be pleasd that to your here vouchsaf't abod
We may give sacred rites, and offer Gold
To do us favour.' He replied: 'I hold 240
No deified state. Why put you thus on me
A God's resemblance? I am onely he
That beares thy Father's name, for whose lov'd sake
Thy youth so grieves, whose absence makes thee take
Such wrongs of men.' Thus kist he him, nor could 245
Forbeare those teares that in such mighty hold
He held before—still held, still yssuing ever—
And now (the shores once broke) the springtide never
Forbore earth from the cheekes he kist. His sonne
(By all these violent arguments not wonne 250
To credit him his Father) did deny
His kinde assumpt, and said some Deity
Fain'd that joye's cause to make him grieve the more,
Affirming that no man, whoever wore
The garment of mortality, could take 255
(By any utmost power his soule could make)
Such change into it—since at so much will
Not Jove himselfe could both remove and fill
Old age with youth, and youth with age so spoile
In such an instant. 'You wore all the soile 260
Of age but now and were old, and but now
You beare that yong grace that the Gods indow
Their heaven-borne formes withall.' His father saide:
'Telemachus! Admire, nor stand dismaide,
But know thy solid Father, since within 265
He answeres all parts that adorne his skin.
There shall no more Ulyssesses come heere.
I am the man, that now this twentith yeare
(Stil under sufferance of a world of ill)
My countrey earth recover. 'Tis the will 270
The Prey-professor Pallas puts in act,
Who put me thus together, thus distract
In aged pieces, as even now you saw,
This youth now rendring. 'Tis within the law
Of her free pow'r. Sometimes to shew me pore, 275
Sometimes againe thus amply to restore
My youth and Ornaments, She still would please.
The Gods can raise, and throw men downe, with ease.'
This said, he sat, when his Telemachus pour'd

Ulysses to Telemachus.

Telemachus to Ulysses.

Ulysses to his sonne.

Himselfe about him. Teares on teares he shour'd, 280
And to desire of mone increast the cloud:
Both wept and howl'd, and laide out shrieks more loud
Than or the Bird-bone-breaking Eagle reres
Or Brood-kind Vulture with the crooked Seres,
When rusticke hands their tender Aries draw, 285
Before they give their wings their full-plum'd Law.
But miserably pour'd they from beneath
Their lids their teares, while both their breasts did breath
As frequent cries: and to their fervent mone
The light had left the skies, if first the sonne 290
Their dumbe mones had not vented, with demand
What Ship it was that gave the naturall land
To his blest feet. He then did likewise lay
Hand on his passion, and gave these words way:

Ulysses tels his sonne what ship he arriv'd in.

'I'le tell thee truth, my sonne. The men that beare 295
Much fame for shipping my Reducers were
To long-wisht Ithaca, who each man els
That greets their shore give passe to where he dwels.
The Phæacensian Peeres in one night's date
(While I fast slept) fetcht th'Ithacensian state, 300
Grac't me with wealthy gifts, Brasse, store of Gold,
And Robes faire wrought—all which have secret hold
In Caves that, by the God's advice, I chusde.
And now, Minerva's admonitions usde
For this retreat, that we might heere dispose 305
In close Discourse the slaughters of our foes,
Recount the number of the wooers then,
And let me know what name they hold with men,
That my minde may cast over their estates
A curious measure, and conferre the rates 310
Of our two pow'rs and theirs—to try if we
Alone may propagate to victory
Our bold encounters of them all, or prove
The kind assistance of some other's love.'

Telemachus to Ulysses.

'O Father,' he replied, 'I oft have heard 315
Your counsailes, and your force of hand prefer'd
To mighty glory. But your speeches now
Your ventrous minde exceeding mighty show.
Even to amaze they move me, for in right
Of no fitte counsaile should be brought to fight 320
Two men 'gainst th'able faction of a throng.
No one two, no one ten, no twice ten strong
These wooers are, but more by much. For know

That from Dulichius there are fifty two,
All choise yong men, and every one of these 325
Six men attend. From Samos crost the Seas
Twice twelve young Gallants. From Zacynthus came
Twice ten. Of Ithaca, the best of name,
Twice six. Of all which all the State they take
A sacred Poet and a Herald make. 330
Their delicacies two (of speciall sort
In skill of banquets) serve. And all this port
If we shall dare t'encounter, all thrust up
In one strong roofe, have great care lest the cup
Your great mind thirsts exceeding bitter taste, 335
And your retreat commend not to your haste
Your great attempt, but make you say you buy
Their pride's revenges at a price too hy.
And therefore (if you could) t'were well you thought
Of some assistent. Be your spirit wrought 340
In such a man's election as may lend
His succours freely and expresse a Friend.'

Ulysses to Telemachus.

His Father answer'd: 'Let me aske of thee:
Heare me, consider, and then answer me.
Think'st thou, if Pallas and the King of skies 345
We had to Friend, would their sufficiencies
Make strong our part? Or that some other yet
My thoughts must worke for?' 'These,' saide he, 'are set

Telemachus.

Aloft the clouds, and are sound aydes indeed—
As pow'rs not onely that these men exceed, 350
But beare of all men else the high command,
And hold, of Gods, an over-ruling hand.'

Ulysses.

'Well then,' said he, 'not these shall sever long
Their force and ours in fights assur'd and strong.
And then twixt us and them shall Mars prefer 355
His strength, to stand our great distinguisher,
When in mine owne Roofes I am forc't to blowes.
But when the day shall first her fires disclose,
Go thou for home, and troope up with the woo'rs,
Thy wil with theirs joind, pow'r with their rude pow'rs; 360
And after, shall the Herdsman guide to Towne
My steps, my person wholly over-growne
With all apparance of a poore old Swaine,
Heavy and wretched. If their high disdaine
Of my vile presence make them my desert 365
Affect with contumelies, let thy loved heart
Beare in fixt confines of thy bosome still,

And see me suffer patient of their ill—
I, though they drag me by the heeles about
Mine owne free earth, and after hurle me out, 370
Do thou still suffer. Nay, though with their Darts
They beate and bruise me, beare. But these foul parts
Perswade them to forbeare, and by their names
Cal all with kinde words, bidding for their shames
Their pleasures cease. If yet they yeeld not way, 375
There breakes the first light of their fatall day.
In meane space, marke this: When the chiefly wise
Minerva prompts me, I'le informe thine eies
With some given signe, and then all th'armes that are
Aloft thy Roofe in some neere roome prepare 380
For speediest use. If those brave men enquire
Thy end in all, still rake up all thy fire
In faire coole words, and say: "I bring them downe
To scoure the smoke off, being so over-growne
That one would thinke all fumes that ever were 385
Breath'd since Ulysses' losse reflected here.
These are not like the armes he left behinde
In way for Troy. Besides, Jove prompts my minde
In their remove apart thus with this thought,
That if in heighth of wine there should bee wrought 390
Some harsh contention twixt you, this apt meane
To mutual bloodshed may be taken cleane
From out your reach, and all the spoile prevented
Of present Feast—perhaps even then presented
My Mother's Nuptials to your long kinde vowes. 395
Steele it selfe, ready, drawes a man to blowes."
Thus make their thoughts secure; to us alone
Two Swords, two Darts, two shields left, which see done
Within our readiest reach, that at our will
We may resume and charge, and all their skil 400
Pallas and Jove, that all just counsailes breath,
May darken with securenesse to their death.
And let me charge thee now, as thou art mine,
And as thy veines mine owne true blood combine:
Let (after this) none know Ulysses nere, 405
Not any one of all the houshold there,
Not here the Herdsman, not Laertes be
Made privy, nor her selfe Penelope—
But onely let thy selfe and me worke out
The women's thoughts of all things borne about 410
The wooers' hearts; and then thy men approve,

To know who honors, who with reverence love,
Our well-weigh'd Memories, and who is won
To faile thy fit right, though my onely Son.'

Telemachus to his Father.

'You teach,' saide he, 'so punctually now, 415
As I knew nothing, nor were sprung from you.
I hope, heereafter, you shall better know
What soule I beare, and that it doth not let
The least loose motion passe his naturall seat.
But this course you propose will prove, I feare, 420
Small profit to us, and could wish your care
Would weigh it better, as too farre about.
For Time will aske much to the sifting out
Of each man's disposition by his deeds;
And, in the meane time, every wooer feeds 425
Beyond saciety, nor knowes how to spare.
The women yet, since they more easie are
For our enquiry, I would wish you try
Who right your state, who do it injury.
The men I would omit, and these things make 430
Your labour after. But to undertake
The wooers' warre, I wish your utmost speede,
Especially if you could cheere the deed
With some Ostent from Jove.' Thus (as the Sire
Consented to the Son) did heere expire 435
Their mutuall speech. And now the Ship was come
That brought the yong Prince and his soldiers home.
The deepe Haven reacht, they drew the Ship ashore,
Tooke all their Armes out, and the rich Gifts bore
To Clytius' house. But to Ulysses' Court 440
They sent a Herald first, to make report
To wise Penelope that safe at field
Her Son was left; yet, since the Ship would yield
Most hast to her, he sent that first, and them
To comfort with his utmost the extream 445
He knew she suffer'd. At the Court now met
The Herald and the Herdsman, to repeat
One message to the Queene. Both whom (arriv'd
Within the gates) both to be formost striv'd
In that good Newes. The Herald, he for hast 450
Amongst the Maids bestow'd it, thinking plac'st
The Queene amongst them. 'Now,' said he, 'O Queen,
Your lov'd Son is arriv'd.' And then was seene
The Queene her selfe, to whom the herdsman tould
All that Telemachus injoyn'd he should. 455

All which discharg'd, his steps he backe bestowes,
And left both Court and City for his Sowes.
The wooers then grew sad, soule-vext, and all
Made forth the Court—when by the mighty wall
They tooke their severall seate before the gates; 460
To whom Eurymachus initiates
Eurymachus to the rest.
Their utter'd greevance: 'O,' sayd he, 'my Friends,
A worke right great begun as proudly ends.
We said Telemachus should never make
His voyage good, nor this shore ever take 465
For his returne's receipt: and yet we faile,
And he performes it. Come, let's man a Saile
The best in our election, and bestow
Such souldiers in her as can swiftest row,
To tell our friends that way-lay his retreat 470
'Tis safe perform'd, and make them quickly get
Their ship for Ithaca.' This was not said,
Before Amphinomus in Port displaid
The ship arriv'd, her sailes then under stroke,
And Oares resum'd—when laughing, thus he spoke: 475
Amphinomus to the other woers.
'Move for no messenger: these men are come.
Some God hath either told his turning home,
Or they themselves have seene his ship gone by,
Had her in chase, and lost her.' Instantly
They rose, and went to Port, found drawne to Land 480
The Ship, the souldiers taking Armes in hand.
The woo'rs themselves to counsaile went in throng,
And not a man besides, or old or yong,
Let sit amongst them. Then Eupitheus' Sonne,
Antinous to the Wooers.
Antinous, said: 'See what the Gods have done: 485
They onely have delivered from our ill
The men we way-laid; every windy hill
Hath bin their watch-tow'r, where by turns they stood
Continuall Sentinell. And we made good
Our worke as well, for (Sun once set) we never 490
Slept winke ashore all night, but made saile ever
This way and that, even till the morning kept
Her sacred Station, so to intercept
And take his life for whom our ambush lay:
And yet hath God to his returne given way. 495
But let us prosecute with counsailes here
His necessary death, nor any where
Let rest his safety, for, if he survive,
Our sailes will never in wisht Havens arrive,

Since he is wise, hath soule, and counsaile too 500
To worke the people, who will never do
Our faction favour. What we then intend
Against his person give we present end
Before he call a counsaile, which, beleeve,
His spirit will hast, and point where it doth greeve, 505
Stand up amongst them all, and urge his death
Decreed amongst us. Which complaint will breath
A fire about their spleenes, and blow no praise
On our ill labours. Lest they therefore raise
Pow'r to exile us from our Native earth, 510
And force our lives' societies to the birth
Of forreigne countries, let our speeds prevent
His comming home to this austere complaint
(At field and farre from Towne, or in some way
Of narrow passage) with his latest day 515
Shewne to his forward youth, his goods and lands
Left to the free division of our hands,
The Moovables made al his Mother's dowre
And his who-ever Fate affoords the powre
To celebrate with her sweet Hymen's rites. 520
Or if this please not, but your appetites
Stand to his safety, and to give him seate
In his whole birth-right, let us looke to eate
At his cost never more, but every man
Haste to his home, and wed with whom he can 525
At home; and there lay first about for dowre,
And then the woman give his second powre
Of Nuptiall liking, and for last, apply
His purpose with most gifts and destiny.'

This silence caus'd, whose breach, at last, begon 530
Amphinomus, the much renowned Son
Of Nisus, surnam'd Aretiades,
Who from Dulichius (full of flowry Leas)
Led all the wooers; and in chiefe did please
The Queene with his discourse, because it grew 535
From rootes of those good mindes that did indue
His goodly person—who (exceeding wise)
Us'd this speech: 'Friends, I never will advise
The Prince's death, for 'tis a damned thing
To put to death the yssue of a King. 540
First, therefore, let's examine what applause
The Gods will give it. If the equall Lawes
Of Jove approove it, I my selfe will be

φρεσὶ ἀγαθῇσιν—Bonis mentibus, *the plurall number used ever by Homer.*

The man shall kill him, and this companie
Exhort to that minde. If the Gods remaine 545
Adverse and hate it, I advise, refraine.'
  This said Amphinomus, and pleas'd them all:
When all arose, and in Ulysses' Hall
Tooke seate againe. Then to the Queene was come
The wooers' plot to kill her sonne at home 550
Since their abroad designe had mist successe,
The Herald Medon (who the whole addresse
Knew of their counsailes) making the report.
The Goddesse of her sex, with her faire sort
Of lovely women, at the large Hal's dore 555
(Her bright cheekes clouded with a veile shee wore)
Stood, and directed to Antinous
Her sharpe reproofe, which she digested thus:

Penelope to Antinous.

  'Antinous! Composde of injury,
Plotter of mischiefe! Though reports that flye 560
Amongst our Ithacensian people say
That thou, of all that glory in their sway,
Art best in words and counsailes, th'art not so.
Fond, busie fellow, why plott'st thou the wo
And slaughter of my Son, and dost not feare 565
The Presidents of suppliants, when the eare
Of Jove stoopes to them? 'Tis unjust to do
Slaughter for slaughter, or pay woe for wo;
Mischiefe for kindnesse, Death for life sought, then,
Is an injustice to be loath'd of men. 570
Serves not thy knowledge to remember when
Thy Father fled to us? Who (mov'd to wrath
Against the Taphian theeves) pursu'd with scath
The guiltlesse Thesprots, in whose people's feare,
Pursuing him for wreake, he landed here, 575
They after him, professing both their prize
Of all his chiefly valew'd Faculties,
And more priz'd life. Of all whose bloodiest ends
Ulysses curb'd them, though they were his frends.
Yet thou, like one that no Law will allow 580
The least true honor, eat'st his house up now
That fed thy Father, woo'st for love his wife,
Whom thus thou griev'st, and seek'st her sole son's life.
Ceasse, I command thee; and command the rest
To see all thought of these foule fashions ceast.' 585

Eurymachus to Penelope.

  Eurymachus replyed: 'Be confident,
Thou all of wit made, the most fam'd descent

Of King Icarius. Free thy spirits of feare.
There lives not any one, nor shall live here
Now nor hereafter, while my life gives heat 590
And light to me on earth, that dares entreat
With any ill touch thy well-loved Sonne—
But heere I vow, and heere will see it done,
His life shall staine my Lance. If on his knees
Ulysses. The City-racer, Laertiades, 595
Hath made me sit, put in my hand his foode,
And held his red wine to me, shall the bloode
Of his Telemachus on my hand lay
The least pollution that my life can stay?
No: I have ever charg'd him not to feare 600
Death's threat from any. And for that most deare
Love of his Father he shall ever be
Much the most lov'd of all that live to me.
Who kils a guiltlesse man, from Man may flye;
From God his searches all escapes deny.' 605

Thus cheer'd his words, but his affections still
Fear'd not to cherish foule intent to kill
Even him whose life to all lives he prefer'd.

The Queene went up, and to her love appear'd
Her Lord so freshly that she wept, till sleepe 610
(By Pallas forc't on her) her eyes did steepe
In his sweet humor. When the Even was come,
The God-like Herdsman reacht the whole way home.
Ulysses and his Son for supper drest
A yeare-old Swine, and ere their Host and Guest 615
Had got their presence, Pallas had put by
With her faire rod Ulysses' royalty,
And render'd him an aged man againe,
With all his vile Integuments, lest his Swaine
Should know him in his trim and tell his Queene, 620
In these deepe secrets being not deeply seene.

He seene, to him the Prince these words did use:
Telemachus to Eumæus. 'Welcome, divine Eumæus. Now what newes
Imployes the City? Are the wooers come
Backe from their Scout dismaid? Or heere at home 625
Will they againe attempt me?' He replied:
Eumæus to Telemachus. 'These touch not my care. I was satisfied
To do, with most speed, what I went to do—
My message done, returne. And yet, not so
Came my newes first; a Herald (met with there) 630
Fore-stal'd my Tale and told how safe you were.

Besides which meerely necessary thing,
What in my way chanc't I may over-bring,
Being what I know and witnest with mine eyes.
'Where the Hermæan Sepulcher doth rise 635
Above the City, I beheld take Port
A Ship, and in her many a man of sort:
Her freight was shields and Lances; and me thought
They were the wooers, but of knowledge nought
Can therein tell you.' The Prince smil'd, and knew 640
They were the wooers, casting secret view
Upon his Father. But what they intended
Fled far the Herdsman—whose Swaine's labors ended,
They drest the Supper, which, past want, was eat.
When all desire suffic'd, of wine, and meat, 645
Of other humane wants, they tooke supplies
At Sleepe's soft hand, who sweetly clos'd their eies.

The End of the xvi. Booke

THE SEVENTEENTH BOOKE
of
HOMER'S ODYSSES

THE ARGUMENT

Telemachus, return'd to Towne,
Makes to his curious mother knowne,
In part, his Travailes. After whome
Ulysses to the Court doth come
In good Eumæus' guide, and preast 5
To witnesse of the Wooers' Feast—
Whom (though twice ten yeares did bestow
In farre off parts) his Dog doth know.

Another Argument

Pῶ. *Ulysses showes*
through all disguise:
Whom his dog knowes;
who knowing dies.

But when aire's rosie birth, the Morne, arose,
Telemachus did for the Towne dispose
His early steps, and tooke to his command
His faire long Lance, well sorting with his hand,
Telemachus to Eumæus. Thus parting with Eumæus: 'Now, my friend, 5
I must to Towne, lest too farre I extend
My Mother's mone for me, who, till her eyes
Mine owne eyes witnesse, varies teares and cries
Through all extreames. Do then this charge of mine,
And guide to Towne this haplesse guest of thine, 10
To beg else-where his further Festivall.
Give they that please, I cannot give to all:
Mine owne wants take up for my selfe my paine.
If it incense him, he the worst shall gaine;
The lovely truth I love, and must be plaine.' 15

Ulysses to his Son.

'Alas, Friend,' saide his Father, 'nor do I
Desire at all your further charity.
'Tis better beg in Cities than in Fields,
And take the worst a begger's fortune yields.
Nor am I apt to stay in Swine-sties more 20
How ever: ever the great Chiefe before
The poore Rankes must to every step obay.
But goe; your man in my command shall sway
Anon yet too by favor, when your fires
Have comforted the colde heat age expires, 25
And when the Sun's flame hath besides corrected
The early aire abroad—not being protected
By these my bare weeds from the morning's frost;
Which (since so much ground is to be engrost
By my poore feete as you report) may give 30
Too violent charge to th'heat by which I live.'
This saide, his Sonne went on with spritely pace,
And to the wooers studied little grace.
Arriv'd at home, he gave his Javeline stay
Against a lofty Pillar, and bold way 35
Made further in—when, having so farre gone
That he transcended the fayre Porch of Stone,
The first by farre that gave his entry eye
Was Nurse Euryclea, who th'embrodery
Of Stooles there set was giving Cushions faire, 40
Who ranne upon him, and her rapt repaire
Shed teares for joy. About him gather'd round
The other Maides, his head and shoulders croun'd
With kisses and embraces. From above
The Queene her selfe came, like the Queene of Love 45
Or bright Diana, cast about her Sonne
Her kinde embraces, with effusion
Of loving teares kist both his lovely eyes,
His cheekes, and forehead, and gave all supplies

Penelope to Telemachus.

With this entreaty: 'Welcome, sweetest light. 50
I never had conceite to set quicke sight
On thee thus soone, when thy lov'd father's fame
As farre as Pylos did thy spirit enflame,
In that search ventur'd all unknowne to me.
O say, by what power cam'st thou now to be 55
Mine eyes' deare object?' He return'd reply:

Telemachus to his Mother.

'Move me not now, when you my scape descry
From iminent death, to thinke me fresh entrapt,
The fear'd wound rubbing, felt before I scap't.

Double not needlesse passion on a heart 60
Whose joy so greene is, and so apt t'invert—
But, pure weeds putting on, ascend and take
Your women with you, that yee all may make
Vowes of full Hecatombs in sacred fire
To all the God-heads, if their onely Sire 65
Vouchsafe revenge of guest-rites wrong'd, which hee
Is to protect, as being their Deity.
My way shall be directed to the hall
Of common Concourse, that I thence may call
A stranger, who from off the Pylian shore 70
Came friendly with me, whom I sent before
With all my souldiers, but in chiefe did charge
Piræus with him, wishing him t'enlarge
His love to him at home in best affaire
And utmost honors, till mine owne repaire.' 75
  Her Son thus spoken, his words could not beare
The wings too easely through her either eare,
But, putting pure weeds on, made vowes entire
Of perfect Hecatombes in sacred fire
To all the Deities, if their onely Sire 80
Vouchsaft revenge of guest-rites wrong'd, which he
Was to protect, as being their Deity.
  Her Son left house, in his faire hand his Lance,
His dogs attending, and on every glance
His lookes cast from them Pallas put a grace 85
That made him seeme of the celestiall race.
Whom (come to concourse) every man admir'd;
About him throng'd the wooers, and desir'd
All good to him in tongues, but in their hearts
Most deepe ils threatn'd to his most deserts. 90
Of whose huge rout once free, he cast glad eie
On some that, long before his infancie,
Were with his Father great and gracious—
Grave Halitherses, Mentor, Antiphus—
To whom he went, tooke seate by them, and they 95
Enquir'd of all things since his parting day.
To them Piræus came, and brought his Guest
Along the City thither, whom not least
The Prince respected, nor was long before
He rose and met him. The first word yet bore 100
Piræus from them both, whose haste besought
The Prince to send his women, to see brought
The Gifts from his house that Atrides gave—

Piræus to Telemachus.

Which his own roofes he thought wold better save.
Telemachus to Piræus.
The wise Prince answer'd: 'I can scarse conceive 105
The way to these workes. If the wooers reave
By privy Stratagem my life at home,
I rather wish Piræus may become
The Maister of them than the best of these.
But, if I sowe in their fields of excesse 110
Slaughter and ruine, then thy trust imploy
And to me joying bring thou those with joy.'
This said, he brought home his grief-practisd Guest,
Where both put off, both oyl'd, and did invest
Themselves in rich Robes, washt, and sate, and eate. 115
His Mother, in a faire chaire taking seate
Directly opposite, her Loome applied—
Who (when her Son and Guest had satisfied
Penelope to Telemachus.
Their appetites with feast) said: 'O my Sonne,
You know that ever since your Sire was wonne 120
To go in Agamemnon's guide to Troy,
Attempting sleepe, I never did injoy
One night's good rest, but made my quiet bed
A Sea blowne up with sighes, with teares still shed
Embrew'd and troubl'd: yet, though all your misse 125
In your late voyage hath bene made for this,
That you might know th'abode your Father made,
You shun to tell me what successe you had.
Now then, before the insolent accesse
The wooers straight will force on us, expresse 130
What you have heard.' 'I will,' saide he, 'and true.
Telemachus briefely relates his voyage to his Mother.
We came to Pylos, where the studious due
That any Father could affoord his Son
(But new arriv'd from some course he had ron
To an extreame length, in some voyage vow'd) 135
Nestor, the Pastor of the people, showed
To me arriv'd in turrets thrust up hye,
Where not his brave Sons were more lov'd than I.
Yet of th'unconquer'd-ever-Sufferer
Ulysses never he could set his eare, 140
Alive or dead, from any earthy man.
But to the great Lacedemonian
(Atrides, famous for his Lance) he sent,
With horse and Chariots, me, to learne th'event
From his Relation—where I had the view 145
Of Argive Helen, whose strong beauties drew
(By wils of Gods) so many Grecian States

And Troyans under such laborious Fates.
Where Menelaus ask't me what affaire
To Lacedemon render'd my repaire. 150
I told him all the truth, who made reply:
Menelaus to Telemachus.
"O deed of most abhor'd indecency!
A sort of Impotents attempt his bed
Whose strength of minde hath Cities levelled?
As to a Lyon's den when any Hinde 155
Hath brought her yong Calves, to their rest inclinde,
When he is ranging hils and hearby dales,
To make of Feeders there his Festivals,
But turning to his luster Calves and Dam,
He shewes abhorr'd death in his anger's flame: 160
So (should Ulysses finde this rabble housd
In his free Turrets, courting his espousd)
Foule death would fall them. O, I would to Jove,
Phœbus and Pallas that (when he shall prove
The broad report of his exhausted store 165
True with his eyes) his Nerves and Sinewes wore
That vigor then that in the Lesbian Tow'rs
(Provok't to wrastle with the iron powrs
Philomelides vanted) he approv'd—
When downe he hurl'd his Challenger and mov'd 170
Huge shouts from all the Achives then in view.
If, once come home, he all those forces drew
About him there to worke, they all were dead,
And should finde bitter his attempted bed.
But what you aske and sue for, I (as far 175
As I have heard the true-spoke Marinar)
Will tell directly, nor delude your eare.
He told me that an Island did enspheare
(In much discomfort) great Laertes' sonne,
And that the Nymph Calypso (over-ronne 180
With his affection) kept him in her Caves,
Where men nor Ship, of pow'r to brook the waves,
Were neere his convoy to his countrie's Shore,
And where her selfe importun'd evermore
His quiet stay—which, not obtain'd, by force 185
She kept his person from all else recourse."
'This told Atrides, which was all he knew;
Nor staid I more, but from the Gods there blew
A prosperous winde, that set me quickly heere.'
This put his Mother quite from all her cheere, 190
When Theoclymenus the Augure said:

Theoclymenus to Penelope.

'O woman, honour'd with Ulysses' bed,
Your Son, no doubt, knowes cleerely nothing more.
Heare me yet speake, that can the truth uncore,
Nor will be curious. Jove, then, witnesse beare, 195
And this thy Hospitable Table heere,
With this whole houshold of your blamelesse Lord,
That, at this houre, his royall feete are shor'd
On his lov'd countrey earth, and that even heere,
Comming or creeping, he will see the cheere 200
These wooers make, and in his soule's field sow
Seeds that shall thrive to all their overthrow.
This, set a ship boord, I knew sorted thus,
And cried it out to your Telemachus.'

Penelope to Theoclymenus.

Penelope replied: 'Would this would prove, 205
You well should witnesse a most friendly love
And gifts such of me as encountring Fame
Should greete you with a blessed Mortal's name.'
This mutuall speech past, all the wooers were
Hurling the stone and tossing of the Speare 210
Before the Pallace, in the paved Court,
Where other-whiles their petulant resort
Sate plotting injuries. But when the hower
Of Supper enter'd, and the feeding power
Brought sheepe from field, that fil'd up every way 215
With those that usde to furnish that purvay,

Medon the Herald calls of the Wooers to supper.

Medon the Herald (who of all the rest
Pleasd most the wooers and at every Feast
Was ever neere) said: 'You whose kind consort
Make the faire branches of the Tree our Court, 220
Grace it within now, and your Suppers take.
You that for health and faire contention's sake
Wil please your minds, know, bodies must have meat:
Play's worse than idlenesse in times to eate.'
This said, all left, came in, cast by on Thrones 225
And Chaires their garments. Their provisions
Were Sheepe, Swine, Goats, the chiefly great and fat,
Besides an Oxe, that from the Herd they gat.
And now the King and Herdsman, from the field,
In good way were to Towne, twixt whom was held 230
Some walking conference, which thus begun

Eumæus to Ulysses.

The good Eumæus: 'Guest, your will was wun
(Because the Prince commanded) to make way
Up to the City, though I wisht your stay
And to have made you Guardian of my stall: 235

But I, in care and feare of what might fall
In after anger of the Prince, forbore.
The checkes of Princes touch their subjects sore.
But make we hast, the day is neerely ended,
And cold ayres still arc in the Even extended.' 240

Ulysses to Eumæus.

'I know't,' said he, 'consider all; your charge
Is given to one that understands at large.
Haste then: heereafter you shall leade the way;
Affoord your Staffe too, if it fit your stay,
That I may use it, since you say our passe 245
Is lesse friend to a weake foot than it was.'
Thus cast he on his necke his nasty Scrip,
All patcht and torne, a cord that would not slip,
For knots and bracks, about the mouth of it
Made serve the turne; and then his Swaine did fit 250
His forc't state with a staffe. Then plied they hard
Their way to towne, their Cottage left in guard
To Swaines and Dogs. And now Eumæus led
The King along, his garments to a thred
All bare and burn'd, and he himselfe hard bore 255
Upon his staffe, at all parts like a pore
And sad old begger. But when now they got
The rough high-way, their voyage wanted not

The washing Fount of the Citty.

Much of the City: where a Fount they reacht
From whence the Towne their choisest water fetcht, 260
That ever over-flow'd, and curious Art
Was shewne about it: in which three had part,
Whose names Neritus and Polyctor were,
And famous Ithacus. It had a Sphere
Of poplar, that ranne round about the wall, 265
And into it a lofty Rocke let fall
Continuall supply of coole cleare streame—
On whose top to the Nymphs that were supreme
In those parts' loves a stately Altar rose,
Where every Travailer did still impose 270
Devoted sacrifice. At this fount found
These silly Travailers a man renown'd
For guard of Goats, which now he had in guide,
Whose huge-stor'd Herd two herdsmen kept beside,
For all Herds it exceld and bred a feed 275
For wooers onely. He was Dolius' seede,
And call'd Melanthius—who, casting eye
On these two there, he chid them terribly,
And so past meane that even the wretched fate

Now on Ulysses he did irritate. 280
His fume to this effect he did pursue:

Melanthius to Eumæus and Ulysses.

'Why so, 'tis now at all parts passing true,
That ill leades ill, good evermore doth traine
With like his like. Why, thou unenvied Swaine,
Whither dost thou leade this same victles Leager, 285
This bane of banquets, this most nasty begger?—
Whose sight doth make one sad, it so abhorres,
Who with his standing in so many doores
Hath broke his backe, and all his beggery tends
To beg base crusts but to no manly ends, 290
As asking swords, or with activity
To get a Caldron. Wouldst thou give him me
To farme my Stable, or to sweepe my yarde,
And bring brouse to my kids, and that prefer'd
He should be at my keeping for his paines, 295
To drinke as much whey as his thirsty veynes
Would still be swilling (whey made all his fees)
His monstrous belly would oppresse his knees.
But he hath learn'd to leade base life about,
And will not worke, but crouch among the rout 300
For broken meate to cram his bursten gut.
Yet this I'le say, and he will finde it put
In sure effect, that, if he enters where
Ulysses' roofes cast shade, the stooles will there
About his eares flye; all the house wil throw, 305
And rub his ragged sides with cuffes enow.'

Past these reviles his manlesse rudenesse spurn'd
Divine Ulysses, who at no part turn'd
His face from him, but had his spirit fed
With these two thoghts—if he should strike him dead 310
With his bestowed staffe, or at his feete
Make his direct head and the pavement meete.
But he bore all, and entertain'd a brest
That in the strife of all extremes did rest.

Eumæus curseth Melanthius for his rude usage of Ulysses.

Eumæus, frowning on him, chid him yet, 315
And, lifting up his hands to heaven, he set
This bitter curse at him: 'O you that beare
Faire name to be the race of Jupiter,
Nymphes of these Fountaines! If Ulysses ever
Burn'd thighes to you that hid in fat, did never 320
Faile your acceptance of or Lambe or Kid,
Grant this grace to me—let the man thus hid
Shine through his dark fate, make som God his guide,

Intending his fat Herd, kept onely for the wooers' daintie Pallats.

That to thee, Goat-herd, this same Pallat's pride
Thou driv'st afore thee he may come and make 325
The scatterings of the earth, and over-take
Thy wrongs with forcing thee to ever erre
About the City, hunted by his feare.
And, in the meane space, may some slothfull Swaines
Let lowsie sicknesse gnaw thy Cattel's Vaines.' 330

Melanthius' answer to Eumæus.

'O Gods!' replyed Melanthius, 'what a curse
Hath this dog barkt out, and can yet do wurse?
This man shall I have given into my hands,
When in a well-built Ship to farre-off Lands
I shall transport him, that (should I want here) 335
My sale of him may finde me victels there.
And, for Ulysses, would to heaven his joy
The Silver-bearing-bow-God would destroy
This day within his house, as sure as he
The day of his returne shall never see.' 340
This said, he left them, going silent on;
But he out-went them, and tooke straight upon
The Pallace royall, which he enter'd straight,
Sat with the wooers, and his Trencher's fraight
The Kervers gave him of the flesh there vented, 345
But bread the reverend Buttleresse presented.
He tooke against Eurymachus his place,
Who most of all the wooers gave him grace.
And now Ulysses and his Swaine got nere,
When round about them visited their eare 350
The hollow Harpe's delicious-stricken string,
To which did Phemius (neere the wooers) sing.
Then by the hand Ulysses tooke his Swaine,
And saide: 'Eumæus! One may heere see plaine

Ulysses.

(In many a grace) that Laertiades 355
Built heere these Turrets, and (mongst others these)
His whole Court arm'd with such a goodly wall,
The Cornish and the Cope Majesticall,
His double gates and Turrets built too strong
For force or vertue ever to expugne. 360
I know the Feasters in it now abound,
Their Cates cast such a savour, and the sound
The Harpe gives argues an accomplisht Feast:
The Gods made Musicke, Banquet's deerest Guest.'
'These things,' said he, 'your skill may tell with ease, 365
Since you are grac't with greater knowledges.
But now consult we how these workes shall sort,

If you will first approch this praised Court
And see these wooers (I remaining here),
Or I shall enter and your selfe forbeare. 370
But be not you too tedious in your stay,
Lest thrust ye be and buffeted away:
Braine hath no fence for blowes; looke too't I pray.'
'You speake to one that comprehends,' said he,
'Go you before, and heere adventure me. 375
I have of old bene usde to cuffes and blowes;
My minde is hardn'd, having borne the throwes
Of many a soure event in waves and wars,
Where knockes and buffets are no Forreinars.
And this same harmefull belly by no meane 380
The greatest Abstinent can ever weane:
Men suffer much Bane by the Bellie's rage,
For whose sake Ships in all their equipage
Are arm'd and set out to th'untamed Seas,
Their bulkes full fraught with ils to enemies.' 385
Such speech they chang'd: when in the yeard there lay
A dogge call'd Argus, which, before his way

Ulysses' dog, called Argus.

Assum'd for Ilion, Ulysses bred,
Yet stood his pleasure then in little sted
(As being too yong), but, growing to his grace, 390
Yong men made choise of him for every Chace,
Or of their wilde Goats, of their Hares, or Harts.
But, his King gone, and he now past his parts,
Lay all abjectly on the Stable's store,
Before the Oxe-stall and Mules' stable dore, 395
To keepe the clothes cast from the Pessants' hands,
While they laide compasse on Ulysses' Lands,
The Dog with Tickes (unlook't to) over-growne.
But by this Dog no sooner seene but knowne
Was wise Ulysses, who (new enter'd there) 400
Up went his Dog's laide eares, and (comming nere)
Up he himselfe rose, fawn'd, and wag'd his Sterne,
Coucht close his eares, and lay so—nor descerne

The Dog dyed as soone as hee had seen Ulysses.

Could evermore his deere-lov'd Lord againe.
Ulysses saw it, nor had powre t'abstaine 405
From shedding tears—which (far-off seeing his Swain)
He dried from his sight cleane, to whom he thus
His griefe dissembled: ''Tis miraculous
That such a Dog as this should have his laire
On such a dunghill, for his forme is faire. 410
And yet I know not if there were in him

Good pace or parts for all his goodly lim,
Or he liv'd empty of those inward things,
As are those trencher-Beagles tending Kings,
Whom for their pleasures or their glorie's sake, 415
Or fashion, they into their favours take.'

Eumæus' Description of Ulysses' Dogge.

"This Dog,' said he, 'was servant to one dead
A huge time since. But if he bore his head
(For forme and quality) of such a hight
As when Ulysses (bound for th'Ilian fight, 420
Or quickly after) left him, your rapt eyes
Would then admire to see him use his Thyes
In strength and swiftnes. He would nothing flye,
Nor any thing let scape. If once his eye
Seiz'd any wilde beast, he knew straight his scent: 425
Go where he would, away with him he went.
Nor was there ever any Savage stood
Amongst the thickets of the deepest wood
Long time before him, but he pull'd him downe—
As well by that true hunting to be showne 430
In such vaste coverts, as for speed of pace
In any open Lawne; for in deepe chace
He was a passing wise and well-nos'd Hound.
And yet is all this good in him uncroun'd
With any grace heere now, nor he more fed 435
Than any errant Curre. His King is dead
Farre from his country, and his servants are
So negligent, they lend his Hound no care.
Where Maysters rule not but let Men alone,
You never there see honest service done. 440
That Man's halfe vertue Jove takes quite away,
That once is Sun-burn'd with the servile day.'

This said, he enter'd the well-builded Towers,
Up bearing right upon the glorious wooers,
And left poore Argus dead. His Lord's first sight, 445
Since that time twenty yeares, bereft his light.

Telemachus did farre the first behould
Eumæus enter, and made signes he should
Come up to him. He (noting) came and tooke
On earth his seate. And then the Maister Cooke 450
Serv'd in more banquet—of which, part he set
Before the wooers, part the Prince did get,
Who sate alone, his Table plac't aside,
To which the Herald did the bread divide.

Ulysses' ruthfull fashion of entrie to his own Hal.

After Eumæus enter'd straight the King, 455

Like to a poore and heavy aged thing,
Bore hard upon his staffe, and was so clad
As would have made his meere beholder sad.
Upon the Ashen floore his limbes he spred,
And gainst a Cypresse threshold staid his head, 460
The tree wrought smooth and in a line direct
Tried by the Plumbe and by the Architect.
The Prince then bad the Herdsman give him bread
The finest there, and see that prostrated
At-all-parts plight of his given all the cheare 465
His hands could turne to: 'Take,' saide he, 'and beare
These cates to him, and bid him beg of all
These wooers heere, and to their feastivall
Beare up with all the impudence he can:
Bashfull behaviour fits no needy Man.' 470

He heard, and did his will: 'Hold, Guest,' saide he,
'Telemachus commends these cates to thee,
Bids thee beare up, and all these woo'rs implore:
Wit must make Impudent whom Fate makes pore.'

'O Jove,' said he, 'do my poore pray'rs the grace 475
To make him blessed'st of the mortall race,
And every thought now in his generous heart
To deeds that further my desires convert.'

Thus tooke he in with both his hands his store,
And in the uncouth Scrip that lay before 480
His ill-shod feete repos'd it, whence he fed
All time the Musicke to the Feasters plaid.
Both joyntly ending, then began the woo'rs
To put in old act their tumultuous pow'rs—
When Pallas, standing close, did prompt her frend 485
To prove how farre the bounties would extend
Of those proud wooers, so to let him try
Who most, who least, had learn'd humanity.
However, no thought toucht Minerva's minde
That any one should scape his wreake design'd. 490
He handsomly became all, crept about
To every wooer, held a forc't hand out,
And all his worke did in so like a way
As he had practis'd begging many a day.
And though they knew all beggers could do this, 495
Yet they admir'd it as no deede of his,
Though farre from thought of other, us'd expence
And pitty to him, who he was, and whence,
Enquiring mutually. Melanthius then:

'Heare me, ye wooers of the farre-fam'd Queen, 500
About this begger: I have seene before
This face of his, and know for certaine more—
That this Swaine brought him hither. What he is,
Or whence he came, flies me.' Reply to this
Antinous made, and mockt Eumæus thus: 505
'O thou renowned Herdsman, why to us
Brought'st thou this begger? Serves it not our hands
That other Land-leapers and Cormorands
(Prophane poore knaves) lye on us unconducted,
But you must bring them? So amisse instructed 510
Art thou in course of thrift as not to know
Thy Lord's goods wrackt in this their over-flow?
Which thinkst thou nothing, that thou calst in these?'
Eumæus answer'd: 'Though you may be wise,
You speak not wisely. Who cals in a Guest 515
That is a guest himselfe? None cal to Feast
Other than men that are of publique use—
Prophets or Poets, whom the Gods produce,
Physitians for men's ils, or Architects.
Such men the boundlesse earth affoords respects 520
Bounded in honour, and may call them wel:
But poore men who cals? Who doth so excell
In other's good to do himselfe an ill?
But all Ulysses' servants have bene still
Eye-sores in your waie more than all that woo, 525
And cheefly I. But what care I for you,
As long as these roofes hold as thrals to none
The wise Penelope and her God-like Sonne?'
'Forbeare,' said he, 'and leave this tongue's bold ill,
Antinous' uses to be crossing still, 530
And give sharpe words: his blood that humor beares,
To set men stil together by the eares.
But' (turning then t'Antinous) 'O,' saide he,
'You entertaine a Father's care of me,
To turne these eating guests out. Tis advise 535
Of needful use for my poore faculties.
But God doth not allow this. There must be
Some care of poore men in humanitie.
What you your selves take, give; I not envy,
But give command that hospitality 540
Be given al strangers. Nor shal my pow'rs feare,
If this mood in me reach my Mother's eare,
Much lesse the servants, that are heere to see

Ulysses' house kept in his old degree.
But you beare no such mind, your wits more cast 545
To fill your selfe than let another tast.'
  Antinous answer'd him: 'Brave spoken man!
Whose mind's free fire see check't no vertue can.
If all we wooers heere would give as much
Intending Ulysses. As my minde serves, his Larges should be such 550
As would for three months serve his farre off way
From troubling your house with more cause of stay.'
  This said, he tooke a stoole up that did rest
Beneath the boord his spangled feete at feast,
And offer'd at him. But the rest gave all, 555
And fil'd his fulsome Scrip with Festivall.
And so Ulysses for the present was,
And for the future, furnisht, and his passe
Bent to the doore to eate—yet could not leave
Ulysses to Antinous. Antinous so, but said: 'Do you too give, 560
Lov'd Lord, your presence makes a shew to me
As you not worst were of the company,
But best, and so much that you seeme the King—
And therefore you should give some better thing
Than bread, like others. I will spred your praise 565
Through all the wide world, that have in my daies
Kept house my selfe, and trod the wealthy waies
Of other men even to the Title Blest;
And often have I given an erring Guest
(How meane soever) to the utmost gaine 570
Of what he wanted, kept whole troopes of men,
And had all other commings in with which
Men live so well and gaine the fame of Rich.
Yet Jove consum'd all: he would have it so:
To which, his meane was this—he made me go 575
Farre off, for Egypt, in the rude consort
Of all-waies-wandring Pyrats, where in Port
I bad my lov'd men draw their Ships ashore,
And dwell amongst them, sent out some t'explore
Up to the Mountaines, who (intemperate, 580
And their inflam'd bloods bent to satiate)
Forrag'd the rich fields, hal'd the women thence,
And unwean'd children, with the foule expence
Both of their fames and bloods. The cry then flew
Straight to the City, and the great fields grew 585
With horse and foot, and flam'd with iron armes—
When Jove (that breaks the Thunder in Alarmes)

An ill flight cast amongst my men, not one
Inspir'd with spirit to stand and turne upon
The fierce pursuing foe: and therefore stood 590
Their ill fate thicke about them, some in blood,
And some in bondage, toiles led by constraint
Fastning upon them. Me along they sent
To Cyprus with a stranger Prince they met,
Dmetor Iasides, who th'Imperiall seat 595
Of that sweete Island swaid in strong command.
And thus feele I heere Need's contemned hand.'
'And what God sent,' saide he, 'this suffering bane
To vex our banquet? Stand off, nor prophane
My boord so boldly, lest I shew thee here 600
Cyprus and Egypt made more soure than there.
You are a sawcy set-fac't Vagabond.
About with all you go, and they beyond
Discretion give thee, since they finde not heere
The least proportion set downe to their cheere. 605
But every Fountaine hath his under floods:
It is no Bounty to give others' goods.'
'O Gods,' replied Ulysses, 'I see now
You beare no soule in this your goodly show.
Beggers at your boord, I perceive, should get 610
Scarse salt from your hands, if themselves broght meat,
Since, sitting where another's boord is spread,
That flowes with feast, not to the broken bread
Will your allowance reach.' 'Nay then,' said he,
And look't austerely, 'if so saucy be 615
Your suffer'd language, I suppose that cleere
You shall not scape without some broken cheere.'
Thus rapt he up a stoole, with which he smit
The King's right shoulder 'twixt his necke, and it.
He stood him like a rocke: Antinous' dart 620
Not stirr'd Ulysses, who in his great hart
Deepe ils projected, which, for time yet, close
He bound in silence, shooke his head, and went
Out to the Entry, where he then gave vent
To his full scrip, sate on the earth, and eate, 625
And talk't still to the wooers: 'Heare me yet,
Ye wooers of the Queene. It never greeves
A man to take blowes, where for Sheepe, or Beeves,
Or other maine possessions, a man fights:
But for his harmefull belly this man smites, 630
Whose love to many a man breeds many a wo.

And if the poore have Gods, and Furies too,
Before Antinous weare his Nuptiall wreath
He shall be worne upon the dart of death.'
'Harsh Guest,' saide he, 'sit silent at your meate, 635
Or seeke your desperate plight some safer seate,
Lest by the hands or heeles youths drag your yeares,
And rend your rotten ragges about your eares.'
This made the rest as highly hate his folly
As he had violated something holy— 640
When one (even of the proudest) thus began:
'Thou dost not nobly thus to play the man
On such an errant wretch. O ill dispos'd!
Perhaps some sacred God-head goes enclos'd
Even in his abject outside. For the Gods 645
Have often visited these rich abods
Like such poore stranger Pilgrims, since their pow'rs
(Being al wayes shapefull) glide through Townes and Tow'rs,
Observing as they passe stil who they be
That piety love, and who impiety.' 650
This all men said, but he held sayings cheape.
And all this time Telemachus did heape
Sorrow on sorrow on his beating hart
To see his Father stricken, yet let part
No teare to earth, but shooke his head, and thought 655
As deepe as those ils that were after wrought.
The Queen now, hearing of her poore guest's stroke,
Said to her Maid (as to her wooer she spoke):
'I wish the famous for his Bow, the Sun,
Would strike thy heart so.' Her wish (thus begun) 660
Her Lady, faire Eurynome, pursude
Her execration, and did thus conclude:
'So may our vowes call downe from heaven his end,
And let no one life of the rest extend
His life till morning.' 'O Eurynome,' 665
Replied the Queene, 'may all Gods speake in thee,
For all the wooers we should rate as foes,
Since all their weales they place in others' woes.
But this Antinous we past all should hate,
As one resembling blacke and cruell Fate. 670
A poor strange wretch beg'd here, compel'd by need,
Askt all, and every one gave in his deed,
Fill'd his sad Scrip and eas'd his heavy wants:
Onely this man bestow'd unmanly tants,
And with a cruell blow (his force let flye) 675

'Twixt necke and shoulders shew'd his charity.'
These minds (above) she and her Maids did show,
While at his scrip Ulysses sate below.
In which time she Eumæus call'd, and said:
'Go, good Eumæus, and see soone convaid 680
The stranger to me. Bid him come and take
My salutations for his welcome's sake,
And my desire serve, if he hath not heard
Or seene distrest Ulysses—who hath err'd
Like such a man, and therefore chance may fall 685
He hath by him bene met, and spoke withall.'
'O Queene,' saide he, 'I wish to heaven your eare
Were quit of this unreverend noise you heare
From these rude wooers, when I bring the guest:
Such words your eare would let into your brest 690
As would delight it to your very heart.
Three nights and dayes I did my Roofe impart
To his fruition (for he came to me
The first of all men since he fled the Sea)
And yet he had not given a perfect end 695
To his relation of what woes did spend
The spight of Fate on him. But as you see
A Singer breathing out of Deity
Love-kindling lines, when all men seated nere
Are rapt with endlesse thirst to ever heare: 700
So sweetn'd he my bosome at my meate,
Affirming that Ulysses was in Crete,
Where first the memories of Minos were,
A Guest to him there dwelling, then as deare
As his true Father; and from thence came he 705
Tir'd on with sorrowes, tost from sea to sea,
To cast himselfe in dust and tumble heere
At wooers' feete, for blowes and broken cheere.
But of Ulysses (where the Thesprots dwell,
A wealthy people) Fame, he sayes, did tell 710
The still survivall—who his Native light
Was bound for now with treasure infinite.'
'Call him,' sayd she, 'that he himselfe may say
This over to me. We shall soone have way
Given by the wooers. They, as well at Gate 715
As set within doores, use to recreate
Their high-fed spirits. As their humors leade
They follow—and may well, for still they treade
Uncharg'd waies here, their own welth lying unwasted

Simile—in which Ulysses is compared with a Poet for the sweetnesse of his speech.

In poore-kept houses; onely something tasted 720
Their bread and wine is by their houshold Swaines,
But they themselves let loose continuall Reines
To our expences, making slaughter still
Of Sheepe, Goats, Oxen, feeding past their fill,
And vainly lavishing our richest wine, 725
All these extending past the sacred line.
For here lives no man like Ulysses now
To curbe these ruines. But should he once show
His country light his presence, he and his
Would soone revenge these wooers' injuries.' 730
This said, about the house in ecchoes round
Neezing a good Omen. Her Son's strange Neesings made a horrid sound,
At which, the Queene yet laught, and said: 'Goe call
The stranger to me. Heardst thou not to all
My words last utter'd what a Neesing brake 735
From my Telemachus? From whence I make
This sure conclusion—that the death and fate
Of every wooer heere is neere his date.
Call then the Guest; and if he tel as trew
What I shal aske him, cote, cloke, all things new 740
These hands shal yeeld him.' This said, down he went
And told Ulysses that the Queene had sent
To call him to her, that she might enquire
About her husband what her sad desire
Urg'd her to aske; and, if she found him true, 745
Both cote, and cassocke (which he needed) new
Her hands would put on him, and that the Bread
Which now he begg'd amongst the commune tread
Should freely feed his hunger now from her,
Who all he wisht would to his wants prefer. 750
His answer was: 'I will with fit speed tell
The whole truth to the Queene. For passing well
I know her Lord, since he and I have shar'd
In equall sorrowes. But I much am scar'd
With this rude multitude of wooers here, 755
The rage of whose pride smites heaven's brazen sphere—
Of whose rout when one strooke me for no fault,
Telemachus, nor none else, turn'd th'assault
From my poore shoulders. Therfore, though she hast,
Beseech the Queene her patience will see past 760
The daye's broad light, and then may she enquire.
'Tis but my closer preasing to the fire
In th'Evening's cold, because my weeds, you know,

Are passing thin—for I made bold to show
Their brackes to you, and pray'd your kinde supply.' 765
He heard, and hasted, and met instantly
The Queene upon the pavement in his way,
Who askt: 'What? Bringst thou not? What cause of stay
Finde his austere supposes? Takes he feare
Of th'unjust wooers? Or thus hard doth beare 770
On any other doubt the house objects?
He does me wrong, and gives too nice respects
To his fear'd safety.' 'He does right,' said he,
'And what he feares should move the policie
Of any wise one, taking care to shun 775
The violent wooers. He bids bide, til Sun
Hath hid his broad light: and, beleeve it, Queene,
T'will make your best course, since you two unseene
May passe th'encounter—you to speake more free,
And he your eare gaine lesse distractedly.' 780
'The Guest is wise,' said she, 'and well doth give
The right thought use. Of all the men that live
Life serves none such as these proud wooers are
To give a good man cause to use his care.'
Thus (all agreed) amongst the wooers goes 785
Eumæus to the Prince, and (whispering close)
Said: 'Now, my Love, my charge shall take up me,
Your goods, and mine. What here is, you must see
In fit protection. But, in chiefe, regard
Your owne deere safegard, whose state study hard, 790
Lest sufferance seize you. Many a wicked thought
Conceale these wooers—whom just Jove see brought
To utter ruine, ere it touch at us.'
'So chance it, Friend,' replyed Telemachus,
'Your Bever taken, go: in first of day 795
Come and bring sacrifice, the best you may.
To me, and to th'immortals, be the care
Of whatsoever heere the safeties are.'
This said, he sate in his elaborate Throne.
Eumæus (fed to satisfaction) 800
Went to his charge, left both the Court and wals,
Full of secure and fatall Festivals,
In which the wooers' pleasures still would sway.
And now begun the Even's nere-ending day.

The End of the Seaventeenth Booke of Homer's Odysses

THE EIGHTEENTH BOOKE
of
HOMER'S ODYSSES

THE ARGUMENT

Ulysses and Rogue Irus fight.
Penelope vouchsafes her sight
To all her Wooers, who present
Gifts to her, ravisht with content.
A certain Parle then we sing 5
Betwixt a Wooer and the King.

Another Argument

Σίγμα. { *The Begger's glee,*
the King's high fame;
Gifts given to see
a vertuous Dame. }

There came a commune Begger to the Court,
Who in the City begg'd of all resort,
Excell'd in madnesse of the gut, drunke, eate
Past intermission, was most hugely great;
Yet had no fivers in him, nor no force: 5
In sight a Man, in mind a living Corse.
His true name was Arnæus, for his mother
Impos'd it from his birth. And yet another
The City youth would give him (from the course
He after tooke, deriv'd out of the force 10
That Need held on him, which was up and downe
To run on all men's errands through the Towne)
Which sounded Irus. When whose gut was come,
He needs would barre Ulysses his owne home,
And fell to chiding him: 'Old man,' saide he, 15
'Your way out of the Entry quickly see
Be with faire Language taken, lest your stay

But little longer see you dragg'd away.
See, Sir. Observe you not how all these make
Direct signes at me, charging me to take 20
Your heeles and drag you out? But I take shame.
Rise yet, y'are best, lest we two play a game
At cuffes together.' He bent browes, and saide:
'Wretch! I do thee no ill, nor once upbraide
Thy presence with a word, nor what mine eye 25
By all hands sees thee given one thought envy:
Nor shouldst thou envy others. Thou mayst see
The place will hold us both, and seem'st to me
A Begger like my self—which who can mend?
The Gods give most to whom they least are Friend: 30
The cheefe goods Gods give is in good to end.
But to the hands' strife, of which y'are so free,
Provoke me not, for feare you anger me,
And lest the old man, on whose scorne you stood,
Your lips and bosome make shake hands in blood. 35
I love my quiet well, and more will love
Tomorrow than to day. But if you move
My peace beyond my right, the warre you make
Will never after give you will to take
Ulysses' house into your begging walke.' 40
'O Gods,' saide he, 'how volubly doth talke
This eating gulfe! And how his fume breakes out,
As from an old crackt Oven! Whom I will clout
So bitterly, and so with both hands mall
His chaps together, that his teeth shall fall 45
As plaine seene on the earth as any Sowe's
That ruts the Corne-fields or devoures the Mowes.
Come, close we now, that all may see what wrong
An old man tempts that takes at cuffes a yong.'
Thus in the entry of those lofty Tow'rs, 50
These two with al splene spent their jarring pow'rs.
Antinous tooke it, laught, and saide: 'O Friends,
We never had such sport. This Guest contends
With this vaste Begger at the Buffet's fight.
Come, joyne we hands, and screw up all their spight.' 55
All rose in Laughters, and about them bore
All the ragg'd rout of beggers at the dore.
Then mov'd Antinous the victor's hire
To all the woo'rs thus: 'There are now at fire
Two brests of Goat, both which let Law set downne 60
Before the man that wins the daye's renowne,

With all their fat and greavie. And of both
The glorious Victor shal preferre his tooth
To which he makes his choise of from us all,
And ever after banquet in our Hall 65
With what our boords yeeld—not a Begger more
Allow'd to share, but all keepe out at dore.'
This he proposd, and this they all approv'd,
To which Ulysses answer'd: 'O most lov'd,
By no meanes should an old man, and one old 70
In chiefe with sorrowes, be so over-bold
To combat with his yonger. But, alas,
Man's owne-ill-working belly needs will passe
This worke upon me, and enforce me too
To beate this fellow. But then you must doo 75
My age no wrong, to take my yonger's part
And play me foule play, making your stroke's smart
Helpe his to conquer—for you easly may
With your strengths crush me. Do then right, and lay
Your Honors on it in your oaths, to yield 80
His part no aide, but equall leave the field.'
All swore his will. But then Telemachus
His Father's scoffes with comforts serious
Could not but answer, and made this reply:
'Guest! If thine owne powers cheere thy victory, 85
Feare no man's else that will not passe it free:
He fights with many that shall touch but thee.
I'le see thy guest-right paide. Thou heere art come
In my protection, and to this the summe
Of all these wooers (which Antinous are 90
And King Eurymachus) conjoyne their care.'
Both vow'd it—when Ulysses, laying by
His upper weed, his inner beggery
Nere shew'd his shame, which he with rags prevented
Pluckt from about his Thighes, and so presented 95
Their goodly sight, which were so white and great,
And his large shoulders were to view so set
By his bare rags, his armes, his breast and all
So broad and brawny (their grace naturall
Being helpt by Pallas, ever standing nere) 100
That all the wooers his admirers were
Beyond all measure, mutuall whispers driven
Through all their cluster, saying: 'Sure as heaven,
Poore Irus pull'd upon him bitter blowes.
Through his thin Garment what a Thigh he showes!' 105

They said, but Irus felt. His Cow-herd minde
Was mov'd at roote. But now he needs must finde
Facts to his brags, and forth at all parts fit
The servants brought him, all his artires smit
With ſeares and tremblings—which Antinous saw, 110
And saide: 'Nay, now too late comes feare. No Law
Thou shouldst at first have given thy braggart vaine,
Nor should it so have swell'd, if terrors straine
Thy spirits to this passe for a man so old
And worne with penuries that still lay hold 115
On his ragg'd person. Howsoever, take
This vow from me for firme—that if he make
Thy forces stoope and prove his owne supreame,
I'le put thee in a Ship, and downe the streame
Send thee ashore where King Echetus raignes 120
(The roughest tyrant that the world containes)
And he will slit thy Nostrils, crop each eare,
Thy shame cut off and give it dogges to teare.'
This shook his Nerves the more. But both were now
Brought to the Lists, and up did either throw 125
His heavy fists—Ulysses, in suspence
To strike so home that he should fright from thence
His Cow-herd soule (his trunke laide prostrate there),
Or let him take more leisure to his feare
And stoope him by degrees. The last shew'd best, 130
To strike him slightly, out of feare the rest
Would else discover him. But (peace now broke)
On his right shoulder Irus laide his stroke.
Ulysses strooke him just beneath the eare,
His jaw-bone broke, and made the blood appeare— 135
When straight he strew'd the dust, and made his crie
Stand for himselfe, with whom his teeth did lie,
Spit with his blood out; and against the ground
His heeles lay sprawling. Up the hands went round
Of all the wooers, all at point to dye 140
With violent laughters. Then the King did ply
The Begger's feete, and dragg'd him forth the Hall
Along the Entry to the gates and wall—
Where leaving him, he put into his hand
A Staffe, and bad him there use his command 145
On Swine and Dogs, and not presume to be
Lord of the guests or of the Beggery,
Since he of all men was the scum and curse—
And so bad please with that, or fare yet wurse.

The buffet fight betwixt Ulysses and Irus.

Then cast he on his scrip, all patcht and rent, 150
Hung by a rotten cord, and backe he went
To greete the Entrie's threshold with his seat.
The wooers throng'd to him, and did entreat
With gentle words his conquest, laughing still,
Pray'd Jove and all the Gods to give his will 155
What most it wisht him and would joy him most,
Since he so happily had cleer'd their cost
Of that unsavoury morsell—whom they vow'd
To see with all their utmost haste bestow'd
Aboord a ship and for Epirus sent 160
To King Echetus, on whose Throne was spent
The worst man's seat that breath'd. And thus was grac't
Divine Ulysses, who with joy embrac't
Even that poore conquest. Then was set to him
The goodly Goat's breast promist (that did swim 165
In fat and greavy) by Antinous.
And from a Basket (by Amphinomus)
Was two Breads given him, who (besides) renown'd
His banquet with a golden Goblet cround,
And this high salutation: 'Frolicke, Guest, 170
And be those riches that you first possest
Restor'd againe with full as many joyes
As, in your poore state, I see now annoyes.'
'Amphinomus,' saide he, 'you seeme to me
Exceeding wise, as being the progeny 175
Of such a Father as autentique Fame
Hath told me was so—one of honour'd name
And great revennues in Dulichius;
His faire name, Nisus. He is blazon'd thus,
And you to be his Sonne, his wisedome heyring 180
As well as wealth, his state in nought empairing.
To prove which all waies, let me tell you this
(As warning you to shun the miseries
That follow full states, if they be not held
With wisedome still at full, and so compeld 185
To courses that abode not in their browes
By too much swindge their sodaine overthrowes)—
Of all things breathing, or that creepe on earth,
Nought is more wretched than a humane Birth.
Bless'd men thinke never they can cursed be, 190
While any power lasts to move a knee.
But when the blest Gods make them feele that smart,
That fled their Faith so as they had no hart,

They beare their sufferings, and what wel they might
Have cleerly shun'd they then meet in despight. 195
The Minde of Man flyes stil out of his way,
Unlesse God guide and prompt it every day.
I thought me once a blessed man with men,
And fashion'd me to all so counted then—
Did all injustice like them, what for Lust 200
Or any pleasure, never so unjust,
I could by powre or violence obtaine,
And gave them both in all their powres the raigne,
Bold of my Fathers and my Brothers still;
While which held good, my Arts seem'd never ill. 205
And thus is none held simply good or bad,
But as his will is either mist or had.
Al goods God's gifts man cals, how ere he gets them,
And so takes all, what price so ere God sets them—
Saies nought how ill they come, nor will controule 210
That Ravine in him, though it cost his soule.
And these parts here I see these wooers play,
Take all that fals, and all dishonors lay
On that man's Queen, that (tell your frends) doth bear
No long time's absence, but is passing neare. 215
Let God then guide thee home, lest he may meete
In his returne thy undeparted feete.
For when he enters and sees men so rude,
The quarrell cannot but in blood conclude.'
This said, he sacrific'd, then drunke, and then 220
Referr'd the given Boule to the guide of men—
Who walk't away afflicted at his heart,
Shook head, and fear'd that these facts wold convert
To ill in th'end. Yet had not grace to flie:
Minerva staid him, being ordain'd to die 225
Upon the Lance of yong Ulyssides.
So downe he sate; and then did Pallas please
T'incline the Queene's affections to appeare
To all the wooers, to extend their cheare
To th'utmost lightning that still ushers death, 230
And made her put on all the painted sheath
That might both set her wooers' fancies hye,
And get her greater honor in the eye
Even of her Son and Soveraigne than before.
Who laughing yet (to shew her humor bore 235
No serious appetite to that light show)
She told Eurynome that not till now

She ever knew her entertaine desire
To please her wooers' eyes, but oft on fire
She set their hate in keeping from them still; 240
Yet now she pleas'd t'appeare, though from no will
To do them honor, vowing she would tell
Her son that of them that should fit him well
To make use of—which was, not to converse
Too freely with their pride, nor to disperse 245
His thoughts amongst them, since they us'd to give
Good words, but through them ill intents did drive.
  Eurynome replied: 'With good advise
You vow his counsaile and your open guise.
Go then, advise your Son; nor keepe more close 250
Your cheekes, stil drown'd in your eyes' overflowes,
But bathe your body, and with Balmes make cleere
Your thickn'd count'nance: *Uncomposed cheare*
And ever mourning will the Marrow weare.
Nor have you cause to mourn; your Son hath now 255
Put on that vertue which (in chiefe) your vow
Wisht (as your blessing) at his birth, might decke
His blood and person.' 'But forbeare to speake
Of Baths, or Balmings, or of beauty, now,'
The Queene replyed, 'lest (urging comforts) you 260
Discomfort much, because the Gods have wonne
The spoile of my lookes since my Lord was gone.
But these must serve. Cal hither then to me
Hippodamia and Autonoe,
That those our traine additions may supply 265
Our owne deserts. And yet besides, not I
(With all my age) have learn'd the boldnesse yet
T'expose my selfe to men, unlesse I get
Some other Gracers.' This said, forth she went
Eurynome.
To call the Ladies, and much spirit spent 270
To make their utmost speed: for now their Queene
Would both her selfe shew and make them be seene.
  But now Minerva other projects laid,
Penelope.
And through Icarius' daughter's Veines convaid
Sweet sleepe's desire—in whose soft fumes involv'd 275
She was as soone as laid, and quite dissolv'd
Were all her Lineaments. The Goddesse then
Bestow'd immortall gifts on her, that men
Might wonder at her beauties, and the beames
That glister in the deified supreames 280
She cleer'd her mourning count'nance up withall—

Even such a radiance as doth round empall
Venus. Crown'd Cytherea, when her order'd paces
Conduct the Bevy of the dancing Graces,
She added to her owne, more plumpe, more hie, 285
And fairer than the polisht Ivory
Rendring her parts and presence. This grace done,
Away the Deity flew; and up did ronne
Her lovely-wristed Ladies with a noise
That blew the soft chaines from her sleeping joyes— 290
When she her faire eyes wip't, and (gasping) saide:
'O me unblest! How deep a sweet sleepe spread
His shades about me! Would Diana pleas'd
To shoot me with a death no more diseas'd
As soone as might be, that no more my mone 295
Might waste my blood in weepings never done,
For want of that accomplisht vertue spher'd
In my lov'd Lord, to all the Greekes prefer'd.'
Then she descended with her Maids, and tooke
Place in the Portall, whence her beamy looke 300
Reacht ev'ry wooer's heart. Yet cast she on
So thin a veyle that through it quite there shone
A grace so stolne, it pleasd above the cleere,
And sunke the knees of every wooer there.
Their minds so melted in love's vehement fires, 305
That to her bed she heightn'd all desires.
The Prince then coming neere, she said: 'O Son,
Thy thoughts and judgements have not yet put on
That constancy in what becomes their good,
Which all expect in thee. Thy yonger blood 310
Did sparkle choicer spirits, but, arriv'd
At this ful growth, wherein their Forme hath thriv'd
Beyond the bounds of child-hood, and when now
Beholders should affirme: "This man doth grow
Like the rare son of his so matchles Sire 315
(His goodlinesse, his beauty, and his fire
Of soule aspir'd to)"—thou mak'st nothing good
Thy Fate, nor fortune, nor thy height of blood
In manage of thy actions. What a deed
Of foule desert hath thy grosse sufferance freed 320
Beneath thine owne Roofe? A poore stranger here
Us'd most unmanly! How will this appeare
To all the world, when Fame shall trumpet out
That thus and thus are our guests beate about
Our Court unrighted? Tis a blaze will show 325

Extreamly shamefull to your name and you.'
'I blame you not, O Mother,' he replide,
'That this cleere wrong sustain'd by me you chide:
Yet know I both the good and bad of all,
Being past the yeares in which yong errors fall. 330
But (all this knowne) skill is not so exact
To give (when once it knowes) things fit their fact.
I wel may doubt the prease of strangers here,
Who, bent to ill, and onely my Nerves nere,
May do it in despight. And yet the jarre 335
Betwixt our guest and Irus was no warre
Wrought by the wooers, nor our guest sustain'd
Wrong in that action, but the conquest gain'd.
And would to Jove, Minerva, and the Sun
That all your woo'rs might serve Contention 340
For such a purchase as the Begger made,
And wore such weak heads. Some should death invade
Strew'd in the Entry, some imbrew the hall,
Till every man had vengeance capitall;
Sattl'd like Irus at the Gates, his head 345
Every way nodding like one forfeited
To reeling Bacchus, knees nor feete his owne
To beare him where hee's better lov'd or knowne.'

Eurymachus' court-ship of the supposed Widdow Queene.

Their speeches given this end, Eurymachus
Began his Court-ship, and exprest it thus: 350
'Most wise Icarius' daughter, if all those
That did for Colchos ventrous saile dispose
For that rich purchase had before but seene
Earth's richer prize in th'Ithacensian Queene,
They had not made that voyage, but to you 355
Would all their vertues and their Beings vow.
Should all the world know what a worth you store,
To morrow than to day, and next light more,
Your Court should banquet—since to all Dames you
Are far preferr'd both for the grace of show, 360
In Stature, Beauty, Forme in every kinde
Of all parts outward, and for faultlesse minde.'

Penelope's answer.

'Alas,' said she, 'my Vertue, Body, Forme,
The Gods have blasted with that onely storme
That ravisht Greece to Ilion, since my Lord 365
(For that warre ship't) bore all my goods abord.
If he (return'd) should come, and governe here
My life's whole state, the grace of all things there
His guide would heighten, as the spirit it bore—

Which, dead in me, lives, given him long before. 370
A sad course I live now; heaven's sterne decree
With many an ill hath numb'd and deaded me.
He tooke life with him, when he tooke my hand
In parting from me to the Troyan strand.

Ulysses' words to his wife at parting.

These words my witnesse: "Woman! I conceive 375
That not all th'Achives bound for Troy shall leave
Their Native earth their safe returned bones,
Fame saying that Troy traines up approved sonnes
In deeds of Armes, brave putters off of shafts,
For winging Lances Maisters of their crafts, 380
Unmatched Riders, swift of foot, and streight
Can arbitrate a warre of deadliest weight.
Hope then can scarse fill all with life's supply,
And of all any failing, why not I?
Nor do I know if God hath marshall'd me 385
Amongst the safe-return'd, or his decree
Hath left me to the thraldome order'd there.
However, all cares be thy burthens here:
My Sire and Mother tend as much as now;
I further off, more neere in cares be you. 390
Your Son, to man's state grown, wed whom you will,
And (you gone) his care let his houshold fill."
Thus made my Lord his will, which heaven sees prov'd
Almost at all parts—for the Sun, remov'd
Downe to his set, ere long wil leade the night 395
Of those abhorred Nuptials that should fright
Each worthy woman, which her second are
With any man that breaths, her first Lord's care
Dead, because he to flesh and blood is dead—
Which, I feare, I shal yeeld to, and so wed 400
A second husband; and my reason is
Since Jove hath taken from me all his blisse.
Whom God gives over, they themselves forsake;
Their greefes their joyes, their God their devill make.
And 'tis a great griefe, nor was seene till now 405
In any fashion of such men as woo
A good and wealthy woman and contend
Who shal obtaine her, that those men should spend
Her Beeves and best Sheepe as their cheefest ends;
But rather that her selfe and all her friends 410
They should with Banquets and rich gifts entreat:
Their life is death that live with others' meat.'

Divine Ulysses much rejoyc't to heare

His Queene thus fish for gifts and keepe in cheare
Their hearts with hope that she would wed againe, 415
Her minde yet still her first intent retaine.
Antinous saw the wooers won to give,
And said: 'Wise Queene, by all your meanes receive
What ever bounty any woo'r shall use:
Gifts freely given 'tis folly to refuse. 420
For know that we resolve not to be gone
To keepe our owne roofes, till of all some One
Whom best you like your long-woo'd love shal win.'
This pleas'd the rest, and every one sent in
His present by the Herald. First had place 425
The Wooers' Gifts. Antinous' gift, a robe of speciall grace,
Exceeding ful and faire, and twenty hewes
Chang'd luster to it—to which, choise of shewes,
Twelve massy plated Buttons all of Gold
Enricht the substance, made to fairly hold 430
The Robe together, all lac'd downe before,
Where Keepes and Catches both sides of it wore.
Eurymachus a golden Tablet gave,
In which did Art her choisest workes engrave,
And round about an Amber verge did run, 435
That cast a radiance from it like the Sun.
Eurydamas two servants had, that bore
Two goodly Earings, whose rich hollowes wore
Three Pearles in either, like so many eyes,
Reflecting glances radiant as the skies. 440
The King Pisander, great Polyctor's heire,
A Casket gave exceeding rich and faire.
The other, other wealthy gifts commended
To her faire hand, which took, and straight ascended
This Goddesse of her sex her upper State, 445
Her Ladies all her gifts elaborate
Up bearing after. All to dancing then
The wooers went, and song's delightfull straine,
In which they frolickt till the Evening came:
And then rais'd sable Hesperus his flame, 450
When, for their Lights within, they set up there
Three Lampes, whose weekes were wood exceeding sere
And passing porous, which they causd to burne,
Their matter ever minister'd by turne
Of several Hand-maids. Whom Ulysses (seeing 455
Too conversant with wooers, ill agreeing
With guise of maids) advisd in this faire sort:

Ulysses to his Wive's women.

'Maids of your long-lackt King, keepe you the port
Your Queene's chast presence beares? Go, up to her,
Imploy your Loomes or Rockes, and keepe ye there: 460
I'le serve to feed these lamps, shold these Lords' dances
Last til Aurora cheer'd us with her glances.
They cannot weary me, for I am one
Borne to endure when all men else have done.'
They wantonly brake out in Laughters all, 465
Look't on each other, and to termes did fall
Cheek-proud Melantho, who was Dolius' seed,
Kept by the Queene—that gave her dainty breed
Fit for her daughter, and yet won not so
Her heart to her, to share in any wo 470
She suffer'd for her Lord. But she was great
With great Eurymachus, and her love's heat
In his bed quenched. And this cholericke thing
Bestow'd this railing Language on the King:

Melantho to Ulysses.

'Base Stranger, you are taken in your braine, 475
You talke so wildely. Never you againe
Can get where you were borne, and seeke your bed
In some Smithe's Hovill or the Market sted,
But heere you must take confidence to prate
Before all these, for feare can get no state 480
In your wine-hardy stomacke—or, 'tis like,
To prove your native garbe, your tongue will strike
On this side of your mouth still, being at best.
Is the man idle-brain'd for want of rest?
Or proud, because he beate the roguish begger? 485
Take heed, Sir, lest some better man beleager
Your eares with his fists, and set headlong hence
Your bold abode heere with your blood's expence.'
He, looking sternly on her, answer'd her:
'Dog! What broad Language giv'st thou? I'le prefer 490
Your usage to the Prince, that he may fall
Foule on your faire limbes, til he tel them all.'
This fray'd the wenches, and al straight got gone
In feare about their businesse, every one
Confessing he saide well. But he stood now 495
Close by the Cressets, and did lookes bestow
On all men there, his Braine employd about
Some sharper businesse than to dance it out—
Which had not long to go. Nor therefore would
Minerva let the wooers' spleenes grow cold 500
With too good usage of him, that his hart

Might fret enough and make his choller smart.
Eurymachus provok't him first, and made
His fellows laugh with a conceit he had
Fetcht farre from what was spoken long before, 505
That his poore forme perhaps some Deity bore.
'It well may chance,' said he, 'some God doth beare
This man's resemblance. For, thus standing nere
The glistering Torches, his slick't head doth throw
Beames round about it as those Cressets do— 510
For not a haire he hath to give it shade.
Say, wil thy heart serve t'undertake a Trade
For fitting wages? Should I take thee hence
To walke my grounds and looke to every Fence,
Or plant high trees, thy hire should raise thy forces, 515
Food store, and cloaths. But these same ydle courses
Thou art so prompt in that thou wilt not worke,
But forrage up and downe, and beg, and lurke
In every house whose Roofes hold any will
To feed such fellowes. That thy gut may fil 520
Gives end to all thy Beeing.' He replyed:
'I wish at any worke we two were tryed,
In hight of Spring time, when heaven's lights are long—
I a good crook'd Sithe that were sharpe and strong,
You such another, where the grasse grew deepe, 525
Up by day breake, and both our labours keepe
Up til slow darknes eas'd the labouring light,
Fasting all day, and not a crum til night.
We then should prove our either workmanship.
Or if (againe) Beeves, that the goad or whip 530
Were apt t'obey before a tearing Plow,
Big, lusty beasts, alike in bulke and brow,
Alike in Labour and alike in strength,
Our taske foure Acres to be Till'd in length
Of one sole day—againe then you should try 535
If the dul glebe before the Plough should flye,
Or I a long Stitch could beare cleane and even.
Or lastly, if the guide of earth and heaven
Should stir sterne war up, either here or there,
And that at this day I had double Speare, 540
And Shield, and steele Caske fitting for my browes—
At this work likewise, midst the foremost blowes,
Your eyes should note me, and get little cause
To twit me with my bellie's sole applause.
But you affect t'affect with injurie, 545

Your minde ungentle, seeme in valour hie,
Because, 'gainst few, and those not of the best,
Your conversation hath bene still profest.
But if Ulysses (landed on his earth,
And enter'd on the true right of his birth) 550
Should come and front ye, straight his ample Gates
Your feete would hold too narrow for your Fates.'
He frown'd, rag'd, call'd him wretch, and vow'd
To be his death, since he durst prove so proud
Amongst so many to tell him so home 555
What he affected, askt if overcome
With wine he were, or (as his Minion said)
Talk't stil so idlely and were palsied
In his mind's instruments, or was proud because
He gat from Irus off with such applause? 560
With all which, snatching up a stoole, he threw,
When old Ulysses to the knees withdrew
Of the Dulichian Lord Amphinomus,
As if he fear'd him. His dart missing thus
His aged object, and his Page's hand 565
(A Boy that waited on his cup's command,
Now holding of an Ewre to him) he smit.
Downe fel the sounding Ewre, and after it
The guiltlesse Page lay sprawling in the dust,
And crying out—when all the wooers thrust 570
A tumult up amongst them, wishing all
The rogue had perisht in some Hospitall
Before his life there stirr'd such uprores up,
And with rude speeches spice their pleasure's cup—
And all this for a Begger, to fulfill 575
A filthy Proverbe: *Good still yeelds to ill.*

Telemachus mockes the wooers, yet wins their praise.

The Prince cried out on them, to let the bad
Obscure the good so, told them they were mad,
Abusd their banquet, and affirm'd some God
Tried maisteries with them, bad them take their load 580
Of food and wine, sit up or fal to bed
At their free pleasures—and since he gave head
To all their freedomes, why should they mistake
Their owne rich humors for a Begger's sake?
All bit their lips to be so taken downe 585
And taught the course that shold have bin their own,
Admir'd the Prince, and saide he bravely spoke.
But Nisus' Son then stroke the equall stroke,
And saide: 'O Friends, let no man here disdaine

To put up equall speeches, nor maintaine 590
With serious words an humor, nor with stroke
A Stranger in another's house provoke,
Nor touch the meanest servant, but confine
All these dissentions in a bolle of wine—
Which fill us, Cup-bearer, that, having done 595
Our nightly sacrifice, we may attone
Our powres with sleepe, resigning first the guest
Up to the Prince, that holds all interest
In his disposure here, the House being his
In just descent, and all the faculties.' 600
This all approv'd; when Noble Mulius
(Herald in chiefe to Lord Amphinomus)
The Wine distributed with reverend grace
To ev'ry wooer—when the Gods given place
With service fit, they serv'd themselves and tooke 605
Their parting Cups, till (when they all had shooke
The angry humor off) they bent to rest,
And every Wooer to severall Roofes addrest.

The End of the Eighteenth Booke of Homer's Odysses

THE NINETEENTH BOOKE
of
HOMER'S ODYSSES

THE ARGUMENT

Ulysses and his Son eschew
Offending of the Wooers' view
With any Armour. His Birth's seate,
Ulysses tels his Queene, is Crete.
Euryclea the truth yet found, 5
Discover'd by a scar-heal'd wound,
Which in Parnassus' tops a Bore
(Strooke by him in his Chace) did gore.

Another Argument

Ταῦ. *The King still hid*
by what he said,
By what he did
informes his maid.

Yet did Divine Ulysses keepe his Roofe,
And with Minerva plotted still the proofe
Of al the wooers' deaths—when thus his Son
He taught with these fore-counsailes: 'We must ron
A close course with these Armes, and lay them by, 5
And to the wooers make so faire a sky
As it would never thunder. Let me then
(That you may wel retaine) repeate agen
What in Eumæus' Cottage I advis'd.
If when they see your leysure exercis'd 10
In fetching downe your Armes, and aske what use
Your minde will give them, say 'tis their abuse
With smoke and rust that makes you take them down,
This not being like the Armory well knowne
To be the leavings of Laertes' Son, 15
Consorting the designe for Ilion.

Ulysses' former counsaile to his Son, for disposing the Armes, repeated.

Your eyes may see how much they are infected,
As all fire's vapors ever since reflected
On those sole Armes. Besides, a graver thought
Jove graves within you, lest (their spirits wrought 20
Above their pitch with wine) they might contend
At some high banquet, and to wounds transcend,
Their Feast inverting—which perhaps may be
Their Nuptiall feast with wise Penelope.
The ready weapon when the bloud is up 25
Doubles the uprore heightned by the Cup.
Wrath's meanes for Act curbe all the wayes ye can;
As Loadstones draw the steele, so steele draws Man.
Retaine these words, nor what is good think, thus
Receiv'd at second hand, superfluous.' 30
The Sonne, obeying, did Euryclea call,
And bad her shut (in the utter Porches) all
The other women, till himselfe brought downe
His Father's Armes, which all were over-growne
By his neglect with rust, his Father gone, 35
And he too childish to spend thoughts upon
Those manly Implements; but he would now
Reforme those yong neglects, and th'armes bestow
Past reach of smoke. The loving Nurse replide:
'I wish, O Son, your powers would once provide 40
For wisedome's habit, see your houshold were
In thrifty mannage, and tend all things there.
But if these armes must downe, and every Maide
Be shut in utter roomes, who else should aide
Your worke with light?' He answer'd: 'This my guest. 45
There shal not one in my house tast my Feast,
(Or joyne in my Nave) that shall ydlely live,
How ever farre hence he his home derive.'
He said, and his words stood. The doores she shut
Of that so wel-fill'd house. And th'other put 50
Their thoghts in act, bost Shields, Helmes, sharpned Lances
Brought downe; and Pallas before both advances
A golden Cresset, that did cast a Light
As if the Day sate in the Throne of Night.
When (halfe amaz'd) the Prince said: 'O my Father, 55
Mine eyes my soule's pow'rs all in wonder gather,
For though the wals and goodly wind-beames here,
And all these Pillars, that their heads so rere,
Are all of Firre, they seeme yet all of fire.
Some God is surely with us.' His wise Sire 60

χοίνικος ἅπτηται—*They wil needs turne this:* Quadram *(for* Modium) gustet—*though the words beare no such signification: But give a Proverb then in use Repetition: which was, Hee shall not joyn or make a spoke in the Nave of my chariot, or Chariot wheele,* χοίνικον *or* χοίνικις *signifying* Modiolus Rotæ, *and* ἅπτω, Necto.

Bad peace, and keepe the counsailes of the Gods,
Nor aske a word: 'These Pow'rs that use abods
Above the starres have power from thence to shine
Through night and all shades to earth's inmost Mine.
Go thou for sleepe, and leave me here to wake 65
The women and the Queene, whose heart doth ake
To make enquiry for my selfe of me.'
He went to sleepe, where lights did endlesly
Burne in his Night-roomes, where he feasted Rest
Til daye's faire weed did all the world invest. 70
Thus was divine Ulysses left alone
With Pallas, plotting foule confusion
To all the wooers. Forth then came the Queene;
Phœbe, with golden Cytherea seene,
Her Port presented. Whom they set a Chaire 75
Aside the fire, the fashion circulare,
The substance Silver and rich Elephant,
Whose Fabricke did the cunning finger vant
Of great Icmalius, who besides had done
A footstoole for her that did sute her Throne— 80
On which they cast an ample skin, to be
The Cushion for her other Royalty.
And there she sate—about whom came her Maids,
Who brought upon a Table store of Breads
And Bolles that with the wooers' wine were cround. 85
The Embers then they cast upon the ground
From out the Lampes and other Fuell added,
That still with cheereful flame the sad house gladded.
Melantho, seeing still Ulysses there,
Thus she held out her spleene: 'Still, stranger, here? 90
Thus late in night? To see what Ladies do?
Avant, you wretch: hence. Go without doores, go—
And quickly, too, lest ye be sindg'd away
With burning fire-brands.' He (thus seeing their fray
Continu'd by her with such spleene) replide: 95
'Minion! What makes your angry blood thus chide
My presence still? Is it because you see
I shine not in your wanton bravery,
But weare these rags? It fits the needy Fate
That makes me beg thus of the commune state. 100
Such poore soules, and such beggers, yet are men;
And even my meane meanes, means had to maintain
A wealthy house, and kept a manly prease,
Was counted blessed, and the poore accesse

Of any Begger did not scorne, but feede 105
With often hand, and any man of neede
Releev'd as fitted; kept my servants, too,
Not few, but did with those additions go
That call choise men The Honest, who are stild
The rich, the great. But what such great ones build 110
Jove oft puls downe, as thus he ruin'd me;
His will was such, which is his equity.
And therefore, woman, beare you fitting hand
On your behaviour, lest your spirit, thus mann'd
And cherisht with your beauties (when they wane), 115
Comes down, your pride now being then your bane.
And in the meane space shun the present danger,
Lest your bold fashion breed your Soveraign's anger—
Or lest Ulysses come, of whom even yet
Hope finds some life in fate. Or, be his seat 120
Amongst the meerly ruin'd, yet his Sonne
(Whose life's heate Phœbus saves) is such a one
As can discover who doth well deserve
Of any woman heere. His yeares now serve.'

The Queen gave eare, and thus supprest the flame: 125
'Thou quite without a brow, past female shame,
I heare thy monstrous boldnesse, which thy head
Shall pay me paines for. Thou hast heard it said,
And from my selfe too; and at every part
Thy knowledge serves thee, that (to ease my hart 130
So punisht in thy witnesse) my desire
Dwelt on this Stranger, that I might enquire
My lost friend's Beeing. But 'tis ever tride—
Both Man and God are still forgot with Pride.
Eurynome! Bring heere this Guest a seat 135
And Cushion on it, that we two may treat
Of the affaire in question. Set it neare,
That I may softly speake, yet he well heare.'

She did this little freely, and he sat
Close by the Queen, who askt him, whence, and what 140
He was himselfe? And what th'inhabited place?
Where liv'd his parents? Whence he fetcht his race?

Ulysses to his Queene.

'O woman,' he replyed, 'with whom no man
That moves in earth's unbounded circle can
Maintaine contention for true honor geven, 145

οὐρανὸν εὐρὺν.

Whose fame hath reacht the fairely-flowing heaven,
Who like a never-ill-deserving King
That is well spoke of, first, for worshipping

And striving to resemble God in Empire,
Whose equall hand impartially doth temper 150
Greatnesse and Goodnesse—to whom therefore beares
The blacke earth store of all graine, Trees conferres
Cracking with burthen, long-liv'd Herds creates,
All which the Sea with her sorts emulates—
And all this feeds beneath his powrefull hand 155
Men, valiant, many, making strong his Land
With happy lives led—nothing else the cause
Of all these blessings but well-order'd Lawes.
Like such a King are you, in Love, in Fame,
And all the blisse that deifies a Dame. 160
And therefore do not mixe this with a mone
So wretched as is now in question.
Aske not my Race nor Countrey, lest you fill
My heart yet fuller with repeated ill:
For I must follow it with many teares; 165
Though 'tis not seemly to sit wounding eares
In publique Roofes with our particular life:
Time's worst expence is still-repeated Griefe.
I should be irkesome to your Ladies here,
And you your selfe would say you urg'd your eare 170
To what offends it, my still-broken eine
Supposing wounded with your too much wine.'
'Stranger,' said she, 'you feare your owne excesse,
With giving me too great a noblenesse.
The Gods my person, Beauty, Vertue too, 175
Long since subverted, when the Ilian wo
The Greeke designe attempted in which went
My praise and honor. In his government
Had I deserv'd your utmost grace; but now
Sinister Deity makes dishonor woo 180
(In shew of grace) my ruine. All the Peres
Sylvane Zacynthus and Dulichius Spheres,
Samos and Ithaca, strange strifes have showne
To win me, spending on me all mine owne,
Will wed me in my spite. And these are those 185
That take from me all vertue to dispose
Or Guest or Suppliant, or take any course
Amongst my Heralds (that should all disburse)
To order any thing. Though I neede none
To give me greefe at home. Abroad erres one 190
That my veins shrink for, whom these, holding gone,
Their Nuptials hasten, and find me as slow.

Good spirits prompted me to make a show
Of undertaking a most curious taske
That an unmeasur'd space of time would aske, 195
Which they, enduring long, would often say,
When ends thy worke? I soone had my delay,
And prai'd their stay. For, though my Lord wer dead,
His Father's life yet matter ministred
That must imploy me, which, (to tell them true) 200
Was that great worke I nam'd. For now nere drew
Laertes' death, and on my hand did lye
His funerall Robe, whose end (being now so nye)
I must not leave, and lose so much begun—
The rather, lest the Greeke Dames might be wun 205
To taxe mine honor, if a man so great
Should greet his grave without his winding sheet.
Pride made them credulous, and I went on—
When whatsoever all the day had done
I made the night helpe to undo againe, 210
Though oyle and watch it cost, and equall paine.
Three yeares my wit secur'd me undiscern'd,
Yet, when the fourth came, by my Maids discern'd
(False carelesse wenches) how they were deluded—
When (by my light descern'd) they all intruded, 215
Us'd threatning words, and made me give it end.
And then could I to no more length extend
My linger'd Nuptials; not a counsaile more
Was to be stood upon; my Parents bore
Continuall hand on me to make me wed; 220
My Sonne grew angry that so ruined
His goods were by them. He is now a man,
Wise in a great degree, and one that can
Himselfe give order to his houshold fare;
And Jove give equal glory to his care. 225
But thus you must not passe me: I must know,
(It may be for more end) from whence doth grow
Your race and you—for I suppose you none
Sprung of old Oake or justl'd out of stone.'
He answer'd: 'O Ulysses' reverend wife! 230
Yet hold you purpose to enquire my life?
I'le tell you, though it much afflict me more
Than all the sorrowes I have felt before—
As worthily it may, since so long time
As I have wandred from my Native Clime 235
Through humane Cities, and in sufferance stil,

To rip all wounds up (though of all their ill
I touch but part) must actuate all their paine.
But aske you still; I'le tell, though stil sustaine.

Ulysses' fain'd relation of himself to his wife.

'In middle of the sable Sea there lies 240
An Isle cal'd Crete, a ravisher of eyes,
Fruitfull, and mann'd with many an infinite store,
Where ninety Cities crowne the famous shore.
Mixt with all-languag'd men, there Greekes survive,
There the great-minded Eteocretans live, 245
There the Dorensians, never out of war,
The Cydons there, and there the singular
Pelasgian people. There doth Cnossus stand,
That mighty City, where had most command
Great Jove's Disciple, Minos, who nine yeares 250
Conferr'd with Jove, both great familiares
In mutual counsailes. And this Minos' Son,
The mighty-minded King Deucalion,
Was Sire to me and royall Idomen,
Who with Atrides went to Ilion then, 255
My elder Brother and the better man;
My name Aethon. At that time began
My knowledge of Ulysses, whom my home
Receiv'd with guest-rites. He was thither come
By force of weather, from the Malean coast 260
But new got off, where he the Navy lost
Then under saile for Troy, and wind-bound lay
Long in Amnisus—hardly got away
From horrid stormes, that made him anchor there
In Havens that sacred to Lucina were, 265
Dreadfull and dangerous, in whose bosome crept
Lucina's Caverne. But in my roofe slept
Ulysses, shor'd in Crete—who first enquir'd
For royall Idomen, and much desir'd
To taste his guest-rites, since to him had bene 270
A welcome Guest my Brother Idomen.
The tenth or leventh light on Ulysses shin'de
In stay at Crete, attending then the winde
For threatn'd Ilion—all which time my house
With love and entertainments curious 275
Embrac't his person, though a number more
My hospitable roofes receiv'd before.
His men I likewise call'd, and from the store
Allow'd them meale and heat-exciting wine,
And Oxen for their slaughter, to confine 280

In my free hand the utmost of their need.
Twelve daies the Greeks staid ere they got them freed;
A gale so bitter blew out of the North
That none could stand on earth, being tumbled forth
By some sterne God. But on the thirteenth day 285
The tempest ceast, and then went Greekes their way.'
Thus many tales Ulysses told his wife,
At most but painting, yet most like the life—
Of which her heart such sense took through hir eares,
It made her weepe as she would turne to teares. 290
And as from off the Mountaines melts the snow
Which Zephyr's breath congeald, but was made flow
By hollow Eurus, which so fast poures downe
That with their Torrent floods have over-flowne:
So downe her faire cheekes her kinde tears did glide, 295
Her mist Lord mourning, set so neere her side.
Ulysses much was mov'd to see her mourne,
Whose eies yet stood as dry as Iron or Horne
In his untroubl'd lids, which, in his craft
Of bridling passion, he from issue saf't. 300
When she had given her moane so many teares
That now 'twas satiate, her yet loving feares
Askt thus much further: 'You have thus farre tried
My love's credulity, but if gratified
With so long stay he was with you, you can 305
Describe what weede he wore, what kinde of man
Both he himselfe was and what Followers
Observ'd him there.' 'Alas,' sayd he, 'the yeares
Have growne so many since (this making now
Their twentith revolution) that my show 310
Of these slight notes will set my memory sore—
But (to my now remembrance) this he wore:
A double purple Robe, drawne close before
With golden Buttons, pleated thicke, and bore
A facing where a hundred colours shinde; 315
About the skirts a Hound a freckl'd Hinde
In full course hunted; on the fore-skirts yet
He pincht, and pull'd her downe, when with hir feet,
And all her force, she struggl'd hard for flight.
Which had such life in Gold that to the sight 320
It seem'd the Hinde it selfe for every hiew,
The Hound and al so answering the view
That all admir'd all. I observ'd beside
His inner weed, so rarely beautifide

Ulysses' description of his apparell going for Troy.

That dumbe amaze it bred, and was as thin 325
As any dry and tender Onion skin:
As soft 'twas, too, and glister'd like the Sun.
The women were to loving wonder wun
By him and by his weeds. But (by the way)
You must excuse me that I cannot say 330
He brought this suite from home, or had it there
Sent for some Present, or perhaps elsewhere
Receiv'd it for his guest-gift. For your Lord
Had Friends not few: the Fleete did not afford
Many that had not fewer. I bestow'd 335
A well-edg'd sword on him, a Robe that flow'd
In foulds and fulnesse, and did reach his feete,
Of richest purple, brought him to his Fleete
With all my honor. And besides (to add
To all this sifted circumstance) he had 340
A Herald there, in height a little more
Put from the earth, that thicker shoulders wore,
A swarth complexion, and a curled head;
His name Eurybates; and much in stead
He stood your King, imploy'd in most command, 345
Since most of all his minde could understand.'

When all these signes she knew for chiefly trew,
Desire of moane upon her beauties grew,
And yet (even that desire suffic'd) she said:

'Till this, my Guest, a wretched state arraid 350
Your ill-usd person, but from this houre forth
You shalbe honor'd, and finde all the worth
That fits a friend. Those weeds these hands bestow'd
From out my wardrobe, those gold buttons sow'd
Before for closure and for Ornament. 355
But never more must his returne present
The person that gave those adornments State.
And therefore under an abhorred Fate
Was he induc't to feed the commune fame,
To visit vile Troy—aye, too vile to name.' 360

'No more yet mourne,' said he, 'nor thus see pinde
Your lovely person: *Weeping wasts the Minde.*
And yet I blame you not; for any Dame
That weds one yong and brings to him his name,
(What ever man he is) will mourne his losse. 365
Much more respectfull then must shew your woes,
That weepe thus for Ulysses, who (Fame saies)
Was equal with the Gods in all his waies.

But where no cause is, there must be no mone:
And therefore heare me; my Relation 370
Shal lay the cleere truth naked to your view.
I heard amongst the Thesprots for most trew
That Lord Ulysses liv'd, and stood just now
On his returne for home; that wealth did flow
In his possession, which he made not knowne, 375
But begg'd amongst the people, since alone
He quite was left—for all his men were lost
In getting off from the Thrinacian Coast;
Jove and the Sun was wroth with them for rape
Made of his Oxen, and no man let scape 380
The rugged deepes of Neptune. Onely he,
The Ship's Keele onely keeping, was by Sea
Cast on the faire Phæacian Continent,
Where men survive that are the Gods' descent
And like a God receiv'd him, gave him heapes 385
Of wealthy gifts, and would conduct his steps
Themselves safe home—which he might long ago
His pleasure make, but profit would not so.
He gather'd going, and had mighty store
Of Gold in safegard: so beyond the Shore 390
That commune sailes kept, his high flood of wit
Bore glorious top, and all the world for it
Hath farre exceeded. All this Pheidon told,
That doth the Scepter of Thesprotia hold,
Who swore to me, in houshold sacrifice, 395
The Ship was lancht and men to man the prise,
That soone should set him on his countrey earth—
Shew'd me the goods, enow to serve the birth
That in the tenth age of his seed shold spring,
Yet in his Court contain'd. But then the King 400
(Your husband) for Dodona was in way,
That from th'oraculous Oake he might display
Jove's will, what course for home would best prevaile—
To come in pompe, or beare a secret saile.
But me the King dispatcht in course before, 405
A Ship then bound for the Dulichian shore.
So thus you see his safety whom you mourne,
Who now is passing neere, and his returne
No more will punish with delayes, but see
His friends and country. All which truth to thee 410
I'le seale with sacred Oath. Be witnesse Jove,
Thou first and best of all the Thron'd above,

And thou house of the great Laertes' heire,
To whose high roofes I tender my repaire,
That what I tell the Queene event shall crowne: 415
This yeare Ulysses shall possesse his owne—
Nay, ere the next month ends shall heere arrive;
Nay, ere it enters, heere abide alive.'
'O may this prove,' saide she, 'gifts, friendship, then
Should make your name the most renown'd of men. 420
But 'tis of me receiv'd, and must so sort,
That nor my Lord shall ever see his Court,
Nor you gaine your deduction thence—for now
The alter'd house doth no such man allow
As was Ulysses (if he ever were) 425
To entertaine a reverend Passenger,
And give him faire dismission. But, Maids, see
Ye bathe his feete, and then with Tapistry,
Best sheets, and blanquets make his bed, and lay
Soft wascotes by him, that (lodg'd warme) he may 430
Even till the golden-seated morning's ray
Enjoy good rest; and then, with her first light,
Bathe, and give balmes, that cherisht appetite
He may apply within our Hall and sit
Safe by Telemachus. Or if th'unfit 435
And harmfull minde of any be so base
To greeve his age againe, let none give grace
Of doing any deed he shall command
(How wroth so ever) to his barbarous hand.
For how shall you, guest, know me for a Dame 440
That passe so far—nay, turne and winde the Fame
Of other Dames for wisedome and the frame
Of houshold usage—if your poore thin weeds
I let draw on you, want, and worser deeds,
That may, perhaps, cause heere your latest day? 445
The life of Man is short and flyes away.
And if the Ruler's selfe of housholds be
Ungentle, studying inhumanity,
The rest prove worse. But he beares all the blame:
All men will, living, vow against his name 450
Mischiefes and miseries, and (dead) supply
With bitter Epitaphes his memory.
But if himselfe be noble (noble things
Doing and knowing) all his Underlings
Will imitate his Noblesse, and all guests 455
Give it, in many, many interests.'

'But, worthiest Queen,' said he, 'where you command
Baths and rich beds for me, I scorne to stand
On such state now, nor ever thought it yet,
Since first I left the snowy hils of Crete. 460
When once I fell a ship-boord, those thoughts fled;
I love to take now (as long since) my bed,
Though I began the use with sleeplesse nights—
I, many a darknesse with right homely rites
Have spent ere this houre; and desir'd the Morne 465
Would come, and make sleepe to the world a scorne.
Nor run these dainty Bathes in my rude head;
Nor any handmaid (to your service bred)
Shal touch my ill-kept feete, unlesse there live
Some poore old drudge here, that hath learnd to give 470
Old men good usage, and no worke wil fly,
As having suffer'd ill as much as I.
But if there live one such in your command,
I wil not shame to give my foot her hand.'
She gave this answere: 'O my loved Guest, 475
There never enter'd these kinde Roofes, for rest,
Stranger or Friend that so much wisedome laide
In gage for Guest-rites as your lippes have paide.
There lives an old maide in my charge, that knowes
The good you speake of by her many woes, 480
That nourisht and brought up with curious care
Th'unhappy man, your old familiar,
Even since his Mother let him view the light,
And oft hath felt in her weake armes his weight.
And she (though now much weaker) shal apply 485
Her Maiden service to your modesty.
Euryclea, rise, and wash the feete of one
That is of one age with your Soveraigne gone—
Such hands, such feet hath, though of alter'd grace:
Much griefe in men wil bring on change apace.' 490
She (from her aged slumber wak't) did cleare
Her heavy eyes, and instantly (to heare
Her Soveraigne's name) had worke enough to dry
Her cheekes from teares, and to his memory
These Mones did offer: 'O my Son,' saide she, 495
'I never can take greefe enough for thee,
Whom Goodnes hurts, and whom even Jove's high spleen
(Since thou art Jove-like) hates the most of men.
For none hath offer'd him so many Thyes,
Nor such whole Hecatombes of sacrifice, 500

Fat and selected, as thy zeale hath done—
For all but praying that thy noble Sonne
Thy happy age might see at state of man.
And yet hath Jove with Mists Cimmerian
Put out the light of his returning day. 505
And as your selfe, O Father, in your way
Tooke these faire roofes for hospitable rights,
Yet finde (for them) our dogged women's spights,
So he (in like course), being driven to proofe
(Long time ere this) what such a royall Roofe 510
Would yeeld his miseries, found such usage there.
And you (now flying the foule Language here,
And many a filthy fact of our faire Dames)
Fly me like them, and put on causlesse shames
To let me clense your feet. For not the cause 515
The Queene's command yeelds is the pow'r that drawes
My will to wash your feete. But what I do
Proceeds from her charge, and your reverence too,
Since I in soule am stricken with a ruth
Of your distresses, and past show of truth— 520
Your strangenesse claiming little interest
In my affections, and yet many a Guest
Of poore condition hath bene harbour'd here,
But never any did so right appeare
Like King Ulysses as your selfe, for state, 525
Both of your stature, voice, and very gate.'

Intending with Trueth it selfe, not his shew onely.

'So all have said,' said he, 'that ever yet
Had the proportions of our figures met
In their observances; so right your eye
Proves in your soule your judging faculty.' 530
Thus tooke she up a Caldron brightly scour'd
To clense his feete in, and into it pour'd
Store of cold wave, which on the fire she set,
And therein bath'd (being temperatly heat)
Her Soveraign's feet—who turnd him from the light, 535
Since sodainly he doubted her conceit
(So rightly touching at his state before),
A scar now seeing on his foot that bore
An old note to discerne him, might descry
The absolute truth, which (witnest by her eye) 540
Was straite approv'd. He first receiv'd this sore
As in Parnassus' tops a white-tooth'd Bore
He stood in chace withall—who stroke him there,
At such time as he liv'd a sojourner

With his grand Sire, Autolycus, who th'Art 545
Of Theft and swearing (not out of the hart,
But by equivocation) first adorn'd
Your witty man withall, and was suborn'd
By Jove's descent, ingenious Mercurie—
Who did bestow it, since so many a Thie 550
Of Lambes and Kids he had on him bestow'd
In sacred flames, who therefore, when he vow'd,
Was ever with him. And this man impos'd
Ulysses' name, the light being first disclos'd
To his first sight then, when his grand Sire came 555
To see the then preferrer of his fame,
His loved daughter. The first supper done,
Euryclea put in his lap her Sonne,
And pray'd him to bethinke and give his name,
Since that desire did all desires inflame. 560

Autolycus gives his Grand child Ulysses his name, from whence the Odysses *is derivd,* 'Οδυσσεύς *deriv'd of* ὀδύζομαι, ex ὀδύνη, factum: *signifying* dolorem proprie corporis, nam ira ex dolore oritur.

'Daughter and Son-in-Law,' sayd he, 'let then
The name that I shall give him stand with men,
Since I arriv'd here at the houre of paine
In which mine owne kinde entrailes did sustaine
Moane for my daughter's yet unended throes, 565
And when so many men's and women's woes,
In joynt compassion met of humane birth,
Brought forth t'attend the many feeding earth.
Let Odysseus be his name, as one
Exposd to just constraint of all men's mone. 570
When heere at home he is arriv'd at state
Of man's first youth, he shall initiate
His practisd feete in travaile made abrode,
And to Parnassus, where mine owne abode
And chiefe meanes lye, addresse his way, where I 575
Will give him from my opened treasury
What shall returne him well, and fit the Fame
Of one that had the honor of his name.'

For these faire gifts he went, and found all grace
Of hands and words in him and all his race. 580
Amphithea (his Mother's mother) too
Applied her to his love with all to-do
In Grandame's welcomes, both his faire eyes kist
And browes, and then commanded to assist
Were all her sonnes by their respected Sire 585
In furnishing a Feast; whose eares did fire
Their minds with his command, who home straite led
A five-yeares-old male Oxe, feld, slew, and flead,

Gather'd about him, cut him up with Art,
Spitted and roasted, and his every part 590
Divided orderly. So all the day
They spent in feast: no one man went his way
Without his fit fill. When the Sun was set
And darknesse rose, they slept, till daye's fire het
Th'enlightned earth, and then on hunting went 595
Both Hounds and all Autolycus' descent.
In whose guide did divine Ulysses go,
Climb'd steepe Parnassus, on whose forehead grow
All sylvan off-springs round. And soone they rech't
The Concaves, whence ayr's sounding vapors fetcht 600
Their loud descent. As soone as any Sun
Had from the Ocean (where his waters run
In silent deepnesse) rais'd his golden head,
The early Huntsmen all the hill had spread
Their Hounds before them on the searching Traile, 605
They neere, and ever eager to assaile,
Ulysses brandishing a lengthfull Lance,
Of whose first flight he long'd to prove the chance.
Then found they lodg'd a Bore of bulke extreame
In such a Queach, as never any beame 610
The Sun shot pierc'st, nor any passe let finde
The moist impressions of the fiercest winde,
Nor any storme the sternest winter drives,
Such proofe it was: yet all within lay leaves
In mighty thicknesse, and through all this flew 615
The hounds' loud mouthes. The sounds, the tumult threw.
And all together rouz'd the Bore, that rusht
Amongst their thickest: all his brissels pusht
From forth his rough necke, and with flaming eyes
Stood close, and dar'd all. On which horrid prise 620
Ulysses first charg'd, whom above the knee
The savage strooke, and rac't it crookedly
Along the skin, yet never reacht the bone.
Ulysses' Lance yet through him quite was throwne,
At his right shoulder entring: at his left, 625
The bright head passage to his keennesse cleft,
And shew'd his point gilt with the gushing gore.
Downe in the dust fell the extended Bore,
And forth his life flew. To Ulysses round
His Unckle drew, who (wofull for his wound) 630
With all Art bound it up, and with a charme
Staid straight the blood, went home, and when the harm

Receiv'd full cure with gifts and all event
Of joy and love, to his lov'd home they sent
Their honor'd Nephew—whose returne his Sire 635
And reverend Mother tooke with joyes entire,
Enquir'd all passages; all which he gave
In good relation, nor of all would save
His wound from utterance: by whose scar he came
To be discovered by this aged Dame. 640

Which when she clensing felt and noted well,
Downe from her Lap into the Caldron fell
His weighty foot, that made the Brasse resound,
Turn'd all aside, and on th'embrewed ground
Spilt all the water. Joy and griefe together 645
Her brest invaded, and of weeping weather
Her eyes stood full; her small voice stucke within
Her part expressive; till at length his chin
She tooke, and spake to him: 'O Sonne,' saide she,
'Thou art Ulysses, nor canst other be: 650
Nor could I know thee yet, till all my King
I had gone over with the warmed Spring.'

Then look't she for the Queene to tell her all;
And yet knew nothing sure, thogh nought could fall
In compasse of all thoughts to make her doubt. 655
Minerva that distraction strooke throughout
Her mind's rapt forces, that she might not tell.
Ulysses, noting yet her aptnesse well,
With one hand tooke her chin, and made all shew
Of favour to her, with the other drew 660
Her offer'd parting closer—askt her why
She, whose kinde breast had nurst so tenderly
His infant life, would now his age destroy,
Though twenty yeares had held him from the joy
Of his lov'd country. But since onely she 665
(God putting her in minde) now knew 'twas he,
He charg'd her silence, and to let no eare
In all the Court more know his being there,
Lest, if God gave into his wreakfull hand
Th'insulting wooers' lives, he did not stand 670
On any partiall respect with her,
Because his Nurse, and to the rest prefer
Her safety therefore, but, when they should feele
His punishing finger, give her equall steele.

'What words,' said she, 'flye your retentive pow'rs? 675
You know you locke your counsailes in your Tow'rs

In my firme bosome, and that I am farre
From those loose frailties. Like an Iron barre
Or bolt of solidst stone, I will containe,
And tell you this besides—that if you gaine, 680
By God's good aide, the wooers' lives in yours,
What Dames are heere their shamelesse Paramours
And have done most dishonor to your worth,
My information well shall paint you forth.'
'It shal not neede,' saide he, 'my selfe will soone 685
(While thus I maske heere) set on every one
My sure observance of the worst and best.
Be thou then silent, and leave God the rest.'
This said, the old Dame for more water went;
The rest was all upon the Pavement spent 690
By knowne Ulysses' foot. More brought (and he
Supplied besides with sweetest Oyntments) he
His seate drew neere the fire to keepe him warme,
And with his peec't rags hiding close his harme.
The Queene came neere, and said: 'Yet, guest, afford 695
Your further patience, till but in a word
I'le tell my woes to you. For well I know
That Rest's sweet Houre her soft foote orders now,
When all poore men, how much soever griev'd,
Would gladly get their wo-watcht pow'rs reliev'd. 700
But God hath given my griefe a heart so great
It will not downe with rest. And so I set
My judgement up to make it my delight.
All day I mourne, yet nothing let the right
I owe my charge, both in my worke and Maids; 705
And when the night brings rest to others' aides,
I tosse my bed, Distresse with twenty points
Slaught'ring the pow'rs that to my turning joynts
Convey the vitall heate. And as all night
Pandareus' daughter, poore Edone, sings, 710
Clad in the verdure of the yearly Springs,
When she for Itylus, her loved Sonne
(By Zethus' issue, in his madnesse done
To cruell death) poures out her hourely mone,
And drawes the eares to her of every one: 715
So flowes my mone, that cuts in two my minde,
And here and there gives my discourse the winde,
Uncertain whether I shal with my Son
Abide still heere the safe possession
And guard of all goods, reverence to the bed 720

Of my lov'd Lord, and, too, my far-off spred
Fame with the people putting still in use—
Or follow any best Greeke I can chuse
To his fit house, with treasure infinite
Won to his Nuptials. While the infant plight 725
And want of judgement kept my Son in guide,
He was not willing with my being a Bride,
Nor with my parting from his Court; but now
(Arriv'd at man's state) he would have me vow
My love to some one of my wooers heere 730
And leave his Court, offended that their cheere
Should so consume his free possessions.
To settle then a choice in these my mones,
Heare and expound a dreame that did engrave
My sleeping fancy. Twenty Geese I have; 735
All which, me thought, mine eye saw tasting wheate
In water steep't, and joy'd to see them eate—
When straight a crooke-beak't Eagle from a hill,
Stoop't, and trust all their neckes, and all did kill;
When (all left scatter'd on the Pavement there) 740
She tooke her wing up to the Gods' faire sphere.
I, even amid my Dreame, did weepe and mourne
To see the Eagle with so shrew'd a turne
Stoope my sad turrets—when, me thought, there came
About my mournings many a Grecian Dame 745
To cheere my sorrowes, in whose most extreame
The Hawke came back, and on the prominent beame
That crost my Chamber fell, and us'd to me
A humane voice that sounded horribly,
And saide: "Be confident, Icarius' seed. 750
This is no dreame, but what shall chance indeed.
The Geese the wooers are; the Eagle, I
Was heeretofore a Fowle, but now imply
Thy husband's Beeing, and am come to give
The wooers death, that on my Treasure live." 755
With this Sleepe left me, and my waking way
I tooke to try if any violent prey
Were made of those my Fowles—which well enough
I (as before) found feeding at their Trough
Their yoted wheate.' 'O woman,' he replide, 760
'Thy dreame can no interpretation bide
But what the Eagle made, who was your Lord,
And saide himselfe would sure effect afford
To what he told you—that confusion

To all the wooers should appeare, and none 765
Escape the Fate and death he had decreed.'
She answer'd him: 'O Guest, these dreames exceede
The Art of man t'interpret, and appere
Without all choise, or forme, nor ever were
Perform'd to all at all parts. But there are 770
To these light Dreames, that like thin vapors fare,
Two two-leav'd gates, the one of Ivory,
The other Horne. Those dreames that Fantasie
Takes from the polisht Ivory Port delude
The Dreamer ever, and no truth include: 775
Those that the glittering Horn-gate lets abrode
Do evermore some certaine truth abode.
But this my dreame I hold of no such sort
To flye from thence; yet, which soever Port
It had accesse from, it did highly please 780
My Son and me. And this my thoughts professe—
That Day that lights me from Ulysses' Court
Shall both my infamy and curse consort.
I therefore purpose to propose them now
In strong Contention Ulysses' Bow— 785
Which he that easly drawes, and from his draft
Shoots through twelve Axes (as he did his shaft,
All set up in a rowe, and from them all
His stand-farre-off kept firme) my fortunes shall
Dispose, and take me to his house from hence, 790
Where I was wed a Maide in confluence
Of feast and riches, such a Court heere then
As I shall ever in my dreames reteine.'
'Do not,' said he, 'deferre the gamefull prise,
But set to taske their importunities 795
With something else than Nuptials. For your Lord
Will to his Court and Kingdome be restor'd,
Before they thred those steeles or draw his Bow.'
'O Guest,' repli'de Penelope, 'would you
Thus sit and please me with your speech, mine eares 800
Would never let mine eye-lids close their Spheares!
But none can live without the death of sleepe;
Th'Immortals in our mortall memories keepe
Our ends and deaths by sleepe, dividing so
(As by the Fate and portion of our wo) 805
Our times spent heere—to let us nightly try
That while we live, as much as live, we dye.
In which use I will to my bed ascend,

The two parts of Dreames.

The proposition of Ulysses' Bow to the Wooers, determined by Penelope.

Which I bedeaw with tears and sigh past end
Through all my houres spent since I lost my joy 810
For vile, lew'd, never-to-be-named Troy.
Yet there I'le prove for sleepe, which take you here—
Or on the earth, if that your custome were,
Or have a bed dispos'd for warmer rest.'
Thus left she with her Ladies her old Guest, 815
Ascended her faire chamber and her bed;
Whose sight did ever duly make her shed
Teares for her Lord, which still her eyes did steepe
Till Pallas shut them with delightsome sleepe.

The End of the Nineteenth Booke of Homer's Odysses

THE TWENTIETH BOOKE
of
HOMER'S ODYSSES

THE ARGUMENT

Ulysses, in the Wooers' Beds
Resolving first to kill the Maids;
That sentence giving off, his care
For other Objects doth prepare.

Another Argument

Ψ. *Jove's thunder chides,*
but cheers the king,
The Wooers' prides
discomfiting.

Ulysses in the Entry laide his head,
And under him an Oxe-hide newly flead,
Above him Sheep-fels' store; and over those
Eurynome cast Mantles. His repose
Would bring no sleepe yet, studying the ill 5
He wisht the wooers—who came by him still
With all their wenches, laughing, wantoning
In mutuall lightnesse: which his heart did sting,
Contending two wayes, if (all patience fled)
He should rush up and strike those Strumpets dead, 10
Or let that night be last, and take th'extreme
Of those proud wooers that were so supreme
In pleasure of their high-fed fantasies.
His heart did barke within him to surprize
Their sports with spoiles. No fell shee-Mastive can 15
Amongst her whelpes flye eagrer on a man
She doth not know, yet sents him something neare,
And faine would come to please her tooth and teare,
Than his disdaine, to see his Roofe so fil'de

With those fowle fashions, grew within him wilde 20
To be in blood of them. But, finding best
In his free judgement to let passion rest,
He chid his angry spirit, and beate his brest,
And said: 'Forbeare, my minde, and thinke on this:
There hath bene time when bitter agonies 25
Have tried thy patience. Call to minde the day
In which the Cyclop, which past manly sway
Of violent strength devour'd thy friends; thou then
Stoodst firmely bold, till from that hellish den
Thy wisedome broght thee off, when nought but death 30
Thy thoughts resolv'd on.' This discourse did breath
The fiery boundings of his heart, that still
Lay in that æsture, without end, his ill
Yet manly suffering. But from side to side
It made him tosse apace. You have not tride 35
A fellow roasting of a Pig before
A hasty fire (his belly yeelding store
Of fat and blood) turne faster, labour more
To have it roast and would not have it burne,
Than this and that way his unrest made turne 40
His thoughts and body, would not quench the fire,
And yet not have it heighten his desire
Past his discretion, and the fit enough
Of hast and speed, that went to all the proofe
His well-laid plots and his exploits requir'd— 45
Since he, but one, to all their deaths aspir'd.

Pallas appeares to Ulysses.

In this contention Pallas stoop't from heaven,
Stood over him, and had her presence given
A woman's forme, who sternly thus began:
'Why, thou most sowre and wretched-fated man 50
Of all that breath, yet liest thou thus awake?
The house in which thy cares so tosse and take
Thy quiet up is thine: thy wife is there;
And such a Son as, if thy wishes were
To be suffic'd with one, they could not mend.' 55
'Goddesse,' said he, 'tis true. But I contend
To right their wrongs, and (though I bee but one)
To lay unhelpt and wreakfull hand upon
This whole resort of impudents that here
Their rude assemblies never will forbeare. 60
And yet a greater doubt imployes my care,
That if their slaughters in my reaches are
And I performe them (Jove and you not pleas'd)

How shall I flye their friends? And would stand seas'd
Of counsaile to resolve this care in me.' 65
'Wretch,' she replied, 'a friend of worse degree
Might win thy credence, that a mortall were
And us'd to second thee, though nothing nere
So powerfull in performance nor in care—
Yet I, a Goddesse, that have still had share 70
In thy atchievements and thy person's guard,
Must still be doubted by thy Braine—so hard
To credit any thing above thy powre,
And that must come from heaven, if every houre
There be not personall apparance made 75
And aide direct given, that may sense invade.
I'le tell thee therefore cleerely. If there were
Of divers-languag'd men an Army here
Of fifty Companies, all driving hence
Thy Sheepe and Oxen, and with violence 80
Offer'd to charge us and besiedge us round,
Thou shouldst their prey reprize and them confound.
Let sleepe then seize thee: *To keepe watch all Night*
Consumes the spirits, and makes dull the sight.'
Thus pour'd the Goddesse sleepe into his eyes, 85
And re-ascended the Olympian skies.
When care-and-lineament-resolving sleepe
Had laide his temples in his golden steepe,
His wise-in-chast-wit-worthy wife did rise:
(First sitting up in her soft bed) her eyes 90
Opened with teares in care of her estate,
Which now her friends resolv'd to terminate
To more delaies, and make her marry one.
Her silent teares then ceast, her Orizon
This Queene of women to Diana made: 95
'Reverend Diana, let thy Darts invade
My wofull bosome and my life deprive
Now at this instant, or soone after drive
My soule with Tempests forth, and give it way
To those farre-off darke Vaults where never day 100
Hath powre to shine, and let them cast it downe
Where refluent Oceanus doth crowne
His curled head, where Pluto's Orchard is
And entrance to our after miseries.
As such sterne whirlewinds ravisht to that streame 105
Pandareus' daughters, when the Gods to them
Had reft their parents and them left alone

(Poore orphan children) in their Mansion—
Whose desolate life did love's sweet Queene incline
To nurse with pressed Milke and sweetest wine, 110
Whom Juno deckt beyond all other Dames
With wisedome's light and beautie's moving flames,
Whom Phœbe goodlinesse of stature render'd,
And to whose faire hands wise Minerva tender'd
The Loome and Needle in their utmost skill— 115
And, while Love's Empresse skal'd th'Olympian hill
To beg of Lightning-loving Jove (since hee
The meanes to all things knowes, and doth decree
Fortunes, infortunes, to the mortall Race)
For those poore virgins the accomplisht grace 120
Of sweetest Nuptials, the fierce Harpyes prey'd
On every good, and miserable Maid
And to the hatefull Furies gave them all
In horrid service—yet may such Fate fall
From steepe Olympus on my loathed head, 125
Or faire-hair'd Phœbe strike me instant dead,
That I may undergo the gloomy Shore
To visit great Ulysses' soule, before
I sooth my idle blood and wed a wurse.
And yet beneath how desperate a curse 130
Do I live now? It is an ill that may
Be well indur'd, to mourne the whole long day,
So night's sweete sleepes (that make a man forget
Both bad and good) in some degree would let
My thoughts leave greeving. But both day and night 135
Some cruell God gives my sad memory sight.
This night (me thought) Ulysses grac't my bed
In all the goodly state with which he led
The Grecian Army—which gave joyes extreame
To my distresse, esteeming it no dreame 140
But true indeed, and that conceite I had,
That when I saw it false, I might be mad.
Such cruell Fates command in my life's guide.'
By this the morning's Orient dewes had di'de
The earth in all her colours, when the King, 145
In his sweet sleepe, suppos'd the sorrowing
That she us'd waking in her plaintiffe bed
To be her mourning, standing by his head,
As having knowne him there—who straight arose,
And did againe within the Hall dispose 150
The Carpets and the Cushions, where before

They serv'd the seats. The Hide without the dore
He carried backe; and then with held-up hands
He pray'd to him that heaven and earth commands:
'O Father Jove, if through the moyst and dry 155
You (willing) brought me home, when misery
Had punisht me enough by your free doomes,
Let some of these within those inner roomes
(Startl'd with horror of some strange Ostent)
Come heere, and tell me that great Jove hath bent 160
Threatnings without at some lewd men within.'
To this his pray'r Jove shooke his sable chin,
And thunder'd from those pure clouds that (above
The breathing aire) in bright Olympus move.
Divine Ulysses joy'd, to heare it rore— 165
Report of which a woman Miller bore
Straight to his eares. For neere to him there ground
Milles for his Corne, that twice six women found
Continuall motion, grinding Barley meale
And wheat (man's Marrow). Sleepe the eies did seale 170
Of all the other women, having done
Their usuall taske, which yet this Dame alone
Had scarce given end to, being of al the rest
Least fit for labour. But when these sounds prest
Her eares above the rumbling of her Mill, 175
She let that stand, look't out, and heaven's steepe hill
Saw cleere and temperate—which made her (unware
Of giving any comfort to his care
In that strange signe he pray'd for) thus invoke:

The Miller-woman's prayer to Jove, in satisfaction of Ulysses' prayer.

'O King of men and Gods, a mighty stroke 180
Thy thundring hand laide on the cope of starres,
No cloud in all the aire; and therefore warres
Thou bidst to some men in thy sure Ostent.
Performe to me (poore wretch) the maine event,
And make this day the last and most extream 185
In which the wooers' pride shall solace them
With whoorish Banquets in Ulysses' Roofe—
That with sad toyle to grinde them meale enough
Have quite dissolv'd my knees. Vouchsafe then now
Thy thunders may their latest Feast foreshow.' 190

Viz. That some from within might yssue and witnesse in his hearing some wreakefull Ostent to his enemies from heaven.

This was the Boone Ulysses begg'd of Jove,
Which (with his Thunder) through his bosom drove
A joy, that this vant breath'd: 'Why, now these men
(Despite their pride) will Jove make pay me paine.'
By this had other Maids than those that lay 195

Mixt with the wooers made a fire like day
Amidst the harth of the illustrious Hall:
And then the Prince, like a Celestiall,
Rose from his bed, to his embalm'd feete tied
Faire shooes, his sword about his breast applied, 200
Tooke to his hand his sharp-pil'd Lance, and met
Amidst the Entry his old Nurse, that set
His hast at sodaine stand—to whom he said:
'O, my lov'd Nurse, with what grace have you laid
And fed my guest heere? Could you so neglect 205
His age, to lodge him thus? Though all respect
I give my Mother's wisedome, I must yet
Affirme it fail'd in this. For she hath set
At much more price a man of much lesse worth
Without his person's note, and yet casts forth 210
With ignominious hands (for his Forme sake)
A man much better.' 'Do not faulty make,
Good Son, the faultlesse. He was given his seat
Close to her side, and food till he would eat,
Wine til his wish was serv'd. For she requir'd 215
His wants, and will'd him all things he desir'd,
Commanded her chiefe Maides to make his bed;
But he (as one whom sorrow onely fed
And all infortune) would not take his rest
In bed and coverings fit for any Guest, 220
But in the Entry, on an Oxe's hide
Never at Tanners, his old Limbes implide
In warme Sheep-fels; yet over all we cast
A mantle fitting for a man more grac'st.'
He tooke her answere, left the house, and went 225
(Attended with his dogges) to sift th'event
Of private Plots betwixt him and his Sire
In commune counsaile. Then the crue entire
Of al the houshold Maids, Euryclea bad
Bestir them through the house, and see it clad 230
In all best Forme; gave all their parts; and one
She set to furnish every seate and Throne
With Needle-workes and purple clothes of State,
Another set to scoure and cleanse the Plate,
Another all the Tables to make proud 235
With porous Sponges, others she bestow'd
In all speed to the Spring, to fetch from thence
Fit store of water; all at all expence
Of paines she will'd to be—for this to all

Should be a day of commune Festivall, 240
And not a wooer now should seeke his home
Else where than there. But all were bid to come
Exceeding early, and be rais'd to heaven
With all the entertainment could be geven.
They heard with greedy eares, and every thing 245
Put straight in practise. Twenty to the Spring
Made speed for water; many in the house
Tooke paines; and all were both laborious
And skill'd in labour. Many fell to Fell
And cleave their wood, and all did more than well. 250
Then troop't the lusty wooers in, and then
Came all from Spring—at their heeles loaded men
With slaughter'd Brawnes, of all the Herd the prize,
That had bene long fed up in severall Sties.
Eumæus and his men convei'd them there. 255
He (seeing now the King) began to chere,
And thus saluted him: 'How now, my Guest?
Have yet your vertues found more interest
In these great wooers' good respects? Or still
Pursue they you with all their wonted ill?' 260
'I would to heaven, Eumæus,' he replide,
'The Deities once would take in hand their pride,
That such unseemly fashions put in frame
In others' Roofes as shew no sparke of shame.'
Thus these; and to these came Melanthius, 265
Great guardian of the most egregious
Rich wooers' Herds, consisting all of Goats,
Which he, with two more, drave, and made their coats
The sounding Porticos of that faire Court.
Melanthius (seeing the King) this former sort 270
Of upland Language gave: 'What? Still stay heere
And dull these wooers with thy wretched cheere?
Not gone for ever, yet? Why, now I see
This strife of cuffes betwixt the beggery
(That yesterday assaid to get thee gone) 275
And thy more roguery needs wil fall upon
My hands to arbitrate. Thou wilt not hence
Till I set on thee—thy ragg'd impudence
Is so fast-footed. Are there not beside
Other great Banquetants, but you must ride 280
At anchor stil with us?' He nothing said,
But thought of ill enough, and shooke his head.
Then came Philœtius (a chiefe of men)

That to the wooers' all-devouring den
A barren Stere drave and fat Goats; for they 285
In custome were with Traffiquers by sea,
That who they would sent, and had utterance there.
And for these likewise, the faire Porches were
Hurdles and Sheep-pens, as in any Faire.
Philœtius tooke note in his repaire 290
Of seene Ulysses, being a man as well
Given to his mind's use as to buy and sell,
Or do the drudgery that the blood desir'd—
And (standing neere Eumæus) this enquir'd:
'What Guest is this that makes our house of late 295
His entertainer? Whence claimes he the state
His birth in this life holds? What Nation?
What race? What country stands his speech upon?
Ore hardly portion'd by the terrible Fates,
The structure of his Lineaments relates 300
A King's resemblance in his pompe of reigne,
Even thus in these rags. But poore erring men
That have no firme homes but range here and there
As Need compels, God keepes in this earth's sphere
As under water; and this tune he sings 305
When he is spinning even the cares of Kings.'

Thus comming to him, with a kinde of feare
He tooke his hand, and (touch't exceeding neare
With meere imagination of his worth)
This salutation he sent lowdly forth: 310

'Health! Father stranger! In another world
Be rich and happy, though thou here art hurld
At feete of never such insulting Neede.
O Jove, there lives no one God of thy seede
More ill to man than thou. Thou tak'st no ruth 315
(When thou thy selfe hast got him in most truth)
To wrap him in the straites of most distresse
And in the curse of others' wickednesse.
My browes have swet to see it, and mine eyes
Broke all in teares, when, this being still the guise 320
Of worthiest men, I have but onely thought
That downe to these ils was Ulysses wrought,
And that (thus clad) even he is error driven,
If yet he lives and sees the light of heaven.
But, if now dead and in the house of hell— 325
O me! O good Ulysses, that my weale
Did ever wish, and when but halfe a man

Amongst the people Cephallenian,
His bounty to his Oxen's charge preferr'd
One in that youth—which now is growne a Herd 330
Unspeakeable for number, and feede there
With their broad heads as thicke as of his eare
A Field of Corne is to a man: yet these
Some men advise me that this noted prease
Of wooers may devoure, and wish me drive 335
Up to their Feasts with them—that neither give
His Son respect, though in his owne free roofe,
Nor have the wit to feare th'infallible proofe
Of heavenly vengeance, but make offer now
The long-lack't King's possessions to bestow 340
In their selfe shares. Me thinkes, the minde in me
Doth turne as fast as (in a flood, or Sea)
A raging whirlepit doth, to gather in
To fishy death those swimmers in their sin,
Or feeds a motion as circulare 345
To drive my Herds away. But while the Son
Beares up with life, t'were hainous wrong to ron
To other people with them, and to trust
Men of another earth: and yet more just
It were to venture their Lawes, the maine right 350
Made stil their Maisters, than at home lose quite
Their right and them, and sit and greeve to see
The wrong authoriz'd by their gluttonie.
And I had long since fled, and tried th'event
With other proud Kings (since more insolent 355
These are than can be borne), but that even stil
I had a hope that this (though borne to ill)
Would one day come from some coast, and their last
In his roofes strew with ruines red and vast.'
'Hersman,' said he, 'because thou art in show 360
Nor lewd nor indiscreete, and that I know
There rules in thee an understanding soule,
I'le take an oath that in thee shall controule
All doubt of what I sweare: be witnesse, Jove,
That swai'st the first Seate of the thron'd above, 365
This hospitable Table and this house
That still holds title for the strenuous
Sonne of Laertes, that (if so you please)
Your eyes shall witnesse Laertiades
Arriv'd at home, and all these men that raigne 370
In such excesses heere shall heere lye slaine.'

He answer'd: 'Stranger! would just Jove wold signe
What you have sworne, in your eyes' beams should shine
What powers I mannage, and how these my hands
Would rise and follow where he first commands.' 375
So said Eumæus, praying all the Sky
That wise Ulysses might arrive and trie.
Thus while they vow'd, the wooers sat as hard
On his Son's death—but had their counsels skar'd,
For on their left hand did an Eagle sore, 380
And in her seres a fearefull Pigeon bore.
Which seene, Amphinomus presag'd: 'O friends,
Our Counsailes never will receive their ends
In this man's slaughter: let us therefore plie
Our bloody feast, and make his Oxen die.' 385
Thus came they in, cast off on seates their cloakes,
And fell to giving sacrificing strokes
Of Sheepe and Goates, the cheefely fat and great,
Slew fed-up Swine and, from the Heard, a Neate.
The inwards (roasted) they dispos'de betwixt 390
Their then observers, wine in Flaggons mixt.
The bolles Eumæus brought, Philœtius bread;
Melanthius fill'd the wine. Thus dranke and fed
The feastfull wooers. Then the Prince (in grace
Of his close project) did his Father place 395
Amids the paved Entrie, in a Seate
Seemelesse and abject, a small boord and meate
Of th'onely inwards. In a cup of gold
Yet sent him wine, and bad him now drinke bolde;
All his approches he himselfe would free 400
Gainst all the wooers, since he would not see
His Court made populare, but that his Sire
Built it to his use. Therefore all the fire
Blowne in the wooers' spleenes he bad suppresse,
And that in hands nor words they should digresse 405
From that set peace his speech did then proclaime.
They bit their lips, and wondred at his aime
In that brave Language, when Antinous saide:
'Though this speech, Grecians, be a meere upbraide,
Yet this time give it passe. The will of Jove 410
Forbids the violence of our hands to move—
But of our tongues we keepe the motion free,
And, therefore, if his further jollity
Tempt our encounter with his Braves, let's checke
His growing insolence, though pride to speake 415

The Feast that Euryclea spoke of before, returned unto.

Fly passing high with him.' The wise Prince made
No more spring of his speech, but let it fade.
And now the Heralds bore about the Towne
The sacred Hecatombe, to whose renowne
The faire-haird Greekes assembl'd; and beneath 420
Apollo's shady wood the holy death
They put to fire, which (made enough) they drew,
Divided all, that did in th'end accrew
To glorious satisfaction. Those that were
Disposers of the Feast did equall cheere 425
Bestow on wretched Laertiades
With all the wooers' soules. It so did please
Telemachus to charge them. And for these
Minerva would not see the malices
The wooers bore too much contain'd, that so 430
Ulysses' mov'd heart yet might higher flow
In wreakfull anguish. There was wooing there
(Amongst the rest) a Gallant, that did beare
The name of one well learn'd in jests prophane,
His name Ctesippus, borne a Samian: 435
Who, proud because his Father was so rich,
Had so much confidence as did bewitch
His heart with hope to wed Ulysses' wife;
And this man said: 'Heare me, my Lords, in strife
For this great widdow. This her guest did share 440
Even feast with us, with very comely care
Of him that order'd it. For 'tis not good
Nor equall to deprive Guestes of their food,
And specially what ever guest makes way
To that house where Telemachus doth sway. 445
And therefore I will adde to his receipt
A gift of very hospitable weight,
Which he may give againe to any Maide
That baths his grave feete, and her paines see paide,
Or any servant else that the divine 450
Ulysses' lofty Battlements confine.'
Thus snatcht he with a valiant hand from out
The poore folke's commune basket a Neat's foot,
And threw it at Ulysses, who his head
Shrunke quietly aside, and let it shed 455
His malice on the wall—the suffering man
A laughter raising most Sardinian,
With scorne and wrath mixt, at the Samian—
Whom thus the Prince reprov'd: 'Your valour wan

Much grace, Ctesippus, and hath eas'd your minde 460
With mighty profit: yet you see it finde
No marke it aim'd at; the poore stranger's part
Himselfe made good enough to scape your Dart.
But should I serve thee worthily, my Lance
Should strike thy heart through, and (in place t'advance 465
Thy selfe in Nuptials with his wealth) thy Sire
Should make thy toomb heere, that the foolish fire
Of all such valors may not dare to show
These foule indecencies to me. I now
Have yeares to understand my strength, and know 470
The good and bad of things, and am no more
At your large sufferance, to behold my store
Consum'd with patience, see my Cattell slaine,
My wine exhausted, and my Bread in vaine
Spent on your license. For to one then yong 475
So many enemies were match too strong—
But let me never more be witnesse to
Your hostile minds, nor those base deeds ye do:
For, should ye kill me in my offred wreake,
I wish it rather, and my death would speake 480
Much more good of me than to live and see
Indignity upon indignity,
My Guests provok't with bitter words and blowes,
My women servants dragg'd about my house
To lust and rapture.' This made silence seize 485
The house throughout, till Damastorides
At length the calme brake, and said: 'Friends, forbeare
To give a just speech a disdainfull eare,
The Guest no more touch, nor no servant here.
My selfe will to the Prince and Queene commend 490
A motion gratefull, if they please to lend
Gratefull receite. As long as any hope
Left wise Ulysses any passage ope
To his returne in our conceits, so long
The Queene's delayes to our demands stood strong 495
In cause and reason; and our quarrels thus
With guests, the Queene, or her Telemachus
Set never foote amongst our liberall Feast.
For should the King returne, though thought deceast,
It had bene gaine to us, in finding him, 500
To lose his wife. But now, since nothing dim
The daie breakes out that shewes he never more
Shal reach the deere touch of his countrey shore,

Sit by your Mother, in perswasion
That now it stands her honor much upon 505
To choose the best of us, and who gives most,
To go with him home. For so, all things lost
In sticking on our haunt so you shall cleere
Recover in our no more concourse here,
Possesse your birth-right wholly, eate and drinke, 510
And never more on our disgraces thinke.'
'By Jove, no, Agelaus! For I sweare
By all my Father's sorrowes, who doth erre
Farre off from Ithaca, or rests in death,
I am so farre from spending but my breath 515
To make my Mother any more defer
Her wished Nuptials, that I'le counsaile her
To make her free choise—and, besides, will give
Large gifts to move her. But I feare to drive
Or charge her hence. For God will not give way 520
To any such course, if I should assay.'
At this Minerva made for foolish joy
The wooers mad, and rouz'd their late annoy
To such a laughter as would never downe.
They laught with others' cheeks, eate meat oreflowne 525
With their owne bloods, their eies stood full of teares
For violent joyes: their soules yet thought of feares—
Which Theoclymenus exprest, and said:
'O wretches! Why? Sustaine ye (well apaid)
Your imminent ill? A night, with which Death sees 530
Your heads and faces hide beneath your knees;
Shriekes burn about you, your eies thrust out teares,
These fixed wals and that maine Beame that beares
The whole house up in bloody torrents fall;
The Entry full of ghosts stands: full the Hall 535
Of passengers to hel; and, under all
The dismall shades, the Sun sinkes from the Poles,
And troubl'd aire poures bane about your soules.'
They sweetly laught at this. Eurymachus
To mocks dispos'd, and saide: 'This new-come-t'us 540
Is surely mad; conduct him forth to light
In th'open Market place—he thinkes 'tis night
Within the house.' 'Eurymachus,' said he,
'I will not aske for any guide of thee:
I both my feete enjoy, have eares and eies, 545
And no mad soule within me: and with these
Will I go forth the doores, because I know

That imminent mischiefe must abide with you—
Which not a man of all the wooers here
Shall flye or scape. Ye all too highly beare 550
Your uncurb'd heads. Impieties ye commit,
And every man affect with formes unfit.'
This said, he left the house, and tooke his way
Home to Piræus, who as free as day
Was of his welcome. When the wooers' eyes 555
Chang'd lookes with one another, and, their guise
Of laughters still held on, still eas'd their brests
Of will to set the Prince against his guests,
Affirming that of all the men alive
He worst lucke had, and prov'd it worst to give 560
Guests entertainment—for he had one there,
A wandring Hunter out of provendere,
An errant Begger every way, yet thought
(He was so hungry) that he needed nought
But wine and Victuals, nor knew how to do, 565
Nor had a spirit to put a knowledge to,
But liv'd an idle burthen to the earth.
Another then stept up, and would lay forth
His lips in phrophesie thus: 'But (would he heare
His friends' perswasions) he should finde it were 570
More profit for him to put both abord
For the Sicilian people, that afford
ἀνδραποδισταί. These feete of men good price, and this would bring
Good meanes for better guests.' These words made wing
To his eares idlely, who had still his eye 575
Upon his Father, looking fervently
When he would lay his long-withholding hand
On those proud wooers. And, within command
Of all this speech that past, Icarius' heire
(The wise Penelope) her royall chaire 580
Had plac't of purpose. Their high dinner then
With all pleas'd palates these ridiculous men
Fell sweetly to, as joying they had slaine
Such store of banquet. But there did not raigne
A bitterer banquet Planet in all heaven 585
Than that which Pallas had to that day driven,
And with her able friend now meant t'appose,
Since they till then were in deserts so grose.

The End of the Twentieth Booke of Homer's Odysses

THE XXI BOOKE
of
HOMER'S ODYSSES

THE ARGUMENT

Penelope proposeth now
To him that drawes Ulysses' Bow
Her instant Nuptials. Ithacus,
Eumæus and Philœtius
Gives charge for guarding of the Gates, 5
And he his shaft shoots through the plates.

Another Argument

Φι. *The Nuptiall vow*
and Game reherst:
Drawne is the Bow,
the steeles are pierst.

Pallas (the Goddesse with the sparkling eyes)
Excites Penelope t'object the prise
(The Bow and bright steeles) to the wooers' strength;
And here began the strife and blood at length.
She first ascended by a lofty staire 5
Her utmost chamber; of whose doore her faire
And halfe transparent hand receiv'd the Key,
Bright, brazen, bitted passing curiously,
And at it hung a knob of Ivory.
And this did leade her where was strongly kept 10
The treasure Royall, in whose store lay heap't
Gold, Brasse, and Steele, engraven with infinite Art,
The crooked Bowe and Arrowy quiver part
Of that rich Magazin. In the Quiver were
Arrowes a number, sharpe, and sighing gere. 15
The Bow was given by kinde Eurytides

(Iphitus, fashion'd like the Deities)
To yong Ulysses, when within the Roofe
Of wise Ortilochus their passe had proofe
Of mutuall meeting in Messena; where 20
Ulysses claim'd a debt, to whose pay were
The whole Messenian people bound, since they
From Ithaca had forc't a wealthy prey
Of Sheepe and Sheepherds. In their ships they thrust
Three hundred Sheepe together; for whose just 25
And instant rendry old Laertes sent
Ulysses his Ambassador, that went
A long way in the Ambassie, yet then
Bore but the formost Prime of yongest men—
His Father sending first to that affaire 30
His gravest Counsailors, and then his heire.
Iphitus made his way there, having lost
Twelve female horse and Mules commended most
For use of burthen, which were after cause
Of death and Fate to him. For (past all Lawes 35
Of hospitality) Jove's mighty Son
(Skill'd in great Acts) was his confusion
Close by his house, though at that time his guest,
Respecting neither the apposed Feast
And hospitable Table that in love 40
He set before him, nor the voyce of Jove—
But, seizing first his Mares, he after slew
His host himselfe. From those Mares' serch now grew
Ulysses knowne t'Iphitus; who that Bow
At their encounter did in love bestow, 45
Which great Eurytus' hand had borne before
(Iphitus' Father) who (at death's sad dore)
In his steepe Turrets left it to his Son.
Ulysses gave him a keene Faulchion
And mighty Lance, and thus began they there 50
Their fatall Loves. For after never were
Their mutuall Tables to each other knowne,
Because Jove's Son th'unworthy part had showne
Of slaughtering this God-like loving man,
Eurytus' Son, who with that Bow began 55
And ended love t'Ulysses—who so deare
A gift esteem'd it that he would not beare
In his black Fleete that guest-rite to the war,
But, in fit memory of one so farre
In his affection, brought it home and kept 60

ἵππους δώδεκα θήλειαι— Equas duodecem fœminæ.

Hercules.

His treasure with it, where till now it slept.
  And now the Queene of women had intent
To give it use; and therefore made ascent
Up all the staire's height to the chamber dore,
Whose shining leaves two bright Pilasters bore 65
To such a Close, when both together went,
It would resist the Aire in their consent.
The Ring she tooke then, and did draw aside
A barre that ran within, and then implide
The Key into the Locke—which gave a sound 70
(The Bolt then shooting) as in pasture ground
A Bull doth Low and make the valleys ring:
So loud the Locke humm'd, when it loosd his Spring,
And ope the doores flew. In she went along
The lofty chamber, that was boorded strong 75
With heart of Oake, which many yeares ago
The Architect did smooth and polish so
That now as then he made it freshly shine,
And tried the evennesse of it with a Line.
  There stood in this roome Presses that enclos'd 80
Robes odoriferous, by which repos'd
The Bow was upon pins, nor from it farre
Hung the round Quiver, glittering like a Starre—
Both which her white extended hand tooke downe.
Then sate she low, and made her lap a Crowne 85
Of both those Reliques, which she wept to see,
And cried quite out with loving memory
Of her deare Lord: to whose worth paying then
Kinde debts enow, she left, and to the men
Vow'd to her wooing brought the crooked Bow 90
And shaft-receiving Quiver, that did flow
With arrowes, beating sighes up where they fell.
Then with another Chist, repleate as well
With Games won by the King of Steele and Brasse,
Her Maids attended—past whom making passe 95
To where her wooers were, she made her stay
Amids the faire Hall doore, and kept the ray
Of her bright count'nance hid with veyles so thin
That, though they seem'd t'expose, they let love in.
Her Maids on both sides stood, and thus she spake: 100
  'Heare me, ye wooers, that a pleasure take
To do me sorrow and my house invade
To eate and drinke, as if 'twere onely made
To serve your Rapines—my Lord long away,

And you allow'd no colour for your stay 105
But his still absence, striving who shall frame
Me for his wife; and (since 'tis made a game)
I heere propose divine Ulysses' Bow
For that great Maister-peece to which ye vow.
He that can draw it with least show to strive, 110
And through these twelve Ax-heads an arrow drive,
Him will I follow, and this house forgo
That nourisht me a Maid, now furnisht so
With all things fit, and which I so esteeme
That I shall still live in it in my dream.' 115
This said, she made Eumæus give it them.
He tooke, and laide it by, and wept for wo,
And like him wept Philœtius, when the Bow
Of which his King was bearer he beheld.
Their teares Antinous' manhood much refeld, 120
And said: 'Ye rustick fooles! that still each day
Your minds give over to this vaine dismay,
Why weepe ye, wretches, and the widdowe's eyes
Tempt with renew'd thought, that would otherwise
Depose her sorrowes, since her Lord is dead 125
And teares are idle? Sit, and eate your bread,
Nor whisper more a word; or get ye gone,
And weepe without doores. Let this Bow alone
To our out-matcht contention. For I feare
The Bow will scarse yeeld draught to any heere. 130
Heere no such man lives as Laertes' Son
Amongst us all. I knew him; thought puts on
His looke's sight now, me thinkes, thogh then a child.'
Thus shew'd his words doubt, yet his hopes enstild
His strength the stretcher of Ulysses' string 135
And his steele's piercer. But his shaft must sing
Through his piercst Pallat first, whom so he wrong'd
In his free roofe, and made the rest ill tongu'd
Against his vertues. Then the sacred heat
That spirited his Son did further set 140
Their confidence on fire, and said: 'O Frends,
Jove hath bereft my wits. The Queene intends
(Though I must grant her wise) ere long to leave
Ulysses' Court, and to her bed receave
Some other Lord: yet, notwithstanding, I 145
Am forc't to laugh and set my pleasures hye
Like one mad sicke. But, wooers, since ye have
An object for your trials now so brave

As all the broad Achaian earth exceeds,
As sacred Pylos, as the Argive breeds, 150
As blacke Epirus, as Mycena's birth,
And as the more-fam'd Ithacensian earth,
All which your selves well know, and oft have saide
(For what neede hath my Mother of my aide
In her advancement?)—tender no excuse 155
For least delay, nor too much time profuse
In stay to draw this Bow; but draw it straight,
Shoot, and the steeles pierce, make all see how sleight
You make these poore barres to so rich a prise.
No eagrer yet? Come on. My faculties 160
Shall try the Bowe's strength and the pierced steele.
I will not for my reverend Mother feele
The sorrowes that I know will seize my heart,
To see her follow any and depart
From her so long-held home, but first extend 165
The Bow and Arrow to their tender'd end.
For I am onely to succeede my Sire
In guard of his games, and let none aspire
To their besides possession.' This said,
His purple Robe he cast off. By he laide 170
His well-edg'd sword; and first, a severall pit
He digg'd for every Axe, and strengthen'd it
With earth close ramm'd about it—on a rew
Set them of one height, by a Line he drew
Along the whole twelve, and so orderly 175
Did every deed belonging (yet his eye
Never before beholding how 'twas done)
That in amaze rose all his lookers on.
Then stood he neere the doore, and prov'd to draw
The stubborne Bow—thrice tried, and thrice gave Law 180
To his uncrown'd attempts, the fourth assay
With all force offering, which a signe gave stay
Given by his Father, though hee shew'd a minde
As if he stood right heartily inclinde
To perfect the exploite, when all was done 185
In onely drift to set the wooers on.
His weaknesse yet confest, he said: 'O shame!
I either shall be ever of no name,
But prove a wretch; or else I am too yong,
And must not now presume on pow'rs so strong 190
As sinewes yet more growing may ingraft,
To turne a man quite over with a shaft.

Besides, to men whose Nerves are best prepar'd,
All great Adventures at first proofe are hard.
But come, you stronger men, attempt this Bow, 195
And let us end our labour.' Thus below
A well-joyn'd boord he laide it, and close by
The brightly-headed shaft, then thron'd his Thie
Amidst his late-left seate. Antinous then
Bad all arise; but first, who did sustaine 200
The cup's state ever, and did sacrifice
Before they eate still, and that man bad rise,
Since on the other's right hand he was plac't,
Because he held the right hand's rising grac't
With best successe still. This direction wun 205
Supreame applause, and first rose Œnops' Son,
Leodes, that was Priest to all the rest,
Sate lowest with the Cup still, and their jest
Could never like, but ever was the man
That checkt their follies: and he now began 210
To taste the Bow, the sharpe shaft tooke, tug'd hard,
And held aloft, and, till he quite had marr'd
His delicate tender fingers, could not stir
The churlish string—who therefore did refer
The game to others, saying that same Bow 215
(In his presage) would prove the overthrow
Of many a chiefe man there, nor thought the Fate
Was any whit austere, since Death's short date
Were much the better taken than long life
Without the object of their amorous strife, 220
For whom they had burn'd out so many dayes
To finde still other, nothing but delayes
Obtaining in them; and affirm'd that now
Some hop't to have her, but, when that tough Bow
They all had tried, and seene the utmost done, 225
They must rest pleasd to cease, and wow some one
Of all their other faire veyl'd Grecian Dames
With gifts and dow'r and Hymeneal Flames—
Let her love light to him that most will give,
And whom the Nuptiall destiny did drive. 230
Thus laid he on the well-joyn'd polisht Bord
The Bow and bright-pil't shaft, and then restor'd
His seate his right. To him Antinous
Gave bitter language, and reprov'd him thus:
'What words, Leodes, passe thy speeche's guard, 235
That 'tis a worke to beare? And set so hard,

They set up my disdaine. This Bow must end
The best of us, since thy armes cannot lend
The string least motion? Thy Mother's throwes
Brought never forth thy armes to draught of Bowes 240
Or knitting shafts off. Though thou canst not draw
The sturdy Plant, thou art to us no law.
Melanthius! Light a fire, and set thereat
A chaire and cushions, and that masse of fat
That lyes within bring out, that we may set 245
Our Pages to this Bow, to see it heat
And suppl'd with the suet—and then wee
May give it draught, and pay this great decree
Utmost performance.' He a mighty fire
Gave instant flame, put into act th'entire 250
Command layd on him, chaire and cushions set,
Laid on the Bow, which straight the Pages het,
Chaft, suppl'd with the Suet to their most;
And still was all their Unctuous labour lost,
All wooers' strengths too indigent and pore 255
To draw that Bow. Antinous' armes it tore,
And great Eurymachus' (the both cleere best)—
Yet both it tir'd and made them glad to rest.
Forth then went both the Swaines, and after them
Divine Ulysses—when, being past th'extreme 260
Of all the Gates, with winning words he tride
Their loves, and this askt: 'Shall my counsailes hide
Their depths from you? My mind would gladly know
If sodainly Ulysses had his Vow
Made good for home, and had some God to guide 265
His steps and strokes to wreak these wooers' pride,
Would your aids joyne on his part, or with theirs?
How stand your hearts affected?' They made prayr's
That some God would please to returne their Lord;
He then should see how farre they would affoord 270
Their lives for his. He, seeing their truth, replied:
'I am your Lord, through many a sufferance tried,
Arriv'd now heere, whom twenty yeares have held
From foorth my Country: yet are not conceal'd
From my sure knowledge your desires to see 275
My safe returne. Of all the company
Now serving heere besides, not one but you
Mine eare hath witnest willing to bestow
Their wishes of my life, so long held dead.
I therefore vow (which shall be perfected) 280

That if God please beneath my hand to leave
These wooers livelesse, ye shall both receive
Wives from that hand, and meanes, and neere to me
Have houses built to you, and both shall be
As friends and brothers to my onely Sonne. 285
And that ye well may know me, and be wonne
To that assurance, the infallible Signe
The white-tooth'd Bore gave this markt knee of mine,
When in Parnassus he was held in chase
By me and by my famous Grandsire's race, 290
I'le let you see.' Thus sever'd he his weede
From that his wound, and every word had deed
In their sure knowledges—which made them cast
Their armes about him, his broade brest imbrac't,
His necke and shoulders kist. And him, as well, 295
Did those true powers of humane love compell
To kisse their heads and hands, and to their mone
Had sent the free light of the cheerefull Sunne
Had not Ulysses broke the ruth, and saide:
'Cease teares and sorrowes, lest wee prove displaide 300
By some that issue from the house, and they
Relate to those within. Take each his way,
Not altogether in, but one by one,
First I, then you. And then see this be done:
The envious wooers will by no meanes give 305
The offer of the Bow and Arrow leave
To come at me; spight then their pride, do thou,
My good Eumæus, bring both shaft and Bow
To my hand's proofe, and charge the maides before
That instantly they shut in every doore, 310
That they themselves (if any tumult rise
Beneath my Roofes by any that envies
My will to undertake the Game) may gaine
No passage forth, but close at worke containe
With all free quiet, or, at least, constrain'd. 315
And therefore, my Philœtius, see maintain'd
(When close the gates are shut) their closure fast,
To which end be it thy sole worke to cast
Their chaines before them.' This said, in he led,
Tooke first his seate, and then they seconded 320
His entry with their owne. Then tooke in hand
Eurymachus the Bow, made close his stand
Aside the fire, at whose heate here and there
He warm'd and suppl'd it, yet could not stere

To any draught the string, with all his Art; 325
And therefore sweld in him his glorious heart,
Affirming that himselfe and all his friends
Had cause to greeve, not onely that their ends
They mist in marriage (since enow besides
Kinde Grecian Dames there liv'd to be their Brides 330
In Ithaca and other bordering Townes)
But that to all times future their renownes
Would stand disparag'd, if Ulysses' Bow
They could not drawe, and yet his wife would woo.
  Antinous answer'd that there could ensue 335
No shame at all to them, for well he knew
That this day was kept holy to the Sunne
By all the City, and there should be done
No such prophane act; therefore bad lay by
The Bow for that day; but the maistery 340
Of Axes that were set up still might stand,
Since that no labour was, nor any hand
Would offer to invade Ulysses' house
To take, or touch with surreptitious
Or violent hand, what there was left for use. 345
He therefore bad the Cup-bearer infuse
Wine to the Bolles, that so with sacrifice
They might let rest the shooting exercise,
And in the morning make Melanthius bring
The cheefe Goats of his Herd, that to the King 350
Of Bowes and Archers they might burne the Thyes
For good successe, and then attempt the prize.
  The rest sate pleasd with this: the Heralds straite
Pour'd water on their hands: each Page did waite
With his crown'd cup of wine, serv'd every man 355
Till all were satisfied: and then began
Ulysses' plot of his close purpose, thus:
'Heare me, ye much renown'd Eurymachus,
And King Antinous, in cheefe, who well,
And with decorum sacred, doth compell 360
This daye's observance, and to let lay downe
The Bow all this light, giving Gods their owne.
The morning's labour God the more wil blesse,
And strength bestow, where he himselfe shall please.
Against which time, let me presume to pray 365
Your favours with the rest, that this assay
May my olde armes proove, trying if there lye
In my poore powers the same activity

That long since crown'd them—or if needy fare
And desolate wandring have the web worne bare 370
Of my life's thred at all parts, that no more
Can furnish these affaires as heeretofore.'
This heat their spleens past measure, blown with fear
Lest his loth'd temples would the garland weare
Of that Bowe's draught, Antinous using speech 375
To this sowre purpose: 'Thou most arrant wretch
Of all guests breathing, in no least degree
Grac't with a humane soule! It serves not thee
To feast in peace with us, take equall share
Of what we reach to, sit and all things heare 380
That we speake freely (which no begging guest
Did ever yet), but thou must make request
To mixe with us in merit of the Queene.
But wine enflames thee, that hath ever beene
The bane of men, whoever yet would take 385
Th'excesse it offers, and the meane forsake.
Wine spoilde the Centaur great Eurytion
In guest-rites with the mighty-minded Son
Of bolde Ixion, in his way to warre
Against the Lapithes; who, driven as farre 390
As madnesse with the bold effects of wine,
Did outrage to his kinde hoast, and decline
Other Heroes from him feasted there
With so much anger that they left their cheere,
And dragg'd him forth the fore-court, slit his nose, 395
Cropt both his eares; and in the ill dispose
His minde then sufferd, drew the fatall day
On his head with his hoast. For thence the fray
Betwixt the Centaurs and the Lapithes
Had mortall act. But he, for his excesse 400
In spoile of wine, far'd worst himselfe—as thou
For thy large cups, if thy armes draw the Bow,
My minde foretels shalt feare; for not a man
Of all our Consort, that in wisedome can
Boast any fit share, will take prayers then, 405
But to Echetus, the most sterne of men,
A blacke Saile freight with thee, whose worst of ill,
Be sure, is past all ransome. Sit then still,
Drinke temperately, and never more contend
With men your yongers.' This the Queene did end 410
With her defence of him, and told his Foe
It was not faire nor equall t'overcrow

The poorest Guest her sonne pleas'd t'entertaine
In his free Turrets, with so proud a straine
Of threats and bravings—asking if he thought 415
That, if the stranger to his armes had brought
The stubborne Bow downe, he should marry her
And beare her home? And said himself should erre
In no such hope; nor of them all the best
That greev'd at any good she did her guest 420
Should banquet there, since it in no sort show'd
Noblesse in them, nor paid her what she ow'd
Her owne free rule there. This Eurymachus
Confirm'd and saide: 'Nor feeds it hope in us,
Icarius' daughter, to solemnize Rites 425
Of Nuptials with thee, nor in noblest sights
It can shew comely; but to our respects
The rumor both of sexes and of Sects
Amongst the people would breede shame and feare,
Lest any worst Greeke said: "See, men that were 430
Of meane deservings will presume t'aspire
To his wive's bed whom all men did admire
For fame and merit—could not draw his Bow,
And yet his wife had foolish pride to woo:
When straight an errant Begger comes and drawes 435
The Bow with ease, performing all the Lawes
The game beside contain'd." And this would thus
Prove both indignity and shame to us.'

The Queene replied: 'The fame of men I see
Beares much price in your great suppos'd degree; 440
Yet who can prove (amongst the people great)
That of one so esteem'd of them the seat
Doth so defame and ruine? And, beside,
With what right is this guest thus vilefied
In your high censures, when the man in blood 445
Is well composd and great, his parents good?
And therefore give the Bow to him, to try
His Birth and breeding by his Chevalry.
If his armes draw it, and that Phœbus stands
So great a glory to his strength, my hands 450
Shall adde this guerdon—every sort of weed,
A two-edg'd Sword and Lance to keepe him freed
From Dogs and Men hereafter, and dismis
His worth to what place tends that heart of his.'

Her sonne gave answere, that it was a wrong 455
To his free sway, in all things that belong

Εὐπηγής—
Bene compactus et coagmentatus.

To guard of that house, to demand the Bow
Of any wooer, and the use bestow
Upon the stranger. For the Bow was his
To give or to with-hold, no maisteries 460
Of her proposing giving any power
T'empaire his right in things for any wower,
Or any that rough Ithaca affords,
Any that Elis; of which no man's words
Nor pow'rs should curbe him (stood he so enclin'd) 465
To see the Bow in absolute gift resign'd
To that his guest to beare and use at will.
And therefore bad his Mother keepe her still
Amongst her women at her Rocke and Loome;
Bowes were for men, and this Bow did become 470
Past al men's his disposure, since his Sire
Left it to him, and all the house entire.
She stood dismaid at this, and in her minde
His wise words laide up, standing so inclinde
As he had will'd—with all her women going 475
Up to her chamber, there her teares bestowing
(As every night she did) on her lov'd Lord,
Til sleepe and Pallas her fit rest restor'd.
The Bow Eumæus tooke, and bore away—
Which up in tumult, and almost in fray, 480
Put all the wooers, one enquiring thus:
'Whether, rogue, abject, wilt thou beare from us
That Bow proposd? Lay downe, or I protest
Thy dogs shal eate thee, that thou nourishest
To guard thy Swine, amongst whom (left of all) 485
Thy life shal leave thee, if the Festivall
We now observe to Phœbus may our zeales
Grace with his aide, and all the Deities else.'
This threat made good Eumæus yeelde the Bow
To his late place, not knowing what might grow 490
From such a multitude. And then fell on
Telemachus with threats, and saide: 'Set gon
That Bow yet further: tis no servant's part
To serve too many Maisters: raise your hart
And beare it off, lest (though your yonger) yet 495
With stones I pelt you to the field with it.
If you and I close, I shal proove too strong.
I wish as much too hard for all this throng
The Gods would make me! I should quickly send
Some after with just sorrow to their end, 500

They waste my victles so, and ply my cup,
And do me such shrewd turnes still.' This put up
The wooers all in Laughters, and put downe
Their angers to him, that so late were growne
So grave and bloody—which resolv'd that feare 505
Of good Eumæus, who did take and beare
The King the Bow, call'd Nurse, and bad her make
The doores all sure, that, if men's tumults take
The eares of some within, they may not fly,
But keepe at worke still close and silently. 510
These words put wings to her, and close she put
The chamber doore. The Court gates then were shut
By kind Philœtius, who straight did go
From out the Hall, and in the Portico
Found laid a Gable of a Ship, compos'd 515
Of spongy Bulrushes—with which hee clos'd
(In winding round about them) the Court gates,
Then tooke his place againe, to view the Fates
That quickly follow'd. When he came, he saw
Ulysses viewing, ere he tried to draw, 520
The famous Bow, which every way he mov'd,
Up and downe turning it—in which he prov'd
The plight it was in, fearing chiefly lest
The hornes were eate with wormes in so long rest.
But what his thoughts intended, turning so, 525
And keeping such a search about the Bow,
The wooers, little knowing, fell to jest,
And said: 'Past doubt, he is a man profest
In Bowyer's craft, and sees quite through the wood,
Or something (certaine) to be understood 530
There is in this his turning of it still.
A cunning Rogue he is at any ill.'
Then spake another proud one: 'Would to heaven
I might (at will) get Gold, till he hath geven
That Bow his draught!' With these sharp jests did these 535
Delightsome woo'rs their fatall humors please.
But when the wise Ulysses once had laide
His fingers on it, and to proofe survaide
The stil sound plight it held, as one of skill
In song and of the Harpe doth at his will, 540
In tuning of his Instrument, extend
A string out with his pin, touch all, and lend
To every wel-wreath'd string his perfect sound,
Strooke all togither—with such ease drew round

The King the Bow. Then twang'd he up the string, 545
That as a Swallow in the aire doth sing
With no continu'd tune, but (pausing still)
Twinkes out her scatter'd voice in accents shrill—
So sharpe the string sung when he gave it touch,
Once having bent and drawne it. Which so much 550
Amaz'd the wooers, that their colours went
And came most grievously. And then Jove rent
The aire with thunder, which at heart did chere
The now-enough-sustaining Traveller,
That Jove againe would his attempt enable. 555
Then tooke he into hand from off the Table
The first drawne arrow—and a number more
Spent shortly on the wooers—but this one
He measur'd by his arme (as if not knowne
The length were to him), nockt it then, and drew, 560
And through the Axes, at the first hole, flew
The steele-chardg'd arrow—which when he had done,
He thus bespake the Prince: 'You have not wonne
Disgrace yet by your Guest, for I have strook
The marke I shot at, and no such toile tooke 565
In wearying the Bow with fat and fire
As did the wooers. Yet reserv'd entire
(Thanke heaven) my strength is, and my selfe am tried
No man to be so basely vilified
As these men pleas'd to thinke me. But free way 570
Take that, and all their pleasures: and while Day
Holds her Torch to you, and the howre of feast
Hath now full date, give banquet and the rest
(Poeme and Harpe) that grace a wel-fill'd boorde.'
  This saide, he beckn'd to his Sonne, whose sword 575
He straight girt to him, tooke to hand his Lance,
And, compleate arm'd, did to his Sire advance.

The End of the XXI. Booke of Homer's Odysses

THE XXII. BOOKE
of
HOMER'S ODYSSES

THE ARGUMENT

The Wooers in Minerva's sight
Slaine by Ulysses, all the light
And lustfull Huswives by his Sonne
And servants are to slaughter done.

Another Argument

Xī. *The end of Pride*
and lawlesse Lust
Is wretched tried
with slaughters just.

The upper rags that wise Ulysses wore
Cast off, he rusheth to the great Hall dore
With Bow and Quiver full of shafts, which downe
He pour'd before his feet, and thus made known
His true state to the wooers: 'This strife thus 5
Hath harmlesse bene decided. Now for us
There rests another marke more hard to hit,
And such as never man before hath smit,
Whose full point likewise my hands shall assay,
And try if Phœbus will give me his day.' 10
He said, and off his bitter Arrow thrust
Right at Antinous; that strooke him just
As he was lifting up the Bolle, to show
That 'twixt the cup and lip much ill may grow.
Death toucht not at his thoughts at Feast: for who 15
Would thinke that he alone could perish so
Amongst so many? And he best of all?
The Arrow in his throate tooke full his fall,
And thrust his head farre through the other side:

Downe fell his cup, downe he, downe all his pride. 20
Straight from his Nostrils gusht the humane gore,
And as he fell his feete farre overbore
The feastfull Table, all the Rost and Bread
About the house strew'd. When his high-born head
The rest beheld so low, up rusht they all, 25
And ransack't every Corner of the Hall
For Shields and Darts, but all fled farre their reach.
Then fell they foule on him with terrible speach,
And told him it should prove the deerest shaft
That ever past him, and that now was saf't 30
No shift for him but sure and sodaine death;
For he had slaine a man whose like did breath
In no part of the Kingdome, and that now
He should no more for Game strive with his Bow,
But Vultures eate him there. These threats they spent, 35
Yet every man beleev'd that sterne event
Chanc't 'gainst the author's will. O Fooles, to thinke
That all their rest had any cup to drinke
But what their great Antinous began.
He (frowning) saide: 'Dogs, see in me the man 40
Ye all held dead at Troy. My house it is
That thus ye spoile, that thus your Luxuries
File with my women's rapes, in which ye woo
The wife of one that lives, and no thought show
Of man's fit feare, or God's, your present Fame, 45
Or any faire sence of your future name.
And therefore present and eternal death
Shall end your base life.' This made fresh feares breath
Their former boldnesse: every man had eye
On all the meanes, and studied wayes to flye 50
So deepe deaths imminent. But, seeing none,
Eurymachus began with suppliant mone
To moove his pitty, saying: 'If you be
This Ile's Ulysses, we must all agree
In grant of your reproofe's integrity. 55
The Greekes have done you many a wrong at home,
At field as many. But of all, the summe
Lies heere contract in death—for onely he
Imposd the whole ill Offices that we
Are now made guilty of, and not so much 60
Sought his endevours, or in thought did touch
At any Nuptials, but a greater thing
Employ'd his forces. For to be our King

Was his cheefe object: his sole plot it was
To kil your Son, which Jove's hand would not passe, 65
But set it to his owne most merited end.
In which end your just anger, nor extend
Your sterne wreake further. Spend your royal pow'rs
In milde ruth of your people; we are yours.
And whatsoever waste of wine or food 70
Our Liberties have made, wee'le make all good
In restitutions: call a Court, and passe
A fine of twenty Oxen, Gold, and Brasse
On every Head, and raise your most rates still,
Till you are pleasd with your confessed fill— 75
Which if we faile to tender, all your wrath
It shalbe justice in our bloods to bathe.'
'Eurymachus,' saide he, 'if you would give
All that your Fathers hoord to make ye live,
And all that ever you your selves possesse 80
Or shal by any industry increase,
I would not cease from slaughter, till your bloods
Had bought out your intemperance in my Goods.
It rests now for you that you either fight
That will scape death, or make your way by flight— 85
In whose best choise my thoughts conceive not one
Shall shun the death your first hath undergone.'
This quite dissolv'd their knees. Eurymachus,
Enforcing all their feares, yet counsail'd thus:
'O Friends! This man, now he hath got the Bow 90
And Quiver by him, ever will bestow
His most inaccessible hands at us
And never leave, if we avoide him thus,
Til he hath strew'd the pavement with us all:
And therefore joyne we swords, and on him fall 95
With Tables forc't up, and borne in opposd
Against his sharpe shafts; when, being round enclosd
By all our on-sets, we shall either take
His horrid person, or for safety make
His rage retire from out the Hall and Gates: 100
And then, if he escape, wee'l make our states
Knowne to the City by our generall cry.
And thus this man shal let his last shaft fly
That ever his hand vanted.' Thus he drew
His sharpe-edg'd sword, and with a table flew 105
In on Ulysses with a terrible throte,
His fierce charge urging. But Ulysses smote

The boord, and cleft it through from end t
Borne at his breast, and made his shaft extend
His sharp head to his Liver, his broad breast
Pierc't at his Nipple—when his hand releast
Forthwith his sword, that fel and kist the ground,
With cups and victles lying scattered round
About the pavement: amongst which his brow
Knockt the embrued earth, while in paines did flow 115
His vitall spirits til his heeles shooke out
His feastful life, and hurl'd a Throne about
That way-laide death's convulsions in his feete,
When from his tender eyes the light did fleet.
  Then charg'd Amphinomus with his drawne blade 120
The glorious King, in purpose to have made
His feete forsake the house. But his assay
The Prince prevented; and his Lance gave way
Quite through his shoulder at his backe, his brest
The fierce pile letting forth. His ruine prest 125
Grones from the pavement, which his forhead strook.
  Telemachus his long Lance then forsooke
(Left in Amphinomus) and to his Sire
Made fiery passe, not staying to acquire
His Lance againe—in doubt that, while he drew 130
The fixed pile, some other might renew
Fierce charge upon him and his unarm'd head
Cleave with his back-drawne sword: for which he fled
Close to his Father, bad him arme, and he
Would bring him Shield and Javelins instantly, 135
His owne head arming; more armes laying by
To serve the Swine-herd and the Oxen-herd.
Valour well arm'd is ever most preferd.
  'Run then,' saide he, 'and come before the last
Of these auxilliary shafts are past, 140
For feare lest (left alone) they force my stand
From forth the Ports.' He flew, and brought to hand
Eight Darts, foure Shields, foure Helmes. His owne parts then
First put in armes, he furnisht both his men,
That to their King stood close. But he, as long 145
As he had shafts to friend, enough was strong
For all the wooers, and some one man still
He made make even with earth, till all a hill
Had raisd in th'even floor'd Hall. His last shaft spent,
He set his Bow against a beame, and went 150
To arme at all parts, while the other three

Kept off the wooers, who, unarm'd, could be
No great assailants. In the well-built wall
A window was thrust out, at end of all
The house's Entry, on whose utter side 155
There lay a way to Towne; and in it wide
And two-leav'd folds were forg'd, that gave fit meane
For flyers out; and therefore at it then
Ulysses plac't Eumæus in close guard,
One onely passe ope to it—which (prepar'd 160
In this sort by Ulysses 'gainst all passe)
By Agelaus' tardy memorie was
In question call'd, who bad some one ascend
At such a window, and bring straight to frend
The City with his clamor, that this man 165
Might quickly shoot his last. 'This no one can
Make safe accesse to,' saide Melanthius,
'For 'tis too neere the Hal's faire doores, whence thus
The man afflicts ye. For from thence there lies
But one streight passage to it, that denies 170
Accesse to all, if any one man stand
(Being one of courage) and will countermand
Our offer to it. But I know a way
To bring you armes from where the King doth lay
His whole munition, and beleeve there is 175
No other place to all the Armories
Both of himselfe and Sonne.' This saide, a paire
Of lofty Staires he climb'd, and to th'affaire
Twelve Shields, twelve Lances broght, as many casks
With horse-haire Plumes—and set to bitter tasks 180
Both Son and Sire. Then shrunke Ulysses' knees
And his lov'd heart, when thus in armes he sees
So many wooers, and their shaken darts:
For then the worke shew'd as it askt more parts
To safe performance—and he tolde his Sonne 185
That or Melanthius or his maides had done
A deed that foule warre to their hands conferd.
'O Father,' he replyed, 'tis I have err'd
In this caus'd labour—I, and none but I,
That left the doore ope of your Armory. 190
But some (it seemes) hath set a sharper eye
On that important place. Eumæus! hast
And shut the doore, observing who hath past
To this false action, any maide, or one
That I suspect more, which is Dolius' Sonne.' 195

While these spake thus, Melanthius went againe
For more faire armes; whom the renowned Swaine
Eumæus saw, and tolde Ulysses straight
It was the hatefull man that his conceite
Before suspected who had done that ill; 200
And (being againe there) askt if he should kill
(If his power serv'd) or he should bring the Swaine
To him, t'inflict on him a severall paine
For every forfeite he had made his house.
He answer'd: 'I and my Telemachus 205
Will heere containe these proud ones in despite,
How much soever these stolne armes excite
Their guilty courages, while you two take
Possession of the Chamber. The doores make
Sure at your backe, and then (surprising him) 210
His feete and hands binde, wrapping every lim
In pliant chaines; and with a halter cast
Above the winde-beame (at himselfe made fast)
Aloft the Column draw him—where alive
He long may hang, and paines enow deprive 215
His vexed life before his death succeede.'
This charge (soone heard) as soone they put to deed,
Stole on his stealth, and at the further end
Of all the chamber saw him busily bend
His hands to more armes, when they (still at dore) 220
Watcht his returne. At last he came, and bore
In one hand a faire Helme, in th'other held
A broad and ancient rusty-rested Shield,
That old Laertes in his youth had worne,
Of which the cheeke-bands had with age bin torne. 225
They rusht upon him, caught him by the haire,
And dragg'd him in againe, whom (crying out)
They cast upon the pavement, wrapt about
With sure and pinching cords both foote and hand,
And then (in full acte of their King's command) 230
A pliant chaine bestow'd on him, and hal'd
His body up the columne, till he scal'd
The highest wind-beame. Where, made firmly fast,
Eumæus on his just infliction past
This pleasurable cavill: 'Now you may 235
All night keepe watch heere, and the earliest day
Discerne (being hung so high) to rouse from rest
Your dainty Cattle to the wooers' Feast.
There (as befits a man of meanes so faire)

Soft may you sleepe, nought under you but aire; 240
And so, long hang you.' Thus they left him there,
Made fast the doore, and, with Ulysses, were
All arm'd in th'instant. Then they all stood close,
Their minds fire breath'd in flames against their foes—
Foure in th'Entry fighting all alone, 245
When from the Hall charg'd many a mighty one.
But to them then Jove's seede (Minerva) came,
Resembling Mentor both in voice and frame
Of manly person. Passing well apaide
Ulysses was, and saide: 'Now, Mentor, aide 250
Gainst these odde mischiefes: call to memory now
My often good to thee, and that we two
Of one yeare's life are.' Thus he said, but thought
It was Minerva, that had ever brought
To her side safety. On the other part, 255
The wooers threatn'd, but the chiefe in heart
Was Agelaus, who to Mentor spake:
'Mentor! Let no words of Ulysses make
Thy hand a fighter on his feeble side
Gainst al us wooers: for we firme abide 260
In this perswasion—that, when Sire and Son
Our swords have slaine, thy life is sure to ron
One fortune with them. What strange acts hast thou
Conceit to forme here? Thy head must bestow
The wreake of theirs on us. And when thy powrs 265
Are taken downe by these fierce steeles of ours,
All thy possessions, in doores and without,
Must raise on heape with his, and all thy rout
Of sons and daughters in thy Turrets bleed
Wreake-offerings to us, and our Towne stand freed 270
Of all charge with thy wife.' Minerva's heart
Was fir'd with these Braves, the approv'd desert
Of her Ulysses chiding, saying: 'No more
Thy force nor fortitude, as heretofore,
Will gaine thee glory. When nine yeares at Troy 275
White-wristed Helen's rescue did imploy
Thy armes and wisedome still, and ever usde
The bloods of thousands through the field diffusde
By thy vaste valor, Priam's broad-waide Towne
By thy grave parts was sackt and overthrowne— 280
And now, amongst thy people and thy goods,
Against the wooers' base and petulant bloods
Stint'st thou thy valour? Rather mourning here

Than manly fighting? Come, Friend, stand we nere
And note my labour, that thou maist discerne 285
Amongst thy foes how Mentor's Nerves will erne
All thy old Bounties.' This she spake, but staide
Her hand from giving each-way-often-swaide
Uncertaine conquest to his certaine use,
But still would try what selfe-pow'rs would produce 290
Both in the Father and the glorious Son.
Then on the wind-beame, that along did ron
The smoaky roofe, transform'd Minerva sat
Like to a Swallow, sometimes cuffing at
The swords and Lances, rushing from her seate, 295
And up and downe the troubl'd house did beate
Her wing at every motion. And as she
Had rouz'd Ulysses, so the enemy
Damastor's sonne excited, Polybus,
Amphimedon and Demoptolemus, 300
Eurynomus and Polyctorides—
For these were men that of the wooing prease
Were most egregious and the clearly best
In strength of hand of all the desperate rest
That yet surviv'd, and now fought for their soules— 305
Which straight swift arrowes sent among the Fouls.
But first Damastor's sonne had more spare breath
To spend on their excitements ere his death,
And saide that now Ulysses would forbeare
His dismall hand, since Mentor's spirit was there 310
And blew vaine vants about Ulysses' eares;
In whose trust he would cease his Massacres,
Rest him, and put his friend's huge boasts in proofe;
And so was he beneath the Entrie's roofe
Left with Telemachus and th'other two— 315
'At whom,' saide he, 'discharge no Darts, but thro
All at Ulysses, rousing his faint rest;
Whom if we slaughter, by our interest
In Jove's assistance, all the rest may yield
Our pow'rs no care, when he strowes once the field.' 320
As he then will'd, they all at randon threw
Where they supposd he rested; and then flew
Minerva after every Dart, and made
Some strike the threshold, some the wals invade,
Some beate the doores, and all acts rendred vaine 325
Their grave steele offer'd—which escap't, againe
Came on Ulysses, saying: 'O that we

The wooers' troope with our joynt Archerie
Might so assaile, that where their spirits dream
On our deaths first, we first may slaughter them.' 330
Thus the much sufferer said; and all let fly,
When everie man strooke dead his enemy:
Ulysses slaughtred Demoptolemus;
Euryades by yong Telemachus
His death encounter'd. Good Eumæus slew 335
Elatus, and Philœtius overthrew
Pisander: all which tore the paved floore
Up with their teeth. The rest retir'd before
Their second charge to inner roomes, and then
Ulysses follow'd, from the slaughter'd men 340
Their darts first drawing. While which worke was done,
The wooers threw, with huge contention
To kill them all—when with her Swallow wing
Minerva cufft, and made their Javelins ring
Against the doores and thresholds as before. 345
Some yet did graze upon their markes. One tore
The Prince's wrist, which was Amphimedon,
Th'extreame part of the skin but toucht upon.
Ctesippus over good Eumæus' Shield
His shoulder's top did taint, which yet did yield 350
The Lance free passe, and gave his hurt the ground.
Againe then charg'd the wooers, and girt round
Ulysses with their Lances; who turn'd head,
And with his Javelin strooke Eurydamas dead.
Telemachus disliv'd Amphimedon; 355
Eumæus, Polybus; Philœtius won
Ctesippus' bosome with his dart, and said
(In quittance of the Jester's part he plaid,
The Neats-foot hurling at Ulysses): 'Now,
Great Sonne of Polytherses, you that vow 360
Your wit to bitter taunts, and love to wound
The heart of any with a jest, so crown'd
Your wit be with a laughter never yeilding
To fooles in folly, but your glory building
On putting downe in fooling, spitting forth 365
Puft words at all sorts. Cease to scoffe at worth,
And leave revenge of vile words to the Gods,
Since their wits beare the sharper edge by ods;
And in the meane time take the Dart I drave
For that right hospitable foote you gave 370
Divine Ulysses, begging but his owne.'

φιλοκέρτομος—amans cor alcui scindere maledicentia.

Thus spake the black-Ox-hersman; and straight down
Ulysses strooke another with his Dart,
Damastor's son. Telemachus did part
Just in the midst the belly of the faire 375
Euenor's sonne, his fierce Pile taking aire
Out at his backe. Flat fell he on his face,
His whole browes knocking, and did marke the place.
And now man-slaughtering Pallas tooke in hand
Her Snake-frindg'd shield, and on that beam took stand 380
In her true forme, where Swallow-like she sat.
And then in this way of the house and that
The wooers (wounded at the heart with feare)
Fled the encounter. As in Pastures, where
Fat Herds of Oxen feede, about the field 385
(As if wilde madnesse their instincts impeld)
The high-fed Bullockes flye, whom in the Spring
(When dayes are long) Gadbees or Breezes sting,
Ulysses and his sonne the Flyers chac'st;
As when with crooked Beakes and Seres a cast 390
Of hill-bred Eagles, cast off at some game,
That yet their strengths keepe, but (put up) in flame
The Eagles' stoopes—from which along the field
The poore Foules make wing, this and that way yield
Their hard-flowne Pinions, then the clouds assay 395
For scape or shelter, their forlorne dismay
All spirit exhaling all wings' strength to carry
Their bodies forth; and (trust up) to the Quarry
Their Faulconers ride in, and rejoyce to see
Their Hawkes performe a flight so fervently: 400
So (in their flight) Ulysses with his Heire
Did stoope and cuffe the wooers, that the aire
Broke in vaste sighes—whose heads they shot and cleft,
The Pavement boyling with the soules they reft.
Leodes (running to Ulysses) toke 405
His knees, and thus did on his name invoke:
'Ulysses! Let me pray thee, to my place
Affoord the reverence, and to me the grace,
That never did or saide to any Dame
Thy Court contain'd, or deede or word to blame. 410
But others so affected I have made
Lay downe their insolence; and if the trade
They kept with wickednesse have made them still
Despise my speech and use their wonted ill,
They have their penance by the stroke of death, 415

Which their desert divinely warranteth.
But I am Priest amongst them; and shall I,
That nought have done worth death, amongst them dy?
From thee this Proverbe then will men derive:
Good turnes do never their meere deeds survive.' 420
He (bending his displeased forehead) saide:
'If you be Priest amongst them, as you pleade,
Yet you would marry, and with my wife too,
And have descent by her. For all that woo
Wish to obtaine, which they should never doo, 425
Dames' husbands living. You must therefore pray
Of force, and oft in Court heere, that the day
Of my returne for home might never shine;
The death to me wish't therefore shall be thine.'
This said, he tooke a sword up that was cast 430
From Agelaus, having strooke his last,
And on the Priest's mid necke he laide a stroke
That strooke his head off, tumbling as he spoke.
Then did the Poet Phemius (whose sur-name
Was call'd Terpiades, who thither came 435
Forc't by the woo'rs) fly death; but, being nere
The Court's great gate, he stood, and parted there
In two his counsailes—either to remove
And take the Altar of Herceian Jove
(Made sacred to him, with a world of Art 440
Engraven about it, where were wont t'impart
Laertes and Ulysses many a Thye
Of broad-brow'd Oxen to the Deity),
Or venture to Ulysses, claspe his knee,
And pray his ruth. The last was the decree 445
His choise resolv'd on. Twixt the royall Throne
And that faire Table that the Bolle stood on
With which they sacrific'd, his Harpe he laide
Along the earth, the King's knees hugg'd, and saide:
'Ulysses! Let my prayers obtaine of thee 450
My sacred skil's respect, and ruth to mee.
It will heereafter grieve thee to have slaine
A Poet, that doth sing to Gods and men.
I of my selfe am taught: for God alone
All sorts of song hath in my bosome sowne. 455
And I, as to a God, will sing to thee.
Then do not thou deale like the Priest with me.
Thine owne lov'd sonne Telemachus will say
That not to beg heere, nor with willing way,

Was my accesse to thy high Court addrest 460
To give the wooers my song after Feast.
But being many, and so much more strong,
They forc't me hither, and compell'd my Song.'
  This did the Prince's sacred vertue heare,
And to the King his Father said: 'Forbeare 465
To mixe the guiltlesse with the guilties' blood.
And with him, likewise, let our mercies save
Medon the Herald, that did still behave
Himselfe with care of my good from a childe—
If by Eumæus yet he be not kild, 470
Or by Philœtius, nor your fury met
While all this blood about the house it swet.'
  This Medon heard as lying hid beneath
A Throne set neere, halfe dead with feare of death,
A new-flead Oxe-hide (as but there throwne by) 475
His serious shroud made, he lying there to fly.
But hearing this, he quickly left the Throne,
His Oxe-hide cast as quickly, and as soone
The Prince's knees seiz'd, saying: 'O my love,
I am not slaine, but heere alive, and move. 480
Abstaine your selfe, and do not see your Sire
Quench with my cold blood the unmeasur'd fire
That flames in his strength, making spoile of me,
His wrath's right, for the wooers' injury.'
  Ulysses smil'd, and said: 'Be confident 485
This man hath sav'd and made thee different,
To let thee know and say, and others see,
Good life is much more safe than villany.
Go then, sit free without from death within.
This much renowned Singer from the sin 490
Of these men likewise quit. Both rest you there,
While I my house purge, as it fits me here.'
  This saide, they went and tooke their seat without
At Jove's high Altar, looking round about,
Expecting still their slaughter—when the King 495
Searcht round the Hall, to try life's hidden wing
Made from more death. But all laid prostrate there
In blood and gore he saw: whole sholes they were,
And lay as thicke as in a hollow creake
Without the white Sea, when the Fishers breake 500
Their many-meshed Draught-net up, there lye
Fish frisking on the Sands, and faine the dry
Would for the wet change. But th'al-seeing beam

The Sun exhales hath suckt their lives from them;
So, one by other, spraul'd the wooers there. 505
Ulysses and his Son then bid appeare
The Nurse Euryclea, to let her heare
His minde in something fit for her affaire.
He op't the doore, and call'd, and said: 'Repaire,
Grave Matron, long since borne, that art our Spy 510
To all this house's servile huswifery.
My Father cals thee to impart some thought
That askes thy action.' His word found in nought
Her slacke observance, who straight op't the dore
And enter'd to him, when himselfe before 515
Had left the Hall. But there the King she view'd
Amongst the slaine, with blood and gore embrew'd.
And as a Lyon sculking all in Night
Farre off in Pastures, and come home all dight
In jawes and brest-lockes with an Oxe's blood, 520
New feasted on him, his lookes full of mood:
So look't Ulysses, all his hands and feete
Freckl'd with purple. When which sight did greete
The poore old woman (such workes being for eyes
Of no soft temper) out she brake in cries, 525
Whose vent, though throughly opened, he yet closd,
Cal'd her more neere, and thus her plaints composd:
'Forbeare, nor shrieke thus. But vent joyes as loud;
It is no piety to bemone the proud.
Though ends befall them moving neere so much, 530
These are the portions of the Gods to such.
Men's owne impieties, in their instant act,
Sustaine their plagues, which are with stay but rackt.
But these men Gods nor men had in esteeme;
Nor good nor bad had any sence in them. 535
Their lives directly ill were therefore cause
That Death in these sterne formes so deepely drawes.
Recount then to me those licentious Dames
That lost my honor, and their sexe's shames.'
'I'le tell you truly,' she replied. 'There are 540
Twice five and twenty women here that share
All worke amongst them; whom I taught to Spin
And beare the just bands that they suffer'd in.
Of all which onely there were twelve that gave
Themselves to impudence and light behave, 545
Nor me respecting, nor herselfe (the Queene).
And for your Son he hath but lately bene

Of yeares to rule, nor would his Mother beare
His Empire where her women's labors were.
But let me go, and give her notice now 550
Of your arrivall. Sure some God doth show
His hand upon her in this rest she takes,
That all these uprores beares, and never wakes.'
'Nor wake her yet,' said he, 'but cause to come
Those twelve light women to this utter roome.' 555
She made all utmost haste to come and go,
And bring the women he had summon'd so.
Then both his Swaines and Son he bad go call
The women to their aide, and cleere the Hall
Of those dead bodies, clense each boord and Throne 560
With wetted Sponges: which with fitnesse done,
He bad take all the Strumpets 'twixt the wall
Of his first Court and that roome next the Hall
In which the vessells of the house were scour'd—
And in their bosomes sheath their every sword, 565
Till all their soules were fled, and they had then
Felt 'twas but paine to sport with lawlesse men.
This said, the women came, all drown'd in mone,
And weeping bitterly. But first was done
The bearing thence the dead—all which beneath 570
The Portico they stow'd, where death on death
They heap't together—then tooke all the paines
Ulysses will'd. His Sonne yet and the Swaines
With paring shovels wrought. The women bore
Their parings forth, and al the clotter'd gore. 575
The house then clensd, they brought the women out,
And put them in a roome, so wall'd about
That no meanes serv'd their sad estates to flye.
Then saide Telemachus: 'These shall not dye
A death that lets out any wanton blood, 580
And vents the poison that gave Lust her foode,
The body clensing; but a death that chokes
The breath and all together, that provokes
And seemes as Bellowes to abhorred Lust—
That both on my head pour'd depraves unjust 585
And on my Mother's, scandaling the Court
With men debaucht in so abhorr'd a sort.'
This said, a Halser of a ship they cast
About a crosse beame of the roofe, which fast
They made about their neckes, in twelve parts cut, 590

And hal'd them up so high they could not put
Their feete to any stay. As which was done,
Looke how a Mavis, or a Pygeon,
In any Grove caught with a Sprindge or Net,
With strugling Pinions 'gainst the ground doth beat 595
Her tender body, and that then-streight bed
Is sowre to that swindge in which she was bred:
So striv'd these taken Birds, till every one
Her pliant halter had enforc't upon
Her stubborne necke, and then aloft was haul'd 600
To wretched death. A little space they sprauld,
Their feet fast moving, but were quickly still.
Then fetcht they downe Melanthius, to fulfill
The equall execution—which was done
In Portall of the Hall, and thus begun. 605
They first slit both his Nosethrils, cropt each eare,
His Members tugg'd off, which the dogges did teare
And chop up bleeding sweet; and while red hot
The vice-abhorring blood was, off they smote
His hands and feet, and there that worke had end. 610
Then washt they hands and feet, that blood had steind,
And tooke the house againe. And then the King
(Euryclea calling) bad her quickly bring
All-ill-expelling Brimstone and some fire,
That, with perfumes cast, he might make entire 615
The house's first integrity in all
And then his timely will was she should call
Her Queene and Ladies, still yet charging her
That all the Handmaids she should first confer.
She said he spake as fitted; but, before, 620
She held it fit to change the weeds he wore,
And she would others bring him—that not so
His faire broad shoulders might rest clad, and show
His person to his servants was to blame.
'First bring me Fire,' said he. She went, and came 625
With fire and sulphure straight—with which the hall
And of the huge house all roomes capitall
He throughly sweetned. Then went Nurse to call
The Handmaid servants downe; and up she went
To tell the newes, and will'd them to present 630
Their service to their Soveraigne. Downe they came,
Sustaining Torches all, and pour'd a flame
Of Love about their Lord with welcomes home,

With huggings of his hands, with laborsome
Both head's and fore-head's kisses and embraces; 635
And plyed him so with all their loving graces
That teares and sighes tooke up his whole desire;
For now he knew their hearts to him entire.

The End of the XXII. Booke of Homer's Odysses

THE XXIII. BOOKE
of
HOMER'S ODYSSES

THE ARGUMENT

Ulysses to his wife is knowne:
A briefe sum of his Travailes showne.
Himselfe, his Son, and Servants go
T'approve the Wooers' overthrow.

Another Argument

Ψι. *For all annoyes*
sustain'd before,
The true wive's joyes
now made the more.

The servants thus inform'd, the Matron goes
Up where the Queene was cast in such repose,
Affected with a fervent joy to tell
What all this time she did with paine conceale.
Her knees revokt their first strength, and her feete 5
Were borne above the ground with wings, to greete
The long-greev'd Queene with newes her King was come;
And (neere her) said: 'Wake! Leave this withdrawne roome,
That now your eyes may see at length, though late,
The man return'd which, all the heavy date 10
Your woes have rackt out, you have long'd to see:
Ulysses is come home, and hath set free
His Court of all your wooers, slaughtering all
For wasting so his goods with Festivall,
His house so vexing, and for violence done 15
So all waies varied to his onely sonne.'
She answer'd her: 'The Gods have made thee mad,
Of whose pow'r now, thy pow'rs such proof have had.
The Gods can blinde with follies wisest eies

And make men foolish, so to make them wise. 20
For they have hurt even thy grave braine, that bore
An understanding spirit heretofore.
Why hast thou wak't me to more teares, when Mone
Hath turn'd my minde with teares into her owne?
Thy madnesse much more blamefull, that with lyes 25
Thy haste is loaden, and both robs mine eyes
Of most delightsome sleepe, and sleepe of them,
That now had bound me in his sweet extream
T'embrace my lids and close my visual Spheres.
I have not slept so much this twenty yeares, 30
Since first my dearest sleeping-Mate was gone
For that too-ill-to-speake-of Ilion.
Hence take your mad steps backe; if any Maid
Of all my traine besides a part had plaid
So bold to wake and tell mine eares such lies, 35
I had return'd her to her huswiferies
With good proofe of my wrath to such rude Dames.
But go, your yeares have sav'd their yonger blames.'
She answer'd her: 'I nothing wrong your eare,
But tell the truth: your long-mist Lord is heere, 40
And with the wooers' slaughter his owne hand
(In chiefe exploit) hath to his owne command
Reduc't his house; and that poore Guest was he
That all those wooers wrought such injurie.
Telemachus had knowledge long ago 45
That 'twas his Father, but his wisedome so
Observ'd his counsailes, to give surer end
To that great worke to which they did contend.'
This call'd her spirits to their conceiving places.
She sprung for joy from blames into embraces 50
Of her grave Nurse, wip't every teare away
From her faire cheekes, and then began to say
What Nurse said, over thus: 'O Nurse, can this
Be true thou sayst? How could that hand of his
Alone destroy so many? They would still 55
Troope all together. How could he then kill
Such numbers so united?' 'How?' said she,
'I have nor seene nor heard, but certainly
The deed is done. We sate within in feare,
The doores shut on us, and from thence might heare 60
The sighes and grones of every man he slew—
But heard nor saw more, till at length there flew
Your sonne's voice to mine eare, that call'd to me,

And bad me then come foorth: and then I see
Ulysses standing in the midst of all 65
Your slaughtred wooers, heap't up like a wall
One on another, round about his side.
It would have done you good to have descride
Your conqu'ring lord, al smeard with blood and gore
So like a Lyon. Straight then off they bore 70
The slaughtred carkasses, that now before
The fore-Court gates lye, one on other pilde.
And now your victor all the Hall (defilde
With stinch of hot death) is perfuming round,
And with a mighty fire the harth hath crown'd. 75
'Thus, all the death remov'd and every roome
Made sweet and sightly, that your selfe should come
His pleasure sent me. Come then, take you now
Your mutuall fils of comfort. Griefe on you
Hath long and many sufferings laid; which length, 80
Which many suffrings, nowe your vertuous strength
Of uncorrupted chastnesse hath conferr'd
A happy end to. He that long hath err'd
Is safe arriv'd at home, his wife, his sonne,
Found safe and good; all ill that hath bene done 85
On all the dooers' heads (though long prolong'd)
His right hath wreak't, and in the place they wrong'd.'
She answer'd: 'Do not you now laugh, and bost
As you had done some great act, seeing most
Into his Being. For, you know, he won 90
(Even through his poore and vile condition)
A kind of prompted thought that there was plac't
Some vertue in him, fit to be embrac't
By all the house, but, most of all, by me
And by my Son, that was the progenie 95
Of both our loves. And yet it is not he,
For all the likely proofes ye plead to me.
Some God hath slaine the wooers, in disdaine
Of the abhorred pride he saw so raigne
In those base workes they did. No man alive, 100
Or good, or bad, whoever did arrive
At their abodes once, ever could obtaine
Regard of them: and therefore their so vaine
And vile deserts have found as vile an end.
But, for Ulysses, never will extend 105
His wisht returne to Greece, nor he yet lives.'
'How strange a Queen are you,' said she, 'that gives

No truth your credit—that your husband, set
Close in his house at fire, can purchase yet
No faith of you, but that he still is farre 110
From any home of his! Your wit's at warre
With all credulity ever. And yet now
I'le name a signe shall force beleefe from you:
I bath'd him lately, and beheld the scar
That still remaines a marke too ocular 115
To leave your heart yet blinded; and I then
Had run and told you, but his hand was feine
To close my lips from th'acclamation
My heart was breathing, and his wisedome won
My still retention, till he gave me leave 120
And charge to tell you this. Now, then, receave
My life for gage of his returne—which take
In any cruell fashion, if I make
All this not cleere to you.' 'Lov'd Nurse,' said she,
'Though many things thou knowst, yet these things be 125
Veil'd in the counsailes th'uncreated Gods
Have long time maskt in, whose darke periods
Tis hard for thee to see into. But come,
Let's see my son, the slaine, and he by whom
They had their slaughter.' This said, down they went— 130
When on the Queen's part divers thoghts wer spent,
If (all this given no faith) she still should stand
Aloofe and question more, or his hugg'd hand
And loved head she should at first assay
With free-given kisses. When her doubtfull way 135
Had past the stony pavement, she tooke seate
Against her husband, in the opposite heate
The fire then cast upon the other wall,
Himselfe set by the Columne of the Hall,
His lookes cast downwards, and expected still 140
When her incredulous and curious will
To shun ridiculous error, and the shame
To kisse a Husband that was not the same,
Would downe, and win enough faith from his sight.
She silent sate, and her perplexed plight 145
Amaze encounter'd. Sometimes she stood cleare
He was her Husband: sometimes the ill weare
His person had put on transform'd him so,
That yet his stampe would hardly currant go.
Her son, her strangenesse seeing, blam'd her thus: 150
'Mother, ungentle Mother! tyrannous!

In this too curious modesty you show,
Why sit you from my Father, nor bestow
A word on me, t'enquire and cleere such doubt
As may perplexe you? Found man ever out 155
One other such a wife that could forbeare
Her lov'd Lord's welcome home, when twenty yeare
In infinite sufferance he had spent apart:
No Flint so hard is as a woman's hart.'
'Son,' she replied, 'amaze containes my minde, 160
Nor can I speake and use the commune kind
Of those enquiries, nor sustaine to see
With opposite lookes his countenance. If this be
My true Ulysses now return'd, there are
Tokens betwixt us of more fitnesse farre 165
To give me argument he is my Lord;
And my assurance of him may afford
My proofes of joy for him from all these eies
With more decorum than object their guise
To publique notice.' The much-Sufferer brake 170
In laughter out, and to his Son said: 'Take
Your Mother from the prease, that she may make
Her owne proofes of me, which perhaps may give
More cause to the acknowledgements that drive
Their shew thus off. But now, because I goe 175
So poorely clad, she takes disdaine to know
So loath'd a creature for her loved Lord.
Let us consult then how we may accord
The Towne to our late action. Some one slaine
Hath made the all-left slaughterer of him faine 180
To fly his friends and country. But our swords
Have slaine a Citie's most supportfull Lords,
The chiefe Peeres of the kingdome: therefore see
You use wise meanes t'uphold your victorie.'
'See you to that, good Father,' saide the Son, 185
'Whose counsailes have the soveraigne glory won
From all men living. None will strive with you,
But with unquestion'd Girlands grace your brow—
To whom, our whol alacrities we vow
In free attendance. Nor shall our hands leave 190
Your onsets needy of supplies to give
All the effects that in our pow'rs can fall.'
'Then this,' said he, 'to me seemes capitall
Of all choise courses. Bathe we first, and then
Attire we freshly, all our Maides and men 195

Enjoyning likewise to their best attire.
The sacred Singer then let touch his Lire,
And go before us all in gracefull dance,
That all without, to whose eares shal advance
Our cheerefull accents (or of Travailers by, 200
Or firme inhabitants) solemnity
Of frolicke Nuptials may imagine heere.
And this performe we, lest the massakere
Of all our wooers be divulg'd about
The ample City ere our selves get out 205
And greet my Father in his Grove of Trees—
Where, after, we will prove what policies
Olympius shall suggest to overcome
Our latest toiles and crowne our welcome home.'
 This all obey'd, bath'd, put on fresh attire 210
Both men and women did. Then tooke his Lire
The holy singer, and set thirst on fire
With songs and faultlesse dances: all the Court
Rung with the footings that the numerous sport
From jocund men drew and faire-girdl'd Dames— 215
Which (heard abroad) thus flew the commune fames:
 'Thus sure the day is when the much-woo'd Queen
Is richly wed. O wretch! that hath not beene
So constant as to keepe her ample house
Til th'utmost houre had brought her formost spouse.' 220
 Thus some conceiv'd, but little knew the thing.
And now Eurynome had bath'd the King,
Smooth'd him with Oyles, and he himselfe attir'd
In vestures royall. Her part then inspir'd
The Goddesse Pallas, deck't his head and face 225
With infinite beauties, gave a goodly grace
Of stature to him, a much plumper plight
Through all his body breath'd. Curles soft and bright
Adorn'd his head withall, and made it show
As if the flowry Hyacinth did grow 230
In all his pride there, in the generall trim
Of every locke, and every curious lim.
Looke how a skilfull Artizan, well seene
In all Arts Metalline, as having beene
Taught by Minerva and the God of fire, 235
Doth Gold with Silver mix so that entire
They keepe their selfe distinction, and yet so
That to the Silver from the Gold doth flow
A much more artificiall luster than his owne,

And thereby to the Gold it selfe is growne 240
A greater glory than if wrought alone,
Both being stuck off by either's mixtion:
So did Minerva hers and his combine;
He more in Her, She more in Him did shine.
Like an Immortall from the Bath he rose, 245
And to his wife did all his grace dispose,
Encountring this her strangenesse: 'Cruell Dame
Of all that breathe, the Gods past steele and flame
Have made thee ruthlesse. Life retaines not one
Of all Dames else that beares so over-growne 250
A minde with abstinence, as twenty yeares
To misse her husband, drown'd in woes and teares,
And, at his comming, keepe aloofe, and fare
As of his so long absence and his care
No sense had seisd her. Go, Nurse, make a bed, 255
That I alone may sleepe; her heart is dead
To all reflection.' To him thus replied
The wise Penelope: 'Man halfe deified,
'Tis not my fashion to be taken streight
With bravest men—nor poorest use to sleight. 260
Your meane apparance made not me retire,
Nor this your rich shew makes me now admire,
Nor moves at all. For what is all to me,
If not my husband? All his certainty
I knew at parting, but (so long apart) 265
The outward likenesse holds no full desart
For me to trust to. Go, Nurse, see addrest
A soft bed for him, and the single rest
Himselfe affects so. Let it be the bed
That stands within our Bridal Chamber-sted, 270
Which he himself made. Bring it forth from thence,
And see it furnisht with magnificence.'
 This said she to assay him, and did stir
Even his establisht patience, and to hir,
Whom thus he answerd: 'Woman! your words prove 275
My patience strangely. Who is it can move
My Bed out of his place? It shall oppresse
Earth's greatest under-stander; and, unlesse
Even God himselfe come, that can easely grace
Men in their most skils, it shall hold his place. 280
For Man—he lives not that (as not most skill'd,
So not most yong) shall easely make it yield,
If (building on the strength in which he flowes)

He addes both Levers too, and Iron Crowes.
For in the fixure of the Bed is showne 285
A Maister-peece, a wonder: and 'twas done
By me, and none but me, and thus was wrought.
There was an Olive tree that had his grought
Amidst a hedge, and was of shadow proud,
Fresh, and the prime age of his verdure show'd, 290
His leaves and armes so thicke that to the eye
It shew'd a columne for solidity.
To this had I a comprehension
To build my Bridall Bowre, which all of stone,
Thicke as the Tree of leaves, I raisde, and cast 295
A Roofe about it nothing meanly grac'st,
Put glew'd doores to it, that op't Art enough.
Then from the Olive every broad-leav'd bough
I lopt away, then fell'd the Tree, and then
Went over it both with my Axe and Plaine, 300
Both govern'd by my Line. And then I hew'd
My curious Bed-sted out, in which I shew'd
Worke of no commune hand. All this, begon,
I could not leave till to perfection
My paines had brought it—tooke my Wimble, bor'd 305
The holes as fitted, and did last afford
The varied Ornament which shew'd no want
Of Silver, Gold, and polisht Elephant.
An Oxe-hide Dide in purple then I threw
Above the cords. And thus to curious view 310
I hope I have objected honest signe,
To prove I author nought that is not mine.
But if my bed stand unremov'd or no,
O woman, passeth humane wit to know.'
This sunk her knees and heart, to heare so true 315
The signes she urg'd; and first did teares ensue
Her rapt assurance; then she ran and spread
Her armes about his necke, kist oft his head,
And thus the curious stay she made excusde:
'Ulysses! Be not angry that I usde 320
Such strange delayes to this, since heretofore
Your suffering wisedome hath the Gyrland wore
From all that breath: and 'tis the Gods that, thus
With mutuall misse so long afflicting us,
Have causd my coynesse—to our youths envied 325
That wisht society that should have tied
Our youths and yeares together: and, since now

Judgement and Duty should our age allow
As full joyes therein as in youth and blood,
See all yong anger and reproofe withstood 330
For not at first sight giving up my armes,
My heart still trembling, lest the false alarmes
That words oft strike up should ridiculize me.
Had Argive Helen knowne credulity
Would bring such plagues with it, and her againe 335
(As aucthresse of them all) with that foule staine
To her and to her countrey, she had staid
Her love and mixture from a stranger's bed.
But God impell'd her to a shamelesse deede,
Because she had not in her selfe decreed 340
Before th'attempt that such acts still were shent
As simply in themselves as in th'event.
By which not onely she her selfe sustaines,
But we, for her fault, have paid mutuall paines.
Yet now, since these signes of our certaine bed 345
You have discover'd and distinguished
From all earth's others, no one man but you
Yet ever getting of it th'onely show,
Nor one of all Dames but my selfe, and she
My Father gave, old Actor's progenie 350
(Who ever guarded to our selves the dore
Of that thick-shaded chamber) I no more
Will crosse your cleere perswasion—though till now
I stood too doubtfull and austere to you.'
These words of hers, so justifying her stay, 355
Did more desire of joyfull mone convay
To his glad minde than if at instant sight
She had allow'd him all his wishes' right.
He wept for joy t'enjoy a wife so fit
For his grave minde, that knew his depth of wit, 360
And held chaste vertue at a price so high.
And as sad men at Sea, when shore is nigh,
Which long their hearts have wisht (their ship quite lost
By Neptune's rigor, and they vext and tost
Twixt winds and black waves, swimming for their lives, 365
A few escap't, and that few that survives
All drencht in fome and brine) craule up to Land
With joy as much as they did worlds command:
So deare to this wife was her husband's sight—
Who still embrac't his necke, and had (til light 370
Displaid her silver Ensigne) if the Dame

That beares the blew sky entermixt with flame
In her faire eyes had not infixt her thought
On other joyes, for loves so hardly brought
To long'd-for meeting: who th'extended night 375
With-held in long date, nor would let the light
Her wing-hoov'd horse joyne (Lampus, Phaeton),
Those ever Colts that bring the morning on
To worldly men, but, in her golden chaire,
Downe to the Ocean by her silver haire 380
Bound her aspirings. Then Ulysses said:
'O wife! Nor yet are my contentions staid;
A most unmeasur'd labour, long and hard,
Askes more performance—to it being prepar'd
By grave Tiresias, when downe to hell 385
I made darke passage, that his skill might tell
My men's returne, and mine. But come, and now
Enjoy the sweet rest that our Fates allow.'
'The place of rest is ready,' she replyed,
'Your will at full serve, since the deified 390
Have brought you where your right is to command.
But since you know (God making understand
Your searching mind) informe me, what must be
Your last set labour? Since 'twill fall to me
(I hope) to heare it after, tell me now: 395
The greatest pleasure is before to know.'
'Unhappy!' said Ulysses, 'To what end
Importune you this labour? It will lend
Nor you nor me delight; but you shall know
I was commanded yet more to bestow 400
My yeares in travaile, many Cities more
By Sea to visit: and, when first for shore
I left my shipping, I was will'd to take
A navall Oare in hand, and with it make
My passage forth till such strange men I met 405
As knew no Sea, nor ever salt did eat
With any victles, who the purple beakes
Of Ships did never see, nor that which breakes
The waves in curles, which is a Fan-like Oare,
And serves as wings with which a ship doth soare. 410
To let me know, then, when I was arriv'd
On that strange earth where such a people liv'd,
He gave me this for an unfailing signe:
When any one that tooke that Oare of mine
Borne on my shoulder for a Corne-clense Fan 415

I met ashore, and shew'd to be a man
Of that Land's labour, there had I command
To fixe mine Oare, and offer on that strand
T'imperiall Neptune (whom I must implore)
A Lambe, a Bull, and Sow-ascending Bore— 420
And then turne home, where all the other Gods
That in the broad heaven made secure abods
I must solicite (all my curious heed
Given to the severall rites they have decreed)
With holy Hecatombes. And, then, at home 425
A gentle death should seize me, that would come
From out the Sea and take me to his rest
In full ripe age, about me living blest
My loving people—to which (he presag'd)
The sequell of my fortunes were engag'd.' 430
'If then,' saide she, 'the Gods will please t'impose
A happier Being to your fortune's close
Than went before, your hope gives comfort strength
That life shall lend you better dayes at length.'
While this discourse spent mutual speech, the bed 435
Eurynome and Nurse had made and spred
With richest Furniture, while Torches spent
Their parcell-gilt thereon. To bed then went
The aged Nurse, and where their Soveraignes were
Eurynome (the Chamber maid) did beare 440
A Torch, and went before them to their rest;
To which she left them, and for hers addrest.
The King and Queene, then, now (as newly wed)
Resum'd the old Lawes of th'embracing bed.
Telemachus and both his Herdsmen then 445
Dissolv'd the dances both to Maids and men,
Who in their shady roofes tooke timely sleepe.
The Bride and Bridegroome, having ceast to keepe
Observed Love-joyes, from their fit delight
They turn'd to talke. The Queene then did recite 450
What she had suffer'd by the hatefull rout
Of harmfull wooers, who had eate her out
So many Oxen and so many Sheepe,
How many Tun of wine their drinking deepe
Had quite exhausted. Great Ulysses, then, 455
What ever slaughters he had made of men,
What ever sorrowes he himselfe sustain'd,
Repeated amply, and her eares remain'd
With all delight attentive to their end,

Nor would one winke sleepe till he told her all— 460
Beginning where he gave the Cicons fall;
From thence his passe to the Lotophagi;
The Cyclop's acts; the putting out his eye,
And wreake of all the Souldiers he had eate,
No least ruth shewne to all they could entreate. 465
His way to Æolus; his prompt receit,
And kinde dismission; his inforc't retreate
By sodaine Tempest to the fishy maine,
And quite distraction from his course againe;
His landing at the Læstrygonian Port, 470
Where ships and men in miserable sort
Met all their spoiles, his ship and he alone
Got off from the abhorr'd confusion;
His passe to Circe, her deceits, and Arts;
His thence descension to th'infernall parts; 475
His life's course of the Theban Prophet learn'd,
Where all the slaughter'd Grecians he descern'd,
And loved Mother; his astonisht eare
With what the Sirens' voices made him heare;
His scape from th'erring Rockes, which Scylla was 480
And rough Charybdis, with the dangerous passe
Of all that toucht there; his Sicilian
Offence given to the Sun, his every man
Destroy'd by thunder vollied out of heaven,
That split his Ship; his owne endevours driven 485
To shift for succours on th'Ogygian shore,
Where Nimph Calypso such affection bore
To him in his arrivall that with feast
She kept him in her Caves, and would have blest
His welcome life with an immortall state, 490
Would he have staid and liv'd her Nuptiall mate,
All which she never could perswade him to.
His passe to the Phæacians, spent in wo,
Their hearty welcome of him, as he were
A God descended from the starry Sphere; 495
Their kinde dismission of him home with Gold,
Brasse, Garments, all things his occasions would.
  This last word usde, sleepe seiz'd his weary eye,
That salves all care to all mortality.
  In meane space, Pallas entertain'd intent 500
That, when Ulysses thought enough time spent
In love-joyes with his wife, to raise the Day,
And make his grave occasions call away.

The Morning rose, and he, when thus he saide:
'O Queene! Now satiate with afflictions laide 505
On both our bosomes (you oppressed heere
With cares for my returne, I every where
By Jove and all the other Deities tost
Even till all hope of my returne was lost)
And both arriv'd at this sweet Haven, our Bed, 510
Be your care usde to see administred
My house-possessions left. Those Sheepe that were
Consum'd in surfets by your wooers heere
I'le forrage to supply with some; and more
The suffering Grecians shall be made restore, 515
Even till our stalles receive their wonted fill.
'And now, to comfort my good Father's ill
Long suffer'd for me, to the many-tree'd
And ample Vineyard grounds it is decreed
In my next care that I must haste and see 520
His long'd-for presence. In the meane time, be
Your wisedome usde, that, since (the Sun ascended)
The fame will soone be through the Town extended
Of those I heere have slaine, your selfe (got close
Up to your chamber) see you there repose, 525
Cheer'd with your women, and nor looke afford
Without your Court, nor anie man a word.'
This said, he arm'd, to arms both Son and Swain
His powre commanding, who did entertaine
His charge with spirit, op't the gates, and out, 530
He leading all. And now was hurl'd about
Aurora's ruddie fire, through all whose light
Minerva led them through the Towne from sight.

The End of XXIII. Booke of Homer's Odysses.

THE XXIIII. BOOKE
of
HOMER'S ODYSSES

THE ARGUMENT

By Mercury the Wooers' soules
Are usher'd to th'Infernall Pooles.
Ulysses with Laertes met,
The people are in uprore set
Against them, for the wooers' ends— 5
Whom Pallas stayes, and renders Frends.

Another Argument

Ω. { *The uprore's fire,*
the People's fall:
The Grandsire, Sire,
and Son, to all. }

Cyllenian Hermes with his golden rod
The wooers' soules (that yet retain'd abod
Amids their bodies) call'd in dreadfull rout
Forth to th'Infernals, who came murmuring out.
And as amids the desolate retreate 5
Of some vaste Caverne (made the sacred seate
Of austere spirits) Bats with Brests and wings
Claspe fast the wals, and each to other clings,
But, swept off from their coverts, up they rise
And flye with murmures in amazefull guise 10
About the caverne: so these (grumbling) rose
And flockt together. Downe before them goes
None-hurting Mercury to hel's broad waies;
And straight to those streights where the Ocean staies
His lofty current in calme deepes they flew. 15
Then to the snowy rocke they next withdrew,
And to the close of Phœbus' orient gates,

The Nation then of Dreames; and then the states
Of those soules' Idols that the weary dead
Gave up in earth, which in a flowry Mead 20
Had habitable situation.
And there they saw the soule of Thetis' son,
Of good Patroclus, brave Antilochus,
And Ajax, the supremely strenuous
Of all the Greeke hoast next Peleion— 25
All which assembled about Maia's son.
And to them (after) came the mournfull Ghost
Of Agamemnon, with all those he lost
In false Ægisthus' Court. Achilles then
Beholding there that mighty King of men, 30
Deplor'd his plight, and said: 'O Atreus' Son!
Of all Heroes all Opinion
Gave thee for Jove's most lov'd, since most command
Of all the Greekes he gave thy eminent hand
At siedge of Ilion, where we suffer'd so. 35
And is the issue this? That first in wo
Sterne Fate did therefore set thy sequell downe?
None borne past others' Fates can passe his owne.
I wish to heaven that in the heighth of all
Our pompe at Ilion Fate had sign'd thy fall, 40
That all the Greekes might have advanc't to thee
A famous Sepulcher, and Fame might see
Thy Son given honor in thy honour'd end;
But now a wretched death did Fate extend
To thy confusion and thy Issue's shame.' 45
'O Thetis' Son,' said he, 'the vitall flame
Extinct at Ilion, far from th'Argive fields,
The stile of blessed to thy vertue yields.
About thy fall the best of Greece and Troy
Were sacrific'd to slaughter, thy just joy 50
Conceiv'd in battell, with some worth forgot,
In such a death as great Apollo shot
At thy encounters. Thy brave person lay
Hid in a dusty whirlewinde, that made way
With humane breaths, spent in thy ruine's state; 55
Thou, great, wert greatly valew'd in thy Fate.
All day we fought about thee, nor at all
Had ceast our conflict had not Jove let fall
A storme, that forc't off our unwilling feete.
But, having brought thee from the fight to fleete, 60
Thy glorious person (bath'd and balm'd) we laide

Aloft a bed, and round about thee paide
The Greekes warme teares to thy deplor'd decease,
Quite danted, cutting all their curles' increase.
Thy death drave a divine voice through the Seas, 65
That started up thy Mother from the waves,
And all the Marine Godheads left their caves,
Consorting to our fleet her rapt repaire.
The Greekes stood frighted to see Sea and Aire
And Earth combine so in thy losse's sence, 70
Had taken ship, and fled for ever thence,
If old much-knowing Nestor had not staide
Their rushing off—his counsailes having swaide
In all times former with such cause their courses—
Who bad containe themselves and trust their forces; 75
For all they saw was Thetis come from Sea,
With others of the watry progenie,
To see and mourne for her deceased Son;
Which staid the feares that all to flight had won.
And round about thee stood th'old Sea-god's seedes, 80
Wretchedly mourning, their immortall weeds
Spreading upon thee; all the sacred Nine
Of deathlesse Muses paid thee dues divine,
By varied turnes their heavenly voyces venting,
All in deepe passion for thy death consenting. 85
And then of all our Army not an eye
You could have seene undrown'd in misery,
The moving Muse so rul'd in every minde.
Full seventeene dayes and nights our teares confin'd
To celebration of thy mourned end, 90
Both men and Gods did in thy moane contend.
The eighteenth day we spent about thy heape
Of dying fire. Blacke Oxen, fattest Sheepe
We slew past number. Then the precious spoile
(Thy Corse) wee tooke up, which with floods of oile 95
And pleasant Hony we embalm'd, and then
Wrapt thee in those Robes that the Gods did raine—
In which we gave thee to the hallowed flame.
To which a number of heroicall name,
All arm'd, came rushing in in desperate plight, 100
As prest to sacrifice their vitall right
To thy dead ruines while so bright they burn'd;
Both foote and horse brake in, and fought, and mourn'd
In infinite tumult. But when all the night
The rich flame lasted, and that wasted quite 105

Thy body was with the enamor'd fire,
We came in early Morne, and an entire
Collection made of every Ivorie bone—
Which, washt in wine and given fit unction,
A two-ear'd Bolle of Gold thy Mother gave, 110
By Bacchus given her, and did forme receave
From Vulcan's famous hand, which, O renown'd
Great Thetis' Son, with thy faire bones we crown'd,
Patroclus. Mixt with the Bones of Menœtiades,
And brave Antilochus, who, in decease 115
Of thy Patroclus, was thy favour's Deere.
About thee then a matchlesse Sepulchere
The sacred hoast of the Achaians raisd
Upon the Hellespont, where most it seisd
(For height and conspicuity) the eies 120
Of living men and their posterities.
Thy Mother then obtain'd the Gods' consent
To institute an honor'd game, that spent
The best approvement of our Grecian Fames:
In whose praise, I must say that many games 125
About Heroes' Sepulchers mine eyes
Have seene perform'd, but these bore off the prize
With myracles to me from all before—
In which thy Silver-footed Mother bore
The Institution's name, but thy desarts 130
(Being great with heaven) caus'd al the eminent parts.
And thus through all the worst effects of Fate
Achilles' Fame even Death shall propagate:
While any one shall lend the light an eye
Divine Æacides shal never dye. 135
But wherein can these comforts be conceiv'd
As rights to me?—when, having quite atchiev'd
An end with safety, and with Conquest too
Of so unmatcht a warre, what none could do
Of all our enemies there, at home a Friend 140
And Wife have given me inglorious end.'
While these thus spake, the Argus-killing spy
Brought neere Ulysses' noble victory
To their renew'd discourse, in all the ends
The wooers suffer'd, and shew'd those his Frends, 145
Whom now amaze invaded with the view,
And made give backe: yet Agamemnon knew
Melanthius' heyre, much-fam'd Amphimedon,
Who had in Ithaca Guest favours shown

To great Atrides—who first spake, and saide: 150
'Amphimedon, what sufferance hath bene laide
On your alive parts that hath made you make
This land of darknesse the retreat you take
So all together, all being like in yeeres,
Nor would a man have choosd, of all the Peeres 155
A City honors, men to make a part
More strong for any object? Hath your smart
Bene felt from Neptune, being at Sea—his wrath
The winds and waves exciting to your scath?
Or have offensive men imposd this Fate, 160
Your Oxen driving, or your flocke's estate?
Or for your City fighting, and your wives,
Have deaths untimely seiz'd your best-tim'd lives?
Informe me truly: I was once your Guest,
When I and Menelaus had profest 165
First armes for Ilion, and were come ashore
On Ithaca, with purpose to implore
Ulysses' aide, that City-racing man,
In wreake of the adulterous Phrygian.
Retaine not you the time? A whole month's date 170
We spent at Sea, in hope to instigate
In our arrivall old Laertes' Son,
Whom (hardly yet) to our designe we won.'
The Soule made answer: 'Worthiest King of men,
I well remember every passage then 175
You now reduce to thought, and will relate
The truth in whole forme of our timelesse Fate.
'We woo'd the wife of that long absent King,
Who (though her second marriage were a thing
Of most hate to her) she would yet deny 180
At no part our affections, nor comply
With any in performance: but decreed
In her delayes the cruell Fates we feed.
Her craft was this. She undertooke to weave
A Funerall garment, destin'd to receave 185
The corse of old Laertes, being a taske
Of infinite labour, and which Time would aske.
In midst of whose attempt, she causd our stay
With this attraction: "Youths, that come in way
Of honor'd Nuptials to me! Though my Lord 190
Abide amongst the dead, yet cease to bord
My choise for present Nuptials, and sustaine
(Lest what is past me of this web be vaine)

Till all receive perfection. 'Tis a weede
Dispos'd to wrap in, at his Funerall neede, 195
The old Laertes, who (possessing much)
Would (in his want of rites as fitting) touch
My honor highly with each vulgar Dame."
Thus spake she, and perswaded; and her Frame
All day she labour'd, her daye's worke not small, 200
But every night time, she unwrought it all—
Three yeares continuing this imperfect taske;
But when the fourth year came, her slights could mask
In no more covert, since her trusted Maid
Her whole deceite to our true note betraid. 205
With which surpriz'd, she could no more protract
Her worke's perfection, but gave end exact
To what remain'd, washt up, and set thereon
A glosse so bright that like the Sun and Moon
The whole worke shew'd together. And when now 210
Of meere necessity her honour'd vow
She must make good to us, ill fortune brought
Ulysses home—who yet gave none one thought
Of his arrivall, but far-off at field
Liv'd with his Herdsman, nor his trust would yield 215
Note of his person, but liv'd there as Guest,
Ragg'd as a begger, in that life profest.
At length Telemachus left Pylos' sand,
And with a Ship fetcht soone his native Land—
When yet, not home he went, but laid his way 220
Up to his Herdsman, where his Father lay,
And where both laide our deaths—to town then bore
The Swine-herd and his King, the Swaine before.
Telemachus, in other wayes, bestow'd
His course home first, t'associate us that woo'd. 225
The Swaine the King led after, who came on
Ragged and wretched, and still lean'd upon
A borrow'd staffe. At length he reacht his home,
Where (on the sodaine and so wretched come)
Nor we, nor much our elders, once did dreame 230
Of his returne there, but did wrongs extreame
Of words and blowes to him, all which he bore
With that old patience he had learn'd before.
But when the minde of Jove had rais'd his owne,
His son and he fetcht all their Armour downe, 235
Fast lockt the doores, and (to prepare their use)
He will'd his wife (for first meane) to produce

His Bow to us to draw; of which no one
Could stir the string. Himselfe yet set upon
The deadly strength it held, drew all with ease, 240
Shot through the steeles, and then began to sease
Our armelesse bosomes, striking first the brest
Of King Antinous, and then the rest
In heapes turn'd over, hopefull of his end
Because some God (he knew) stood firme his frend. 245
Nor prov'd it worse with him, but all in flood
The Pavement straight blusht with our vitall blood.
And thus our soules came heere, our bodies laid
Neglected in his roofes, no word convaid
To any friend to take us home and give 250
Our wounds fit balming, nor let such as live
Entombe our deaths, and, for our fortunes, shed
Those teares and dead rites that renowne the dead.'
  Atrides' Ghost gave answere: 'O blest Son
Of old Laertes, thou at length hast won 255
With mighty vertue thy unmatched wife!
How good a knowledge, how untoucht a life
Hath wise Penelope! How well she laide
Her husband's rights up, whom she lov'd a Maid!
For which her vertues shall extend applause 260
Beyond the circles fraile mortality drawes,
The deathlesse in this vale of death comprising
Her praise in numbers into infinites rising.
The daughter Tyndarus begat begot
No such chaste thoughts, but cut the virgin knot 265
That knit her spouse and her with murtherous swords.
For which posterities shall put hatefull words
To notes of her, that all her Sex defam'd,
And for her ill shall even the good be blam'd.'
  To this effect these these digressions made 270
In hell, Earth's darke and ever-hiding shade.
  Ulysses and his Son (now past the Towne)
Soone reacht the field, elaborately growne
By old Laertes' labour, when, with cares
For his lost Son, he left all Court affaires 275
And tooke to this rude upland, which, with toile,
He made a sweet and habitable soile—
Where stood a house to him, about which ran,
In turnings thicke and Labyrinthian,
Poore Hovels, where his necessary men 280
That did those workes (of pleasure to him then)

Might sit, and eate, and sleepe. In his owne house
An old Sicilian Dame liv'd, studious
To serve his sowre age with her cheerefull paines.
  Then saide Ulysses to his Son and Swaines: 285
'Go you to Towne, and for your dinner kill
The best Swine ye can choose; my selfe will still
Stay with my father and assay his eye,
If my acknowledg'd truth it can descry,
Or that my long time's travaile doth so change 290
My sight to him that I appeare as strange.'
Thus gave he armes to them, and home they hied.
Ulysses to the fruitfull field applied
His present place, nor found he Dolius there,
His sonnes, or any servant, any where 295
In all that spacious ground; all, gone from thence,
Were dragging bushes to repaire a Fence,
Old Dolius leading all. Ulysses found
His father farre above in that faire ground,
Employd in proyning of a Plant, his weeds 300
All torne and tatter'd, fit for homely deeds,
But not for him. Upon his legs he wore
Patcht boots, to guard him from the brambles' gore;
His hands had thorne-proofe hedging Mittens on,
His head a Goats-skin Caske—through all which shone 305
His heart given over to abjectest mone.
  Him when Ulysses saw consum'd with age,
And all the Ensignes on him that the rage
Of griefe presented, he brake out in teares,
And (taking stand then, where a tree of Peares 310
Shot high his forehead over him) his minde
Had much contention—if to yeeld to kinde,
Make straight way to his father, kisse, embrace,
Tell his returne, and put on all the face
And fashion of his instant-told returne, 315
Or stay th'impulsion, and the long day burne
Of his quite losse given in his Father's feare
A little longer, trying first his cheare
With some free dalliance, th'earnest being so neare.
  This course his choise preferr'd, and forth he went, 320
His Father then his aged shoulders bent
Beneath what yeares had stoop't, about a Tree
Busily digging: 'O, old man,' said he,
'You want no skill to dresse and decke your ground,
For all your Plants doth order'd distance bound: 325

No Apple, Peare, or Olive, Fig, or Vine,
Nor any plat or quarter you confine
To grasse or flow'rs, stands empty of your care,
Which shewes exact in each peculiare:
And yet (which let not move you) you bestow 330
No care upon your selfe, though to this show
Of outward irksomnesse to what you are,
You labour with an inward froward care,
Which is your age, that should weare all without
More neate and cherishing. I make no doubt 335
That any sloth you use procures your Lord
To let an old man go so much abhord
In all his weeds, nor shines there in your looke
A fashion and a goodlinesse so tooke
With abject qualities to merit this 340
Nasty entreaty. Your resemblance is
A very King's and shines through this retreate.
You looke like one that, having washt and eate,
Should sleepe securely, lying sweet and neate.
It is the ground of Age, when cares abuse it, 345
To know life's end; and, as 'tis sweet, so use it.
'But utter truth and tell: what Lord is he
That rates your labour and your liberty?
Whose Orchard is it that you husband thus?
Or quit me this doubt—for if Ithacus 350
This kingdome claimes for his, the man I found
At first arrivall heere is hardly sound
Of braine or civill, not induring stay
To tell, nor heare me my enquiry out
Of that my friend—if stil he bore about 355
His life and Being, or were div'd to Death
And in the house of him that harboureth
The soules of men. For once he liv'd my guest,
My Land and house retaining interest
In his abode there, where there sojourn'd none, 360
As guest, from any forreigne Region
Of more price with me. He deriv'd his race
From Ithaca, and said his Father was
Laertes, surnam'd Arcesiades.
I had him home, and all the offices 365
Perform'd to him that fitted any friend,
Whose proofe I did to wealthy gifts extend—
Seven Talents Gold, a Bolle all silver, set
With pots of flowers, twelve robes, that had no pleat,

Twelve cloakes (or mantles) of delicious dye, 370
Twelve inner weeds, twelve sutes of Tapistry.
I gave him likewise women skill'd in use
Of Loome and Needle, freeing him to chuse
Foure the most faire.' His Father (weeping) saide:
'Stranger! The earth to which you are convaide 375
Is Ithaca, by such rude men possest,
Unjust and insolent, as first addrest
To your encounter; but the gifts you gave
Were given (alas) to the ungratefull grave.
If with his people, where you now arrive, 380
Your Fate had bene to finde your friend alive,
You shold have found like Guest-rites from his hand,
Like gifts, and kinde passe to your wished land.
But how long since receiv'd you as your guest
Your Friend, my Son, who was th'unhappiest 385
Of all men breathing, if he were at all?
O, borne when Fates and ill Aspects let fall
A cruell influence for him, farre away
From Friends and Countrey, destin'd to alay
The Sea-bred appetites, or (left ashore) 390
To be by Fowles and upland Monsters tore—
His life's kinde authors nor his wealthy wife
Bemoning (as behoov'd) his parted life,
Nor closing (as in honour's course it lyes
To all men dead) in bed his dying eyes. 395
But give me knowledge of your name and race.
What City bred you? Where the anchoring place
Your ship now rides at lies, that shor'd you here?
And where your men? Or if a passenger
In others' Keeles you came, who (giving Land 400
To your adventures heere, some other Strand
To fetch in further course) have left to us
Your welcome presence?' His reply was thus:
'I am of Alybande, where I hold
My name's chief house, to much renowne extold. 405
My Father Aphidantes, fam'd to spring
From Polypemon, the Molossian King:
My name, Eperitus. My taking land
On this faire Isle was rul'd by the command
Of God or Fortune, quite against consent 410
Of my free purpose, that in course was bent
For th'Isle Sicania. My Ship is held
Farre from the City, neere an ample field.

And, for Ulysses, since his passe from me
'Tis now five yeares. Unblest by Destiny, 415
That all this time hath had the Fate to erre!
Though at his parting good Birds did augure
His putting off, and on his right hand flew,
Which to his passage my affection drew,
His spirit joyfull; and my hope was now 420
To guest with him and see his hand bestow
Rights of our friendship.' This a cloud of griefe
Cast over all the forces of his life.
With both his hands the burning dust he swept
Up from the earth, which on his head he heapt, 425
And fetcht a sigh, as in it life were broke—
Which greev'd his Son, and gave so smart a stroke
Upon his nosethrils with the inward stripe
That up the Veine rose there; and weeping ripe
He was to see his Sire feele such woe 430
For his dissembl'd joy—which now (let goe)
He sprung from earth, embrac't and kist his Sire,
And said: 'O Father, he of whom y'enquire
Am I my selfe, that (from you twenty yeares)
Is now return'd. But do not breake in teares, 435
For now we must not formes of kinde maintaine,
But haste and guard the substance. I have slaine
All my wive's wooers, so revenging now
Their wrong so long time suffer'd. Take not you
The comfort of my comming, then, to heart 440
At this glad instant; but, in prov'd desert
Of your grave judgement, give mone glad suspence,
And on the sodaine put this consequence
In act as absolute, as all time went
To ripening of your resolute assent.' 445
All this haste made not his staide faith so free
To trust his words, who said: 'If you are he,
Approve it by some signe.' 'This scar then see,'
Replied Ulysses, 'given me by the Bore
Slaine in Parnassus, I being sent before 450
By yours and by my honour'd Mother's will,
To see her Sire Autolycus fulfill
The gifts he vow'd at giving of my Name.
I'le tel you, too, the Trees (in goodly frame
Of this faire Orchard) that I askt of you 455
Being yet a childe, and follow'd for your show
And name of every Tree. You gave me then

Of Figge-trees forty, Apple-bearers ten,
Peare-trees thirteene, and fifty rankes of Vine,
Each one of which a season did confine 460
For his best eating. Not a Grape did grow
That grew not there, and had his heavy brow
When Jove's faire daughters (the all-ripening how'rs)
Gave timely date to it.' This charg'd the pow'rs
Both of his knees and heart with such impression 465
Of sodaine comfort that it gave possession
Of all to Trance—the signes were all so true,
And did the love that gave them so renue.
He cast his armes about his sonne, and sunke,
The cicle slipping to his feete, so shrunke 470
Were all his age's forces with the fire
Of his yong love rekindl'd. The old Sire
The Son tooke up quite livelesse, but his breath
Againe respiring, and his soule from death
His bodie's pow'rs recovering, out he cried, 475
And said: 'O Jupiter! I now have tried
That still there live in heaven remembring Gods
Of men that serve them; though the periods
They set to their apparances are long
In best men's sufferings, yet as sure as strong 480
They are in comforts, be their strange delayes
Extended never so from dayes to dayes.
Yet see the short joyes, or the soone-mixt feares
Of helpes with-held by them so many yeares—
For, if the wooers now have paide the paine 485
Due to their impious pleasures, now againe
Extreame feare takes me, lest we straight shall see
Th'Ithacensians here in mutinie,
Their Messengers dispatcht to win to friend
The Cephallenian Cities.' 'Do not spend 490
Your thoughts on these cares,' saide his suffering son,
'But be of comfort, and see that course ron
That best may shun the worst. Our house is nere,
Telemachus and both his Herdsmen there
To dresse our supper with their utmost hast; 495
And thither haste we.' This saide, forth they past,
Came home, and found Telemachus at feast
With both his Swaines: while who had done, all drest
With Baths and Balmes and royally arraid
The old King was by his Sicilian Maid— 500
By whose side Pallas stood, his crookt-age streitning,

His flesh more plumping and his looks enlightning,
Who yssuing then to view, his son admir'd
The God's Aspects into his forme inspir'd,
And said: 'O Father, certainly some God 505
By your addression in this state hath stood,
More great, more reverend, rendring you by farre
At all your parts than of your selfe you are.'
'I would to Jove,' said he, 'the Sun and She
That beares Jove's shield, the state had stood with me 510
That helpt me take in the wel-builded Tow'rs
Of strong Nericus (the Cephallian pow'rs
To that faire City leading) two dayes past,
While with the wooers thy conflict did last;
And I had then bene in the wooers' wreake! 515
I should have helpt thee so to render weake
Their stubborne knees that in thy joye's desert
Thy breast had bene too little for thy heart.'
This said, and supper order'd by their men,
They sate to it, old Dolius entring then, 520
And with him (tyr'd with labour) his sonnes came,
Call'd by their Mother, the Sicilian dame
That brought them up and drest their Father's fare—
As whose age grew, with it encreast her care
To see him serv'd as fitted. When (thus set) 525
These men beheld Ulysses there at meate,
They knew him, and astonisht in the place
Stood at his presence—who, with words of grace
Call'd to olde Dolius, saying: 'Come and eate,
And banish all astonishment: your meate 530
Hath long bene ready and our selves made stay,
Expecting ever when your wished way
Would reach amongst us.' This brought fiercely on
Old Dolius from his stand, who ran upon
(With both his armes abroad) the King, and kist 535
Of both his rapt up hands the either wrist,
Thus welcomming his presence: 'O my Love,
Your presence heere (for which all wishes strove)
No one expected. Even the Gods have gone
In guide before you to your mansion. 540
Welcom, and all joyes to your heart contend.
Knowes yet Penelope? Or shall we send
Some one to tell her this?' 'She knowes,' said he,
'What need these troubles, Father, touch at thee?'
Then came the Sonnes of Dolius, and againe 545

Went over with their Father's entertaine,
Welcom'd, shooke hands, and then to feast sate down—
About which while they sate, about the Towne
Fame flew and shriek't about the cruell death
And Fate the wooers had sustain'd beneath 550
Ulysses' roofes. All heard; together all
From hence and thence met in Ulysses' Hall,
Short-breath'd and noisefull, bore out all the dead
To instant buriall, while their deaths were spread
To other Neighbor-Cities, where they liv'd— 555
From whence in swiftest Fisher-boats arriv'd
Men to transfer them home. In meane space, here
The heavy Nobles all in counsaile were,
Where (met in much heape) up to all arose
Extremely-greev'd Eupeithes so to lose 560
His Son Antinous, who first of all
By great Ulysses' hand had slaughtrous fall—
Whose Father (weeping for him) saide: 'O Friends,
This man hath author'd workes of dismall ends,
Long since conveying in his guide to Troy 565
Good men and many, that did ships employ:
All which are lost, and all their Souldiers dead.
And now the best men Cephallenia bred
His hand hath slaughter'd. Go we then (before
His scape to Pylos or the Elean Shore 570
Where rule the Epeans) 'gainst his horrid hand:
For we shall grieve, and infamy will brand
Our Fames for ever, if we see our Sons
And Brothers end in these confusions,
Revenge left uninflicted. Nor will I 575
Enjoy one daye's life more, but greeve and die
With instant onset. Nor should you survive
To keepe a base and beastly name alive.
Haste then, lest flight prevent us.' This with teares
His griefes advisd, and made all sufferers 580
In his affliction. But by this was come
Up to the Counsaile from Ulysses' home
(When sleep had left them, which the slaughters there
And their selfe dangers from their eyes in feare
Had two nights intercepted) those two men 585
That just Ulysses sav'd out of the slaine—
Which Medon and the sacred Singer were.
These stood amidst the Counsaile, and the feare
The slaughter had imprest in either's looke

Stucke stil so gastly that amaze it strooke 590
Through every there beholder—to whose eares
One thus enforc't, in his fright, cause of theirs:
'Attend me, Ithacensians. This sterne fact
Done by Ulysses was not put in act
Without the Gods' assistance. These selfe eies 595
Saw one of the immortall Deities
Close by Ulysses, Mentor's forme put on
At every part: and this sure Deity shone
Now neere Ulysses, setting on his bold
And slaughterous spirit, now the points controll'd 600
Of all the wooers' weapons, round about
The arm'd house whisking, in continuall rout
Their party putting, till in heapes they fell.'
This newes new fears did through their spirits impel,
When Halitherses (honor'd Mastor's sonne, 605
Who of them all saw onely what was done
Present and future) the much-knowing man
And aged Heroe, this plaine course ran
Amongst their counsailes: 'Give me likewise eare,
And let me tell ye, Friends, that these ils beare 610
On your malignant spleenes their sad effects,
Who not what I perswaded gave respects,
Nor what the people's Pastor, Mentor, saide—
That you should see your issues' follies staid
In those foule courses, by their petulant life 615
The goods devouring, scandaling the wife
Of no meane person, who (they still would say)
Could never more see his returning day:
Which yet appearing now, now give it trust,
And yeeld to my free counsailes: Do not thrust 620
Your owne safe persons on the acts your Sons
So deerely bought, lest their confusions
On your lov'd heads your like addictions draw.'
This stood so farre from force of any Law
To curbe their loose attempts, that much the more 625
They rusht to wreake, and made rude tumult rore.
The greater part of all the Court arose:
Good counsaile could not ill designes dispose.
Eupeithes was perswader of the course,
Which (compleate arm'd) they put in present force: 630
The rest sate still in counsaile. These men met
Before the broad Towne in a place they set,
All girt in armes, Eupeithes choosing Chiefe

To all their follies, who put griefe to griefe,
And in his slaughter'd son's revenge did burne. 635
But Fate gave never feete to his returne,
Ordaining there his death. Then Pallas spake
To Jove, her Father, with intent to make
His will high Arbiter of th'act design'd,
And askt of him what his unsearched mind 640
Held undiscover'd—if with Armes, and ill,
And grave encounter, he would first fulfill
His sacred purpose, or both parts combine
In peacefull friendship? He askt: 'Why incline
These doubts thy counsailes? Hast not thou decreed 645
That Ithacus should come and give his deed
The glory of revenge on these and theirs?
Performe thy will; the frame of these affaires
Have this fit issue—when Ulysses' hand
Hath reacht full wreake, his then renown'd command 650
Shall reigne for ever, faithfull Truces strooke
'Twixt him and all, for every man shall brooke
His Sons' and Brothers' slaughters by our meane
To send Oblivion in, expugning cleane
The Character of enmity in all, 655
As in best Leagues before. *Peace, Feastivall*
And Riches in abundance be the state
That crownes the close of Wise Ulysses' Fate.'
This spurr'd the Free, who from heaven's Continent
To th'Ithacensian Isle made straight descent. 660
Where (dinner past) Ulysses said: 'Some one
Looke out to see their neerenesse.' Dolius' sonne
Made present speed abroad, and saw them nie,
Ran backe, and told, bad Arme; and instantlie
Were all in armes. Ulysses' part was foure, 665
And sixe more sons of Dolius—all his powre
Two onely more, which were his aged Sire
And like-year'd Dolius, whose lives' slaked fire
All white had left their heads, yet, driven by Neede,
Made Souldiers both of necessary deede. 670
And now, all girt in armes, the Ports set wide,
They sallied forth, Ulysses being their guide.
And to them, in the instant, Pallas came,
In forme and voice like Mentor, who, a flame
Inspir'd of comfort in Ulysses' hart 675
With her seene presence. To his Son, apart,
He thus then spake: 'Now, Son, your eyes shall see

(Expos'd in slaughterous fight) the enemy,
Against whom who shall best serve will be seene:
Disgrace not then your race, that yet hath beene 680
For force and fortitude the formost tried
Of all earth's off-springs.' His true Son replied:
'Your selfe shall see, lov'd Father, if you please,
That my deservings shall in nought digresse
From best fame of our Race's formost merit.' 685
The old King sprung for joy to heare his spirit,
And said: 'O lov'd Immortals, what a day
Do your cleere bounties to my life display?
I joy past measure to behold my Son
And Nephew close in such contention 690
Of vertues martiall.' Pallas (standing neere)
Said: 'O my Friend! Of all, supreamly deere
Seed of Arcesius, pray to Jove and her
That rules in Armes (his daughter) and a dart
(Spritefully brandisht) hurle at th'adverse part.' 695
This said, he pray'd; and she a mighty force
Inspir'd within him, who gave instant course
To his brave-brandisht Lance, which strook the brasse
That cheek't Eupeithes' Caske, and thrust his passe
Quite through his head; who fell, and sounded falling, 700
His Armes the sound againe from earth recalling.
Ulysses and his Son rusht on before,
And with their both-way-headed Darts did gore
Their enemies' breasts so thicke that all had gone
The way of slaughter, had not Pallas throwne 705
Her voice betwixt them, charging all to stay
And spare expence of blood. Her voice did fray
The blood so from their faces that it left
A greenish palenesse. All their hands it reft
Of all their weapons, falling thence to earth, 710
And to the commune Mother of their Birth
(The City) all fled, in desire to save
The lives yet left them. Then Ulysses gave
A horrid shout, and like Jove's Eagle flew
In fiery pursuite, till Saturnius threw 715
His smoaking lightning twixt them, that had fall
Before Minerva—who then out did call
Thus to Ulysses: 'Borne of Jove! Abstaine
From further bloodshed: Jove's hand in the slaine
Hath equall'd in their paines their prides to thee. 720
Abstaine then, lest you move the Deity.'

Againe, then, twixt both parts the seed of Jove,
Athenian Pallas, of all future love
A league compos'd; and for her forme tooke choice
Of Mentor's likenesse both in Limb and Voice. 725

The End of the XXIIII. and last Booke of Homer's Odysses.

So wrought divine Ulysses through his woes,
So croun'd the Light with him his Mother's Throes,
As through his great Renowner I have wrought,
And my safe saile to sacred Anchor brought.
Nor did the Argive ship more burthen feele, 5
That bore the Care of all men in her Keele,
Than my adventurous Barke—the Colchian Fleece
Not halfe so precious as this soule of Greece—
In whose songs I have made our shores rejoyce,
And Greeke it selfe veile to our English voyce. 10
Yet this inestimable Pearle wil all
Our Dunghil Chanticheres but obvious call,
Each Moderne scraper this Gem scratching by,
His Oate preferring far. Let such let ly:
So scorne the stars the clouds, as true-soul'd men 15
Despise Deceivers. For, as Clouds would faine
Obscure the Stars, yet (Regions left below
With all their envies) bar them but of show,
For they shine ever, and wil shine when they
Dissolve in sinckes, make Mire, and temper Clay: 20
So puft Impostors (our Muse-vapours) strive,
With their selfe-blowne additions, to deprive
Men solid of their full, though infinite short
They come in their compare and false report
Of levelling or touching at their light, 25
That still retaine their radiance and cleere right,
And shal shine ever—when, alas, one blast
Of least disgrace teares downe th'Impostor's Mast,
His Tops, and Tacklings, his whole Freight and He
Confiscate to the Fishy Monarchy, 30
His trash, by foolish Fame bought now, from hence
Given to serve Mackarell forth, and Frankincence.

Such then, and any too soft-ey'd to see
Through workes so solid any worth, so free
Of all the learn'd professions as is fit 35
To praise at such price, let him thinke his wit
Too weake to rate it, rather than oppose
With his poore pow'rs Ages and Hosts of Foes.

To the Ruines of Troy and Greece.

Troy rac't, Greece wrackt, who mournes? Ye both may bost,
Else th'*Iliads* and *Odysses* had bene lost.

Ad Deum.

The onely true God (betwixt whom and Me
I onely bound my comforts, and agree
With all my actions) onely truly knowes
And can judge truly me, with all that goes
To all my Faculties. In whose free grace 5
And inspiration I onely place
All meanes to know (with my meanes, Study, praire,
In and from his word taken) staire by staire,
In all continual contentation, rising
To knowledge of his Truth, and practising 10
His wil in it with my sole Saviour's aide,
Guide, and enlightning—nothing done, nor saide,
Nor thought that good is, but acknowledg'd by
His inclination, skill, and faculty.
By which to finde the way out to his love 15
Past all the worlds the sphere is, where doth move
My studies, prai'rs, and pow'rs—no pleasure taken
But sign'd by his: for which, my blood forsaken,
My soule I cleave to and what (in his blood
That hath redeem'd, cleansd, taught her) fits her good. 20

Deo opt. Max. gloria.

FINIS

TEXTUAL NOTES

TEXTUAL NOTES

For certain pages where the marginal glosses are carried on below the text, references are given to the last line of text, followed by the line of the gloss (as in Book 1, 122,4 and 122,7). '*Odysses 12*' refers to the separate issue of the first twelve books.

Dedicatory Epistle

9 and	*Odysses 12*—&
thunder	*Odysses 12*—thũder
10 and	*Odysses 12*—&
18 no blacke	No blacke
no Nation	No Nation
39 Odyssean	Odyssæan
82 *this*	*Odysses 12—these*
87 *Longinus*	Longimus
89 *or to*	*Or to*
92 *when*	*When*
96 *where*	*Where*
98 *well-bounded*	*well bounded*
108 *wherein*	*Wherein*
134 *there*	*There*
138 et	&
142 et	&
143 *one*	*One*
148 *against*	*Against*
150 *Epicharmus*	Epichar:
155 *the*	*The*
156 *their infected*	*Their infected*
200 farre-off	farre off
232 Rout State-engrost	*Rout: State* engrost
239 when	When

Book 1

Argument

7 *Mentas'*	Menta's

Text

4,4 [gloss] et	&
[gloss] verum	veram

7	at	At
43	to	To
60	[gloss] *the*	*The*
95	evermore	Euermore
105	Did	did
117	[gloss] *deciphering*	*Deciphering*
122	Phorcys'	*Phorcis*
122,4	[gloss] et	&
122,7	[gloss] *the*	*The*
139	Let	let
222	Powr'd	Prowr'd
229	when	When
275	I'le	Ile
280	having	Hauing
282	other-languag'd	other languag'd
290	Rhethrus	*Rethrus*
294	Heroe	Herœe
306	I'le	Ile
329	when	When
334	with all	withall
349	What's	what's
375	Harpies	*Harpies*
402	Centaur	*Centaure*
422	Heroes	*Heroes*
463	I'le	Ile
515	Troy's	*Trois*
543	in	In
544	[gloss] *information*	*informatiõ*
564	Much	much
565	Sit	sit
572	glance	light [Loane]
573	I'le	Ile
592	Eupitheus'	*Eupytheus*
602	[gloss] *from*	*frõ*
604	[gloss] *and*	*&*
605	[gloss] *commandingly*	*cõmandingly*
613	[gloss] asperitatem	asperitatẽ
614	[gloss] dictum	dictũ
623	off of	of, of
627	From	from
	And	and
629	His	his
634	[gloss] et	&
657	Euryclea	*Euryclæa*

659 Pisenorides	*Pysenorides*
660 who	Who
672 the	The

Book 2

Argument

6 *Euryclea*	Euryclæa

Text

22 Heroe	*Heroe*
24 who	Who
63 Pisenor	*Pysenor*
154 Heroe	*Heroe*
243 Heroe	*Heroe*
327 Amathoan	*Amathoon*
329 long-lackt	long lackt
369 Leocritus	*Liocritus*
[gloss] *Leocritus*	*Liocritus*
426 true-borne	true borne
453 I'le	Ile
466 steepe	sleepe
500 bowls	bow'ls
508 while	While
522 Her	her
536 Whither	whithur
538 And	and
566 Nocmon	*Normon*

Book 3

Argument

10 [gloss] *and*	*&*

Text

5 ever-tredders	ever tredders
53 tooke	Tooke
54 their	Their
55 in	In
57 Thrasymed	*Thrasimed*
59 kerv'd	Keru'd
151 the in-counsell-like-the-Gods	the-in-counsell-like the-Gods
211 But	but
216 abundant-in-all-counsels	abundant in all counsels
222 Tydides	*Tidides*
228 Psyria	*Psiria*

244 fore-right	fore right
251 mightie-soul'd	mightie sould
253 Pœan's	*Pæans*
254 Idomeneus	*Idomenæus*
307 not	Not
316 car'd-for	car'd for
332 I'le	Ile
344 How	how
350 I'le	Ile
365 to	too
383 Sunium	*Sunius*
385 Augur	*Augur*
396 wine-hewd	wind-hewd
398 [gloss] vinum	vinũ
404 Crete	*Creete*
425 eighth	eight
434 Good-at-a-martiall-shout	good at a martiall shout
459 ever-blest	euer blest
463 they	They
495 Great-soul'd	Great-sould
520 brode-headed	brode headed
557 Thrasymed	*Thrasimed*
598 Thrasymed	*Thrasimed*
607 Thrasymed	*Thrasimed*
623 five-pointed	fine-pointed [Loane]

Book 4

6 Megapenthes	*Megapenthe*
8 when Helen	When *Hellen*
37 Boethides	*Beotides*
[gloss] *servant*	*seruãt*
49 at	At
71 And	and
101 eighth	eight
103 Sidonia	*Sydonia*
104 farre-off	farre off
117 from	From
155 Helen	*Hellen*
156 Alcippe	*Alcyppe*
158 Phylo	*Philo*
165 Helen	*Hellen*
173 [gloss] *Helen*	*Hellen*
193 continuall	continnall
228 whither	Whither
231 here	him

243	Helen	*Hellen*
248	[gloss] *remembrance*	*remẽbrance*
251	there	There
276	right-borne	right borne
286	But	[new paragraph in original]
290	This said	[no new paragraph in original]
293	Helen	*Hellen*
294	[gloss] *Helen's*	*Hellens*
302	Helen	*Hellen*
310	Helen	*Hellen*
312	[gloss] *Helen*	*Hellen*
338	talkt	Talkt
	but	But
340	and	And
362	[gloss] *Helen*	*Hellen*
382	[gloss] *Helen*	*Hellen*
404	Helen	*Hellen*
	handmaids	handmaid [Loane]
405	Portico	*Portico*
410	Portico	*Portico*
412	forth	for [Loane]
423	some	Some
	publicke cause	publicke [Loane]
469	I'le	Ile
474	I'le	Ile
496	Idothea	*Edothea*
516	I'le	Ile
526	God-preserv'd	God preseru'd
536	I'le	Ile
546	I'le	Ile
550	I'le	Ile
579	Idothea	*Edothea*
594	Ambrosia	*Ambrosia*
616	too	to
630	the	The
651	I'le	Ile
688	Oiliades	*Oileades*
694	Affected	Afflicted [Loane]
695	Malian	*Malean*
700	Thyestes	*Thiestes*
701	Thyestiades	*Thiestiades*
717	Plebeians	*Plebeians*
733	O	ô
761	Elysian	*Elisian*
	[gloss] *Elysium*	*Elisium*

765	Zephyr	*Zephyre*
767	Helen	*Hellen*
785	I'le	Ile
802	Cypers	*Cypers*
813	What	what
862	Let	let
867	Who	who
869	He	he
942	Why	why
992	Euryclea	*Euryclæa*
993	[gloss] *Euryclea's*	*Euryclæas*
994	I'le	Ile
1048	Who	who
1070	so	So
1085	[gloss] et	&
1128	Daigne	daigne
1143	wayes	waues [Loane]

Book 5

Another Argument

3	*Glassie*	*Gassie*

Text

33	Hast	hast
69	Pieria	*Pierea*
116	Thou	thou
124	Nectar	*Nectar*
216	I'le	Ile
263	Nectar	*Nectar*
	Ambrosia	*Ambrosia*
268	So	so
295	I'le	Ile
305	out weed	out-weed
306	Graces	*Graces*
325	looke	tooke
345	the	The
363	Now	now
377	Zephyr	*Zephire*
	North making-faire	*North*-making faire
430	Zephyr	*Zephire*
	made pursue	made it pursue
472	I'le	Ile
546	death-fast-following	death-fast following
551	wave-beate	way-beate [Loane]
572	Polypus	*Polypus*

592 rocks	Rocks
596 Whatever	whatever
610 voice	Voice
612 [gloss] ὠδίνω	ὀδίνω
628 The	the
669 Delicacies	*Delicacies*

Book 6

4 [gloss] et	&
23 a	A
29 neare	Neare
53 Grace	*Grace*
67 and	And
80 Senate	*Senate*
81 [gloss] *and*	*&*
138 Nausicaa	*Nausicae*
141 Nausicaa	*Nausicae*
150 amongst	Amongst
162 lovely-sighted	louely sighted
173 [gloss] *Spondanus*	*Spond.*
174 Or	or
175 Like	like
180 I'le	Ile
186 weather-beaten-hewd	weather-beaten hewd
247 Phane	*Phane*
324 [gloss] et	&
329 From	from
336 [gloss] et	&
349,1 [gloss] *as recusing*	*As receiuing* [Loanc]
351 I'le	Ile
356 broad soild shoulders	broad-soild-shoulders
376 to	To
427 So	so
428 Where	where
465 where	Where
482 seated	Seated

Book 7

14 [gloss] Spondanus	Spond.
29 stood	Stood
40 The	the
48 [gloss] ὡς εἰ	οσεις
60 Heroes	*Heroes*
73 The	the

Line	Reading	Original
84	[gloss] *Diagram*	*Diagrã*
	grac't	glac't
106	left	Left
107	out	Out
110	Erechtheus	*Erectheus*
162	Zephyr	*Zephire*
179	And	and
196	when	When
216	Echeneus	*Echinæus*
	Heroe	*Heroe*
219	And	and
220	[gloss] *Echeneus*	*Echinæus*
	It	it
224	A	a
256	minds wine	minds*-wine
265	[gloss] et	&
295	[gloss] *Alcinous*	*Antinous*
299	[gloss] *and*	*&*
306	[gloss] *and*	*&*
311	[gloss] *Alcinous*	*Antinous*
317	[gloss] *appearance*	*appearãce*
323	when	When
340	Laertiades	*Laertides*
366	eighth	eight
422	too	to
443	your	you
472	Portico	*Portico*
482	Portico	*Portico*

Book 8

Argument

Line	Reading	Original
5	*Which*	*which*
8	*Demodocus*	Demodecus

Text

Line	Reading	Original
14	Peers Phæacensian	*Peers Phæacensian'*
15	All	all
32	[gloss] *reliefe*	*beliefe*
56	Some other	[new paragraph in original]
60	This said	[no new paragraph in original]
70	Porticos	*Porticos*
78	who	Who
	men	mean
101	Augur	*Augur*
104	Pytho	*Pythia*
128	which	Which

131 brake	Brake
154 Anchialus	*Anchyalus*
156 Ponteus	*Pontæus*
157 Polyneus	*Polinius*
163 [gloss] summa	sũma
Anabesineus	*Anabesinzus*
166 Clytoneus	*Clytonæus*
170 Clytoneus	*Clytonæus*
176 at	At
206 [gloss] aliquando	aliquandiu
254 I'le	Ile
301 I'le	Ile
311 Eurytus	*Euritus*
318 I'le	Ile
336 Heroes	*Heroes*
346 for	For
348 Poesie, Musique, Dancing, Baths and Beds	*Poesie, Musique, Dancing, Baths,* and *Beds*
375 [gloss] *twinckld*	*twinckd*
380 [gloss] *fire*	*first* [Loane]
409 Love	*Loue*
419 both-foote-crook't	Both-foot cook't
433 all-things-making-come-to-nought	All things-making-come to nought
453 She-Deitie	She Deity
454 All	all
455 Stood	stood
465 [gloss] *them*	*thẽ*
477 but	But
488 Your word	[no new paragraph in original]
492 she	She
Grove	*Groue*
531 Twelve	twelue
539 Our	One
567 And	and
583 Hymne	*Hymne*
602 Reverend-for-her-wisedome	Reverend for her wisedome
622 varied-in-all-counsels	varied in all counsels
629 I'le	Ile
638 grac't-with-wisedome	grac't with wisedome
648 The Muse	*The Muse*
679 where	Where
700 Ilian	*Ilion*
705 and	And
721 [gloss] *Metaphorically*	Metaph.
723 [gloss] tabesco	tabeseo

736	sufferance	sufferanc
	so	So
778	[gloss] *strange*	*strãge*
787	harbor	habor
795	both from whence	both whence
802	Why	why

Book 9

Argument

4	*Lotophagi*	Lotophagie

Another Argument

2	*Lotophagi*	Lotophagie

Text

11	when	When
16	tables	Tables
44	[gloss] quædam	quędam
68	much-distress-conferring facts	much-distrest-conferring-facts
111	our	Our
137	Cythera	*Cythæra*
139	Lotophagi	*Lotophagie*
145	[gloss] *Lotophagi*	*Lotophagie*
146	Lotophagi	*Lotophagie*
217	And	and
238	allotted it	allotted
355	Whence	whence
365	[gloss] *and*	*&*
384	[gloss] *observation*	*obseruatiõ*
386	[gloss] *and*	*&*
394	ship	ships
416	when	When
420	more	More
491	Cyclops	*Cylops*
495	Nectar and Ambrosia	*Nectar* and *Ambrosia*
499	Cyclop	*Cylop*
500	I'le	Ile
	tell my	tell thee my
505	I'le	Ile
530	Augur's	*Augurs*
533	so	So
560	No-Man	No man
	Right	right
581	learn'd-in-villanie	learn'd in villanie
607	Thou	thou

615 But	but
674 [gloss] *insolence*	*insolēce*
678 [gloss] *his Epithetes*	*Epithetes*
683 Augur	*Augur*
684 Eurymides	*Eurymedes*
685 Augurie	*Augurie*
686 Truth	*Truth*

Book 10

Argument

6 *Zephyr*	Zephyre
13 *Læstrygonians*	Læstrigonians
23 *Moly*	Moly

Text

3 Hippotades	*Hippotydes*
5 wave-beat-smooth rocke	waue-beat-smooth-rocke
15 each	Each
19 of	Of
49 and	And
51 whatsoever	Whatsoeuer
52 How	how
74 where	Where
80 What	what
91 But	but
97 Foorth	foorth
105 the	The
Læstrygonian	*Laestrigonian*
114 that's	thats
123 [gloss] et	&
127,1 [gloss] *Homer*	*Hom.*
140 Læstrygonian	*Laestrigonian*
176 Æetes'	*Æætas*
186 in	I
233 huge-bodied	hugebodied
246 [gloss] *Polypheme*	*Polyph.*
267 Læstrygonian	*Laestrigonian*
366 manie	maine
373 Thou no-place-finding-for-repose	Thou-no-place-finding-for repose
380 like	Like
381 I'le	Ile
387 Shee'le	Sheele
391 when	When
406 with	With

407	and	And
419	[gloss] quidem	quidẽ
427	to	To
428	Out	out
430	when	When
432	Of	of
433	Whence?	whence?
	What	what
484	eye-meate	eye meate
487	than	the [Loane]
491	Out	out
530	circl'd	Circl'd
539	unlookt-for	vnlookt for
	that	That
548	Why	why
550	transforme	tranforme
565	our	Our
569	select	secret [Loane]
632	Pyriphlegethon	*Pyriphlegiton*
635	Heroe	*Heroe*
660	[gloss] advocat	adnocet
662	Grave	*Graue*
702	Austere	*Austere*

Book 11

Title

	ELEVENTH	XI.

Argument

6	*Heroes and Heroesses*	Heroes *and* Heroesses

Text

23	Perimedes	*Persimedes*
103	Autolycus	*Antolicus*
104	Anticlea	*Anticlæa*
	whom	Whom
111	Circe	*Circes*
162	Countrey	Countey
207	that	That
214	Grecian	*Græcian*
245	when	When
341	Amphitryo	*Amphytrio*
344	Creon's	*Cræons*
367	Minyæan	*Myniæan*
368	Pylian	*Pylean*
371	Periclymenus	*Peryclimenus*
382	Iphicles	*Iphiclus*

399	Iphicles	*Iphiclus*
402	Leda	*Læda*
408	after	After
414	[gloss] *Iphimedea*	*Iphemedea*
	Iphimedea	*Iphemedea*
	Leda	*Læda*
443	Eriphyle	*Eryphile*
445	[gloss] *whom*	*whõ*
	Heroesses	*Heroesses*
447	Ambrosian	*Ambrosian*
450	My	my
464	Heroe	*Heroe*
483	[gloss] et	&
493	You	you
501	Consorts	*Consorts*
509	Times	*Times*
513	[gloss] *relation*	*relatiõ*
520	Ægisthus'	*Ægysthus*
535	Or	or
539	Ægisthus	*Ægysthus*
544	as	As
560	when	When
566	when	When
577	be	Be
586	who	Who
592	when	When
604	Or	or
605	Yet	yet
646	throne	thone
658	Ilian	*Ilion*
673	[gloss] *Achilles*	*Aehilles*
692	Eurypylus	*Eurypilus*
706	Epeus'	*Epæus*
751	What?	what?
	Not	not
759	who	Who
794	Panopeus	*Panopæus*
833	Art	*Art*
855	Heroes	*Herœes*

Book 12

Title

	TWELFTH	XII.

Text

3	Pallace	*Pallace*
5	Active	*Actiue*

17	whose	Whose
50	when	When
103	Ambrosia	*Ambrosia*
115	Th' Argive	*Th' Argiue*
117	Æeta	*Areta*
123	[gloss] *interpreting*	*Interpreting*
126	not	Not
126,8	[gloss] νηῦς	νευς
126,9	[gloss] omnibus heroibus	omnib^{9} heroib^{9}
126,10	[gloss] *preservation*	*preseruatiõ*
126,13	[gloss] *being*	Being
126,19	[gloss] *by*	*By*
	[gloss] et	&
142	[gloss] *no*	*No*
143	looke	lookt
152	If got	got
157	a	A
157,3	[gloss] λάσκω	ληχεο
157,5	[gloss] *because*	*Because*
157,6	[gloss] *imagining*	*Imagining*
157,7	[gloss] *And*	*and*
164	drinkes	drinking [Loane]
184	her	their
194	Triangulare	*Triangulare*
216	long'd-for	long'd for
246	ship	ships [Loane]
268	Rowd	[new paragraph in original]
276	*ravishd*	*rauish*
309	that	That
415	wilt	wet
423	hest	best
438	severest	seuerst
445	Tempest	Tempst
450	ship	ships
456	Herds	*Herds*
	Flocks	*Flocks*
473	Retreate	*Retreate*
518	about	About
538	Lampetie	*Lempetie*
540	Ambassadresse	*Ambassadresse*
543	ever-living	euer liuing
548	I'le	Ile
575	Zephyr	*Zephyre*
578	tackle	cattle [Loane]
579	Pylot's	*Pylots*
609	Clambring	Chambring

618	So	so
633	abode	about [Loane]
635	where	Where

Book 13

Argument

9	*and*	*And*

Text

1	and	And
22	[gloss] *and*	*&*
32	and	&
35	that	y^{t}
66	[gloss] *Ulysses to Alcinous*	Vlysses to Alcinous
	of	Of
86	[gloss] *Alcinous to the Herrald*	Alcinous to the Herrald
97	to	To
98	[gloss] *Ulysses to Arete*	Vlysses to Arete
115	with	With
127	[gloss] *Similitude*	Similitude
135	nor	Nor
136	Faulcon	Faulcou
157	sacred	Sacred
167	but	But
173	bed	Bed
187	[gloss] *Neptune to Jupiter*	Neptune *to* Iupiter
191	[gloss] *from Neptune*	*frō* Neptune
195	Yet	yet
210	for	For
213	if	If
245	all	All
246	and	&
253	[gloss] *tels . . . Stone*	[in roman]
269	Mountaine	Mouutaine
286	the	The
287	the	The
	wayes	waues [Loane]
291	and	&
308	heere	Heere
328	Kings'	King
329	Athwart	A'thwart
333	be	Be
340	and	And

343	[gloss] *Pallas*	Pallas
	[gloss] *Ulysses*	Vlysses
354	[gloss] jejunaque	Ieiunaq
387	but	But
400	Epeians	*Epeyans*
403	from	frõ
413	Sidon	*Sydon*
426	[gloss] et	&
	though	Though
427	but	But
428	that	That
443	onely	Onely
448	nor	Nor
479	nor	Nor
505	if	If
507	that	That
516	I'le	Ile
518	this	This
526	Neritus	*Nerytus*
532	and	&
537	rejoyce	Reioyce
539	if	If
551	and	&
575	Ilian	*Ilion*
583	combine	cõbine
588	thy	Thy
632	brown	brow
	and	&
638	a	A

Book 14

31	their	Their
36	three	Three
42	[gloss] latrandum	latrandū
	Odysseus	*Odyssæus*
91	a	A
94	and	And
101	Helen	*Hellen*
108	a	A
112	then	Then
113	sate	Sate
	and	&
136	but	But
145	Heroe	*Heroe*
148	no	No
150	I'le	Ile

152	no	No
158	an	An
166	[gloss] *Ulysses*	Vlysses
176	whose	Whose
177	Grecian	*Græcian*
230	I'le	Ile
243	I'le	ile
277	I'le	Ile
285	I'le	Ile
318	sad	Sad
335	Idomen	*Idomene*
371	and	&
408	Libya	*Lybia*
440	Pheidon	Phidon
443	where	Where
444	and	&
453	a	A
454	and	&
	and	&
463	if	If
496	thus-made scape	thus-made-scape
508	And	and
509	since	Since
515	which	w^{c}
522	I'le	Ile
525	circularly-witted	circularly witted
530	some	Some
534	Ætolian	*Etolian*
589	and	&
598	that	rhat
650	[gloss] μέγας αἰὲν	αιεν
	th'	Th'
651	Zephyr	*Zephyre*
658	I'le	Ile
668	Ilian	*Ilion*
703	no	No
710	We	we
714	whose	Whose
715	which	Which
722	fits	fit's
753	sharpe-edg'd	sharpe edg'd

Book 15

4	[gloss] possunt	possũt
21	too	to
39	I'le	Ile

61	chains	chain's
63	that	y^{t}
64	Night	night
78	Helen's	*Hellens*
80	on	On
86	My	[new paragraph in original]
87	[gloss] *Menelaus'*	*Menel.*
95	loves	loue's
96	likes	like's
98	which	Which
100	I'le	Ile
103	too	to
108	I'le	Ile
	and	&
117	[gloss] et	&
119	hop't-for	hop't for
133	Megapenthes	*Megapenthe*
151	presented	Presented
152	Heroe	*Heroe*
	Sidonia's	*Sydonia's*
156	Megapenthes	*Megapenthe*
158	Helen	*Hellen*
162	Helen's	*Hellens*
166	and	And
180	Eteoneus	*Eteonæus*
181	Megapenthes	*Megapenthe*
184	Portico	*Portico*
185	when	When
188	horse	Gods [Loane]
191	Ilian	*Ilion*
207	and	&
	a	A
214	[gloss] *his*	His
217	Helen	*Hellen*
219	[gloss] *Helen*	Hellen
230	[gloss] *Telemachus*	*Telem.*
	[gloss] *Helen*	*Hellen*
248	[gloss] *Telemachus*	*Telem.*
	[gloss] *Pisistratus*	*Pisist.*
249	We	we
265	his	His
267	Helen's	*Hellens*
273	that	That
274	all	All
282	while	While

286	to	To
301	Erinnys	*Erynnis*
314	Oicleus	*Oiclæus*
	Oicleus	*Oiclæus*
318	held	hel'd
	yet	Yet
322	Alcmæon	*Alcinaon*
324	but	But
340	by	By
344	nor	Nor
366	[gloss] *Telemachus'*	*Telem.*
383	Epean	*Epian*
389	their	Her
403	I'le	Ile
406	I'le	Ile
410	I'le	Ile
452	I'le	Ile
479	Ctimene	*Ctimie*
487	but	But
490	which	Which
507	from	From
	Pray	pray
512	set	Set
522	away	Away
527	and	&
537	and	&
544	and	&
551	Phœnicians	*Phænissians*
555	Phœnician	*Phænissian*
557	Phœnician	*Phænissian*
	layer	lai're
558	[gloss] admodum	admodũ
560	[gloss] et	&
568	Sidons	*Sydons*
587	to	To
593	I'le	Ile
595	I'le	Ile
603	she	She
	they	there [Loane]
608	Phœnician	*Phænissian*
609	brought	bought
620	Portico	*Portico*
630	Phœnician	*Phænissian*
631	tooke	Tooke
	and	And

632	waies	waues [Loane]
633	but	But
672	Whose	whose
676	I'le	Ile
684	I'le	Ile
685	that's	thats
701	this	This
709	and	&
711	[gloss] *Telemachus*	*Tele.*
	Piræus	*Pyræus*
	Clytius'	*Clytus*
712	[gloss] *Piræus*	*Pyræus*
716	and	&
719	[gloss] *Piræus'*	*Pyræus*
	If	if
720	I'le	Ile

Book 16

3	and	And
17	did	Did
18	both	Both
19	and	And
25–6	divin'd-So-much-for-forme	diuin'd So much for forme
26	divine-for-mind	diuine for mind
28	Whom	Whõ
40	[gloss] *and*	*&*
48	[gloss] *the*	*The*
52	from	From
55	saying	Saying
57	other	othet
65	when	When
67	Pray	pray
68	What	what
	seamen	seaman [Loane]
70	Who	who
71	I'le	Ile
73	and	And
77	I'le	Ile
79	to	To
90	or	Or
92	least	lest
95	I'le	Ile
97	fit	Fit
100	I'le	Ile

Textual Notes

108	although	Although
112	[gloss] *Telemachus*	*Telẽ.*
113	I'le	Ile
122	which	wͨ
127	Would	would
129	Yet-never-toucht	Yet neuer toucht
142	wrong'd	wrõg'd
	and	&
145	food	Food
149	I'le	Ile
151	nor	Nor
164	Dulichius	*Dulychius*
165	or	Or
182	[gloss] *Eumæus*	*Eum.*
183	[gloss] *Telemachus*	*Telem.*
186	Who	who
191	but	But
197	[gloss] *Telemachus*	*Telem.*
198	[gloss] *Eumæus*	*Eum.*
203	[gloss] *from*	*frõ*
209	[gloss] *Laertes*	*La rtes*
217	where	Where
220	utter	Vtter
223	affirming	Affirming
232	and	&
235	other	Other
241	[gloss] *Telemachus*	*Tele.*
252	some	Some
	[gloss] *Telemachus*	*Tel.*
261	and	And
264	[gloss] *Ulysses*	*Vlys.*
282	and	&
	and	&
289	and	&
295	I'le	Ile
302	all	All
310	and	&
315	[gloss] *Telemachus*	*Telem.*
316	[gloss] *Ulysses*	*Vlys.*
322	no	No
324	Dulichius	*Dulychius*
343	[gloss] *Ulysses*	*Vlys.*
344	[gloss] *Telemachus*	*Telem.*
348	[gloss] *Telemachus*	*Telemachu.*
356	strength	strengrh

378	I'le	Ile
379	and	&
398	which	$\overset{c}{\text{w}}$
400	and	And
407	not	Not
437	and	&
449	both	Both
454	to	To
459	when	When
475	when	When
477	[gloss] *other*	oth r
484	Eupitheus'	*Eupitheus*
490	for	For
491	but	But
500	too	to
505	and	&
528	and	And
533	Dulichius	*Dulychius*
559	[gloss] *Penelope*	*Penel:*
	[gloss] *Antinous*	*Antin.*
	Composde	composde
563	th'	Th'
572	Who	who
583	and	&
586	[gloss] *Eurymachus*	*Eurym:*
587	[gloss] *Penelope*	*Penel*
620	and	&
623	[gloss] *Telemachus*	*Telem.*
624	[gloss] *Eumæus*	*Eum.*
627	[gloss] *Eumæus*	*Eum.*
628	[gloss] *Telemachus*	*Telem.*

Book 17

5	[gloss] *Telemachus*	*Telem.*
6	[gloss] *Eumæus*	*Eum.*
16	[gloss] *Ulysses*	*Vlys.*
24	too	to
36	when	When
46	cast	Cast
50	[gloss] *Penelope*	*Penel.*
51	[gloss] *Telemachus*	*Telem.*
55	by	By
57	[gloss] *Telemachus*	*Telem.*
65	if	If

73	Piræus	*Pyræus*
83	in	In
94	Halitherses	*Halytherses*
95	and	And
97	Piræus	*Pyræus*
98	least	lest
101	[gloss] *Piræus*	*Pyræ.*
	Piræus	*Pyræus*
102	[gloss] *Telemachus*	*Telem.*
105	[gloss] *Telemachus*	*Telem.*
106	[gloss] *Piræus*	*Pyræ.*
108	Piræus	*Pyræus*
119	[gloss] *Penelope*	*Penel.*
120	[gloss] *Telemachus*	*Telem.*
132	[gloss] *Telemachus*	*Telemachu*
144	me	Me
146	Helen	*Hellen*
152	[gloss] *Menelaus*	*Men.*
153	[gloss] *Telemachus*	*Telem.*
205	[gloss] *Penelope*	*Penel.*
206	[gloss] *Theoclymenus*	*Theoc.*
218	[gloss] *calls*	*ca l*
227	and	&
230	twixt	Twixt
232	[gloss] *Eumæus*	*Eumæ.*
	[gloss] *Ulysses*	*Vlyss.*
241	[gloss] *Ulysses*	*Vlyss.*
	[gloss] *Eumæus*	*Eumæ.*
244	too	to
248	a	A
252	their	Their
262	in	In
277	who	Who
278	On	One
279	wretched	wrethed
302	I'le	Ile
310	if	If
316	[gloss] *Melanthius*	*Melan.*
331	[gloss] *Melanthius'*	*Melan.*
335	that	That
352	Phemius	*Phæmius*
403	nor	Nor
420	Ilian	*Ilion*
432	for	For
435	nor	Nor

451 of	Of
479 both	hoth
483 then	Then
489 Minerva's	*Mineruaes*
559 yet	Yet
560 too	to
561 [gloss] *Antinous*	*Altin.*
579 sent	Sent
588 not	Not
592 toiles	Toiles
611 themselves	thẽselues
615 if	If
626 Heare	heare
632 too	to
648 al wayes	alwayes [Loane]
651 but	But
697 [gloss] *Simile*	Simil.
[gloss] *in*	*In*
729 he	He
737 that	That
740 cote	Cote
747 and	And
756 brazen	brazẽ
764 for	For
768 What	what
Bringst	bringst
What	what

Tail-line

Seaventeenth	*Seauententh*

Book 18

6 in	In
20 charging	Charging
43 Whom	whom
66 not	Not
73 Man's owne-ill-working	Man's-owne-ill-working
79 and	&
88 I'le	Ile
92 when	When
94 prevented	preuẽted
106 but	But
110 which	Which
117 that	That
119 I'le	Ile

162 that	y[t]
177 one	One
178 Dulichius	*Dulychius*
220 and	&
234 and	&
249 and	&
252 and	&
258 and	&
264 and	&
Autonoe	*Antonoe*
266 not	Not
272 and	&
275 in	In
283 paces	places [Loane]
308 and	&
310 Thy	thy
311 but	But
315 so matchles	matchles
347 knees	Knees
349 [gloss] *Eurymachus'*	*Eurym.*
351 if	If
352 [gloss] *Queene*	*Qu ene*
363 [gloss] *Penelope's*	*Penel*
379 brave	Braue
386 or	Or
393 which	w[c]
418 Wise	wise
428 to	To
441 Pisander	*Pysander*
452 Three	3.
461 I'le	Ile
481 or	Or
490 I'le	Ile
494 every	Euery
504 fellows	fellow [Loane]
505 Fetcht	fetch
516 and	&
532 alike	Alike
535 againe	Againe
538 and	&
551 and	&
556 askt	Askt
563 Dulichian	*Dulychian*
570 when	When
577 [gloss] *Telemachus*	*Telem*

578 told	Told
580 bad	Bad
581 sit	Sit
591 nor	Nor
600 and	&
601 This	Thls

Book 19

3 when	When
4 We	we
5 and	&
11 and	&
12 say	Say
13 and	&
22 and	&
28 *draws*	*draw's*
29 Retaine	[new paragraph in original]
31 The	[no new paragraph in original]
41 see	See
48 [gloss] *though*	*Though*
50 And	and
51 bost	Best [Loane]
58 And	All
59 Are	And
74 Phœbe	*Phæbe*
76 the	The
107 too	to
116 your	Your
125 and	&
140 whence	Whence
and	&
142 Whence	whence
146 fairely-flowing	fairely flowing
148 first	First
151 to	To
153 long-liv'd	Long-liu'd
157 nothing	Nothing
158 well-order'd	well order'd
171 my	My
175 too	to
176 Ilian	*Ilion*
177 in	In
179 but	But
182 Dulichius	*Dulychius*
191 whom	whõ

218	not	Not
228	for	For
232	I'le	Ile
239	I'le	Ile
240	[gloss] *Ulysses'*	*Vlys:*
244	all-languag'd	all Languag'd
	there	There
248	Cnossus	*Gnossus*
251	both	Both
254	and	&
266	in	In
271	Idomen	*Idomene*
274	all	All
286	and	&
292	Zephyr's	*Zephyres*
	congeald	conceald [Loane]
304	but	But
316	a	A
317	on	On
334	the	The
338	brought	Brought
362	*wasts*	*wast's*
374	that	That
378	Thrinacrian	*Trinacryan*
393	Pheidon	*Phædon*
406	Dulichian	*Dulychian*
411	I'le	Ile
433	balmes	almes [Loane]
451	and	And
465	and	&
471	and	&
497	and	&
	whom	whõ
504	Cimmerian	*Cimmerean*
516	that	$\overset{t}{y}$
518	too	to
525	for	For
535	who	Who
542	white-tooth'd	white tooth'd
574	Parnassus	*Pernassus*
581	too	to
582	with all to-do	withall, to do [Loane]
588	five-yeares-old male	fiue-yeares old-male
592	no	No
611	nor	Nor
618	all	All

632 and	&
638 nor	Nor
639 by	By
647 her	Her
661 askt	Askt
673 but	But
680 that	That
692 he	she [Loane]
697 I'le	Ile
698 Rest's sweet Houre	*Rests sweete Houre*
713 Zethus'	*Zetus*
720 reverence	Reuerence
721 too	to
728 but	But
788 and	And
812 I'le	Ile

Book 20

Title	
TWENTIETH	TWENTITH
Argument	
3 *his*	*His*
Text	
3 and	&
13 high-fed	high fed
15 shee-Mastive	shee Mastiue
20 grew	Grew
30 when	whẽ
35 You	you
64 And	&
77 I'le	Ile
78 divers-languag'd	diuers languag'd
82 and	&
89 worthy wife	worthy-wife
113 Phœbe	*Phæbe*
121 the	The
122 and	&
124 yet	Yet
126 faire-hair'd	faire-chair'd [Loane]
149 who	Who
153 and	&
held-up	held vp
154 and	&
155 if	If

160	and	&
189	Vouchsafe	vouchsafe
191	[gloss] *and*	*&*
194	[gloss] *from*	*frõ*
203	to	To
225	left	Left
236	others	Others
239	for	For
247	many	Many
250	and	&
252	at	At
268	and	&
269	Porticos	*Porticos*
271	Still	still
273	Why	why
279	fast-footed	fast footed
283	Philœtius	*Philætius*
290	Philœtius	*Philætius*
292	and	&
296	Whence	whence
297	What	what
298	What	what
311	In	in
326	that	That
328	Cephallenian	*Cephalenian*
356	but	But
358	and	&
363	I'le	Il'e
389	fed-up	fed vp
392	Philœtius	*Philætius*
393	Melanthius	*Melanthus*
408	In	Iu
	Antinous	*Antinons*
435	Samian	*Samiane*
443	Guestes	Gustes
449	baths	bath's
456	the	The
465	and	&
473	see	See
478	nor	Nor
487	Friends	Friend [Loane]
492	As	as
502	daie	daies
517	that	That
	I'le	Ile

518	and	And
527	their	Their
531	hide	hides
535	full	Full
536	and	And
537	the	The
554	Piræus	*Pyræus*
561	for	For

Tail-line

Twentieth	*Twəntith*

Book 21

Argument

4	*Philœtius*	Philætius

Text

3	and	&
16	Eurytides	*Eurythides*
19	Ortilochus	*Ortilocus*
21	to	To
81	odoriferous	odorferous
82	nor	Nor
88	to	To
89	she	She
95	past	Past
96	she	She
104	my	My
111	arrow	aɹrow
118	Philœtius	*Philætius*
132	thought	Thought
151	Epirus	*Epyrus*
155	tender	Tender
165	but	But
173	on	On
179	and	&
180	thrice	Thrice
	and	&
189	or	Or
207	Leodes	*Liodes*
220	object	ohject
226	wow	now [Loane]
235	Leodes	*Liodes*
244	and	&
251	chaire	Chaire
266	to	to, to

291	I'le	Il'e
293	which	Which
304	And	and
316	Philœtius	*Philætius*
328	not	Not
335	that	That
336	for	For
360	decorum	*decorum*
369	or	Or
387	Centaur	*Centaure*
399	Centaurs	*Centaures*
400	But	but
401	as	As
424	Nor	nor
426	nor	Nor
437	And	and
447	[gloss] et	&
448	[gloss] coagmentatus	coagmentatis
451	every	Euery
455	that	That
460	no	No
481	one	One
482	rogue	Rogue
513	Philœtius	*Philætius*
514	Portico	*Portico*
535	With	with
539	as	As
558	but	But
	one	One
562	when	whē
567	Yet	yet
568	and	&

Book 22

Argument

1	*Minerva's*	Mineruaes
2	*all*	*All*

Another Argument

2	*and*	*&*

Text

3	which	w^{c}
4	and	&
14	and	&
58	for	For

105	sharpe-edg'd	sharpe edg'd
143	foure	4.
148	till	Till
157	two-leav'd	two leau'd
194	one	One
209	The	the
261	that	That
263	What	what
270	Wreake-offerings	Wreake offerings
271	Minerva's	*Mineruaes*
276	Helen's	*Hellens*
284	stand	Stand
300	Amphimedon	*Amphinomus* [Loane]
309	that	That
326	againe	Againe
336	and	And
	Philœtius	*Philætius*
337	Pisander	*Pysander*
341	which	w^{c}
356	Philœtius	*Philætius*
372	and	&
380	and	&
389	Ulysses	[new paragraph in original]
392	but	But
393	from	From
395	then	Then
403	and	&
405	Leodes	*Liodes*
418	them	thē
434	Phemius	*Phæmius*
471	Philœtius	*Philætius*
495	when	When
540	I'le	Ile
548	nor	Nor
560	clense	Clense
	and	&
564	vessells	vessell
571	Portico	*Portico*
572	then	Then
611	and	&
614	All-ill-expelling	All ill-expelling
620	but	But
624	to	too
626	and	&
629	and	&

Book 23

29 visual	vsuall
32 too-ill-to-speake-of	too-ill-to-speake of
69 and	&
85 and	&
106 nor	Nor
108 that	That
110 but	But
111 Your	your
112 And	and
113 I'le	Ile
129 Let's	Lets
133 or	Or
153 nor	Nor
156 that	That
160 amaze	Amaze
169 decorum	*decorum*
210 bath'd	Bath'd
216 commune	cõmune
218 that	That
228 and	&
231 in	In
260 nor	Nor
284 too	to
305 tooke	Tooke
315 and	&
317 then	Then
325 to	To
334 Helen	*Hellen*
341 that	That
347 no	No
365 and	&
379 but	But
417 there	There
425 Hecatombes	*Hectatombes*
429 to	To
438 parcell-gilt	parcell gilt
461 Cicons	*Cacons*
462 Lotophagi	*Lotophagie*
470 Læstrygonian	*Læstrigonian*
476 Theban	*Thebane*
478 his	His
479 Sirens'	*Syrens*
482 his	His
483 his	His

488 that	That
514 I'le	Ile
518 to	To
525 repose	tepose
528 to	To
530 op't	Op't
532 Aurora's	*Auroraes*

Book 24

Another Argument

Ω	ω

Text

11 so	So
13 None-hurting	*None-hurting*
25 Peleion	*Plebeian*
29 Ægisthus'	*Ægysthus*
50 thy	Thy
72 old much-knowing Nestor	old-much-knowing-*Nestor*
73 his	His
103 and	&
and	&
114 Menœtiades	*Mænetiades*
126 Heroes'	*Heroes*
127 but	But
154 all	All
158 his	His
215 nor	Nor
218 sand	sank
222 to	To
240 drew	Drew
266 and	&
292 they	he [Loane]
312 if	If
315 instant-told	instant told
332 Of	f
350 for	For
371 twelve	Twelue
385 th'unhappiest	Th' nhappiest
388 farre	Farre
452 her	your [Loane]
454 I'le	Ile
467 the	The
469 He	His
470 cicle	Circle
so	So

473	but	But
475	out	Out
486	now	Now
496	forth	Forth
512	Cephallian	*Cephalian*
547	and	&
553	bore	Bore
560	Eupeithes	*Eupitheus*
568	Cephallenia	*Cephalenia*
572	infamy	*infamy*
576	but	But
579	lest	let
583	them	thẽ
591	to	To
600	now	Now
629	Eupeithes	*Eupitheus*
633	Eupeithes	*Eupitheus*
641	if	If
644	Why	why
649	when	When
651	faithfull	Faithfull
652	for	For
664	bad	Bad
666	all	All
693	pray	Pray
696	he	He
699	Eupeithes'	*Eupitheus*
700	and	&
718	Abstaine	abstaine

Verses

2	*his*	*His*
7	*the*	*The*
	Colchian	Colchean
12	*Chanticheres*	Chanticheres
21	*Muse-vapours*	Muse-vapours
27	*when*	*When*
29	*his*	*His*
32	*Mackarell*	Mackarell
	Frankincence	Frankincence

To the Ruines of Troy and Greece

2	*Iliads*	*Ilyads*

Ad Deum

8	*and*	*&*
12	*nothing*	*Nothing*
17	*no*	*No*

COMMENTARY

COMMENTARY

Epistle Dedicatory

232 *Rout*	I am not sure of the proper reading here. The original has *'Rout: State* engrost,' but there seems to be no meaning of 'rout' which would fit an interpretation as 'Rout-State engrost.' It seems best to treat 'rout' as a verb.

Book 1

76 *convert*	In the sense of 'be converted, turned': 'may all the pains . . . be turned . . . to revenge.'
94 *this homelesse-driven*	'This man driven about away from his home.'
99 *Manage . . . home*	Textual corruption is to be suspected here. The general sense down to this line is: 'Calypso . . . always pouring forth her soft and winning speeches which have the effect of abusing Ulysses' mind, of making him languish, of setting back his thoughts of return.' But the word 'manage' will not fit in here.
104 *converted on his thrall*	'Turned, or made to desist, from making him your victim.'
116 *That holds . . . knees*	Neptune.
140 *Argicides*	Mercury.
154 *epithete*	Because it gives the adjective to Pylos.
167–8 *if her ire . . . inflame*	'If their crimes arouse her anger.'
385 *now*	Loane suggests that this is in error for 'wow,' meaning 'woo'; and it is likely that his suggestion is correct. I have, however, retained 'now,' since it gives perfect sense.

Book 2

47 *thus*	Loane suggests the deletion of this word, for the sake of the rhythm.
308 *Gods*	Loane proposes to read 'goods.'.

Book 3

106 *which*	Refers back to the device. 'Girlonds' here practically means 'objects.'
210 *time's*	Loane proposes to read 'home's,' which is probably correct.
216–8 *Which were . . . flie*	There is probably corruption here. The folio reads 'men' in l. 216 and this agrees with 'were'; but the reference seems definitely to be to Ulysses, here, as in l. 217.
258 *farre off dwellers*	This should possibly be hyphenated; it means, of course, 'you who dwell so far off from his home.'
302 *their seeking marriages*	'The marriage that they seek.'
425 *his affrighting fate*	Almost signifies 'to his alarm and destined to bring death to him.'
461 *light . . . date*	'The sun has set and the light has ended.'

Book 4

83 *They . . . plac't*	If the text is right, it is hard to see precisely what Chapman intends—unless he means 'they saw that the food on the table was set for them.'
93–4 *How many . . . sights*	'To what infinite admiration are not all men aroused by seeing it.'
168 *ribd*	Loane suggests reading 'rimm'd' or 'brim'd.'
231 *Inhabited about*	In this rather difficult construction Chapman was evidently following Spondanus—'una urbe euacuata earum, Quae circum habitantur.'
551 *take all the sights of*	'Scrutinise.'
576 *firme at every force*	'Steadfast on all occasions.'
802 *men-fed*	'Men-feeding,' i.e., 'which feeds men.'
898 *his Father saf't*	It is to be suspected that 'saf't' comes in here simply because of the need of a rime for 'craft.' The phrase seems quite meaningless, although Chapman may have thought he was saying 'for his father whom he hoped he would find saved.'
1114–5 *the men . . . be*	This also is obscure. Perhaps Chapman intends: 'the men accompanying him who may become his enemies.'

1124 *thy delight's defeate*	'The trouble that destroys your happiness.'

Book 5

35 *addresse*	Loane suggests reading 'redresse,' but the construction may well be Chapman's, in the sense of: 'apply himself to the wrongs the wooers have done him.'
140 *roy*	Loane suggests reading 'coy,' but 'roy' may be used for 'king.'
335 *they*	Loane proposes reading 'she,' but Chapman may be thinking of Calypso and her maids.
591 *Callicoe's flood*	It has been noted that Chapman has here created a name for a river not named in Homer. The text reads: ποταμοῖο κατὰ στομα καλλιρόοιο 'against the mouth of a fair-flowing river.' Evidently the poet took καλλιρόοιο as a proper name (although the Latin is 'pulcrifluentis'); presumably he wrote 'Calliroe.'

Book 6

54 *ow'st thy selfe a race*	This apparently means: 'You acknowledge yourself born of this country.'
121–3 *did more . . . not seen*	A typical tortured sentence: 'the waters were the better able to remove stains the more stains were washed away by their purity.'
164 *his return advance*	'Find means for his returning to his home.'
191 *in his beasts' attempt*	'In attempting to slay his (i.e., the herdsman's) cattle.'

Book 7

48 *they cut . . . thought*	Chapman's rather strained rendering, meaning that they are like birds in flight, swift as thought.
126 *knowing inwards*	'Skilful mind.'
171 *A large . . . had*	It is to be suspected that there is something wrong with the text here.
267–8 *under hand . . . deduction*	'By the means we provide to send him home.'
310–11 *will not . . . wound*	Presumably 'kind' means 'nature' and hence 'body,' the phrase signifying: 'will not grievously injure their bodies.'

362 *on her stayes*	'By her forcible detention.'
414 *grow*	Loane wishes to read 'glow,' but one may believe that Chapman intended 'blood' to mean 'strength'—and, if so, 'grow' is right.

Book 8

36–7 *doth beare . . . Peere*	'Wishes to put it forward for the consideration of every peer.'
398 *bespent*	Loane would read 'besprent,' but the original gives perfectly good sense.
457–8 *That which . . . end*	Presumably meaning: 'that which occasioned them to declare that no impious action can conclude fortunately.'
476 *watry state*	'Lord of the seas,' Neptune.

Book 9

56 *with horror*	Presumably applied to Ulysses—'against my will.'
238 *ten onely mine*	'Mine alone being granted ten goats.'
457 *made*	Loane is probably right in suggesting that Chapman wrote 'bade' here, but I have retained 'made' since it makes sense.

Book 10

558 *gash*	Loane proposes to read 'dash,' but this seems to be a typical Chapman construction.

Book 11

3 *Up our sailes*	Loane is no doubt right in thinking that 'our sailes' is an error for 'our selues.'
175 *onely-earnest-prayr-vow'd*	No doubt 'pray' should be, as Loane thinks, 'pray'r.'
457–8 *all you . . . doth us*	'You all share in the renown his visit brings us.'
753 *in thine owne One*	It is strongly to be suspected that the text is corrupt here.

791–4 *offring to enforce . . . Panopeus* — 'Offring' refers to Tityus, 'his love' is 'Jove's beloved'; 'in the close recourse she usde' evidently means 'as she was going secretly.'

839 *in this heart* — This does not seem to give good sense and the text may be corrupt.

Book 12

194 *Ile Triangulare* — Translating 'Thrinacriam . . . ad insulam'—Θρινακρίην δ' ἐς νῆσον. Evidently Chapman believed the word came from τρεῖς ἄκραι.

517–8 *They took . . . eminent* — Seemingly 'took of sence' means 'killed.'

Book 13

178–9 *since he . . . Minerva* — 'Since he showed so much wisdom.'

541 *my sav'd decease* — A strained phrase evidently meaning 'to me, saved from death.'

596 *wife* — Loane conjectures that we should read 'wise' here.

Book 14

138–41 *There is . . . spoile of* — 'No day passes but they profane by killing, not merely one or two beasts, but many.'

506 *chang'd relation* — Presumably meaning: 'the other part of your story.'

621–2 *of that King . . . string* — I am not sure of the exact construction here, but the general sense is obvious.

Book 15

393–6 *To try . . . to Towne* — 'To try if he still wanted him to remain there or if he would urge him to go to the city.'

506 *of a little one* — 'From the time you were a child.'

510–11 *Where dwelt . . . there* — 'Where dwelt your father and mother and where you were spared' is apparently the sense.

Book 16

184 *all in one yet* — Apparently meaning 'in spite of what you have said.'

248–9 *the springtide . . . kist* — 'He kissed the cheeke from which a flow of tears continuously poured on the earth.'

Book 18

157–8 *had cleer'd their cost . . . morsell*	In former editions 'cost' is changed to 'coast,' but the sense is more likely to be 'cleared them of the cost, or expense.'
186–7 *that abode . . . overthrowes*	The general sense is clear but the particular construction is almost inexplicable.
191 *While any . . . knee*	'While they have power to move.'
193 *That fled . . . hart*	I take this to mean: 'who act irreligiously as if they were deprived of human faculties.'
248–9 *With good advise . . . guise*	This is no doubt intended to be a direct rendering of Eurynome's words in the original: 'What you say is good. Go and speak to your son and do not make any concealment.'
303 *above the cleere*	'Beyond any unveiled display.'
442 *Casket*	Loane proposes to read 'Carknet.'

Book 19

18–19 *As all . . . Armes*	'For ever since that time the fires have been shining on these weapons.'

Book 20

145–9 *when the King . . . there*	This is a typically involved sentence: all that Homer says and Chapman means is that Ulysses hears her weeping and thinks that even now she knows him and stands at his head.
285–7 *for they . . . there*	It is to be feared that Chapman quite misunderstood this passage: the reference is simply to ferrymen.
327–30 *and when . . . youth*	Something seems to be wrong here: the meaning is simply that as a lad Philœtius was made an ox-herd by Ulysses.

Book 21

232–3 *and then . . . right*	'Returned to his seat.'

Book 22

306 *Fouls*	I assume here that 'Fouls' is 'fowls,' i.e. 'birds of prey, vultures'; but the phrase is a peculiar one.

Book 24

51 *with some worth forgot* — Perhaps Chapman misconstrued the original: 'oblitus equitatus' as it appears in Spondanus — λελασμένος ἱπποσυνάων.

369 *pots* — Loane conjectures that this should be 'plots.'

591–2 *To whose ears . . . theirs* — It is to be suspected that the text is corrupt here.

GLOSSARY

GLOSSARY

[Like the glossary to the *Iliads,* this glossary to the *Odysses* is intended merely as a guide for the reader. No attempt has been made to list all the words that Chapman uses in peculiar senses. Those words or meanings which I have not found recorded before 1614–15, as well as some characteristic usages, are marked by an *.]

abet	support, uphold
abject	low; low-lying, despicable, worthless
able	endow with strength (but in 12. 413 'thou ablest us to' the sense seems to be rather 'you force us beyond our weaker powers')
abode	forebode
abodes	1) fates
	2) abidings, stays (as in 3. 471, 'provokt thus their abodes')
	* 3) place of stay (as in 13. 166 'bore no abodes for earthy men' i.e. mortal men were prohibited from staying or entering there)
abstinent	one who abstains, one who fasts
acceptation	acceptance
access	1) approach, arrival
	* 2) gateway, entrance hall
accessless	* inaccessible, that cannot be reached
accomplished	complete, perfect
accost	approach, draw near
act	put into act
active	* suited or fitted for action (as in 1. 166, active lance)
addiction	inclination
address	1) make ready, prepare
	2) advance, direct (one's course)
address	* tone, tenour (as in 16. 552, 'the whole addresse Knew of their counsailes')
addressed	made ready, prepared
addression	* 1) direction of one's course
	* 2) action of going to a place
adherent	follower, supporter
admire	wonder at
advance	further, promote, aid

adventure		venture (in 17. 375 'adventure me' means almost 'let me remain')
advise		notify, warn
aesture	*	swelling tide
affect		show an inclination or liking for
affection		passion, emotion, desire
affects		emotions, passions
afflict	*	(There is no sense of the word in *NED* which explains 'whatever came in reach of hand or hook the belly's flame afflicted to it,' where it appears to mean 'attracted' i.e. made them seize it)
agreement		harmony
aid		1) assistance 2) assistant, ally
alienation		madness
ambassadress		female ambassador
ambient	*	revolving
ambrosian	*	divinely fragrant (as in 'th' ambrosian shade of night'; Chapman here perhaps has the sense of 'immortal' in mind)
amplify		increase
anger		make angry
annoy		vexation, trouble, grief
apaid (appaid)		satisfied, content
appal		shock, dismay
apply		set oneself closely to, pursue
appose		place in front of
apprehensive		capable of apprehending, perceptive
approbation		approval
arbitry		decision, award
arew		in a row
arrive		arrival
arrowy	*	full of arrows (as in 'arrowy quiver')
artfully		with skill
artificial		artful, artistic
artires	*	arteries, used for ligaments
artist	*	artificer, craftsman (used for Vulcan)
artly	*	skilful, ingenious
ascent	*	1) going up or reaching shore
	*	2) high pitch (apparently in 'which . . . Ulysses amplified to this ascent')
assay		endeavour
associate		associate with
assume		take up, carry, bear
assumpt		assumption

asteep		steeped
attain		arrive, reach
attone		atone, unite, make one
attraction	*	speech (as in 24. 189 'with this attraction')
augur		seer, diviner; used for Apollo
austere	*	fierce (of dogs)
author		originate, instigate, be responsible for (used also as in 15. 321, 'two sonnes author'd his posterity')
author		one who originates anything
avail		worth, estimation
bace		run
baine		bain, bath (at 10. 567 'in severall baine' means 'each in a bath')
banquetants	*	This sounds as though it should mean 'banqueter' but it is a rendering of the original 'feasts'
bawdrick		belt
beamy		bright, shining
beat		cheapen (as in 15. 613, 'the price beat')
bedfere		bedfellow
behave	*	behaviour
bent		inclination
besides	*	(Used as an adjective in 21. 169, 'to their besides possession' i.e. possession by anyone else)
besogne	*	rogue, low worthless fellow
bespent	*	spent, devoted to (as at 8. 398)
bestowed	*	(Used as adjective in 17. 311, 'his bestowed staffe' i.e. the staff he might bestow on a person)
bever		evening meal
bevy		company
bewraid		made known, displayed
bewray		make known, display, reveal
bird-eyd	*	(In the gloss 12. 126,14 this seems to mean 'timorous')
birth		offspring, child
bits and knocks	*	(There is a peculiar use of this phrase in 4. 724, 'gave him bits and knocks,' meaning 'slew him')
bitted	*	provided with bits (of a key)
bittour		bittern
blame		fault, culpability
blanch		put a fair appearance on
blatter		speak volubly, blazon
blore		1) blast of wind
	*	2) air (as in 4. 1138)
board		accost, address

boot	booty
bord	(see board)
born	borne
bounder	that which bounds
bracks	1) broken parts 2) rags, tatters
braid	brayed, chewed up
brave	well-clad, gallantly dressed
brave	boast
brawn	hog
bray	chew or pound up
breeze	gadfly
broad house, in	* openly
brouse	brose
brow, without a	* shameless
browse	fodder for animals
brush	* buffet (as in 14. 540)
bubble	* idle, worthless opinion
built	build (as in 11. 146, 'of forreigne built')
bursten	burst, bursting
butleress	* female butler
cantles	portions, parts
capital	most serious
care-nurse	nurse of care (applied to night in 5. 627)
cast	pair (of eagles)
catches	fastenings on a robe
cates	delicacies
cavill	* cavil, insulting speech
cavy	* formed of a cave
censure	opinion
character	essential nature
chist	chest, treasury
cincture	* circumference, enclosure
circular	perfect
circularly-witted	* most wise
circumfluous	* surrounded by water, sea-girt
circumvent	outwit, 'get round,' beguile
cliffy	having cliffs
close	* 1) closure (of a door) * 2) lock
close	secret
clout	beat
coarse	corse
coats	cotes (sheep-cotes)

coily	*	coyly, disdainfully
collection	*	accumulation (as in 1. 104, gloss, where 'generall collection' seems to mean the general run of human misfortune)
commixtion		mixture
commodity		thing of use
commune		common
compell		(In 21. 360 'doth compell this daye's observance' ought to mean 'decrees that for today the archery should cease')
composure		composition
conceit		1) think of, consider 2) think highly of
conceit		idea, concept
conclude		1) include, comprise 2) end
confer		1) talk, hold conversation 2) compare
confine		put an end to, terminate
confirm		strengthen
confirmance		confirmation, strengthening
confluence		flowing together
consent	*	(In 21. 67 'in their consent' refers to the close meeting together of two leaves of a door)
consent to	*	(In 16. 435 'consented to' ought to mean 'conferred with' or 'gave advice to')
considerate		prudent
consort		1) associate oneself with (as in 'consorting the design for Ilion' = 'joining in the Trojan expedition')
	*	2) summon into association (as in 2. 9)
consort		1) company
	*	2) companion, associate
conspicuity		conspicuousness
contain		hold back
contempt	*	contemptuous remark, critical objection
contend to		strive for
contention		striving
continent	*	(In 12. 323 'the Continent that all our spirits convaid' the word means 'ship,' a special sense not covered in the *NED*)
continuate		continuing, long enduring
contracting		summarising, epitomising
convent	*	(In 13. 540 'convent my person home' the word seems to mean 'convey')
convert		turn

cope	covering ('cope of light' is the heavens)
core	heart
cormorand	cormorant; greedy person
cornish	cornice
cote	outstrip, pass by
counterfeit	(In 8. 685 used for the Trojan horse i.e. something other than it seemed)
countermine	(There is a peculiar use of the word at 4. 535, 'countermine with God' i.e. contend secretly with)
court	* majesty
cow-herd	coward
cresset	torch
crown	fill to overflowing
cruse	container for oil
curious	painstaking, artful, ingenious
cypers grass	galingale
dancery	* dancing
date	period, limit of a period (The phrase 'in long date dead' means 'dead long ago')
deaded	benumbed
decipher	indicate, reveal
decline	1) turn aside (In 21. 392 'did decline other Heroes from him . . . with so much anger' means 'so much angered the others'; in 4. 470 'decline a thought' signifies 'leave one thought out') 2) bend down, lower (as in 5. 66, 'with which he declin'd the eyes of any waker' i.e. put them to sleep)
deduction	* sending or guiding back, conveyance home
deedless	inactive
deepsome	* deep
defame	dishonour, disgrace
defer	postpone
degenerately	* in a degenerate manner
deified	divine
deject	cast down
dejection	* lamentation
delayful	delighting in delay
delicious	delicate
depeople	depopulate, kill the people off
deplore	weep, grieve
depopulation	* laying waste, ravaging
depose	put down, back or aside
deprave	detraction, defamation

depraver	one who defames, scorner
descent	progeny, offspring
desert	deserted, abandoned
desert, have	deserve
desertful	deserving, meritorious
desherit	disherit (q.v.)
deviceful	ingenious, artfully fashioned, full of devices
dide	dyed
difference	(In 4. 337 applied to a disguised appearance—'through all this difference')
different	distinguished from others
digest	* (In 16. 558 'which she digested thus' almost means 'which she thus expressed or phrased')
dignified	* rendered worthy
disbord	* disboard, disembark
disease	trouble, unrest
disease	put out of ease, waken (a sleeper)
diseased	tired out, wearied
disgrace	be unkind to
dishelm	take off one's helmet
disherit (desherit)	* (In 9. 3 'desherit' = 'disherit' is used for taking something away from the joy of a feast)
dislive	deprive of life, kill
dismal	terrible, dire
disperple	sprinkle
display	see, discern, view
dissite	lying or situate apart
dissolve	1) cut, set free 2) soften (as in 4. 1072, where 'dissolving humor' is applied to sleep)
dissundered	separated, divided
disterminate	* separated, set far apart
distinguisher	* one who singles out a person for special aid
distractions	conflicting thoughts
distrustful	suspicious, incredulous
diversory	way-side inn
divined	made divine
doctrinal	instructive
domage	damage, injury, misfortune
doom	decision, decree
dop-chick	dab-chick
doubtless	free from doubt or fear
down	keep or put down
dread	dreariness, gloom (In 1.403 'watrie dreads' means 'terrible wastes of waters')

drench	drown
drift	current, moving mass (as in 3. 410, 'drift of waves')
dubbed	smeared with fat
dwarfy	dwarfish
eager	keen, biting
earthy	earthly, mortal; dwelling on earth
egregious	prominent
egregiously	a great deal, much, excessively
egression	departure from or entry into
eine	eyne, eyes
election, in our	at our discretion
elephant	ivory
embossed	foaming at the mouth
embrew	imbrue (q.v.)
embrodery	embroidery
empair	impair (q.v.)
empale	impale (q.v.)
empall	cover or surround as with a cloak
empery	sovereign authority
enable	strengthen, make competent or capable
enchace	* enshrine, enclose
enchac't	enchased, set as a jewel
encounter	* (There is no sense in the *NED* that covers the use of this word in 7. 136, 'encounter feast with houswifry,' where it seems to mean 'supplement')
endless	eternal, immortal
endue	indue (q.v.)
enflame	set on fire
enflower	adorn with flowers
enforce	(It is hard to determine what sense the word has in 22. 89, 'enforcing all their feares'—possibly 'strengthening')
enform	inform (q.v.)
enfranchise	set free
engine	(Applied to the Trojan horse, 'device' or 'contrivance')
enginous	ingenious
engross	1) heap up * 2) cover (as by writing—17. 29, 'so much ground is to be engrost by my poore feete') 3) occupy entirely

engrost	engrossed
ensphere	* encircle, enclose
enstild	(In all probability the word signifies 'enstyled' in 21. 134, 'his hopes enstild his strength the stretcher of Ulysses' string' i.e. his hope nominated him the person strong enough to draw Ulysses' bow)
entercourse	intercourse (q.v.)
entire	complete
entitle	bestow as a title, give a title
entreat	treat, deal with
envy	1) feel ill will towards 2) grudge, deny
equal	just, impartial
equity	sense of justice
erected	uplifted (as in 'erected voice,' 12. 268)
err	1) deviate from 2) wander
error	wandering
error-driven	* driven wandering
eruption	issuing or bursting forth
estrang'd	(The sense in 4. 1115 is difficult to determine; possibly it means 'become his enemies')
eternify	make eternal
eternise	* make eternal
ethereal	* heavenly
event, have	apply to
exciteful	* likely to excite or arouse
excruciate	* tormented, tortured
exempt	cut or pick out
exempt	removed from (in 6. 35 'from comparison exempt' means 'beyond comparison')
exhale	breathe out
expect	wait for
expectance	state of waiting
expire (exspire)	breathe out
exposure	action of leaving without shelter; casting out, driving forth
expressive	* concerned with expression (as in 19. 648, 'her part expressive' i.e. her mouth)
expressor	* one who expresses, poet
expressure	* expression, revelation
expugn	overpower, wipe out
expugner	razer (of a city)
exquire	search out, seek out, explore
exspire	expire (q.v.)

extracts	chief parts drawn from anything
extreme	extremity, dire strait
extreme, stand so	be so utterly opposed
fact	deed, action
faculties	means, resources, property
fame	report
familiar	friend, associate
fantasies	(In 4. 391 the sense is almost that of 'desires')
fantastic	born of the fantasy, unreal
farrow	bring forth
far-shot	far shooting
fatal	fated, destined by fate
faultful	faulty, culpable
fawn	fawning
fawn	* entice by fawning or sweet trickery
fearful	timid
feastful	* worthy of a banquet
feed	encourage
fel, fell	skin
fervency	* intensity, severity
fetch	reach, arrive at
fewell	fuel
fibres	fivers (q.v.)
fictive	fictitious
fil'd	filed, refined, polished
file	defile
fill	satisfaction, repletion
fish for	seek, angle for
fishy	abounding in fish
fivers (fibres)	* sinews
flat	prosaic, uninspired
flaw	* rolling wave
flea	flay
fled	avoided, feared
flitting	* rolling, constantly moving
fluent	flowing
fly	* 1) fail to reach 2) escape
foil	overthrow, injury
foody	supplying food
footmanship	skill in walking or running
forceful	* powerful, strong
fore-gale	* favouring wind
foreright	right forwards (of winds)

foresend		send before
forewhile	*	intervening time
forewind	*	favouring wind
forger	*	cheat (used for Proteus in 4. 609)
frame		action of shaping or framing
fray'd		fraid, frightened
free		(In 24. 659 'the Free' is used for Minerva, meaning 'the noble goddess')
freight		freighted, laden
frequent		common, frequently seen
frontless		shameless, audacious
froofe	*	handle of an auger
fruit		offspring
fruition		pleasurable possession
fulsome		nasty
fume		anger
gaberdine		coarse cloak or smock
gables		cables
gadbee		gadfly
gadding		wandering, straying
gasp	*	breath of wind
gate, at		outside a house, not bidden to come in
gaze, at		(The phrase, as in the *Iliads,* suggests a state of silent wonder or contemplation)
gere		(In 21. 15 'sighing gere' evidently means 'sighing gear' and seems to be intended to mean 'arrows winged for death' i.e. weapons that cause sighs)
girlond		garland, crown
glad		make glad
glibness		glossiness, slipperiness
glister		glitter
glorious		1) vain-glorious, boasting 2) seeking glory
glose		speak fair, flatter, deceive
glose		flattery, deceit
gobbets		pieces
grace of, in		having in view, for the prosecution of
grave		heavy, ponderous
gray	*	gray-eyed
greavie		gravy
green		fresh, new
grone		groan
grought		growth
guard		guarding

guestive	* suitable for guests
guide	guiding, guidance
gulphie	gulfy, with gulfs or pools
halser (halster)	hawser
hard-hit	hard to recognise (of a face disguised)
haulk	hawk
hearby	herby (q.v.)
hearers	* ears
hearty	1) heart-felt
	* 2) vigorous, vehement, keenly animated
heavy	sorrowing, sorrowful
helm	handle
herby	1) full of herbs, grassy
	* 2) made of herbs
heroess	female hero
heroical	heroic
het	heated, warmed
high-gone	high-going (of the sun)
high-spoke	speaking high or shrilly
hin-deck	hind deck, rear deck
hir	her
hire	reward, prize
hoise (hoice)	hoist
homicide	killer of men (used in the phrase 'homicide of warre' for Mars)
honorary	* honouring gift
humorous	watery, moist
hyacinthian	* pertaining to the hyacinth
idol	image, figure
ignorant	ignorant person
ilander	islander
ile	1) isle
	2) aisle, alley
illation	conclusion, deduction
illustrate	illuminate, light up
illustrated	illuminated
illustrious	glowing with light
imbost	embost, covered with foam
imbrew (embrew)	sprinkle
immane	monstrous, cruel
immartial	1) not trained for war
	* 2) peaceable

impair (empair)	injure, hurt
impale (empale)	encircle, surround
imply	1) twist round (of a veil) 2) involve
impose	place or put in or on
impostorous	* full of imposture
imprest	1) enlisted, compelled to serve 2) imprinted
impudency	shamelessness
impulsion	impulse
in	inner
inaccessible	1) beyond reach 2) invincible
incense	set on fire
incessancy	* unbroken continuance
incline	concern, apply to
inclose	put in harness
incorruptible	that cannot decay
indecent	unbecoming
induction	introduction
indue (endue)	put on, dress
inexciteable	* from which one cannot be roused
influent	* (There is apparently an unrecorded sense in the 'influent stone' of the Dedication, where the phrase is applied to a magnet)
infold	enclose, cover
inform (enform)	* 1) delineate, describe 2) gain information regarding
infortune	misfortune
infuse	bring or pour into
infusion	imparting of divine (poetic) concepts
ingenious	having genius
ingenuous	frank, honest
ingression	entry, entrance
innative	native
inquest	search
in-room	inner room
instant	pressing, insistent
instill	produce
instruct	put in order, equip
insultance	* insulting speech
integuments	wrappings (of a beggar)
intend	1) attend to, superintend 2) signify, have for its purpose
intentively	heedfully, intently

intercourse (entercourse)	*	(There is a peculiar use of the word in the Argument to Book 8: 'the entercourse of acts,' where the phrase seems to mean no more than 'the series of actions')
interest		to invest with a share in (as in 15. 326, 'interested him amongst the Gods')
interminate		interminable, very lengthy
interprease	*	interpose, intercept, intervene
inveagle (inveigle)		beguile, deceive
invert		(In 17. 61 'so apt t' invert' seems to mean 'so apt to be changed')
invitement		invitation
iterate		repeat
jejune	*	flat, poor, uninteresting
jet		strut
junkets		sweetmeats
justle	*	(There is a peculiar unrecorded sense in 19. 229, 'justl'd out of stone' i.e. produced by chance out of a poor stock)
justs		games, tournaments
keel		ship
keep in	*	dwell in, have residence in
keeps	*	fastenings on a robe
kerve		carve
kind		nature
kitling		kitten
knit	*	project (as in 21. 241, 'knitting shafts off' i.e. projecting arrows)
laborious		hard-working, strong
laboursome		hard-working
lackey		go on foot
lanch		launch
land-leaper		vagabond
leager	*	(Used in 17. 285 as a term of abuse in 'victles Leager,' which evidently means, more or less, 'scrounger')
league	*	(In 10. 214 used for a continuous rope placed round a hart)
learned		well-instructed, skilful
least		lest
lengthful		lengthy, long

let		hindrance
liberal		unrestrained (as in 'liberall safetie')
lien		lain
lift		lifted
light		day (as in 'all this light')
liking	*	(There appears to be no recorded sense that fits 6. 142, 'Nausicaa . . . the liking stroke strooke')
linage		lineage
list		wish
liver		living creature (as in 5. 274, 'be a liver ever' i.e. be immortal)
lode		load
loiterer		vagabond
lote		lotus
lust		wish
luster	*	den, cave
magnitude		magnanimity
main		sea
maine		(In 11. 459 this may be intended for 'meane' = 'means' or else refer to 'main' in the sense of 'main object')
maisteries		masteries (q.v.)
mall		beat
manless		inhuman, brutal
mann'd		(It is almost impossible to determine what is meant, in 19. 114, by the phrase 'lest your spirit thus mann'd and cherisht with your beauties.' Perhaps Chapman intends: 'lest your pride, encouraged now because wooers flock to you on account of your beauty')
marine		of the sea
maritimal		of the sea
market sted		market place
massie		massive
masteries with, try		exercise skill on, play tricks with
mate		check, oppose, confront
maund		basket
mechanical		mechanic
men-fed		eaten by men
mere (meere)		entire, whole, pure
merely (meerely)		entirely
mervail		marvel, sense of wonder
metalline	*	relating to metals (as in 23. 234, 'arts metalline')
mind	*	significance, meaning

Minerva	* wisdom
misease	distress, discomfiture, pain
miss	absence, loss
miss	want, require
mixtion	mixing, mixture
mix with	(In 19. 243 'Cities . . . mixt with all-languag'd men' means 'inhabited diversely by men of many tongues')
moan	lament for
moist	* of the sea (as in 6. 311, 'moist man')
moist	sea
moly	fabulous herb (μῶλυ)
mote	* (In 4. 690, 'the rough waves of the world's vast mote' is hard to interpret; perhaps 'mote' is used in the sense of 'motion' and thence transferred to 'sea')
naked	bare (as in 'naked truth' i.e. actual fact)
native	(In 9. 66 'from our native' may refer back to 'roofs,' but it looks as though Chapman is using the word for 'native country' or 'home')
natural	native
nave	central block of a wheel (see Chapman's gloss to 19. 55)
neesing	sneezing
nephew	grandson
noiseful	full of noise, noisy
object	put over against, place before
obliquely	* (In the Dedication this word seems to have an unrecorded sense of 'evilly' in 'madness obliquely and degenerately proceeding from man')
obscureness	obscurity, darkness
observe	keep, retain
observed	* well worthy observation, beautiful
occurrent	occurrence, fact
ocular	performed by the eye (In 15. 610 'this had ocular view' means 'this was seen')
odd	1) peculiar, rare 2) unequalled, peerless
odoriferous	sweet-smelling, fragrant
Odyssean	* having the characteristics of Odysseus; wise, skilful
officious	busy
often	(In 19. 106 'with often hand' means 'with open hand,' i.e. giving alms frequently)

omnisufficient	* fitting in all things
one-hooved	(Used in the sense of 'whole-hooved' = whole-hoofed)
only (onely)	alone
opportune	fit, convenient
opposite	opposed, in opposition
opposure	opposition
op't	opened, displayed
optimate	prince, potentate
oraculous	oracular
ore	oar
ossifrage	* osprey
ostent	prodigy, omen
ostentful	* full of omen
other	(Frequently used for 'others')
outstrive	get the better of
overbring	* bring over (in sense of 'relate,' 'tell,' 'carry news')
overcome	complete, bring to an end
overcrow	crow or exult over
owe	own, possess
ower	oar
painted	adorned, resplendent
pale	frontier, rampart, fence
paramore	paramour
parcel-gilt	* glittering shimmer (used of torch-light radiance)
paring	refuse (In 22. 574 'paring shovels' are shovels with which to clean floors)
parricide	one who slays a relation
pass	come on (almost in sense of 'deserve')
pass	passport, allowance or permission to pass
past	surpassing
penury	(In 16. 45 'in penury of' means 'in want of')
period	course of time (Chapman uses this word usually in the plural and often gives it the sense of 'time that has come to an end'—as in 'periods of all thy labours' i.e. destined ends and 'past periods' i.e. enduring endlessly or for a very long time)
perspicuity	clarification, lucidity
petulant	insolent, rude
phane	fane
phrase	* perform (of a musical dance)
pile	point of a weapon
pinch	afflict, harass
placeful	* in their proper place
plainer	plane

plebeian	commonplace or vulgar person
plight	physical condition
plume	pluck the feathers from
policy	scheme, stratagem
pompous	splendid, magnificent
popular	of public resort, hence unruly
porous	* (Apparently in 14. 200 'porous skin' means 'skin having pores')
port	fine appearance
portly	majestic, imposing
pourvaid	purveyed, furnished with food
prease	press, press on
prease	crowd
precinct	quarters (for sheep)
prefer	put forward, advance (In 14. 337 'so prefer'd was . . . the rumour' means 'the people's voice was so strong')
premonition	notification
presage	prognostication
prest	1) ready 2) hired or pressed into service
presume to	dare to go to
pretie	(In 5. 353 'did a pretie figure yeeld' 'pretie' seems to be 'pretty,' but the sense of the Greek is 'dark' or 'shadowy')
prevention	* (In 9. 69 the sense seems to be 'command' or 'anticipatory action'—the reverse of the familiar significance)
prey-professor	* one who professes to seek prey (translating ἀγελείη 'driver of the spoil')
priority	precedence, preeminence
private	* private sailor
prize	booty ('Men of prize' are 'pirates')
profest	(In 13. 381 'profest men for the race' means 'men who are acknowledged to be excellent runners')
profuse	pour forth, waste
profuse of	full of, lavish of
proin	prune
proller	prowler, vagabond
propagate	multiply, spread (In the Dedication 'life doth into Ages propagate' means 'eternises')
propitiate	inclined to plead
proposition	concept, 'thesis' of a work
proser	* prosaic critic

proud	luxuriant
proud, make	make polished, clean (of tables)
prove	1) try, attempt 2) be shown
provoke	(In 3. 471 'provokt thus their abodes' evidently means 'thus urged them to remain')
provoked	* excited, aroused, anxious
puft	* puffed or idle (of words)
quaint	delicate, neat
queach	thicket
quern	hand-mill
race	offspring
race	erase, raze, destroy
rampant	fierce, greedy (In 8. 219 'rampant Gaine' translates 'greedily gotten')
rampire	rampart
randon	random (In 14. 224 'at needy randon' means 'lightly, carelessly')
rapting	ravishing, entrancing
rapture	* rape
rare	early
rate	(In 24. 348 'That rates your labour and your liberty' means 'who pays you for your labour and is your master')
rate, past	(In 2. 228 'past rate' is 'excessive'; in 8. 542 'past our rate' is 'beyond our custom')
rates, confer the	compare the weights
ravish	snatch fiercely, carry away
rear	animate, encourage
rear-feast	latter portion of a feast
reave	take away by violence
receit	1) receipt, capacity 2) acceptance 3) inner room
reciprocal	having backwards and forwards motion (In 5. 615 'when breath did find a passe reciprocall' means 'when he recovered his breath')
reclaime	(It is almost impossible to determine the meaning of this word in 8. 565, 'in my reclaime'; probably the sense is 'in your endeavour to call me back to friendship')
recollect	recover

recomfort	console
recourse	go back, journey
rectify	(In the Dedication this word seems to mean 'point out rightly')
recuse	refuse, reject
redemption	ransom
redition	return
redound	come back to
reduce	bring back or in
reducer	one who leads or conveys back
reduction	conveyance back
refell	force back
refer	give back
refluent	* flowing back (of the sea)
regality	royal behaviour
regress	return
regular	* well-ordered, well-behaved
reines, adde more	(In 1. 585 this means 'give fuller scope to')
relater	one who relates an event
remember	remind ('Remembered of' is 'reminded, brought to mind')
remorse	pity
remorseful	compassionate
rendry	surrender
repair	1) arrival, resort 2) act of repairing or mending
reparance	* (In the gloss to 4. 155 this seemingly means 'arrival.' Presumably it is a noun, formed from 'repair')
repose	replace, place or lay up. (But the meaning of 'up arose Aurora, that the Golden hils repose' in 15. 75 is doubtful. Perhaps Chapman was thinking of the dawn replacing gold on the mountains)
representment	* mental image (as in 1. 185)
reputatively	* by reputation
require	seek, inquire into, find out
rer'd	reared
rere	rear
reremouse	bat
resignment	act of resigning or leaving
respectless	unheeding, without paying attention to anything
respire	breathe
resume	take up (as in 13. 218, 'resumes act from thy speech')
retreat	* return, revenge

retriv'd	retrieved
return	restore, bring back
revoke	call back
rew	rue, lament
ridiculise	* make ridiculous
ring-leader	leader, chief authority
rock	distaff with wool attached
rod	(In 12. 390 this might stand for either 'rowed' or 'rode')
rode	road (In 6. 436 'lie at rode' means 'remain peace ful and content' i.e. like a ship at anchor)
rome	roam
roy	(For this word see the commentary on 5. 140: it may stand for 'king')
rub	* (In the Dedication the phrase 'none loved but those that rub them' seems to demand a sense of 'flatter')
ruffled	* agitated, disturbed (of the sea)
rumour	voices of the crowd
ruthful	compassionate
saciety	satiety
saft	saved
saker	falcon
salve	soothe
Sardinian	* sardonic
sattled	settled
scandal	defame, put shame on
sceptre-state	chief king
scout	* scouting expedition
scrip	small bag or wallet
seasd, sease	1) seized, seize (q.v.)
	2) grasp, take (as in 11. 683, 'the prease of great or common he would never sease,' meaning 'he would never seek protection by hanging back among a crowd')
second	support, act as assistant
secret	* (In 10. 649 'secret Rites' apparently means 'sepa-rate rites')
secure	having a sense of security
seed	offspring
seele	seel, close the eyes of
seemless	unseemly (although perhaps the sense here may be an unrecorded one—'not conspicuous')
seize	put in possession

self-tyre	* (The meaning of this word, as applied to dogs, is hard to determine. R. B. le Page suggests to me that Chapman may intend 'self-attired' i.e. not needing to put on dress as the shepherds do)
sent	scent
sere	talon
serviceable	* (In the Dedication 'serviceable sea' seems to mean 'tributary sea')
set-up-on-end	arouse
several	(See the commentary on 7. 171)
sewer	server, butler
shapeful	* having or taking any shape
she	showy exterior
shent	* disgraceful
shittle	shuttle
shore	take or place on shore
shore, flow past	exceed, excel or abound in
shot	share (as when guests pay shares in a feast)
show	appear
shrewdly-bitten	keenly biting
side	support, act as companion to
sideling	on a side-saddle
sigh	speak with a sigh (transitive use)
silly	poor, simple, weak
skall	scale
slaughterous	destructive
sleight	skill
slickt	sleeked, made smooth
smoke	discover, find out
sod	seethed
sodainly	suddenly
solemnise	dignify, honour (In 1. 35 'solemniz'd a retreate' means 'make a formal journey')
solid	(Used in connection with the body, as in 'solid lineaments' and 'solid father' i.e. 'father in the flesh')
sorcerous	pertaining to sorcery
sort	crowd
sorted	fated, decreed
souc't	soused (see souse)
soundful	* full of sound, tuneful
souse	steep, soak, make wet
spangled	* sleek (as applied to feet in 17. 554, translating λιπαροὺς πόδας)

spelt		kind of grain
sphere		circle
spiced		over-particular, scrupulous
spie		spy
spleenless	*	mild, gentle
spring		(Transitive use as in 'spring your joy in children')
staid		discreetly behavioured
staies		stays (q.v.)
stakes with, part		fight with (as in 'he must part stakes with the herdsmen')
stand in hand		befit, become (as in 'stands you more in hand' i.e. 'is more proper')
stand on the maid		remain a virgin, unmarried
stand upon		pay attention to, esteem
start		started
starter		one who starts at or is frightened of something
state		1) prince, ruler of a state 2) royal entry
statist	*	ruler of a state, lord
stays, on the		(Nautical term for arrangement of ships' tackle so that it does not move forward)
stead, in		(In 19. 344 'much in stead he stood your king' translates 'the king honoured him')
stere		1) stir 2) steer
sterve		starve, die
stich		furrow
still		distil
stock		race, lineage
stool-ball		a kind of ball game
stoop		1) swoop down on 2) make to bend
strain		family, race, descent
strange		alien, unknown
streak		stretch
strenuous		vigorous, strong
stupid		astonished
stupidity		stupor, astonishment
stuse		stews
suborn		prepare in a stealthy manner
substanced	*	furnished with wealth
sufferance		suffering, injury
summe	*	chief (as in 18. 89, 'the summe Of all these wooers')
supereminent		exalted above all

supply	1) something to make up a deficiency
	* 2) (There seems to be an unrecorded sense in 17. 49, 'gave all supplies with this entreaty,' evidently signifying 'uttered her full heart')
supportful	affording support
suppose	supposition, thought
supremes	* gods
suspense, in	debating, in debate
swet	sweated
swift-hov'd	with swift hoofs or hooves
swinge	forcible movement
sylvan	1) covered with trees, woody
	2) made of wood
take-in	capture
tarriance	tarrying, delay
taste	try by touch, handle
terms with, affect	vie with
terms, stand on	hang back
thickened	clouded (of a face stained with tears)
thickening	darkening
thin	* piercing, bitter
thrall	thraldom
thralled	kept as a thrall
three-aged	* living through three generations
throat (throte)	loud cry, shout
throat-brisk	* part of the brisket near the throat
throte	throat (q.v.)
thrust	crowd (In 3. 52 'in thrust' means 'in a crowd')
timed	(It is not certain whether, in 12. 50, 'timed powres' stands for 'timid' or is an error for 'tired')
timeless	untimely
to-be-studied	worthy of being closely examined
toil	subject to toil
trace	* 1) follow, pursue
	* 2) afflict (as in 10. 417, 'tract with some distraction')
tract	traced (q.v.)
train	trick, stratagem
transcend	rise up to, climb
transgress	go or travel beyond
transparent	apparent or visible through (the water)
tread	* common run of people
tredders	treaders

triangulare	(See commentary on 12. 194)
trim	1) gear
	2) dress
trundlebed	trucklebed
tumble	bow down
twink	twitter (of a bird)
Ulyssean	* characteristic of Ulysses
unaltered	* unalterable
unclose	* detach, unharness
uncore	* reveal, open from the heart
underdive	* dive down into
undigested	* (There is an unrecorded sense in 15. 469, where 'undigested age' means 'old age brought on before its time')
unequal	unjust
unmatched	matchless
unmeasured	immeasurable
unpacified	never quiet
unpassionate	impartial
unpeered	unequalled, without rival
unreconciled	* (In 15. 226 the word seems to have the sense of 'angry at heart')
unrest	torment, trouble
unruled	ungoverned, unruly
unseen	unskilled, inexperienced
unsighted	* deprived of sight
unsilenced	* not to be silenced
upland	living in a remote place; uncivilised
utmost	uttermost, extreme
utter	outer
vail	lower in sign of submission
vaine	vein
vegetant	proceeding from plants
vent	1) utter, give expression to
	2) let loose
vertue	virtû, valour, strength
victles leager	(See leager; apparently 'victles' is 'victuals')
virulency	* virulence
visual	* (In 4. 773 'visuall light' is the light seen by the eyes)
voiceful	stentorian, with loud voice
voluntary	one voluntarily serving as a soldier

vow	dedicate oneself
wan	1) won
	2) wand, oar
want	absence
waterish	aquatic
water-treader	* ship
wayless	trackless
weed	garment
weekes	wicks
weight, of	important, great
whorlbat (whoorlbat)	whirlbat, hurling club
whuling	whine
wimble	gimlet
wine-heat	heated by wine
wishful	desirable
with	withe, rope made of osiers
woon	won
wow	woo
wrackful	causing ruin or shipwreck
wrastle	wrestle
wreak	revenge
wreakful	avenging, vengeful
wrung	(It is not certain whether this word in 9. 747 stands for 'wronged' or means 'pressed hardly')
wunt	wont, fashion, appearance
yote	* soak

THE LESSER HOMERICA

INTRODUCTION

In Chapman's *Iliads* breathes a vigorous, impetuous spirit, the excitement of a poet who sees in Achilles a prime representative of the manly virtues. The atmosphere of the *Odysses* is more placid, in keeping with the translator's double discovery that not all which had seemed virtuous in Achilles was indeed so and that a nobler soul might be found in the sorely-tried Ulysses, the man made wise through suffering. Even although he has infused into both these works much of his own changing philosophy and has departed from or added to his original, Chapman deserves Keats' praise for both. Here is the realm of gold expressed in Elizabethan terms.

Perhaps not so much may be said for the *Batrachomyomachia,* the *Hymns* and the *Epigrams*. The noticeable decline in poetic inspiration manifest in these poems seems to be due to several things. First, we get the impression that in essaying the translation of the lesser poems, Chapman was not truly impelled to his task, but was intent merely on 'finishing off' his Homer. Secondly, it is obvious that he could find here no opportunity for interpreting the original Greek in his own characteristic way; there was no hero with whom he could identify himself. Thirdly, we feel that, despite his philosophical tendencies, Chapman's genius found finest scope in the narrative and dramatic kinds, particularly when the subject-matter permitted a rich flow of noble rhetoric. His hand was too heavy to deal successfully with the light burlesque of the battle of the frogs and mice, and in the *Hymns* and *Epigrams* he was given but little opportunity for the telling of a story. A fourth element of weakness is to be traced in his actual understanding of the Greek original. He had made some mistakes in the *Iliads* and the *Odysses,* but most of his deviations from the original were deliberate. Again and again we get the impression not so much of a man uncertain concerning the true meaning of the Greek, but sure in his own soul that by inspiration he has divined a sense which has passed the scholars by. In the later poems only too often we watch Chapman utterly mistaking the original sense or so baffled that he can wrest no sense whatsoever from the Greek lines. Finally, it must be admitted that the stylistic crabbedness which is to be discerned in all his writings increased as the years went by, and even when he knew clearly what he wanted to say he now found his means of expression inadequate to convey his thoughts. Favourite words and expressions are now tortured almost beyond belief, and sometimes the simplest thoughts are forced to assume circumlocutionary forms which at first reading, sometimes even at later readings, seem meaningless.

Perhaps the most interesting aspect of this work is the way in which it demonstrates Chapman's self-identification with Homer. The dedicatory verses addressed to the Earl of Somerset and the final lines in which he provides a valedictory to his self-assumed task indicate this most clearly, but repeatedly in the translations the same note is struck. Accepting the universal view that the *Hymns* and the *Epigrams* were genuinely the work of Homer, he seizes every opportunity of identifying his fate with the presumed lot of the Greek poet—a man of supreme greatness whose words had not been given their due meed of praise, who had been neglected by the rabble and who had moved through life poverty-stricken and esteemed only by an intellectual few. The manner in which Chapman's verses strike sudden fire whenever he comes to a passage which permits him to express contempt and detestation of his detractors tells its own story.

Precisely when *The Crowne of all Homers Workes* appeared or was written is difficult to determine, but certainly several years must have elapsed after the *Odysses* of 1614 before it was completed. Perhaps 1624 is as near a guess as we can make to its date of publication. Although he was a chronic grumbler, in one thing Chapman must always have considered himself fortunate. His *Iliads* and *Odysses* are handsome volumes, and for his *Crowne* he found an important printer-bookseller willing to produce an equally handsome folio, on the whole carefully printed and amply—indeed, perhaps over-amply—spaced. The volume has an elaborate engraved title page which must have pleased the author greatly, for it shows a laurel-crowned Homer, heavy-bearded, and, directly below, a portrait of an equally heavily bearded Chapman, the latter even more prominent than the former. Homer is backed by a trio of deities—Apollo holding a musical instrument, Hermes with his caduceus, and a buxom Pallas. The lower frame of the title page, besides Chapman's portrait, with the motto '*Conscium evasi diem*', surrounded by clouds, has illustrations of the battle of the frogs and the mice, eagles flying above, and the title itself:

the

CROWNE of all HOMERS WORKES

Batrachomyomachia

Or the Battaile of Frogs and Mise.

His Hymn's —— *and* —— Epigrams

Translated according to yᵉ Originall

By George Chapman.

At the foot is the bookseller's announcement: London, *Printed by* Iohn

Bill, *his* MAIESTIES *Printer. 'Pass: fecit'* appears at the bottom of the frame to the right, indicating that this engraving was the work of William Pass (Willem van de Passe).

The volume itself, apart from the title page, consists of 100 leaves, with signatures ¶4, A—Z4, Aa2. For the dedicatory verses a roman font is used; the rest, except for the Latin prayer at the end and for proper names, is in large italic. In some copies 'WORKES' appears as 'WORCKES.'

The Widener Library at Harvard University possesses a copy which has a manuscript dedication in Chapman's own hand:

In loue and honor of ye Righte Virtuouse and
worthie Gent: Mr Henry Reynolds,
And to crowne all his deseruings
wth eternall Memorie
Geo: Chapman
Joines this Crowne and Conclusion
of all the Homericall Meritts wth his
Accomplisht Improuements;
Aduising
That if at first sighte he seme darck
Or too fierie He will yet holde
him fast (like Proteus)
Till he appere in his propper similitude
And he will then shewe him
self—Vatem egregiũ cui non sit publica Vena
Qui Nihil expositum soleat deducere; nec qui
Communi feriat Carmen triuiale moneta.

Two corrections of the text in Chapman's hand have been incorporated in the present edition.

In general, the same principles have been employed here as were applied for the texts of the *Iliads* and the *Odysses,* except that the introductory verses have been printed in italic and the italic text in roman. The punctuation of the original has been entirely abandoned, since it is hopelessly erratic and in numerous passages rather puzzling. Two examples will serve. The first is *A Hymne to Hermes,* ll. 98–104:

His word,
And worke, had individuall accord.
All being as swiftly to perfection brought;
As any worldly mans, most rauisht thought,
Whose minde, Care cuts, in an infinity
Of varied parts, or passions instantly;
Or as the frequent twincklings of an eye.

The same hymn, ll. 379–82, provides another example:

But last Euening late,
I sawe a Thing, that shew'd of childish state;
To my ould lights; and seem'd as he pursude
A Herd of Oxen.

Instead of an attempt to modify the original, it seemed better boldly to repunctuate the entire text.

As in the second part of the *Odysses,* a few possessive nouns have apostrophes in the original, and, for the sake of completeness of record, these are noted here: *An Hymne to Apollo,* l. 52 'Ida's', l. 154 'Saturnia's', l. 609 'Delphusa's', l. 834 'Latona's'; *A Hymne to Hermes,* l. 142 'Pieria's', l. 192 'Phoebus-Apollo's', l. 299 'Latona's', l. 300 'Apollo's', l. 333 'Latona's', l. 353 'Latona's', l. 419 'Maia's', l. 426 'Apollo's', l. 463 'Latona's', l. 504 'Apollo's', l. 899 'Mercurie's', ll. 911, 967, 992 and 1001 'Maia's'; *To Mars,* l. 9 *'Fortitud's'; To Castor and Pollux,* l. 4 'Leda's'; *To Mercurie,* l. 11 'Iuno's', l. 15 'Maia's'; *To Diana,* l. 35 'Latona's'; *To Pallas,* l. 1 'Pallas-Minerua's'; *To Men of Hospitalitie,* l. 5 'Pluto's'; *Cuma refusing his Offer,* l. 28 'Cuma's'. All the other possessive apostrophes in the present text have been inserted.

No attempt has been made to follow the typographical setting out of the titles and end-lines of the separate poems. Rather irregularly the words 'he' and 'all' are printed in Chapman's text as 'He' and 'All': for the most part the capitals have been retained, but in a few instances, where confusion might arise, the capitals have been reduced to lower case and have been so marked in the notes.

A number of brackets indicating triple rhymes, omitted in the original text, have been added; and in one instance such a bracket in the original has been omitted because, in fact, four rhymes, not three, are concerned.

The Crowne of All Homers Workes

TO
MY EVER
MOST-WORTHIE-TO-BE-MOST-HONOR'D LORD
THE EARLE OF SOMERSET, &c

Not forc't by fortune, but since your free minde
(Made by affliction) rests in choice resign'd
To calme Retreate, laid quite beneath the winde
Of Grace and Glory, I well know, my Lord,
You would not be entitl'd to a word 5
That might a thought remove from your Repose
To thunder and spit Flames, as Greatnesse does,
For all the Trumps that still tell where he goes.
Of which Trumps Dedication being One,
Me thinks I see you start to heare it blowne. 10
But this is no such Trump as summons Lords
Gainst Envie's steele to draw their leaden swords,
Or gainst Hare-lipt Detraction, Contempt,
All which from all Resistance stand exempt,
It being as hard to sever Wrong from Merit 15
As meate-indude from blood, or blood from spirit.
Nor in the spirit's Chariot rides the soule
In bodies chaste with more divine controule,
Nor virtue shines more in a lovely Face,
Than true desert is stuck off with Disgrace. 20
And therefore truth it selfe, that had to blesse
The merit of it all, Almightinesse,
Would not protect it from the Bane and Ban
Of all Moodes most distraught and Stygian—
As counting it the Crowne of all Desert, 25
Borne to Heaven, to take of Earth no part
Of false Joy here, for Joyes-there-endlesse troth,
Nor sell his Birthright for a messe of Broth,
But stay and still sustaine, and his Blisse bring,
Like to the hatching of the Black-thorne's spring, 30
With bitter frosts and smarting haile-stormes, forth.
Fates love Bees' labors; onely Paine crownes Worth.
This Dedication calls no Greatnes then

To patrone this Greatnes-creating Penn,
Nor you to add to your dead calme a breath; 35
For those arm'd Angells, that in spight of death
Inspir'd those flowrs that wrought this poet's wreath,
Shall keepe it ever Poesie's steepest Starr,
As, in Earth's flaming wals, Heaven's sevenfold Carr
(From all the wildes of Neptune's watrie sphere) 40
For ever guards the Erymanthian Beare.
Since then your Lordship settles in your shade
A life retir'd, and no Retreate is made
But to some strength (for else tis no Retreate,
But rudely running from your Battaile's heate), 45
I give this as your strength: your strength, my Lord,
In Counsailes and Examples, that afford
More Guard than whole Hosts of corporeal powre,
And more deliverance teach the fatall Howre.
Turne not your medcine then to your disease, 50
By your too set and sleight repulse of these,
The Adjuncts of your matchlesse Odysses;
Since on that wisest minde of Man relies
Refuge from all Live's Infelicities.
Nor sing these such division from them, 55
But that these spinn the thred of the same streame
From one selfe Distaff's stuff: for Poesie's Pen
(Through al theames) is t'informe the lives of Men,
All whose Retreates neede strengths of all degrees—
Without which (had you even Herculean knees) 60
Your foes' fresh Charges would at length prevaile,
To leave your Noblest suff'rance no least saile.
Strength then the Object is of all Retreates;
Strength needes no friend's trust, strength your foes defeates.
Retire to strength, then, of eternall things, 65
And y'are eternall; for our knowing Springs
Flow into those things that we truely know,
Which (being Eternall) we are render'd so.
And though your high-fixt Light passe infinite farr
Th'advicefull Guide of my still-trembling Starr, 70
Yet heare what my dischardg'd Peece must foretell,
Standing your Poore and Perdue Sentinell.
Kings may perhaps wish even your Beggar's Voice
To their Eternities, how skorn'd a choice
Soever now it lies; And (dead) I may 75
Extend your life to light's extreamest Raie.
If not, your Homer yet past doubt shall make
Immortall, like himselfe, your Bountie's stake

Put in my hands, to propagate your Fame;
Such virtue reigns in such united Name. 80

A simile illustrating the most renownd service of Generall Noris in his Retreate before Gant, never before made sacred to Memorie.

Retire to him then for advice and skill
To know things call'd worst Best, and Best most ill.
Which knowne, truths best chuse, and retire to still.
And as our English Generall (whose Name
Shall equall interest finde in th'House of Fame 85
With all Earth's great'st Commanders), in Retreate
To Belgian Gant, stood all Spaine's Armies' heate
By Parma led, though but one thousand strong;
Three miles together thrusting through the throng
Of th'Enimies' Horse (still pouring on their Fall 90
Twixt him and home) and thunderd through them al;
The Gallick Monsiour standing on the wall,
And wondring at his dreadfull Discipline,
Fir'd with a Valor that spit spirit Divine;
In five Battaillons randging all his Men, 95
Bristl'd with Pikes, and flanck't with Flanckers ten;
Gave fire still in his Rere; retir'd and wrought
Downe to his fixt strength still, retir'd and fought;
All the Battaillons of the Enemie's Horse
Storming upon him still their fieriest Force; 100
Charge upon Charge laid fresh; he, fresh as day,
Repulsing all, and forcing glorious way
Into the Gates, that gaspt (as swounes for Ayre)
And tooke their life in with untoucht Repaire:
So fight out, sweet Earle, your Retreate in Peace; 105
No ope-warr equalls that where privie Prease
Of never-numberd odds of Enimie,
Arm'd all by Envie, in blinde Ambush lie,
To rush out like an open threatning skie,
Broke al in Meteors round about your eares. 110
Gainst which (though far from hence) through al your Reres
Have fires prepar'd; wisdome with wisdome flanck,
And all your forces randge in present ranck;
Retiring as you now fought in your strength,
From all the Force laid, in time's utmost length, 115
To charge, and basely come on you behind.
The Doctrine of all which you here shall finde,
And in the true Glasse of a humane Minde—
Your Odysses—the Body letting see
All his life past, through Infelicitie, 120
And manage of it all. In which to friend,
The full Muse brings you both the prime and end
Of all Arts ambient in the Orbe of Man;

Which never darknesse most Cimmerian
Can give Eclipse, since (blinde) He all things sawe, 125
And to all, ever since, liv'd Lord and Lawe.
And though our mere-learn'd men, and Modern wise,
Taste not poore Poesie's Ingenuities,
Being crusted with their covetous Leprosies,
But hold her paines worse than the spider's worke, 130
And lighter than the shadowe of a Corke,
Yet th'ancient learn'd, heat with celestiall fire,
Affirmes her flames so sacred and entire
That not without God's greatest grace she can
Fall in the wid'st Capacitie of Man. 135

Ut non sine Maximo favore Dei comparari queat. Pla. in Ione.

If yet the vile Soule of this Verminous time
Love more the Sale-Muse, and the Squirrel's chime,
Than this full sphere of Poesie's sweetest Prime,
Give them unenvied their vaine veine and vent,
And rest your wings in his approv'd Ascent 140
That yet was never reacht, nor ever fell
Into affections bought with things that sell,
Being the Sunn's Flowre, and wrapt so in his skie
He cannot yeeld to every Candle's eye.

Whose most worthy Discoveries to your
Lordship's Judiciall Perspective in most
subdude Humilitie submitteth,

GEORGE CHAPMAN

To the Earle of Somerset

The Occasion of this Impos'd

CROWNE

After this not onely Prime of Poets, but Philosophers, had
written his two great Poems of Iliads and Odysses—which
(for their first Lights borne before all Learning) were
worthily call'd the Sunne and Moone of the Earth—(finding
no compensation) he writ in contempt of Men this ridiculous 5
Poem of Vermin, giving them Nobility of Birth, valorous
elocution not inferior to his Heroes. At which the Gods
themselves, put in amaze, call'd Counsailes about their
assistance of either Armie, and the justice of their Quarrels,
even to the mounting of Jove's Artillery against them, and 10
discharge of his three-forckt flashes: and all for the drowning
of a Mouse. After which sleight and onely recreative touch,
hee betooke him seriously to the honor of the Gods, in
Hymns resounding all their peculiar Titles, Jurisdiction, and
Dignities; which hee illustrates at all parts as he had been 15
continually conversant amongst them: and whatsoever
autentique Poesie he omitted in the Episods contained in his
Iliads and Odysses, he comprehends and concludes in his
Hymns and Epigrams. Al his observance and honor of the
Gods rather mov'd their envies against him than their re- 20
wards, or respects of his endevours. And so like a Man
verecundi ingenii (which he witnesseth of himselfe) he liv'd
unhonord and needie till his death; yet notwithstanding all
men's servile and manacled Miseries to his most absolute and
never-equall'd Merite—yea even bursten profusion to Im- 25
posture and Impiety—heare our ever-the-Same intranced and
never-sleeping Master of the Muses, to his last accent in-
comparablie singing.

BATRACHOMYOMACHIA

Entring the fields, first let my Vowes call on
The Muses' whole Quire out of Helicon
Into my Heart, for such a Poem's sake
As lately I did in my Tables take,
And put into report upon my knees— 5
A fight so fierce as might in all degrees
Fit Mars himselfe and his tumultuous hand,
Glorying to dart to th'eares of every land
Of all the voice-devided, and to show
How bravely did both Froggs and Mise bestow 10
In glorious fight their forces, even the deedes
Daring to imitate of earth's Giant seedes.
Thus, then, men talkt; this seede the strife begat:
The Mouse, once drie, and scap't the dangerous Cat,
Drench't in the neighbour lake her tender berde, 15
To taste the sweetnesse of the wave it rer'de.
The farre-fam'de Fen-affecter (seeing him) said:
'Ho! Stranger! what are you? And whence, that tred
This shore of ours? Who brought you forth? Replie
What truth may witnesse, lest I finde you lie. 20
If worth fruition of my love and me,
I'le have thee home, and Hospitalitie
Of feast and gift, good and magnificent,
Bestow on thee. For all this Confluent
Resounds my Royaltie; my Name, the great 25
In blowne-up count'nances and lookes of threat,
Physignathus, ador'd of all Frogs here
All their daies' durance, and the Empire beare
Of all their Beings—mine owne Beeing begot
By royall Peleus, mixt in nuptiall knot 30
With faire Hydromedusa, on the Bounds
Nere which Eridanus his Race resounds.
And Thee mine Eie makes my Conceipt enclinde
To reckon powerfull, both in forme and Minde,
A Scepter-bearer, and past others farre 35
Advanc't in all the fiery Fights of warre.
Come then, Thy race to my renowne commend.'
The Mouse made answer: 'Why enquires my friend
For what so well know men and Deities,
And all the wing'd affecters of the skies? 40

[9] *Intending Men, being divided from all other creatures by the voice,* μέροψ *being a periphrasis signifying* voce divisus, *of* μείρω, divido, *and* ὕψ, ὀπός, vox.

[27] φυσίγναθος, Genas et buccas inflans.

[30] Πηλεύς, qui ex luto nascitur.

[31] Ὑδρομέδουσα, Aquarum Regina.

[32] *The river Po, in Italie.*

[41] Ψιχάρπαξ, *Gather-crum, or ravish-crum.*

[41] *Sheare-crust.*

[43] *Lick-mill.*

[44] *Bacon-flitch-devourer, or gnawer.*

[57] Τανύπεπλος, Extenso et promisso Peplo amictus. *A metaphor taken from ladies' veiles, or traines, and therefore their names are here added.*

[58] Ἤπατα λευκοχίτωνα, *Livering puddings white skind.*

[64] Παντοδαποῖσιν,—*Whose common exposition is onely* Varijs *when it properly signifies,* Ex omni solo.

[81] Στονόεσσαν, *of* στενός, *Angustus.*

Psicharpax, I am calld, Troxartes' seede,
Surnam'de the Mighty-Minded. She that free'd
Mine eyes from darknesse was Lichomyle,
King Pternotroctes' Daughter, shewing me
Within an aged hovell the young light— 45
Fed me with figges and nuts, and all the height
Of varied viands. But unfolde the cause,
Why, 'gainst similitude's most equall lawes
(Observ'd in friendship) thou makst me thy friend?
Thy life, the waters only helpe t'extend. 50
Mine, whatsoever men are us'd to eat
Takes part with them at shore: their purest cheat,
Thrice boulted, kneaded, and subdu'd in past,
In cleane round kymnels, cannot be so fast
From my approches kept, but in I eat; 55
Nor Cheesecakes full of finest Indian wheat,
That Crustie-weedes weare, large as Ladies' traines;
Lyvrings (white-skind as Ladies); nor the straines
Of prest milke, renneted; nor collups cut
Fresh from the flitch; nor junkets such as put 60
Palats divine in Appetite; nor any
Of all men's delicates, though ne're so many
Their Cookes devise them, who each dish see deckt
With all the dainties all strange soiles affect.
Yet am I not so sensuall to flie 65
Of fields embattaild the most fiery crie,
But rush out strait, and with the first in fight
Mixe in adventure. No man with affright
Can daunt my forces, though his bodie bee
Of never so immense a quantitie, 70
But making up, even to his bed, accesse,
His fingers' ends dare with my teeth compresse,
His feet taint likewise, and so soft sease both
They shall not tast th'Impression of a tooth.
Sweet sleepe shall hold his owne in every eie 75
Where my tooth takes his tartest libertie.
But two there are that alwaies, far and neare,
Extremely still controule my force with feare,
The Cat and Night-Hawke, who much skathe confer
On all the Outraies where for food I erre— 80
Together with the streights-still-keeping Trap,
Where lurkes deceiptfull and set-spleend Mishap.
But most of all the Cat constraines my feare,
Being ever apt t'assault me everywhere;
For by that hole that hope saies I shall scape, 85
At that hole ever she commits my Rape.

The best is yet, I eat no pot-herb grasse,
Nor Raddishes, nor Coloquintidas,
Nor Still-greene Beetes, nor Parsley—which you make
Your dainties still, that live upon the lake.' 90
The Frog replide: 'Stranger, your boasts creepe all
Upon their bellies, though to our lives fall
Much more miraculous meates, by lake and land,
Jove tendring our lives with a twofold hand,
Enabling us to leape ashore for food, 95
And hide us strait in our retreatfull flood—
Which, if your will serve, you may prove with ease.
I'le take you on my shoulders—which fast sease,
If safe arrivall at my house y'intend.'
He stoopt, and th'other spritelie did ascend, 100
Clasping his golden necke, that easie seat
Gave to his sallie; who was jocund yet,
Seeing the safe harbors of the King so nere,
And he a swimmer so exempt from Pere.
But when he sunke into the purple wave, 105
He mournd extremely, and did much deprave
Unprofitable penitence; his haire
Tore by the roots up, labord for the aire,
With his feet fetcht up to his belly close:
His heart within him panted out repose 110
For th'insolent plight in which his state did stand,
Sigh'd bitterly, and long'd to greete the land,
Forc't by the dire Neede of his freezing feare.
First, on the waters he his taile did stere
Like to a Sterne, then drew it like an ore, 115
Still praying the Gods to set him safe ashore;
Yet sunke he midst the red waves more and more,
And laid a throat out to his utmost height.
Yet in forc'd speech he made his perill sleight,
And thus his glorie with his grievance strove: 120
'Not in such choice state was the charge of love
Borne by the Bull, when to the Cretane shore
He swumme Europa through the wavie rore,
As this Frog ferries me, his pallid brest
Bravely advancing, and his verdant crest 125
(Submitted to my seat) made my support,
Through his white waters, to his royall Court.'
But on the sudden did apparance make
An horrid spectacle—a water-snake
Thrusting his freckeld necke above the lake. 130
Which seene to both, away Physignathus
Div'd to his deepes, as no way conscious

Of whom he left to perish in his lake,
But shunn'd blacke fate himselfe, and let him take
The blackest of it—who amids the Fenn 135
Swumme with his brest up, hands held up in vaine,
Cried 'Peepe', and perisht; sunke the waters oft,
And often with his sprawlings came aloft;
Yet no way kept downe death's relentlesse force,
But (full of water) made an heavie Corse. 140
Before he perisht yet, he threatned thus:
'Thou lurk'st not yet from heaven, Physignathus,
Though yet thou hid'st here, that hast cast from thee
(As from a Rocke) the shipwrackt life of mee.
Though thou thy selfe no better was than I 145
(O worst of things) at any facultie,
Wrastling or race: but for thy perfidie
In this my wracke Jove beares a wreakefull eie,
And to the Hoast of Mise thou paines shalt pay
Past all evasion.' This his life let say, 150
And left him to the waters. Him beheld,
Lichopinax, plac't in the pleasing fielde,

[152] *Lick-dish.*

Who shrick't extremely, ranne and told the Mise;
Who having heard his watry destinies,
Pernicious anger pierst the hearts of all, 155
And then their Heralds forth they sent to call
A councell early, at Troxartes' house,
Sad father of this fatall shipwrack't Mouse,
Whose dead Corpse upwards swum along the lake,
Nor yet (poore wretch) could be enforc'd to make 160
The shore his harbour, but the mid-Maine swum.
When now (all haste made) with first morne did come
All to set councell; in which first rais'd head
Troxartes, angrie for his sonne, and said:
'O Friends, though I alone may seeme to beare 165
All the infortune, yet may all mette here
Account it their case. But tis true, I am
In chiefe unhappy, that a triple flame
Of life feele put forth in three famous sonnes:
The first, the chiefe in our confusions, 170
The Cat, made rape of, caught without his hole;
The second, Man, made with a cruell soule,
Brought to his ruine with a new-found sleight,
And a most woodden engine of deceipt,
They terme a Trap, mere Murthresse of our Mise; 175
The last, that in my love held speciall prise
And his rare mother's, this Physignathus

[175] 'Ολέτειρα, Interfectrix, Perditrix.

(With false pretext of wafting to his house)
Strangl'd in chiefe deepes of his bloudy streame.
Come then, haste all, and issue out on them, 180
Our bodies deckt in our Dædalean armes.'
  This said, his words thrust all up in alarmes;
And Mars himselfe, that serves the cure of war,
Made all in their Appropriats circular.
First on each leg the greene shales of a Beane 185
They clos'd for Bootes, that sat exceeding cleane:
The shales they broke ope, Bootehaling by night,
And eat the beanes. Their Jacks Art exquisite
Had showne in them, being Cats-skins, every where
Quilted with quills. Their fencefull bucklers were 190
The middle rounds of Can'sticks; but their speare
A huge long Needle was, that could not beare
The braine of any but be Mars his owne
Mortall invention. Their heads' arming Crowne
Was vessel to the kirnell of a nut. 195
And thus the Mise their powers in armour put.
  This the frogs hearing, from the water all
Issue to one place, and a councell call
Of wicked war, consulting what should be
Cause to this murmure and strange mutinie. 200
While this was question'd, neere them made his stand
An Herald with a Scepter in his hand
(Embasichytrus calld) that fetcht his kinde
From Tyroglyphus with the mightie minde,
Denouncing ill-nam'd war in these high termes: 205
  'O Frogs! the Mise sends threats to you of armes
And bid me bid ye Battell and fixt fight;
Their eies all wounded with Psicharpax' sight
Floting your waters, whom your king hath kild.
And therefore all prepare for force of field, 210
You that are best borne whosoever held.'
This said, he sever'd; his speech firing th'eares
Of all the Mise, but frees'd the Frogs with feares,
Themselves conceiting guiltie; whom the King
Thus answer'd (rising): 'Friends! I did not bring 215
Psicharpax to his end. He, wantoning
Upon our waters, practising to swimme,
Ap'te us, and drown'd without my sight of him.
And yet these worst of Vermine accuse me,
Though no way guiltie. Come, consider we 220
How we may ruine these deceiptfull Mise.
For my part, I give voice to this advise,

[186] Εὖ τ'ἀσκήσαντες, ab ἀσκέω, Elaboratè concinno.

[203] *Enter-pot, or Serch-pot.*

[204] *Cheese-miner.* Qui caseum rodendo cavat.

[218] Μιμούμενος, *Aping or imitating us.*

As seeming fittest to direct our deeds:
Our bodies decking with our arming weeds,
Let all our Pow'rs stand rais'd in steep'st repose 225
Of all our shore; that, when they charge us close,
We may the helms snatch off from all so deckt,
Daring our onset, and them all deject
Downe to our waters—who, not knowing the sleight
To dive our soft deeps, may be strangl'd streight, 230
And we triumphing may a Trophey rere
Of all the Mise that we have slaughter'd here.'

These words put all in armes; and mallow leaves
They drew upon their leggs for arming Greaves.

[234] *Boots of warre.*

Their Curets, broad greene Beetes; their bucklers were 235
Good thick-leav'd Cabbadge, proofe gainst any spe're;
Their speares, sharpe Bullrushes, of which were all
Fitted with long ones. Their parts Capitall
They hid in subtle Cockleshels from blowes.
And thus all arm'd, the steepest shores they chose 240
T'encamp themselves, where lance with lance they lin'd,
And brandisht bravelie, each Frogg full of Minde.

Then Jove calld all Gods in his flaming Throne,
And shewd all all this preparation
For resolute warre—these able soldiers, 245
Many and great, all shaking lengthfull spe'res,
In shew like Centaures, or the Gyants' Host.
When (sweetlie smiling) he enquir'd who, most
Of all th'Immortalls, pleas'd to adde their aide
To Froggs or Mise; and thus to Pallas said: 250

'O daughter! Must not you needs aid these Mise,
That, with the Odors and meate sacrifice
Us'd in your Temple, endlesse triumphs make,
And serve you for your sacred victles' sake?'

Pallas repli'd: 'O Father, never I 255
Will aid the Mise in anie miserie.
So many mischiefes by them I have found,
Eating the Cotten that my distaffs crown'd,
My lamps still hanting to devoure the oyle.
But that which most my minde eates is their spoile 260
Made of a veile, that me in much did stand;
On which bestowing an elaborate hand,
A fine woofe working of as pure a thredd,
Such holes therein their Petulancies fed
That, putting it to darning, when t'was done, 265
The darner a most deare paie stood upon
For his so deare paines, laid downe instantlie,

[258] Στέμματα, Lanas, eo quod colus cingant seu coronent. *Which our learned sect translate eating the crownes that Pallas wore.*

[268] Τόκος, Partus et id quod partu edidit Mater. Metap. hic appellatur fœnus quod ex usura ad nos redit.

Or (to forbeare) exacted usurie.
So, borrowing from my Phane the weed I wove,
I can by no meanes th'usurous darner move 270
To let me have the mantle to restore.
And this is it that rubs the angrie sore
Of my offence tooke at these petulant Mise.
Nor will I yeeld the Froggs' wants my supplies,
For their infirme mindes that no confines keepe; 275
For I from warre retir'd, and wanting sleepe,
All lept ashore in tumult, nor would staie
Till one winck seas'd myne eyes; and so I laie
Sleeplesse, and pain'de with headach, till first light
The Cock had crow'd up. Therefore, to the fight 280
Let no God goe assistent, lest a lance
Wound whosoever offers to advance
Or wishes but their aid, that skorne all foes,
Should any God's accesse their spirits oppose.
Sit we then pleas'd to see from heaven their fight.' 285
She said, and all Gods join'd in her delight.
And now both Hosts to one field drew the jarre,
Both Heralds bearing the ostents of warre.

[289] Κώνωψ, Culex vinarius.

And then the wine-Gnats, that shrill Trumpets sound,
Terriblie rung out the encounter round. 290

[292] *Lowd-mouth.*

[292] *Kitchen-vessell licker.*

Jove thundred; all heaven sad warr's signe resounded.
And first Hypsiboas Lichenor wounded,
Standing th'impression of the first in fight.
His lance did in his Lyver's midst's alight,
Along his bellie. Downe he fell; his face 295
His fall on that part swaid, and all the grace

[298] *Hole-dweller.* Qui foramina subit.

[299] *Mud-borne.*

[301] *Beet-devourer.*

[302] *The great bread-eater.*

[303] *The great Noise-maker, shrill or bigg-voic't.*

Of his soft hayre fil'd with disgracefull dust.
Then Troglodytes his thick javeline thrust
In Pelion's bosome, bearing him to ground,
Whom sad death seas'd; his soule flew through his wound. 300
Seutlæus next Embasichytros slew,
His heart through thrusting. Then Artophagus threw
His lance at Polyphon, and strooke him quite
Through his midd-bellie: downe he fell upright,
And from his fayre limms took his soule her flight. 305

[306] *The lake-lover.*

Limnocharis, beholding Polyphon
Thus done to death, did, with as round a stone
As that the mill turnes, Troglodytes wound
Neare his mid-neck, ere he his onset found—

[310] Qui lambit culinaria vasa.

Whose eyes sad darknes seas'd. Lichenor cast 310
A flying dart off, and his ayme so plac't

[312] Τιτύσκομαι, intentissime dirigo ut certum ictum inferam.
[315] *The cabbage-eater.*
[323] Paludis incola, *Lake-liver.*
[325] Qui in Calamintha, herba palustri, habitat.
[326] *Bacon-eater.*
[328] Qui Aquis delectatur.
[329] *Collup-devourer.*
[334] *Mudd-sleeper.*
[336] *Leeke or scalion lover.*
[337] *Kitchin-smell hanter, or hunter.*
[341] *Fennstalker.*
[344] Qui per lutum it.
[355] *Vociferator.*

Upon Limnocharis, that Sure he thought
The wound he wisht him; nor untruely wrought
The dire successe, for through his Lyver flew
The fatall lance; which when Crambophagus knew, 315
Downe the deepe waves neare shore he, diving, fled;
But fled not fate so; the sterne enimie fed
Death with his life in diving: never more
The ayre he drew in; his Vermilian gore
Staind all the waters, and along the shore 320
He lay extended; his fat entrailes laie
(By his small guts' impulsion) breaking waie
Out at his wound. Limnisius neare the shore
Destroid Tyroglyphus: which frighted sore
The soule of Calaminth, seeing comming on 325
(For wreake) Pternoglyphus; who got him gon
With large leapes to the lake, his Target throwne
Into the waters. Hydrocharis slew
King Pternophagus, at whose throte he threw
A huge stone, strooke it high, and beate his braine 330
Out at his nostrills: earth blusht with the staine
His blood made on her bosom. For next Prise,
Lichopinax to death did sacrifice
Borborocœtes' faultlesse faculties;
His lance enforc't it; darknes clos'd his eyes. 335
On which when Prassophagus cast his looke,
Cnissodioctes by the heeles he tooke,
Dragg'd him to fenn from off his native ground,
Then seas'd his throate, and souc't him till he droun'd.
But now Psicharpax wreakes his fellows' deaths, 340
And in the bosome of Pelusius sheathes
(In center of his Lyver) his bright lance.
He fel before the Author of the chance;
His soule to hell fled. Which Pelobates
Taking sad note of, wreakefully did sease 345
His hand's gripe full of mudd, and all besmear'd
His forhead with it so, that scarce appeard
The light to him. Which certainely incenst
His fierie splene; who with his wreake dispenst
No point of tyme, but rer'd with his strong hand 350
A stone so massie it opprest the land,
And hurld it at him; when below the knee
It strooke his right legge so impetuouslie
It peece-meale brake it; he the dust did sease,
Upwards everted. But Craugasides 355
Revendg'd his death, and at his enimie

Dischardg'd a dart that did his point implie
In his mid-bellie. All the sharp-pil'de speare
Got after in, and did before it beare
His universall entrailes to the earth, 360
Soone as his swolne hand gave his javeline birth.

[362] *Eate-corne.*

Sitophagus, beholding the sad sight
Set on the shore, went halting from the fight,
Vext with his wounds extremelie; and to make
Waie from extreme fate, lept into the lake. 365
Troxartes strooke, in th'instep's upper part,
Physignathus; who (privie to the smart
His wound imparted) with his utmost hast
Lept to the lake, and fled. Troxartes cast
His eye upon the foe that fell before, 370
And (see'ng him halfe-liv'de) long'd againe to gore
His gutlesse bosome, and (to kill him quite)
Ranne fiercely at him. Which Prassæus' sight
Tooke instant note of, and the first in fight

[373] *Scallian-devourer.*

Thrust desp'rate way through, casting his keene lance 375
Off at Troxartes, whose shield turn'd th'advance
The sharpe head made, and checkt the mortall chance.
Amongst the Mise fought an Egregiouse
Young springall, and a close-encountring Mouse,
Pure Artepibulus-his deare descent, 380
A Prince that Mars himselfe shewd where he went
(Call'd Meridarpax), of so huge a might,
That onely He still dominer'd in fight
Of all the Mouse-Host. He, advancing close
Up to the Lake, past all the rest arose 385
In glorious object, and made vant that He
Came to depopulate all the progenie
Of Froggs, affected with the lance of warre.
And certainely he had put on as farre
As he advanc't his vant—he was indude 390
With so unmatcht a force and fortitude—
Had not the Father both of Gods and Men
Instantly knowne it, and the Froggs (even then
Given up to ruine) rescude with remorse:
Who (his head moving) thus began discourse: 395
'No meane amaze affects me, to behold
Prince Meridarpax rage so uncontrold,
In thirst of Frogg-blood, all along the lake.
Come therefore still, and all addression make,
Dispatching Pallas, with tumultuous Mars, 400
Downe to the field, to make him leave the wars,

[380] *Bread-betraier.*

[382] *Scrap or broken-meat-eater.*

[402] Κρατερός, Validus seu potens in retinendo.

How Potently soever he be said
Where he attempts once to uphold his head.'
Mars answered: 'O Jove, neither she nor I
(With both our aides) can keepe depopulacie 405
From off the Froggs. And therefore arme we all,
Even thy lance letting brandish to his call
From off the field, that from the field withdrew
The Titanois, the Titanois that slew,
Though most exempt from match of all earth's seedes, 410
So great and so inaccessible deeds
It hath proclaim'd to men; bound hand and foot
The vast Enceladus, and rac't by th'root
The race of upland Gyants.' This speech past,
Saturnius a smoking lightening cast 415
Amongst the armies, thundring then so sore
That with a rapting circumflexe he bore
All huge heaven over. But the terrible ire
Of his dart, sent abroad all wrapt in fire
(Which certainely his very finger was), 420
Amazde both Mise and Froggs. Yet soone let passe
Was all this by the Mise, who much the more
Burnd in desire t'exterminate the store
Of all those lance-lov'd souldiers. Which had beene,
If from Olympus Jove's eye had not seene 425
The Froggs with pittie, and with instant speede
Sent them assistents. Who (ere any heede
Was given to their approch) came crawling on
With Anviles on their backs, that (beat upon
Never so much) are never wearied yet; 430
Crook-pawd, and wrested on with foule cloven feet,
Tongues in their mouths, brick-backt, all over bone,
Broade-shoulderd, whence a ruddie yellow shone;
Distorted, and small thigh'd; had eyes that saw
Out at their bosomes; twice foure feet did draw 435
About their bodies; strong neckt, whence did rise
Two heads; nor could to any hand be Prise;
They call them Lobsters, that eat from the Mise
Their tailes, their feet, and hands, and wrested all
Their lances from them so that cold Appall 440
The wretches put in rout, past all returne.
And now the Fount of light forbore to burne
Above the earth, when (which men's lawes commend)
Our Battaile in one daie tooke absolute end.

[429] Νωτάκμονες, Incudes ferentes: *Or Anvile-back't.* Ἄκμων, Incus, dicta pro syncopen quasi nullis ictibus fatigetur.

[432] Ψαλίδοοστμος, Forcipem in ore habens.

THE END OF HOMER'S BATTAILE OF FROGGES AND MISE

AL THE HYMNES OF HOMER

AN HYMNE TO APOLLO

I will remember and expresse the praise
Of heaven's far-darter, the faire King of daies,
Whom even the Gods themselves feare when he goes
Through Jove's high house; and when his goodly bowes
He goes to bend, all from their Thrones arise, 5
And cluster neare t'admire his faculties.
Onely Latona stirs not from her seate
Close by the Thunderer, till her sonne's retreat
From his dread archerie; but then she goes,
Slackens his string, and shuts his Quiver close, 10
And (having taken to her hand his bowe
From off his able shoulders) doth bestowe
Upon a Pinne of gold the glorious Tiller,
The Pinne of gold fixt in his Father's Piller.
Then doth she to his Throne his state uphold, 15
Where his great Father in a cup of gold
Serves him with Nectar, and shews all the grace
Of his great sonne. Then th'other gods take place,
His gracious mother glorying to beare
So great an Archer and a sonne so cleare. 20
All haile (O blest Latona!) to bring forth
An issue of such All-out-shining worth,
Royall Apollo, and the Queene that loves
The hurles of darts. She in th'Ortygian groves,
And he in cliffie Delos, leaning on 25
The loftie Oros, and being built upon
By Cynthus' Prominent, that his head reares
Close to the Palme that Inops' fluent cheares.
How shall I praise thee, farre being worthiest praise,
O Phœbus, to whose worth the law of layes 30
In all kindes is ascrib'de? If feeding flocks
By Continent or Ile, all eminen'st rocks
Did sing for joy, Hill-tops, and floods in song
Did breake their billows, as they flow'd along
To serve the sea. The shores, the seas, and all 35
Did sing as soone as from the lap did fall
Of blest Latona thee, the joy of Man.

Her Child-bed made the mountaine Cynthian
In rockie Delos, the sea-circled Ile,
On whose all sides the black seas brake their Pile 40
And over-flowd for joy, so franck a Gale
The singing winds did on their waves exhale.
  Here borne, all mortalls live in thy commands,
Who ever Crete holds, Athens, or the strands
Of th'Ile Ægina, or the famous lands 45
For ships, Eubœa, or Eresia,
Or Peparethus, bordring on the sea,
Ægas, or Athos, that doth Thrace divide
And Macedon, or Pelion, with the pride
Of his high forehead, or the Samian Ile, 50
That likewise lies neare Thrace, or Scyrus' soile,
Ida's steepe tops, or all that Phocis fill,
Or Autocanes, with the heaven-high hill,
Or populous Imber, Lemnos without Ports,
Or Lesbos, fit for the divine resorts, 55
And sacred soile of blest Æolion;
Or Chius that exceeds comparison
For fruitfulnes, with all the Iles that lie
Embrac't with seas, Mimas, with rocks so hie,
Or Loftie-crownd Corycius, or the bright 60
Charos, or Æsagæus' dazeling height,
Or waterie Samos; Mycale, that beares
Her browes even with the circles of the spheares,
Miletus, Cous, that the Citie is
Of voice-divided-choice humanities, 65
High Cnidus, Carpathus, still strooke with winde,
Naxus, and Paros, and the rockie-min'd
Rugged Rhenæa. Yet through all these parts,
Latona, great-growne with the King of darts,
Travailde, and tried if any would become 70
To her deare birth an hospitable home—
All which extremely trembled (shooke with feare),
Nor durst endure so high a birth to beare
In their free States, though, for it, they became
Never so fruitfull; till the reverend Dame 75
Ascended Delos, and her soile did sease
With these wing'd words: 'O Delos! would'st thou please
To be my sonne Apolloe's native seat,
And build a welthie Phane to one so great,
No one shall blame or question thy kinde deede. 80
Nor think I, thou dost Sheepe or Oxen feede
In any such store, or in vines exceede,

Nor bring'st forth such innumerable Plants
(Which often make the rich Inhabitants
Careles of Deitie). If thou then should'st rere 85
A Phane to Phœbus, all men would confer
Whole Hecatombs of beeves for sacrifice,
Still thronging hither. And to thee would rise
Ever unmeasur'd Odors, should'st thou long
Nourish thy King thus; and from forreigne wrong 90
The Gods would guard thee, which thine owne addresse
Can never compasse for thy barrennesse.'
She said, and Delos joi'd, replying thus:
'Most happie sister of Saturnius!
I gladly would with all meanes entertein 95
The King your sonne, being now despis'de of men,
But should be honord with the greatest then.
Yet this I feare, nor will conceale from thee:
Your Sonne (some say) will author miserie
In many kindes, as being to sustein 100
A mightie empire over Gods and Men
Upon the holie-gift-giver, the earth.
And bitterly I feare that, when his birth
Gives him the sight of my so barren soile,
He will contemne, and give me up to spoile, 105
Enforce the sea to me, that ever will
Oppresse my heart with many a watrie hill.
And therefore let him chuse some other land,
Where he shall please to build at his command
Temple and Grove, set thick with many a Tree. 110
For wretched Polypusses breed in me
Retyring chambers, and black sea-calves Den
In my poore soile, for penurie of Men.
And yet, O Goddesse, would'st thou please to sweare
The Gods' great oath to me, before thou beare 115
Thy blessed Sonne here, that thou wilt erect
A Phane to him, to render the effect
Of men's demands to them before they fall,
Then will thy sonne's renowne be generall,
Men will his name in such varietie call, 120
And I shall, then, be glad his birth to beare.'
This said, the Gods' great oath she thus did swere:
'Know this, O earth! broad heaven's inferior sphere!
And of blacke Styx the most infernall lake!—
Which is the gravest oath the Gods can take— 125
That here shall ever rise to Phœbus' Name
An odorous Phane and Altar; and thy fame

Honor, past all Iles else, shall see him emploid.'
  Her oath thus tooke and ended, Delos joi'd
In mightie measure that she should become 130
To farr-shot Phœbus' birth the famous home.
  Latona then nine daies and nights did fall
In hopeles labor; at whose birth were all
Heaven's most supreame and worthie Goddesses,
Dione, Rhea, and th'Exploratresse 135
Themis, and Amphitrite, that will be
Pursu'd with sighs still—every Deitie
Except the snowie-wristed wife of Jove,
Who held her moodes aloft, and would not move.
Onely Lucina (to whose virtue vowes 140
Each Child-birth patient) heard not of her throwes,
But sat (by Juno's counsaile) on the browes
Of broad Olympus, wrapt in clouds of gold;
Whom Jove's proud wife in envie did with-hold,
Because bright-lockt Latona was to beare 145
A Sonne so faultles and in force so cleare.
The rest Thaumantia sent before to bring
Lucina to release the envied King,
Assuring her that they would strait confer
A Carquenet, nine cubits long, on her, 150
All woven with wires of Gold. But chargd her, then,
To call apart from th'Ivorie-wristed Queene
The child-birth-guiding Goddesse, for just feare
Lest, her charge utter'd in Saturnia's eare,
She, after, might disswade her from descent. 155
  When winde-swift-footed Iris knew th'intent
Of th'other Goddesses, away she went,
And instantly she past the infinite space
Twixt Earth and Heaven; when, comming to the place
Where dwelt th'Immortals, strait without the gate 160
She gat Lucina, and did all relate
The Goddesses commanded, and enclin'd
To all that they demanded her deare Minde.
And on their way they went, like those two Doves
That, walking high-waies, every shadow moves 165
Up from the earth, forc't with their naturall feare:
When entring Delos, she that is so deare
To Dames in labor made Latona strait
Prone to deliverie, and to weild the wait
Of her deare burthen with a world of ease. 170
When with her faire hand she a Palme did sease,
And (staying her by it) stucke her tender knees

Amidst the soft meade, that did smile beneath
Her sacred labor; and the child did breath
The aire in th'instant. All the Goddesses 175
Brake in kinde teares and shrikes for her quicke ease,
And Thee, O Archer Phœbus, with waves cleere
Washt sweetly over, swadled with sincere
And spotlesse swath-bands; and made then to flow
About thy breast a mantle, white as snow, 180
Fine, and new made; and cast a Veile of Gold
Over thy forehead. Nor yet forth did hold
Thy mother for thy foode her golden brest,
But Themis, in supply of it, addrest
Lovely Ambrosia, and drunke off to thee 185
A Bowle of Nectar, interchangeablie
With her immortall fingers serving thine.
And when, O Phœbus, that eternall wine
Thy tast had relisht, and that foode divine,
No golden swath-band longer could containe 190
Thy panting bosome; all that would constraine
Thy soone-easd God-head, every feeble chaine
Of earthy Child-rights, flew in sunder all.
And then didst thou thus to the Deities call:
'Let there be given me my lov'd Lute and Bow; 195
I'le prophecie to men, and make them know
Jove's perfect counsailes.' This said, up did flie
From brode-waide Earth the unshorne Deitie,
Far-shot Apollo. All th'Immortalls stood
In steepe amaze to see Latonae's brood. 200
All Delos, looking on him, all with gold
Was loden strait, and joi'd to be extold
By great Latona so, that she decreed
Her barrennesse should beare the fruitfulst seed
Of all the Iles and Continents of earth, 205
And lov'd her from her heart so for her birth.
For so she florisht as a hill that stood
Crownd with the flowre of an abundant wood:
And thou, O Phœbus, bearing in thy hand
Thy silver bow, walk'st over every land, 210
Sometimes ascend'st the rough-hewne rockie hill
Of desolate Cynthus, and sometimes tak'st will
To visit Ilands, and the Plumps of men.
And manie a Temple, all wayes, men ordein
To thy bright God-head; Groves, made darke with Trees, 215
And never shorne, to hide ye Deities,
All high-lov'd Prospects, all the steepest browes

Of farr-seene Hills, and every flood that flowes
Forth to the sea, are dedicate to Thee.
But most of all thy minde's Alacritie 220
Is rais'd with Delos; since to fill thy Phane
There flocks so manie an Ionian,
With ample Gownes that flowe downe to their feet,
With all their children, and the reverend Sweet
Of all their pious wives. And these are they 225
That (mindefull of thee) even thy Deitie
Render more spritelie with their Champion fight,
Dances, and songs, perform'd to glorious sight,
Once having publisht and proclaim'd their strife.
And these are acted with such exquisite life 230
That one would say, 'Now, the Ionian straines
Are turn'd Immortalls, nor know what Age meanes.'
His minde would take such pleasure from his eye,
To see them serv'd by all Mortalitie,
Their men so humane, women so well-grac't, 235
Their ships so swift, their riches so encreast,
Since thy observance, who (being all before
Thy opposites) were all despis'd and poore.
And to all these this absolute wonder add,
Whose praise shall render all posterities gladd: 240
The Delian Virgines are thy handmaides, All,
And, since they serv'd Apollo, jointly fall
Before Latona, and Diana too,
In sacred service, and doe therefore know
How to make mention of the ancient Trimms 245
Of men and women in their well-made Hymns,
And soften barbarous Nations with their songs,
Being able, all, to speake the severall tongu's
Of forreine Nations, and to imitate
Their musiques there, with art so fortunate 250
That one would say, there every one did speake,
And all their tunes in naturall accents breake,
Their songs so well compos'd are, and their Art
To answer all soundes is of such Desart.
  But come, Latona, and thou king of Flames, 255
With Phœbe, Rectresse of chaste thoughts in Dames,
Let me salute ye, and your Graces call
Hereafter to my just memoriall.
  And you, O Delian Virgins, doe me grace,
When any stranger of our earthie Race 260
Whose restlesse life Affliction hath in chace
Shall hither come and question you: 'Who is,

To your chaste eares, of choicest faculties
In sacred Poesie, and with most right
Is Author of your absolut'st delight?' 265
Ye shall your selves doe all the right ye can
To answer for our Name: 'The sightlesse man
Of stonie Chios. All whose Poems shall
In all last Ages stand for Capitall.'
This for your owne sakes I desire; for I 270
Will propagate mine owne precedencie
As far as earth shall well-built cities beare,
Or humane conversation is held deare—
Not with my praise direct, but praises due,
And men shall credit it because tis true. 275
How ever, I'le not cease the praise I vow
To farre-shot Phœbus with the silver bow,
Whom lovely-hair'd Latona gave the light.
O King! both Lycia is in Rule thy Right,
Faire Mœonie, and the Maritimall 280
Miletus, wisht to be the seate of all.
But chiefely Delos, girt with billowes round,
Thy most respected empire doth resound—
Where thou to Pythus wentst, to answer there
(As soone as thou wert borne) the burning eare 285
Of many a far-come to heare future deeds,
Clad in divine and odoriferous weeds,
And with thy Golden Fescue plaidst upon
Thy hollow Harp, that sounds to heaven set gone.
Then to Olympus swift as thought hee flew 290
To Jove's high house, and had a retinew
Of Gods t'attend him. And then strait did fall
To studie of the Harp and Harpsicall
All th'Immortalls. To whom every Muse
With ravishing voices did their answers use, 295
Singing th'eternall deeds of Deitie,
And from their hands what Hells of miserie
Poore Humanes suffer, living desperate quite,
And not an Art they have, wit, or deceipt,
Can make them manage any Act aright, 300
Nor finde, with all the soule they can engage,
A salve for Death, or remedie for Age.
But here the fayre-hayrd graces, the wise Howres,
Harmonia, Hebe, and sweet Venus' powres,
Danc't, and each other's Palme to Palme did cling, 305
And with these danc't not a deformed thing,
No forspoke Dwarfe, nor downeward witherling,

But all with wondrous goodly formes were deckt,
And mov'd with Beauties of unpris'd aspect.
  Dart-deare-Diana (even with Phœbus bred) 310
Danc't likewise there; and Mars a march did tred
With that brave Bevie. In whose consort fell
Argicides, th'ingenious Sentinell.
Phœbus-Apollo toucht his Lute to them
Sweetely and softly, a most glorious beame 315
Casting about him as he danc't and plaid,
And even his feet were all with raies araide.
His weede and all, of a most curious Trymm,
With no lesse Luster grac't and circled him.
  By these Latona, with a hayre that shin'd 320
Like burnisht gold, and (with the Mightie Minde)
Heaven's Counsailor, Jove, sat with delightsome eyes,
To see their Sonne new rankt with Deities.
  How shall I praise thee, then, that art all praise?
Amongst the Brides shall I thy Deitie raise? 325
Or being in love, when, sad, thou wentst to wowe
The Virgin Aza, and didst overthrowe
The even-with-Gods, Elation's Mightie seed,
That had of goodly horse so brave a breed,
And Phorbas, sonne of soveraigne Triopus, 330
Valiant Leucippus, and Ereutheus,
And Triopus himselfe, with equall fall,
Thou but on foot, and they on horsebacke all?
  Or shall I sing thee, as thou first didst grace
Earth with thy foot, to finde thee forth a place 335
Fit to pronounce thy Oracles to Men?
First from Olympus thou alightedst then
Into Pieria, passing all the land
Of fruitles Lesbos, chok't with drifts of sand,
The Magnets likewise, and the Perrhæbes; 340
And to Iolcus variedst thy accesse,
Cenæus' Topps ascending, that their Base
Make bright Eubœa, being of ships the Grace,
And fixt thy faire stand in Lelantus' field,
That did not yet thy minde's contentment yeeld 345
To raise a Phane on, and a sacred Grove.
  Passing Euripus then, thou mad'st remove
Up to earth's ever-greene and holyest Hill,
Yet swiftly thence, too, thou transcendedst still
To Mycalessus, and did'st touch upon 350
Teumessus, apt to make greene couches on,
And flowrie field-bedds. Then thy Progresse found

Thebes out, whose soile with onely woods was crown'd.
For yet was sacred Thebes no humane seate,
And therefore were no Paths nor high waies beat 355
On her free bosome, that flowes now with wheat,
But then she onely wore on it a wood.
  From hence (even loth to part, because it stood
Fit for thy service) thou put'st on Remove
To greene Onchestus, Neptune's glorious Grove, 360
Where new-tam'd horse, bredd, nourish nerves so rare
That still they frolick, though they travaild are
Never so sore, and hurrie after them
Most heavie Coches, but are so extream
(In usuall-travaile) fierie-and-free 365
That, though their cochman ne're so masterlie
Governes their courages, he sometimes must
Forsake his seat, and give their spirits their lust—
When after them their emptie coach they drawe,
Foming and Neighing, quite exempt from awe. 370
And if their Cocheman guide through any Grove
Unshorne, and vow'd to any Deitie's Love,
The Lords encocht leap out, and all their care
Use to allaie their fires, with speaking faire,
Stroking and trimming them, and in some queach 375
(Or strength of shade) within their nearest reach
Reigning them up, invoke the deified King
Of that unshorne and everlasting spring,
And leave them then to her preserving hands
Who is the Fate that there the God commands. 380
And this was first the sacred fashion there.
From hence thou wentst, O thou in shafts past Pere,
And found'st Cephissus with thy all-seeing beames,
Whose flood affects so many silver streames,
And from Lilæus poures so bright a wave. 385
  Yet forth thy foot flew, and thy faire eyes gave
The view of Ocale, the rich in towrs;
Then to Amartus, that abounds in flowrs,
Then to Delphusa putt'st thy progresse on,
Whose blessed soile nought harmefull breeds upon. 390
And there thy pleasure would a Phane adorne,
And nourish woods whose shades should ne're be shorne.
Where this thou told'st her, standing to her close:
'Delphusa, here I entertaine suppose
To build a farr-fam'd Temple, and ordein 395
An Oracle t'informe the mindes of Men,
Who shall for ever offer to my love

Whole Hecatombs—even all the men that move
In rich Peloponnesus, and all those
Of Europe, and the Iles the seas enclose, 400
Whom future search of Acts and Beings brings—
To whom I'le prophecie the truths of things
In that rich Temple where my Oracle sings.'
This said, the all-bounds-reacher with his bowe
The Phane's divine foundations did foreshowe; 405
Ample they were, and did huge length impart,
With a continuate Tenour, full of Art.
But when Delphusa look't into his end,
Her heart grew angrie, and did thus extend
It selfe to Phœbus: 'Phœbus, since thy minde 410
A farr-fam'd Phane hath in it selfe design'd
To beare an Oracle to men in me,
That Hecatombs may put in fire to thee,
This let me tell thee, and impose for staie
Upon thy purpose: th'Inarticulate neye 415
Of fire-hov'd horse will ever disobaie
Thy numerous eare, and mules will for their drinke
Trouble my sacred springs, and I should thinke
That any of the humane Race had rather
See here the hurreys of rich Coches gather, 420
And heare the haughtie Neys of swift-hov'd horse,
Than (in his pleasure's place) convert recourse
T'a Mightie Temple; and his wealth bestow
On Pieties, where his sports may freely flow,
Or see huge wealth that he shall never owe. 425
And therefore (wouldst thou heare my free advise,
Though Mightier farre thou art, and much more wise,
O King, than I, thy powre being great'st of all),
In Crissa, underneath the bosome's fall
Of steepe Parnassus, let thy minde be given 430
To set thee up a Phane, where never driven
Shall glorious Coches be, nor horses' Neys
Storme neare thy well-built Altars, but thy praise
Let the faire race of pious Humanes bring
Into thy Phane, that Io-Pæans sing. 435
And those gifts onely let thy Deified minde
Be circularlie pleas'd with, being the kinde
And fayre-burnt-offrings that true Deities binde.'
With this, his minde she altered, though she spake
Not for his good, but her owne glorie's sake. 440
From hence, O Phœbus, first thou mad'st retreat,
And of the Phlegians reacht the walled seat,

Inhabited with contumelious Men,
Whoe, sleighting Jove, tooke up their dwellings then
Within a large Cave neare Cephissus' Lake. 445
Hence, swiftly moving, thou all speed didst make
Up to the tops intended, and the ground
Of Crissa, under the with-snowe-still-croun'd
Parnassus, reacht, whose face affects the west;
Above which hangs a rock that still seemes prest 450
To fall upon it, through whose brest doth runn
A rockie Cave, neare which the King the Sunn
Cast to contrive a Temple to his minde,
And said: 'Now heere stands my conceipt inclin'd
To build a famous Phane, where still shall be 455
An Oracle to Men, that still to me
Shall offer absolute Hecatombs, as well
Those that in rich Peloponnesus dwell
As those of Europe, and the Iles that lie
Walld with the sea, that all their paines applie 460
T'employ my counsailes. To all which will I
True secrets tell, by way of Prophesie,
In my rich Temple, that shall ever be
An Oracle to all Posteritie.'
This said, the Phane's forme he did strait present, 465
Ample, and of a length of great extent;
In which Trophonius and Agamede
(Who of Erginus were the famous seed)
Impos'd the stonie Entrie, and the Heart
Of every God had for their excellent Art. 470
About the Temple dwelt of humane Name
Unnumbred Nations, it acquir'd such Fame,
Being all of stone, built for eternall date.
And neare it did a Fountaine propagate
A fayre streame farr away; when Jove's bright seed, 475
The King Apollo, with an arrow, freed
From his strong string, destroid the Dragonesse
That Wonder nourisht, being of such excesse
In size and horridnesse of monstrous shape,
That on the forc't earth she wrought many a rape, 480
Many a spoile made on it, many an ill
On crooke-hancht Herds brought, being impurpl'd still
With blood of all sorts; having undergone
The charge of Juno, with the golden Throne,
To nourish Typhon, the abhorr'd affright 485
And bane of mortalls—whom into the light
Saturnia brought forth, being incenst with Jove,

Because the most renowm'd fruit of his love,
Pallas, he got, and shooke out of his braine.
For which Majestique Juno did complaine 490
In this kinde to the blest Court of the skies:
'Know all ye sex-distinguisht Deities,
That Jove (assembler of the cloudie throng)
Beginns with me first and affects with wrong
My right in him, made by himselfe his wife, 495
That knowes and does the honor'd marriage life
All honest offices; and yet hath he
Undulie got, without my companie,
Blew-eyd Minerva, who of all the skie
Of blest Immortalls is the absolute Grace; 500
Where I have brought into the heavenly Race
A Sonne, both taken in his feet and head
So oughly, and so farr from worth my bedd,
That (ravisht into hand) I tooke and threw
Downe to the vast sea his detested view; 505
Where Nereus' Daughter, Thetis, who her waie
With silver feet makes, and the faire araie
Of her bright sisters sav'd, and tooke to guard.
But would to heaven, another yet were spar'd
The like Grace of his God-head. Craftie mate, 510
What other scape canst thou excogitate?
How could thy heart sustaine to get alone
The grey-eyd Goddesse? Her conception
Nor bringing forth had any hand of mine,
And yet know all the Gods I goe for thine 515
To such kinde uses. But I'le now employ
My braine to procreate a masculine Joy,
That 'mongst th'Immortalls may as eminent shine,
With shame affecting nor my bedd nor thine.
Nor will I ever touch at thine againe, 520
But farr fly it and thee; and yet will raigne
Amongst th'Immortalls ever.' This spleene spent,
(Still yet left angrie) farre away she went
From all the Deathlesse, and yet praid to all,
Advanc't her hand, and e're she let it fall 525
Us'd these excitements: 'Heare me now, O Earth!
Brode Heaven above it, and beneath, your birth,
The Deified Titanois, that dwell about
Vast Tartarus, from whence sprung all the Rout
Of Men and Deities! Heare me all, I say, 530
With all your forces, and give instant way
T'a sonne of mine, without Jove, who yet may

Nothing inferiour prove in force to him,
But past him spring as farre in able lim
As he past Saturne.' This pronounc't, she strooke 535
Life-bearing Earth so strongly, that she shooke
Beneath her numb'd hand—which when she beheld,
Her bosome with abundant comforts sweld,
In hope all should to her desire extend.
From hence the Yeare that all such proofes gives end 540
Grew round; yet all that time the bed of Jove
Shee never toucht at, never was her love
Enflam'd to sit nere his Dædalian Throne,
As she accustomed, to consult upon
Counsells kept darke with many a secret skill, 545
But kept her Vow-frequented Temple still,
Pleas'd with her sacrifice; till now, the Nights
And Daies accomplish't, and the yeare's whole rights
In all her revolutions being expir'de,
The Howres, and all, run out that were requir'd 550
To vent a Birth-right, she brought forth a Sonne,
Like Gods or Men in no condition,
But a most dreadfull and pernicious thing
Call'd Typhon, who on all the humane Spring
Confer'd confusion—which receiv'd to hand 555
By Juno, instantly she gave command
(Ill to ill adding) that the Dragonesse
Should bring it up; who tooke, and did oppresse
With many a misery (to maintaine th'excesse
Of that inhumane Monster) all the Race 560
Of Men that were of all the world the grace—
Till the farre-working Phœbus at her sent
A fierie Arrow, that invok't event
Of death gave to her execrable life.
Before which yet she lay in bitter strife, 565
With dying paines groveling on earth, and drew
Extreme short respirations; for which flew
A shout about the aire, whence no man knew
But came by power divine. And then she lay
Tumbling her Truncke, and winding every way 570
About her nastie Nest, quite leaving then
Her murtherous life, embru'd with deaths of Men.
  Then Phœbus gloried, saying: 'Thy selfe now lie
On Men-sustaining Earth, and putrifie,
Who first of Putrifaction was inform'd. 575
Now on thy life have Death's cold vapors stormd,
That stormd'st on Men the Earth-fed so much death,

In envie of the Of-spring they made breathe
Their lives out on my Altars. Now from thee
Not Typhon shall enforce the miserie 580
Of merited death, nor shee whose name implies
Such scath, Chimæra, but blacke earth make prise
To putrifaction thy Immanities,
And bright Hyperion, that light all eyes showes,
Thyne with a night of rottennesse shall close.' 585
Thus spake he glory'ng; and then seas'd upon
Her horrid heape, with Putrifaction,
Hyperion's lovely powrs; from whence her name
Tooke sound of Python, and heaven's soveraigne flame
Was surnam'd Pythius, since the sharp-eyd Sunn 590
Affected so with Putrifaction
The hellish Monster. And now Phœbus' minde
Gave him to know that falsehood had strooke blinde
Even his bright eye, because it could not finde
The subtle Fountaine's fraud—to whom he flew, 595
Enflam'd with anger, and in th'instant drew
Close to Delphusa, using this short vow:
'Delphusa! you must looke no longer now
To vent your frauds on me; for well I know
Your scituation to be lovely worth 600
A Temple's Imposition, it poures forth
So delicate a streame. But your renowne
Shall now no longer shine here, but mine owne.'
This said, he thrust her Promontorie downe,
And damn'd her fountaine up with mightie stones, 605
A Temple giving consecrations
In woods adjoining. And in this Phane all
On him, by surname of Delphusius, call,
Because Delphusa's sacred flood and fame
His wrath affected so, and hid in shame. 610
And then thought Phœbus what descent of Men
To be his Ministers he should retein,
To doe in stonie Pythos sacrifice.
To which his minde contending, his quicke eies
He cast upon the blew Sea, and beheld 615
A ship, on whose Masts sailes that wing'd it sweld,
In which were men transferr'd, many and good,
That in Minoian Cnossus eate their food,
And were Cretensians; who now are those
That all the sacrifising dues dispose, 620
And all the lawes deliver to a word
Of Daie's great King, that weares the golden sword,

And Oracles (out of his Delphian Tree
That shrowds her faire armes in the Cavitie
Beneath Parnassus' Mount) pronounce to Men. 625
These, now his Priests, that liv'd as Merchants then,
In trafficks and Pecuniarie Rates
For sandie Pylos and the Pylian States
Were under saile. But now encounterd them
Phœbus Apollo, who into the streame 630
Cast himselfe headlong, and the strange disguise
Tooke of a Dolphine of a goodly sise—
Like which He leapt into their ship, and lay
As an Ostent of infinite dismay,
For none with any strife of Minde could looke 635
Into the Omen. All the shipmasts shooke,
And silent all sate with the feare they tooke,
Arınd not, nor strooke they saile, but as before
Went on with full Trim; and a foreright Blore,
Stiff and from forth the South, the ship made flie. 640
When first they stript the Malean Promont'rie,
Toucht at Laconia's soile, in which a Towne
Their ship ariv'd at, that the Sea doth Crowne,
Call'd Tenarus, a place of much delight
To men that serve Heaven's Comforter of sight, 645
In which are fed the famous flocks that beare
The wealthie Fleeces, on a delicate Laire
Being fed, and seated—where the Merchants faine
Would have put in, that they might out againe
To tell the Miracle that chanc't to them, 650
And trie if it would take the sacred streame,
Rushing far forth, that he againe might beare
Those other Fishes that abounded there
Delightsome companie, or still would stay
Abord their drie ship. But it failde t'obay, 655
And for the rich Peloponnesian shore
Steer'de her free saile; Apollo made the Blore
Directly guide it. That, obaying still,
Reacht drie Arena, and (what wish doth fill)
Faire Argyphæa, and the populous height 660
Of Thryus, whose streame (siding her) doth weight
With safe passe on Alphæus, Pylos' sands
And Pylian dwellers; keeping by the strands
On which th'Inhabitants of Crunius dwell,
And Helida, set opposite to Hell; 665
Chalcis and Dymes reach't, and happily
Made saile by Pheras—all being over-joide

With that francke Gale that Jove himselfe emploid.
And then amongst the cloudes they might descrie
The Hill that far-seene Ithaca calls her Eie, 670
Dulichius, Samos, and, with timber grac't,
Shadie Zacynthus. But when now they past
Peloponnesus all, and then when show'de
The infinite Vale of Crissa, that doth shroud
All rich Morea with her liberall brest, 675
So francke a Gale there flew out of the West
As all the skie discovered; twas so great,
And blew so from the verie Counsell seat
Of Jove himselfe, that quickly it might send
The ship through full Seas to her journey's end. 680
From thence they saild, quite opposite, to the East,
And to the Region where light leaves his rest,
The Light himselfe being sacred Pylot there,
And made the Sea-trod ship arive them nere
The Grapefull Crissa, where he rest doth take 685
Close to her Port and sands. And then forth brake
The far-shot King, like to a starre that strowes
His glorious forehead where the Mid-day glowes,
That all in sparkles did his state attire,
Whose Luster leapt up to the spheare of fire. 690
He trodd where no waie op'te, and pierst the place
That of his sacred Tripods held the grace,
In which he lighted such a fluent flame
As guilt all Crissa; in which every Dame
And Dame's faire daughter cast out vehement cries 695
At those fell fires of Phœbus' Prodigies,
That shaking feares through all their fancies threw.
Then (like the minde's swift light) againe he flew
Backe to the ship, shap't like a youth in Height
Of all his graces, shoulders broad and streit, 700
And all his haire in golden currls enwrapt;
And to the Merchants thus his speech he shap't:
'Ho! strangers! what are you? and from what seat
Saile ye these waies that salt and water sweat?
To traffick justlie? or use vagrant scapes 705
Voyde of all rule, conferring wrongs and Rapes
(Like Pyrats) on the men ye never sawe,
With mindes project, exempt from list or Lawe?
Why sit ye heere so stupified, nor take
Land while ye may, nor deposition make 710
Of Navall Arms, when this the fashion is
Of men Industrious, who (their faculties

Wearied at sea) leave ship, and use the land
For foode, that with their healths and stomacks stand?'
  This said, with bold mindes he their brest suppli'd, 715
And thus made answer the Cretensian guide:
  'Stranger! because you seeme to us no seed
Of any mortall, but celestiall breed
For parts and person, Joy your steps ensue,
And Gods make good the blisse we thinke your due. 720
Vouchsafe us true relation, on what land
We here arive, and what men here command.
We were for well-knowne parts bound, and from Crete
(Our vanted countrie) to the Pylian seat
Vow'd our whole voyage. Yet arive we here, 725
Quite crosse to those wills that our motions stere,
Wishing to make returne some other way,
Some other course desirous to assaie,
To pay our lost paines. But some God hath fill'd
Our frustrate sayles, defeating what we will'd.' 730
  Apollo answerd: 'Strangers! though before
Yee dwelt in wooddie Cnossus, yet no more
Yee must be made your owne Reciprocalls
To your lov'd Cittie and faire severalls
Of wives and houses. But ye shall have here 735
My wealthie Temple, honord farre and nere
Of many a Nation; for my selfe am Son
To Jove himselfe, and of Apollo won
The glorious Title, who thus safelie through
The sea's vast billows still have held your plough, 740
No ill intending, that will let ye make
My Temple here your owne, and honors take
Upon your selves, all that to me are given.
And more, the counsailes of the King of Heaven
Your selves shall know, and with his will receive 745
Ever the honors that all men shall give.
Doe as I say then instantly: strike saile,
Take downe your Tackling, and your vessell hale
Up into land; your goods bring forth, and all
The instruments that into sayling fall; 750
Make on this shore an Altar, fire enflame,
And barley white cakes offer to my name.
And then (environing the Altar) pray,
And call me (as ye sawe me in the day
When from the windie seas I brake swift way 755
Into your ship) Delphinius, since I tooke
A Dolphin's forme then. And to every looke

That there shall seeke it, that my Altar shall
Be made a Delphian memoriall
From thence for ever. After this, ascend 760
Your swift black ship and sup, and then intend
Ingenuous Offerings to the equall Gods
That in celestiall seates make blest abods—
When (having staid your helthfull hunger's sting)
Come all with me, and Io-Pæans sing 765
All the waie's length, till you attaine the state
Where I your oppulent Phane have consecrate.'
To this they gave him passing diligent eare,
And vow'd to his obedience all they were.
First, striking sayle, their tacklings then they los'd, 770
And (with their Gables stoop't) their mast impos'd
Into the Mast roome. Forth themselves then went,
And from the sea into the Continent
Drew up their ship, which farr up from the sand
They rais'd with ample rafters. Then in hand 775
They tooke the Altar, and inform'd it on
The sea's nere shore, imposing thereupon
White cakes of barley, fire made, and did stand
About it round, as Phœbus gave command,
Submitting Invocations to his will; 780
Then sacrifis'd to all the heavenly Hill
Of powrefull God-heads. After which they eat
Abord their ship, till with fit food repleat
They rose, nor to their Temple us'd delay.
Whom Phœbus usherd, and toucht all the way 785
His heavenly Lute with Art above admir'd,
Gracefully leading them. When all were fir'd
With zeale to him, and follow'd wondring, all,
To Pythos; and upon his name did call
With Io-Pæans, such as Cretans use. 790
And in their bosomes did the deified Muse
Voices of honey-Harmonie infuse.
With never-wearie feet their way they went,
And made with all alacritie ascent
Up to Parnassus, and that long'd-for place 795
Where they should live, and be of men the Grace.
When, all the way, Apollo shew'd them still
Their farr-stretcht valleys, and their two-topt Hill,
Their famous Phane, and all that all could raise
To a supreame height of their Joy, and praise. 800
And then the Cretan Captaine thus enquir'd
Of King Apollo: 'Since you have retir'd,

O Soveraigne, our sad lives so farr from friends
And native soile (because so farr extends
Your deare minde's pleasure) tell us how we shall 805
Live in your service. To which question call
Our provident mindes, because we see not croun'd
This soile with store of vines, nor doth abound
In welthie meddows, on which we may live,
As well as on men our attendance give.' 810
He smil'd, and said: 'O men, that nothing know
And so are follow'd with a world of woe,
That needs will succour care and curious mone,
And poure out sighs without cessation,
Were all the riches of the earth your owne! 815
Without much busines, I will render knowne
To your simplicities an easie way
To wealth enough. Let every man purvaie
A skeane (or slaugh'ring steele) and his right hand
(Bravely bestowing) evermore see mann'd 820
With killing sheepe, that to my Phane will flowe
From all farr Nations. On all which bestowe
Good observation, and all else they give
To me make you your owne all, and so live.
For all which watch before my Temple well, 825
And all my counsailes, above all, conceale.
If any give vaine language, or to deeds,
Yea, or as farr as injurie proceedes,
Know that (at losers' hands) for those that gaine,
It is the lawes of Mortalls to sustaine. 830
Besides, yee shall have Princes to obay,
Which still yee must, and (so yee gaine) yee may.
All, now, is said; give all thy memorie's stay.'
And thus to thee, Jove and Latona's Sonne,
Be given all grace of salutation. 835
Both thee and others of th'Immortall state
My song shall memorize to endlesse date.

THE END OF THE HYMNE TO APOLLO

A HYMNE TO HERMES

Hermes, the Sonne of Jove and Maia, sing,
O Muse, th'Arcadian and Cyllenian King,
They rich in flocks, he heaven enriching still
In Messages return'd with all his will—
Whom glorious Maia, the Nimph rich in haire, 5
Mixing with Jove in amorous affaire,
Brought forth to him, sustaining a retreat
From all th'Immortalls of the blessed seat,
And living in the same darke Cave where Jove
Inform'd at mid-night the effect of love, 10
Unknowne to either man or Deitie,
Sweet sleepe once having seas'd the jelous eye
Of Juno, deckt with wrists of ivorie.
But when great Jove's high minde was consummate,
The tenth moneth had in heaven confin'de the date 15
Of Maia's Labour, and into the sight
She brought, in one birth, Labours infinite:
For then she bore a sonne, that all tried waies
Could turne and winde to wisht events assaies,
A faire tongu'd, but false-hearted, Counsellor, 20
Rector of Ox-stealers, and for all stealths bore
A varied finger; Speeder of Night's spies
And guide of all her dreames' obscurities;
Guard of dore-Guardians; and was borne to be
Amongst th'Immortalls that wing'd Deitie 25
That in an instant should doe acts would aske
The Powres of others an Eternall Taske.
Borne in the Morne, he form'd his Lute at Noone,
At Night stole all the Oxen of the Sunne;
And all this in his Birth's first day was done, 30
Which was the fourth of the encreasing Moone.
Because Celestiall lims sustain'd his straines,
His sacred swath-bands must not be his chaines.
So (starting up) to Phœbus' Herde he stept,
Found strait the high-roof't Cave where they were kept, 35
And (th'entrie passing) he th'invention found
Of making Lutes; and did in wealth abound

By that Invention, since he first of all
Was author of that Engine Musicall,
By this meane mov'd to the ingenious worke: 40
Nere the Cave's inmost overture did lurke
A Tortois, tasting th'odoriferous grasse,
Leisurely moving; and this Object was
The motive to Jove's Sonne (who could convert
To profitablest uses all desert 45
That nature had in any worke convaid)
To forme the Lute; when (smiling) thus he said:
'Thou mov'st in me a note of excellent use,
Which thy ill forme shall never so seduce
T'evert the good to be inform'd by it, 50
In pliant force of my forme-forging wit.'
Then the slowe Tortois, wrought on by his minde,
He thus saluted: 'All joy to the kinde
Instinct of nature in thee, borne to be
The spirriter of Dances, companie 55
For feasts and following Banquets, grac't and blest
For bearing light to all the interest
Claim'd in this Instrument—from whence shall spring
Play faire and sweet, to which may Graces sing.
A prettie painted cote thou putt'st on here, 60
O Tortois, while thy hill-bred vitall sphere
Confines thy fashion; but (surpris'd by me)
I'le beare thee home, where thou shalt ever be
A Profit to me; and yet nothing more
Will I contemne thee in my merited store. 65
Goods, with good parts got, worth and honour gave;
Left goods and honors every foole may have.
And since thou first shalt give me meanes to live,
I'le love thee ever. Virtuous qualities give
To live at home with them enough content, 70
Where those that want such inward ornament
Fly out for outward, their life made their lode:
Tis best to be at home; Harme lurks abroad.
And certainely thy vertue shall be knowne
Gainst great-yll-causing incantation 75
To serve as for a Lance or Ammulet.
And where, in comfort of thy vitall heat,
Thou now breathst but a sound confus'd for song,
Expos'd by nature, after death, more strong
Thou shalt in sounds of Art be, and command 80
Song infinite sweeter.' Thus with either hand
He tooke it up, and instantly tooke flight

Back to his Cave with that his home-delight—
Where (giving to the Mountaine Tortois vents
Of life and motion) with fit Instruments 85
Forg'd of bright steele he strait inform'd a Lute,
Put neck and frets to it, of which a sute
He made of splitted quills, in equall space
Impos'd upon the neck, and did embrace
Both backe and bosome. At whose height (as gynns 90
T'extend and ease the strings) he put in pynns.
Seven strings, of severall tunes, he then applied,
Made of the Entrailes of a sheepe well dried,
And throughly twisted. Next he did provide
A Case for all, made of an Oxe's Hyde, 95
Out of his counsailes to preserve as well
As to create. And all this Action fell
Into an instant consequence. His word
And worke had individuall accord,
All being as swiftly to perfection brought 100
As any worldly man's most ravisht thought,
Whose minde Care cuts in an infinity
Of varied parts or passions instantly,
Or as the frequent twincklings of an eye.
And thus his House-delight given absolute end, 105
He toucht it, and did every string extend
(With an exploratorie spirit assaid)
To all the parts that could on it be plaid.
It sounded dreadfully; to which he sung,
As if from thence the first and true force sprung 110
That fashions Virtue. God in him did sing.
His play was likewise an unspeakable thing,
Yet, but as an extemporall Assay
Of what showe it would make, being the first way,
It tryed his hand; or a tumultuous noise 115
Such as at feasts the first-flowr'd spirits of Boies
Poure out in mutuall contumelies still,
As little squaring with his curious will,
Or was as wanton and untaught a Store.
Of Jove and Maia, that rich shooes still wore, 120
He sung; who sufferd ill reports before,
And foule staines under her faire titles bore.
But Hermes sung her Nation, and her Name
Did itterate ever—all her high-flowne fame
Of being Jove's Mistresse; celebrating all 125
Her traine of servants, and collaterall
Sumpture of Houses; all her Tripods there,

And Caldrons huge, encreasing every yeare.
All which she knew, yet felt her knowledge stung
With her fame's losse, which (found) she more wisht sung. 130
But now he in his sacred cradle laid
His Lute so absolute, and strait convaid
Himselfe up to a watch-towre forth his house,
Rich and divinely Odoriferous,
A loftie wile at worke in his conceipt, 135
Thirsting the practise of his Empire's height.
And where Impostors rule (since sable Night
Must serve their deeds) he did his deeds their right—
For now the never-resting Sunne was turn'd
For th'under earth, and in the Ocean burn'd 140
His Coch and Coursers. When th'ingenious spie
Pieria's shadie hill had in his eye,
Where the immortall Oxen of the Gods
In ayre's flood solac't their select Abods,
And earth's sweet greene floure, that was never shorne, 145
Fed ever downe. And these the wittie-borne
Argicides set serious spie upon,
Severing from all the rest and setting gone
Full fiftie of the violent Bellowers.
Which driving through the sands, he did reverse 150
(His birth's-craft strait remembring) all their hoves,
And them transpos'd in opposite removes,
The fore behinde set, the behinde before,
T'employ the eyes of such as should explore.
And he himselfe (as slye-pac't) cast away 155
His sandalls on the sea-sands; past display
And unexcogitable thoughts in Act
Putting, to shunn of his stolne steps the Tract,
Mixing both Tamrisk and like-Tamrisk sprayes
In a most rare confusion, to raise 160
His footsteps up from earth. Of which sprayes he
(His armefull gathering fresh from off the Tree)
Made for his sandalls Tyes, both leaves and tyes
Holding together; and then fear'd no eyes
That could affect his feet's discoveries. 165
The Tamrisk boughs he gather'd, making way
Backe from Pieria, but as to convaie
Provision in them for his journey fit,
It being long and, therefore, needing it.
An ould man, now at labour nere the field 170
Of greene Onchestus, knew the verdant yield
Of his fayre armefull; whom th'ingenious Sonne

Of Maia, therefore, salutation
Did thus beginn to: 'Ho! ould man! that now
Art crooked growne with making Plants to grow, 175
Thy nerves will farr be spent, when these boughs shall
To these their leaves confer me fruit and All.
But see not thou what ever thou dost see,
Nor heare, though heare; but all as touching me
Conceale, since nought it can endamage thee.' 180
  This and no more he said, and on drave still
His brode-browd Oxen. Many a shadie Hill,
And many an echoing valley, many a field
Pleasant and wishfull, did his passage yield
Their safe Transcension. But now the divine 185
And black-browd Night (his Mistresse) did decline
Exceeding swiftly, Daie's most earely light
Fast hasting to her first point, to excite
Worldlings to worke; and in her Watch-towre shone
King Pallas-Megamedes' seed, the Moone; 190
When through th'Alphæan flood Jove's powerfull Sonne
Phœbus-Apollo's ample-foreheaded Herd
(Whose necks the laboring yoke had never spher'd)
Drave swiftly on; and then into a stall
(Hillie, yet past to through an humble vale 195
And hollow Dells, in a most lovely Meade)
He gatherd all, and them divinely fedd
With Odorous Cypresse and the ravishing Tree
That makes his Eaters lose the memorie
Of name and countrie. Then he brought, withall, 200
Much wood, whose sight into his serch let fall
The Art of making fire—which thus he tried:
He tooke a branch of Lawrell, amplified
Past others both in beautie and in sise,
Yet lay next hand, rubb'd it, and strait did rise 205
A warme fume from it, Steele being that did raise
(As Agent) the attenuated Baies
To that hot vapor. So that Hermes found
Both fire first, and of it the seede close bound
In other substances; and then the seed 210
He multiplied, of sere-wood making feed
The apt heat of it, in a pile Combin'de
Laid in a lowe Pit, that in flames strait shin'de,
And cast a sparkling crack up to the Skye,
All the drie parts so fervent were, and hye 215
In their combustion. And how long the force
Of glorious Vulcan kept the fire in course,
So long was he in dragging from their stall

Two of the crook-hancht Herd, that ror'd withall,
And rag'd for feare t'approch the sacred fire, 220
To which did all his dreadfull powrs aspire.
When (blustring forth their breath) he on the soile
Cast both at length, though with a world of toile,
For long he was in getting them to ground
After their through-thrust and most mortall wound. 225
But worke to worke he join'd, the flesh and cut
Coverd with fat, and (on treene broches put)
In peeces rosted. But in th'Intestines
The black blood, and the honorarie chines,
Together with the carcases, lay there 230
Cast on the cold earth, as no Dieties' chere.
The Hydes upon a rugged rock he spred.
And thus were these now all in peeces shred,
And undistinguisht from Earth's common herd,
Though borne for long date and to heaven endeard, 235
And now must ever live in dead event.
But Hermes, herehence having his content,
Car'd for no more, but drew to places even
The fat-works, that, of force, must have for heaven
Their capitall ends, though stolne; and therefore were 240
In twelve parts cut, for twelve choice Deities' chere,
By this devotion. To all which he gave
Their severall honors, and did wish to have
His equall part thereof, as free and well
As th'other Deities; but the fattie smell 245
Afflicted him, though he immortall were,
Play'ng mortall parts, and being like mortalls here.
Yet his proud minde nothing the more obayde
For being a God himselfe, and his owne aide
Having to cause his due, and though in heart 250
Hee highly wisht it; but the weaker part
Subdu'd the stronger and went on in ill.
Even heavenly Powre had rather have his Will
Than have his Right; and will's the worst of All,
When but in least sort it is criminall, 255
One Taint being Author of a Number still.
And thus (resolv'd to leave his hallow'd Hill)
First, both the fat parts and the fleshie All
Taking away, at the steepe-entryed stall
He laid all, all the feet and heads entire, 260
And all the sere-wood, making cleare with fire.
And now, he leaving there then all things done
And finisht in their fit perfection
(The Coles put out, and their black Ashes throwne

From all discoverie by the lovely light 265
The cherefull Moone cast, shyning all the Night)
He strait assum'd a novell voice's note,
And in the whirle-pit-eating flood aflote
He set his sandalls. When now, once againe
The that-morne-borne Cyllenius did attaine 270
His Home's divine height; all the farr-stretcht waie
No one blest God encountring his assaie,
Nor Mortall Man; nor any Dogg durst spend
His borne-to-barke mouth at him; till in th'end
He reacht his Cave, and at the Gate went in 275
Crooked, and wrapt into a fold so thin,
That no eye could discover his repayre
But as a darkness of th'Autumnall ayre.
When, going on fore-right, he strait arriv'd
At his rich Phane, his soft feet quite depriv'd 280
Of all least noise of one that trod the earth,
They trod so swift to reach his roome of Birth.
Where in his swath-bands he his shoulders wrapt,
And (like an Infant, newly having scap't
The teeming streights) as in the Palms he lay 285
Of his lov'd Nurse. Yet instantly would play
(Freeing his right hand) with his bearing cloth
About his knees wrapt, and strait (loosing both
His right and left hand) with his left he caught
His most-lov'd Lute. His Mother yet was taught 290
His wanton wiles, nor could a God's wit lie
Hid from a Goddesse, who did therefore trye
His answer thus: 'Why, thou made all of sleight,
And whence ariv'st thou in this rest of Night?
Improvident Impudent! In my conceipt 295
Thou rather shouldst be getting forth thy Gate,
With all flight fit for thy endanger'd State
(In merit of th'Inevitable bands
To be impos'd by vext Latona's hands,
Justly incenst for her Apollo's harms) 300
Than ly thus wrapt, as ready for her arms,
To take thee up and kisse thee. Would to heaven
(In crosse of that high grace) Thou hadst beene given
Up to Perdition, ere poore mortalls beare
Those blacke banes that thy father Thunderer 305
Hath planted thee of purpose to confer
On them and Deities!' He return'd replie:
'As Master of the feates of Policie,
Mother, why ayme you thus amisse at me,

As if I were a Sonne that Infancie 310
Could keepe from all the skill that Age can teach,
Or had in cheating but a childish reach,
And of a Mother's mandats fear'd the breach?
I mount that Art at first, that will be best
When all times consummate their cunningest, 315
Able to counsaile now my selfe and thee
In all things best, to all Eternitie.
We cannot live like Gods here without gifts,
No, nor without corruption and shifts,
And, much lesse, without eating—as we must 320
In keeping thy rules and in being Just,
Of which we cannot undergoe the lodes.
Tis better here to Imitate the Gods,
And wine or wench out all time's Periods,
To that end growing rich in readie heapes, 325
Stor'de with Revennews, being in corne-fielde reapes
Of infinite Acres, than to live enclos'd
In Caves, to all Earth's sweetest ayre expos'd.
I as much honor hold as Phœbus does;
And if my Father please not to dispose 330
Possessions to me, I my selfe will see
If I can force them in, for I can be
Prince of all Theeves. And if Latona's Sonne
Make after my stealth Indignation,
I'le have a Scape as well as he a Serch, 335
And overtake him with a greater lurch—
For I can post to Pythos, and breake through
His huge house there, where harbors wealth enough,
Most precious Tripods, Caldrons, Steele, and Gold,
Garments rich wrought, and full of liberall fold, 340
All which will I at pleasure owne, and thow
Shalt see all, wilt thou but thy sight bestow.'
Thus chang'd great words the Gote-hyde-wearer's Sonne,
And Maia of Majestique fashion.
And now the Ayre-begot Aurora rose 345
From out the Ocean great-in-ebbs-and-flows,
When, at the never-shorne, pure-and-faire Grove
Onchestus, consecrated to the love
Of round-and-long-neckt Neptune, Phœbus found
A man whom heavie yeares had prest halfe round, 350
And yet at worke in plashing of a Fence
About a Vineyeard, that had residence
Hard by the high-way; whom Latona's Sonne
Made it not strange, but first did question

And first saluted: 'Ho! you! Aged syre 355
That here are hewing from the Vine the Bryre,
For certaine Oxen I come here t'enquire
Out of Pieria; femalls All, and rer'd
All with hornes wreath'd, unlike the common Herde;
A Cole-black Bull fed by them all alone; 360
And all observ'd for preservation
Through all their foodie and delicious Fen
With foure fierce Mastifs, like one-minded men.
These left their Doggs and Bull (which I admire)
And when was nere set Daie's eternall fire, 365
From their fierce Guardians, from their delicate fare,
Made clere departure. To me then declare,
O ould man, long since borne, if thy grave raie
Hath any man seene making stealthfull waie
With all those Oxen.' Th'Olde man made replie: 370
'Tis hard, O friend, to render readily
Account of all that may invade mine eye,
For many a Travailer this high-way tredds,
Some in much ill's serch, some in noble thredds
Leading their lives out; but I this young Day, 375
Even from her first point, have made good display
Of all men passing this abundant hill
Planted with Vines, and no such stealthfull ill
Her light hath showne me. But last Evening late
I sawe a Thing that shew'd of childish state 380
To my ould lights, and seem'd as he pursude
A Herd of Oxen with brave Heads indude—
Yet but an Infant, and retainde a Rodd,
Who warilie both this and that way trodd,
His head still backwards turn'd.' This th'ould Man spake; 385
Which he well thought upon, and swiftly brake
Into his Pursuit with abundant wing,
That strooke but one plaine ere he knew the thing
That was the Theefe to be th'Impostor borne,
Whom Jove yet with his Sonne's name did adorne. 390
In studie and with Ardor then the King,
Jove's dazeling Sonne, plac't his exploring wing
On sacred Pylos for his forced Heard,
His ample shoulders in a cloud enspheard'd
Of fierie chrimsine. Strait the steps he found 395
Of his stolne Herd, and said: 'Strange sights confound
My apprehensive powers, for here I see
The Tracts of Oxen, but aversivelie
Converted towards the Pierian Hills,

As Tredding to their Meade of Daffodills; 400
But nor mine eye Men's feet nor Women's drawes,
Nor hoarie Wolves', nor Beares', nor Lyons' Paws,
Nor thick-neckt Bulls' they show. But hee that does
These monstrous Deeds, with never so swift shooes
Hath past from that howre hither, but from hence 405
His foule course may meete fouler consequence.'
With this tooke Phœbus wing, and Hermes still
(For all his Threats) secure lay in his Hill
Wall'd with a woodd; and more, a Rock, beside,
Where a Retreat rann, deepely multiplide 410
In blinding shadows, and where th'endlesse Bride
Bore to Saturnius his Ingenious Sonne—
An Odor, worth a Heart's desire, being throwne
Along the Heaven-sweet Hill, on whose Herb fedd
Rich flocks of sheepe, that bow not where they tredd 415
Their horney Pasterns. There the light of Men,
Jove's Sonne Apollo, strait descended then
The Marble Pavement in that gloomie Den.
On whom when Jove and Maia's Sonne set eye,
Wroth for his Oxen, on then instantly 420
His Odorous swath-bands flew; in which as close
Th'Impostor lay, as in the coole repose
Of cast-on Ashes Harths of burning Coles
Ly in the woods hidd, under the Controules
Of skilfull Colyers: even so close did lie 425
Inscrutable Hermes in Apollo's eye,
Contracting his great God-head to a small
And Infant likenesse, feet, hands, head and All.
And as a Hunter hath beene often viewd,
From Chace retir'd, with both his hands embrewd 430
In his Game's blood, that doth for water call
To clense his hands, and to provoke withall
Delightsome sleepe, new washt and laid to rest;
So now lay Hermes in the close comprest
Chace of his Oxen, his New-found-out Lute 435
Beneath his arme held, as if no pursuite
But that Prise, and the virtue of his play,
His heart affected. But to Phœbus lay
His close Heart open; and he likewise knew
The brave Hyll-Nymph there and her deare Sonne, new- 440
Borne, and as well wrapt in his wiles as weeds.
All the close shrouds, too, for his Rapinous deedes
In All the Cave he knew; and with his key
He open'd three of them, in which there lay

Silver and Gold-heapes, Nectar infinite store, 445
And Deare Ambrosia; and of weedes she wore
(Pure white, and Purple) a rich Wardrobe shin'de,
Fit for the blest States of powrs so divin'de.
All which discoverd, thus to Mercurie
He offerd Conference: 'Infant! you that lie 450
Wrapt so in swath-bands, instantly unfold
In what conceald Retreats of yours you hold
My Oxen stolne by you; or strait we shall
Jarr, as beseemes not powrs Celestiall.
For I will take and hurle Thee to the Deepes 455
Of dismall Tartarus, where ill Death keepes
His gloomie and inextricable fates,
And to no Eye that light Illuminates
Mother nor Father shall returne thee free,
But under Earth shall Sorrow fetter thee, 460
And few repute thee their Superiour.'
  On him replied Craft's subtlest Counsailor:
'What cruell speech hath past Latona's Care!
Seekes he his stolne-wilde-Cows where Deities are?
I have nor seene nor heard, nor can report 465
From others' mouthes one word of their resort
To any stranger. Nor will I, to gaine
A base Reward, a false Relation faine.
Nor would I, could I tell. Resemble I
An Ox-Theefe, or a Man? Especiallie 470
A man of such a courage, such a force
As to that labour goes, that violent course?
No Infant's worke is That. My powres aspire
To sleepe and quenching of my hunger's fire
With Mother's Milke, and gainst cold shades to arme 475
With Cradle-cloths my shoulders, and Baths warme,
That no man may conceive the warr you threat
Can spring in cause from my so peacefull heat.
And even amongst th'Immortalls it would beare
Event of absolute Miracle, to heare 480
A new-borne Infant's forces should transcend
The limits of his Dores, much lesse contend
With untam'd Oxen. This speech nothing seemes
To savour the Decorum of the Beames
Cast round about the Ayre Apollo breakes, 485
Where his divine minde her intention speakes.
I brake but yesterday the blessed wombe;
My feet are tender, and the common Tombe
Of men (the Earth) lies sharpe beneath their tred.

But, if you please, even by my Father's head 490
I'le take the great Oath, that nor I protest
My selfe to Author on your Interest
Any such usurpation, nor have I
Seene any other that felloniously
Hath forc't your Oxen. Strange thing! What are those 495
Oxen of yours? Or what are Oxen? Knowes
My rude minde, thinke you? My eares onely touch
At their renowne, and heare that there are such.'
This speech he past; and ever as he spake
Beames from the hayre about his eye-lidds brake, 500
His eye-brows up and downe cast, and his eye
Every way look't askans and careleslie,
And he into a loftie whistling fell,
As if he idle thought Apollo's spell.
Apollo (gently smiling) made Replie: 505
'O thou Impostor! whose thoughts ever lye
In labour with Deceipt! For certaine, I
Retaine Opinon that thou (even thus soone)
Hast ransackt many a House, and not in one
Night's-worke alone, nor in one Countrie neither, 510
Hast beene beseeging House and Man together,
Rigging and rifeling all waies, and no Noise
Made with thy soft feete, where it all destroies.
Soft, therefore, well, and tender thou maist call
The feet that thy stealths goe and fly withall; 515
For many a field-bredd Herdsman (unheard still)
Hast thou made drowne the Caverns of the Hill
Where his Retreates lie with his helplesse teares,
When any flesh-stealth thy desire endeares,
And thou encountrest either flocks of sheepe 520
Or Herds of Oxen! Up then! doe not sleepe
Thy last Nap in thy Cradle, but come downe
(Companion of black Night) and for this Crowne
Of thy young Rapines beare (from all) the state
And stile of Prince Theefe into endlesse Date.' 525
This said, he tooke the Infant in his Armes,
And with him the remembrance of his harmes,
This Præsage utt'ring, lifting him aloft:
'Be ever more the miserablie-soft
Slave of the bellie, Pursuivant of all, 530
And Author of all mischiefs Capitall.'
He scorn'd his Prophesie so he Nees'd in's face
Most forciblie, which hearing, his embrace
He loth'd, and hurl'd him gainst the ground; yet still

Tooke seate before him; though (with all the ill 535
He bore by him) he would have left full faine
That Hewer of his heart so into twaine.
Yet salv'd all thus: 'Come, you so swadl'd thing!
Issue of Maia and the Thunder's King,
Be confident I shall hereafter finde 540
My brode-browd Oxen, my Prophetique minde
So farr from blaming this thy course that I
Foresee thee in it to Posteritie
The guide of All Men, All waies, to their ends.'
This spoken, Hermes from the Earth Ascends, 545
Starting Aloft, and as in Studie went,
Wrapping himselfe in his Integument;
And thus askt Phœbus: 'Whither force you Me,
Farr-shot and farr most powrefull Deitie?
I know (for all your fayning) y'are still wroth 550
About your Oxen, and suspect my Troth.
O Jupiter! I wish the generall Race
Of all Earth's Oxen rooted from her face.
I steale your Oxen? I againe professe
That neither I have stolne them, nor can ghesse 555
Who else should steale them. What strange Beasts are these
Your so-lov'd Oxen? I must say (to please
Your humor thus farr) that even My few Hoowres
Have heard their fame. But be the sentence yours
Of the Debate betwixt us, or to Jove 560
(For more indifferencie) the Cause remove.'
Thus when the Solitude-affecting God
And the Latonian seede had laid abroad
All things betwixt them, (though not yet agreed,
Yet might I speake) Apollo did proceede, 565
Nothing unjustly, to charge Mercurie
With stealing of the Cows he does denie.
But his Profession was, with filed speach
And Craft's faire Complements, to overreach
All, and even Phœbus. Who because he knew 570
His Trade of subtletie, he still at view
Hunted his Foe through all the sandie waie
Up to Olympus—nor would let him straie
From out his sight, but kept behinde him still.
And now they reacht the Odoriferous Hill 575
Of high Olympus, to their Father Jove,
To Arbitrate the Cause in which they strove.
Where, before both, Talents of justice were
Propos'd for him whom Jove should sentence Clere

In cause of their contention. And now 580
About Olympus (ever-crown'de with snow)
The rumor of their controversie flew.
All the Incorruptible, to their view,
On heaven's steepe Mountaine made return'd repaire.
  Hermes and He that light hurls through the ayre 585
Before the Thunderer's knees stood; who begunn
To question thus farr his Illustrious Sonne:
'Phœbus! To what end bringst thou Captive here
Him in whom my Minde putts delights so deare?
This New-borne Infant, that the place supplies 590
Of Herrald yet to all the Deities?
This serious busines you may witnesse drawes
The Deities' whole Court to discusse the cause.'
  Phœbus replied: 'And not unworthie is
The cause of all the Court of Deities. 595
For you shall heare it comprehends the weight
Of Devastation, and the verie height
Of spoile and rapine, even of Deities' rights.
Yet you (as if my selfe lov'd such delights)
Use words that wound my heart. I bring you here 600
An Infant that, even now, admits no Pere
In rapes and robb'ries. Finding out his Place
(After my measure of an infinite space)
In the Cyllenian Mountaine, such a one
In all the Art of opprobration 605
As not in all the Deities I have seene,
Nor in th'Oblivion-marckt whole Race of men.
In Night he drave my Oxen from their Leas,
Along the loftie rore-resounding Seas,
From out the Rode way quite; the steps of them 610
So quite transpos'd as would amaze the beame
Of any minde's eye, being so infinite much
Involv'd in doubt as showd a Deified touch
Went to the work's performance—all the way
Through which my cross-hov'd Cows hee did convaie 615
Had dust so darklie-hard to serch, and He
So past all measure wrapt in subtiltie:
For nor with feet nor hands he form'd his steps
In passing through the drie waie's sandie heaps,
But us'd another counsaile to keepe hidd 620
His monstrous Tracts, that showd as one had slid
On Oke or other Boughs, that swept out still
The footsteps of his Oxen and did fill
Their prints up ever, to the Daffodill

(Or daintie feeding Meddow) as they trodd, 625
Driven by this cautelous and Infant God.
'A Mortall Man yet saw him driving on
His Prey to Pylos. Which when he had done
And got his Passe sign'd, with a sacred fire,
In peace and freely (though to his desire, 630
Not to the Gods, he offerd part of these
My ravisht Oxen) he retires, and lies
Like to the gloomie Night in his dimm Denn,
All hid in darknesse; and in clouts againe
Wrapt him so closely that the sharpe-seene eye 635
Of your owne Eagle could not see him lye.
For with his hands the ayre he rarified
(This way and that mov'd) till bright gleames did glide
About his Being, that, if any eye
Should dare the Darknesse, Light appos'd so nie 640
Might blinde it quite with her Antipathie—
Which wile he wove in curious care t'illude
Th'Extreame of any eye that could intrude.
On which relying, he outrageouslie
(When I accus'd him) trebled his replie: 645
"I did not see, I did not heare, nor I
Will tell at all, that any other stole
Your brode-browd Beeves. Which an Impostor's soule
Would soone have done, and any Author faine
Of purpose onely a Reward to gaine." 650
And thus he colourd truth in every lie.'
This said, Apollo sate; and Mercurie
The Gods' Commander pleas'd with this replie:
'Father! I'le tell the truth (for I am true
And farr from Art to lie). He did pursue 655
Even to my Cave his Oxen this selfe daie,
The Sunn new raising his illustrious raie;
But brought with him none of the Bliss-indu'd,
Nor any ocular witnesse, to conclude
His bare assertion. But his owne command 660
Laid on with strong and necessarie hand,
To showe his Oxen, using Threats to cast
My poore and Infant powrs into the Vast
Of ghastlie Tartarus, because he beares
Of strength-sustayning youth the flaming yeares, 665
And I but yesterday produc'd to light.
By which it fell into his owne fre sight
That I in no similitude apper'd
Of powre to be the forcer of a Herde.

And credite me, O Father, since the Grace 670
Of that name in your stile you please to place,
I drave not home his Oxen, no, nor preast
Past mine owne threshold; for tis manifest
I reverence with my soule the Sunn, and all
The knowing dwellers in this heavenly Hall, 675
Love you, observe the least; and tis most cleare
In your owne knowledge that my Merits beare
No least guilt of his blame. To all which I
Dare adde heaven's great oath, boldly swearing by
All these so well-built Entries of the Blest. 680
And therefore when I saw my selfe so prest
With his reproches, I confesse I burn'd
In my pure gall, and harsh replie return'd.
Adde your aid to your Yonger then, and free
The scruple fixt in Phœbus' Jelousie.' 685
 This said, he winckt upon his Sire, and still
His swath-bands held beneath his arme—no Will
Discernd in him to hide, but have them showne.
 Jove laught aloud at his Ingenious Sonne,
Quitting himselfe with Art, so likely wrought 690
As showd in his heart not a rapinous thought;
Commanding Both to beare attoned mindes
And seeke out th'Oxen; in which serch he bindes
Hermes to play the Guide, and show the Sunn
(All grudge exilde) the Shrowd to which he wunn 695
His fayre-eyd Oxen. Then his forehead bow'd
For signe it must be so, and Hermes show'd
His free obedience. So soone he enclin'd
To his perswasion and command his minde.
 Now, then, Jove's Jarring Sonnes no longer stood, 700
But sandie Pylos and th'Alphæan flood
Reacht instantly, and made as quick a fall
On those rich-feeding fields and loftie stall
Where Phœbus' Oxen Hermes safelie kept,
Driven in by night. When sodainely he stept 705
Up to the stonie Cave, and into light
Drave forth the Oxen. Phœbus at first sight
Knew them the same, and saw apart dispread
Upon a high-rais'd rock the hydes new flead
Of th'Oxen sacrifis'd. Then Phœbus said: 710
'O thou in craftie counsailes undisplaid!
How couldst thou cut the throtes and cast to Earth
Two such huge Oxen, being so young a birth
And a mere Infant? I admire thy force

And will, behinde thy back. But this swift course 715
Of growing into strength, thou hadst not need
Continue any long Date, O thou seed
Of honor'd Maia!' Hermes (to shew how
He did those Deedes) did forthwith cut and bow
Strong Osiers in soft folds, and strappl'd strait 720
One of his hugest Oxen, all his weight
Lay'ng prostrate on the earth at Phœbus' feet,
All his foure cloven hoves easly made to greete
Each other upwards, all together brought.
In all which bands yet all the Beast's powres wrought 725
To rise and stand; when all the Herd about
The mighty Hermes rusht in, to help out
Their fellow from his fetters. Phœbus' view
Of all this up to Admiration drew
Even his high forces. And sterne lookes he threw 730
At Hermes for his Herd's wrong and the place
To which he had retir'd them, being in grace
And fruitfull riches of it so entire;
All which set all his force on envious fire,
All whose heat flew out of his eyes in flames, 735
Which faine he would have hidd, to hide the shames
Of his ill govern'd passions. But with ease
Hermes could calme them, and his humors please
Still at his pleasure, were he ne're so great
In force and fortitude, and high in heat. 740
In all which he his Lute tooke, and assaid
A Song upon him, and so strangely plaid
That from his hand a ravishing horror flew—
Which Phœbus into laughter turn'd, and grew
Pleasant past measure; Tunes so artfull clere 745
Strooke even his heart-strings, and his minde made heare.
His Lute so powerfull was in forcing love
(As his hand rul'd it) that from him it drove
All feare of Phœbus; yet he gave him still
The upper hand; and (to advance his skill) 750
To utmost Miracle he plaid sometimes
Single awhile; in which, when all the Clymes
Of rapture he had reacht (to make the Sunn
Admire enough) O then his voice would runn
Such points upon his play, and did so move, 755
They tooke Apollo Prisoner to his love.
And now the deathlesse Gods and deathfull Earth
He sung, beginning at their either's Birth
To full extent of all their Emperie.

And, first, the honor to Mnemosyne, 760
The Muses' Mother, of all Goddesse states
He gave, even forc't too't by the equall fates.
And then (as it did in Prioritie fall
Of Age and Birth) He celebrated All.
And with such Elegance and Order sung 765
(His Lute still toucht, to stick more off his tongue)
That Phœbus' heart with infinite love he eate.
Who, therefore, thus did his Deserts entreate:
'Master of Sacrifice! chiefe soule of feast!
Patient of all paines! Artizan so blest 770
That all things thou canst doe in any One!
Worth fiftie Oxen is th'Invention
Of this one Lute. We both shall now, I hope,
In firme peace worke to all our wishes' scope.
Informe me (thou that every way canst winde, 775
And turne to Act, all wishes of thy minde)
Together with thy birth came all thy skill?
Or did some God, or God-like man, instill
This heavenly song to thee? Me thinks I heare
A new voice, such as never yet came nere 780
The brest of any, either Man or God,
Till in thee it had Prime and Period.
What Art, what Muse that medcine can produce
For cares most curelesse, what inveterate use
Or practise of a virtue so profuse 785
(Which three doe all the contribution keepe
That Joy or Love conferrs, or pleasing Sleepe)
Taught thee the soveraigne facture of them all?
I of the Muses am the capitall
Consort or follower; and to these belong 790
The grace of dance, all worthie waies of song
And ever-florishing verse, the delicate Set
And sound of Instruments. But never yet
Did anything so much affect my minde
With joy and care to compasse as this kinde 795
Of Song and Play, that for the spritely feast
Of florishing assemblies are the best
And aptest works that ever Worth gave Act.
My powres with admiration stand distract
To heare with what a hand to make in love 800
Thou rul'st thy Lute. And (though thy yongst howres move
At full art in ould counsailes) here I vow
(Even by this Cornell Dart I use to throw)
To thee, and to thy Mother, I'le make thee

Amongst the Gods of glorious degree, 805
Guide of Men's waies and Theirs; and will impart
To thee the mightie Imperatorie Art,
Bestowe rich gifts on thee, and in the end
Never deceive thee.' Hermes (as a friend
That wrought on all advantage, and made gaine 810
His Capitall object) thus did entertaine
Phœbus Apollo: 'Doe thy Dignities,
Farr-working God and circularlie wise,
Demand my vertues? Without envie I
Will teach thee to ascend my facultie. 815
And this Day thou shalt reach it—finding me
In Acts and Counsailes all waies kinde to thee,
As one that all things knows, and first tak'st seat
Amongst th'Immortalls, being good, and great,
And therefore to Jove's love mak'st free accesse, 820
Even out of his accomplisht Holinesse.
Great gifts he likewise gives thee; who, fame saies,
Hast wunn thy greatnesse by his will, his waies,
By him know'st all the powers Propheticall,
O thou farr-worker, and the fates of all. 825
Yea, and I know thee rich, yet apt to learne,
And even thy Wish dost but discerne and earne.
And since thy soule so burns to know the way
To play and sing as I doe, sing and play—
Play, and perfection in thy play employ; 830
And be thy care to learne things good, thy Joy.
Take thou my Lute, My Love, and give thou me
The glorie of so great a facultie.
This sweet-tun'd consort, held but in thy hand,
Sing, and perfection in thy song command. 835
For thou alreadie hast the way to speake
Fayrely and elegantly, and to breake
All eloquence into thy utterd minde.
One gift from heaven found, may another finde.
Use then securely this thy gift, and goe 840
To feasts and dances that enamour so,
And to that covetous sport of getting glory,
That Day nor Night will suffer to be sory.
Whoever does but say in verse, sings still;
Which he that can of any other skill 845
Is capable, so he be taught by Art
And wisedome, and can speake at every part
Things pleasing to an understanding Minde;
And such a one that seekes this Lute shall finde.

Him still it teaches easely, though he plaies 850
Soft voluntaries onely, and assaies
As wanton as the sports of children are,
And (even when he aspires to singular
In all the Mast'ries he shall play or sing)
Findes the whole worke but an unhappie thing, 855
He, I say, sure shall of this Lute be King.
But he, whoever rudely sets upon
Of this Lute's skill th'Inquest or Question
Never so ardently and angrilie,
Without the aptnesse and habilitie 860
Of Art and Nature fitting, never shall
Aspire to this, but utter triviall
And idle accents, though sung ne're so lowd,
And never so commended of the Crowde.
But thee I know, O Eminent Sonne of Jove, 865
The fiery Learner of what ever Love
Hath sharpn'd thy affections to achive.
And thee I give this Lute. Let us now live
Feeding upon the Hill-and-horse-fed Earth
Our never-handled Oxen; whose deare Birth 870
(Their femalls fellowd with their Males) let flowe
In store enough hereafter; nor must you
(However cunning-hearted your wits are)
Boile in your Gall a Grudge too circulare.'
Thus gave he him his Lute, which he embrac't, 875
And gave againe a Gode, whose bright head cast
Beames like the light forth; leaving to his care
His Oxen's keeping—which, with joyfull fare,
He tooke on him. The Lute Apollo tooke
Into his left hand, and aloft he shooke 880
Delightsome sounds up, to which God did sing.
Then were the Oxen to their endlesse Spring
Turn'd; and Jove's Two illustr'ous Off-springs flew
Up to Olympus, where it ever snew,
Delighted with their Lute's sound all the way— 885
Whom Jove much joi'd to see, and endlesse stay
Gave to their knot of friendship. From which date
Hermes gave Phœbus an eternall state
In his affection, whose sure pledge and signe
His Lute was, and the Doctrine so divine 890
Jointly conferd on him—which well might be
True Symbole of his Love's simplicitie.
On th'other part, Apollo in his friend
Form'd th'Art of Wisedome, to the binding end

Of his vow'd friendship; and (for further meede) 895
Gave him the farr-heard fistularie Reede.
 For all these forms of friendship, Phœbus yet
Feard that both forme and substance were not mett
In Mercurie's intentions; and, in plaine,
Said (since he saw him borne to craft and gaine, 900
And that Jove's will had him the honor done
To change at his will the possession
Of others' Goods) he fear'd his breach of vowes
In stealing both his Lute and curving Bowes,
And therefore wisht that what the Gods affect 905
Himselfe would witnesse, and to his request
His head Bow, swearing by th'Impetuous flood
Of Styx that of his whole possessions not a Good
He would diminish, but therein maintaine
The full content in which his Minde did raigne. 910
And then did Maia's Sonne his fore-head bow,
Making, by all that he desir'd, his vow
Never to prey more upon any Thing
In just possession of the farr-shot King,
Nor ever to come neare a House of his. 915
 Latonian Phœbus bowd his Brow to this
With his like promise, say'ng: 'Not any One
Of all the Gods, nor any Man, that Sonne
Is to Saturnius is more deare to me,
More trusted, nor more honord, is than thee— 920
Which yet with greater Gifts of Deitie
In future I'le confirme, and give thy state
A Rodd that riches shall accumulate,
Nor leave the bearer thrall to Death, or fate,
Or any sicknesse. All of Gold it is, 925
Three-leav'd, and full of all felicities.
And this shall be thy Guardian; this shall give
The Gods to thee in all the truth they live.
And finally, shall this the Tutresse be
Of all the words and workes informing me 930
From Jove's high counsailes, making knowne to thee
All my instructions. But to Prophesie,
O best of Jove's belov'd, and that high skill
Which to obtaine lies burning in thy will,
Nor thee, nor any God, will Fate let learne. 935
Onely Jove's minde hath insight to discerne
What that importeth; yet am I allowd
(My knowne faith trusted, and my forhead bowd,
Our great Oath taken, to resolve to none

Of all th'Immortalls the restriction 940
Of that deepe knowledge) of it All the Minde.
Since then it sits in such fast bounds confinde,
O Brother, when the Golden rodd is held
In thy strong hand, seeke not to have reveal'd
Any sure fate that Jove will have conceald— 945
For no man shall, by know'ng, prevent his fate.
And therefore will I hold in my free state
The powre to hurt and helpe what man I will,
Of all the greatest, or least toucht with ill,
That walke within the Circle of mine eye, 950
In all the Tribes and Sexes it shall trye.
'Yet, truely, any man shall have his will
To reape the fruites of my Prophetique skill,
Whoever seekes it by the voice or wing
Of Birds, borne truely such events to sing. 955
Nor will I falsly, nor with fallacies,
Infringe the truth on which his faith relies;
But he that Truths in chattering plumes would finde
(Quite opposite to them that prompt my Minde)
And learne by naturall forgers of vaine lyes 960
The more-than-ever-certaine Deities,
That man shall Sea-waies tred that leave no Tracts,
And false or no guide finde for all his facts.
And yet will I his Gifts accept as well
As his to whom the simple Truth I tell. 965
'One other thing to thee I'le yet make knowne,
Maia's exceedingly renowned sonne
And Jove's, and of the Gods' whole session
The most ingenious Genius. There dwell
Within a crooked Crannie, in a Dell 970
Beneath Parnassus, certaine sisters borne,
Call'd Parcæ, whom extreame swift wings adorne,
Their Number three, that have upon their heads
White Barly floure still sprinckled, and are maids;
And these are schoole-Mistresses of things to come, 975
Without the gift of Prophecie; of whom
(Being but a boy, and keeping Oxen nere)
I learn'd their skill, though my great Father were
Careless of it, or them. These flying from home
To others' roofes, and fedd with Hony-come, 980
Command all skill, and (being enraged then)
Will freely tell the Truths of things to Men.
But if they give them not that Gods' sweete meat,
They then are apt to utter their deceit,

And leade Men from their way. And these will I 985
Give thee hereafter, when their scrutinie
And truth thou hast both made and learn'd; and then
Please thy selfe with them, and the Race of men
(Wilt thou know any) with thy skill endeare—
Who will (be sure) afford it greedie eare, 990
And heare it often if it prove sincere.
'Take these, O Maia's Sonne, and in thy care
Be Horse and Oxen, all such Men as are
Patient of labour, Lyons, white-tooth'd Bores,
Mastifs, and flocks that feede the flowrie shores, 995
And every foure-foot Beast—all which shall stand
In awe of thy high Imperatory hand.
Be thou to Dis, too, sole Ambassador,
Who (though all gifts and bounties he abhor)
On thee he will bestowe a wealthie One.' 1000
Thus King Apollo honor'd Maia's Sonne
With all the rights of friendship—all whose love
Had Imposition from the Will of Jove.
And thus with Gods and Mortalls Hermes liv'd,
Who truely helpt but few, but all deceiv'd 1005
With an undifferencing respect, and made
Vaine words and false perswasions his Trade.
His Deeds were all associats of the Night,
In which his close wrongs car'd for no man's Right.
So all salutes to Hermes that are due, 1010
Of whom, and all Gods, shall my Muse sing true.

THE END OF THE HYMNE TO HERMES

A HYMNE TO VENUS

The force, O Muse, and functions now unfold
Of Cyprian Venus, grac't with Mines of Gold,
Who even in Deities lights Love's sweet desire,
And all Death's kindes of men makes kisse her fire,
All Ayre's wing'd Nation, all the Belluine 5
That or the Earth feedes or the Seas confine—
To all which appertaine the love and care
Of well-crown'd Venus' works. Yet three there are
Whose mindes she neither can deceive nor move—
Pallas, the seede of Ægis-bearing Jove, 10
Who still lives Indevirginate, her eyes
Being blew and sparkling like the freezing skies,
Whom all the Gold of Venus never can
Tempt to affect her facts with God or Man.
She loving strife, and Mars-his working Banes, 15
Pitcht fields and fights, and famous Artizanes,
Taught earthie men first all the Arts that are,
Charriots, and all the frames vehiculare,
Chiefely with brasse arm'd and adorn'd for warre
Where Venus onely soft-skinnd wenches fills 20
With wanton House-works, and suggests those skills
Still to their studies. Whom Diana neither,
That beares the Golden distaff, and together
Calls Horns and Hollows, and the cries of Houndes,
And ownes the Epithete of loving sounds 25
For their sakes, springing from such spritely sports,
Can catch with her kinde Lures—but hill resorts
To wilde-Beasts' slaughters, accents farr-off heard
Of Harps and Dances, and of woods unsheard
The sacred shades she loves, yet likes as well 30
Citties where good men and their off-spring dwell.
The third whom her kinde Passions nothing please
Is Virgine Vesta, whom Saturnides
Made reverend with his counsailes, when his Sire
That advers counsailes agitates life's fire 35
Had kindled in her, being his last begot—

Whom Neptune wow'd to knit with him the knot
Of honord Nuptialls, and Apollo too;
Which, with much vehemence she refus'd to doe,
And sterne Repulses put upon them both, 40
Adding to all her vows the Gods' great Oath,
And touching Jove's chynn (which must consummate
All vows so bound) that she would hold her state,
And be th'Invincible Maid of Deities
Through all her daies' dates. For Saturnides 45
Gave her a faire gift in her Nuptialls' stedd,
To sit in midst of his house and be fedd
With all the free and richest feast of Heaven,
In all the Temples of the Gods being given
The prise of honor. Not a mortall Man 50
(That either, of the powrs Olympian
His half-birth having, may be said to be
A mortall of the Gods, or else that he
(Deities' wills doings) is of Deitie)
But gives her honor of the amplest kinde. 55
Of all these Three can Venus not a Minde
Deceive, or set on forces to reflect.
Of all powrs els yet not a sex nor sect
Flies Venus—either of the blessed Gods,
Or Men confin'de in mortall Periods. 60
But even the Minde of Jove she doth seduce,
That chides with Thunder so her lawlesse use
In humane Creatures, and by lot is given
Of all most honor, both in Earth and Heaven.
And yet even his all-wise and mightie Minde 65
She, when she lists, can forge affectes to blinde,
And mixe with mortall Dames his Deitie,
Conceald at all parts from the jelous eye
Of Juno, who was both his sister borne
And made his wife, whom beautie did adorne 70
Past all the Bevie of immortall Dames,
And whose so chiefely-glorified Flames
Crosse-counsailde Saturne got, and Rhea bore,
And Jove's pure counsailes (being Conqueror)
His wife made of his sister—I, and more, 75
Cast such an amorous fire into her minde
As made her (like him) with the Mortall kinde
Meete in unmeete bedd; using utmost haste,
Lest she should know that he liv'd so unchaste,
Before her selfe felt that fault in her heart, 80
And gave her tongue too just edge of Desert

To tax his lightnes. With this End, beside,
Lest laughter-studying Venus should deride
The Gods more than the Goddesses, and say
That shee the Gods commixt in amorous play 85
With mortall Dames, begetting mortall seede
T'Immortall sires, and not make Goddesses breede
The like with mortall Fathers, but t'acquite
Both Gods and Goddesses of her despite,
Jove tooke (even in her selfe) on him her powre, 90
And made her with a mortall Paramoure
Use as deform'd a mixture as the rest;
Kindling a kinde affection in her brest
To God-like-limm'd Anchises, as he kept
On Ida's top-on-top-to-heaven's-Pole-heapt 95
Amongst the manie fountaines there his Herd;
For after his brave Person had apper'de
To her bright eye, her heart flew all on fire,
And (to amaze) she burn'd in his desire,
Flew strait to Cyprus, to her odorous Phane 100
And Altars that the people Paphiane
Advanc't to her. Where (soone as entred) shee
The shyning gates shut, and the Graces three
Washt, and with Oiles of everlasting sent
Bath'd, as became her deathlesse lyneament. 105
Then her Ambrosian Mantle she assum'd,
With rich and odoriferous Ayres perfum'd—
Which being put on, and all her Trimms beside
Fayre, and with all allurements amplified,
The All-of-Gold-made laughter-loving Dame 110
Left odorous Cyprus, and for Troy became
A swift Contendresse, her Passe cutting All
Along the cloudes, and made her instant fall
On fountfull Ida, that her Mother-Brests
Gives to the Preyfull broode of savage Beasts. 115
And through the Hill she went the readie way
T'Anchises' Oxstall, where did fawne and play
About her blessed feet Wolves grislie-gray,
Terrible Lyons, many a Mankind Beare,
And Lybberds swift, insatiate of red Deare— 120
Whose sight so pleas'd that ever as she past
Through every Beast a kindely Love she cast,
That in their Denns, obscur'd with shadowes deepe,
Made all, distinguisht in kinde Couples, sleepe.
And now she reacht the rich Pavilion 125
Of the Heroe, in whom heavens had showne

[95] 'Ακροπόλος, Altissimum habens verticem, cujus summitas ipsum polum attingit.

A fayre and goodly Composition
And whom she in his Oxstall found alone,
His Oxen feeding in fat Pastures by,
He walking up and downe, sounds clere and hye 130
From his harp striking. Then before him shee
Stood like a Virgine that invinciblie
Had borne her beauties, yet alluringly
Bearing her person, lest his ravisht eye
Should chance t'affect him with a stupid feare. 135
Anchises seeing her, all his senses were
With wonder stricken, and high-taken heeds
Both of her forme, brave stature, and rich weedes.
For, for a vaile, she shin'd in an Attire
That cast a radiance past the Ray of fire. 140
Beneath which wore she, guirt to her, a Gowne
Wrought all with growing-rose-budds, reaching downe
T'her slender smalls, which buskinns did divine,
Such as taught Thetis' silver Feete to shine.
Her soft white neck rich Carquenets embrac't, 145
Bright, and with gold in all variety grac't,
That, to her brests let downe, lay there and shone
As, at her joyfull full, the rising Moone.
Her sight show'd miracles. Anchises' Heart
Love tooke into his hand, and made him part 150
With these high Salutations: 'Joy, O Queene!
Whoever of the Blest thy beauties beene
That light these Entries! Or the Deitie
That Darts affecteth, or that gave the eye
Of Heaven his heat and Luster! Or that moves 155
The hearts of all with all-commanding Loves!
Or generous Themis! Or the blew-eyd Maid!
Or of the Graces any that are laid
With all the Gods in comparable skales,
And whom Fame up to Immortalitie calles! 160
Or any of the Nymphs that unshorne Groves
Or that this fayre Hill-habitation loves,
Or valleys flowing with earth's fattest Goods,
Or Fountaines pouring forth eternall floods!
Say which of all thou art, that in some place 165
Of circular prospect, for thine eyes' deare grace
I may an Altar build, and to thy Powres
Make sacred all the yeare's devoted Howres
With consecrations sweet and oppulent.
Assur'd whereof, be thy benigne Minde bent 170
To these wisht blessings of me: give me parts

Of chiefe attraction in Troyan hearts;
And after give me the refulgencie
Of most renownd and rich Posteritie,
Long and free life, and Heaven's sweet light as long, 175
The people's blessings, and a health so strong
That no disease it let my life engage,
Till th'utmost limit of a humane Age.'
To this Jove's seede this answer gave againe:
'Anchises! happiest of the humane straine! 180
I am no Goddesse. Why, a thrall to Death,
Think'st thou like those that immortality breath!
A woman brought me forth; my Father's Name
Was Otreus (if ever his high fame
Thine eares have witnest, for he governd all 185
The Phrygian State, whose every Towne a wall
Impregnable embrac't). Your tongue, you heare,
I speake so well that in my naturall spheare
(As I pretend) it must have taken prime.
A woman, likewise of the Troyan clime, 190
Tooke of me in her house the Nurse's care
From my deare Mother's Bosome; and thus are
My words of equall accent with your owne.
How here I come (to make the reason knowne)—
Argicides, that beares the Golden Rod, 195
Transferd me forciblie from my Abod
Made with the Maiden Traine of her that joies
In Golden shafts, and loves so well the noise
Of Hounds and Hunters (Heaven's pure-living powre)
Where many a Nymph and maid of mighty Dowre 200
Chast sports emploid, all circkl'd with a Crowne
Of infinite Multitude, to see so showne
Our maiden Pastimes. Yet from all the Fayre
Of this so forcefull concourse, up in Ayre
The Golden-Rodd-sustaining Argus' Guide 205
Rapt me in sight of all, and made me ride
Along the Clouds with him, enforcing me
Through many a labour of Mortalitie,
Through many an unbuilt Region and a rude,
Where savage Beasts devour'd Preys warme and crude, 210
And would not let my feares take one foot's tred
On her by whom are all Lives comforted;
But said my Maiden State must grace the Bed
Of King Anchises, and bring forth to thee
Issue as faire as of divine Degree. 215
Which said, and showing me thy moving Grace,

Away flew he up to th'Immortall Race.
And thus came I to thee, Necessitie
With her steele stings compelling me t'applie
To her high Powre my will. But You must I 220
Implore by Jove, and all the reverence due
To your deare Parents, who (in bearing you)
Can beare no meane saile, leade me home to them
An untoucht Maid, being brought up in th'extreme
Of much too cold simplicitie to know 225
The fiery cunnings that in Venus glow.
Show me to them then, and thy Brothers borne:
I shall appeare none that parts disadorne,
But such as well may serve a Brother's wife;
And show them now, even to my future life, 230
If such or no my Present will extend.
To Horse-Breede-vary'ng Phrygia likewise send
T'Informe my Sire and Mother of my State,
That live for me extreame disconsolate—
Who Gold enough and well-woven weedes will give— 235
All whose rich Gifts in my Amends receive.
All this perform'd, adde celebration then
Of honord Nuptialls, that by God and Men
Are held in reverence.' All this while she said,
Into his bosome jointly she convaid 240
The fires of love; when (all enamourd) He
In these terms answered: 'If Mortalitie
Confine thy Fortunes, and a woman were
Mother to those attractions that appeare
In thy admir'd forme, thy great Father given 245
High Name of Otreus, and the Spie of Heaven
(Immortall Mercurie) th'enforce-full cause
That made thee lose the Prize of that applause
That modestie immaculate Virgines gives,
My wife thou shalt be call'd through both our lives. 250
Nor shall the powrs of Men nor Gods withhold
My fiery resolution to enfold
Thy bosome in mine armes—which here I vow
To firme performance, past delay and Now.
Nor (should Apollo with his silver Bow 255
Shoote me to instant death) would I forbeare
To doe a deede so full of cause so deare.
For with a Heaven-sweet woman I will ly,
Though strait I stoope the house of Dis, and die.'
This said, he tooke her hand, and she tooke way 260
With him, her bright eyes casting round—whose stay

She stuck upon a bed that was before
Made for the King, and wealthie coverings wore.
On which Beares' Hydes and bigg-voic't Lyons' lay,
Whose Preyfull lives the King had made his Prey, 265
Hunting th'Idalian Hills. This Bed when they
Had both ascended, first he tooke from her
The fierie weede that was her utmost weare,
Unbutton'd her next rosie Robe, and los'd
The Gyrdle that her slender wast enclos'd, 270
Unlac't her buskinns, all her Jewellrie
Tooke from her neck and brests, and all lay'd by
Upon a Golden-studded Chaire of State.
Th'Amaze of all which being remov'd, even Fate
And counsaile of the equall Gods gave way 275
To this, that with a Deathlesse Goddesse lay
A deathfull Man, since what his love assum'd
Not with his conscious knowledge was presum'd.
Now when the shepherds and the Herdsmen, all,
Turnd from their flowrie Pasture to their Stall 280
With all their Oxen, fat and frolick sheepe,
Venus into Anchises cast a sleepe,
Sweet and profound; while with her owne hands now
With her rich weeds she did her selfe indow,
But so distinguisht that he clere might know 285
His happie Glories. Then (to her desire
Her heavenly Person put in Trimms entire)
Shee by the bed stood of the well-built Stall,
Advanc't her head to State Celestiall,
And in her cheekes arose the radiant hew 290
Of rich-cround Venus to apparant view.
And then she rous'd him from his rest, and said:
'Up, my Dardanides, forsake thy bed.
What pleasure, late emploid, letts Humor steepe
Thy lidds in this inexcitable sleepe? 295
Wake, and now say if I appeare to thee
Like her that first thine eyes conceited me.'
This started him from sleepe, though deepe and deare,
And passing promptlie he enjoy'd his eare.
But when his eye saw Venus' neck and eyes, 300
Whose beauties could not beare the Counterprise
Of any other, downe his owne eyes fell,
Which pallid feare did from her view repell,
And made him with a maine respect beside
Turne his whole person from her state, and hide 305
(With his rich weede appos'd) his royall face,

These wing'd words using: 'When at first thy Grace
Mine eyes gave entertainment, well I knew
Thy state was Deified; but thou told'st not true;
And therefore let me pray thee (by thy Love 310
Borne to thy Father, Ægis-bearing Jove)
That thou wilt never let me live to be
An abject, after so divine degree
Taken in fortune, but take ruth on me.
For any Man that with a Goddesse lies, 315
Of interest in immortalities,
Is never long liv'd.' She replied: 'Forbeare,
O happiest of Mortall Men, this feare,
And rest assur'd that (not for me, at least)
Thy least ills feare fits—no, nor for the rest 320
Of all the Blessed; for thou art their friend,
And so farr from sustaining instant end
That to thy long-enlarg'd life there shall spring
Amongst the Troyans a deare Sonne, and King,
To whom shall many a Sonne and Sonne's Sonne rise 325
In everlasting-great Posterities,
His Name Æneas—therein keeping life
For ever in my much-conceipted griefe,
That I (immortall) fell into the bed
Of one whose blood Mortality must shed. 330
But rest thou comforted, and all the Race
That Troy shall propagate in this high grace—
That past all Races else the Gods stand nere
Your glorious Nation, for the formes ye beare
And Natures so ingenuous and sincere. 335
For which, the great in counsailes, Jupiter,
Your Gold-lockt Ganymedes did transfer
(In rapture farr from men's depressed fates)
To make him Consort with our Deified states,
And skale the Tops of the Saturnian skies, 340
He was so meere a Marveile in their eyes.
And therefore from a Bolle of Gold he fills
Redd Nectar, that the rude distension kills
Of windes that in your humane stomacks breede.
But then did Languor on the Liver feede 345
Of Tros, his Father, that was King of Troy,
And ever did his memorie employ
With losse of his deare bewtie so bereven,
Though with a sacred whirlewinde rapt to heaven.
But Jove (in pittie of him) saw him given 350
Good compensation, sending by Heaven's Spye

[345] ἄληστος, Cujus memoria erit perpetua.

White-swift-hov'd Horse, that Immortality
Had made firme spirrited; and had (beside)
Hermes to see his Ambassie supplied
With this vow'd Bountie (using all at large 355
That his unaltered counsailes gave in charge)
That he himselfe should Immortality breath,
Expert of Age and Woe as well as Death.
'This Ambassie exprest, he mourn'd no more,
But up with all his inmost minde he bore, 360
Joying that he upon his swift-hov'd Horse
Should be sustain'd in an eternall course.
'So did the golden-thron'de Aurora raise
Into her Lap another that the praise
Of an Immortall fashion had in Fame, 365
And of your Nation bore the Noble Name—
His Title Tithon, who, not pleas'd with her
As she his lovely Person did transfer,
(To satisfie him) she bad aske of Jove
The Gift of an Immortall for her Love. 370
Jove gave, and bound it with his bowed Brow,
Performing to the utmost point his vow.
Foole that she was, that would her love engage,
And not as long aske from the Bane of Age
The sweet exemption, and Youth's endlesse flowre! 375
Of which as long as both the grace and powre
His person entertainde, she lov'd the Man,
And (at the fluents of the Ocean
Nere Earth's extreame bounds) dwelt with him: but when
(According to the course of aged Men) 380
On his faire head and honorable Beard
His first gray hayres to her light eyes apperd,
She left his bed, yet gave him still for food
The Gods' Ambrosia, and attire as good—
Till even the hate of Age came on so fast 385
That not a lyneament of his was grac't
With powre of Motion, nor did still sustaine
(Much lesse) the Vigor had t'advance a vaine,
The virtue lost in each exhausted limm
That (at his wish) before would answer him; 390
All Powrs so quite decaid that, when he spake,
His voice no perceptible accent brake:
Her counsaile then thought best to strive no more,
But lay him in his bed and lock his Dore.
Such an Immortall would not I wish thee, 395
T'extend all daies so to Eternitie.

But if, as now, thou couldst performe thy course
In Grace of Forme and all corporeall force
To an eternall Date, Thou then should'st beare
My Husband's worthie Name, and not a Teare 400
Should I neede raine for thy deserts declinde,
From my All-clouded bitternesse of minde.
But now the sterne storme of relentlesse Age
Will quickly circkle thee, that waites t'engage
All Men alike, even Lothsomnesse and Bane 405
Attending with it every humane wane,
Which even the Gods hate. Such a Penance lies
Impos'd on flesh and blood's infirmities.
Which I my selfe must taste in great degree,
And date as endlesse, for consorting thee. 410
All the Immortalls with my opprobrie
Are full by this time; on their Hearts so lie
(Even to the sting of Feare) my cunnings us'd,
And wiving conversations infus'd
Into the bosomes of the best of them 415
With women that the fraile and mortall stream
Doth daily ravish—all this long since done,
Which now no more but with effusion
Of teares, I must in Heaven so much as name,
I have so forfaited in this my Fame, 420
And am impos'd paine of so great a kinde
For so much erring from a Goddesse' Minde.
For I have put beneath my Gyrdle here
A Sonne whose sire the humane mortall sphere
Gives Circumscription. But when first the light 425
His eyes shall comfort, Nymphs that hant the height
Of Hills, and Brests have of most deepe receit,
Shall be his Nurses; who inhabit now
A Hill of so vast and divine a Brow
As Man nor God can come at their Retreates; 430
Who live long lives, and eat immortall Meates,
And with Immortalls in the exercise
Of comely Dances dare contend, and rise
Into high Question which deserves the Prise.
The light Sileni mix in love with These, 435
And of all Spies the Prince, Argicides,
In well-trymmd Caves their secret meetings made.
And with the lives of these doth life invade
Or odorous firre Trees, or high-forheaded Okes,
Together taking their begetting strokes, 440

And have their lives and deaths of equall Dates,
Trees bearing lovely and Delightsome states,
Whom Earth first feedes, that Men initiates.
On her high Hills she doth their states sustaine,
And they their owne heights raise as high againe. 445
'Their Growghts together made, Nymphs call their Groves
Vowd to th'Immortalls' services and loves—
Which men's steeles therefore touch not, but let grow.
But when wise Fates times for their fadings know,
The faire Trees still before the faire Nymphs die, 450
The Bark about them growne corrupt and drie,
And all their boughs (falne) yeeld to Earth her right;
And then the Nymphs' lives leave the lovely Light.
'And these Nymphs in their Caves shall nurse my Son,
Whom (when in him Youth's first grace is begun) 455
The Nymphs, his Nurses, shall present to thee,
And shew thee what a Birth thou hast by Me.
And (sure as now I tell thee all these things)
When earth hath cloth'd her plants in five faire springs,
My selfe will make returne to this Retreate, 460
And bring that Flowre of thy enamour'd heate;
Whom when thou then seest, Joy shall fire thine eyes,
He shall so well Present the Deities.
And then into thine owne care take thy Sonne
From his calme seat to windie Ilion, 465
Where if strickt question be upon thee past,
Asking what Mother bore beneath her wast
So deare a Sonne, answer, as I afford
Fit admonition, nor forget a word:
"They say a Nymph, call'd Calucopides, 470
That is with others an inhabitresse
On this thy wood-crownd Hill, acknowledges
That she his life gave." But if thou declare
The Secret's truth, and art so mad to dare
(In glory of thy fortunes) to approve 475
That rich-crownd Venus mixt with thee in love,
Jove (fir'd with my aspersion so dispred)
Will with a wreakefull lightning dart thee dead.
'All now is told thee; comprehend it All.
Be Master of thy selfe, and doe not call 480
My Name in question; but with reverence vow
To Deities' angers all the awe ye owe.'
This said, shee reacht Heaven, where ayres ever flowe.
And so, O Goddesse, ever honord be

In thy so Odorous Cyprian Emperie!
My Muse, affecting first thy Fame to raise,
Shall make Transcension now to others' Praise.

THE END OF THE FIRST HYMNE TO VENUS

TO THE SAME

The Reverend Rich-crownd, and Faire Queene I sing,
Venus, that owes in Fate the fortressing
Of all Maritimall Cyprus—where the force
Of gentle-breathing Zephyr sterde her Course
Along the waves of the resounding Sea, 5
While, yet unborne, in that soft fome she laie
That brought her forth; whom those faire Howrs that beare
The Golden-bridles joyfully stood nere,
Tooke up into their armes, and put on her
Weeds of a never corruptible weare. 10
On her immortall head a Crowne they plac't,
Elaborate, and with all the beauties grac't
That Gold could give it; of a weight so great
That, to impose and take off, it had set
Three Handles on it, made, for endlesse hold, 15
Of shyning Brasse and all adorn'd with Gold.
Her soft neck all with Carquenets was grac't,
That stoop't, and both her silver brests embrac't,
Which even the Howrs themselves weare in resort
To Deities' Dances and her Father's Court. 20
Grac't at all parts, they brought to Heaven her graces;
Whose first sight seene, all fell into embraces,
Hugg'd her white hands, saluted, wishing all
To weare her Maiden Flowre in festivall
Of sacred Hymen, and to leade her home— 25
All, to all admiration, overcome
With Cytheræa with the violet Crowne.
So to the black-Browd-sweet-spoke All Renowne!
Prepare my Song, and give me, in the end,
The victory to whose Palme all contend! 30
So shall my Muse for ever honour thee,
And (for thy sake) thy faire Posteritie.

BACCHUS,

or

The Pyrats

Of Dionysus (Noble Semele's Son)
I now intend to render Mention,
As on a prominent shore his person shone,
Like to a Youth whose flowre was newly blone.
Bright azure Tresses plaid about his head, 5
And on his bright brode shoulders was dispred
A purple Mantle. Strait he was descride
By certaine Manly Pyrats, that applide
Their utmost speede to prise him, being abord
A well-built Barck, about whose brode sides ror'd 10
The wine-black Tyrrhene Billows. Death as black
Brought them upon him in their future wrack.
For soone as they had purchast but his view,
Mutuall signes past them, and ashore they flew,
Tooke him, and brought him instantly aborde, 15
Soothing their Hopes to have obtain'd a Horde
Of riches with him—and a Jove-kept King
To such a Flowre must needes be naturall spring.
And therefore strait strong Fetters they must fetch,
To make him sure. But no such strength would stretch 20
To his constrain'd Powrs. Farr flew all their Bands
From any least force done his feet or hands.
But he sate casting smiles from his black eyes
At all their worst. At which Discoveries
Made by the Master, he did thus dehort 25
All his Associats: 'Wretches! Of what sort
Hold ye the Person ye assaie to binde?
Nay, which of all the Powre fully-divin'de
Esteeme ye him, whose worth yeelds so much weight
That not our well-built Barck will beare his freight? 30
Or Jove himselfe he is, or he that beares
The silver Bowe, or Neptune. Nor appeares

In him the least resemblance of a Man,
But of a straine at least Olympian.
Come! Make we quick dismission of his state, 35
And on the black-soild earth exonerate
Our sinking vessell of his Deified Lode,
Nor dare the touch of an intangible God,
Lest windes outragious and of wrackfull scath,
And smoking Tempests, blowe his fiery wrath.' 40
This well-spoke Master the Tall captaine gave
Hatefull and horrible language; call'd him slave,
And bad him mark the prosperous gale that blew,
And how their vessell with her maine saile flew;
Bade all take armes, and said their workes requir'de 45
The cares of Men, and not of an inspir'de
Pure zealous Master—his firme hopes being fir'de
With this Opinion, that they should arive
In Ægypt strait, or Cyprus, or where live
Men whose brave breaths above the Northwinde blowe— 50
Yea, and perhaps beyond their Region too;
And that he made no doubt but in the end
To make his Prisoner tell him every friend
Of all his off-spring, Brothers, Wealth, and All;
Since that Prise, certaine, must some God let fall. 55
This said, the Mast and maine-saile up he drew,
And in the maine saile's midd'st a franck Gale blew;
When all his ship tooke arms to brave their Prise.
But strait strange works apperde to all their eyes:
First, sweete wine through their swift-black Barck did flow, 60
Of which the Odors did a little blowe
Their fiery spirits, making th'Ayre so fine
That they in flood were there as well as wine.
A meere Immortall-making savour rose,
Which on the Ayre the Deitie did Impose. 65
The Sea-Men see'ng All, Admiration seas'd.
Yet instantly their wonders were encreas'd,
For on the Top saile there rann, here and there,
A Vine that Grapes did in abundance beare,
And in an instant was the ship's maine Mast 70
With an obscure-greene Ivie's armes embrac't,
That florisht strait and were with Buries grac't;
Of which did Gyrlonds circle every brow
Of all the Pirats, and no One knew how.
Which when they sawe, they made the Master stere 75
Out to the shore; whom Bacchus made forbeare,
With showing more wonders. On the Hatches He

Apper'd a terrible Lyon, horriblie
Roring; and in the Mid-deck a Male Beare,
Made with a huge Mane; making all for feare 80
Crowd to the sterne about the Master there,
Whose Minde he still kept dantlesse and sincere,
But on the Captaine rusht and rampt, with force
So rude and sodaine that his maine recours
Was to the Maine-Sea strait; and after him 85
Leapt all his Mates, as trusting to their swimm
To fly foule Death—but so found what they fled,
Being all to Dolphinns metamorphosed.
The Master he tooke Ruth of, sav'd, and made
The blessedst Man that ever tried his Trade, 90
These few words giving him: 'Be confident,
Thou God-inspired Pylot! in the Bent
Of my affection, readie to requite
Thy late-to-me-intended benefite.
I am the Roring God of spritely Wine, 95
Whom Semele (that did even Jove incline
To amorous Mixture, and was Cadmus' care)
Made issue to the Mighty Thunderar.'
And thus all Excellence of Grace to thee,
Sonne of sweete-count'nance-cary'ng Semele. 100
I must not thee forget in least Degree;
But pray thy spirit to render so my song
Sweete, and all waies in order'd furie strong.

TO MARS

Mars, Most-strong, Gold-helm'd, making Chariots crack;
Never without a shield cast on thy back;
Minde-master, towne-guard, with darts never driven;
Strong-handed, All armes, fort and fence of heaven;
Father of Victory with faire strokes given; 5
Joint surrogate of Justice, lest she fall
In unjust strifes a Tyrant; Generall
Onely of Just Men justly; that dost beare
Fortitud's Scepter; to Heaven's fiery sphere
Giver of circulare motion, betweene 10
That and the Pleiads that still wandring bene;
Where thy still-vehemently-flaming Horse
About the third Heaven make their fiery course;
Helper of Mortalls; Heare! As thy fires give
The faire and present boldnesses that strive 15
In Youth for Honor, being the sweete-beamd Light
That darts into their lives, from all thy Height,
The Fortitudes and Fortunes found in fight;
So would I likewise wish to have the Powre
To keepe off from my head thy bitter Howre, 20
And that false fire, cast from my soule's lowe kinde,
Stoope to the fit rule of my highest Minde,
Controuling that so eager sting of wrath
That styrrs me on still to that horrid scath
Of Warr, that God still sends to wreake his splene 25
(Even by whole Tribes) of proud injurious Men.

But O thou ever-blessed! Give me still
Presence of minde to put in Act my will,
Varied, as fits, to all Occasion;
And to live free, unforc't, unwrought upon, 30
Beneath those Lawes of Peace that never are
Affected with Pollutions Populare
Of unjust hurt, or losse to any One;
And to beare safe the burthen undergone
Of Foes inflexive and inhumane hates, 35
Secure from violent and harmefull Fates.

TO DIANA

Diana praise, Muse, that in Darts delights,
Lives still a Maid, and had nutritiall rights
With her borne-Brother, the farr-shooting Sunn—
That doth her all-of-Gold-made Chariot runn
In Chace of Game, from Meles that abounds 5
In black-browd Bull-rushes (and where her Hounds
She first uncouples, joyning there her Horse)
Through Smyrna, carried in most fiery course
To Grape-rich Claros, where (in his rich home,
And constant expectation she will come) 10
Sits Phœbus, that the silver Bowe doth beare,
To meete with Phœbe, that doth Darts transferre
As farr as He his shafts. As farr then be
Thy chaste Fame shot, O Queene of Archerie!
Sacring my song to every Deitie. 15

TO VENUS

To Cyprian Venus, still my verses vow,
Who Gifts as sweete as honey doth bestow
On all Mortality; that ever smiles,
And rules a face that all foes reconciles;
Ever sustaining in her hand a Flowre 5
That all desire keepes ever in her Powre.
Haile then, O Queene of well-built Salamine
And all the state that Cyprus doth confine!
Informe my song with that celestiall fire
That in thy beauties kindles all desire. 10
So shall my Muse for ever honour Thee,
And any other thou commend'st to Me.

TO PALLAS

Pallas Minerva onely I beginne
To give my song; that makes warr's terrible Dinne,
Is Patronesse of Citties, and with Mars
Marshall'd in all the care and cure of wars,
And in everted Citties, fights and Cries— 5
But never doth her selfe set downe or rise
Before a Cittie, but at both times Shee
All injur'de people sets on foot and free.
Give, with thy warr's force, Fortune then to Me,
And, with thy Wisedome's force, Felicity. 10

TO JUNO

Saturnia and her Throne of Gold I sing,
That was of Rhea the eternall spring,
And Empresse of a beautie never yet
Equall'd in height of Tincture—of the great
Saturnius (breaking Ayre in awfull Noise) 5
The farr-fam'd wife and sister, whom in joies
Of high Olympus all the blessed Love
And Honour equall with unequall'd Jove.

TO CERES

The Rich-hayr'd Ceres I assaie to sing;
A Goddesse in whose Grace the naturall spring
Of serious Majestie it selfe is seene;
And of the wedded, yet in grace stil green,
Proserpina, her Daughter, that displaies 5
A Beautie casting every way her Raies.
All Honor to thee, Goddesse! Keepe this Towne,
And take thou chiefe charge of my song's Renoune!

TO THE MOTHER OF THE GODS

Mother of All, both Gods and Men, Commend,
O Muse, whose faire Forme did from Jove descend;
That doth with Cymball sounds delight her life,
And tremulous divisions of the Fife,
Love's dreadfull Lyons' Rores, and Wolves' hoarse Houles, 5
Sylvane Retreates, and Hills whose hollow knoules
Raise repercussive soundes about her eares.
And so may Honour ever crowne thy yeares
With All-else Goddesses, and ever be
Exalted in the Muses' Harmonie! 10

TO LYON-HEARTED HERCULES

Alcides, (Force-fullest of all the Broode
Of Men enforc't with neede of earthie foode)
My Muse shal memorise; the son of Jove,
Whom, in faire seated Thebs (commixt in love

With great Heaven's sable-cloude-assembling state) 5
Alcmena bore to him, and who (in date
Of daies forepast) through all the Sea was sent
And Earth's inenarrable Continent,
To Acts that King Eurystheus had decreede;
Did many a Petulant and Imperious Deede 10
Himselfe, and therefore suffer'd many a Toile;
Yet now inhabites the illustrious Soile
Of white Olympus, and Delights his life
With still young Hebe, his well-anckled wife.
Haile, King, and Sonne of Jove! Vouchsafe thou Me 15
Virtue, and her Effect, Felicitie!

TO ÆSCULAPIUS

With Æsculapius, the Phisition,
That cur'd all sicknesse, and was Phœbus' Sonne,
My Muse makes Entrie; to whose life gave yield
Divine Coronis in the Dotian field,
King Phlegius' Daughter, who much Joy on Men 5
Conferd in deare Ease of their yrkesome Paine—
For which, my salutation, worthy King,
And vowes to thee paid, ever when I sing!

TO CASTOR AND POLLUX

Castor and Pollux, the Tyndarides,
Sweete Muse illustrate; that their Essences
Fetch from the high forms of Olympian Jove,
And were the faire fruits of bright Leda's Love,
Which shee produc't beneath the sacred shade 5
Of steepe Taygetus, being subdu'd and made
To serve th'Affections of the Thunderer.
And so all Grace to you, whom all Aver
(For skill in Horses and their Manage geven)
To be the bravest Horsemen under Heaven! 10

TO MERCURIE

Hermes I honor, the Cyllenian Spie,
King of Cyllenia and of Arcadie
With flocks abounding; and the Messenger
Of all th'Immortalls, that doth still inferre
Profites of infinite valew to their store; 5
Whom to Saturnius bashfull Maia bore,
Daughter of Atlas, and did therefore flie
Of all th'Immortalls the Societie
To that darcke Cave where, in the dead of Night,
Jove joind with her in Love's divine Delight, 10
When Golden sleepe shut Juno's jealous eye,
Whose arms had wrists as white as Ivorie,
From whom and all, both Men and Gods beside,
The faire-hayrd Nymph her scape kept undescride.
Joy to the Jove-got then, and Maia's Care, 15
Twixt Men and Gods the generall Messenger,
Giver of good Grace, Gladnesse, and the Flood
Of all that Men or Gods account their Good!

TO PAN

Sing, Muse, this chiefe of Hermes' love-got Joies,
Goate-footed, Two-horn'd, amorous of noise,
That through the faire-Greenes, al adorn'd with Trees,
Together goes with Nymphs, whose nimble knees
Can every Dance foot, that affect to scale 5
The most inaccessible Tops of all
Uprightest rocks, and ever use to call
On Pan, the bright-hayr'd God of Pastorall—
Who yet is leane and lovelesse, and doth owe
By lot all loftiest Mountaines crown'd with snowe; 10

All Tops of Hills and cliffie Highnesses,
All Silvan Copses, and the Fortresses
Of Thorniest Queaches, here and there doth rove,
And sometimes (by allurement of his love)
Will wade the watrie softnesses. Sometimes 15
(In quite oppos'de Capriccios) he climes
The hardest Rocks and highest, every way
Running their Ridges. Often will convaie
Himselfe up to a watch Towr's Top, where sheepe
Have their Observance; oft through Hills as steepe 20
His Gotes he runns upon, and never rests.
Then turns he head, and flies on savage Beasts,
Mad of their slaughters—so most sharpe an eye
Setting upon them as his Beames let flie
Through all their thickest Tapistries. And then 25
(When Hesp'rus calls to folde the flocks of Men)
From the greene Clossets of his loftiest Reedes
He rushes forth, and Joy with Song he feedes—
When (under shadow of their motions set)
He plaies a verse forth so profoundly sweet 30
As not the Bird that in the flowrie Spring
(Amidds the leaves set) makes the Thickets ring
Of her sowre sorrowes, sweetened with her song,
Runns her divisions varied so and strong.
And then the sweete-voic't Nymphs that crowne his
mountaines 35
(Flockt round about the deepe-black-watred fountaines)
Fall in with their Contention of song,
To which the Echoes all the Hills along
Their repercussions add. Then here and there
(Plac't in the midd'st) the God the Guide doth beare 40
Of all their Dances, winding in and out,
A Lynce's Hide (besprinckled round about
With blood) cast on his shoulders. And thus He
With well-made songs maintaines th'alacritie
Of his free minde, in silken Meddows crownde 45
With Hyacynths and Saffrons, that abound
In sweete-breath'd Odors, that th'unnumber'd grasse
(Besides their sents) give as through all they passe.
And these, in all their pleasures, ever raise
The blessed Gods' and long Olympus' praise; 50
Like zealous Hermes, who (of all) I said
Most Profits up to all the Gods convaide.
Who, likewise, came into th'Arcadian state
(That's rich in Fountaines, and all celebrate

For Nurse of flocks) where he had vowd a Grove 55
(Surnam'd Cyllenius) to his God-head's love.
Yet even himselfe (although a God he were),
Clad in a squallid sheepskinn governd there
A Mortall's sheepe. For soft Love, entring him,
Conformd his state to his conceipted Trimm, 60
And made him long in an extreame degree
T'enjoy the fayre-hayrd Virgine Dryope.
Which, ere he could, she made him consummate
The florishing Rites of Hymen's honord State,
And brought him such a peece of Progenie 65
As showd (at first sight) monstrous to the eye,
Gote-footed, Two-horn'd, full of noise even then,
And (opposite quite to other children)
Told (in sweete laughter) he ought death no Teare.
Yet strait his Mother start, and fled in feare 70
The sight of so unsatisfying a Thing,
In whose face put forth such a bristled spring.
Yet the most usefull Mercurie embrac't,
And tooke into his armes, his homely-fac't,
Beyond all measure joyfull with his sight; 75
And up to heaven with him made instant flight,
Wrapt in the warme skinne of a Mountaine Hare,
Set him by Jove, and made most merrie fare
To all the Deities else with his Sonne's sight,
Which most of all fill'd Bacchus with delight; 80
And Pan they call'd him, since he brought to All
Of Mirth so rare and full a Festivall.
 And thus, all honor to the shepherds' King!
 For Sacrifice to Thee my Muse shall sing!

TO VULCAN

Praise Vulcane, now, Muse; whom Fame gives the Prise
For Depth and Facture of al Fordge devise;
Who, with the skie-eyd Pallas, first did give
Men rules of buildings, that before did live
In Caves and Denns and Hills like savage Beasts; 5
But now, by Art-fam'd Vulcan's Interests

In all their civill Industries, waies cleare
Through th'All-things-bringing-to-their-Ends, the yeare,
They worke out to their Ages' ends, at ease
Lodg'd in safe Roofes from Winter's utmost prease. 10
But, Vulcan, stand propitious to Me,
Virtue safe granting, and Felicitie!

TO PHŒBUS

O Phœbus! Even the Swann from forth her wings
(Jumping her proyning-banck) thee sweetly sings,
By bright Peneus' whirle-pit-making streames.
Thee that thy Lute mak'st sound so to thy Beames,
Thee, first and last, the sweete-voic't singer still 5
Sings, for thy song's all-songs-transcending skill.
Thy Pleasure then shall my song still supply,
And so salutes thee, King of Poësie.

TO NEPTUNE

Neptune, the mighty Marine God, I sing,
Earth's mover, and the fruitles Ocean's king,
That Helicon and th'Ægean Deepes dost hold.
O thou Earth-shaker! Thy Command two-fold
The Gods have sorted, making thee of Horses 5
The awfull Tamer, and of Navall Forces
The sure Preserver. Haile, O Saturns Birth!
Whose gracefull greene hayre circkles all the Earth.
Beare a benigne minde, and thy helpfull hand
Lend All submitted to thy drad Command. 10

TO JOVE

Jove now I sing, the greatest and the best
Of al these Powrs that are with Deitie blest,
That farr-off doth his dreadfull Voice diffuse,
And (being King of All) doth all conduce
To all their Ends. Who (shut from all Gods else 5
With Themis, that the lawes of all things tells)
Their fit Composures to their Times doth call,
Wedds them together, and preserves This All.
Grace then, O Farr-heard Jove, the grace t'hast geven,
Most glorious, and most great of Earth and Heaven. 10

TO VESTA

Vesta, that (as a servant) Oversees
King Phœbus' hallowd house, in all degrees
Of Guide about it, on the sacred shore
Of heavenly Pythos, and hast evermore
Rich balms distilling from thy Odorous hayre, 5
Grace this House with thy huswifely repaire!
Enter, and bring a Minde that most may move,
Conferring even the great in counsailes, Jove;
And let my verse taste of your either's love.

TO THE MUSES AND APOLLO

The Muses, Jove and Phœbus, now I sing;
For from the farr-off-shooting Phœbus spring
All Poets and Musitions, and from Jove
Th'Ascents of Kings. The Man the Muses love,

Felicitie blesses, Elocution's choice — 5
In Syrrup lay'ng, of sweetest breath, his voice.
Haile, Seede of Jove, my song your honors give,
And so in Mine shall yours and others' live.

TO BACCHUS

Ivie-Crown'd Bacchus Iterate in thy Praises,
O Muse, whose Voice all loftiest Echoes raises;
And He with all th'illustrous seede of Jove
Is joinde in honor, being the fruite of Love
To him and Semele the-great-in-graces; — 5
And from the King his Father's kinde embraces
By faire-hayrde Nymphs was taken to the Dales
Of Nyssa, and with curious Festivals
Given his faire Grought, far from his Father's view,
In Caves from whence eternall Odors flew, — 10
And in high number of the Deities plac't.
Yet when the many-Hymne-given God had past
His Nurses' Cares, in Ivies and in Baies
All over Thicketed, his varied waies
To sylvan Coverts evermore he tooke — 15
With all his Nurses, whose shrill voices shooke
Thickets in which could no foote's Entrie fall,
And he himself made Captaine of them All.
And so, O Grape-abounding Bacchus, be
Ever saluted by my Muse and Me! — 20
Give us to spend with spirit our Howres out here,
And every Howre extend to many a Yeare.

TO DIANA

Diana (that the Golden Spyndle moves,
And loftie soundes as wel as Bacchus loves,
A bashfull Virgine, and of fearefull hearts
The Death-affecter with delighted Darts,

By Sire and Mother Phœbus' Sister borne, 5
Whose Thigh the Golden Falchion doth adorne)
I sing; who, likewise over Hills of shade
And Promontories that vast windes invade,
(Amorous of Hunting) bends her all-gold Bowe,
And sigh-begetting Arrows doth bestowe 10
In fates so dreadfull that the Hill-Tops quake,
And Bristlde woods their leavie foreheads shake,
Horrors invade Earth, and the fishie Seas
Impassiond furies; nothing can appease
The dying Braies of Beasts, and her Delight 15
In so much Death affects so with affright
Even all inanimate natures. For while shee
Her sports applies, their generall Progenie
Shee all waies turnes upon, to All their Banes.
Yet when her fierie Pleasures finde their wanes, 20
(Her yeelding Bowe unbent) to th'ample House
(Seated in Delphos, rich and Populous)
Of her deare Brother her Retreats advance—
Where th' Instauration of delightsome Dance
Amongst the Muses and the Graces shee 25
Gives forme; in which her selfe the Regencie
(Her unbent Bowe hung up, and casting on
A gracious Robe) assumes, and first sets gone
The Dance's Entrie; to which all send forth
Their heavenly voices, and advance the worth 30
Of her faire-anckl'd Mother, since to light
Shee Children brought the farr most exquisite
In Counsailes and Performances of all
The Goddesses that grace the heavenly Hall.
Haile then, Latona's faire-hayrd seede, and Jove's! 35
My song shall ever call to Minde your Loves.

TO PALLAS

Pallas-Minerva's Deitie, the renown'd,
My Muse in her variety must resound;
Mightie in counsailes; whose Illustrous Eyes
In all resemblance represent the skies.

A reverend Maid of an inflexible Minde; 5
In Spirit and Person strong; of Triple kinde;
Fautresse of Citties that just Lawes maintaine;
Of Jove-the-great-in-counsaile's very Braine
Tooke Prime existence; his unbounded Brows
Could not containe her, such impetuous Throws 10
Her Birth gave way to that abrode she flew,
And stood in Gold arm'd in her Father's view,
Shaking her sharpe Lance. All Olympus shooke
So terriblie beneath her that it tooke
Up in amazes all the Deities there; 15
All Earth resounded with vociferous Feare;
The Sea was put up all in purple Waves,
And settld sodainly her rudest Raves;
Hyperion's radiant Sonne his swift-hov'd Steedes
A mighty Tyme staid, till her arming weedes, 20
As glorious as the Gods', the blew-eyd Maid
Tooke from her Deathlesse shoulders. But then staid
All these distempers, and heaven's counsailor, Jove,
Rejoic't that all things else his stay could move.
So I salute thee still; and still in Praise 25
Thy Fame, and others', shall my Memorie raise.

TO VESTA AND MERCURIE

Vesta I sing, who, in Bequest of Fate,
Art sorted out an everlasting State
In all th'Immortals' high-built roofes, and all
Those of Earth-dwelling Men, as generall
And ancient honors given thee for thy gift 5
Of free-liv'd Chastitie and precious Thrift.
Nor can there amongst Mortalls Banquets be
In which, both first and last, they give not Thee
Their endlesse Gratitudes in pourd-out wine,
As gracious sacrifice to thy divine 10
And usefull virtues; being invok't by All,
Before the least Taste of their Festivall
In wine or foode affect their appetites.
And thou that of th'adorn'd with all Delights

Art the most usefull Angell, borne a God 15
Of Jove and Maia, of Heaven's golden Rodd
The sole Sustainer, and hast powre to blesse
With All good All Men, great Argicides,
Inhabit all Good houses, see'ng no wants
Of mutuall mindes' love in th'inhabitants, 20
Joine in kinde blessing with the bashfull Maid
And all-lov'd Virgin, Vesta—either's aid
Combin'd in every Hospitable House,
Both being best seene in all the gracious
House-works of Mortalls. Jointly follow then, 25
Even from their youths, the mindes of dames and men.
Haile then, ould Daughter of the ouldest God,
And thou great bearer of Heaven's golden Rodd!
Yet not to you alone my vowes belong;
Others as well claime t'Homage of my song. 30

TO EARTH THE MOTHER OF ALL

Mother of all things, the well-founded Earth,
My Muse shall memorise; who al the birth
Gives foode that al her upper regions breede,
All that in her divine diffusions feede
In under Continents, all those that live 5
In all the Seas, and All the ayre doth give
Wing'd expeditions, of thy bounties eate;
Faire Children, and faire fruites, thy labor's sweate,
O great in reverence, and referd to thee
For life and death is all the Pedigree 10
Of Mortall humanes. Happie then is He
Whom the innate Propensions of thy Minde
Stand bent to honor. He shall all things finde
In all abundance; all his Pastures yield
Herds in all plenties; all his roofes are fill'd 15
With rich possessions; He, in all the swaie
Of Lawes best orderd, cuts out his owne way
In Citties shining with delicious Dames,
And takes his choice of all those striving Flames.
High happinesse and riches (like his Traine) 20
Follow his Fortunes, with delights that raigne

In all their Princes. Glorie invests his Sonnes;
His Daughters, with their croun'd selections
Of all the Cittie, frolick through the Meades,
And every one her calld-for Dances treads 25
Along the soft-flowre of the claver Grasse.
All this, with all those, ever comes to passe
That thy love blesses, Goddesse full of grace,
And treasurous Angell t'all the humane Race.
Haile then, Great Mother of the Deified kinde, 30
Wife to the Cope of Starrs! Sustaine a Minde
Propitious to me for my Praise, and give
(Answering my minde) my vows fit Meanes to live.

TO THE SUN

The radiant Sun's divine renowne diffuse,
Jove's Daughter, great Calliope, my Muse—
Whom Ox-ey'd Euryphaessa gave Birth
To the bright seede of starrie Heaven and Earth.
For the farr-fam'd Hyperion tooke to Wife 5
His Sister Euryphaessa, that life
Of his high Race gave to these lovely Three:
Aurora with the Rosie-wrists, and shee
That ownes th'enamouring tresses, the bright Moone,
Together with the never-wearied Sunne, 10
Who (his Horse mounting) gives both Mortalls light
And all th'immortalls. Even to horror, bright
A blaze burns from his Golden Burgonet,
Which to behold exceeds the sharpest set
Of any eye's intention, beames so cleare 15
It all waies powres abroade. The glorious cheare
Of his farr-shining Face up to his Crowne
Casts circular Radiance, that comes streaming downe
About his Temples, his bright Cheeks, and all,
Retayning the refulgence of their Fall. 20
About his bosome flowes so fine a Weede
As doth the thynnesse of the winde exceede
In rich context; beneath whose deepe folds flie
His Masculine Horses round about the skie,

Till in this Hemisphere he renders staie 25
T'his gold-yo'kt Coch and Coursers; and his way
(Let downe by Heaven) the heavenly Cocheman makes
Downe to the Ocean, where his rest he takes.
My Salutations then, faire King, receive,
And in propitious returnes Relieve 30
My life with Minde-fit means, and then from Thee
And all the race of compleate Deitie
My song shall celebrate those halfe-God states
That yet sad death's condicion circulates,
And whose brave Acts the Gods shew men, that they 35
As brave may ayme at, since they can but die.

TO THE MOONE

The Moone, now, Muses, teach me to resound,
Whose wide wings measure such a world of ground—
Jove's Daughter, deckt with the mellifluous Tongue,
And seene in All the sacred Art of Song;
Whose deathles Brows, when shee from Heaven displaies, 5
All Earth she wraps up in her Orient Raies.
A Heaven of Ornament in Earth is rais'd
When her Beames rise. The subt'le Ayre is sais'd
Of delicate splendor from her Crowne of Gold
And, when her silver Bosome is extoll'd, 10
Washt in the Ocean. In Daies equall'd Noone
Is Mid-night seated; but when shee puts on
Her farr-off-sprinckling-Luster Evening weedes,
(The Moneth in two cut, her high-brested Steedes
Man'de All with curl'd flames, put in Coch and All 15
Her huge Orb fill'd) her whole Trimms then exhall
Unspeakable splendors from the glorious skie.
And out of that State Mortall Men implie
Many Prædictions. And with Her then
(In Love mixt) lay the King of Gods and Men, 20
By whom (made fruitfull) she Pandea bore
And added her State to th'immortall Store.
Haile, queene and Goddesse, th'ivorie-wristed Moone
Divine, Prompt, faire-hayr'd. With thy grace begun,

My Muse shall forth and celebrate the praise 25
Of Men whose states the Deities did raise
To Semideities; whose deedes t'endlesse Date
Muse-lov'd and sweete-sung Poets celebrate.

TO CASTOR AND POLLUX

Jove's faire Sonnes, Father'd by th'Oebalian King,
Muses well-worth-All-Men's-beholdings, sing—
The Deare Birth that Bright-Anckl'd Leda bore,
Horse-taming Castor, and the Conqueror
Of Tooth-tongu'd Momus, Pollux: whom beneath 5
Steepe-Browd Taygetus she gave half-God breath,
In Love mixt with the black-cloudes King of heaven;
Who both of Men and ships (being Tempest driven,
When Winter's wrathfull Empire is in force
Upon th'Implacable Seas) preserve the course. 10
For when the Gusts beginn, (if nere the shore)
The Sea-Men leave their ship, and (evermore
Bearing two milke-white Lambs aboard) they now
Kill them ashore, and to Jove's Issue vow,
When though their ship (in height of all the rore 15
The windes and waves confound) can live no more
In all their hopes; then sodainely appeare
Jove's saving Sonnes, who both their Bodies beare
Twixt yellowe wings, downe from the sparkling Pole,
Who strait the rage of those rude Winds controle, 20
And all the high-waves couch into the Brest
Of t'hoarie Seas. All which sweete signes of rest
To Sea-Men's labors their glad soules conceive,
And End to all their yrckesome grievance give.
So (once more) to the swift-horse-riding Race 25
Of Royall Tyndarus, eternall Grace!

TO MEN OF HOSPITALITIE

Reverence a Man with use Propitious
That Hospitable rights wants; and a house
(You of this Cittie with the seate of State
To Ox-eyd Juno vowd) yet situate
Nere Pluto's Region—at the extreame Base 5
Of whose so high-hayrd Cittie, from the Race
Of blew-wav'd Hebrus' lovely Fluent, (grac't
With Jove's begetting) you divine Cups Tast.

CERTAINE EPIGRAMMS
AND OTHER POEMS OF HOMER

TO CUMA

Lend hospitable Rights and house-respect,
You that the Virgine with the faire eys deckt
Make Favtresse of your stately-seated Towne
At foot of Sardes, with the high-haird Crowne,
Inhabiting rich Cuma: where ye Taste 5
Of Hermus' heavenly Fluent, all embrac't
By curld-head whyrlpits, and whose waters move
From the divine seede of immortall Jove.

IN HIS RETURNE

To Cuma

Swiftlie my feete sustaine me to the Towne
Where Men inhabit whom due Honors Crowne,
Whose Mindes with free-given faculties are mov'd,
And whose grave Counsailes best of Best approv'd.

UPON THE SEPULCHER OF MIDUS,

Cut in Brasse in the Figure of a Virgine

A Maid of Brasse I am, Infixed here
T'Eternise Honest Midus' Sepulcher,
And while the streame her fluent seede receives,
And steepe trees curle their verdant brows with leaves,

While Phœbus rais'd above the Earth gives sight, 5
And t'humorous Moone takes Luster from his light,
While floods beare waves, and Seas shall wash the shore,
At this his Sepulcher, whom all deplore,
I'le constantly Abide, all passers by
Informing: *'Here doth Honest Midus Lie.'* 10

CUMA
REFUSING HIS OFFER T'ETERNISE THEIR STATE,
though brought thither by the Muses

O to what Fate hath father Jove given O're
My friendles life, borne ever to be Pore?
While in my Infant state he pleas'd to save Mee,
Milke on my reverend Mother's knees he gave Me
In delicate and curious Nurserie— 5
Æolian Smyrna, seated neare the Sea,
(Of glorious Empire, and whose bright sides
Sacred Meletus' silver Current glides)
Being native Seate to me. Which (in the force
Of farr-past Time) the Breakers of wilde Horse, 10
Phriconia's Noble Nation, girt with Towres,
Whose Youth in fight put on with fiery Powres.
From hence, (the Muse-maids, Jove's illustrous seede,
Impelling me) I made impetuous speede,
And went with them to Cuma, with Intent 15
T'Eternise all the sacred Continent
And State of Cuma. They (in proud Ascent
From off their Bench) refus'd with usage fierce
The sacred voice which I averre is Verse.
Their follies yet, and madnesse borne by Me, 20
Shall by some Powre be thought on futurely,
To wreake of him whoever whose tongue sought
With false empaire my fall. What fate God brought
Upon my Birth I'le beare with any paine,
But undeserv'd Defame, unfelt, sustaine. 25
Nor feeles my Person (deare to me, though Pore)
Any great lust to linger any more

In Cuma's holy Highwaies; but my Minde
(No thought empaird for cares of any kinde
Borne in my body) rather vowes to trie 30
The Influence of any other skie,
And spirits of People bredd in any Land,
Of ne're so slender and obscure Command.

AN ASSAIE OF HIS BEGUNNE ILIADS

Ilion, and all the brave-Horse-breeding Soile,
Dardania, I sing; that many a Toile
Impos'd upon the Mighty Grecian Powrs,
Who were of Mars the manlie Servitours.

TO THESTOR'S SONNE,

Inquisitive of HOMER ABOUT THE CAUSES OF THINGS

Thestorides! Of all the skills unknowne
To errant Mortals, there remains not One
Of more inscrutable Affaire to finde
Than is the true State of a humane Minde.

Homer intimated in this his Answer to Thestorides—A will to have him learne the knowledge of himselfe, before hee enquir'd so curiously the causes of other things. And from hence had the great Peripatetique, Themistius, his most grave Epiphoneme, Anima quæ seipsam ignorat, quid sciret ipsa de alijs?*—and therefore (according to Aristotle) advises all Philosophicall Students to beginne with that Studie.*

TO NEPTUNE

Heare, Powreful Neptune, that shak'st Earth in Ire,
King of the great Greene where dance All the Quire
Of faire-hayr'd Helicon; give prosperous Gales
And good passe to these Guiders of our sailes,
Their Voyage rendring happily directed, 5
And their Returne with no ill Fate affected.
Grant, likewise, at rough Mimas' lowest rootes
(Whose strength up to her Tops prærupt rocks shootes),
My Passage safe arrivall; and that I
My bashfull disposition may applie 10
To Pious Men, and wreake my selfe upon
The Man whose verball circumvention
In Me did wrong t'Hospitious Jove's whole state,
And t'Hospitable Table violate.

TO THE CITTIE ERYTHRÆA

Worshipfull Earth, giver of all things good!
Giver of even Felicitie, whose flood
The Minde all-over steepes in honey Dewe,
That to some Men dost infinite kindenesse shew,
To others that despise thee art a Shrew, 5
And giv'st them Gamesters' galls—who, once their Maine
Lost with an ill chance, fare like Abjects slaine.

TO MARINERS

Ye wave-trod Watermen, as ill as shee
That all the Earth in Infelicitie
Of Rapine plunges; who upon youre Fare
As sterv'd-like-ravenous as Cormorants are;

The lives ye leade (but in the worse Degree) 5
Not to be envied more than Misery—
Take shame, and feare the Indignation
Of him that Thunders from the highest Throne,
Hospitious Jove, who at the Back prepares
Paines of abhord effect of him that dares 10
The Pieties breake of his Hospitious squares.

THE PINE

Any Tree else beares better Fruit than Thee
That Ida's Tops sustaine, where every Tree
Beares up in aire such perspirable Heights,
And in which Caves and sinuous Receipts
Creepe in such great abundance. For about 5
Thy rootes (that ever all thy Fruites put out
As nourisht by them equall with thy Fruites)
Poure Mars his Iron-Mines their accurst pursuites.
So that when any Earth-encroching Man
Of all the Martiall Broode Cebrenian 10
Plead neede of Iron, they are certaine still
About thy Rootes to satiate every Will.

TO GLAUCUS, WHO WAS SO MISERABLIE SPARING THAT HE FEARED ALL MEN'S ACCESSE TO HIM

Glaucus! though wise enough, yet one word more
Let my advice add to thy wisedome's store,
For t'will be better so. Before thy Dore

Give still thy Mastifs Meate, that will be sure
To lie there, therefore, still, and not endure 5
(With way-laid eares) the softest foot can fall,
But Men and Beasts make fly Thee and thy stall.

AGAINST THE SAMIAN MINISTRESSE OR NUNNE

Heare Me, O goddesse, that invoke thine eare,
Thou that dost feede and forme the youthfull Yeare,
And grant that this Dame may the loves refuse
And Beds of Young Men, and affect to use
Humanes whose Temples hoary hayres distaine, 5
Whose Powrs are passing coye, whose Wils would faine.

WRITTEN ON THE COUNSAILE CHAMBER

Of Men, Sonnes are the Crownes of Citties' Towres;
Of Pastures, Horse are the most bewtious Flowres;
Of Seas, ships are the Grace; and Money still
With Traines and Titles doth the Family fill.
But Royall Counsailors, in Counsaile set, 5
Are Ornaments past All, as clearely great
As Houses are that shining fires enfolde,
Superior farr to Houses nak't and colde.

THE FORNACE, CALL'D IN TO SING BY POTTERS

If ye deale freely, O my fierie Friends,
As ye assure, I'le sing, and serve your Ends.
Pallas! Vouchsafe thou here invok't Accesse,
Impose thy hand upon this Fordge, and blesse

All Cups these Artists earne so, that they may 5
Looke black still with their depth, and every way
Give all their Vessels a most sacred Sale.
Make all well burn'd, and Estimation call
Up to their Prices. Let them marcket well,
And in all high-waies in abundance sell, 10
Till Riches to their utmost wish arise—
And as thou mak'st them rich, so make me wise.
But if ye now turne all to Impudence,
And think to pay with lies my Pacience,
Then will I summon gainst your Fornace All 15
Hell's harmefull'st spirits; Maragus I'le call,
Sabactes, Asbett, and Omadamus,
Who ylls against your Art Innumerous
Excogitates, supplies, and multiplies.
Come, Pallas, then, and all command to rise, 20
Infesting Fordge and house with fire, till All
Tumble together and to Ashes Fall,
These Potters' selves dissolv'd in Teares as small.
And as a Horse-cheeke chides his foming Bit,
So let this Fordge murmure in fire and flit, 25
And all this stuffe to ashie ruines runne.
And thou, O Circe, Daughter of the Sunne,
Great-many-Poison-Mixer, come, and poure
Thy cruell'st Poisons on this Potters' floore,
Shivering their vessells; and themselves affect 30
With all the Mischiefes possible to direct
Gainst all their Beings, urdg'd by all thy feends.
Let Chiron likewise come, and all those friends,
The Centaures, that Alcides' fingers fled,
And All the rest too that his hand strooke dead 35
(Their Ghosts excited), come and macerate
These Earthen Men; and yet with further Fate
Affect their Fornace, all their teare-burst Eyes
Seeing and mourning for their Miseries,
While I looke on, and laugh their blasted Art 40
And them to Ruine. Lastly, if, apart
Any lies lurking, and sees yet, his Face
Into a Cole let th'angrie fire embrace,
That all may learne by them, in all their lust,
To dare Deedes Great, to see them great and Just. 45

EIRESIONE,

or

The Olive Branch

The Turrets of a Man of infinite Might,
Of infinite Action, substance Infinite,
Wee make accesse to; whose whole Being rebounds
From Earth to Heaven, and nought but Blisse resounds.
Give entrie then, ye Dores; more riches yet 5
Shall enter with me, all the Graces met
In joy of their fruition, perfect Peace
Confirming All—All crown'd with such encrease,
That every emptie Vessell in your House
May stand repleate with all thing precious. 10
Elaborate Ceres may your Larders fill
With all deare Delicates, and serve in still.
May for your Sonne a Wife make wisht approch
Into your Towrs, and rapt in in her Coch
With strong-kneed Mules. May yet her state prove staid 15
With honord Huswiferies, her faire hand laid
To artfull Loomeworks, and her nak't feet treade
The Gumme of Amber to a Golden Beade.
But I'le returne. Returne, and yet not presse
Your bounties now assaid with oft Accesse, 20
Once a yeere onely, as the Swallow prates
Before the welthie Spring's wide open Gates.
Meane time I stand at yours, nor purpose stay
More time t'entreate. Give, or not give, away
My feet shall beare me, that did never come 25
With any thought to make your House my Home.

TO CERTAINE FISHER-BOYES PLEASING HIM WITH INGENIOUS RIDDLES

Yet from the bloods even of your-selfe-like sires
Are you descended, that could make ye heires
To no huge hords of Coine, nor leave ye Able
To feede Flocks of innumerable Rabble.

THE END OF ALL THE ENDLESS WORKS OF HOMER

The Worke that I was borne to doe is done.
Glory to Him that the Conclusion
Makes the beginning of my life; and Never
Let me be said to live, till I live Ever.
Where's the outliving of my Fortunes then, 5
Ye errant vapors of Fame's Lernean Fenn,
That (like possest stormes) blast all not in Herde
With your abhorr'd heads; who, because casher'de
By Men for Monsters, thinck Men Monsters All
That are not of your pyed Hood and your Hall— 10
When you are nothing but the scumm of things,
And must be cast off—Drones, that have no stings,
Nor any more soule than a stone hath wings.
Avant ye Haggs! Your Hates and Scandalls are
The Crownes and Comforts of a good Man's Care; 15
By whose impartiall Perpendiculare,
All is extuberance and tumor All,
That you your Ornaments and glories call.
Your wrie Mouthes censure right! your blister'd Tongues
That licke but itches, and whose ulcerous Lungs 20
Come up at all things permanent and sound!
O you (like flies in Dreggs) in Humors droun'd,
Your loves, like Atoms, lost in gloomie Ayre,
I would not retrive with a wither'd Haire!
Hate, and cast still your stings then, for your kisses 25
Betray but Truth, and your Applauds are Hisses.
To see our supercilious wizerds frowne,
Their faces falne like Foggs, and, coming downe,
Stincking the Sunn out, make me shine the more,
And like a checkt flood beare above the shore 30
That their prophane Opinions faine would set
To what they see not, know not, nor can let.
Yet then our learn'd Men with their Torrents come
Roring from their forc't Hills, all crown'd with fome,
That one not taught like them should learne to know 35
Their Greeke rootes, and from thence the Groves that grow,
Casting such rich shades, from great Homer's wings,
That first and last command the Muses' springs—

Though he's best Scholler that, through paines and vows
Made his owne Master onely, all things knows. 40
Nor pleades my poore skill forme, or learned Place,
But dantlesse labor, constant Prayer, and Grace.
And what's all their skill but vast varied reading?
As if brode-beaten High-waies had the leading
To Truth's abstract, and narrow Path and Pit, 45
Found in no walke of any worldly wit.
And without Truth, all's onely sleight of hand,
Or our Law-learning in a Forraine Land,
Embroderie spent on Cobwebs, Braggart show
Of Men that all things learne and nothing know. 50
For Ostentation humble Truth still flies,
And all confederate fashionists defies.
And as some sharpe-browd Doctor (English borne)
In much learn'd Latine Idioms can adorne
A verse with rare Attractions, yet become 55
His English Muse like an Arachnean Loome
Wrought spight of Pallas, and therein bewraies
More tongue than truth, beggs, and adopts his Bayes:
So Ostentation, bee hee never so
Larded with labour to suborne his showe, 60
Shall soothe within him but a bastard soule,
No more Heaven heyring than Earth's sonne, the Moule.
But as in dead Calmes emptiest smokes arise
Uncheckt and free, up strait into the skies:
So drousie Peace, that in her humor steepes 65
All she affects, lets such rise while she sleepes.
Many and most Men have of wealth least store,
But None the gracious shame that fits the Pore;
So most learn'd Men enough are Ignorant,
But few the grace have to confesse their want, 70
Till Lives and Learnings come concomitant.
For from Men's knowledges their Lives'-Acts flowe;
Vaineglorious Acts then vaine prove all they know.
As Night the life-enclining starrs best showes,
So lives obscure the starriest soules disclose. 75
For me, let just Men judge by what I show
In Acts expos'd how much I erre or knowe;
And let not Envie make all worse than nought
With her meere headstrong and quite braineles thought,
Others, for doing nothing, giving All, 80
And bounding all worth in her bursten Gall.
God and my deare Redeemer, rescue Me
From Men's immane and mad Impietie,

And by my life and soule (sole knowne to them)
Make me of Palme, or Yew, an Anadem.
And so, my sole God, the thrice sacred Trine,
Beare all th' Ascription of all Me and Mine.

Supplico tibi, Domine, Pater et Dux rationis nostræ, ut Nostræ Nobilitatis recordemur quâ tu nos ornasti; et ut tu nobis prestò sis, ut iis qui per sese moventur; ut et à Corporis contagio, Brutorumque affectuum repurgemur, eosque superemus, atque regamus; et sicut decet, pro instrumentis iis utamur. Deinde, ut nobis Adiumento sis, ad accuratam rationis nostræ correctionem, et coniunctionem cum iis qui verè sunt per lucem veritatis. Et tertiùm, Salvatori supplex oro, ut ab oculis animorum nostrorum, caliginem prorsus abstergas, ut norimus bene qui Deus, aut Mortalis, habendus. Amen.

SINE HONORE VIVAM, NULLOQUE NUMERO ERO

TEXTUAL NOTES

TEXTUAL NOTES

Dedication

Heading

MOST-WORTHIE-TO-BE-MOST-HONOR'D	MOST-WORTHIE-TO-BE-MOST HONOR'D
26 *to Heaven*	[The Harvard copy is corrected: to All Heauen]
66 *Springs*	Spring's
85 *th'House*	T'House
90 *th'Enimies'*	Th' Enimies
91 *and*	&
and	&
111 *from hence*	frõ hẽce
127 *men, and*	mẽ; &

The Occasion

2 and	*&*
11 drowning	*deuouring* [manuscript correction by Chapman in the Harvard copy]
14 Hymns	*Hymn's*
19 Hymns	*Hym'ns*
26 our ever-the-Same	*our-euer-the Same*

Batrachomyomachia

9 and	*And*
19 Who	*who*
Replie	*replie*
22 I'le	*Ile*
27 [note] et	*&*
28 and	*And*
29 mine	*Mine*
31 on	*On*
35 and	*And*
38 Why	*why*
41 Psicharpax	Psycharpax
57 [note] et	*&*

59 nor	*Nor*
60 nor	*Nor*
62 though	*thought*
64 [note] *common*	commõ
74 th'	*Th'*
88 Coloquintidas	*Coloquintida's*
98 I'le	*Ile*
100 th'other	*thither*
107 his	*His*
124 his	*His*
167 tis	*ti's*
181 Dædalean	Dedalean
197 from	*From*
208 Psicharpax'	Psycharpax
216 Psicharpax	Psycharpax
225 Pow'rs	*'Powr's*
229 who	*Who*
234 [note] *Boots*	Boot's
245 these	*These*
292 Lichenor	Lychenor
301 Seutlæus	Sentlæus
302 Then	*then*
306 Limnocharis	Lymnocharis
310 Lichenor	Lychenor
312 Limnocharis	Lymnocharis
315 Crambophagus	Crambaphagus
323 Limnisius	Lymnisius
336 Prassophagus	Brassophagus
336 [note] Leeke or	Leeke-or
337 Cnissodioctes	Cnisodioctes
340 Psicharpax	Psycharpax
364 and	*And*
377 and	*&*
382 of	*Of*
432 brick-backt	*Brick-backt*
all	*All*
435 twice	*Twice*
436 strong	*Strong*
443 when	*When*

An Hymne to Apollo

Heading

Hymne	Hymnc
45 lands	*land*
49 or	*Or*

50	or	*Or*
52	or	*Or*
64	that	*That*
70	if	*If*
82	or	*Or*
98	nor	*Nor*
	thee	*theee*
135	Rhea	Rhæa
137	every	*Euery*
192	every	*Euery*
237	who	*Who*
247	songs	*song's*
279	both	*Both*
296	th'	*Th'*
338	passing	*Passing*
340	Perrhæbes	Perrhabes
347	Euripus	Eurypus
351	Teumessus	Teucmessus
383	Cephissus	Cephyssus
385	Lilæus	Lylæus
398	even	*Euen*
399	Peloponnesus	Peloponesus
404	the	*The*
415	th'	*Th'*
430	Parnassus	Paranassus
439	his	*His*
445	Cephissus'	Cephyssus
448	the with-snowe-still-croun'd	*the-with-snowe-still croun'd*
458	Peloponnesus	Peloponessus
460	that	*That*
483	having	*Hauing*
486	whom	*Whom*
513	Her	*her*
528	Titanois	Titanoys
543	Dædalian	Dedalian
582	Chimæra	Chymæra
595	to	*To*
599	frauds	*fraud's*
601	it	*It*
618	Cnossus	Gnossus
628	Pylian	Pylean
638	but	*But*
639	and	*And*
641	Malean	Mal e
644	a	*A*

647 on	*On*
654 or	*Or*
656 Peloponnesian	Peloponesian
659 and	*And*
660 Argyphæa	Aryphæa
and	*And*
666 and	*And*
667 all	*All*
673 Peloponnesus	Peloponesus
and	*And*
675 Morea	Moræa
694 in	*In*
698 like	*lik*
againe	*Againe*
705 or	*Or*
706 conferring	*Conferring*
710 nor	*Nor*
732 Cnossus	Gnossus
759 a	*A*
778 fire	*Fire*
783 food	*foot*
788 all	*All*
799 that all	*that All*
815 your	*yonr*
824 all	*All*
827 If	[new paragraph]
831 Besides	[new paragraph]
833 all	*All*

A Hymne to Hermes

2 and	*&*
5 the	*The*
16 and	*And*
28 he	*He*
38 since	*Since*
he	*He*
54 borne	*Borne*
58 from	*From*
76 or	*Or*
97 And	*and*
124 all	*All*
153 the	*The*
156 past	*Past*
174 that	*That*

179 but	*But*
202 which	*Which*
222 he	*He*
250 and	*And*
260 all	*All*
268 whirle-pit-eating flood	*whirle-pit-eating-flood*
270 The that-morne-borne Cyllenius	*The-that-morne-borne-*Cyllenius
274 His borne-to-barke mouth	*His-borne-to-barke-mouth*
283 in	*In*
316 now	*Now*
346 Ocean great-in-ebbs-and-flows	*Ocean-great-in-ebbs-and flows*
349 round-and-long-neckt	*round and long-neckt*
368 if	*If*
396 and	*And*
420 on	*On*
422 as	*As*
425 even	*Euen*
432 and	*And*
435 his	*His*
436 as	*As*
439 and	*And*
441 weeds	*weed's*
442 shrouds	*shroud's*
444 in	*In*
447 a	*A*
449 thus	*Thus*
451 instantly	*Instantly*
453 or	*Or*
469 could	*Could*
470 or	*Or*
472 that	*That*
491 that	*That*
493 nor	*Nor*
495 What	*what*
496 Knowes	*knowes*
521 Up	*vp*
541 my	*My*
560 or	*Or*
570 and	*And*
571 he	*He*
573 nor	*Nor*
604 such	*Such*

607	Oblivion-marckt whole	*Obliuion-marckt-whole*
614	all	*All*
619	heaps	*heap's*
622	that	*That*
662	using	*Vsing*
693	in	*In*
746	and	*&*
752	in	*In*
792	And	*and*
802	here	*Here*
806	and	*And*
814	Without	*without*
818	and	*And*
868	Let	*let*
873	However cunning-hearted	*How-euer-cunning hearted*
878	which	*Which*
891	which	*Which*
903	Goods	*Gods*
904	curving	*cumming*

A Hymne to Venus

10	Ægis-bearing Jove	*Ægis-bearing*-Ioue
19	and	*&*
27	but	*But*
73	Rhea	Rhæa
88	but	*But*
95	Ida's top-on-top-to-heaven's-Pole-heapt	Idas-*top-on-top-to-heauens-Pole heapt*
	[note] verticem	*virticem*
110	All-of-Gold-made laughter-loving	*All-of-Gold-made-laughter-louing*
123	Denns, obscur'd	*Denns-obscur'd*
126	in	*In*
137	high-taken heeds	*high-taken-heed's*
172	Troyan	Troian
181	Why	*why*
184	if	*If*
189	it	*It*
190	Troyan	Troian
199	and	*&*
201	all	*All*
205	Golden-Rodd-sustaining Argus'	*Golden-Rodd-sustaining*-Argus
214	and	*And*

224 brought	*broisght*
269 Unbutton'd	*Vnbutto'nd*
296 if	*If*
324 Troyans	Troians
362 sustain'd	*stustain'd*
367 Tithon	Tython
417 all	*All*
426 Nymphs	*Nymps* [the Harvard copy reads, correctly: *Nymphs*]
475 to	*te*

To the Same

3 where	*Where*
4 Zephyr	Zephire
10 Weeds	*Weed's*
13 of	*Of*

Bacchus

3 prominent	*prominẽt*
19 therefore strait	*therefore-strait*
31 or	*Or*
32 or	*Or*
47 his	*His*
71 obscure-greene Ivie's	*obscure-greene-Iuies*
87 but	*But*
92 inspired	*inspir'd*
in	*In*

To Mars

1 Mars, Most-strong	MArs-*Most-strong*
8 that	*That*
9 to	*To*
11 Pleiads	Pleiad's

To Diana

2 and	*&*
4 all-of-Gold-made Chariot	*all of Gold-made-Chariot*
9 where	*Where*

To Venus

3 that	*That*

To Pallas

1 onely	*Onely*

To Juno

2 Rhea	Rhæa
4 of	*Of*

To Ceres

7 Keepe	*keepe*

To Lyon-hearted Hercules

1 Alcides	ALlcides
6 and	*And*
15 Vouchsafe	*vouchsafe*

To Pan

5 that	*That*
23 so	*So*
55 where	*Where*
67 then	*Then*

To Vulcan

2 and	*&*

To Phœbus

3 whirle-pit-making streames	*whirle-pit-making-streames*
6 song's all-songs-transcending	*songs-all-songs-transcending*

To Neptune

2 and	*&*
3 Ægean Deepes	Ægan *Depees*

To Jove

1 and	*&*
10 and	*&*
and	*&*

Textual Notes

To Bacchus

5 Semele the-great-in-graces	Semele-*the-great-in-graces*

To Diana

13 the fishie	*fishie*
18 their	*Their*
24 th'	*Th'*
26 in	*In*
35 and	*&*

To Pallas

10 Throws	*Throw's*
13 All	*all*
22 But	*but*

To Vesta and Mercurie

3 and	*&*
4 as	*As*
20 th'	*Th'*
30 t'	*T'*

To Earth

5 all	*All*
7 of	*Of*
14 all	*All*
15 all	*All*
31 Sustaine	*sustaine*

To the Sun

12 th'	*Th'*
15 beames	*Beames*
31 and	*&*

To the Moone

13 farr-off-sprinckling-Luster Evening	*farr-off-sprinckling-Luster-Euening*
16 then	*Then*
21 Pandea	Pandæa
23 and	*&*

To Castor and Pollux

1	th'	*Th'*
2	Muses well-worth-All-Men's-beholdings	*Muses-well-worth-All Mens beholdings*
3	Leda	Læda
22	t'	*T'*

To Men of Hospitalitie

5	at	*At*

To Cuma

7	and	*And*

Upon the Sepulcher of Midus

6	t'	*T'*
9	all	*All*

Cuma refusing his Offer

1	to	*To*
24	I'le	*Iile*

To Thestor's Sonne

1	[note] *the*	*The*
4	[note] *and*	*And*

To Neptune

14	t'	*T'*

To the Cittie Erythræa

7	chance	*cãhce*

To Mariners

1	as	*As*
3	who	*Who*

The Pine

11	they	*They*

Textual Notes

The Fornace

28 Great-many-Poison-Mixer	*Great-many-Poison Mixer*
38 all	*All*
40 on	*On*

Eiresione

4 and	*&*
6 all	*All*
16 her	*Her*

[*Final verses*]

2 Him	*him*
14 Your	*your*
17 tumor	*excretion*
26 Applauds	*Applaud's*
36 and	*&*
40 knows	*know's*

[*Latin prayer*]

6 *Adiumento*	Adiuneto

COMMENTARY

COMMENTARY

The Occasion

24–7 notwithstanding . . . Impiety	I take this as meaning: 'in spite of the fact that all men, servile and hidebound in their opinions, miserably ignored his great and unequalled merit, while at the same time they overflowed in their welcome of imposture and impiety.'

Batrachomyomachia

91–2 your boasts . . . bellies	'Your boasts are all concerned with matters relating to the stomach'—translating λίην αὐχεῖς ἐπι γαστέρι.
100 th'other	The text reads *'thither,'* but the sense needs a definite reference to the mouse.
106–7 did much . . . penitence	'Did much, unprofitably, blame himself for the penance he was undergoing.'
111 in which his state did stand	'In which he found himself.'
119–20 Yet in forc'd speech . . . strove	'Yet when he did speak, he minimised his sense of danger, since his desire to be esteemed brave strove with his fear.'
150 Past all evasion	'However much you try to evade them.'
154 his watry destinies	'His fatal end in the water.'
170 the chief in our confusions	'Our principal bane.'
184 Made all . . . circular	'Equipped them all completely in appropriate armour.'
192–3 that could not beare thc braine of any	'That could not have been invented by any brain.'
218 without my sight of him	'Without my seeing him,' translating οὐδὲ κατεῖδον ὀλλύμενον.
261 that me in much did stand	'That I much valued,' or 'On which I had devoted much toil.'
266–71 The darner . . . mantle to restore	It is doubtful whether Chapman himself knew precisely what he wanted to express here. The sense of the original is that Pallas had borrowed money in order to make the veil and now cannot repay:— ὁ δ' ἠπητής μοι ἐπέστη καὶ πράσσει με τόκον . . . χρησαμένη γὰρ ὕφανα καὶ οὐκ ἔχω ἀνταποδοῦναι.

280–4 Therefore, to the fight . . . oppose	The general sense is: 'Let no god assist in the fight, for if he enters the battle or even just tries to aid them, they are so fierce against their enemies that they might dare to attack him.'
293 Standing . . . fight	'Meeting the first shock of the foe.'
295–6 his face . . . swaid	'He fell on his face.'
361 Soone as . . . birth	I have no idea what Chapman intends here.
402–3 How Potently . . . his head	Another of Chapman's peculiarly involved phrases, meaning—it would seem—simply: 'However powerfully he may fight.'
408 that	Refers to *'thy lance'*: 'getting him out of the battle by using the lance that slew the Titans.'

An Hymne to Apollo

113 for penurie of Men	'Because of the lack of men,' translating χήτεϊ λαῶν.
117–8 to render . . . they fall	'To prophesy coming events' when men demand an oracle.
147 Thaumantia	Iris.
224 Sweet	In all probability this is 'suite,' so spelt to rime with 'feet.'
227 Champion fight	Evidently 'boxing,' translating πυγμαχίῃ.
289 that sounds . . . set gone	'Which sends its harmonies up to heaven.'
401 Whom future . . . brings	'Who are brought here in search of information concerning the future.'
422 in his pleasure's place	'In the place of this pleasure.'
473 built for eternall date	'Built to last for ever.'
563–4 that invok't . . . gave	Apparently this simply means, 'which brought death, as he had intended it to.'
579–81 Now from thee . . . death	This translates οὐδὲ τί τοι θανατόν γε δυσηλεγέ' οὔτε Τυφωεὺς ἀρκέσει οὔτε Χίμαιρα δυσώνυμος, and seems to mean 'Neither Typhon nor Chimæra will be of any power to avert death from you.'
645 Heaven's Comforter of sight	The Sun.

655 it failde t'obay	'The ship failed to answer to the rudder.'
714 that with . . . stand	'Which their health and stomachs need.'
732–4 Yet no more . . . lov'd Cittie	'Yet you must return no more to your beloved city.'
734–5 severalls . . . and houses	'Your individual wives and houses.'
829–30 Know that . . . sustaine	It is almost impossible to determine what precisely Chapman meant here. The original text says that they will lose their privileges and be subdued.

A Hymne to Hermes

14 when great . . . consummate	'When the purpose of great Jove was fulfilled.'
19 Could turne . . . assaies	'Could turn and twist so as to bring about what he desired.'
21–2 bore a varied finger	Evidently this means 'had various devices.'
49–51 Which . . . wit	Apparently meaning, 'which your ill form will not prevent me, by my skill, from making use of you.'
136 Thirsting . . . height	'Anxious to attempt some extraordinary thing.'
144 In ayre's . . . Abods	This simply means, 'they dwelt in the open air.'
167–9 but as . . . needing it	Here Chapman seemingly got lost in the Greek text, οἶά τ'ἐπειγόμενος δολιχὴν ὁδόν, αὐτοτροπήσας—which is confessedly puzzling. Presumably he intended the meaning to be, 'but as if he were merely collecting food for his journey, since he had a long way to go and needed to carry provisions with him.'
249–50 and his owne . . . due	Once again Chapman seems to have been uncertain about what he intended to express.
267 a novell voice's note	Presumably, 'a new device.'
326–7 being . . . Acres	The sense is clear, but the grammar—and the precise usage of 'reapes'—is obscure: 'having the benefit of the corn cut in a great number of acres.'
343 the Gote-hyde-wearer's Sonne	The son of Zeus.

353–4	whom Latona's . . . strange	'Whom Apollo did not refrain from saluting.'
388	That strooke but one plaine	It is to be suspected that Chapman could make no clear sense of the Greek, ὃ δὲ θᾶσσον ὁδὸν κίε μῦθον ἀκούσας· οἰωνὸν δ'ἐνόει τανυσίπτερον, αὐτίκα δ'ἔγνω φηλητὴν γεγαῶτα Διὸς παῖδα Κρονίωνος.
435	Chace	Probably, 'closely concealing the theft of the oxen.'
468	a false Relation faine	'Present a false report.'
603	After . . . infinite space	'After I had travelled far.'
612–3	being so . . . in doubt	'Being so skilfully designed to deceive.'
629	got his Passe sign'd	'Finished his journey.'
658	Bliss-indu'd	'Gods.'
763–4	as it . . . Birth	'According to their order of age and birth.'
826	And even . . . earne	'And no sooner do you desire it than it is done.'
853–4	even when . . . sing	'Even when he aims at singular virtue in what he plays or sings.'
904	curving	The text reads *'cumming,'* but presumably Chapman wrote *'curving,'* translating καμπύλα τόξα.
905–6	what . . . witnesse	'Would take the oath the Gods use.'
921	Gifts of Deitie	'Divine gifts.'

A Hymne to Venus

153–4	the Deity that Darts affecteth	Artemis.
154–5	that gave the eye of Heaven his heat	Latona (Leto).
155–6	that moves The hearts of all	Venus.
157	the blew-eyd Maid	Athene.
171–2	give me . . . hearts	'Make the Trojans love me.'
197–8	her . . . shafts	Artemis.
201–2	all circkl'd . . . Multitude	'Surrounded by a large crowd,' translating ἀμφὶ δ' ὅμιλος ἀπείριτος ἐστεφάνωτο.

208 a labour of Mortalitie	'A work of man,' translating πολλὰ δ'ἔπ' ἤγαγεν ἔϱγα καταθνητῶν ἀνθϱώπων.
212 On her . . . comforted	The earth.
299 he enjoy'd his eare	'He listened.'

Bacchus

55 Since that Prise . . . let fall	Apparently, 'since some God certainly put this prize in our way'—ἐπεὶ ἡμῖν ἔμβαλε δαίμων.

To Pan

70 start	'Started.'

To Earth

23 with their croun'd selections	'With the suitors whom they have chosen.'

To the Moone

2 Whose wide . . . ground	Translating 'long-winged,' τανυσίπτεϱον.

To Cuma

6–7 all embrac't . . . whyrlpits	Since Chapman is fond of using the word 'whirlpit' in connection with streams, it is interesting to note that the whole phrase here means nothing more than 'eddying,' δινήεντος.

[*Final verses*]

17 tumor	Chapman's own correction of '*excretion*' in the printed text.

GLOSSARY

GLOSSARY

So strange became Chapman's use of language that there are scores of words and phrases which, in bold terms or more subtly, appear in these translations with significances not commonly assigned to them. The present glossary aims merely at giving aid to the reader of the poems, with an asterisk indicating usages or meanings for which he individually seems to have been responsible. Included also are words spelt, often for rime's sake, in peculiar ways.

abject	abject creature
abode	[This is frequently used in peculiar phrases, as in 'solac't Abods,' meaning 'dwelt']
absolute	complete, perfect
access	entry, movement towards, approach
acquite	acquit
address	1) bring forward 2) skill, effort (as in 'thine own address,' meaning 'your own efforts')
addression	direction of one's course
admire	wonder at
advance	put forward (as in 'that they advanc't to her,' meaning 'which they built for her')
adversively	* adversely, in an opposite direction
affect	1) turn towards (as in 'whose face affects the west') 2) possess (as in 'whose flood affects so many silver streames') 3) touch, or infect 4) effect
affected	1) touched 2) afflicted (as in 'affected with the lance of war')
affecter	one who has an affection for, user
all-else	* all other
ambient	revolving
amends	dowry (as in 'in my Amends,' meaning 'as a dowry')
amplified	['Amplified past others' means 'outstanding']
angel	1) messenger 2) blesser, protector
antipathy	* anything opposite to another

appall	fear
apparance	appearance
appose	place to or on
appropriats	* appropriate things
approve	declare
ap'te	aped
arrive	cause to arrive
as	[Frequently meaning 'as if']
ascend	rise to, attain
attoned	reconciled
attraction	* ornament
autentique	authentic
author	1) originate, be the cause of 2) one who originates anything
ayre	air (often used as 'wind')
beam	* [Used in various senses, once evidently as 'song']
bear . . . . a finger	[See Commentary, *A Hymne to Hermes,* ll. 21–2]
belluine	* the race of animals
bene	been
bequest	that which is bestowed ('in Bequest of Fate' means 'according to fate's decrees')
berde	beard
beseeging	besieging (sometimes used almost in the sense of 'afflicting')
birth	race, animals
blame	blaming ('of his blame' means 'of what he accuses me')
blone	blown
blore	gale
bolle	bowl
boote haling	carrying away of booty, foraging
borne	born
broch	* broach, branch
bryre	briar
burgonet	helmet
can'stick	candlestick
carquenet	carcanet, chain of jewels
cautelous	wily
cheat	bread
chrimsine	crimson
circular	complete, perfect
circularly	completely
circulate	encircle, bind
circumflex	bending round

circumvention	[Used in a peculiar phrase, 'verbal circumvention in me,' meaning 'deceiving me']
claver grass	clover
clear	noble
close	secret (as in 'close Heart')
closset	close or secret place, lair
clymes	[In *Hermes,* ll. 552–3 'the Clymes of rapture,' the word may be intended for either 'climes' or 'climbs']
coch	coach
collateral	equal, corresponding
coloquintida	bitter apple
come up at	attack
composure	* fulfilment
concelpt	conceit
conceit	think, consider
conclude	* [In *Hermes,* ll. 659–60 'conclude his bare assertion,' the word seems to mean 'back up, support']
concomitant	concurrent
confer	* 1) agree or harmonise with (in *Vesta,* l. 8 'conferring . . . Jove' translates ἔν' ἔρχεο θυμὸν ἔχουσα σὺν Διὶ μητιόεντι) * 2) bring, impose (as in 'conferring wrongs')
confluent	* water, pond (without any implication of streams flowing together)
contendresse	one who urges her way or hastens towards (as in 'for Troy became a swift Contendresse')
contention	endeavour (in *Pan,* l. 37 'contention of song' means simply 'melody, chant')
contumelious	presumptuous, insolent (translating ὑβριστάων)
convert	turn or turn to (as in 'convert recourse to')
cornel	[In *Hermes,* l. 803 'cornel dart' apparently means 'cornelled' or 'embattled']
counterprise	* comparison ('bear the Counterprise' means 'be compared with')
covetous	eager, striving, involving competition (as in 'covetous sport of getting glory')
crown	1) end, conclusion 2) chief effort 3) ring (of people)
crustie-weeds	* [Apparently the frillings on a cake]
cure	care (as in 'cure of war')
Dædalian	ingenious, formed by art ('Dædalian Throne' translates πολυδαίδαλον)

date	duration ('long date' means 'a long time,' 'endless date' is 'eternity' and 'to endless date' is 'continually')
deceiptfull	deceitful
dehort	exhort against
deified	divine
deject	cast down
delighted	affording delight
delightsome	delighted
den	make a den
denounce	announce (as in 'denouncing ill-nam'd war')
depopulacy	* depopulated condition, depopulation
deposition	placing or putting down
deprave	vilify, abuse (but it is difficult to give an exact meaning for the word as used in *Batrachomyomachia,* ll. 106–7, 'did much deprave Unprofitable penitence')
desire	satisfaction (as in 'to her desire')
disgraceful	unpleasing
dismission	sending away
display	* what has ever been seen (as in 'past display')
display, make	* look at or watch
dispose	[In *Hermes,* ll. 330–1 'dispose Possessions to me' means 'give me possessions']
dispred	spread out
distinguished	separated
divine	make divine
divined	divine
doctrine	training, skill
drad	dread
ease	easing
eat	ate
egregious	noble, eminent
elaborate	* elaborating, adorning (as in 'bestowing an elaborate hand')
either	both (as in 'either hand,' meaning 'both hands')
empair	1) impairment 2) hurt or damage
emperie	empire
employed	* brought to pass, caused to be
enamour	give delight or charm
encline	persuade
endless	immortal
enforce	produce by force, accomplish
ensue	follow or pursue

entertain	*	answer
entreat	*	address
equal		that is equal to ('cqual Gods' means 'Gods who are my equals')
err		wander
errant		wandering
event		[Used in various peculiar phrases: 'dead event' is 'death,' 'bear event of' is 'be regarded as']
evert		turn ('evert the good' means 'turn the good aside')
everted	*	sacked (of cities)
excitement		incitement
excogitate		think up
exempt		free from (as in 'exempt from Pere,' 'exempt from match,' which mean 'peerless,' 'matchless')
exile		set apart or dismiss
exonerate		lighten
expert		free from
exploratoric	*	exploring, searching (as in 'exploratorie spirit')
explore		search
extuberancc		something that swells up
eye		sight (as 'in Apollo's eye')
fact		action, deed
facture		1) the action of making a thing
	*	2) craft
fall		descent ('make a fall' means 'descend' and 'still pouring on their fall' is used of one army bearing down on another)
far-come	*	far-comer, comer from afar
far-shot		far-shooting
fashionist	*	one who follows current fashions
fautress		patroness
fenceful	*	giving defence
fervent	*	quick to burn (as applied to dry wood)
fescue	*	plcctrum
filed		1) defiled
		2) deceitful
fire-hov'd		fire-hoofed
fistularie	*	['Fistularie Reede' means a 'pipe']
fixed fight		battle
flame	*	woman in love
flead		flayed
flit	*	[Apparently in *The Fornace,* l. 25 this means 'dust,' according to the original πάντ' ἔντοσθ' αὐτῆς κεϱαμήια λεπτὰ ποιοῦσα]

flood	['Ayre's flood' means 'the air']
floting	floating on
floure	1) flower
	* 2) herbage (as in 'greene floure,' meaning 'grass')
fluent	1) river
	* 2) flowing or flaring (used for flames)
forc't	enforced, despoiled
fordge	forge (used in adjectival sense)
fore-right	straight forwards
forspoke	forespoke, bewitched
fortressing	turning into a fortress
free	set free or dismiss
fully-divin'de	completely divine
futurely	in the future
gable	cable (of a ship)
ghesse	guess
glory	1) boasting
	2) fame
gode	goad
grievance	sense of grief, terror
grought, growght	growth
guilt	gilt, gilded
gynn	gin, device, instrument
gyrlond	garland
hair	head of hair
hant	haunt, dwell on
hanting	haunting
harpsical	* kind of harp
heed	attention, observation
height	[Used peculiarly in phrases such as 'to his utmost height,' meaning 'to the best of his ability']
herd, in	* in line with
herehence	from this
heyring	heiring, being the heir of, coming from
hill-bred	bred on the hills
hollow	shout
honorarie	* honourable, worthy of honour
humorous	watery
humour	liquid
hurreys	* hurries, hastenings (of coaches)
ill-named	* called or styled ill
illude	cheat
illustrate	make to shine, glorify
immane	monstrous
immanitie	monstrous deed

imperatorie	* concerned with ruling ('imperatorie art' is the 'art of government')
imply	* place (as in 'did his point implie in')
impose	place, set, up or on
impression	* [Used in peculiar phrases such as 'standing th' impression of the first in fight,' meaning 'getting the first shock of the onset']
inaccessible	unreachable, unmatchable
indevirginate	* unravished, virgin
indifferencie	absence of bias
indifferencing	* impartial
inexcitable	from which one cannot be roused (as in 'inexcitable sleepe')
infer	introduce, bring
inflexive	* inflexible
inform	1) make, form out of, construct 2) inspire
infortune	misfortune
ingenuities	* beauties, things of skill (as in 'Poesie's ingenuities')
ingenuous	noble
inhabitresse	one who inhabits
innumerous	without number
inquest	question, finding out
insolent	strange, terrible
instauration	start, beginning
interest	matter of concern (as in 'of interest in,' meaning 'concerned or associated with'; 'your interest,' meaning 'things concerned with you')
invention, find the	invent
inveterate	old-standing
jack	buff jerkin
jarre	battle
jointly	at the same time
kind	nature, race (as in 'fetcht his kinde from,' meaning 'was descended from')
kirnell	kernel
knoule	knoll
kymnel	tub
languor	grief
lay abroad	* debate
lengthful	lengthy
Lernean	* vile, monstrous
list	limit, check (as in 'list or Lawe')
livrings	liver puddings

los'd	loosed
lurch	deceit
lust	will, desire
lybberd	leopard
lynce	lynx
man'de	maned, having a mane
mankind	fierce
manly	bold
manned	* occupied with (as in 'mann'd with sheepe')
mastery	work of distinction
mere	simple, pure
mere-learn'd	learned men who have no other virtues
merit	* ['In merit of' means 'because of, through']
mind	* 1) knowledge ('uttered minde' is 'speech') * 2) courage (as in 'each Frogg full of Minde')
mind-master	* spirit of courage
miseries	* [In 'Miseries to his Merite' the sense seems to be 'miserable treatment' and hence 'neglect of']
moule	mole
murmur	noise
mutiny	warlike preparation
neese	sneeze
next	that which was next
neye	neigh
note	benefit, use (in *Hermes,* l. 48 'Thou mov'st in me a note of excellent use' means 'You are of benefit to me by showing how you can be put to good use')
numerous	rhythmical, musical
nursery	process of nursing
nutritial	* concerned with nursing or fostering
offspring	[Used in *Apollo,* l. 578 for animals sacrificed at the altar]
ope-war	open, or openly declared, war
opprobation	* impertinence (spelt 'opprobation' in the original, but possibly intended for 'opprobration')
opprobrie	condemnation, reproach
op'te	oped, opened
ostent	outward sign
oughly	ugly
ought	owed, owned
outray	* outgoing, expedition ('on all the Outraies where for food I erre' means 'in all the expeditions when I wander about seeking food')
overture	* innermost part (of a cave)

owe	own
past	paste
pecuniarie	* having to do with money ('pecuniarie Rates' means 'commerce')
pedigree	race
penurie	lack, destitution
perdue	lying in ambush
pere	peer
perpendicular	* virtue
perspective	* sight, view
perspirable	* airy, hence lofty (as in 'perspirable heights')
petulant	wanton, bold
phane	fane
plash	* plashed thicket
plume	* bird
plump	crowd
possest	possessed, demonic
prærupt	steep, precipitous
prease	press
preast	pressed
present	[In *Venus*, l. 463 'so well Present the Deities' means 'be so god-like in appearance']
prest	ready
prise	take as a prize
project	abandoned, abject, base
propension	inclination, tendency
proyning-bank	* [This seems to mean a bank where a bird preens itself]
prime	first ('tooke Prime existence' means 'was born')
purvaie	* take
queach	thicket
rac't	razed
raie	ray
rapting	ravishing
rapture	seizing away
ray	* vision, glance
receipt	* cave, cavern
receit	receipt
reciprocal	* one who is sent back (as in 'You must be made your own Reciprocalls to,' meaning 'You must be sent back')
recourse	[See under 'convert']
recreative	humorous, amusing
rector	chief
refulgency	* refulgence, glory

regency	act of ruling
relation	account
rely	[Perhaps in the dedicatory verses ll. 53–4 'relies Refuge' means 'reposes relief, or release']
remove	* [Used peculiarly in such phrases as 'in opposite removes,' meaning 'in reverse,' and 'thou put'st on Remove,' meaning 'you removed, or moved, over']
repair	* return
repose	* [None of the usual senses fit 'his heart within him panted out repose,' apparently meaning simply 'palpitated' (i.e. was agitated), and 'in steep'st repose,' which seems to mean 'in the highest position']
rer'de	reared
restriction	* transference
retire	cause to retire, conceal
retreatful	* acting as a retreat
retrive	retrieve
rigging	* trickery
rore	['Wavie rore' means 'roaring waves']
rumour	word, report
sacring	consecrating
sail, bear no mean	* be base or inglorious
sais'd	seised, put in possession
sale-muse	* muse put out for sale
salve	explain away
saving	bringing safety or salvation
scath	scathe, hurt, damage
scruple	doubt, uncertainty
sease	seize
seed	child, offspring ('while the streame her fluent seede receives' evidently means 'while the waters flow,' translating ἔστ' ἂν ὕδωρ τε νάῃ)
sensual	addicted to merely sensuous pleasures
sent	scent
set	1) [In *Hermes,* l. 792 this seems to mean 'playing' (of an instrument)] 2) sat 3) fixing
set-spleend	* set down with spleen
sever	1) break up 2) bring a speech to an end
several	something belonging to an individual
sex-distinguish't	* of both sexes

sharp-seen	* seeing keenly
shew, in	in appearance
shrick't	shricked
shrike	shriek
shroud	place of concealment, recess
sight	power of seeing
simplicity	sincerity
sincere	pure, unmixed
singular	* [In *Hermes,* l. 853 'aspires to singular' seems to mean 'aims at singularity']
skeane	dagger or sword
sleight	slight, device, trick
snew	snowed
solace	[See under 'abode']
sort	decree of fate
souc't	soused
spell	talk
spring	1) race, progeny
	* 2) father, begetter
springal	youth
spritclie	sprightly
square	* law
state	[This seems to be used almost as 'position' in 'thy endanger'd State' and 'an eternall state in his affection']
stealth	stealing
stere	1) stir
	2) steer (as in *Batrachomyomachia,* l. 114 where the Greek has οὐρὴν μὲν προπέτασσεν ἐφ' ὕδασιν, ἠύτε κώπην σύρων)
stern	rudder
sterved-like-raven-ous	* rapacious, rapaciously
stick off	* set off
storm	bring upon violently
strain	family, descent
striving	competing with one another
submitted	['Submitted to my seat' means 'which he has given to me as my seat']
sumpture	* splendour
supplies	help
supply	['In supply of it' means 'in its place']
surrogate	deputy
sustain	['Sustaining a retreat' is simply 'retreating']

swim	swimming, power of swimming
taint	touch
talents of justice	scales of justice
tapistries	* [In *Pan,* l. 25 this clearly means 'hiding places'; the word may be formed from the verb 'tapis' or 'tapish']
taught	made aware of
thirst	thirst for
throat	loud cry
tiller	part of a bow
transcension	carrying or driving over
transfer	throw, cast
treble	speak in a treble, whine
treen	belonging to trees
trim	manners, fashion, equipage
tumble	tumble or throw down
tutress	female instructor
unexcogitable	* unthinkable
universal	prevalent over all (in 'his universall entrailes' it simply means 'all')
unpris'd	unpriced, priceless
useful	* use or luck bringing (translating ἐριούνιος)
utmost	outermost
vaine	* [There seems no known sense of 'vain' or 'vein' which fits 't'advance a vaine,' meaning 'to lift or rise up']
vanted	vaunted
vehicular	* provided with wheels
vent	* ['Giving vents of life and motion' means 'killing']
view, at	* in full sight ('to their view' is 'to see them')
voluntary	a piece of music
weeds	garments
whirlpit	whirlpool
wishful	delightful
witherling	* twisted, emaciated creature
without	outside of
wiving	* ['Wiving conversations' means 'ideas about marriage']
wowe	woo
wreakful	full of vengeance
yrckesome	irksome